TEACHING IN THE MIDDLE AND SECONDARY SCHOOLS

■ EIGHTH EDITION

Richard D. Kellough

California State University, Sacramento

Jioanna Carjuzaa

Linfield College

PEARSON

Merrill
Prentice Hall

Upper Saddle River, New Jersey
Columbus, Ohio

Library of Congress Cataloging-in-Publication Data

Kellough, Richard D. (Richard Dean)
    Teaching in the middle and secondary schools / Richard D. Kellough, Jioanna Carjuzaa—
8th ed.
        p. cm.
    Rev. ed of: Teaching in the middle and secondary schools / Joseph F. Callahan,
Leonard H. Clark, Richard D. Kellough. 7th ed. c2002.
    Includes bibliographical references and index.
    ISBN 0-13-119373-2
    1. High school teaching—United States. 2. Middle schools—United States. I. Carjuzaa,
Jioanna. II. Callahan, Joseph F. Teaching in the middle and secondary schools. III. Title.

LB1737.U6C27 2006
373.1102—dc22

373.1102
.T253
2006

2004065648

Vice President and Executive Publisher: Jeffery W. Johnston
Executive Editor: Debra A. Stollenwerk
Senior Editorial Assistant: Mary Morrill
Production Editor: Kris Roach
Production Coordination: Amy Gehl, Carlisle Publishers Services
Design Coordinator: Diane C. Lorenzo
Cover Designer: Jeff Vanik
Cover Image: Corbis
Photo Coordinator: Maria B. Vonada
Production Manager: Susan Hannahs
Director of Marketing: Ann Castel Davis
Marketing Manager: Darcy Betts Prybella
Marketing Coordinator: Brian Mounts

This book was set in Minion by Carlisle Communications, Ltd. It was printed and bound by Banta Harrisonburg Book Group. The cover was printed by Coral Graphic Services, Inc.

Photo Credits: Larry Hamill/Merrill, p. 55; Anthony Magnacca/Merrill, p. 169; Anne Vega/Merrill, p. 253; Todd Yarrington/Merrill, p. 1.

Pearson Education Ltd.
Pearson Education Singapore Pte. Ltd.
Pearson Education Canada, Ltd.
Pearson Education—Japan

Pearson Education Australia Pty. Limited
Pearson Education North Asia Ltd.
Pearson Educación de Mexico, S.A. de C.V.
Pearson Education Malaysia Pte. Ltd.

10 9 8 7 6 5 4 3 2 1
ISBN: 0-13-119373-2

Preface

As its primary purpose, this textbook provides a practical, concise, criterion-referenced, performance-based, mastery learning model for college or university students who are in a general secondary or middle school methods course or in the field component of teacher education. The modular organization of this textbook shows instructors of methods courses how to provide enough basic instruction that they can individualize their instruction and devote their time and attention to specific learning activities. Others who will find it useful are experienced teachers who desire to continue developing their teaching skills, and curriculum specialists and school administrators, who desire to have a current, practical, and concise book of methods about teaching for reference.

The book is organized around four developmental components: *why*—the rationale to support the components that follow; *what*—what you will be teaching; *how*—how you will teach it; and *how well*—how well you are teaching it. These components are represented by the four parts of the book. Each part begins with a statement of its major objectives and with quotations relevant to topics addressed in its modules.

Throughout the text we consistently provide information useful for a decision-making teacher. We also provide frequent exercises for practice in handling concepts in ways that facilitate metacognitive thinking. All exercises require the user to deal in some descriptive, analytical, or self-reflective manner with text concepts and actual practice. Most exercises are adaptable for cooperative or collaborative group processing.

■ PART 1: INTRODUCTION TO TEACHING AND LEARNING IN MIDDLE AND SECONDARY SCHOOLS

The two modules of Part 1 are written to reflect the reality and challenge of teaching today; to provide the rationale, or the *why*, to support the organization and details of the components that follow. While Module 1 presents an important overview of that reality and challenge, Module 2 addresses developments in cognitive science and constructivism that enhance and celebrate the differences among students and their learning styles and capacities. It provides specific guidelines for meeting that challenge with specific groups of learners.

■ PART 2: PLANNING FOR INSTRUCTION

The three modules of Part 2 are designed to reflect the *what* component. Because teachers must have the students' attention before they can effectively implement any instructional plan, guidelines for establishing and maintaining a psychologically and intellectually safe and supportive learning environment are presented in Module 3. Along with providing important rationale and guidelines for selecting and using content and textbooks and preparing instructional objectives, Module 4 also presents information about the national standards for subject areas in the curriculum. Module 5 provides straightforward information on the use and preparation of various types of units and for lesson planning as is relevant for today's teaching.

■ PART 3: SELECTING AND IMPLEMENTING INSTRUCTIONAL STRATEGIES

Part 3 is the *how* component and consists of three modules. Module 6 focuses attention on grouping students for learning, using assignments, ensuring equality in the classroom, using project-centered teaching, and writing across the curriculum. Module 7 provides guidelines for using teacher talk, demonstrations, thinking, inquiry, and games.

Intricately interwoven with teaching and learning is the teacher's use of fundamental classroom tools (e.g., writing board and overhead projector) and the selection and use of media, aids, and resources. The use of these tools is the focus of Module 8, the final module of Part 3.

■ PART 4: ASSESSMENT OF TEACHING AND LEARNING

Part 4 focuses on the fourth component of competent teaching—*how well* the students are learning and how well the teacher is doing. Module 9 examines the assessment of what students know or think they know before, during, and after the instruction. The module also provides practical guidelines for parent-teacher collaboration and for grading and reporting student achievement.

Module 10, considered an important module by student users and sometimes even studied first, provides an emphasis on how well the teacher is doing—the assessment of teaching effectiveness, as well as guidelines and resources for ongoing professional development.

Module 10 also provides guidelines and resources for student teaching and for finding a teaching position. These guidelines—and this book in general—have proven to be useful as references for years beyond the current methods course.

■ NEW TO THIS EDITION

Changes for this eighth edition are as follows:

- In keeping with the book's long-standing title, we strive throughout for an improved balance of content between middle and secondary schools, emphasizing the middle school as uniquely different from both the high school and the traditional junior high school, and pre- and early adolescence as different from late adolescence.

- Every module of the book was reviewed, updated, and tweaked to reduce wordiness and update content, figures, and exercises.

- Current updated Internet references and resources appear throughout.

- The text was carefully updated to reflect the cultural sensitivity of the authors and issues of diversity were integrated throughout the textbook. Current terminology for describing various groups was updated (for example: LEP (Limited English Proficient) students were changed to ELL (English Language Learner) students; special needs students were changed to exceptional students and so forth).

- Module 1 was rewritten to strengthen it as an introductory module, providing a contextualized framework for secondary and middle schools, especially with respect to historical foundations, as well as organizational and structural provisions for student differences; the purpose of school and recent and current reform efforts; fundamental characteristics of exemplary education; the roles of telecommunications, the community, and parent organizations; key trends and practices; and problems and issues that plague the nation's schools.

- Module 2 addresses the diversity of students in our pluralistic society and highlights strategies for increasing self- and other awareness. Cultural competence and multicultural education are described in detail. A focus on adolescent development, the changes that take place in Stevenson's five domains, and the implications in the teaching/learning process are provided, as are guidelines for addressing the needs of a variety of students with special needs. These guidelines can serve as *best practices* for meeting the needs of all students.

- Module 3, "Establishing and Maintaining a Safe and Supportive Classroom Learning Environment," was revised to expand on preemptive steps teachers can take to gain student cooperation. Guidelines emphasize ways to help teachers establish a welcoming classroom climate conducive to learning where all students are encouraged to fulfill their academic potential.

- Module 5 has added a more detailed lesson plan template including a category on accommodating students with special needs, as well as separate categories for both assessment of students and teacher reflection and evaluation. A variety of lesson plan samples from many disciplines are provided from pre-service and in-service teachers, as well as model lesson plans from teacher educators.

- For Module 6, "Student-Centered Instructional Strategies," we strengthened the sections about intelligent behavior, the teaching of thinking skills, and educational games and simulations. Cooperative instructional strategies are stressed throughout.

- Module 7, "Teacher-Centered Instructional Strategies," contains a new section titled "Giving Students a Second Chance."

- Module 8, "Media, Aids, and Resources," with all new updated lists of resources, continues as strong support for Modules 4 through 7. It also contains a new section on distance learning, document cameras, and multimedia programs.

- Module 9 was revised to emphasize an eclectic approach to assessment.

- Module 10, "Self-Assessment of Teaching and Continued Professional Development," was updated to encourage educators to take advantage of a variety of professional development opportunities.

- Posttest questions, endnotes, and suggested reading lists have been updated for each module.
- The textbook has been reformatted to make the content visually more appealing and easier to read.
- Exercises will be included on the Companion Website for this textbook so that students can complete them with the aid of a computer. The exercises are still included in a reduced format in the textbook so that they can be referred to in class.

FEATURES OF THE TEXT

- The four parts serve as advance organizers—that is, they establish a mind-set.
- To promote mastery learning, we employ a competency-based modular format. Each module contains (a) an opening list of specific learning objectives (or learning targets) for that module, (b) a presentation of content as related to those objectives, (c) an integration of practice and reinforcement in each module, and, at the completion of the module, (d) a posttest assessment of how well the opening targets have been achieved. For self-assessment, there is an answer key to the Posttest questions on the Companion Website.
- Exercises for active learning are found within each module. The exercises are designed to have the teacher candidate continually assess his or her progress in the understanding and skill development of teaching and involve the candidates in active and collaborative learning. (*Note:* Because some exercises necessitate a visit to a school to have dialogue with students and staff, exercises should be reviewed early so that you can plan your visits and work schedule. In fact, because certain exercises build upon previous ones or suggest that help be obtained from teachers in the field, we advise that all exercises be reviewed at the beginning of the course. Because it is unlikely that all exercises could [or should] be completed in a one-semester course, you will have to decide which exercises will be done.)
- Performance assessment, rather than paper-and-pencil testing of teaching skills development, is encouraged by the micro peer-teaching exercises found in Modules 1, 7, and 10. Indeed, Exercise 10.2 is designed to be useful as a performance as-

sessment at the conclusion of the course for which this textbook is used.

- Suggested readings at the conclusion of each module offer additional sources, both classic and current, that can deepen and broaden understandings of particular topics.
- Posttest questions at the end of each module can serve as an assessment of the module and as springboards for further discussion.
- The text concludes with a glossary of terms, an author index, and a subject index.
- **The Online Instructor's Manual** provides instructors with a variety of useful resources and is available to instructors who adopt the text. To request information, please contact your local Prentice Hall sales representative. If you do not know how to contact your sales representative, please call Faculty Service at 1-800-526-0485 for assistance.

ACKNOWLEDGMENTS

Although teaching and learning in middle and secondary schools have become increasingly complex—with many new and exciting things happening as schools continue to restructure their efforts to provide the best learning for today's youth—we strive to keep the text at a reasonable length and to keep it user friendly. We thank all the persons who helped in its development. We thank those who contributed and who are acknowledged at appropriate places throughout, as well as our friends and highly competent professionals at Merrill/Prentice Hall, who have maintained their belief in and support for this book.

In our preparation of this eighth edition, we carefully heeded the recommendations made by users and reviewers of the previous edition. We acknowledge and offer a sincere thank you for the cogent reviews and recommendations made by Cynthia G. Kruger, University of Massachusetts, Dartmouth; Mary-Beth Muskin, Creighton University; Geoff Quick, Central Michigan University; and Noell Reinhiller, Concordia College.

Although this edition is the result of the contributions of many professionals, we, as always, assume full responsibility for its shortcomings. Our aspiration for this eighth edition is that it will spark reflective thinking about your teaching and that you will find it stimulating and professionally rewarding.

Discover the Companion Website Accompanying This Book ҪШ

■ THE PRENTICE HALL COMPANION WEBSITE: A VIRTUAL LEARNING ENVIRONMENT

Technology is a constantly growing and changing aspect of our field that is creating a need for content and resources. To address this emerging need, Prentice Hall has developed an online learning environment for students and professors alike—Companion Websites—to support our textbooks.

In creating a Companion Website, our goal is to enhance and build on what the textbook already offers. For this reason, the content of each user-friendly website is organized by chapter and provides professors and students with a variety of meaningful resources.

■ For the Professor—

Every Companion Website integrates **Syllabus Manager**™, an online syllabus creation and management utility.

- **Syllabus Manager**™ provides you, the instructor, with an easy, step-by-step process to create and revise syllabi, with direct links into the Companion Website and other online content without having to learn HTML.

- Students may log on to your syllabus during any study session. All they need to know is the web address for the Companion Website and the password you have assigned to your syllabus.

- After you have created a syllabus using **Syllabus Manager**™, students may enter the syllabus for their course section from any point in the Companion Website.

- By clicking on a date, students can see the list of activities for an assignment. The activities for each assignment are linked directly to actual content, saving students' time.

- You can add assignments by clicking on the desired due date and filling in the details of the assignment: name of the assignment, instructions, and whether it is a one-time or repeating assignment.

- You can also easily create links to other activities. If an activity is online, you can enter a URL in the space provided, which will be automatically linked in the final syllabus.

- Your completed syllabus is hosted on Prentice Hall's servers, allowing convenient updates from any computer on the Internet. Changes you make to your syllabus are immediately available to your students at their next logon.

To take advantage of the many available resources, please visit the text's Companion Website at *www.prenhall.com/kellough.*

■ For the Student—

- *Exercises and PostTests* at the end of each chapter are also available online, for you to complete.

- *PostTest Answer Keys* provide solutions to the PostTest questions.

- *Electronic Bluebook* allows you to electronically send homework answers to your instructor.

- *Chat* room offers real-time communication regarding the text's topic areas.

- *Message Board* allows you to post and respond to questions and comments from a national audience.

To take advantage of the many available resources, please visit the *Teaching in the Middle and Secondary Schools* Companion Website at *www.prenhall.com/kellough.*

Brief Contents

EDUCATOR LEARNING CENTER: AN INVALUABLE ONLINE RESOURCE

Merrill Education and the Association for Supervision and Curriculum Development (ASCD) invite you to take advantage of a new online resource, one that provides access to the top research and proven strategies associated with ASCD and Merrill—the Educator Learning Center. At **www.educatorlearningcenter.com,** you will find resources that will enhance your students' understanding of course topics and of current educational issues, in addition to being invaluable for further research.

■ HOW THE EDUCATOR LEARNING CENTER WILL HELP YOUR STUDENTS BECOME BETTER TEACHERS

With the combined resources of Merrill Education and ASCD, you and your students will find a wealth of tools and materials to better prepare them for the classroom.

Research

- More than 600 articles from the ASCD journal Educational Leadership discuss everyday issues faced by practicing teachers.

- A direct link on the site to Research Navigator™ gives students access to many of the leading education journals, as well as extensive content detailing the research process.

- Excerpts from Merrill Education texts give your students insights on important topics of instructional methods, diverse populations, assessment, classroom management, technology, and refining classroom practice.

Classroom Practice

- Hundreds of lesson plans and teaching strategies are categorized by content area and age range.

- Case studies and classroom video footage provide virtual field experience for student reflection.

- Computer simulations and other electronic tools keep your students abreast of today's classrooms and current technologies.

- The Educator's Learning Center is a joint website with the Association for Supervision and Curriculum Development (ASCD) and Merrill Education. The site offers a link to Research Navigator for educational journals, articles from the ASCD journal *Educational Leadership,* lesson plans and teaching strategies categorized by content area and age range, excerpts from Merrill education texts on important topics, as well as classroom videos, case studies, and computer simulations. See **www.educatorlearningcenter.com.**

■ LOOK INTO THE VALUE OF EDUCATOR LEARNING CENTER YOURSELF

A four-month subscription to Educator Learning Center is $25 but is FREE when packaged with any Merrill Education text. In order for your students to have access to this site, you must use this special value-pack ISBN number WHEN placing your textbook order with the bookstore: 0-13-168668-2. Your students will then receive a copy of the text packaged with a free ASCD pincode. To preview the value of this website to you and your students, please go to **www.educatorlearningcenter.com** and click on "Demo."

Contents

Note: Every effort has been made to provide accurate and current Internet information in this book. However, the Internet and information posted on it are constantly changing, so it is inevitable that some of the Internet addresses listed in this textbook will change.

Introduction to Teaching and Learning in Middle and Secondary Schools

Part 1 Overview

To prepare you to teach in a middle or secondary school, the two modules of Part 1 will introduce you to the purpose, organization, and structure of our schools at the middle and secondary levels, current re-form efforts, the complex world of students ages 10 to 18, and the plethora of unprecedented diversity you will encounter in today's classrooms. Although this book is designed to explain the practical *know-how* of the teaching and learning process more than the *why*, an understanding of the school context, and the theory behind the *whys*, is necessary to use teaching methods well. Consequently, the two mod-ules of Part 1 review fundamental concepts that serve as a foundation for the selection of instructional strategies. Module 1 provides an overview of middle schools and secondary schools; Module 2 provides an overview of students of those schools and how they best learn. By reading the first two modules, you'll be introduced to the following:

- The issues facing educators in public middle and secondary schools.
- The teaching and learning process.
- The importance of an eclectic teaching style.
- Information about learning styles.
- Guidelines for recognizing and providing for student differences.
- Home, school, and community connections.

Wherever and however the students are housed, and regardless of other responsive practices, in the end it is the dedication, commitment, and nature of the understanding of the involved adults—the teachers, administrators, bus drivers, cooks, grounds crew, security staff, custodial staff, and support personnel—that remains the incisive element that determines an exemplary educational program.

—Joseph F. Callahan,
Leonard H. Clark, and
Richard D. Kellough
(7th edition)

Today's Middle and Secondary Schools: Purpose, Organization, Structure, and Reform

"If we value independence, if we are disturbed by the growing conformity of knowledge, of values, of attitudes, which our present system induces, then we may wish to set up conditions of learning which make for uniqueness, for self-direction, and for self-initiated learning."[1]

—Carl Rogers

Module 1 Overview

In this module we will define secondary schools and discuss the development of high schools, junior high schools, and middle schools. Our reasons for reviewing the milestones in the secondary school movement and the many variables that impact the teaching/learning process are simple: to be a competent teacher, you must not only know *how* schools are designed to facilitate student learning but you must also understand *why* an eclectic teaching style is the best way for you to meet the varied needs of *all* of your students. To accomplish this goal, you need to understand your options. The material in Part 1 provides a basis for selecting the instructional strategies and techniques presented in subsequent modules.

Specific Objectives

At the completion of this module, you should be able to:

- Define and differentiate middle schools and secondary schools.
- Describe similarities and differences between the exemplary middle school and the traditional junior high school.
- Describe the purpose, organization, and structure of the various schools at the secondary and middle school levels.
- Demonstrate an understanding of the importance of an eclectic teaching style.
- Describe current trends, challenges, and issues in public school education in the United States.
- Describe efforts being made by educators to enhance the connections among the home, school, local, and global communities to promote the success of all students.

Introduction

Because schools are microcosms representative of the complexity of the larger society, the rapid and dramatic demographic changes occurring in the United States today are reflected in our middle and secondary schools. In addition, recent discoveries about the teaching and learning process influence our pedagogy. Consequently, the school in which you soon will be teaching most likely will differ dramatically from the secondary school from which you graduated—in its curriculum, its student body, its methods of instruction, or its physical appearance. Before we go any further, let us define what is meant by the term **secondary school.** Then we will briefly review the inception and growth of secondary and middle schools in the United States. We will also highlight the key issues driving the current middle and secondary education reform movements.

MIDDLE AND SECONDARY SCHOOLS

A *secondary school* is any school that houses students in some combination of what traditionally have been known as grades 7 through 12. However, because **middle schools,** which may begin with students in the sixth and even fifth grades, as discussed later in the module, usually house students through the eighth-grade level, we use both terms—*middle school* and *secondary school*—in this book's title and throughout the text. Although covered in detail in foundations courses, we will take a quick look at when and how secondary schools came to be. We will also describe transitional schools by highlighting how junior highs and middle schools differ.

COLONIAL EDUCATION: THE FIRST SCHOOLS

Many of the same issues we currently face in our schools were controversial from the beginning. Although today the separation of church and state in schools is protected by law, religion played a key role in education in colonial New England. The Puritans, having been persecuted for their religious beliefs in England, were determined to secure the power of their church by providing their children with an education grounded in their protestant beliefs.

Education started in the home where parents were responsible for overseeing their children's moral development and teaching them how to read the Bible. As the vocational and other skills young people needed became more specialized, **dame schools** formed.[2] Women, dedicated to teaching reading, writing, and basic math skills, started these schools in their homes where they prepared youngsters for a fee.

After completing one to three years of study, boys would complete an apprenticeship to master a trade. From the beginning, everyone did not benefit from the same educational opportunities—a reality that many claim persists today. One's socioeconomic status determined his or her opportunity; the wealthier the family, the more desirable the apprenticeship the boys could choose. Some efforts to educate the disadvantaged did take place, but they were minimal. Gender differences also existed. After one or two years of reading and writing basics, girls focused on homemaking skills. Race and religion dictated educational opportunity as well. African Americans and Native Americans were prohibited from seeking an education. As more religiously diverse settlers came to the New World, several religious schools were founded so parents could exercise control over their children's religious instruction.

Colonial education varied tremendously. In an effort to standardize the education students received, Massachusetts checked in on masters training apprentices and parents who were homeschooling their children. Once towns grew to more than 50 households, the inhabitants were required by law to hire a teacher. When the town doubled in size, they had to establish a secondary school. Local control determined the curriculum, and property taxes funded the schools.

THE ADVENT OF SECONDARY EDUCATION: THE FORERUNNERS OF TODAY'S HIGH SCHOOLS

The early secondary schools fell into one of three categories: **Latin grammar schools, academies,** and **English classical schools.**[3] The first secondary school was established in Massachusetts, which was also the site of the first elementary school. As mentioned earlier, elementary education in the Colonial Era was limited. Boys of poorer families, females, and nonwhite children had limited educational opportunities. However, for the children of the privileged class who were expected to pursue a university education, attending elementary school was considered inadequate preparation.

Latin Grammar Schools

To meet the needs of these wealthier students, the first secondary schools were founded. In 1635, only 15 years after the Puritans arrived in America, the Boston Latin Grammar School opened. In the Latin grammar schools young boys between 7 and 14 years of age received an education focusing on the classics. During the seven to eight years students spent in these secondary schools, they mastered Latin. After they graduated from one of these prep schools, the students were expected to attend college to pursue a career in politics or the ministry. One year after the Boston Latin Grammar School was founded, Harvard College, America's first college, was established to prepare ministers.[4] As colonies were established along the eastern seaboard and more individuals completed an elementary education, more colleges were established. As a result, more secondary schools were created.

Academies

More than 100 years after the first Latin grammar school was established, a new kind of private secondary school, the academy, opened. The first of its kind, the Franklin Academy, bears the name of its founder, Benjamin Franklin. Established in Philadelphia in 1751, this school's curriculum was free of religious influence and much more practical in its offerings than what the standard Latin grammar school curriculum included. The academies prepared students for a number of fields. Students could select from a variety of courses including such electives as "mathematics, astronomy, athletics, navigation, dramatics, and bookkeeping."[5] These schools charged tuition like the Latin grammar schools, but unlike them, the majority of these private academies welcomed both girls and boys. The academies became very popular, with over 6,000 established. Still there were limited options for children of middle or working class families, and the pursuit of a secondary education often remained a distant dream.

Horace Mann is credited with reforming education and leading the effort to establish formal, free public education for *all* students. He attempted to promote moral development and encourage tolerance by educating the masses, which were representative of tremendous socioeconomic, religious, and ethnic diversity. Although initially it only impacted elementary education, the concept of a free public education spread to **normal schools** (schools designed to prepare teachers for the public elementary schools), and then to secondary schools. Mann believed in a humane, practical education that would better prepare individuals to enter the workforce and participate in a democratic society. The spread of the Common School Movement went hand-in-hand with Westward expansion.[6]

English Classical Schools: The First American Public High Schools

A third secondary school model, the English grammar school, provided a free public education for all students. The English Classical School, later renamed the English High School, first opened in Boston in 1821. These types of high schools offered a practical curriculum including courses in everything from navigation to foreign languages. In fact, boys enrolled in the English grammar schools often studied to become mechanics and merchants. Five years after the boys' school was founded, a public high school for female students was established in the same city, but the girls' high school only remained open for two years. Students were eager to attend, but taxpayers were reluctant to foot the bill.

FUNDING FOR PUBLIC SECONDARY EDUCATION

Most of the other secondary schools that were established throughout the nation in the early 1800s charged tuition and fees, and shared little resemblance to the public secondary schools of this century. Just as the Deluder Satan Act required Massachusetts' residents to financially support elementary education as early as 1647, new legisla-

tion in 1827 required that communities with 500+ families establish publicly funded high schools.[7] With some local financial support, public high schools spread, although slowly at first. By 1860, there were approximately 40 public high schools in the United States. Then in 1874 the Kalamazoo, Michigan Case[8] provided state governments with the ability to levy taxes to support high schools; by 1900, there were over 6,000. Public high schools continued to open; in the 1930s there were approximately four million high school students. By the 1960s, that number increased to over ten million students. Today, there are over 14 million students in America's high schools.[9]

THE CREATION OF JUNIOR HIGH SCHOOLS

Even with an expanded education, all students' needs were not being met by the elementary-secondary school configuration. Although intermediate schools were established on the east coast at the beginning of the 20th century, the first notable junior high school was founded in Berkeley, California, in 1909.[10] Its curriculum resembled the discipline organization of the traditional high schools. In fact, junior highs were established to help prepare students for the academic rigor demanded of them as high school students. Junior high schools, initially housing students in grades seven, eight, and nine, sprang up throughout the country. These in-between schools caught on; by 1930 there were over 2,000 junior highs in the country, and in the 1970s there were over 8,000.[11] Some felt the junior highs were the answer to bridging elementary and high school education, and making the transition of the students "caught in the middle" easier.

THE CREATION OF MIDDLE SCHOOLS

Forty years after the first junior high schools were established, middle schools, created to better meet the unique academic and psychosocial needs of pre- and early adolescents, gained popularity. Schools at the middle level, between elementary and secondary schools, have a specialized mission, structure, and organization. Middle schools expanded the seventh- to ninth-grade span of the junior high schools to include fifth and sixth graders. When the awarding of Carnegie Units became a popular way to determine credit earned toward graduation from high school, the ninth-grade link to grades 10 to 12 was emphasized.[12]

Some combination of grades five through eight, interdisciplinary teaching teams, integrated curriculum, age-appropriate student-centered instructional strategies, block scheduling, and teacher advising programs are the foundation of the middle school philosophy

TABLE 1.1	Summary of Differences Between Junior High Schools and Middle Schools	
	Junior High School	**Middle School**
Most common grade span	7–8 or 7–9	6–8
Scheduling	Traditional	Flexible, usually block
Subject organization	Departmentalized	Integrated and thematic; interdisciplinary; usually language arts, math, science, and social studies
Guidance/counseling	Separate advising by full-time counselor on individual or "as-needed" basis	Advisor-advisee relationship between teacher and student within a home base or homeroom
Exploratory curriculum	Electives by individual choice	Common "wheel" of experiences for all students
Teachers	Subject-centered; grades 7–12 certification	Interdisciplinary teams; student-centered; grades K–8 or 6–8 certification
Instruction	Traditional; lecture; skills and repetition	Thematic units; discovery techniques; "learning how to learn" study skills
Athletics	Interscholastic sports emphasizing competition	Intramural programs emphasizing participation

and characterize today's middle schools. Middle schools were designed to nurture students' developmental needs by providing a community atmosphere and helping them to make a smooth transition between elementary and secondary school. Debates continue as to whether middle grade schooling should focus on the students' academic or affective development. While many agree that we need to nurture adolescent well-being, raising the level of academic performance remains the key focus.[13] (See Table 1.1.)

THE CHANGING PURPOSE OF EDUCATION

The primary role of high schools has been disputed for years. Although today as a nation we aspire to provide all children with equal educational opportunities so they can reach their social and academic potential, this egalitarian philosophy has not always been embraced by everyone.

Schools evolved as our nation developed. The changing social milieu, cultural context, political climate, and economic reality of the United States impacted the secondary school movement. The nature and aims of education have evolved as have our ideas about the best way to organize and structure schools.

Schooling in the Colonial Era sought to support moral development and encourage adherence to religious doctrine, while securing social stability.[14] From the beginning, the reality of differentiated educational opportunities prevailed. The inception of public secondary schools addressed the needs of a very diverse student body—students from a variety of ethnic heritages, religious backgrounds, and socioeconomic realities.

In the 1800s schooling focused on preparing students for the changing economy. Educating only the elite and focusing exclusively on religious instruction was replaced with a more equitable approach and practical application. As we shifted from an agrarian nation to an industrialized economy, our young nation needed better trained work-

ers. To meet the needs of a diverse student body, **comprehensive high schools** offered college preparatory, general, vocational, and agricultural tracks. The high schools of the 20th century, by promoting social harmony and emphasizing citizenry, sought to Americanize the great waves of immigrants by preparing them to participate in our democratic society and helping them to assimilate into the dominant culture.

Some see the current purpose of secondary education as preparing students for work. They believe contemporary high schools should prepare students for a knowledge-driven interdependent global economy.[15] Others believe that a high school curriculum should prepare students for postsecondary education. Although the purpose of school is still debated, there is agreement that serious challenges face our educational system. The growing number of students who are unsuccessful in our schools is of great concern. The achievement gap between wealthy and poor students and white and nonwhite students appears to be widening once again. The disparity in academic performance is alarming.[16] Elliot W. Eisner believes that in order for schools to address this key issue, we have to question several assumptions regarding the education system in this country. Because we are all products of our educational system and our secondary schools are steeped in tradition, transforming high schools is very challenging. Eisner asserts, "Schools have a special difficulty in changing their nature. Part of this difficulty stems from the fact that all of us have served an apprenticeship in them—and from an early age. Indeed, teaching is the only profession I know in which professional socialization begins at age 5 or 6. Students, even those of so tender an age, learn what it takes to 'do school'."[17]

Still, many believe that democratic equality can be realized through educational opportunity and support a free and appropriate education for all children in this nation. Education is seen as the great equalizer; for many, obtaining an education is equated with changing one's economic reality.[18] Next we will highlight some of the more meaningful secondary school reform efforts designed to promote educational equity.

■ REFORM INITIATIVES

Currently there are several reform initiatives in place in America's middle and secondary schools. Some focus on a *policy-oriented approach* while others promote a *student-centered approach.* Both approaches have their strengths and weaknesses. Aligning *content standards* with the curricula and utilizing *high-stakes testing* are variables associated with the policy-oriented approach. Those advocating a student-centered approach suggest, as a starting point, the downsizing of schools in order to cultivate learning environments where students can be nurtured, and as a result thrive.[19] Current reform has focused on the dismantling of large high schools and the creation of smaller, more intimate learning environments. The Bill and Melinda Gates Foundation, Carnegie, Brode, Annenberg, and other philanthropic organizations have been supporting smaller high schools.[20] Small secondary schools that combat the feelings of anonymity that permeate our larger schools have made a big difference in narrowing the achievement gap. One of the nation's largest school districts in New York City is phasing out its lowest-performing high schools and replacing them with smaller schools.[21]

There are two kinds of reform: *systemic reform* and *superficial change.* The former focuses on the most comprehensive school reform and seeks to positively impact all aspects of a school's culture. Systemic local reform efforts usually involve the teachers, administrators, staff, students, parents, and even the greater community in the decision-making process.[22] Involving all of the key players results in greater buy-in, and as a result, systemic reform programs are usually successful, significant, and long-lasting. However, reform efforts generated from a top-down management initiative rarely produce meaningful, sustainable change.

The 40 national organizations that make up the *National High School Alliance* reported that there are many challenges to realizing school reform.[23] The recent formation of *The National Forum to Accelerate Middle Grades Reform* has brought a variety of these issues to the forefront.[24] The effort of trying to reform and restructure the school has been compared to trying to rebuild a jetliner while it's in flight.[25] The challenges have multiplied through the years, but the goal remains consistent: reforming schools to benefit students.

■ EARLY REFORM EFFORTS

From their inception, secondary schools varied greatly. To address this inconsistency, in 1892 the *National Education Association (NEA)* presented the *Committee of Ten,* with the task of establishing a uniform policy for high schools that could be implemented nationally. The college presidents and professors that served on the Committee of Ten sought to standardize the secondary curriculum. Committee consensus identified the purpose of high school as preparation of gifted students (wealthy white males for the most part) for university study. Therefore, the Committee's recommendations promoted a traditional curriculum focusing on the classics; electives were to be kept to a minimum.

In almost every decade since the Committee of Ten published their report back in the late 1800s, several task forces have been formed to evaluate the current state of affairs in public school education and propose recommendations. In 1918, the NEA established a more diverse committee including education professors, high school administrators, and classroom teachers to evaluate the high schools. Unlike the Committe of Ten, which focused on the elite few destined to earn a university degree, these evaluators focused on the needs of the majority of students who would most likely be ending their academic pursuits after high school. They proposed a curriculum that would help high school graduates become self-sufficient, happy, moral citizens in an industrialized economy.

The *comprehensive high school* resulted from the National Education Association's Commission report in 1918. Because there was great debate over whether high schools should offer a college preparatory curriculum or a vocational track, the Commission recommended offering both under the umbrella term *comprehensive high school.* This focus on offering a varied curriculum to meet students' differing needs remains popular today. Comprehensive high schools became popular in the 1940s and 1950s when the curriculum was expanded to include a variety of electives and vocational programs. Despite the growing popularity of the progressive education movement, most high schools remained unchanged in the decade following World War II except for the expansion of the vocational and general curriculum offerings. This focus was redirected when the 1983 National Commission on Educational Excellence published their report. It claimed we were lagging behind other nations in science, math, technology, and business. The push to raise our students' level of performance in these disciplines continues today.

■ GOALS 2000

Since the 1980s, education reform efforts have been national in scope. In 1989, then-President George Bush convened all the governors to discuss the state of education. They developed educational standards and proposed six national education goals known as Education 2000. Under President Clinton these goals were modified and became **Goals 2000.** According to the expecta-

TABLE 1.2	**Summary of Goals 2000: Educate America Act**

"By the Year 2000—

1. All children in America will start school ready to learn.

2. The high school graduation rate will increase to at least 90 percent.

3. All students will leave grades 4, 8, and 12 having demonstrated competency over challenging subject matter including English, mathematics, science, foreign languages, civics and government, economics, the arts, history, and geography, and every school in America will ensure that all students learn to use their minds well, so they may be prepared for responsible citizenship, further learning, and productive employment in our nation's modern economy.

4. United States students will be first in the world in mathematics and science achievement.

5. Every adult American will be literate and will possess the knowledge and skills necessary to compete in a global economy and exercise the rights and responsibilities of citizenship.

6. Every school in the United States will be free of drugs, violence, and the unauthorized presence of firearms and alcohol and will offer a disciplined environment conducive to learning.

7. The nation's teaching force will have access to programs for the continued improvement of their professional skills and the opportunity to acquire the knowledge and skills needed to instruct and prepare all American students for the next century.

8. Every school will promote partnerships that will increase parental involvement and participation in promoting the social, emotional, and academic growth of children."

NOTE: President Clinton signed the original six goals of Goals 2000: Educate America Act into law on March 31, 1994. The last two goals were added later.

SOURCE: U.S. Department of Education. See http://www.ncrel.org/sdrs/areas/issues/envrnmnt/stw/sw0goals.htm

tions, all of America's students were to meet each of the six goals by the beginning of the 21st century. Although 2000 came and went and we were unsuccessful in meeting the guidelines laid out in Goals 2000, this reform effort initiated a critical analysis of the education system. As a result, national and state content standards have been developed for the core curricular areas as well as for all the other disciplines. For a summary of the National Education Goals outlined in Goals 2000: Educate America Act (P.L. 103–277), see Table 1.2.

■ NO CHILD LEFT BEHIND

On January 8, 2002, the **No Child Left Behind (NCLB)** Act became law. This landmark legislation promised to improve student achievement and change the culture of America's schools while providing educational opportunity for all students. President George W. Bush's education reform was built on four common pillars: accountability, scientific research, parental options, and local control and flexibility. This reform effort focused on performance standards and was intended to measure how well students meet the content standards laid out in previous reform efforts.

■ REFORMING MIDDLE SCHOOLS

One of the national goals laid out in the No Child Left Behind Act of 2002 mandates increasing student performance. The legislation requires that by 2014, all students completing eighth grade achieve academic proficiency.[26] In the past decade the founders of the National Forum to Accelerate Middle School Reform and other middle school supporters have advocated substantive systemic reform and recommend increased academic achieve-

ment of middle school students. In order to realize this goal, we continue to examine and modify the organization and structure of our middle and secondary schools.

■ TODAY'S MIDDLE AND SECONDARY SCHOOLS

Let's start by describing the current state of education. During the 2001–2002 academic year, there were a total of 94,112 public elementary and secondary schools in operation across the United States. According to the National Center for Education Statistics, in the fall of 2001 the K–12 public and private schools served a record 54 million students. That marked a 19% increase from 1988 to 2001. The increase in the number of students in grades 9 to 12 during the same timeframe was 17%. Between 2001 and 2013 the total enrollment is expected to climb another 5% and the 9 to 12 enrollment is projected to increase by 4%. Middle schools, ranging from grades four to nine, made up 17% of the 2001 total student population. Migration within the country, immigration (both legal and illegal), and high birth rates are cited as the key factors affecting the increase.[27]

■ ORGANIZING EDUCATION TO MEET STUDENTS' NEEDS

■ Organization

The organization of schools varies greatly throughout the United States. In an attempt to best meet the needs of their youth, communities have organized their schools in a variety of ways. Some districts adhere to an elementary, secondary model 6+6 (six years of elementary school and six years of secondary school) organizational plan. Others follow an elementary, middle, and high school 6+3+3 (six years of elementary school, three years of middle school, and three years of secondary school) or a 5+3+4, or a 6+2+4 configuration. Next, we will discuss how different communities choose to organize schools and the impact the organization has on its students.

The Middle School Concept and Philosophy

Exemplary middle schools, as shown in Table 1.1, are quite different from the traditional junior high schools. To understand the significance of what has become known as the middle school concept, certain background information may prove helpful.

As mentioned earlier, reasons for the reorganization away from the concept of junior high school and the adoption of a middle school education included: to provide a program specifically designed for children in this age group, to set up a better transition between the elementary school and the high school, and to move grade 9 to the high school or, as has happened in some school districts in recent years, to a location designed solely for ninth graders, known as a *ninth-grade center*.[28,29]

Although any combination of grades five through nine may be included in a middle school, the most common configuration is grades six through eight. The trend of including sixth graders and excluding ninth graders is a reflection of the recommendation of the National Middle School Association in its official position paper, *This We Believe*.[30] The trend continues. For example, in California grades six to eight are now the most common grade span included in middle schools in that state.

The term *middle level education* identifies school organizations based on a philosophy that incorporates curricula and instructional practices specifically designed to meet the needs of youngsters between the ages of 10 and 14. This philosophy is often referred to as the *middle school concept*. The notion that greater and more specific attention should be given to the special needs of young adolescents became known as the *middle school movement*. Basic to the movement is the belief that middle school teachers need specialized training to work most effectively with young adolescents.

Middle Schools and Junior High Schools

When you receive your state teaching credentials, you may or may not be certified to teach at the middle school level. In some states a secondary school credential certifies a person to teach a particular subject at any grade level, K through 12. In other states such a credential qualifies a person to teach only grades 7 through 12. At least 33 states provide a middle school teaching credential to candidates who have successfully completed a program specifically designed to prepare teachers for that level.

Organizational Provisions for Student Differences

Today there continues to be an attempt to provide different types of schools for persons with different needs or aspirations. The secondary level includes comprehensive high schools, ninth-grade centers, middle schools, and junior high schools.

A school might be called a **magnet school,** that is, a school that specializes in a particular academic area. For example, Austin High School for Teaching Professions (Houston, TX) specializes in preparing students for the teaching professions; Murry Bergtraum High School (New York, NY) for business careers; Chicago High School (Chicago, IL) for the Agricultural Sciences; and Renaissance High School (Detroit, MI) emphasizes college admissions for all its graduates. Still other magnet schools may specialize in the visual and performing arts, science, mathematics and technology, or in language and international studies. For example, in Norwalk, Connecticut, the Center for Japanese Study Abroad (CJSA) is a magnet program that allows students in a house program for grades 9 to 12 at Brien McMahon High School to become proficient in Japanese language through an interdisciplinary Japanese studies curriculum that includes economics, literature, arts, and music and to obtain firsthand knowledge of the Japanese culture through a two-week experience in Japan.[31]

A school might also be a *comprehensive college preparatory high school*. Other options are (a) a **fundamental school,** that is, a school that specializes in teaching basic skills; (b) a **charter school,** that is, a school that is "an autonomous educational entity operating under a charter, or contract, that has been negotiated between the organizers, who create and operate the school, and a sponsor, who oversees the provisions of the charter"[32]; (c) a **for-profit school,** a public school that is operated by a for-profit company; (d) a **partnership school,** that is, a school that has entered into a partnership agreement with community business and industry to link school studies with the workplace;[33] (e) a **tech prep high school,** that is, one that has a 4–2 coordinated curriculum that is articulated from grades 9 to 12 to the first two years of college, leading to an associate of applied science degree;[34] (f) a **full-service school,** a school that serves as a hub for quality education and comprehensive social services, all under one roof;[35] (g) an **International Baccalaureate School** with a curriculum approved by the International Baccalaureate Organization (IBO), a worldwide nonprofit educational foundation founded in the 1960s and based in Switzerland;[36] (h) a **special transitional school** such as New York City's Liberty High School, a one-year school designed to help recent immigrant students feel welcome and self-assured and to succeed in learning to read and write in English.[37] It might also be a *private school*, a *church-affiliated school*, or a *continuation* or *alternative high school*.[38] Or perhaps it might be another type or a combination of these, such as a *for-profit charter school* or a *charter-magnet-fundamental school*. Although in different ways and with various terminology, the historical practice of providing different routes for students with different needs and different vocational and academic aspirations continues.

■ Curriculum Tracks and Homogeneous Grouping

Some school systems, especially large urban systems, provide different schools for youths planning for different vocations. In most school systems, though, offering a variety of curricula in comprehensive high schools accommodates these differences. By providing a judicious selection of courses, students can prepare themselves for entrance to a four-year college or university or for a specific vocation that may include a continuing postsecondary education vocational program. Such a choice of curricula is probably the most common administrative or organizational means of providing for individual differences at the high school level. Although a student's choice of a curriculum may begin in middle school or junior high school, it usually becomes apparent at the high school level.

Traditionally, and still today, many high schools are organized on the basis of the demonstrated ability of students. For instance, a school may provide one sequence for honors students, a second sequence for college-preparatory students, a third sequence for general students, and a fourth sequence for academically challenged or seemingly unmotivated students. These different sequences—sometimes called *tracks*—may differ from one another in difficulty and complexity of subject content, rate of student progress, and methods of instruction.

As traditionally practiced, ability grouping, or **tracking,** is the assignment of students to curriculum and class groups based on evidence of academic ability. Grouping and tracking do not seem to increase overall achievement of learning, but they do promote inequity. Although many research studies conclude that tracking should be discontinued because of its discriminatory and damaging effects on students, many schools continue using it, either directly, by counseling students into classes according to evidence of ability and the degree of academic rigor of the program, or indirectly, by designating certain classes and programs as *college prep* and others as *noncollege prep* and allowing students some degree of latitude to choose.

Tracks are, in effect, a type of homogeneous grouping. Homogeneous groups are formed by dividing stu-

dents into class sections according to some criterion or a combination of criteria. Usually the criteria include a combination of motivation and prior academic success. Other criteria are educational-vocational goals (e.g., business English or college-preparatory English) or just interest. In any case, the reasons for forming homogeneous groups are to provide for the differences in students and to make teaching more efficient and perhaps easier. Theoretically, when classes are grouped homogeneously, teachers can more easily select content and methods that are suitable for all students in that group.

In some instances and to some degree, tracking according to proven ability and interests works. For example, when all the students in an advanced mathematics class are interested, motivated, and self-confident (and have similar learning capacities, styles of learning, and modality preferences), teaching them is no doubt easier. And finding content, textbooks, and methods suitable for everyone in a class is also easier if the group is homogeneous in these respects. Nevertheless, homogeneous grouping as discussed here is not necessarily the answer to the challenge of addressing individual student differences.

In the first place, homogeneous groups are not truly homogeneous; they are merely attempts to make groups similar, according to certain criteria. All that homogeneous grouping does is to reduce the heterogeneity of classes, making certain aspects of providing for individual differences in students a bit more manageable.

Whatever the advantages of homogeneous grouping, this organizational scheme also has several built-in problems. One occurs when the teacher assumes that all class members are the same. In classes grouped according to demonstrated ability and interest, the range of proven academic ability may be reduced, but the range of interest, ambitions, motivations, and goals is probably just as wide as in any other class. No matter how much a school attempts to homogenize classes—and no matter what plan of grouping is used—you as the teacher will always face the necessity of attending to and providing for individual student differences.

Another very real problem of traditional ability grouping is that students of the less academically rigorous courses may get shortchanged, with little expected of them and with little for them to do. Furthermore, these students have little opportunity to interact with and to learn from their more motivated or more educationally advantaged peers. Students can learn a great deal from one another. When this opportunity for interaction is not provided, classes for the less-motivated and educationally disadvantaged students become educational ghettos. If there is anything that has been learned in recent years, it is that there is no student in a public school who cannot learn when given the proper learning environment, opportunity, and encouragement.

STRUCTURING SCHOOLS TO MEET STUDENTS' NEEDS

The Structure of Middle Schools and High Schools

We begin our quest for understanding how schools are structured by presenting some of the more significant characteristics of today's middle and secondary schools. First we will describe the school calendar year. Next we will look at a typical school day, school start times, teaching teams, and scheduling variations.

The School Calendar Year

Conventional and **year-round school** years vary from state to state, from district to district, and from school to school. Most school years begin in mid- to late August or early September and continue through late May or mid-June. However, to accommodate more students without a significant increase in capital costs and to better sustain student learning, an increasing number of schools are eliminating the traditional long summer break by switching to *year-round education* (YRE), which, by the way, has been around for more than half a century.[39] Whether or not the school follows a year-round schedule, the school year still approximates 180 days for teachers and students in the United States.

Although experts are not in agreement as to how negatively a shortened school year impacts achievement, it is interesting to note that the United States has a shorter school year than many other nations. The following is a list of approximate school days per year in several countries: Japan, 243; West Germany, 240; South Korea, 220; Luxembourg and Israel, 216; Soviet Union, 211; Netherlands, Scotland, and Thailand, 200; Hong Kong, 195; England/Wales and Hungary, 192; Switzerland, 191; Nigeria and Finland, 190; Ontario and France, 185; Ireland, 184; New Brunswick, 182; Quebec, Spain, and the United States, 180; French Belgium, 175; and Flemish Belgium, 160.[40]

In a school with year-round education, a teacher might teach for three-quarters of the year and be off for one-quarter or teach in a 45/15 program, which means nine weeks of school (45 days) "on track" followed by three weeks of school (15 days) "off track" throughout the year. Nearly 70% of YRE schools use the 45/15 plan.[41] In 45/15 arrangements, teachers and students are on tracks, referred to as A track, B track, and so on, with starting and ending times that vary depending on the track and time of year. At any one time there is always at least one track on vacation. "Intersession" programs may be held during off-track time, at which time students might participate in short classes specifically planned for remediation or enrichment.

The School Day

The regular school day begins about 8:00 A.M. and lasts until about 3:00 P.M. In addition to this regular school day, there may be special earlier starting and later ending classes and cocurricular activities. District and state laws vary, but generally teachers are expected to be in the classroom no less than 15 minutes prior to the start of school and to remain in their classrooms no less than 15 minutes after final dismissal of students. Many teachers engage in a variety of other activities or have other commitments, responsibilities, or duties that require them to spend several additional hours per week on the school campus.

Nonstandard Daily Starting Times

Some schools are experimenting with modified starting times, drawing upon studies of adolescent sleep patterns as well as the need to find ways to deal with crowded schools or to cut transportation expenses by reducing the number of busses and drivers needed.[42] For example, a school might not even begin classes until around 9:30 A.M. or midmorning. Or a school might schedule activities or classes such as the visual and performing arts and physical education first, in early morning, to be followed by classes dealing with the core curriculum subjects. Or to allow for adolescent sleep patterns and work schedules, a school may give students the option of attending early day classes or late afternoon and evening classes. Some schools offer a *zero period* where classes meet before the standard bell schedule, sometimes as early as 6:30 A.M.

Teaching Teams

Traditionally, junior and senior high school teachers have taught their subjects five or six times each day, in their own classrooms and fairly isolated from other teachers and school activities. In many schools, that is still the case. Increasingly, however, both middle school and secondary school teachers are finding themselves members of a collaborative **teaching team** in which several teachers from different discipline areas work together to plan the curriculum for a common group of students.

(**Note:** A distinction must be made between *teaching teams* and **team teaching.** Team teaching refers to two or more teachers simultaneously providing instruction to students in the same classroom. Members of a teaching team may participate in team teaching.)

There are several variations on team teaching. Two or more teachers may choose to split the instructional time in many ways. Maybe they share the class time and each instructor is responsible for part of the instruction, maybe they alternate days and/or meetings, or maybe both teachers are present for all class meetings and provide their unique discipline perspective on everything.

The teaching team may comprise only a few teachers, such as high school teachers who teach the same group of eleventh-grade students in English and in world history; they may meet periodically to plan a curriculum and learning activities around a common theme, such as the Elizabethan Era. Often, especially in middle schools, teaching teams comprise one teacher each from English/ language arts, mathematics, science, and history/social studies. These four subject areas are known as the **core curriculum.** In addition to the core-subject teachers, specialty-area teachers may be part of the teaching team, including teachers of physical education, the visual and performing arts, and even special education teachers and at-risk specialty personnel or school counselors. In addition, some teams may invite a community-resource person to be a member. Because the core and specialty subjects cross different disciplines of study, these teams are commonly called **interdisciplinary teaching teams** or simply **interdisciplinary teams.**

■ The School-Within-a-School (SWAS) Concept

As mentioned earlier, the current trend is to personalize schools. There are several strategies for making large schools feel more welcoming. Separate and autonomous units known as **schools-within-a-school** have proven effective in diminishing the isolation students often experience in bigger schools. The Adams Ninth Grade Campus at McMinnville High School in Oregon is an example of a small group functioning within a larger school. Ninth graders spend their mornings taking core curriculum courses and eating lunch in their separate food court before joining the other high school students on the main campus in the afternoon. An interdisciplinary teaching team and its common group of students can be thought of as a school-within-a-school (also referred to as a *village, pod, learning family, academy,* or *house*), where each team of teachers is assigned each day to the same cohort of students for a common block of time. Within this block of time, teachers on the team are responsible for the many professional decisions necessary, such as how school can be made *developmentally responsive,* or most meaningful, to students' lives; what specific responsibilities each teacher has each day; what guidance activities need to be implemented; which accommodations should be made to meet the special needs of students; and how students will be grouped for instruction. Members of such a team get to know their students well and thereby build the curriculum and instruction around their students' interests, perspectives, and perceptions. Because they "turn on" learning, the school and its classrooms become exciting places to be in and to learn in. (In contrast, "symptoms of turned-off learning include students' seeming inabilities to grasp concepts, to exert effort, or to display enthusiasm; repeated late-

ness or absence; boredom; and work that is sloppy or of poor quality.")[43]

The SWAS concept helps students make important and meaningful connections among disciplines. It also provides them with both peer and adult group identification, which provides an important sense of belonging. In some schools, such as Quest High School (Humble, TX), Gnarly High School (Norfolk, VA), and Celebration School (Celebration, FL), using an arrangement called **looping,** the cohort of students and teachers remain together as a group for several or for all the years a student is at that school.[44]

The advantages of being a member of a teaching team in a SWAS environment are numerous. For example, the combined thinking of several teachers creates an expanded pool of ideas, enhances individual capacities for handling complex problems, and provides intellectual stimulation and emotional support. The synergism of talents produces an energy that has a positive impact on the instructional program. A beginning teacher who joins a team has the benefit of support from more experienced teammates. More and better planning for students occurs as teachers discuss, argue, and reach agreement on behavioral expectations, curriculum emphasis, instructional approaches, and materials.

■ Teacher's Daily Schedules

For many middle school and secondary school teachers, the school day consists of the traditional seven or eight periods; each period lasts about 40 to 50 minutes. This traditional schedule includes teaching three or four classes before lunch and three or four following lunch. One period each day is reserved as a *preparation* or *prep period,* referred to sometimes as the *conference* or *planning period.* When a teacher's preparation period falls during either the first or the final period of the day—or just before or after lunch—the teacher is still expected to be present on the campus during that time in order to be available for conferences with students, parents, guardians, counselors, other teachers, or administrators. Most teachers are quite busy during their preparation periods, reading and grading student papers, preparing class materials, meeting in conferences, or preparing for use of media equipment. Sometimes, this is a period when the teacher may prefer to sit and relax over a cup of tea or coffee, perhaps in the pleasant surroundings of the faculty lounge.

■ Common Planning Time for Interdisciplinary Teams

For an interdisciplinary teaching team to plan most effectively and efficiently, members must meet together frequently. This is best accomplished when they share a *common planning time,* preferably no fewer than four hours each week. This means that in addition to each member's preparation period, members of a team share a common planning time to plan curriculum and to discuss the progress and needs of the students within their cohort.[45]

Each teaching team assigns a member to be a *team facilitator* or lead teacher. The lead teacher organizes the meetings and facilitates discussions during the common planning time. Usually, this person also acts as a liaison with the administration in order to ensure that the team has the necessary resources to put its plans into action. A team's lead teacher (or another member designated by the team) may also serve on the *school leadership team*, a group of teachers and administrators, and sometimes students, designated by the principal or elected by the faculty (and student body) to assist in the leadership of the school. Sometimes, in lieu of a traditional site principal, the school leadership team is the leadership for the school.[46]

■ Nontraditional Scheduling

To maximize the learning time, to allow for more instructional flexibility, and to accommodate common planning time for teachers, many schools are using some form of **block scheduling.** Block scheduling means that, for at least part of the school day, or part of the week, blocks of time ranging from 70 to 140 or more minutes replace the traditional structure of the seven- or eight-period day with 40- to 50-minute-long class periods. The possible variations are nearly limitless.

For example, the school year in some schools consists of three 12-week trimesters, and each school day is divided into five 70-minute-long class periods. Such a schedule is referred to as a 5 × 7 *block plan.* Some schools use a 4 × 4 *block plan*, whereby students take four 85- to 90-minute-long *macroperiods* (or *macroclasses*) each day, each semester.[47] Other schools use an A–B, or *alternating day*, block plan, where classes meet every other day for the entire school year for 90-minute blocks.[48]

Using *macroperiods* lengthens the time each day that students are in a course, thereby simultaneously reducing the number of courses taken at one time. The macroperiod allows the teacher to supervise and assist students with assignments and project work and with their reading, writing, thinking, and study skills. Macroperiods provide more time for interactive and interdisciplinary thematic instruction that might otherwise be difficult or impossible to accomplish in shorter class periods.

■ Block Scheduling: Advantages and Disadvantages

Reported advantages of schools using block scheduling includes (a) greater satisfaction among teachers and administrators and (b) improvement in both the behavior and the learning of all students, regardless of ability level, attitude toward school, and degree of school success. Teachers get to know the students better and are there-

fore able to respond to a student's needs with greater care. Consequently, students do more writing, pursue issues in greater depth, enjoy classes more, feel more challenged, and gain deeper understandings.

In evaluating schools using block scheduling, researchers have found more course credits completed, equal or better mastery and retention of content, and a significant reduction in discipline problems and dropout rates. Other reported benefits of the block plans are: In one school year the total hours of instruction are significantly greater; each teacher teaches and is responsible for fewer courses during a semester and is responsible for fewer students; student-teacher interaction is more productive and the school climate is positive, with fewer discipline problems; because planning periods are longer, there is more time for teachers to plan and to interact with parents; and more students can take advanced placement (AP) classes.[49]

There are also benefits to taxpayers. During one school year teachers teach more courses and potentially more students, thereby decreasing the number of faculty needed. In addition, fewer textbooks are needed. For example, instead of all sophomores taking history for an entire year, half of them take it the first semester and half the second, thereby reducing the number of textbooks needed by one-half.

The reduction of bells ringing from as many as eight times a day to perhaps only two or three times a day or not at all creates less disturbance. Because students are not roaming halls for three to five minutes five or six times a day, teachers can more easily supervise unstructured time and thereby have better control over portions of the unplanned and subtle message systems within schools, referred to as the *hidden curriculum.* The messages of the hidden curriculum are the school climate, the feelings projected from the teacher and other adults to students and from the students to one another, not only in classrooms but before and after school, at social events, and in the halls, restrooms, and other areas of the school that are not monitored as closely as the individual classrooms.

Nontraditional school schedules are not without their problems. Problems that sometimes arise from block scheduling are: Content coverage in a course may be less than that which was traditionally covered; there may be a mismatch between content coverage and that expected by state-mandated tests and the dates those tests are given to students; when absent a day from school, a student will miss more in a subject area; and community relations problems may occur, such as when students are out of school and off campus at nontraditional times.

Some schools have successfully used *modified block schedules*, thus satisfying teachers who prefer scheduling and those who prefer a traditional schedule. A modified block schedule can provide both traditional 40-minute periods (sometimes called *split-block periods*) that meet daily (sometimes preferred, especially by teachers of mathematics[50] and foreign languages) and longer blocks. A modified block schedule centers on a seven or eight 45- or 40-minutes-per-period day along with alternate longer blocks. In a modified block schedule all students might start the day with a 30- or 40-minute-long first period, which serves as a homeroom or advisor/advisee time. From there, some students continue the morning attending traditional-length periods while others may move into a morning block class. Throughout the day, teachers and students may pass from block classes to those of traditional length or vice versa.

Some schools use a *flexible block schedule*, such as the following sample. The daily schedule is a seven-period day with all seven classes meeting on Monday. Periods one through four meet for 75 minutes, while periods five through seven meet for 30 minutes. On Tuesdays and Thursdays, periods one through four meet for 105 minutes each, and on Wednesdays and Fridays, periods five through seven meet for 120 minutes each. A 30-minute period after lunch allows students to attend club meetings or pep rallies, to make up tests, or to receive guidance and counseling or tutorial help. In short, there is little doubt that longer blocks of instructional time with students are a positive factor contributing to students' meaningful learning, especially when combined with some form of year-round education, the use of interdisciplinary thematic instruction, and the elimination of curriculum tracking.

MODIFYING THE CURRICULUM TO FACILITATE STUDENT LEARNING

Striving to Present Quality Education for All Students

Nontraditional scheduling is part of the effort to restructure schools to deliver quality learning opportunities to all students. The students of a *quality education school* see the relevancy in what they are learning to their lives. A quality school provides a stimulating learning environment.

Sometimes it may appear that more energy is devoted to organizational change (*how* the curriculum is delivered) than to school curriculum (*what* is taught). School organization has a direct effect on what students learn; if it didn't, educators wouldn't be spending so much valuable time trying to restructure their schools to effect the most productive (and cost-effective) delivery of the curriculum.

School restructuring has been defined as "activities that change fundamental assumptions, practices, and relationships, both within the organization and between the organization and the outside world, in ways leading to improved learning outcomes."[51]

Exemplified by efforts mentioned in the preceding discussions, the movement to year-round education and the redesigning of schools into "houses" represents a movement that is becoming increasingly common across the country. With this redesign, the intention is that

- Advisory programs and adult advocacy relationships for every student.
- Allowing a student to attend a high school class while still in middle school or to attend college classes while still in high school.[52]
- Allowing a student to skip a traditional grade level.
- Community service learning.
- Cooperative learning in the classroom.
- Curriculum compacting.
- High expectations for all students.
- Integrating new technologies into the curriculum.
- Interdisciplinary teaming and thematic instruction.
- Mid-year promotions.
- Multiage grouping.
- Peer and cross-age teaching.
- Problem-centered learning.
- Second opportunity recovery strategies.
- Specialized schools and flexible block scheduling.
- Student-centered projects within-class and across discipline.

FIGURE 1.1 ● Multiple Pathways to Success: Productive Ways of Attending to Student Differences, of Providing a More Challenging Learning Environment, and of Stimulating the Talents and Motivation of Each Student

schools will better address the needs and capabilities of each unique student. To that end, a number of specific trends are shown later in this Module in Figure 1.6.

Providing Challenging Curriculum Options

Consequently, the trend in public schools is to replace both what traditionally were known as general curriculum and the low-level curriculum tracks with more challenging, rigorous, and meaningful curriculum options (see Figure 1.1). For example, dedicated to the premise that all students can learn, Souderton Area High School (Souderton, PA) eliminated its general curriculum track, raised standards for graduation from 17 to 23 credits, and required all students to take four years of mathematics, science, language arts, and social studies. Just five years after making those changes, students' failure rate had dropped from 10% to 3%, suspensions from school declined by 60%, and average daily attendance of students increased from 87% to 93%.[53] With its commitment to higher expectations for all students, Lee County High School (Beattyville, KY) replaced its general track with an integrated curriculum that emphasizes active learning, includes continuous reinforcement of academic content with vocational application, and offers ongoing career planning and preparation with an advisory system to guide students to high achievement.[54] And, at Colonial High School (Orlando, FL), *all* ninth graders start their portfolios that include career assessments and programs of study that lead to enrollment in a postsecondary education program.[55]

■ EMBRACING STUDENT DIVERSITY TO MEET STUDENTS' NEEDS

■ At-Risk Students

The term *at-risk* is used to identify students who have a high probability of not finishing school. Researchers have identified five categories of factors that cause a young person to be at risk of dropping out of school. These categories are personal pain (exemplified by drugs, physical and psychological abuse, suspension from school), academic failure (exemplified by low grades, failure, absences, low self-esteem), family tragedy (exemplified by parent illness or death, health problems), family socioeconomic situation (exemplified by low income, negativism, lack of education), and family instability (exemplified by moving, separation, divorce).[56] Many students experience risk factors from more than one of these categories. A modified school schedule alone, without quality individualized attention to each student, may not be enough to address the needs of students who are at risk of not completing school. It has been estimated that by the year 2020, the majority of students in American public schools will be at risk.[57]

■ Responsive Practices for Helping All Students Succeed in School

Because of the enormous diversity of students, the advantage of using a combination of practices concurrently is the best way to help all students succeed in school. The reorganization of schools and the restructuring of school schedules, then, represent only two aspects of efforts to help all students make successful transitions.[58]

Other important responsive practices (including attitudes) are (a) a perception, shared by all teachers and staff, that all students can learn when they are given adequate support, although not all students need the same amount of time to learn the same thing; (b) high, although not necessarily identical, expectations for all students; (c) personalized and individualized attention, adult advocacy, scheduling, and learning plans to help students learn in a manner by which they best learn—research clearly points out that achievement increases, students learn more, and students enjoy learning and remember more of what they have learned when individual learning styles and capacities are identified and accommodated; (d) engagement of parents and guardians as partners in their child's education; (e) extra time and guided attention to basic skills—such as those of thinking, writing, and reading—rather than on rote memory; (f) specialist teachers and smaller classes; (g) peer tutoring and cross-age coaching; and (h) attention and guidance in the development of coping skills.

■ PREPARING TEACHERS TO TEACH IN A DIVERSE CLASSROOM

■ The Fundamental Characteristic of Exemplary Education

Wherever and however the students are housed, and regardless of other responsive practices, in the end it is the dedication, commitment, and nature of the understanding of the involved adults—the teachers, administrators, bus drivers, cooks, grounds crew, security staff, custodial staff, and support personnel—that remain the incisive element. That, in our opinion, is the fundamental characteristic of exemplary public education: to celebrate and build upon the diverse characteristics and needs of students. That is the essence of the content of Module 2.

■ Committed Teachers

Public teachers are unique individuals. Let us imagine that a teaching colleague mentions that Lou Compton, in room 17, is a "fantastic teacher," "one of the best teachers in the district," "super," and "magnificent." What might be some of the characteristics you would expect to see in Lou's teaching behaviors?

We can expect Lou to (a) be understanding of and committed to the school's statement of philosophy or mission (see Figure 1.2); (b) know the curriculum and how best to teach it; (c) be enthusiastic, motivated, and well organized; (d) show effective communication and interpersonal skills; (e) be willing to listen to the students and to risk trying their ideas; and (f) be warm, caring, accepting, and nurturing of all students.

Students need teachers who are well organized and who know how to establish and manage an active and supportive learning environment (the topic of Module 3), even with its multiple instructional demands. Students respond best to teachers who provide leadership and who enjoy their function as role models, advisors, mentors, and reflective decision makers.

■ Reflective Decision Making and the Locus of Control

During any school day, a teacher makes hundreds of decisions, many of them instantaneously. In addition, in preparation for the day, the teacher will already have made many decisions. Thus, during one school year a teacher makes literally thousands of decisions, many of which can and will affect the lives of students for years to come. For you this should seem an awesome responsibility—which it is. In the nearly poetic words of Brown and Moffett, "We [teachers] influence students in myriad, unperceived ways that affect them and the lives of people with whom they in-

- All students entering *Cape Elizabeth High School* will graduate equipped with a personal plan for the future and with well-rounded skills and knowledge. CEHS will challenge students to reach their potential; to demonstrate self-confidence, respect for others, and responsibility for their community; and to embrace and welcome diversity. (Cape Elizabeth High School, Cape Elizabeth, ME)

- The mission of the *Eugenio Maria DeHostos Community Bilingual Charter School* (hereafter referred to as Hostos Charter School) is to promote excellence by providing middle level students a bilingual, bicultural academically enriched curriculum that draws from the social historical experience of Puerto Rico and Puerto Ricans living in the United States. This curriculum will provide all students a clear sense of their cultural identity, a critical approach to the history of Puerto Rico as part of the Americas and Caribbean, and they will develop a strong social change commitment to their community. The school will provide a rigorous curriculum that will fuse high technology with the arts and project-based instruction. We believe that school should be a place that is characterized by respect, critical thinking, democratic classrooms, and the vigorous challenges that are essential to maximize every student's potential. In addition, at the core of the Hostos Charter School is the unity and empowerment of the community, parents, students, teachers, and staff of the schools. (Eugenio Maria DeHostos Charter School, Philadelphia, PA)

- The staff at *Riverside Middle School* takes a special interest in each student with unique and special ways of caring and nurturing. By using a variety of teaching techniques, the goal of the staff is to focus on the individual learning needs of the pupils. We strive to actively involve students, their families, and their community in their learning experience at Riverside Middle School. (Riverside Middle School, Billings, MT)

- The mission of *Thomas J. Pappas School* is to develop within all students the leadership qualities to fulfill their roles as responsible citizens of a changing world. We provide an equitable education that promotes inquiry, positive decision-making, effective communication, cultural appreciation, and lifelong learning experiences. We provide enrichment opportunities to curtail homelessness. (Thomas J. Pappas Schools for the Homeless, Mesa, AZ)

- The mission of *Paseo Academy of Fine and Performing Arts* is to provide the highest quality education with emphasis on pre-professional training in the creative, visual and performing arts. The program encourages and promotes the academic, creative, artistic, physical, social and emotional development of students within a desegregated atmosphere of true and active racial and socio-economic integration. We strive to develop adults who will become consumers of and contributors to the local, national and global arts community and who will also become actively involved in the issues of their times. (Paseo Academy of Fine and Performing Arts, Kansas City Missouri School District, Kansas City, MO)

FIGURE 1.2 ● Sample Exemplary Mission Statements

SOURCE: Reprinted by Permission.

teract like the widening circles extending from a stone tossed into a tranquil pond."[59]

To be an effectively and positively influential teacher, you must become adept at decision making. You must make decisions developed through careful thinking over time, as well as decisions on the spot that arise from unforeseen circumstances. To make decisions that affect the students in the most positive kinds of ways, you need common sense, intelligence, a background of theory in curriculum and instruction with extended practical experience in working with young people, and the willingness to think about and reflect upon your teaching and to continue learning all that is necessary to become an exemplary classroom teacher.

Initially, of course, you will make errors in judgment, but you will also learn that teenagers are fairly resilient. You will find experts to guide you and help you so you can learn from your errors. Keep in mind that the sheer number of decisions you make each day will mean that not all of them will be the best ones that could have been made if you had more time to think and if you had better resources for planning.

Although effective teaching is based on scientific principles, good classroom teaching is as much an art as it is a science. In fact, the selection of content, instructional objectives, materials for instruction, teaching strategies, responses to inappropriate student behavior, and techniques for assessment are all the result of subjective judgments. Although many decisions may be made unhurried, such as when you plan the instruction, many others must be made on the spur of the moment. At your best, you will base decisions on your knowledge of school policies and your teaching style, as well as on pedagogical research, the curriculum, and the nature of the students in your classroom. You will also base your decisions on instinct, common sense, and reflective judgment.

The better your understanding and experience are with schools, the content of the curriculum, and the students—and the more time you give for thinking and careful reflection—the more likely it will be that your decisions will result in the student learning that you had planned. You will reflect upon concepts developed from one teaching experience and apply them to the next. As your classroom experiences accumulate, your teaching will become more routinized, predictable, and refined.

■ DECISION-MAKING AND THOUGHT-PROCESSING PHASES OF INSTRUCTION

Instruction can be divided into four decision-making and thought-processing phases. These are (a) the planning or *preactive phase*, (b) the teaching or *interactive phase*, (c) the analyzing and evaluating or *reflective phase*, and (d) the application or *projective phase*.[60]

The preactive phase consists of all those intellectual functions and decisions you will make prior to actual instruction. The interactive phase includes all the decisions made during the immediacy and spontaneity of the teaching act. As mentioned before, decisions made during this phase are likely to be more intuitive, unconscious, and routine than those made during the planning phase. The reflective phase is the time you will take to reflect on, analyze, and judge the decisions and behaviors that occurred during the interactive phase. As a result of this reflection, decisions are made to use what was learned in subsequent teaching actions. At this point, you are in the projective phase, abstracting from your reflection and projecting your analysis into subsequent teaching actions.

■ Reflection and the Decision-Making Process

During the reflective phase, teachers have a choice of whether to assume responsibility for the positive instructional outcomes of the planned instruction while placing the blame for the negative outcomes on outside forces (e.g., parents and guardians or society in general, students, other teachers, administrators, textbooks). Where the responsibility for outcomes is placed is referred to as *locus of control*. Just because a teacher thinks that he or she is a competent teacher doesn't mean it is so. If many of a teacher's students are not learning, then that teacher is not competent. In the words of the late Madeline Hunter, "To say that I am an effective teacher, and acknowledge that my students may not be learning is the same as saying I am a great surgeon, but most of my patients die."[61] Competent teachers tend to assume full responsibility for the instructional outcomes, re-

gardless of whether the outcomes are as intended from the planning phase.

■ Developing a Teaching Style

Every teacher develops a personal style of teaching with which she or he feels most comfortable. A teaching style can be defined as the way a teacher teaches, including the teacher's distinctive mannerisms complemented by his or her choices of teaching behaviors and strategies. This style develops both from the teacher's personal traits and from the knowledge and skills the teacher has in methodology, subject matter, and pedagogical theory. The most effective teachers can vary their styles; that is, their styles are flexible enough to encompass many and various strategies. Those teachers, therefore, are prepared to address the students' preferred learning styles.

The most effective teachers can modify their styles by selecting the strategy that is most appropriate for the situation, thus securing active student involvement and the greatest amount of student achievement. Highly effective teaching of this sort requires expertise in a wide variety of methods.[62] It also requires a command of the subject matter and an understanding of the students being taught.

Thus, to be an effective teacher you must accomplish three things: (a) learn as much about your students as you can, including their learning capacities, styles, preferred modalities, and interests; (b) develop an eclectic teaching style accompanied by a large repertoire of strategies and techniques; and (c) develop your knowledge and skills in using instructional media and resources.

■ A Model for Teaching

You should incorporate the following five-step model into your teaching style: (a) diagnosis or preassessment, (b) planning and preparation, (c) guidance of student learning, (d) continual assessment of student learning, and (e) follow-up. The diagnosis is an initial assessment of the students' present knowledge as well as their needs and desires. Through such preassessment you (and the students) can determine what should be accomplished and how it might best be done.

Next, you plan and prepare for the instruction. This step includes planning the units and lessons and the corresponding motivational strategies, preparing instructional activities, gathering materials and equipment, and arranging the environmental setting for instruction. Often these things are done in collaboration with the students.

While steps (a) and (b) are within the preactive phase of the thought-processing and decision-making phases of instruction, step (c), guidance of student learning, is the teaching or interactive phase. It includes implementation of the learning activities, that is, the instruction—showing students how, making information available to students, and providing opportunity for dialogue and constructive feedback to students about their work.

In step (d), assessment, you and the students reflect on and assess the ongoing progress of their learning and, in so doing, the success of the instruction. Assessment provides information to both you and your students about where progress has been made and where it has not. As part of the reflective phase of instructional decision making, those data provide a basis for determining the follow-up, the projective phase.

On the basis of assessment data, you follow up the instruction by helping students fill in what they have missed and by building on what they have learned.

As is true for the four decision-making and thought-processing phases of instruction, these five steps of the model for instruction tend to merge. For example, the assessment and follow-up for one unit or lesson may become the diagnosis, preparation, and guidance phases for the next one. But even when truncated, this five-step model is evident in exemplary teaching.

■ ACCESSING COMMUNITY RESOURCES TO MEET STUDENTS' NEEDS: TELECOMMUNICATIONS NETWORKS, MEMBERS OF THE COMMUNITY, AND PARENT ORGANIZATIONS

■ Vehicles for Obtaining and Sharing Ideas and Information

Today's exemplary educators are making focused efforts to enhance the connections among the home, school, and local and global communities to promote the success of all students.

■ Home and School Connections

It is well known that parents' involvement in their child's education can have a positive impact on their child's achievement at school. For example, when parents of an at-risk student get involved, the student benefits with more consistent attendance at school, more positive attitudes and actions, better grades, and higher test scores. In recognition of the positive effect that parent and family involvement have on student achievement and success, the National PTA published *National Standards for Parent/Family Involvement Programs* in 1997.[63]

Many schools have adopted formal policies about home and community connections. These policies usually emphasize that parents should be included as partners in the educational program, that teachers and administrators will inform parents about their child's progress, about the school's family involvement policy, and about any programs in which family members can participate. Some schools are members of the *National Network of*

> ● **Big Dummy's Guide to Service-Learning**
> <http://www.fiu.edu/~time4chg/Library/bigdummy.html>.
> ● **Campus Compact Service Learning Links**
> <http://www.compact.org/links/service.html>.
> ● **Service Learning Project**
> <http://www.aahe.org/service/srv-links.htm>.
> ● **UCLA Service Learning Clearinghouse**
> <http://www.gseis.ucla.edu/slc/>.

FIGURE 1.3 ● Internet Sources on Community Service Learning

Partnership 2000 Schools. Efforts to foster parent and community involvement are as varied as the people who participate, and include (a) student-teacher-parent contracts and assignment calendars, sometimes available via the school's Web page on the Internet; (b) home visitor programs; (c) involvement of community leaders in the classroom as mentors, aides, and role models;[64] (d) newsletters, workshops,[65] and electronic hardware and software for parents to help their children; (e) homework hotlines; (f) regular phone calls[66] and personal notes home about a student's progress; and (g) involvement of students in community service learning.[67]

■ Community Service Learning

Via service learning, students can learn and develop through active participation in thoughtfully organized and curriculum-connected experiences that meet community needs.[68] (See Figure 1.3 for Internet sources of additional information and descriptions of community service projects.)

Community members, geographic features, buildings, monuments, historic sites, and other places in a school's geographic area constitute some of the richest instructional laboratories that can be imagined. In order to take advantage of this accumulated wealth of resources, as well as to build school-community partnerships, you should start a file of community resources once hired by a school. It is a good idea to start your professional resources file immediately, and maintain it throughout your professional career; for that, see Figure 1.4.

■ Telecommunications Networks

Teachers looking to guide their students toward becoming autonomous thinkers, effective decision makers, and lifelong learners and to make their classrooms more student-centered, collaborative, interdisciplinary, and interactive are increasingly turning to telecommunications networks and the global community. Webs of connected computers allow teachers and students from around the world to reach each other directly and gain access to information previously unimaginable. Students using networks learn and develop new inquiry and analytical skills

A professional resources file is a project that you could begin now and maintain throughout your professional career. Begin your resources file either on a computer database program or on color-coded file cards that list (a) name of resource, (b) how and where to obtain the resource, (c) description of how to use the resource, and (d) evaluative comments about the resource.

Organize the file in a way that makes the most sense to you now. Cross-reference or color-code your system to accommodate the following categories of instructional aids and resources.

- Articles from print sources.
- Compact disc titles.
- Computer software titles.
- Games.
- Guest speakers and other community resources.
- Internet resources.
- Media catalogs.
- Motivational ideas.
- Pictures, posters, graphs, cartoons, quotes.

- Resources to order.
- Sources of free and inexpensive materials.
- Student worksheets.
- Test items.
- Thematic units and ideas.
- Unit and lesson plans and ideas.
- Videocassette titles.
- Videodisc titles.
- Miscellaneous.

FIGURE 1.4 ● Beginning a Professional Resource File

in a stimulating environment, and gain an increased appreciation of their role as world citizens. Sample Web sites and addresses are shown in Figure 1.5. See others elsewhere in this book, especially Figures 8.2 and 8.3 in Module 8.

■ THE EMERGENT OVERALL PICTURE

Certainly, no facet of education receives more attention from the media or causes more concern among parents and teachers than students' achievement in the public schools. Reports are issued, polls taken, debates organized, and blue-ribbon commissions are formed. Community members write letters to local editors about it, news editors devote editorial space to it, television anchors comment about it, and documentaries and specials focus on it in full color. What initiated this attention that began about half a century ago and continues today? We are not sure, but it has never been matched in its political interest and participation, and it has affected and continues to affect both the public schools and programs in higher education that are directly or indirectly related to teacher preparation and certification.[69]

In response to the reports, educators, corporations, local businesspersons, and politicians acted. Around the nation, their actions resulted in:

- Changes in standards for teacher certification. For example, model standards describing what prospective teachers should know and be able to do in order to receive a teaching license were published by the Interstate New Teacher Assessment and Support Consortium (INTASC), a project of the Council of Chief State School Officers (CCSSO), in a document titled *Model Standards for Beginning Teacher Licensing and Development*. Representatives of at least 36 states and professional associations comprise the group, including the *National Education Association (NEA)*, the *American Federation of*

Teachers (AFT), the *American Association of Colleges for Teacher Education (AACTE)*, and the *National Council for the Accreditation of Teacher Education (NCATE)*. The standards are performance-based and revolve around a common core of principles of knowledge and skills that cut across disciplines. *The INTASC standards* were developed to be compatible with the *National Board for Professional Teaching Standards (NBPTS)*.[70] Specifically addressing middle level instruction, the NBPTS in 1997 released 11 categories of standards for certification as a Middle Childhood/Generalist. These 11 categories are knowledge of students, knowledge of content and curriculum, learning environment, respect for diversity, instructional resources, meaningful applications of knowledge, multiple paths of knowledge, assessment, family involvement, reflection, and contributions to the profession.[71] The categories include:

- Emphasis on education for cultural diversity and ways of teaching language minority students.

- Emphasis on helping students make effective transitions from one level of schooling to the next and from school to life, with an increased focus on helping students make connections between what is being learned and real life, as well as connections between subjects in the curriculum and between academics and vocations.

- Emphasis on raising test scores, reducing dropout rates (that is, the rate of students who do not complete high school nor receive the equivalent degree), increasing instructional time, and changing curricula.

- Federally enacted Goals 2000: Educate America Act and the development of national education standards for all major subject areas (see Module 4).

- **ArtFul Minds** <http://faldo.atmos.uiuc.edu/CLA/LESSONS/2226.html>.
- **Beginning Teacher's Tool Box** <http://www.inspiringteachers.com>.
- **Classroom Connect** <http://corporate.classroom.com/>.
- **ClubMid** <http://www.ClubMid.phschool.com>. Middle grades network.
- **Community LearningNetwork** <http://www.cln.org/>.
- **Council of the Great City Schools** <http://www.cgcs.org/urbaneducator/>.
- **EdIndex** <http://www.pitt.edu/~poole>. K–12 education links.
- **Education Links** <http://www.execpc.com/~dboals/k–12.html>. K–12 education links.
- **Education World** <http://www.education-world.com>. Electronic version of *Education Week*.
- **EduServe / GlobaLearn** <http://www.eduserveinc.com/GLN7.htm>.
- **Eisenhower National Clearinghouse for Mathematics and Science (ENC)** <http://www.enc.org>.
- **FedWorld** <http://www.fedworld.gov>. Access to information from government agencies.
- **GEM, the Gateway to Educational Materials** <http://www.thegateway.org/index.html>. National government's effort to provide access to Internet-based educational materials.
- **Global Schoolnet Foundation** <http://www.gsn.org/>. Global resources and links.
- **GLOBE (Global Learning and Observations to Benefit the Environment) Program** <http://www.globe.gov>. An international environmental science and education partnership.
- **Go Math** <http://www.gomath.com>. Online tutoring in math. Resources for teachers.
- **Homeschool Resources** <http://www.teach-at-home.com/>.
- **Homeschool Internet Resource Center** <http://www.rsts.net/>.
- **HomeworkCentral** <http://www.homeworkcentral.com>. For lesson plans and subject research.
- **Kathy Schrock Guide** <http://kathyschrock.net/>.
- **Kathy Schrock's Guide for Educators** <http://www.capecod.net/schrockguide/> for resources and information on education.
- **Library of Congress** <http://lcweb.loc.gov/homepage/lchp.html>. National Digital Library life history manuscripts from the WPA Federal Writers' Folklore Project, Civil War photographs, early motion pictures, legal information, and research sources.
- **I Love Teaching** <http://www.iloveteaching.com>.
- **Microsoft Lesson Connection** <http://www.k12.msn.com>. Lesson plan resources and more.
- **MiddleWeb** <http://www.middleweb.com/>. Middle school focus.
- **National Consortium for School Networking** <http://cosn.org>.
- **PedagoNet** <http://www.pedagonat.com>. Learning Resources Center for exchange of educational resources.
- **Study Web** <http://www.studyweb.com>. Place for students and teachers to research topics.
- **Teachers First** <http://www.teachersfirst.com>. Resources provided by the Network for Instructional TV (NiTV).
- **Teachers Helping Teachers** <http://www.pacificnet.net/~mandel>.
- **Teacher Talk** <http://education.indiana.edu/cas/tt/tthmpg.html>.
- **Too Cool for grownups** <http://gort.ucsd.edu/newjour/t/msg02406.html>.
- **21st Century Teachers** <http://www.21ct.org>. Teachers for teachers exchange.
- **United Nations' CyberSchool Bus** <http://www.un.org/Pubs/CyberSchoolBus/>. Curriculum units and projects, databases on U.N. member states, and global trends.
- **United States Department of Education** <http://www.ed.gov/index.html>.
- **Virtual Reference Desk** <http://www.vrd.org/>.
- **Yahoo Education Index** <http://dir.yahoo.com/Education/>.

FIGURE 1.5 ● Sample Internet Sites for Teachers and Students

- Formation of school-home-community connections.
- New "basics" required for high school graduation.
- School restructuring to provide more meaningful curriculum options.

Key Trends and Practices Today

Key trends and practices today are listed in Figure 1.6.

Problems and Issues That Plague the Nation's Schools

Major problems and issues plague our nation's schools, some of which are listed in Figure 1.7. Some of these are discussed in subsequent modules (see index for topic locations). Perhaps you and members of your class can identify other issues and problems faced by our nation's schools.[72]

- Dividing the student body and faculty into smaller cohort groups and using nontraditional scheduling and interdisciplinary teaching teams.
- Encouraging self-control and problem solving.
- Facilitating students' social skills as they interact, relate to one another, and develop relationships and peaceful friendships.
- Facilitating the developing of students' values as related to families, the community, and schools.
- Holding high expectations, although not necessarily the same expectations, for all students by establishing goals and assessing results against those goals.
- Integrating the curriculum, and introducing reading, thinking, and writing across the curriculum.
- Involving communities in the schools and involving parents and guardians in school decision making.
- Involving students in self-assessment.
- Making multicultural education work for all students.
- Providing meaningful curriculum options with multiple pathways for academic success.
- Providing students with the time and the opportunity to think and to be creative, rather than simply memorizing and repeating information.
- Redefining giftedness to include nonacademic as well as traditional academic abilities.
- Using heterogeneous grouping and cooperative learning, peer coaching, and cross-age tutoring as instructional strategies.
- Using the Internet as a communication tool and learning resource.
- Using occupations to contextualize learning and instruction to vitalize the transition from school to work.

FIGURE 1.6 ● Key Trends and Practices in Today's Middle and Secondary Schools

- A demand for test scores and statistics that can be used to judge schools and their principals.
- Buildings badly in need of repair and upgrading.[73]
- Bullying of students by other students.
- Continuing controversy over books and their content.
- Continuing, long-running controversy over values, morality, and sexuality education.
- Controversy created by the concept of teaching less content but teaching it better.
- Controversy over concept of a national curriculum with national assessments.[74]
- Continued controversy over traditional ability grouping or tracking.
- Identification and development of programs that recognize, develop, and nurture talents in all our youths at all levels of education.[75]
- Retention in grade versus social promotion.[76]
- Scarcity of teachers of color to serve as role models for minority youth.[77]
- School security and the related problem of weapons, crime, violence, and drugs on school campuses and in school neighborhoods.[78]
- Schools that are too large.[79]
- Sexual harassment of students, mostly from other students but sometimes from school employees.
- Shortage of qualified teachers, especially in special education, bilingual education, science, and mathematics, and in schools located in poverty-stricken areas.[80]
- Teaching and assessing for higher-order thinking skills.
- The education of teachers to work effectively with students who may be too overwhelmed by personal problems to focus on learning and to succeed in school.
- The number of students at risk of dropping out of school, especially Hispanics where the dropout rate has remained around 30% for two decades.[81]

FIGURE 1.7 ● Problems and Issues that Plague the Nation's Schools

■ YOUR EMERGING TEACHING STYLE

It is indeed a challenge to teach middle and secondary school students. To help you meet the challenge, there is a wealth of information and resources available. As you build broader frameworks of understanding of teaching and learning, as you practice the development of your instructional skills, and as you reflect upon that experience, you will be well on your way to becoming the most effective teacher you can be by developing your own personal style of teaching. This teaching style will develop from a combination of personal traits; expertise you have in methodology, subject matter, and pedagogical theory; and from your knowledge about your particular group of students.

The most effective teachers are those who can vary their instructional styles. Effective teachers can select and use the strategy that is most appropriate, thus securing active student involvement and the greatest amount of student achievement. Highly effective teaching of this sort requires both expertise in a wide variety of methods and a feeling for the appropriate situation in which to use each method. Such teaching also demands a good command of the subject matter and an understanding of the students being taught.

To be an effective teacher you should (a) develop a large repertoire of techniques in order to be pre-

pared for the many possible contingencies; (b) learn as much about your students as you can; (c) develop an eclectic style of teaching, one that is flexible and adaptable; and (d) build into your teaching use of the five-step model of diagnosis, preparation, guidance of student learning, continual assessment of the learning, and follow-up.

In deciding which methods to use, you will be influenced by a number of factors, each of which is explored further in subsequent modules. To continue your learning about methods available and a teacher's decision-making process, now do Exercises 1.1 to 1.5.

EXERCISE 1.1

■ Methods of Instruction

Instructions: The purpose of this exercise is for you to reflect on how you have been taught (throughout your schooling) and share those reflections with your classmates, looking for differences as well as commonalities.

1. The following is a list of methods of instruction and a variety of tools. Rate each according to your familiarity and experiences with it, using this rating scale: A = very familiar and with good learning experiences, B = somewhat familiar, C = never experienced, D = familiar but with bad learning experiences.

_____ Assignment	_____ Lecture
_____ Audiovisual equipment	_____ Library/resource center
_____ Autotutorial	_____ Metacognition
_____ Coaching	_____ Mock-up
_____ Collaborative learning	_____ Multimedia
_____ Compact disc	_____ Panel discussion
_____ Computer-assisted learning	_____ Periodicals
_____ Cooperative learning	_____ Problem solving
_____ Debate	_____ Project
_____ Demonstration	_____ Questioning
_____ Discovery	_____ Review and practice
_____ Drama	_____ Role-play
_____ Drill	_____ Self-instructional module
_____ Expository	_____ Simulation
_____ Field trip	_____ Study guide
_____ Game	_____ Symposium
_____ Group work	_____ Telecommunication
_____ Guest speaker	_____ Term paper
_____ Homework	_____ Textbook
_____ Individualized instruction	_____ Think-pair-share/Think-write-pair-share
_____ Inquiry	_____ Tutorial
_____ Laboratory investigation	_____ Visual tools
_____ Laser videodisc	

(continued)

2. Now list the methods in four columns according to the rating you gave to each.

      A Methods   *B Methods*   *C Methods*   *D Methods*

3. In small groups (three or four per group), share your columns with your classmates. Are there methods that seem to show up consistently in certain columns? If so, try to analyze why. Questions that you might discuss in your groups are:

   ■ Were certain methods more consistently used at any one level of your education, such as college, high school, junior high, and so forth?
   ■ In what ways have your teachers' teaching styles differed?
   ■ Which have appealed to you most?
   ■ What qualities did they have that you would most like to emulate? Avoid?
   ■ Did they seem to rely more on certain strategies, tactics, and techniques?

 To access this exercise online, go to the Companion Website at **www.prenhall.com/kellough.**

EXERCISE 1.2

■ The Teacher as Reflective Decision-Maker

Instructions: The purpose of this exercise is to learn more about the nature of the decisions and the decision-making process used by teachers. To accomplish this, you are to talk with and observe one middle school or secondary school teacher for one class period. Tabulate as accurately as possible the number of decisions the teacher makes during that time period, and then share the results with your classmates. Obtain permission from a cooperating teacher by explaining the purpose of your observations. You will need to have a follow-up discussion with the cooperating teacher regarding your tabulations. A follow-up thank you letter is appropriate.

School, teacher, and class observed: _____

1. Use the following format for your tabulations. You may first want to make your tabulations on a separate blank sheet of paper and then organize and transfer those tabulations to this page. Tabulate and identify each decision. To tabulate the decisions made before and after instruction, confer with the teacher after class.

Decisions Made Before Instruction
Examples:
■ objectives of lesson
■ amount of time to be devoted to particular activities
■ classroom management procedures

Decisions Made During Instruction
Examples:
■ called on Roberta to answer a question
■ teacher remained silent until students in back corner got quiet
■ talked with tardy student

Decisions Made After Instruction
Examples:
■ to review a particular concept tomorrow
■ to arrange a conference with Sean to talk with him about his hostility in class
■ to make a revision in Friday's homework assignment

(continued)

2. What was the total number of decisions made by this teacher

   before instruction? _____   during instruction? _____   after instruction? _____

   Compare your results with those of others in your class.

3. Did you observe any evidence that this teacher assumed full responsibility for the learning outcomes of this class session? Describe the evidence.

4. What percentage of all decisions by this teacher

   were planned? _____   were spontaneous? _____

5. Did you share your results from this exercise with the cooperating teacher? What was his or her reaction?

6. What are your conclusions from this exercise?

 To access this exercise online, go to the Companion Website at **www.prenhall.com/kellough.**

EXERCISE 1.3

■ The Preactive Phase of Instruction

Instructions: Mentally rehearsing what actions you will take as the teacher before meeting the students is absolutely essential for effective teaching and learning. The purpose of this exercise is to stress the importance of clearly and fully thinking about what you will do and say in the classroom to demonstrate how mental rehearsal of a lesson can identify possible problems. Follow these steps:

1. Select a middle school or secondary school grade level you are currently teaching or that you would like to teach.

2. Note the objective of the lesson: Students will design a name tag for their desks during a 20-minute time frame.

3. Without looking ahead at step 4, write a lesson plan for this activity. (Although you have not yet learned the details of lesson planning, outline the steps you would follow and things you would say to your students in order to accomplish the objective of step 2.)

4. To analyze the thoroughness of your preactive thinking, respond to the following questions.
   a. Are materials listed in your plan?
   b. Are those materials readily available in your classroom?
   c. Will paper or tagboard need to be precut?
   d. How large can the name tags be?
   e. How and where will they be attached to each desk?
   f. Should they be flat or three-dimensional?
   g. Do you have markers or crayons, or are the students expected to have them?
   h. Will students need scissors?
   i. Do you have left-handed scissors available if needed?
   j. Should name tags have first name, last name, last initial?
   k. Can other words or designs be added?
   l. When and how will materials be distributed? Collected?
   m. What plan do you have for absent or tardy students?

(continued)

5. Share the results of your steps 1–4 with others in your class. Did members of your class come up with other questions relevant and necessary to the preplanning for this instructional period? If so, share them with the rest of the class.

Conclusion: A teacher who practices thorough preactive planning should have planned answers for each of these questions.

 To access this exercise online, go to the Companion Website at **www.prenhall.com/kellough.**

EXERCISE 1.4

■ My First Micro Peer-Teaching Demonstration—MPT 1

Instructions: Prepare and present a five-minute micro peer-teaching (MPT) demonstration and present it to your classmates. You may choose any topic and strategy, but the MPT should be video recorded so that you can later compare this first MPT with Exercise 10.1.

 To access this exercise online, go to the Companion Website at **www.prenhall.com/kellough.**

EXERCISE 1.5

■ Reflecting Upon My Own School Experiences

Instructions: The purpose of this exercise is to share with others in your class your reflections on your own middle school and secondary school experiences. We suggest that you do this first in small groups, perhaps no larger than four people, and then share highlights or commonalities of the small group discussion with the whole group.

1. What school(s) did you attend, where, and when? Were they public or private?

2. Describe the school(s)—for example, urban or rural, large or small.

3. What do you remember most from your middle and secondary school experiences?

4. What do you remember most about your teachers?

5. What do you remember most about the other students?

6. What do you remember most about your overall school life?

7. What grade (or class or teachers) do you specifically recall with fondness? Why?

8. What grade (or class or teacher) would you just like to forget? Why?

9. What do you recall about peer and parental pressures?

(continued)

10. What do you recall about your feelings during those years?

11. Is there any other aspect of your life as a middle school or secondary school student you wish to share with others?

 To access this exercise online, go to the Companion Website at **www.prenhall.com/kellough.**

■ SUMMARY

In this module we have reviewed the chronological development of secondary schools. We have distinguished between middle and junior high schools while discussing the changing purpose, organization, and structure of our schools. We have hightlighted key past and current reform efforts. We have also discussed the role teachers, students, parents, administrators, and community members play in a quality education school. We have advocated for an eclectic teaching style as the best approach to meeting the varied needs of our diverse students. In Module 2 we will talk about the many ways students are different while pointing out commonalities. We will also explore ways to leverage the diversity you are likely to find in your classrooms.

■ MODULE 1 **POSTTEST**

Multiple Choice

1. Which were the first public secondary high schools?
   a. common schools
   b. academies
   c. Latin grammar schools
   d. English classical schools

2. Which one of the following is not synonymous with the term *looping*?
   a. multiyear grouping
   b. multiyear instruction
   c. multiyear placement
   d. interdisciplinary teaming
   e. teacher-student progression

3. The core curriculum includes the subject matter areas of
   a. mathematics and science.
   b. English/language arts and history/social studies.
   c. physical education and the visual and performing arts.
   d. English/language arts, mathematics, science, and history/social studies.

4. In the five-step model for teaching, which step(s) are analogous to the preactive phase of decision making and thought processing?
   a. first step
   b. first two steps
   c. third step
   d. fourth step
   e. fifth and first steps

5. Which one of the four decision-making and thought-processing phases of instruction occurs at the time the lesson is being taught?
   a. preactive
   b. reflective
   c. projective
   d. interactive
   e. none of the above

(continued)

6. By definition, a secondary school is any school that houses students in some combination of grades
   a. 6 through 12.
   b. 7 through 12.
   c. 8 through 12.
   d. 9 through 12.
   e. none of the above.

7. _____ is a school with a curriculum that is designed for specialization, such as for humanities and international studies, performing and visual arts, or science and technology.
   a. A charter school
   b. A magnet school
   c. An exemplary school
   d. A fundamentals school
   e. An international baccalaureate school

8. *House, pod, family,* and *village* are terms used when referring to
   a. interdisciplinary teams of teachers.
   b. separate schools within one large multischool district.
   c. academic departments within a large comprehensive high school.
   d. clusters of students and teachers in a school-within-a-school program.

9. _____ assessment is a synonym for preassessment.
   a. Aligned
   b. Formative
   c. Diagnostic
   d. Summative
   e. Alternative

10. You need a large repertoire of teaching strategies so that you can
    a. cover the subject matter.
    b. impress the school principal.
    c. score well on the national teacher examination.
    d. adapt the best and most appropriate teaching methods to specific teaching/learning situations.

Short Explanation

1. Clearly distinguish these types of schools: Middle school, junior high school, high school, secondary school.
2. Distinguish between the terms *teaching team* and *team teaching*.
3. Describe the house concept and its advantages and disadvantages from an educational standpoint.
4. Define school restructuring, describe its purpose, and exemplify some of the results of efforts to restructure schools.
5. Describe the philosophy that drives the middle school movement.
6. Give the authors' description of the fundamental characteristic of exemplary education. Explain why you agree or disagree with their conclusion regarding that characteristic.
7. Describe the meaning of the term *quality education*.
8. Describe ways that schools today attempt to stimulate the talents and motivation of each student.
9. Describe when, if ever, a middle school is not a secondary school.
10. Identify and describe each of the steps of the five-step model for effective teaching.

Essay

1. It has been predicted that by the year 2020, 20% to 30% of the U.S. public schools will be run by for-profit corporations. (See page 67 of the February 7, 2000, issue of *Business Week* magazine.) Are for-profit public schools actually increasing in number from the approximately 200 such schools in the year 2000? Why or why not, do you suppose, is the for-profit public school alternative growing in popularity?
2. From what you now know about middle and secondary schools, at which do you believe you would most like to teach? Explain why.

(continued)

3. How do you explain the phenomenal growth in the number of charter schools since the first charter school opened its doors in Minnesota only about a decade ago? What do you see as the future for the charter school movement?

4. From your current observations and fieldwork (related to your teacher-preparation program), clearly identify one specific example of an educational practice that seems contradictory to exemplary practice or theory as presented in this module. Present your explanation for the discrepancy.

5. Describe any prior concepts you held that changed as a result of your experiences with this module. Describe the changes.

 To access this posttest and the answers online, go to the Companion Website at www.prenhall.com/kellough.

■ SUGGESTED READINGS

Battista, M. T. (1999). The mathematical miseducation of America's youth: Ignoring research and scientific study in education. *Phi Delta Kappan, 80*(6), 425–433.

Beane, J. A. (1999). Middle schools under siege: Responding to the attack. *Middle School Journal, 30*(5), 3–6.

Black, S. (1998). Learning on the block. *American School Board Journal, 185*(1), 32–34.

Brandt, R. S. (Ed.). (2000). *Education in a new era.* Alexandria, VA: Association for Supervision and Curriculum Development.

Brown, B. L. (1998). *Service learning: More than community service.* ERIC Digest Number 198. Columbus, OH: ERIC Clearinghouse on Adult, Career, and Vocational Education.

Brown, J. L., & Moffett, C. A. (1999). *The hero's journey.* Alexandria, VA: Association for Supervision and Curriculum Development.

Capps, W. R., & Maxwell, M. E. (1999). Where everybody knows your name. *American School Board Journal, 186*(9), 35–36.

Cizek, G. J. (1999). Give us this day our daily bread. *Phi Delta Kappan, 80*(10), 737–743.

Clark, R. C., & Smith, W. T. (1999). *Effective professional development schools.* San Francisco: Jossey-Bass.

Cloud, J. P. (1998). School community partnerships that work. *Social Studies Review, 37*(2), 45–48.

Cummings, L., & Winston, M. (1998). Service-based solutions. *Science Teacher, 65*(1), 39–41.

Dryfoos, J. G. (1998). *Full-service schools.* San Francisco: Jossey-Bass.

Fusarelli, L. D. (1999). Reinventing urban education in Texas: Charter schools, smaller schools, and the new institutionalism. *Education and the Urban Society, 31*(2), 214–224.

Gallagher, J. (1999). Teaching in the block. *Middle Ground, 2*(3), 10–15.

Gibbs, W. W., & Fox, D. (1999). The false crisis in science education. *Scientific American, 281*(4), 87–93.

Goldberg, M. F. (1999). Recipes for school success. *Phi Delta Kappan, 80*(10), 770–772.

Hertzog, C. J., & Morgan, P. L. (1999). Making the transition from middle level to high school. *High School Magazine, 6*(4), 26–30.

Kirby, P. C. (1999). First charter school in Louisiana provides an alternative to expulsion for students at risk. *Middle School Journal, 30*(5), 13–22.

Klonsky, S., & Klonsky, M. (1999). Countering anonymity through small schools. *Educational Leadership, 57*(1), 38–41.

Kommer, D. (1999). Is it time to revisit multiage teams in the middle grades? *Middle School Journal, 30*(3), 28–32.

Lawton, M. (1999). For whom the school bell tolls. *School Administrator, 56*(3), 6–12.

Loveless, T. (1998). *The tracking and ability grouping debate.* Washington, DC: Thomas B. Fordham Foundation.

Loveless, T. (1999). Will tracking reform promote social equity? *Educational Leadership, 56*(7), 28–32.

Lucas, S. R. (1999). *Tracking inequality: stratification and mobility in American high schools.* New York: Teachers College Press.

Maeroff, G. I. (Ed.). (1998). *Imaging education: The media and schools in America.* New York: Teachers College Press.

Mills, R. (1998). *Grouping students for instruction in middle schools.* ERIC Digest 419631. Champaign, IL: ERIC Clearinghouse on Elementary and Early Childhood Education.

Nathan, J. (1998). *Charter schools.* San Francisco: Jossey-Bass. National Alliance of Business. (1999). Positive results for all students dispel fears of leaving some behind. *WorkAmerica, 16*(2), 1, 4–5.

Nolan, F. (1998). Ability grouping plus heterogeneous grouping: Win-win schedules. *Middle School Journal, 29*(5), 14–19.

Oakes, J., Quartz, K. H., Ryan, S., & Lipton, M. (1999). *Becoming good American schools.* San Francisco: Jossey-Bass.

Oakes, J., & Wells, A. S. (1998). Detracking for high student achievement. *Educational Leadership, 55*(6), 38–41.

Olson, L. (1998). The new basics in school-to-work. *Educational Leadership, 55*(6), 50–53.

Rudner, L. M. (1999). Scholastic achievement and demographic characteristics of home school students in 1998. *Education Policy Analysis Archives, 7*(8).

Sanders, M. G., & Epstein, J. L. (1998). *School-family-community partnerships in middle and high schools: From theory to practice.* Report Number 22. Baltimore, MD: Center for Research on the Education of Students Placed at Risk.

Sarason, S. B. (1998). *Charter schools: Another flawed educational reform?* New York: Teachers College Press.

Scales, P. C. (1999). Increasing service-learning's impact on middle school students. *Middle School Journal, 30*(5), 40–44.

Schank, R. C. (2000). A vision of education for the 21st century. *T.H.E Journal, 27*(6), 42–45.

Seed, A. (1998). Free at last: Making the most of the flexible block schedule. *Middle School Journal, 29*(5), 20–21.

Smith, D. G., et al. (1998). Flexing the middle school block schedule by adding non-traditional core subjects and teachers to the interdisciplinary team. *Middle School Journal, 29*(5), 22–27.

Treffinger, D. J. (1998). From gifted education to programming for talent development. *Phi Delta Kappan, 79*(10), 752–755.

Wang, M. C., et al. (1998). *Building educational resilience.* Fastback 430. Bloomington, IN: Phi Delta Kappa Educational Foundation.

■ ENDNOTES

[1] Excerpted from C. Rogers, *On Becoming a Person* (Cambridge, MA: Riverside Press, 1961).

[2] See W. J. Urban and J. L. Wagoner, Jr., *American Education: A History* (2nd ed.) (Boston: McGraw-Hill, 2000).

[3] See K. D. Moore, *Middle and Secondary School Instructional Methods* (2nd ed.) (Boston: McGraw-Hill College, 1999).

[4] See J. H. Spring, *The American School, 1642–2000* (5th ed.) (Boston: McGraw-Hill, 2001).

[5] See M. P. Sadker, and D. M. Sadker, *Teachers, Schools and Society* (7th ed.) (Boston, MA: McGraw Hill, 2005).

[6] Ibid., Chapter 8.

[7] See K. D. Moore, *Middle and Secondary School Instructional Methods* (2nd ed.) (Boston: McGraw-Hill College, 1999).

[8] See M. P. Sadker, and D. M. Sadker, *Teachers, Schools and Society* (7th ed.). (Boston, MA: McGraw Hill, 2005).

[9] T. M. Smith, G. T. Rogers, N. Alsalam, M. Perie, R. P. Mahoney, and V. Martin, *The Condition of Education 1994.* (Washington, D.C.: U.S. Department of Education, Office of Educational Research and Improvement, National Center for Education Statistics, 1994).

[10] J. H. Lounsbury, Perspectives on the Middle School Movement. In J. L. Irvin (Ed.), *Transforming Middle Level Education: Perspectives and Possibilities* (Needham Heights, MA: Allyn & Bacon, 1992), 295–313.

[11] Ibid.

[12] See J. H. Spring, *The American School, 1642–2000* (5th ed.) (Boston: McGraw-Hill, 2001).

[13] H. Mizell, *Guiding Questions for Middle School Reform* (2003). Remarks made at a meeting convened by the Los Angeles Unified School District by Hayes Mizell, Director of the Program for Student Achievement at the Edna McConnell Clark Foundation, January 16, 2003.

[14] K. D. Moore, *Middle and Secondary School Instructional Methods* (2nd ed.) (Boston: McGraw-Hill College, 1999).

[15] D. G. Armstrong and T. Savage, *Teaching in the Secondary School* (4th ed.) (Upper Saddle River, NJ: Merrill, 1998).

[16] S. Ansell, *Achievement Gap,* (July 16, 2004). Education Week on the Web: American Education's Online Newspaper of record. http://www.edweek.org/context/topics/issuepage.cfm?id=61.

[17] E. W. Eisner, Questionable Assumptions About Schooling, *Phi Delta Kappan 84*(9), 648–657 (2003).

[18] P. A. Noguera, Beyond Size: The Challenge of High School Reform, *Educational Leadership 59*(5), 60–64.

[19] L. Olson, Report Points Out Lack of Clarity for High School Reforms, *Education Week 23*(37), 18 (May 19, 2004).

[20] A. C. Lewis, High Schools and Reform, *Phi Delta Kappan 85*(8), 563–564 (2004).

[21] C. Hendrie, High Schools Nationwide Paring Down, *Education Week 23*(40), pp. 1, 28–30 (2004).

[22] G. Arriaza, Making Changes That Stay Made: School Reform and Community Involvement, *High School Journal 87*(4), 10–35, (2004).

[23] C. Hendrie, High Schools Nationwide Paring Down, *Education Week 23*(40), pp. 1, 28–30 (2004).

[24] H. Mizell, *Guiding Questions for Middle School Reform* (2003). Remarks made at a meeting convened by the Los Angeles Unified School District by Hayes Mizell, Director of the Program for Student Achievement at the Edna McConnell Clark Foundation, January 16, 2003.

[25] G. A. Donaldson, Jr., Working Smarter Together, *Educational Leadership 51*(2), 12–16 (October 1993).

[26] H. Mizell, *Guiding Questions for Middle School Reform* (2003). Remarks made at a meeting convened by the Los Angeles Unified School District by Hayes Mizell, Director of the Program for Student Achievement at the Edna McConnell Clark Foundation, January 16, 2003.

[27] U.S. Department of Education. National Center for Educational Statistics. (2004, June 1). *Language Minority Students.* Condition of Education 2004. Washington, DC: Author. Retrieved June 8, 2004 from the World Wide Web: http://nces.ed.gov/programs/coe/.

[28] K. Brooks and F. Edwards, *The Middle School in Transition: A Research Report on the Status of the Middle School Movement* (Lexington: College of Education, University of Kentucky, 1978).

[29] See, for example, the story of Oregon City High School, in C. Paglin and J. Fager, *Grade Configuration: Who Goes Where?* (Portland, OR: Northwest Regional Educational Laboratory, 1997), pp. 29–31, and visit the West Orange High School (Orlando, FL) Ninth Grade Center on the Internet at http://www.scott.k12.hy.us/9th/8thhistory.html.

[30] National Middle School Association, *This We Believe* (Columbus, OH: Author, 1982, reissued in 1995).

[31] See W. Jassey, *Center for Japanese Study Abroad, Fastback 386* (Bloomington, IN: Phi Delta Kappa Educational Foundation, 1995).

[32] L. A. Mulholland and L. A. Bierlein, *Understanding Charter Schools, Fastback 383* (Bloomington, IN: Phi Delta Kappa Educational Foundation, 1995), p. 7. See also the theme issue, The Charter School Movement, in the March 1998 *Phi Delta Kappan*, Volume 79, number 7, and the several articles about charter schools in the October 1998 issue of *Educational Leadership*, Volume 56, number 2. Connect to the charter school home pages via the United States Charter School Web site at http://www.uscharterschools.org/. For additional information and for a copy of the *National Charter School Directory*, contact the Center for Education Reform (CER) at 800-521-2118; see the Web site at http://edreform.com/research/css9697.htm.

[33] Some schools belong to the National Network of Partnership 2000 Schools. For information, contact the Center on School, Family, and Community Partnerships, The Johns Hopkins University, 3506 North Charles Street, Baltimore, MD 21216, phone: 410-516-8807 or fax: 410-516-8890. See also M. G. Sanders, Improving School, Family, and

Community Partnerships in Urban Middle Schools, *Middle School Journal 31*(2), 35–41 (November 1999); and W. Johnson et al., Texas Scholars, *Phi Delta Kappan 79*(10), 781–783 (June 1998).

[34]See, for example, B. L. Brown, *Tech Prep: Is It Working? Myths and Realities* (Columbus, OH: ERIC Clearinghouse on Adult, Career, and Vocational Education, 1998).

[35]See, for example, H. Raham, Full-Service Schools, *School Business Affairs 64*(6), 24–28 (June 1998); D. MacKenzie and V. Rogers, The Full Service School: A Management and Organizational Structure for 21st Century Schools, *Community Education Journal 25*(3–4), 9–11 (Spring/Summer 1997); and J. G. Dryfoos, Full Service Schools: Revolution or Fad? *Journal of Research on Adolescence 5*(2), 147–172 (1995).

[36]IBO offers a Primary Years Program (for children ages 3 to 12), a Middle Years Program (for students ages 11 to 16), and a Diploma Program for students in the final two years of high school. See IBO's site on the Internet at **http://www.ibo.org**.

[37]See B. Schnur, A Newcomer's High School, *Educational Leadership 56*(7), 50–52 (April 1999).

[38]See, for example, Alternative Schools: Caring for Kids on the Edge, *Northwest Education 3*(4) (Summer 1998).

[39]See, for example, M. McCord, Bursting at the Seams: Financing and Planning for Rising Enrollments, *School Business Affairs 63*(6), 20–23 (June 1997); B. P. Venable, A School for All Seasons, *Executive Educator 18*(7), 24–27 (July 1996); C. C. Kneese, Review of Research on Student Learning in Year-Round Education, *Journal of Research and Development in Education 29*(2), 60–72 (Winter 1996); and N. R. Brekke, *Year-Round Education: Does It Cost More?* (Madison, WI: Consortium for Policy Research in Education, 1997).

[40]M. Barrett, The Case for More School Days, *The Atlantic Monthly 266*(5) (November 1990), pp. 78–106. Online at **http://www.theatlantic.com/politics/education/barr2f.htm**.

[41]W. D. Gee, The Copernican Plan and Year-Round Education: Two Ideas That Work Together, *Phi Delta Kappan 78*(10), 795 (June 1997).

[42]See, for example, P. L. Kubow, K. L. Wahlstrom, and A. E. Bemis, *Starting Time and School Life: Reflections From Educators and Students*, and K. L. Wahlstrom, The Prickly Politics of School Starting Times, *Phi Delta Kappan 80*(5), 344–347 and 366–371, respectively (January 1999).

[43]The phrases "students of their students" and "turn on learning" are borrowed from *Turning on Learning* (p. 2), by C. A. Grant and C. E. Sleeter, 1989 (Upper Saddle River, NJ: Prentice Hall).

[44]See, for example, L. Kohn, Quest High School's Mission and the 'Fully Functioning Person,' in H. J. Freiberg, *Perceiving, Behaving, Becoming: Lessons Learned* (Alexandria, VA: Association for Supervision and Curriculum Development, 1999), pp. 64–67; and D. K. Schnitzer and M. J. Caprio, Academy Rewards, *Educational Leadership 57*(1), 46–48 (September 1999). Celebration School is a Professional Development School (PDS), founded as a collaboration among the Osceola County School District, Stetson University, and the Walt Disney Company. See the school's Web site at **http://www.cs.osceola.k12.fl.us.**; more about PDSs in Holmes Group, *Tomorrow's Schools: Principles for the Design of Professional Development Schools* (East Lansing, MI: Holmes Group, 1990) and R. E. Ishler and K. M. Edens (Eds.), *Professional Development Schools: What Are They? What Are the Issues and Challenges? How Are They Funded? How Should They Be Evaluated?* (Kingston, RI: Association of Colleges and Schools of Education in State Universities and Land Grant Colleges, 1995).

[45]See, for example, A. C. Howe and J. Bell, Factors Associated With Successful Implementation of Interdisciplinary Curriculum Units, *Research in Middle Level Education Quarterly 21*(2), 39–52 (Winter 1998); and N. Flowers et al., The Impact of Teaming: Five Research-Based Outcomes, *Middle School Journal 31*(2), 57–60 (November 1999).

[46]See, for example, D. Barnett et al., A School Without a Principal, *Educational Leadership 55*(7), 48–49 (April 1998).

[47]See, for example, B. R. Cobb, S. Abate, and D. Baker, Effects on Students of a 4 × 4 Junior High School Block Scheduling Program, *Education Policy Analysis Archives 7*(3) (1999).

[48]See, for example, M. D. DiRocco, How an Alternating-Day Schedule Empowers Teachers, *Educational Leadership 56*(4), 82–84 (December 1998/January 1999).

[49]See, for example, T. L. Shortt and Y. V. Thayer, Block Scheduling Can Enhance School Climate, *Educational Leadership 56*(4), 76–81 (December 1998/January 1999); W. J. Ullrich and J. T. Yeamen, Using a Modified Block Schedule to Create a Positive Learning Environment, *Middle School Journal 31*(1), 14–20 (September 1999); S. Black, Learning on the Block, *American School Board Journal 185*(1), 32–34 (January 1998); and Most Commonly Asked Questions About Block Scheduling, on the Internet site of the National Association of Secondary School Principals, **http://nassp.org/services/blockfaq.htm**. [Online June 8, 1998.]

[50]See, for example, S. L. Kramer, What We Know About Block Scheduling and Its Effects on Math Instruction, Part II, *NASSP (National Association of Secondary School Principals) Bulletin 81*(587), 69–82 (March 1997).

[51]D. T. Conley, Restructuring: In Search of a Definition, *Principal 72*(3), 12–16 (January 1993).

[52]Advanced placement courses are available online. For further information, contact APEX Online Learning, 110–110th Avenue NE, Suite 210, Bellevue, WA 98004, phone: 800-453-1454, **e-mail: inquiries@apexlearning.com**

[53]Southern Regional Education Board, 1995 *Outstanding Practices* (Atlanta, GA: Author, 1995), p. 3.

[54]Southern Regional Education Board, 1995 *Outstanding Practices* (Atlanta, GA: Author, 1995), pp. 9, 10.

[55]Southern Regional Education Board, 1997 *Outstanding Practices* (Atlanta, GA: Author, 1998), p. 20.

[56]P. I. Tiedt and I. M. Tiedt, *Multicultural Teaching: A Handbook of Activities, Information, and Resources,* 5th ed. (Boston: Allyn & Bacon, 1999), p. 35.

[57]R. J. Rossi and S. C. Stringfield, What We Must Do for Students Placed at Risk, *Phi Delta Kappan 77*(1), 73–76 (September 1995).

[58]See, for example, T. L. Williams, *The Directory of Programs for Students at Risk* (New York: Eye on Education, 1999). Visit the home page of The National Institute on the Education of At-Risk Students at **http://www.ed.gov/offices/OERI/**.

[59]J. A. Brown and C. A. Moffett, *The Hero's Journey: How Educators Can Transform Schools and Improve Learning* (Alexandria, VA: Association for Supervision and Curriculum Development, 1999), p. 24.

[60]A. L. Costa, *The School as a Home for the Mind* (Palatine, IL: Skylight Publishing, 1991), pp. 97–106.

[61]In R. A. Villa and J. S. Thousands (Eds.), *Creating an Inclusive School* (Alexandria, VA: Association for Supervision and Curriculum Development, 1995), p. 36.

[62]See, for example, P. Wasley, Teaching Worth Celebrating, *Educational Leadership 56*(8), 8–13 (May 1999).

[63]See P. Sullivan, The PTA's National Standards, *Educational Leadership 55*(8), 43–44 (May 1998). For a copy of the standards contact the National PTA, 330 N. Wabash Ave., Chicago, IL 60611–3690, phone: (312) 670–6782 and fax: (312) 670–6783.

[64]See, for example, the Hand in Hand Web page at **http://www. handinhand.org**.

[65]See, for example, T. Whiteford, Math for Moms and Dads, *Educational Leadership 55*(8), 64–66 (May 1998).

[66]See, for example, C. Gustafson, Phone Home, *Educational Leadership 56*(2), 31–32 (October 1998).

[67]See C. Bodinger-deUriarte et al., A Guide to Promising Practices, *Educational Partnerships* (Washington, DC: ED392980, U.S. Government Printing Office, 1996); the articles in the May 1998 theme issue, Engaging Parents and the Community in School, of *Educational Leadership 55*(8); and W. C. Hope, Service Learning: A Reform Initiative for Middle Level Curriculum, *Clearing House 72*(4), 236–238 (March/April 1999).

[68]See, for example, K. Kesson and C. Oyler, Integrated Curriculum and Service Learning: Linking School-Based Knowledge and Social Action,

English Education 31(2), 135–149 (January 1999); L. Cummings and M. Winston, Service-Based Solutions, *Science Teacher 65*(1), 39–41 (January 1998); J. P. Cloud, School Community Partnerships That Work, *Social Studies Review 37*(2), 45–48 (Spring/Summer 1998); and J. Westheimer and J. Kahne, Service Learning Required: But What Exactly Do Students Learn? *Education Week 19*(20), 32, 52 (January 26, 2000).

[69]See, for example, G. I. Maeroff (Ed.), *Imaging Education: The Media and School in America* (New York: Teachers College Press, 1998).

[70]For copies of the INTASC document, contact CCSSO, One Massachusetts Ave. NW, Suite 700, Washington, DC 20001–1431, phone: 202-408-5505, **http://www.ccsso.org**.

[71]Access the standards via Internet **http://www.nbpts.org/nbpts/standards/mc-gen.html**. You may want to compare the 11 standards of the NBPTS document with the 22 "components of professional practice" in C. Danielson, *Enhancing Professional Practice: A Framework for Teaching* (Alexandria, VA: Association for Supervision and Curriculum Development, 1996).

[72]See D. R. Walling (Ed.), *Hot Buttons: Unraveling 10 Controversial Issues in Education* (Bloomington, IN: Phi Delta Kappa International, 1997).

[73]C. Rowand, *How Old Are America's Public Schools?* (Washington, DC: ED426586, National Center for Education Statistics, 1999).

[74]See, for example, S. Ohanian, Goals 2000: What's in a Name? *Phi Delta Kappan 81*(5), 233–255 (January 2000), and A. Stotkopf, Clio's Lament: Teaching and Learning History in the Age of Accountability. *Education Week 19*(21), 38, 41 (February 2, 2000).

[75]See, for example, J. Fulkerson and M. Horvich, Talent Development: Two Perspectives, and J. Van Tassel-Baska. The Development of Academic Talent, both in *Phi Delta Kappan 79*(10), 756–759 and 760–763 (respectively) (June 1998).

[76]See, for example, K. Kelly, Retention vs. Social Promotion: Schools Search for Alternatives. *The Harvard Education Letter 15*(1), 1–3 (January/February 1999).

[77]See, for example, A. S. Latham et al., What the Tests Tell Us About New Teachers, and M. H. Futrell, Recruiting Minority Teachers, both in *Educational Leadership 56*(8), 23–26 and 30–33 (respectively) (May 1999), and J. Archer, Competition Is Fierce for Minority Teachers, *Quality Counts 2000: Education Week 19*(18), 32–34 (January 13, 2000).

[78]Intended to alert teachers and parents to the warning signs exhibited by troubled children is *Early Warning-Time Response: A Guide to Safe Schools*. Written by the National Association of School Psychologists and released in August 1998, the guide is available free by calling 1-877-4ED-PUBS or from the Internet at **<http://www.ed.gov/offices/OSERS/OSEP/earlywrn.html>**.

[79]Although researchers repeatedly have reported that small schools (less than 800 students for a secondary school) are at least equal to and often superior to large ones on most measures, still in today's urban and suburban settings high school enrollments of 2,000 and more students are common. See K. Cotton, School Size, School Climate, and Student Performance, *Close-Up Number 20* (Portland, OR: Northwest Regional Educational Laboratory, 1996). [Online 2/10/00] **<http://www.nwrel.org/scpd/sirs/10/c020.html>**.

[80]See, for example, R. M. Ingersoll. The Problem of Out-of-Field Teaching. *Phi Delta Kappan 79*(10), 773–776 (June 1998), and L. Olson, Finding and Keeping Competent Teachers, *Quality Counts 2000: Education Week 19*(28), 12–18 (January 13, 2000).

[81]National Center for Education Statistics, *Mini-Digest of Education Statistics 1996* (Washington, DC: Office of Educational Research and Improvement, U.S. Department of Education, 1997), p. 37.

Middle and Secondary School Students

Module 2 Overview

No one is exactly like anyone else. The ways in which individuals differ are innumerable. Not only are there differences in physical appearance and in personality traits, but there are also differences in life experiences and cultural backgrounds. Some students have academic talents that are readily identified, whereas others' gifts are not so apparent; some students seem well-adjusted, whereas others do not appear as resilient; some students are from socioeconomic, religious, or ethnic backgrounds similar to yours, whereas others have drastically different identities.

Some of these differences may be of no consequence as far as school is concerned: whether a student's eyes are blue, hazel, or brown does not really matter. However, other differences are extremely important for teaching, because what passes as sound educational practice for one person may not be as effective for another. Thus, in this module we cover some of the common characteristics and individual differences in students that you will need to consider when planning for instruction, and we provide guidelines for leveraging classroom diversity.

While considering what to teach and how to teach it, you will need to focus on your students and the best way to be responsive to their developmental and individual needs. There is no one best method of teaching. Rather, there are numerous methods that may or may not be effective in a particular situation with particular students.

To be an effective teacher you must select the teaching method that best suits each situation. To be able to select the best teaching method means that you must have a large repertoire from which to choose. In addition to your knowledge of strategies, in deciding which method to use you will be influenced by a number of other factors, including (a) the students and how they learn; (b) the content and objectives of the instruction; and (c) the availability of equipment, materials, and other resources. In this module we explore the nature and diversity of students and how they learn.

> "It is time for the preachers, the rabbis, the priests and pundits, and the professors to believe in the awesome wonder of diversity so that they can teach those who follow them. It is time for parents to teach young people early on that in diversity there is beauty and there is strength. We all should know that diversity makes for a rich tapestry, and we must understand that all the threads of the tapestry are equal in value no matter their color; equal in importance no matter their texture."[1]
>
> —MAYA ANGELOU

Specific Objectives

At the completion of this module, you should be able to:

- Define the terms *cultural competence* and *multicultural education*, and identify skills in recognizing, celebrating, and building upon student diversity.
- Explain the five caveats and five domains used to describe adolescent development.

- Demonstrate an understanding of the significance of the concepts of learning modalities, learning styles, and learning capacities and of their implications for appropriate educational practice.

- Explain the three phases of the learning cycle and the types of learning activities that might occur in each phase.

- Describe appropriate curriculum options and instructional practices for specific groups of learners.

- Apply your developing knowledge of practical ways of recognizing and attending to students' individual differences while working with a cohort of students.

Introduction

Not only is there variation in the purpose, organization, and structure of our middle and secondary schools across America (as discussed in Module 1), but the students of today represent tremendous diversity as well. Although there are many commonalities among adolescents, each student is a unique individual. In fact, adolescent students differ in many ways. In order to teach pre-, early, and late adolescents successfully, you need to understand how they think, what motivates them, and where their interests lie. You also need to know their personal values and beliefs. This information, in addition to knowing what is developmentally appropriate at their age, will help you to make sound instructional decisions and create a classroom climate conducive to learning. This module is designed to help you gather this information and gain this understanding.

■ ADOLESCENCE

■ Characteristics of Middle and Secondary School Students

Middle and secondary school students embark on the journey from childhood to adulthood. In a dramatic growth spurt during the early years of middle school, children begin changing from little boys and girls to awkward adolescents with new secondary sex characteristics and all the problems that come with new life roles. This growing up continues until the adolescent becomes a young adult—a process often not complete until the postsecondary years.

During the middle school years (ages 10 through 14) and throughout late adolescence (ages 15 to 19), individual differences in physical, intellectual, social, and emotional growth are striking. Individuals seem to change markedly from day to day, for this is not only a period of growth but also a period of instability and insecurity.

Although adolescents desire and need opportunities to act independently, they also need and want security and support. Because of these contrasting needs for dependence on and escape from adult domination, young people tend to band together for mutual support as they experiment with new sociosexual roles. To find comfort, they often become conformists, and are extremely susceptible to peer pressure.

Nevertheless, adolescents normally are self-motivated, active, and interested in novelty. Their intellectual growth causes them to be interested in ideas and eventually allows them to cope with formal intellectual operations and abstract ideas. These desires compel some adolescents to adopt idealistic causes and others to try adventures and roles that get them into trouble.

Adolescence, undoubtedly one of the most trying times in life, is a period marked by change and uncertainty. As discussed in Module 1, middle school educators generally have recognized that students in those early adolescent years need a nurturing educational experience to guide them through this unstable period. Educators have learned that to be most effective, school organization and instructional techniques must be quite different from those of the past.

■ Teaching Adolescents

The bell rings, and the students enter your classroom, a kaleidoscope of personalities, each a bundle of eccentricities, different concentrations, different life experiences, and different dispositions and capacities. What a challenge this is—to understand and to teach 30 or so unique individuals, all at once, and to do it for 6 hours a day, 5 days a week, 180 days a year!

So, how do you help each of your students reach his or her potential? Since adolescence is an important stage of identity development where the rite of passage from childhood to adulthood remains unpredictable even if it may be typified, schools and teachers need to provide numerous opportunities for adolescents to explore and experiment in a stable and supportive environment. Adolescents share certain commonalities with their peers, so we can generalize what you need to know about what occurs during adolescence.

As educators, we want to make sure that adolescent learning needs are addressed in their school experiences. Learning is enhanced for adolescents when it is developmentally appropriate. In fact, integrating a combination of developmentally and personally appropriate accommodations is the best way to meet your students' needs.

■ Adolescent Development

In *Teaching Ten to Fourteen Year Olds,* Chris Stevenson highlights five *"givens"* concerning the passage from childhood to adulthood and then expands on what to expect in the five key domains that capture the changes that young adolescents go through.[2] The five caveats Stevenson outlines hold true universally for the adolescent experience. He explains them in the following manner: "1). Early adolescence is a growth period characterized by enormous change and variability among children. 2). Individual schedules of change are idiosyncratic. 3). Home, neighborhood, prevailing gender roles, and racial and ethnic identity influence development. 4). The influences and effects of early adolescent experiences are long-lasting. 5). Young adolescents thrive when their needs are being met."[3]

Summarized, these five truths suggest that even though all individuals go through tremendous changes during adolescence, they do so at their own pace. In addition, the home and school cultures influence the changes that usually result in profound effects. Stevenson's framework for understanding adolescent behavior considers these five truths while looking at five broad domains and the interplay among them. The five areas of adolescent development that he describes are: the introspective domain, the somatic domain, the intellectual domain, the familial domain, and the communal domain.

The central or preeminent area is the introspective domain that revolves around the key question—"who am I?"—where adolescents ponder their personal identity. This domain encompasses all the others and is affected by all perceptions, decisions, and changes in the other domains. During adolescence, students engage in constant self-talk where they weigh, reevaluate, and critically analyze everything.

The somatic domain covers the physical changes that take place during puberty. In addition to being preoccupied with their looks, adolescents also have concerns regarding their sexuality, fitness, drug and alcohol use, personal hygiene, and overall well-being, among other things. Often described as "walking raging hormones," adolescents are prone to mood swings and volatile behavior.

The changes that occur in the intellectual domain are central to any discussion on cognitive development. It is important for you to understand and respect your students' thought processes and require that they engage in learning that they are capable of handling. Most likely, as part of your educational psychology curriculum you will cover Swiss psychologist Jean Piaget's Developmental Stage Theory and focus on the types of activities, questioning, and assignments that are appropriate for students at various ages.

The familial domain looks at how adolescents interact with siblings and the evolving relationship they share with their parents and other family members. Students' relationships with relatives influence their classroom interaction. Changing roles and tensions in the family affect adolescents' self-concept and self-esteem and impact their interpersonal relationships.

We cannot underestimate the power of peer influence during this stage. The communal domain addresses the social aspect of school. Many students attend school eager to socialize. Students want to belong and explore group participation in their school, neighborhood, and local community. During adolescence, young people want to branch out and increase their sense of belonging while examining their place in the world.

Although you may think concentrating on cognitive development and its intersection with the subject you are assigned to teach is your sole responsibility, you have to teach the whole child and not limit your focus to the intellectual domain. Since adolescent students have many concerns, you must be aware of them. It is important to develop a good rapport with your students since connectedness promotes learning. Therefore, it is critical that you understand the social, emotional, and physical challenges that typify this stage in addition to the cognitive changes and limitations.

When asked to reflect on their middle school experiences, most individuals' memories are packed with tales of friendships, love interests, family ties, and other social interactions while the subjects they studied in school are often long forgotten. Truly, adolescence is a time of complex paradoxes and contradictions. In addition to knowing about the profound changes that take place during adolescence, it is important for you to also know about the various microcultures individual students identify with and are members of.

■ CULTURE AND ITS IMPACT ON EDUCATION

■ Cultural Identity

There are many definitions of **culture.** A simple, concise explanation defines culture as shared, learned behavior. We all have a cultural heritage that shapes who we are and helps us to make sense of our world. We are immersed in our cultural way of knowing and it is as natural to us as the air we breathe. The specifics describing the U.S. culture are debated, but most people would agree that we share identifiable cultural patterns that distinguish us from other cultures. By nature of the fact that you are living within the borders of the United States during the 21st century, you share certain characteristics with the dominant U.S. macroculture.

In addition, each of us belongs to many microcultural groups, also referred to as **microcultures,** *subcultures,* or *subsocieties.*[4] Microcultures are distinctive, yet their members share certain cultural patterns with all Americans. As is the case with the many microcultures we each identify with as we move through various life stages, "we feel, think, perceive and behave, in part, because of the age group to which we belong."[5] We saw evidence of a microculture sharing common characteristics in our discussion of adolescence.

Although age is one microculture you may identify with, we often limit our definition of cultural identity to race and/or ethnicity. We confuse biological factors with cultural factors, which leads us to label people based on their race and/or ethnicity, but culture is much more complex than that. Lumping students together and stereotyping them based on their membership in one or two microcultures is confining. Cultural identity is composed of a number of interrelated microcultures including—in addition to one's age, race, and ethnicity—religion, gender, class, ability, and language.[6]

As we did with our discussion of adolescence, we will offer generalizations, not stereotypes, throughout this textbook to help you to understand commonalities shared to some degree by students who belong to various microcultures. Stereotypes can be damaging, but generalizations can shed light on shared characteristics. **Stereotypes,** which are absolute and inflexible, ignore individual differences while **generalizations** simply highlight insights that may prove to be helpful. As a teacher it is important for you to learn about your students and their cultural backgrounds and then reflect that information in your classroom behavior.

Cultural Competence

To uphold our democratic ideals and provide educational opportunities for all students, it is important that school policies are equitably enforced. Therefore, the 1,200 schools of education across this country are revamping pre-service training so you and other education students will be better prepared for the diversity you will encounter in your future classrooms.

To meet the needs of a multicultural student body, some states are expanding licensure requirements to include a cultural competence component. *Cultural competence* focuses on the ability to effectively teach to a cross-cultural group of students. As defined by Diller and Moule, cultural competence "is the ability to successfully teach students who come from cultures other than your own. It entails mastering complex awareness and sensitivities, various bodies of knowledge, and a set of skills that, taken together, underlie effective cross-cultural teaching."[7]

Although there are many similarities across cultures, the differences in values, traditions, beliefs, within groups, and between groups can show up in our schools. To avoid conflict, promote social harmony, and guarantee educational equity, it is important to understand these differences and to model respect for individual differences.

Cultural Sensitivity

To be culturally competent, you first need to learn about your own cultural background and become aware of your own preferences and unconscious biases. Then you need to learn about the cultures of your students. Some of your students' cultures will be more familiar to you than others. Some students will see their home culture reflected in the school culture, while other students' experiences at school might have little in common with their home environments.

In order to increase your cultural sensitivity and provide equal educational opportunity for all students, Gollnick and Chinn make the following suggestions. "To work effectively with the heterogeneous student populations found in schools, educators need to understand and feel comfortable with their own cultural backgrounds. They also must understand the cultural setting in which the school is located to develop effective instructional strategies. They must help their students become aware of cultural differences and inequalities in the nation and in the world. One goal is to help students affirm cultural differences while realizing that individuals across cultures have many similarities."[8]

If you pick up an article addressing the current state of education in this country, you are likely to find the terms *diversity* and *challenge* in the same headline. Instead of viewing diversity in a negative light, we need a paradigm shift that recognizes diversity as the norm. Dr. Mel Levine, professor of pediatric medicine, recently published an article entitled *Celebrating Diverse Minds*. His refreshing approach honors our country's pluralism and rejoices in uncovering each student's unique gifts and talents. Levine explains, ". . . The real challenge for schools rests more with identifying and fortifying individuals' strengths than with caulking academic crevices."[9]

Multicultural Education

The concept of **multicultural education** has been around since the 1920s in this country, but the goals have changed through the years. We have shifted from an emphasis on multiethnic education where information on various racial and ethnic groups was included in the curriculum, to global education that has an international focus, to a multicultural education approach that promotes pluralism and prepares all students to participate in our diverse democratic society.[10]

Since students are not identical, and one's culture permeates every cell of one's being, a one-size-fits-all approach to teaching is not effective. All students have the right to learn, and multicultural education upholds that right by valuing diversity. Gollnick and Chinn define *multicultural education* as, "the educational strategy in which students' cultural backgrounds are used to develop effective classroom instruction and school environments. It is designed to support and extend the concepts of culture, diversity, equality, social justice, and democracy in the formal school setting."[11]

Although often misperceived as an add-on to the standard curriculum, valuable exclusively for students of color and other "multicultural students," or for younger children, or in social studies classes, the truth is a multicultural educational approach is excellent pedagogical practice in all grades, for all students, and in all subject areas.

The goal of multicultural education is to make sure all students "experience an equal opportunity to learn." It is your responsibility to establish a classroom climate that reflects your students' personal experiences and cultural backgrounds as well as aligning with their preferred learning styles. "The core theme of K–12 education in this century should be straightforward: high standards with an unwavering commitment to individuality."[12]

According to Futrell, Gomez, and Bedden, "Student diversity is often viewed as a major problem because of the way American schools are organized. The current organizational structure sorts students so that only about 20% receive what is defined as an excellent education.... Schools of education and school districts need to work together to reverse the proportions so that at least 80% of all students—regardless of language, culture, ethnicity, or socioeconomic status—will receive an excellent education."[13]

We also need to prepare students to make a smooth school-to-work transition since, even though the majority of students say they intend to pursue a postsecondary education, in reality, according to the National Center for Education Statistics, only about 60% of high school students go to college, and a smaller percentage, only 35%, actually earn an undergraduate degree.[14]

■ THE CLASSROOM IN A NATION OF INCREASING DIVERSITY

Our pluralistic society is becoming more and more complex. Demographic changes in the United States have resulted in a very racially, ethnically, religiously, and linguistically heterogeneous student body. In fact, we are one of the most diverse nations worldwide. The projections, based on immigration patterns and birthrates, suggest that we will become even more culturally diverse in the future.

The "melting pot" metaphor, popularized in 1909 by Israel Zangwell's play of the same name,[15] has been replaced with an updated image that honors individual contributions to a diverse mix. The salad bowl, tapestry, orchestra, and mosaic metaphors of today emphasize how each ingredient or component is in itself worthy and valuable but, when combined with other ingredients or components, adds to a new uniquely valuable creation.

As our demographics have changed, we have been reexamining, redefining, and expanding our understanding of the fundamental concepts supporting the teaching/learning process. A multicultural education approach that leverages the diversity we find in our classrooms today by recognizing and embracing student diversity is seen as the most effective model. The goal of this concept is to provide schooling so that all students—male and female students, exceptional students, linguistically diverse students, students of different religious backgrounds, students from the various socioeconomic realities, and students of all racial, ethnic, and cultural heritages—have equal opportunity to achieve academically.[16]

The variety of individual differences among students requires that teachers use teaching strategies and tactics that accommodate those differences. To most effectively teach students who are different from you, you need skills in (a) establishing a classroom climate in which all students feel welcome and where they can learn and are supported in doing so (topic of Module 3); (b) techniques that emphasize cooperative and social-interactive learning and that deemphasize competitive learning (topic of Module 6); (c) building upon students' learning styles, capacities, and modalities; and (d) strategies and techniques that have proven successful for students of specific differences. The last two skills are the focus of this module.

As a licensed teacher you are expected to know it all, or at least to know where you can find all necessary information—and to review it when needed. Fortunately, a wealth of information is available. Certain information you have stored in memory will surface and become useful at the most unexpected times. While concerned about all students' safety and physical well-being, you will want to remain sensitive to each student's attitudes, values, social adjustment, emotional well-being, and cognitive development. You must be prepared not only to teach one or more subjects but also to do it effectively with students of different cultural backgrounds, diverse linguistic abilities, and different learning styles, as well as with students who have been identified as having special needs. It is indeed a challenge! The statistics that follow make this challenge even more obvious.

■ Demographic Changes

The traditional two-parent, two-child family now constitutes only about 6% of U.S. households. Approximately one-half of the children in the United States will spend some years being raised by a single parent. Between one-third and one-fourth of U.S. children go home after school to places devoid of any adult supervision. And, on any given day, it is estimated that as many as 300,000 children have no place at all to call home.

The U. S. population is predicted to reach 404 million by the year 2050 (from 2004's approximately 294 million),[17] a population boom that will be led by Hispanics and Asian Americans. A steady increase in interracial marriages and interracial babies may challenge today's conceptions of multiculturalism and race.[18]

The United States truly is a multilingual, multiethnic, multicultural country. According to the 2000 U. S. Census Bureau and other predictions, approximately half of the school-age population will consist of students of color by the year 2020.[19] In some states, nonwhite students are already in the majority. It is also estimated that more than one in six children between the ages of five and seven speak a language other than English at home. More than one-third have been labeled Limited English Proficient (i.e., conversational speaking ability only). In many large school districts, more than 100 languages are represented, with as many as 20 or more different primary languages found in some classrooms. In addition, as many as one in five children lives in poverty. This increasing ethnic, cultural, linguistic, and socioeconomic diversity is affecting schools all across the country, not only the large urban areas but also traditionally homogeneous suburbs and small rural communities.

The overall picture that emerges is a rapidly changing, diverse student population that challenges teaching skills. Teachers who traditionally have used the lecture and other techniques of direct instruction (see Module 7) as the dominant mode of instruction have done so with the assumption that their students were relatively homogeneous in terms of experience, background, knowledge, motivation, and facility with the English language. However, no such assumption can be made today in classrooms of such cultural, ethnic, and linguistic diversity. As a classroom teacher of today, you must be knowledgeable and skilled in using teaching strategies that recognize, celebrate, and build upon that diversity.

■ STYLES OF LEARNING AND IMPLICATIONS FOR TEACHING

The most effective classroom teachers are those who adapt their teaching styles and methods to their students, using approaches (a) that interest the students, (b) that are neither too easy nor too difficult, (c) that match the students' learning styles and learning capacities, and (d) that are relevant to the students' lives. This adaptation process is further complicated because each student is different from every other one. All have varying interests, abilities, backgrounds, and learning styles and capacities. As a matter of fact, not only do young people differ from one another, but each student can change to some extent from one day to the next. Therefore, you need to consider both the nature of students in general (for example, methods appropriate for a particular seventh-grade class are unlikely to be the same as those that work best for a group of high school seniors)

and each student in particular. Since you probably have already experienced a recent course in the psychology of learning, what follows is only a brief synopsis of relevant knowledge about learning.

■ Learning Modalities

The most basic way that individual students differ is in how they prefer to take in information. **Learning modality** refers to the *sensory portal* (or input channel) by which a learner prefers to receive sensory reception (modality preference), or the actual way a person learns best (modality adeptness). Some students prefer learning by seeing, a *visual modality;* others prefer learning through instruction from others (through talk), an *auditory modality;* while many others prefer learning by doing and being physically involved, the *kinesthetic modality;* and by touching objects, the *tactile modality.* A student's modality preference is not always that student's modality strength.

While primary modality strength can be determined by observing students, it can also be mixed and it can change as the result of experience and intellectual maturity. As one might suspect, *modality integration* (i.e., engaging more of the sensory input channels, using several modalities at once or staggered) has been found to contribute to better achievement in student learning. This concept is described in Part 2 of this book.

Learning modality and its implications for teaching Because many middle school and high school students neither have a preference nor a strength for auditory reception, teachers should severely limit their use of the lecture method of instruction, that is, of too much reliance on formal teacher talk. Furthermore, instruction that uses a singular approach, such as auditory (e.g., talking to the students), cheats students who learn better another way. This difference can affect student achievement. A teacher, for example, who only talks to the students or uses discussions day after day is shortchanging the education of learners who learn better another way, who are, for example, kinesthetic and visual learners. One purpose of Exercises 2.1A and 2.1B is to get you to start integrating all of the learning modalities in your teaching. Do these exercises now.

Finally, if a teacher's verbal communication conflicts with his or her nonverbal messages, students can become confused, and this too can affect their learning. When there is a discrepancy between what the teacher says and what that teacher does, the teacher's nonverbal signal will triumph every time. A teacher, for example, who has just finished a lesson on the conservation of energy and does not turn off the room lights upon leaving the classroom for lunch has, by his or her inappropriate modeling behavior, created cognitive disequilibrium and sabotaged the very purpose for the lesson.

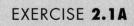

EXERCISE **2.1A**

■ Create an Ice-Breaker Activity Addressing the Learning Modalities

Now practice what you have learned about learning modalities. Middle and high school teachers often have 150+ students each semester or each new school year. It is important for you to learn the names of your students. It is also important for your students to learn each others' names.

Describe an ice-breaker activity that you would use with your class to get to know the names of your students. Be sure to include activities that address each of the learning modalities: visual, auditory, kinesthetic, and tactile.

 To access this exercise online, go to the Companion Website at **www.prenhall.com/kellough.**

EXERCISE **2.1B**

■ Create a Warm-Up Activity Addressing the Learning Modalities

Describe a warm-up activity that you would use with your class so that you could learn some personal information about your students. Be sure to include activities that address each of the learning modalities: visual, auditory, kinesthetic, and tactile.

 To access this exercise online, go to the Companion Website at **www.prenhall.com/kellough.**

Actions do speak louder than words[20] As a general rule, most middle and secondary school students prefer and learn best by touching objects, by feeling shapes and textures, by interacting with each other, and by moving things around. In contrast, learning by sitting and listening are difficult for many of them. At one school, after discovering that nearly two-thirds of its students were either tactile or kinesthetic learners, teachers and administrators grouped the students according to their modality strengths and altered reading instruction schedules every 3 weeks so that each group had opportunities to learn at the best time of day. As a result, student behavior, learning achievement, and attitudes improved considerably.[21]

Certain learning-style traits significantly discriminate between students who are at risk of not finishing school and students who perform well. Students who are underachieving and at-risk need (a) frequent opportunities for mobility; (b) options and choices; (c) a variety of instructional resources, environments, and sociological groupings, rather than routines and patterns; (d) to learn during late morning, afternoon, or evening hours, rather than in the early morning; (e) informal seating, rather than wooden, steel, or plastic chairs; (f) low illumination, because bright light contributes to hyperactivity; and (g) tactile/visual introductory resources reinforced by kinesthetic (i.e., direct experiencing and whole-body activities)/visual resources, or introductory kinesthetic/visual resources reinforced by tactile/visual resources.[22]

Regardless of the grade level and subject(s) you intend to teach, you are advised to use strategies that integrate the modalities. When well-designed, thematic units and project-based learning incorporate modality integration. In conclusion, then, when teaching any group of students of mixed learning abilities, mixed modality strengths, mixed language proficiency, and mixed cultural backgrounds, the integration of learning modalities is a must for the most successful teaching.

■ Learning Styles

Related to learning modality is *learning style,* which can be defined as *independent forms of knowing and processing information.* While some students may be comfortable with beginning their learning of a new idea in the abstract (e.g., visual or verbal symbolization), most need to begin with the concrete (e.g., learning by actually doing it). While some students prosper while working alone, many others prefer working in groups. Some are quick in their studies, whereas others are slow, cautious, and meticulous. Some can sustain attention on a single topic for a long time, becoming more absorbed in their study as time passes. Others are slower starters and more casual in their pursuits but are capable of shifting with ease from subject to subject. Some can study in the midst of music, noise, or movement, whereas others need quiet, solitude, and a desk or table. The point is this: *Students vary in not only their skills and preferences in the way knowledge is received, but also in how they mentally process that information once it has been received.* The latter is a person's style of learning.

Classifications of learning styles It is important to note that learning style is not an indicator of intelligence, but rather an indicator of how a person learns. Although there are probably as many types of learning styles as there are individuals, David Kolb describes two major differences in how people learn: How they perceive situations and how they process information.[23] On the basis of perceiving and processing an earlier work by Carl Jung on psychological types,[24] Bernice McCarthy has described four major learning styles, presented in the following paragraphs.[25]

The *imaginative learner* perceives information concretely and processes it reflectively. Imaginative learners learn well by listening and sharing with others, and integrating the ideas of others with their own experiences. Imaginative learners often have difficulty adjusting to traditional teaching, which depends less on classroom interactions and students' sharing and connecting of their prior experiences. In a traditional classroom, the imaginative learner is likely to be an at-risk student.

The *analytic learner* perceives information abstractly and processes it reflectively. The analytic learner prefers sequential thinking, needs details, and values what experts have to offer. Analytic learners do well in traditional classrooms.

The *commonsense learner* perceives information abstractly and processes it actively. The commonsense learner is pragmatic and enjoys hands-on learning. Commonsense learners sometimes find school frustrating unless they can see immediate use to what is being learned. In the traditional classroom the commonsense learner is likely to be a learner who is at risk of not completing school but of dropping out.

The *dynamic learner* perceives information concretely and processes it actively. The dynamic learner also prefers hands-on learning and is excited by anything new. Dynamic learners are risk takers and are frustrated by learning if they see it as being tedious and sequential. In a traditional classroom the dynamic learner also is likely to be an at-risk student.

■ THE LEARNING CYCLE

To understand conceptual development and change, researchers in the 1960s developed a Piaget-based theory of learning where students are guided from concrete,

hands-on learning experiences to the abstract formulations of concepts and their formal applications. This theory became known as the three-phase learning cycle.[26] Long a popular strategy for teaching science, the learning cycle can be useful in other disciplines as well.[27] The three phases are (a) the *exploratory hands-on phase,* where students can explore ideas and experience assimilation and disequilibrium that lead to their own questions and tentative answers; (b) the *invention or concept development phase,* where, under the guidance of the teacher, students invent concepts and principles that help them answer their questions and reorganize their ideas; that is, the students revise their thinking to allow the new information to fit; and (c) the *expansion or concept application phase,* another hands-on phase where the students try out their new ideas by applying them to situations that are relevant and meaningful to them. During application of a concept the learner may discover new information that causes a change in the learner's understanding of the concept being applied. Thus, the process of learning is cyclical.[28]

There have been more recent interpretations or modifications of the three-phase cycle, such as McCarthy's 4MAT.[29] With the 4MAT system, teachers employ a learning cycle of instructional strategies to try and reach each student's learning style. As stated by McCarthy, in the cycle learners sense and feel, they experience, then they watch, they reflect; then they think, they develop theories, then they try out theories, and they experiment. Finally, they evaluate and synthesize what they have learned in order to apply it to their next similar experience. They get smarter. They apply experience to experiences.[30] And, in this process they are likely to be using all four learning modalities.

To evince constructivist learning theory—that is, that learning is a process involving the active engagement of learners who adapt the educative event to fit and expand their individual worldview (as opposed to the behaviorist pedagogical assumption that learning is something done to learners)[31] and to accentuate the importance of student self-assessment—some variations of the learning cycle include a fourth phase, an *assessment phase.* However, because we, the authors of this book, believe that assessment of what students know or think they know should be a continual process, permeating all three phases of the learning cycle, we reject any treatment of assessment as a self-standing phase.

■ LEARNING CAPACITIES: THE THEORY OF MULTIPLE INTELLIGENCES

In contrast to learning styles, Gardner introduced what he calls *learning capacities* exhibited by individuals in differing ways.[32] Originally, and sometimes still, referred to as multiple intelligences, or even ways of knowing, capacities thus far identified are:

- *Bodily/kinesthetic:* ability to use the body skillfully and to handle objects skillfully.

- *Interpersonal:* ability to understand people and relationships.

- *Intrapersonal:* ability to assess one's emotional life as a means to understand oneself and others.

- *Logical/mathematical:* ability to handle chains of reasoning and to recognize patterns and orders.

- *Musical:* sensitivity to pitch, melody, rhythm, and tone.

- *Naturalist:* ability to draw on materials and features of the natural environment to solve problems or fashion products.

- *Verbal/linguistic:* sensitivity to the meaning and order of words.

- *Visual/spatial:* ability to perceive the world accurately and to manipulate the nature of space, such as through architecture, mime, or sculpture.

Apply the theory of multiple intelligences by completing Exercise 2.2.

EXERCISE 2.2

■ Modify a Lesson Plan to Integrate the Multiple Intelligences

Instructions: Get into small groups of three to five students based on the subject area you plan to teach. Suggested small groups include: English/Language Arts, History/Social Studies, Science, Mathematics, Physical Education, Health, Music, Art, and Foreign Language. If there are fewer than two people in a group, combine groups. In your discipline groups, decide on a course, grade level, and lesson plan. If your entire class consists of students with the same major, break into groups of three to five students each and have each group select a different grade level, course, and/or lesson plan. Review each of the eight multiple intelligences and describe an activity you would include in your lesson to address each one. Record your ideas here.

Now that you have been introduced to Gardner's eight different ways of knowing, or multiple intelligences, you have the opportunity to discuss how you would modify a lesson plan in your discipline to integrate each of the different ways of knowing.

Our lesson plan entitled _____ is designed for _____ graders in a _____ course. Following are the various activities we would include to address the multiple intelligences.

1. Bodily/kinesthetic

2. Interpersonal

3. Intrapersonal

4. Logical/Mathematical

5. Musical

6. Naturalist

7. Verbal/Linguistic

8. Visual/Spatial

(continued)

Now answer the following questions. After you discuss and record your answers in your small groups, be prepared to share your lesson plan activities with the rest of the class. Ask for their input on other activities you could include.

1. Which of the multiple intelligences were easiest for you to use to come up with an activity for your lesson plan? Why?

2. Which of the multiple intelligences were hardest for you to use to come up with an activity for your lesson plan? Why?

 To access this exercise online, go to the Companion Website at **www.prenhall.com/kellough.**

As discussed earlier, and as implied in the presentation of McCarthy's four types of learners, many educators believe that many of the students who are at risk of not completing school are those who may be dominant in a cognitive learning style that is not in sync with traditional teaching methods. Traditional methods are largely of McCarthy's analytic style, where information is presented in a logical, linear, sequential fashion, and of three of the Gardner types: verbal/linguistic, logical/mathematical, and intrapersonal. Consequently, to better synchronize methods of instruction with learning styles, some teachers and schools have restructured the curriculum and instruction around Gardner's learning capacities.[33] See the sample classroom scenario shown in Figure 2.1. Internet resources on learning styles and multiple intelligences are shown in Figure 2.2.

■ Learning Style and Its Implications for Teaching

The importance of the preceding information about learning styles is that you must realize at least two things:

1. *Intelligence is not a fixed or static reality, but can be learned, taught, and developed.* This concept is important for students to understand, too. When students understand that intelligence is incremental, something that is developed through use over time, they tend to be more motivated to work at learning than when they believe intelligence is a fixed entity.[34]

2. *Not all students learn and respond to learning situations in the same way.* A student may learn differently according to the situation or according to

In one middle school classroom, during one week of a 6-week thematic unit on weather, students were concentrating on learning about the water cycle. For this study of the water cycle, with the students' help the teacher divided the class into several groups of three to five students per group. While working on six projects simultaneously to learn about the water cycle: (a) one group of students designed, conducted, and repeated an experiment to discover the number of drops of water that can be held on one side of a new one-cent coin versus the number that can be held on the side of a worn one-cent coin; (b) working in part with the first group, a second group designed and prepared graphs to illustrate the results of the experiments of the first group; (c) a third group of students created and composed the words and music of a song about the water cycle; (d) a fourth group incorporated their combined interests in mathematics and art to design, collect the necessary materials, and create a colorful and interactive bulletin board about the water cycle; (e) a fifth group read about the water cycle in materials they researched from the Internet and various libraries; and (f) a sixth group created a puppet show about the water cycle. On Friday, after each group had finished, the groups shared their projects with the whole class.

FIGURE 2.1 ● Classroom Vignette: Using the Theory of Learning Capacities (Multiple Intelligences) and Multitasking

- **ERIC Link to Multiple Intelligences Resources** <http://reading-indiana.edu>.
- **HG Project Zero** <http://www.pz.harvard.edu/>.
- **Multiple Intelligences** <http://www.education-world.com/a_curr/curr207.shtml>.
- **Resources on Learning Styles** <http://www.support4learning.org.uk/education/lstyles.htm>.

FIGURE 2.2 ● Internet Resources on Learning Styles and Multiple Intelligences

the student's ethnicity, cultural background, or socioeconomic status.[35] A teacher who, for all students, uses only one style of teaching, or who teaches using only one or a few styles of learning, day after day, is short-changing those students who learn better another way. As emphasized by Rita Dunn, when students do not learn the way we teach them, then we must teach them the way they learn.[36]

MEETING THE CHALLENGE: RECOGNIZING AND PROVIDING FOR STUDENT DIFFERENCES

Assume that you are a high school history teacher and that your teaching schedule includes three sections of U.S. history. Furthermore, assume that students at your school are tracked (as they are in many high schools). One of your classes is a so-called college-prep class with 30 students. Another is a regular-education class with 35 students, 3 of whom have special needs because of disabilities. And the third is a sheltered English class with 13 students, 6 Hispanics with limited proficiency in English, 3 students from the former Soviet Union with very limited proficiency in English, and 4 Southeast Asians, 2 with no ability to use English. Again, for all three sections, the course is U.S. history. Will one lesson plan using lecture and teacher-directed discussion as the primary instructional strategies work for all three sections? The answer is an emphatic *no!* How do you decide what to do? Before you finish this book we hope the answer to that question will become clear to you.

First consider the following general guidelines, most of which are discussed in further detail in later modules as designated.

INSTRUCTIONAL PRACTICES THAT PROVIDE FOR STUDENT DIFFERENCES: GENERAL GUIDELINES

To provide learning experiences that are consistent with what is known about ways of learning and knowing, consider the recommendations that follow and refer to them during the preactive phase of your instruction (discussed in Module 1).

- As frequently as is appropriate, and especially for skills development, plan the learning activities so they follow a step-by-step sequence from concrete to abstract.

- With students, collaboratively plan challenging and engaging classroom learning activities and assignments (see Modules 6, 7, and others).

- Concentrate on using student-centered instruction, by using project-centered learning, discovery and inquiry strategies, and simulations and role-play (Module 6).

- Establish multiple learning centers within the classroom (Module 6).

- Maintain high, although not necessarily identical, expectations for every student; establish high standards and teach toward them without wavering (see throughout).

- Make learning meaningful by integrating learning with life, academic with vocational, helping each student successfully make the transitions from one level of learning to the next, one level of schooling to the next, and from school to life (see throughout).

- Provide a structured learning environment with regular and understood procedures (Module 3).

- Provide ongoing and frequent monitoring of individual student learning (formative assessment) (Module 9).

- Provide variations in meaningful assignments, with optional due dates, that are based on individual student abilities and interests (Modules 4 and 7).

- Use direct instruction to teach to the development of observation, generalization, and other thinking and learning skills (Module 6).

- Use reciprocal peer coaching and cross-age tutoring (Module 6).

- Use multilevel instruction (see Figure 2.1 and Module 4).

- Use interactive computer programs and multimedia (Module 8).

- Use small-group and cooperative learning strategies (Module 6).

Because social awareness is such an important and integral part of a student's experience, exemplary school programs and much of their practices are geared toward some type of social interaction. Indeed, learning is a social enterprise among learners and their teachers. Although many of today's successful instructional practices rely heavily on social learning activities and interpersonal relationships, each teacher must be aware of and sensitive to individual student differences.

RECOGNIZING AND WORKING WITH EXCEPTIONAL STUDENTS

If you think of placing students along a continuum, the bulk of students we refer to as *average* or *normal* would collect around the center point. Those students who deviate from the norm (either below or above) would fall somewhere between the center point and either end of the spectrum. The more they deviated from the *norm*, the farther those students would be placed away from the center. To reach their academic potential, these students would need special accommodations. Those students falling outside the *norm* would be classified as **exceptional learners,** also known as *students with special needs.* Included under this broad label are those with disabling conditions or impairments in any one or more of the following categories: mental retardation, hearing, speech or language, visual, emotional, orthopedic, autism, traumatic brain injury, other health impairment, or specific learning disability. Gifted and Talented students fall under this umbrella term as well.

To the extent possible, students with special needs must be educated with their peers in the regular classroom. Public Law 94-142, the Education for All Handicapped Children Act (EAHCA) of 1975, mandates that all children have the right to a free and appropriate education, as well as to nondiscriminatory assessment. (Public Law 94-142 was amended in 1986 by P. L. 99-457. It was again amended in 1990 by P. L. 101-476, at which time its name was changed to Individuals with Disabilities Education Act—IDEA. It was again amended in 1997 by P. L. 105-17 to better ensure that all students are given access to a broad, rich general curriculum.) Emphasizing the normalization of the educational environment for students with disabilities, this legislation requires provision of the **least-restrictive environment (LRE)** for these students. An LRE is an environment that is as normal as possible.

Students identified as having special needs may be placed in the regular classroom for the entire school day, called *full inclusion* (as is the trend).[37] Those students may also be in a regular classroom the greater part of the school day, called *partial inclusion,* or only for designated periods. Although there is no single, universally accepted definition of the term, *inclusion* is the concept that students with disabilities should be integrated into general education classrooms regardless of whether they can meet traditional academic standards.[38] (The term *inclusion* has largely replaced use of an earlier and similar term, *mainstreaming.*) As a classroom teacher you will need information and skills specific to teaching learners with special needs who are included in your classes.

Generally speaking, teaching students who have special needs requires more care, better diagnosis, greater skill, more attention to individual needs, and an even greater understanding of the students. The challenges of teaching students with special needs in the regular classroom are great enough that to do it well you need specialized training beyond the general guidelines presented here.

When a student with special needs is placed in your classroom, your task is to develop an understanding of the general characteristics of different types of special needs learners, identify the student's unique needs relative to your classroom, and design lessons that teach to different needs at the same time (as exemplified in Figure 2.1 and discussed in the section Multitasking at the end of this module). Remember that just because a student has been identified as having one or more special needs does not preclude that person from being gifted or talented.

Congress stipulated in P.L. 94-142 that an Individualized Educational Program (IEP) be devised annually for each child with special needs. According to that law, an IEP is developed for each student each year by a team that includes special education teachers, the child's parents or guardians, and the classroom teachers. The IEP contains a statement of the student's present educational levels, the educational goals for the year, specifications for the services to be provided and the extent to which the student should be expected to take part in the regular education program, and the evaluative criteria for the services to be provided. Consultation by special and skilled support personnel is essential in all IEP models. A consultant works directly with teachers or with students and parents. As a classroom teacher, you may play an active role in preparing the specifications for the students with special needs assigned to your classroom, as well as have major responsibility for implementing the program. Today, some schools report success using personalized learning plans for all students, not only those with special needs.[39]

■ GUIDELINES FOR WORKING WITH STUDENTS WITH SPECIAL NEEDS IN THE REGULAR CLASSROOM

Although the guidelines represented by the paragraphs that follow are important for teaching all students, they are especially important for working with students with special needs. Familiarize yourself with exactly what the special needs of each learner are. Privately ask the student whether there is anything he or she would like for you to know that may help you to facilitate his or her learning while in your class.

Adapt and modify materials and procedures to the special needs of each student. For example, a student who has extreme difficulty sitting still for more than a few minutes will need planned changes in learning activities. When establishing student seating arrangements in the classroom, give preference to students according to their special needs. Try to incorporate into lessons activities that engage all learning modalities—visual, auditory, tactile, and kinesthetic. Be flexible in your classroom procedures. For example, allow the use of tape recorders for note taking and test taking when students have trouble with the written language.

Provide high structure and clear expectations by defining the learning objectives in behavioral terms (discussed in Module 4). Teach students the correct procedures for everything (Module 3). Break complex learning into simpler components, moving from the most concrete to the abstract, rather than the other way around. Check frequently for student understanding of instructions and procedures, and for comprehension of content. Use computers and other self-correcting materials for drill and practice and for provision of immediate and private feedback to the student.

Develop your **withitness,** which is your awareness of everything that is going on in the classroom, at all times, by monitoring students for signs of restlessness, frustration, anxiety, and off-task behaviors. Be ready to reassign individual learners to different activities as the situation warrants. Established classroom learning centers (discussed in Module 6) can be a big help.

Have all students maintain assignments for the week or some other period of time in an assignment book or in a folder that is kept in their notebooks. Post assignments in a special place in the classroom and frequently remind students of these and of assignment deadlines.

Maintain consistency in your expectations and in your responses. Learners with special needs can become frustrated when they do not understand a teacher's expectations and when they cannot depend on a teacher's reactions. Plan interesting bridging activities for learning, activities that help the students connect what is being learned with their real world. Learning that connects what is being learned with the real world helps to motivate students and to keep them on-task.

Plan questions and questioning sequences and write them into your lesson plans (discussed in Module 7). Plan questions that you ask learners with special needs so that they are likely to answer them with confidence. Use signals to let students know that you are likely to call on them in class (e.g., prolonged eye contact or mentioning your intention to the student before class begins). After asking a question, give the student adequate time to think and respond. Then, after the student responds, build upon the student's response to indicate that the student's contribution was accepted as being important.

Provide for and teach toward student success. Offer students activities and experiences that ensure each individual student's success and mastery at some level. Use of student portfolios (discussed in Module 9) can give evidence of progress and help in building student confidence and self-esteem.

Provide guided or coached practice. Provide time in class for students to work on assignments and projects. During this time, you can monitor the work of each student while looking for misconceptions, thus ensuring that students get started on the right track.

Provide help in the organization of students' learning. For example, give instruction in the organization of notes and notebooks. Have a three-hole punch available in the classroom so students can put papers into their notebooks immediately, thus avoiding disorganization and lost papers. During class presentations use an overhead projector with transparencies; students who need more time can then copy material from the transparencies. Ask students to read their notes aloud to each other in small groups, thereby aiding their recall and understanding, and encouraging them to take notes for meaning rather than for rote learning. Encourage and provide for peer support, peer tutoring or coaching, and cross-age teaching (Module 6). Ensure that the learners with special needs are included in all class activities to the fullest extent possible.[40]

■ WORKING WITH CULTURALLY AND LINGUISTICALLY DIVERSE STUDENTS

Quickly determine the language and ethnic groups represented by the students in your classroom. A major problem for recent newcomers, as well as some ethnic groups, is learning a second (or third or fourth) language. While in many schools it is not uncommon for more than half the students to come from homes where the home language is not English, standard English is a necessity in most communities of this country if a person is to become vocationally successful and enjoy a full life.

Learning basic communication skills in English can take an immigrant student at least a year and probably longer; to master English well enough to compete with their English-speaking counterparts in cognitively challenging academic courses it may take English Language Learners (ELLs) up to 7 years. By default, then, an increasing number of teachers are teachers of English Language Learning. Helpful to the success of ELLs is the demonstration of respect for students' cultural backgrounds, long-term teacher-student cohorts (such as, for example, in looping), and the use of active and cooperative learning.[41]

There are numerous programs specially designed for English Language Learners. Students' language skills will vary greatly. Some non-English-speaking students may understand single sentences and speak simple words or phrases in English. Sometimes students who are considered fluent in English may have an excellent command of everyday spoken English, and yet the student's overall academic achievement may still be less than desired because of language or cultural differences.[42]

Some schools use a "pullout" approach, where part of the student's school time is spent in special classes, and the rest of the time the student is placed in regular classrooms. In some schools, English Language Learners are placed in academic classrooms that use a "sheltered" English approach. Regardless of the program, specific techniques recommended for teaching English Language Learners include:

- Allowing more time for learning activities than one normally would.

- Allowing time for addressing language as well as content objectives for each lesson.

A HUMOROUS SCENARIO RELATED TO IDIOMS: A TEACHABLE MOMENT

While Lina was reciting she had a little difficulty with her throat (due to a cold) and stumbled over some words. The teacher jokingly commented, "That's okay Lina, you must have a horse in your throat." Quickly, Monique, a Hispanic student and recent immigrant, asked, "How could she have a horse in her throat?" The teacher ignored Monique's question. Missing a teachable moment, the teacher continued with the planned lesson.

- Avoiding jargon or idioms that might be misunderstood. See the scenario above.

- Dividing complex or extended language discourse into smaller, more manageable units.

- Giving directions in a variety of ways.

- Giving special attention to key words that convey meaning, and writing them on the board.

- Reading written directions aloud, and then writing the directions on the board.

- Speaking clearly and naturally but at a slower than normal pace.

- Using a variety of examples and observable models.

- Using simplified vocabulary without talking down to students.[43]

ADDITIONAL GUIDELINES FOR WORKING WITH ENGLISH LANGUAGE LEARNERS

While they are becoming literate in English language usage, English Language Learners are expected to learn the same curriculum in the various disciplines as native English-speaking students. Although the guidelines presented in the following paragraphs are important for teaching all students, they are especially important when working with non-native-English-speaking students.

Present instruction that is concrete and that includes the most direct learning experiences possible. Use the most concrete (least abstract) forms of instruction.

Build upon (or connect with) what the students already have experienced and know. Building upon what students already know, or think they know, helps them to connect their knowledge and construct their understandings.

Encourage student writing. One way is by using student journals (see Module 6). Two kinds of journals are appropriate when working with English Language Learners: dialogue journals and response journals. Dialogue journals are used for students to write anything that is on their minds, usually on the right page. Teachers, parents, and classmates then respond on the left page, thereby "talking with" the journal writers. Response journals are used for students to write (record) their responses to what they are reading or studying.[44]

Help students learn the vocabulary. Assist the English Language Learners in learning two vocabulary sets: the regular English vocabulary needed for learning and the new vocabulary introduced by the subject content. For example, while learning science a student is dealing with both the regular English language vocabulary and the special vocabulary of science.

Involve parents, guardians, or older siblings. Students whose primary language is not English may have other differences about which you will also need to become knowledgeable. These differences are related to culture, customs, family life, and expectations. To be most successful in working with linguistically different students, you should learn as much as possible about each student. To this end it can be valuable to solicit the help of the student's parent, guardian, or even an older sibling. Parents (or guardians) of new immigrant children are usually truly concerned about the education of their children and may be very interested in cooperating with you in any way possible. In a study of schools recognized for their exemplary practices with language-minority students, the schools were recognized for being "parent friendly," that is, for welcoming parents in a variety of innovative ways.[45]

Plan for and use all learning modalities. As with teaching children in general, in working with linguistically different students in particular you need to use multisensory approaches—learning activities that involve students in auditory, visual, tactile, and kinesthetic learning activities.

Use small-group cooperative learning. Cooperative learning strategies are particularly effective with linguistically different students because they provide opportunities for students to produce language in a setting that is less threatening than is speaking before the entire class.

Use the benefits afforded by modern technology. For example, computer networking allows the linguistically different students to write and communicate with peers from around the world as well as to participate in "publishing" their classroom work.

BEST PRACTICES FOR PROMOTING SUCCESS FOR ALL STUDENTS

To be compatible with, and be able to teach, students who come from backgrounds different from yours, you need to believe that, given adequate support, *all* students *can* learn—regardless of gender, social class, physical characteristics, language, and ethnic or cultural backgrounds. You also need to develop special skills that include those in the following guidelines, each of which is discussed in detail in other modules. To work successfully and most effectively with students of diverse backgrounds, you should:

- Build the learning around students' individual learning styles. Personalize learning for each student, much like what is done by using the IEP with learners with special needs. Involve students in understanding and in making important decisions about their own learning, so that they feel ownership (i.e., a sense of empowerment and connectedness) of that learning.

- Communicate positively with every student and with the student's parents or guardians, learning as much as you can about the student and the student's culture and encouraging family members to participate in the student's learning. Involve parents, guardians, and other members of the community in the educational program so that all have a sense of ownership and responsibility and feel positive about the school program.

- Establish and maintain high expectations, although not necessarily the same expectations, for each student. Both you and your students must understand that intelligence is not a fixed entity, but a set of characteristics that—through a feeling of "I can" and with proper coaching—can be developed.

- Teach to individuals by using a variety of strategies to achieve an objective or by using a number of different objectives at the same time (multilevel teaching).

- Use techniques that emphasize collaborative and cooperative learning—that deemphasize competitive learning.

▬ RECOGNIZING AND WORKING WITH STUDENTS WHO ARE GIFTED

Historically, educators have used the term *gifted* when referring to a person with identified exceptional ability in one or more academic subjects, and have used the term *talented* when referring to a person with exceptional ability in one or more of the visual or performing arts.[46] Today, however, the terms often are used interchangeably, which is how they are used here; that is, as if they are synonymous.

Sometimes, unfortunately, in the regular classroom gifted students are neglected.[47] At least part of the time, it is likely to be because there is no singularly accepted method for identification of these students. For placement in special classes or programs for the Gifted and Talented, school districts traditionally have used grade point averages and standard intelligence quotient (IQ) scores.

However, because IQ testing measures linguistic and logical/mathematical aspects of giftedness (refer to earlier discussion in this module—Learning Capacities: The Theory of Multiple Intelligences), it does not account for others, and thus gifted students sometimes are unrecognized; they also are sometimes among the students most at-risk of dropping out of school.[48] It is estimated that between 10 and 20% of school dropouts are students who are in the range of being intellectually gifted.[49]

To work most effectively with gifted learners, their talents first must be identified. This can be done not only by using tests, rating scales, and auditions but also by observations in the classroom, on the campus, and from knowledge about the student's personal life. With those information sources in mind, here is a list of indicators of superior intelligence:[50]

- Ability to extrapolate knowledge to different circumstances.
- Ability to manipulate a symbol system.
- Ability to reason by analogy.
- Ability to take on adult roles at home, such as managing the household and supervising siblings, even at the expense of school attendance and achievement.
- Ability to think logically.
- Ability to use stored knowledge to solve problems.
- Creativity and artistic ability.
- Leadership ability and an independent mind.
- Resiliency: The ability to cope with school while living in poverty and/or with dysfunctional families.
- Strong sense of self, pride, and worth.
- Understanding of one's cultural heritage.

To assist you in understanding gifted students that may or may not have yet been identified as being gifted, here are some types of students and the kinds of problems to which they may be prone, that is, personal behaviors that may identify them as being gifted but academically disabled, bored, and alienated.

- *Antisocial* students, alienated by their differences from peers, may become bored and impatient troublemakers.
- *Creative, high-achieving* students often feel isolated, weird, and depressed.
- *Divergent thinking* students can develop self-esteem problems when they provide answers that are logical to them but seem unusual and off-the-wall to their peers. They may have only a few peer friends.
- *Perfectionists* may exhibit compulsive behaviors because they feel as though their value comes from their accomplishments. When their accomplishments do not live up to expectations— their own, their parents', or their teachers'—anxiety

and feelings of inadequacy arise. When other students do not live up to the gifted student's high standards, alienation from those other students is probable.

- *Sensitive* students who also are gifted may become easily depressed because they are more aware of their surroundings and of their differences.

- *Students with special needs* may be gifted. Attention deficit disorder, dyslexia, hyperactivity, and other learning disorders sometimes mask giftedness.

- *Underachieving* students can also be gifted students but fail in their studies because they learn in ways that are seldom or never challenged by classroom teachers. Although often expected to excel in everything they do, most gifted students can be underachievers in some areas. As they have high expectations of themselves, underachievers tend to be highly critical of themselves, develop a low self-esteem, and can become indifferent and even hostile.[51]

Guidelines for Working with Gifted Students

When working in the regular classroom with a student who has special gifts and talents, you are advised to:

- Collaborate with students in some planning of their own objectives and activities for learning.

- Emphasize skills in critical thinking, problem solving, and inquiry.

- Identify and showcase the student's special gift or talent.

- Involve the student in selecting and planning activities, encouraging the development of the student's leadership skills.

- Plan assignments and activities that challenge the students to the full extent of their abilities. This does not mean overloading them with homework or giving identical assignments to all students. Rather, carefully plan so that the students' time spent on assignments and activities is quality time on meaningful learning.

- Provide in-class seminars for students to discuss topics and problems that they are pursuing individually or as members of a learning team.

- Provide independent and dyad learning opportunities. Gifted students often prefer to work alone or with another gifted student.

- Use curriculum compacting, which is allowing a student who already knows the material to pursue enriched or accelerated study. Plan and provide optional and voluntary enrichment activities. Learning centers, special projects, and computer and multimedia activities are excellent tools for provision of enriched learning activities.

- Use preassessments (diagnostic evaluation) for reading level and subject content achievement so that you are better able to prescribe objectives and activities for each student.

RECOGNIZING AND WORKING WITH STUDENTS WHO TAKE MORE TIME BUT ARE WILLING TO TRY

Students who take more time to learn typically fall into one of two categories: (a) those who try to learn but simply need more time to do it, and (b) those who do not try, referred to variously as *underachievers, recalcitrant,* or *reluctant learners.* Practices that work well with students of one category are often not those that work well with those of the second. Remember that just because a student is slow to learn doesn't mean that the student is less intelligent; some students just take longer, for any number of reasons. The following guidelines may be helpful when working with a slow student who has indicated a willingness to try:

- Adjust the instruction to the student's preferred learning style, which may be different from yours and from other students in the group.

- Be less concerned with the amount of content coverage than with the student's successful understanding of content that is covered.

- Discover something the student does exceptionally well, or a special interest, and try to build on that.

- Emphasize basic communication skills, such as speaking, listening, reading, and writing, to ensure that the student's skills in these areas are sufficient for learning the intended content.

- Help the student learn content in small sequential steps with frequent checks for comprehension.

- If necessary, help the student to improve his or her reading skills, such as pronunciation and word meanings.

- If using a single textbook, be certain that the reading level is adequate for the student; if it is not, then for that student use other more appropriate reading materials.

- Maximize the use of in-class, on-task work and cooperative learning, closely monitoring the student's progress. Avoid relying too much on successful completion of traditional out-of-class assignments unless the student gets coached guidance by you before leaving your classroom.

- Vary the instructional strategies, using a variety of activities to engage the visual, verbal, tactile, and kinesthetic modalities.

- When appropriate, use frequent positive reinforcement, with the intention of increasing the student's self-esteem.

◼ RECOGNIZING AND WORKING WITH RECALCITRANT STUDENTS

For working with recalcitrant students you can use many of the same guidelines from the preceding list, except that you should understand that the reasons for these students' behaviors may be quite different from those for the other category of slow learners. Slower-learning students who are willing to try are simply that—slower learning. They may be slow because of their learning style or because of genetic reasons, or a combination of the two. But they can and will learn. Recalcitrant learners, however, may be generally quick and bright thinkers but reluctant even to try because of a history of failure, a history of boredom with school, a poor self-concept, severe personal problems that distract from school, or any variety and combination of reasons, many of which are psychological in nature.

Whatever the case, you need to know that a student identified as being a slow or recalcitrant learner might, in fact, be quite gifted or talented in some way, but may have a history of increasingly poor school attendance, poor attention to schoolwork, poor self-confidence, and an attitude problem. Consider the following guidelines when working with recalcitrant learners:

- At the beginning, learn as much about each student as you can. Be cautious in how you do it, though, because many of these students will be suspicious of any genuine interest in them shown by you. Be businesslike, trusting, genuinely interested, and patient. A second caution is to use the past not as ammunition, something to be held against the student, but as insight to help you work more productively with the student.

- Avoid lecturing to these students; it won't work.

- Early in the school term, preferably with the help of adult volunteers (e.g., professional community members as mentors have worked well at helping change the student's attitude from rebellion to one of hope, challenge, and success), work out a personalized education plan with each student.

- Engage the students in learning by using interactive media, such as the Internet.

- Engage the students in active learning with real-world problem solving and perhaps community service projects.

- Forget about trying to "cover the subject," concentrating instead on the student learning some things well. A good procedure is to use thematic teaching and divide the theme into short segments. Because school attendance for these students is sometimes sporadic, try to individualize their assignments so that they can pick up where they left off and move through the course in an orderly fashion even when they have been excessively absent. Try to ensure some degree of success for each student.

- Help students develop their studying and learning skills, such as concentrating, remembering, and comprehending. Mnemonics, for example, is a device these students respond to positively and are often quick to create on their own (for examples, see Module 6).

- If using a single textbook, see if the reading level is appropriate; if it is not, then for that student discard the book and select other more appropriate reading materials.

- Make sure your classroom procedures and rules are understood at the beginning of the school term and be consistent about enforcing them.

- Maximize the use of in-class, on-task work and cooperative learning, with close monitoring of the student's progress. Do not rely on successful completion of traditional out-of-class assignments unless the student gets coached guidance from you before leaving your classroom.

- Use simple language in the classroom. Be concerned less about the words the students use and the way they use them and more about the ideas they are expressing. Let the students use their own idioms without carping too much on grammar and syntax. Always take care, though, to use proper and professional English yourself.

- When appropriate, use frequent positive reinforcement, with the intention of increasing the student's sense of personal worth. When using praise for reinforcement, however, try to praise the deed rather than the student.

◼ TEACHING TOWARD POSITIVE CHARACTER DEVELOPMENT

In the 1930s, again in the late 1960s, and now today, there is a resurgence in interest in the development of students' values, especially those of honesty, kindness, respect, and responsibility. Today this interest is in what some refer to as *character education*. Whether defined as ethics, citizenship, moral values, or personal development, character education has long been part of public education in this country.[52] Stimulated by a perceived need to act to reduce students' antisocial behaviors and to produce more respectful and responsible citizens, many schools and districts today are developing curricula in character education with the ultimate goal of "developing mature adults capable of responsible citizenship and moral action."[53]

You can teach toward positive character development in two general ways: By providing a conducive classroom atmosphere where students actively and positively share in the decision making, and by being a model that students can proudly emulate. Acquiring knowledge and developing understanding can enhance the learning of attitudes. Nevertheless, changing an attitude is often a long and tedious process, requiring the commitment of the teacher and the school, assistance from the community, and the provision of numerous experiences that will guide students to new convictions. Here are some specific practices, most of which are discussed further in later modules:

- Build a sense of community in the school and in the classroom, with shared goals, optimism, cooperative efforts, and clearly identified and practiced procedures for reaching those goals.

- Collaboratively plan with students action- and community-oriented projects that relate to curriculum themes; solicit parent and community members to assist in projects.

- Teach students to negotiate; practice and develop skills in conflict resolution, skills such as empathy, problem solving, impulse control, and anger management.[54]

- Have students research and give a presentation advocating a particular stance on a controversial issue.[55]

- Share and highlight anchor examples of class and individual cooperation in serving the classroom, school, and community.

- Make student service projects visible in the school and community.[56]

- Promote higher-order thinking about value issues through the development of skills in questioning.

- Sensitize students to issues and teach skills of conflict resolution through role-play, simulations, and creative drama. Resources on character education are shown in Figure 2.3.

When compared with traditional instruction, one characteristic of exemplary instruction today is the teacher's encouragement of dialogue among students in the classroom to discuss and to explore their own ideas. Modeling the very behaviors we expect of teachers and students in the classroom is a constant theme throughout this book.

■ MULTITASKING

To personalize the instruction to the extent possible, many teachers use *multilevel instruction* (known also as multitasking). Multitasking involves different students or groups of students working at different tasks to accomplish different objectives or working at different tasks to accomplish the same objective, all with several levels of teaching and learning going on simultaneously. An example is the classroom scenario presented in Figure 2.1.

When integrating student learning, multitasking is an important and useful, perhaps even necessary, strategy. Project-centered teaching (discussed in Module 6) is an instructional method that easily allows for the provision of multilevel instruction. When using multilevel instruction, individual students and small groups will be doing different activities at the same time to accomplish the same or different objectives. While some students may be working independently of the teacher, others may be doing small-group work, while still others are receiving direct instruction.

To most effectively teach any group of students of mixed learning capacities and abilities, modality strengths, language proficiency, and cultural backgrounds, the use of multilevel instruction is necessary.

■ SUMMARY

To teach middle and secondary students effectively it is important for you to know what is developmentally and individually appropriate for your students. You must also be familiar with the different cultural lenses through which your students view the world. As a classroom teacher you must acknowledge that students in your classroom have different ways of receiving information

---

- **Character Education Institute,** 8918 Tesoro Drive, San Antonio, TX 78217 (800-284-0499).
- **Character Education Partnership,** 918 16th Street NW, Suite 501, Washington, DC 20006 (800-988-8081). Web site: <http://www.character.org>.
- **Character Education Resources,** P.O. Box 651, Contoocook, NH 03229.
- **Developmental Studies Center,** 111 Deerwood Place, San Ramon, CA 94583 (415-838-7633).
- **Ethics Resource Center,** 1120 G Street NW, Washington, DC 20005 (202-434-8465).
- **Jefferson Center for Character Education,** 202 S. Lake Avenue, Pasadena, CA 91101 (818-792-8130). Web site: <http://www.jeffersoncenter.org>.
- **Josephson Institute of Ethics,** 310 Washington Boulevard, Marina Del Rey, CA 90292 (310-306-1868).

FIGURE 2.3 ● Selected Resources on Character Education

and different ways of processing that information—different ways of knowing and of constructing their knowledge. These differences are unique and important, and as you will learn in Part 2 of this book, they are central considerations in curriculum development and instructional practice.

You must try to learn as much as you can about how each student learns and processes information. But because you can never know everything about each student, the more you dialogue with your colleagues, vary your teaching strategies, and assist students in integrating their learning, the more likely you are to reach more of the students more of the time. In short, to be an effective classroom teacher you should: (a) learn as much about your students' cultural backgrounds and their preferred styles of learning as you can; (b) develop an eclectic style of teaching, one that is flexible and adaptable; and (c) integrate the disciplines, thereby helping students make bridges or connections between their lives and all that is being learned.

You are now ready to begin learning the specifics of how to establish and maintain a safe and effective classroom environment and plan for instruction, the topics of Part 2.

■ MODULE 2 POSTTEST

Multiple Choice

1. When a teacher is thinking about and assessing a lesson just taught, the teacher is in the _____ phase of instruction.
   a. preactive
   b. reflective
   c. projective
   d. interactive

2. A constructivist view of teaching and learning
   a. emphasizes the importance of covering the subject matter content.
   b. is irrelevant for teaching the diversity of students in today's schools.
   c. relies less on the use of manipulatives and more on the facts of the subject matter content.
   d. emphasizes the importance of preassessing the learners' understandings about the subject matter and then scaffolding or building upon that.

3. Each of the following is a learning modality except one. Which one is not?
   a. visual
   b. tactile
   c. verbal
   d. auditory
   e. kinesthetic
   f. All the above are learning modalities.

4. Assimilation is the mental process of
   a. forming a new schema.
   b. developing a naïve theory.
   c. moving away from an egocentric outlook.
   d. fitting new information into an existing schema.

5. Regarding the three-phase learning cycle, which one of the following is least like the others?
   a. direct learning
   b. exploratory phase
   c. hands-on learning
   d. expository teaching

6. While learning modality has to do with the way knowledge is received, _____ is how the learner mentally processes that information.
   a. looping
   b. learning style
   c. modality integration
   d. learning activity center

(continued)

7. The rate of a child's intellectual development is not fixed by genetics, but is affected by the child's
   a. experiences.
   b. equilibration.
   c. social interactions.
   d. all of the above.

8. Which one of the following learner types is least likely to be at-risk in a traditional classroom?
   a. dynamic
   b. analytic
   c. imaginative
   d. common sense

9. It is the contention of the authors of this textbook that your teaching style should be
   a. eclectic.
   b. student-centered.
   c. teacher-centered.
   d. curriculum-focused.

10. While teaching students about the water cycle, the teacher groups the students. One group is conducting an experiment to find out how many drops of water can be held on the side of a new penny versus how many can be held on the side of a worn penny; another group is composing a song about the water cycle; another group is creating and painting a wall poster about it; another group is reading about the water cycle on computer resources; and another group is creating a drama about the water cycle. When each group is finished, they share their group work with others in the class. This teacher is using a teaching strategy that is
    a. an example of multilevel teaching.
    b. based on Gardner's Theory of Multiple Intelligences.
    c. consistent with what is known about student learning styles.
    d. all of the above.

Short Explanation

1. Give an example of how you would use multilevel teaching in your subject field. Of what benefit is the use of multilevel teaching?
2. Explain why knowledge of teaching styles and student learning styles is important for a teacher in your subject field.
3. Explain why integration of the curriculum is important for learning in the middle and secondary school, and identify some techniques used in middle and secondary schools to integrate the learning.
4. For a concept usually taught in your subject field (your choice), demonstrate specifically how you might help students bridge their learning of that concept with what is going on in their lives and with their learning in other disciplines.
5. Do you believe that middle and secondary school teachers should be concerned about student character development? Explain why or why not. If you believe in the affirmative, explain some specific ways you would address it in your own teaching.
6. Define the concept and goal of multicultural education. Explain why you agree or disagree with the goal.
7. Colleen, a social science teacher, has a class of 33 eighth graders. During her lectures, teacher-led discussions, and recitation lessons, these students are restless and inattentive, creating a major classroom management problem for her. At Colleen's invitation, the school psychologist tests the children for learning modality and finds that 29 of the 33 are predominantly kinesthetic learners. Of what use is this information to Colleen?
8. Describe the concept of inclusion and its importance to the teacher of the regular classroom.
9. Describe when, by whom, and for whom individual education programs are prepared.
10. Describe the concept and importance of the "teachable moment."

Essay

1. Identify the topic of a lesson for middle school or secondary school students in your subject field. Describe how you would present the lesson from a behaviorist viewpoint; then describe how you would present the same lesson from a constructivist viewpoint. Is it possible to design the lesson in a way that encompasses both viewpoints? Explain your response.

(continued)

2. Do you accept the view that learning is the product of creative inquiry through social interaction, with the students as active participants in that inquiry? Explain why you agree or disagree.

3. Assume that you are a high school teacher and that your teaching schedule includes three sections of U.S. history. Furthermore, assume that students at your school are tracked and that one of your classes is a so-called college prep class with 30 students; another is a regular education class with 35 students, 3 of whom have special needs because of disabilities; and the third is a sheltered English class with 13 students; 7 of whom are Hispanics with limited proficiency in English, 2 are from Russia with very limited proficiency in English, and 4 of whom are Southeast Asians, 2 with no ability to use English. Will one lesson plan using lecture and discussion as the primary instructional strategies work for all three sections? If so, explain why. If not, explain what you will have to do and why.

4. From your current observations and fieldwork as related to this teacher preparation program, clearly identify one specific example of educational practice that seems contradictory to exemplary practice or theory as presented in this module. Present your explanation for the discrepancy.

5. Describe any prior concepts you held that changed as a result of your experiences with this module. Describe the changes.

 To access this posttest and the answers online, go to the Companion Website at **www.prenhall.com/kellough.**

■ SUGGESTED READINGS

Armstrong, D. G., & Savage, T. V. (1998). *Teaching in the secondary school: An introduction* (4th ed.). Upper Saddle River, NJ: Merrill/Prentice Hall.

Armstrong, T. (1998). *Awakening genius in the classroom.* Alexandria, VA: Association for Supervision and Curriculum Development.

Baker, J. C., & Martin, F. G. (1998). *A neural network guide to teaching.* Fastback 431. Bloomington, IN: Phi Delta Kappa Educational Foundation.

Beamon, G. W. (2001). *Teaching with adolescent learning in mind.* Arlington Heights, IL: Skylight Professional Development.

Ben-Avie, M. (1998). Secondary education: The school development program at work in three high schools. *Journal of Education for Students Placed at Risk (JESPAR),* 3(1), 53–70.

Brandt, R. (1998). *Powerful learning.* Alexandria, VA: Association for Supervision and Curriculum Development.

Brandt, R., & Perkins, D. N. (2000). The evolving science of learning. In R. S. Brandt (Ed.), *Education in a new era* (pp. 159–189) Alexandria, VA: ASCD Yearbook, Association for Supervision and Curriculum Development.

Caine, R. N., & Caine, G. (1998). How to think about the brain. *School Administrator, 55*(1), 12–16.

Campbell, L., & Campbell, B. (1999). *Multiple intelligences and student achievement: Success stories from six schools.* Alexandria, VA: Association for Supervision and Curriculum Development.

Clark, G., & Zimmerman, E. (1998). Nurturing the arts in programs for gifted and talented students. *Phi Delta Kappan, 79*(10), 747–751.

Fogarty, R. (1998). The intelligence-friendly classroom. *Phi Delta Kappan, 79*(9), 655–657.

Gonzalez, M. L., Huerta-Macias, A., & Tinajero, J. V. (Eds.). (1998). *Educating latino students: A guide to successful practice.* Lancaster, PA: Technomic.

Guild, P. B., & Chock-Eng, S. (1998). Multiple intelligence, learning styles, brain-based education: Where do the messages overlap? *Schools in the Middle, 7*(4), 38–40.

Harrison, A. G., Grayson, D. J., & Treagust, D. F. (1999). Investigating a grade 11 student's evolving conceptions of heat and temperature. *Journal of Research in Science Teaching, 36*(1), 55–87.

Jenkins, J. M. (1999). Strategies for personalizing instruction, part two. *International Journal of Educational Reform, 8*(1), 83–88.

Jensen, E. (1998). *Teaching with the brain in mind.* Alexandria, VA: Association for Supervision and Curriculum Development.

Keller, M. M., & Decoteau, G. T. (2000). *The military child: Mobility and education.* Fastback 463. Bloomington, IN: Phi Delta Kappa Educational Foundation.

Kovalik, S., & Olsen, K. D. (1998). The physiology of learning—Just what does go on in there? *Schools in the Middle, 7*(4), 32–37.

More, K. D. (1999). *Middle and secondary school instructional methods.* Boston, MA: McGraw-Hill College, a Division of the McGraw-Hill Companies, Inc.

Morgan, R. R., Ponticell, J. A., & Gordon, E. E. (2000). *Rethinking creativity.* Fastback 458. Bloomington, IN: Phi Delta Kappa Educational Foundation.

O'Brien, T. C. (1999). Parrot math. *Phi Delta Kappan, 80*(6), 434–438.

Rosenberg, S. L. (1999). The need to belong. *American School Board Journal, 186*(9), 26–28.

Sadker, M. P., & Sadker, D. M. (2005). *Teachers, schools and society* (7th ed.). Boston, MA: McGraw-Hill.

Sizer, T. R. (1999). Michael alone: Anonymity is the curse of the American comprehensive high school. *American School Board Journal, 186*(9), 29–30.

Smutney, J. F. (1998). *Gifted girls.* Fastback 427. Bloomington, IN: Phi Delta Kappa Educational Foundation.

Sprenger, M. (1999). *Learning memory: The brain in action.* Alexandria, VA: Association for Supervision and Curriculum Development.

Sweet, S. S. (1998). A lesson learned about multiple intelligences. *Educational Leadership, 56*(3), 50–51.

Tauber, R. T. (1998). *Good or bad, what teachers expect from students they generally get!* ERIC Digest 426985 98. Washington, DC: ERIC Clearinghouse on Teaching and Teacher Education.

Tiegerman-Farber, E. M. (1998). *Collaborative decision-making: The pathway to inclusion.* Upper Saddle River, NJ: Merrill/Prentice Hall.

Walley, C. W., & Gerrick, W. G. (1999). *Affirming middle grades education.* Boston: Allyn & Bacon.

Williams, C. W., &Hounshell, P. B. (1998). Enabling the learning disabled. *Science Teacher, 65*(1), 29–31.

■ ENDNOTES

[1] Exerpt from *Our Boys* in Maya Angelou, *Wouldn't Take Nothing for My Journey Now* (New York: Random House, 1993), p. 124.

[2] C. Stevenson, *Teaching Ten to Fourteen Year Olds* (3rd ed.) (Boston: Allyn & Bacon, 2002).

[3] Ibid., pp. 77–78.

[4] D. M. Gollnick and P. C. Chinn, *Multicultural Education in* a Pluralistic Society (Upper River Saddle, NJ: Merill/Prentice Hall, 2002).

[5] Ibid., p. 277.

[6] Ibid.

[7] J. V. Diller and J. Moule, *Cultural Competence: A Primer for educators* (Belmont, CA: Thompson Wadsworth, 2005), p. 2.

[8] D. M. Gollnick and P. C. Chinn, *Multicultural Education in a Pluralistic Society* (Upper River Saddle, NJ: Merrill/Prentice Hall, 2002), p. 5.

[9] M. Levine, Celebrating Diverse Minds, *Educational Leadership* (October 2003), p. 14.

[10] K. Koppelman and L. Goodhart, *Understanding Human Differences: Multicultural Education for a Diverse America* (Boston, MA: Pearson Education, Inc., 2005).

[11] D. M. Gollnick and P. C. Chinn, *Multicultural Education in a Pluralistic Society* (Upper River Saddle, NJ: Merrill/Prentice Hall, 2002), p. 5.

[12] M. Levine, Celebrating Diverse Minds, *Educational Leadership* (October 2003), pp. 12–18.

[13] M. H. Futrell, J. Gomez, and D. Bedden, *Teaching the Children of a New America: The Challenge of Diversity, Phi Delta Keepan,* 84(5), p. 283.

[14] National Center for Education Statistics, *The Condition of Education 2003* (NCES 2003-067) (Washington DC: U.S. Department of Education, Institute of Education Sciences, 2003). Retrieved December 4, 2003, from **http://nces.ed.gov/pubs2003/2003067.pdf**.

[15] I. Zangwell, *The Melting-Pot: Drama in Four Acts* (New York: Macmillan, 1909).

[16] J. A. Banks and C. A. McGee Banks (Eds.), *Multicultural Education: Issues and Perspectives* (Boston: Allyn & Bacon, 1989), p. 1.

[17] U.S. Census Bureau, *National Population Projections* (August 18, 2004). *On-line:* **http://ww.census.gov/population/www/projections/natsum-T3.html**

[18] L. Baines, Future Schlock, *Phi Delta Kappan, 78*(7), 497 (March 1997).

[19] U.S. Census Bureau, *National Population Projections* (2000). On-line: **http://www.census.gov/population/www/projections/natsum-T3.html**

[20] T. L. Good and J. E. Brophy, *Looking in Classrooms* (8th ed.) (New York: Addison Wesley Longman, 2000), p. 127.

[21] P. Stone, How We Turned Around a Problem School, *Principal, 72*(2), 34–36 (November 1992). See also B. G. Barron et al., Effects of Time of Day Instruction on Reading Achievement of Below Grade Readers, *Reading Improvement, 31*(1), 59–60 (Spring 1994).

[22] R. Dunn, *Strategies for Educating Diverse Learners,* Fastback 384 (Bloomington, IN: Phi Delta Kappa Educational Foundation, 1995), p. 9.

[23] D. A. Kolb, *Experiential Learning: Experience as the Source of Learning and Development* (Upper Saddle River, NJ: Prentice Hall, 1984).

[24] C. G. Jung, *Psychological Types* (New York: Harcourt Brace, 1923).

[25] See B. McCarthy, A Tale of Four Learners: 4MAT's Learning Styles, *Educational Leadership, 54*(6), 47–51 (March 1997).

[26] See R. Karplus, *Science Curriculum Improvement Study,* Teacher's Handbook (Berkeley: University of California, 1974).

[27] See, for example, A. Colburn and M. P. Clough, Implementing the Learning Cycle, *Science Teacher, 64*(5), 30–33 (May 1997); E. A. Kral, Scientific. Reasoning and Achievement in a High School English Course, *Skeptical Inquirer, 21*(3), 34–39 (May/June 1997); A. C. Rule, *Using the Learning Cycle to Teach Acronyms, a Language Arts Lesson* (ED383000, 1995); J. E. Sowell, Approach to Art History in the Classroom, *Art Education, 46*(2), 19–24 (March 1993); and M. M. Bevevino, J. Dengel, and K. Adams, Constructivist Theory in the Classroom: Internalizing Concepts Through Inquiry Learning, *Clearing House, 72*(5), 275–278 (May/June 1999).

[28] The three phases of the learning cycle are comparable to the three levels of thinking, described variously by others. For example, in E. Eisner's *The Educational Imagination* (New York: Macmillan, 1979), the levels are referred to as *descriptive, interpretive,* and *evaluative.*

[29] For information about 4MAT, contact Excel, Inc., 23385 W. Old Barrington Road, Barrington, IL 60010, phone: (847) 382-7272, or at 6322 Fenworth Ct., Agoura Hills, CA 91301, phone: (818) 879-7442, or via the Internet at **http://www.excelcorp.com/4mataboutlong.html**

[30] B. McCarthy, Using the 4MAT System to Bring Learning Styles to Schools, *Educational Leadership, 48*(2), 33 (October 1990).

[31] R. DeLay, Forming Knowledge: Constructivist Learning and Experiential Education, *Journal of Experiential Education, 19*(2), 76–81 (August/September 1996).

[32] For Gardner's distinction between learning style and intelligences, see H. Gardner, Multiple Intelligences: Myths and Messages, *International Schools Journal, 15*(2), 8–22 (April 1996), and the many articles in the "Teaching for Multiple Intelligences" theme issue of *Educational Leadership, 55*(1) (September 1997).

[33] For example, see G. Gallagher, Multiple Intelligences, *Middle Ground, 1*(2), 10–12 (October 1997).

[34] See, for example, R. J. Marzano, 20th Century Advances in Instruction, in R. S. Brandt (Ed.), *Education in a New Era,* Chap. 4 (Alexandria, VA: ASCD Yearbook, Association for Supervision and Curriculum Development, 2000), p. 76.

[35] See P. Guild, The Culture/Learning Style Connection, *Educational Leadership, 51*(8), 16–21 (May 1994).

[36] Dunn, *Educating Diverse Learners,* p. 30.

[37] See, for example, M. L. Yell, the Legal Basis of Inclusion, *Educational Leadership, 56*(2), 70–73 (October 1998). For information about education law as related to special education students, see the Web site at **http://ww.access.digex.net/~edlawinc/**.

[38] E. Tiegerman-Farber and C. Radziewicz, *Collaborative Decision Making: The Pathway to Inclusion* (Upper Saddle River, NJ: Merrill/Prentice Hall, 1998), pp. 12–13.

[39]Such is the case, for example, for the K–12 Celebration School (Celebration, FL). See the Web site at **http://www.cs.osceola.k12.fl.us.**

[40]See L. Farlow, A Quartet of Success Stories: How to Make Inclusion Work, *Educational Leadership,* 53(5), 51–55 (April 1996), and other articles in the theme issue of *Students with Special-Needs.*

[41]See J. Cummins, *Bilingualism and Special Education: Issues in Assessment and Pedagogy* (San Diego: College-Hill Press, 1984); P. Berman et al., *School Reform and Student Diversity, Volume II: Case Studies of Exemplary Practices for LEP Students* (Berkeley, CA: National Center for Research on Cultural Diversity and Second Language Learning, 1995).

[42]D. R. Walling, *English as a Second Language: 25 Questions and Answers,* Fastback 347 (Bloomington, IN: Phi Delta Kappa Educational Foundation, 1993), pp. 12–13.

[43]Walling, *English as a Second Language,* p. 26.

[44]See K. M. Johns and C. Espinoza, *Mainstreaming Language Minority Children in Reading and Writing,* Fastback 340 (Bloomington, IN: Phi Delta Kappa Educational Foundation, 1992).

[45]C. Minicucci et al., School Reform and Student Diversity, *Phi Delta Kappan,* 77(1), 77–80 (September 1995).

[46]See the discussion in G. Clark and E. Zimmerman, Nurturing the Arts in Programs for Gifted and Talented Students, *Phi Delta Kappan,* 79(10), 747–751 (June 1998).

[47]See, for example, J. F. Feldhusen, Programs for the Gifted Few or Talent Development for the Many? *Phi Delta Kappan,* 79(10), 735–738 (June 1998).

[48]C. Dixon, L. Mains, and M. J. Reeves, *Gifted and at Risk,* Fastback 398 (Bloomington, IN: Phi Delta Kappa Educational Foundation, 1996), p. 7.

[49]S. B. Rimm, Underachievement Syndrome: A National Epidemic, in N. Colangelo and G. A. Davis (Eds.), *Handbook of Gifted Education* (2nd ed.) (Needham Heights, MA: Allyn & Bacon, 1997), p. 416.

[50]S. Schwartz, *Strategies for Identifying the Talents of Diverse Students.* ERIC/CUE Digest, number 122 (New York: ED410323, ERIC Clearinghouse on Urban Education, May 1997).

[51]Adapted from *Gifted and At Risk* (pp. 9–12) by Dixon, Mains, and Reeves (Bloomington, IN: Phi Delta Kappa Educational Foundation, 1996). Copyright 1996 by Phi Delta Kappa Educational Foundation. Adapted with permission. See also K. Checkley, Serving Gifted Students in the Regular Classroom, *ASCDs Curriculum Update,* 5 (Winter 2000).

[52]See K. Burrett and T. Rusnak, *Integrated Character Education,* Fastback 351 (Bloomington, IN: Phi Delta Kappa Educational Foundation, 1993).

[53]Ibid., p. 15.

[54]See D. W. Johnson and R. T. Johnson, *Reducing School Violence Through Conflict Resolution* (Alexandria, VA: Association for Supervision and Curriculum Development, 1995).

[55]Ibid., Chapter 11.

[56]See J. Van Til, Facing Inequality and the End of Work, *Educational Leadership,* 54(6), 78–81 (March 1997).

Planning for Instruction

Part 2 Overview

To be successful in school, students need to know what is expected of them behaviorally and academically. During the first few weeks of a new school year, you will have the opportunity to prepare your students for success. You need them to cooperate. Following the guidelines and procedures you lay out as well as participating in the various learning activities you plan will help them to be successful in your class. We will help you develop your classroom management system, plan for instruction, and design your daily, weekly, and unit lesson plans in the three modules of Part 2.

First, we will review the key components to establishing and maintaining a safe and supportive classroom learning environment. Carefully planned rules and explicitly taught procedures will help you to create an effective management system. Once we review what you need to do to get your classroom organized, and your students ready to follow the guidelines and procedures you present, then it is time for you to turn your attention to instruction. Methods to plan and execute lessons that will promote the learning experiences you want for your students will be covered as well.

Part 2, consisting of three modules, assists with your understanding of:

- Establishing and maintaining an effective learning environment.
- Starting the school year.
- Managing daily class meetings.
- Providing positive modeling behaviors.
- Integrating the curriculum.
- Curriculum standards and their role in instruction.
- Instructional objectives and how they are used.
- Procedures for preparing an instructional unit.
- Unit and lesson plan formats.
- Preparing content sequence.
- Reasons for thoughtfully and thoroughly planning for instruction at three levels.
- How to use student textbooks and other resources for the selection of content.

Learning that is most meaningful to students is not always neat or easily predicted or isolated. Rather than teaching one objective at a time, much of the time, you should direct your teaching toward the simultaneous learning of multiple objectives, understandings, and appreciations. However, when you assess for learning, assessment is cleaner when objectives are assessed one at a time.

—Joseph F. Callahan,
Leonard H. Clark, and
Richard D. Kellough
(7ᵀᴴ edition)

Establishing and Maintaining a Safe and Supportive Classroom Learning Environment

Module 3 Overview

No matter how well-prepared your plans are, those plans will go untaught or poorly taught if presented to students in a classroom that is nonsupportive and poorly managed. Thoughtfully and thoroughly planning your procedures for classroom management is as important a part of your preactive-phase decision making as is preparing units and daily lessons. And for that reason it is a key step for instructional planning. Indeed, classroom management is perhaps the single most important factor influencing student learning. Just as you will learn to do for unit and lesson plans, you should plan and write down your management system long before you meet your first class of students, which you will begin doing in this module. In this, the first module of Part 2, you will learn how to create a supportive classroom environment and manage the classroom effectively, for the most efficient instruction will result in the best student achievement.

Specific Objectives

At the completion of this module, you should be able to:

- Identify characteristics of a classroom environment that is both safe for students and favorable to their learning.

- Explain the difference between direct and indirect intervention to refocus a student and describe situations where you would be most likely to use each, thereby demonstrating that you understand and have begun building your repertoire of a teacher's options to specific classroom situations.

- Describe, by examples, how each of the following contributes to effective classroom control: a well-designed room arrangement, a positive approach, well-planned lessons, a good start in the school term, classroom procedures and rules, consistency but with professional judgment in enforcing procedures and rules, correction of student misbehavior, and classroom management.

- With respect to classroom management, distinguish between the concepts *consequences* and *punishment*.

- Describe ways that you can help students develop self-control.

- Describe steps you should take in preparing for the first few days of school.

Introduction

U.S. citizens have certain inalienable rights that are protected by our Constitution. Those same rights are extended to students entering our schools; however, they do not translate into free license for students to do whatever they want. By law, all students have the right to an equal educational opportunity. With such diversity among our student body, equal educational opportunity does not always result in equitable educational opportunity. Some adjustments must be made to accommodate individual needs. This does not suggest that we should dumb down the curriculum, succumb to grade inflation, avoid distinguishing between right and wrong answers, or accept disrespectful behavior. Equal educational opportunity means that we need to create a welcoming classroom climate built on respect and design instruction in such a way that it meets the needs of *all* of our students and guarantees all students the chance to learn and achieve to the greatest degree possible.[2] This cannot happen in the midst of chaos. It is our duty as educators to provide a safe and supportive environment in which all students can reach their academic potential. Sometimes students' behavior can get in the way and make it difficult for teachers to use class time productively.

New teachers, as well as seasoned professionals, are susceptible to job burnout. Discipline issues can try the patience of even the most dedicated teachers. Educators and the public alike have been concerned about student behavior for many years. In fact, since the inception of the annual Phi Delta Kappa Gallup Poll highlighting the public's attitudes toward the public schools, school discipline has ranked as one of the public's major educational concerns, along with drug use, school funding, and violence. In fact, school discipline was named as the number one problem our schools face 16 times in the 33-year span between 1969 and 2002.[3]

What are the kinds of classroom management issues that arise in the middle and secondary classrooms of today? According to research conducted by Dr. Frederic H. Jones, psychology professor at the University of California at Santa Cruz and classroom management guru, classroom disruptions can be classified into three main categories. Jones claimed that 80% of the disruptions in a typical classroom were due to students talking to their neighbors. In contrast, 15% of the disruptions were the result of students being up and out of their seats while the final 5% were made up of a variety of disruptive behaviors including passing notes, fiddling with pencils, rocking in chairs, and disturbing classmates. Furthermore, while students are engaged in seatwork, on average, one disruption per student every minute was observed in normal classrooms.[4]

In this module we will provide you with skills to avoid or address the disruptions previously described, a history of classroom management approaches, a review of current research and theory, and a variety of methods that you can implement in order to create a welcoming classroom environment conducive to learning.

■ THE IMPORTANCE OF PERCEPTIONS

Unless you believe that each and every one of your students can learn, they will not. Unless you believe that you can teach each and every one of them, you will not. Unless each and every one of your students believe that they can learn and until they want to learn, they will not.

There are many influences on how teachers approach decisions around classroom management. How you go about creating a positive learning environment is greatly influenced by your personal history including how you were disciplined at home and in your past educational experiences as a student. In addition, your personality, your previous teaching experiences with children, your teaching preparation, your personal preferences, and the school context all play a role.[5]

We all know or have heard of teachers who get the very best from all their students, even from those students that many teachers find to be the most challenging to teach. Regardless of individual circumstances, those teachers who (a) provide adequate support to all students so they can learn, (b) expect the best from each student, (c) establish a classroom environment that motivates students to do their best, and (d) manage their classrooms so class time is efficiently used, that is, with the least amount of distraction to the learning process, are the most effective.

Regardless of how well you plan for instruction, certain perceptions by students must be in place to support the successful implementation of those plans. Students must perceive that (a) the classroom environment is supportive of their efforts, (b) you care about their learning and that they are welcome in your classroom, (c) the expected learning is challenging but not impossible, and (d) the anticipated learning outcomes are worthy of their time and effort to try and achieve.

■ CLASSROOM CONTROL: ITS MEANING—PAST AND PRESENT

Classroom control frequently is of the greatest concern to beginning teachers—and they have good cause to be concerned. As previously mentioned, even experienced teachers sometimes find control difficult, particularly at the middle and secondary schools where so many students come to school with so much psychological baggage and have already become alienated as the result of negative experiences in their lives.[6] This module has been thoughtfully designed to help you with your concerns about control.

■ Historical Meaning of Classroom Control

To set the stage for your comprehension, consider what the term *classroom control* has meant historically and what it means today. In the 1800s, educators did not speak of classroom control; instead, they spoke of *classroom discipline*, and that meant *punishment*. Such an interpretation was consistent with the then-popular learning theory that assumed children were innately bad and that inappropriate behavior could be prevented by strictness or treated with punishment. Schools in the mid-1800s have been described as "wild and unruly places," and "full of idleness and disorder."[7]

By the early 1900s, educators were asking, "Why are the children still misbehaving?" The accepted answer was that the children were misbehaving as a result of the rigid punitive system. On this point, the era of progressive education began, providing students more freedom to decide what they would learn. The teacher's job, then, became one of providing a rich classroom of resources and materials to stimulate the students' natural curiosity. And because the system no longer would be contributing to misbehavior, punishment would no longer be necessary. Classes of the 1930s that were highly permissive, however, turned out to cause more anxiety than the restrictive classes of the 1800s.

■ Today's Meaning of Classroom Control and the Concept of Classroom Management

Today, rather than classroom discipline, educators talk of classroom *control*, the process of controlling student behavior in the classroom. The most effective teacher is one who is in control of classroom events rather than controlled by them. Classroom control is an important aspect of the broader concept of classroom management and is part of a management plan designed to (a) prevent inappropriate student behaviors, (b) help students develop self-control, and (c) suggest procedures for dealing with inappropriate student behaviors.

Effective teaching requires a well-organized, businesslike classroom in which motivated students work diligently at their learning tasks, free from distractions and interruptions. Establishing such a setting for learning requires careful thought and preparation and is called effective classroom management. Effective classroom management is the process of organizing and conducting a classroom so that it maximizes student learning.

A teacher's procedures for classroom control reflect that teacher's philosophy about how young people learn and the teacher's interpretation and commitment to the school's stated mission. In sum, those procedures represent the teacher's concept of classroom management. Although often eclectic in their approaches, today's teachers share a concern for selecting management techniques that enhance student self-esteem and that empower students to assume control of their behavior and ownership of their learning.

Although some schools and school districts subscribe heavily to one approach or another, many others are more eclectic, having evolved from the historical works of several leading authorities. Let's consider what some authorities have said. As was said in the preceding paragraph, the guidelines and suggestions that are presented throughout this module represent an eclectic approach, borrowing from many of these authorities.

■ Classroom Management: Contributions of Some Leading Authorities

You are probably familiar with the term *behavior modification*, which describes several high-control techniques for changing behavior in an observable and predictable way; with B. F. Skinner's ideas about how students learn and how behavior can be modified by using reinforcers (rewards); and with how his principles of behavior shaping have been extended by others.[8] Behavior modification begins with four steps: (a) identify the behavior to be modified; (b) record how often and under what conditions that behavior occurs; (c) cause a change by reinforcing a desired behavior with a positive reinforcer (a reward); and (d) choose the type of positive reinforcers to award. At some point, almost all teachers use some type of reinforcer with their students. Following is a list of five different types of reinforcers and examples of each type. Some suggestions may seem more appropriate for middle school students while others may motivate secondary students.

- *Activity or privilege reinforcers,* such as choice of playing a game, running the media equipment for the teacher, caring for a classroom pet, free reading, decorating the classroom, free art time, spending time at a learning center, being free without penalty from doing an assignment or test, running an errand for the teacher;
- *Social reinforcers,* such as verbal attention or praise, nonverbal behavior such as proximity of teacher to student, and facial (such as a wink or smile) or bodily expressions (such as a handshake or pat on the back) of approval;
- *Graphic reinforcers,* such as numerals and symbols like those made by rubber stamps;
- *Tangible reinforcers,* such as candy and other edibles, badges, certificates, stickers, books;
- *Token reinforcers,* such as points, stars, or tickets that can be accumulated and cashed in later for a tangible reinforcer, such as a supervised trip to the pizzeria or ice cream store.

Lee Canter and Marlene Canter developed the *assertive discipline model*. Using an approach that emphasizes both reinforcement for appropriate behaviors and consequences for inappropriate behaviors, their model emphasizes four major points. First, as a teacher, you have professional rights in your classroom and should expect appropriate student behavior. Second, your students have rights to choose how to behave in your classroom, and you should plan limits for inappropriate behavior. Third, an assertive discipline approach means you clearly state your expectations in a firm voice and explain the boundaries for behavior. And fourth, you should plan a system of positive consequences (e.g., positive messages home; awards and rewards; special privileges) for appropriate behavior, and establish consequences (e.g., time-out, withdrawal of privileges, parent conference) for inappropriate student behavior. Consistent follow-through is necessary.[9]

With a *logical consequences* approach, Rudolf Dreikurs emphasized six points. First, be fair, firm, and friendly, and involve your students in developing and implementing class rules. Second, students need to clearly understand the rules and the logical consequences for misbehavior. For example, a logical consequence for a student who has painted graffiti on a school building wall would be to either clean the wall or pay for a school custodian to do it. Third, allow the students to be responsible not only for their own actions but also for influencing others to maintain appropriate behavior in your classroom. Fourth, encourage students to show respect for themselves and for others, and provide each student with a sense of belonging to the class. Fifth, recognize and encourage student goals of belonging, gaining status, and gaining recognition. And sixth, recognize but do not reinforce correlated student goals of getting attention, seeking power, and taking revenge.[10]

Continuing the work of Dreikurs, Linda Albert has developed a detailed and popular system called *cooperative discipline*. The cooperative discipline model makes use of Dreikurs' fundamental concepts, with emphasis added on three C's: capable, connect, and contribute.[11] Also building upon the work of Dreikurs, Jane Nelsen provides guidelines for helping children develop positive feelings of self. Key points made by Nelsen and reflected throughout this book are (a) use natural and logical consequences as a means to inspire a positive classroom atmosphere, (b) understand that children have goals that drive them toward misbehavior (attention, power, revenge, and assumed adequacy), (c) use kindness (student retains dignity) and firmness when administering consequences for a student's misbehavior, (d) establish a climate of mutual respect, (e) use class meetings to give students ownership in problem solving, and (f) offer encouragement as a means of inspiring self-evaluation and focusing on the students' behaviors.[12]

William Glasser developed his concept of *reality therapy* (i.e., the condition of the present, rather than of the past, contributes to inappropriate behavior) for the classroom. Glasser emphasizes that students have a responsibility to learn at school and to maintain appropriate behavior while there. He stresses that with the teacher's help, students can make appropriate choices about their behavior in school—they can, in fact, learn self-control.[13] Glasser suggests holding classroom meetings that are devoted to establishing class rules and to identifying standards for student behavior, matters of misbehavior, and the consequences of misbehavior. Since the publication of his first book in 1965, Glasser has expanded his message to include the student's needs of belonging and love, control, freedom, and fun, asserting that if these needs are ignored and unattended at school, children are bound to fail.[14] Today's commitment to quality education (discussed in Module 1) is largely derived from the recent work of Glasser. In schools committed to quality education, students feel a sense of belonging, enjoy some degree of power, have fun learning, and experience a sense of freedom in the process.

Haim G. Ginott (1922–1973) emphasized ways for teacher and student to communicate—a *communication model*. He advised a teacher to send a clear message (or messages) about situations rather than about the child. And he stressed that teachers must model the behavior they expect from students.[15] Ginott's suggested messages are those that express feelings appropriately, acknowledge students' feelings, give appropriate direction, and invite cooperation.

Thomas Gordon emphasizes influence over control and decries use of reinforcement (i.e., rewards and punishment) as an ineffective tool for achieving a positive influence over a child's behavior.[16] Rather than using reinforcements for appropriate behavior and punishment for inappropriate behaviors, Gordon advocates encouragement and development of student self-control and self-regulated behavior. To have a positive influence and to encourage self-control, the teacher (and school) must provide a rich and positive learning environment, with rich and stimulating learning activities. Specific teacher behaviors include active listening, sending I-messages (rather than you-messages), shifting from I-messages to listening when there is student resistance to an I-message, clearly identifying ownership of problems to the student when such is the case (i.e., not assuming ownership if it is a student's problem), and encouraging collaborative problem solving.

Fredric Jones, who was mentioned in the introduction, also promotes the idea of helping students support their own behavioral self-control. He accomplishes this by using effective nonverbal communication and implementing an incentive system. His incentive system employs a negative reinforcement method in which rewards follow good behavior.[17] Preferred activity time (PAT), for example, is an invention derived from the Jones Model. The Jones Model makes four recommendations.

TABLE 3.1	Comparing Approaches to Classroom Management	
Authority	**To Know What Is Going On**	**To Provide Smooth Transitions**
Canter/Jones	Realize that the student has the right to choose how to behave in your class with the understanding of the consequences that will follow his or her choice.	Insist on decent, responsible behavior.
Dreikurs/Nelsen/Albert	Realize that the student wants status, recognition, and a feeling of belonging. Misbehavior is associated with mistaken goals of getting attention, seeking power, getting revenge, and wanting to be left alone.	Identify a mistaken student goal; act in ways that do not reinforce these goals.
Ginott/Kohn	Communicate with the student to find out his/her feelings about a situation and about his/herself.	Invite student cooperation.
Glasser/Gordon/Rogers/Gathercoal/ Freiberg	Realize that the student is a rational being; he/she can control his or her own behavior.	Help the student make good choices; good choices produce good behavior, and bad choices produce bad behavior.
Kounin	Develop withitness, a skill enabling you to see what is happening in all parts of the classroom at all times.	Avoid jerkiness, which consists of thrusts (giving directions before your group is ready), dangles (leaving one activity dangling in the verbal air, starting another one, and then returning to the first activity), and flip-flops (terminating one activity, beginning another one, and then returning to the first activity you terminated).
Skinner	Realize the value of nonverbal interaction (i.e., smiles, pats, and handshakes) to communicate to students that you know what is going on.	Realize that smooth transitions may be part of your procedures for awarding reinforcers (i.e., points and tokens) to reward appropriate behavior.

SOURCE: Reprinted by Permission.

First, you properly structure your classroom so students understand the rules and procedures. Second, you maintain control by selecting appropriate instructional strategies. Third, you build patterns of cooperative work. Finally, you develop appropriate backup methods for dealing with inappropriate student behavior.

Jacob Kounin is well-known for his identification of the *ripple effect*, or the effect of a teacher's response to one student's misbehavior on students whose behavior was appropriate. Kounin also focused on *withitness*, the teacher's ability to remain alert in the classroom and spot quickly and redirect potential student misbehavior, which is analogous to having "eyes in the back of your head."[18] In addition to being alert to everything that is going on in the classroom, another characteristic of a "withit" teacher is the ability to attend to a disruptive student without neglecting the rest of the class.

Guidelines for developing withitness Consider the following guidelines for developing withitness.

- Avoid spending too much time with any one student or group; longer than 30 seconds may be approaching "too much time."

- Avoid turning your back to all or a portion of the students, such as when writing on the writing board.

- If two or more errant behaviors are occurring simultaneously in different locations, attend to the most serious first, while giving the other(s) a nonverbal gesture showing your awareness (such as by eye contact) and displeasure (such as by a frown).

- Involve all students in your activities, not just any one student or group. Avoid concentrating on only those who appear most interested or responsive, sometimes referred to as the "chosen few."

- Keep students alert by calling on them randomly, asking questions, and calling on an answerer, circulating from group to group during team learning activities and frequently checking on the progress of individual students.

- Maintain constant visual surveillance of the entire class, even when talking to or working with an individual or small group of students and when meeting a classroom visitor at the door.

- Move around the room. Be on top of potential misbehavior and quietly redirect student attention

To Maintain Group Alertness	To Involve Students	To Attend to Misbehavior
Set clear limits and consequences; follow through consistently; state what you expect; state the consequences and why the limits are needed.	Use firm tone of voice; keep eye contact; use nonverbal gestures and verbal statements; use hints, questions, and direct messages in requesting student behavior; give and receive compliments.	Follow through with your promises and the reasonable, previously stated consequences that have been established in your class.
Provide firm guidance and leadership.	Allow students to have a say in establishing rules and consequences in your class.	Make it clear that unpleasant consequences will follow inappropriate behavior.
Model the behavior you expect to see in your students.	Build student's self-esteem.	Give a message that addresses the situation and does not attack the student's character.
Understand that class rules are essential.	Realize that classroom meetings are effective means for attending to rules, behavior, and discipline.	Accept no excuses for inappropriate behavior; see that reasonable consequences always follow.
Avoid slowdowns (delays and time wasting) that can be caused by overdwelling (too much time spent on explanations) and by fragmentation (breaking down an activity into several unnecessary steps). Develop a group focus (active participation by all students in the group) through accountability (holding all students accountable for the concept of the lesson) and by attention (seeing all the students and using unison and individual responses).	Avoid boredom by providing a feeling of progress for the students, offering challenges, varying class activities, hanging the level of intellectual challenge, varying lesson presentations, and using many different learning materials and aids.	Understand that teacher correction influences behavior of other nearby students (the ripple effect).
Set rules, rewards, and consequences; emphasize that responsibility for good behavior rests with each student.	Involve students in "token economies," in contracts, and in charting behavior performance.	Provide tangibles to students who follow the class rules; represent tangibles as "points" for the whole class to use to "purchase" a special activity.

before the misbehavior occurs or gets out of control.

- During direct instruction try to establish eye contact with each student about once every minute. It initially may sound impossible to do, but it is not; this skill can be developed with practice.

A prerequisite to being withit is the skill to attend to more than one matter at a time. This is referred to as the *overlapping ability*. The teacher with overlapping skills uses body language, body position, and hand signals to communicate with students. Consider the following examples of overlapping ability.

- Rather than having students bring their papers and problems to her desk, the teacher expects them to remain seated and to raise their hands as he/she circulates in the room monitoring and attending to individual students.

- The teacher takes care of attendance while visually and/or verbally monitoring the students during their warm-up activity.

- While attending to a messenger who has walked into the room, the teacher demonstrates verbally or by gestures that he expects the students to continue their work.

- While working in a small group, a student raises his hand to get the teacher's attention. The teacher, while continuing to work with another group of students, signals with her hand to tell the student that she is aware that he wants her attention and will get to him quickly, which she does.

- Without missing a beat in her talk, the teacher aborts the potentially disruptive behavior of a student by gesturing, by making eye contact, or by moving closer to the student (proximity control). (See Table 3.1.)

Developing Your Own Effective Approach to Classroom Management

As you review these classic contributions to today's approaches to effective classroom management, the expert opinions as well as the research evidence will remind you of the importance of doing the following: (a) concentrating your attention on desirable student behaviors; (b) quickly and appropriately attending to inappropriate behavior; (c) maintaining alertness to all that is happening in your classroom; (d) providing smooth transitions, keeping the entire class on task, preventing dead time; and (e) involving students by providing challenges, class meetings,[19] ways of establishing rules and consequences, opportunities to receive and return compliments, and chances to build self-control and self-esteem.

Using the criteria of your own philosophy, feelings, values, knowledge, and perceptions, you are encouraged to construct a classroom environment and management system that is explicit, positive, and effective for you and your students and then to consistently apply it.

■ PROVIDING A SUPPORTIVE LEARNING ENVIRONMENT

It is probably no surprise to hear that teachers whose classrooms are pleasant, positive, and challenging but supportive places find that their students learn and behave better than the students of teachers whose classroom atmospheres are harsh, negative, repressive, and unchallenging. What follows now are specific suggestions for making your classroom a pleasant, positive, and challenging place, that is, an environment that supports students in their development of meaningful understandings.

■ Create a Positive Classroom Atmosphere

All students should feel welcome in your classroom and accepted by you as individuals of dignity. Although these feelings and behaviors should be reciprocal—that is, expected of the students as well—they may need your frequent modeling of the behaviors expected of them. You must help students know that any disapproval by you of a specific student's behavior is not a denial of that individual as a worthwhile person. Make it clear that the offending student is still welcomed to come to your class to learn as long as he or she agrees to follow expected procedures. Specific things you can do to create a positive classroom environment, some of which are repeated from preceding modules and others addressed in later modules, are:

- Admonish behavior, not persons.
- Ensure that no prejudice is ever displayed against any individual student.
- Attend to the classroom's physical appearance and comfort. It is your place of work; show pride in that fact.
- Be an interesting person and an optimistic and enthusiastic teacher.

- Encourage students to set high, yet realistic goals for themselves, and then show them how to take the necessary steps toward meeting their goal—letting each know that you are confident in her or his ability to achieve.
- Help students develop their skills in interactive and cooperative learning.
- Involve students in every aspect of their learning, including the planning of learning activities, thereby giving them part ownership and responsibility in their learning.
- Use interesting and motivating learning activities. Make the learning enjoyable, at least to the extent possible and reasonable.
- Send positive messages home to parents or guardians, even if you have to get help, and write the message in the language of the student's home.
- Recognize and reward truly positive behaviors and individual successes, no matter how meager they might seem to you.
- Have fun! Remember you set the tone for your classroom. Enthusiasm is infectious, so be a carrier.

■ Behaviors to Avoid

Two items in the preceding list are statements about giving encouragement. When using encouragement to motivate student learning, you should avoid a few important behaviors because they inhibit learning.

- Avoid comparing one student with another or one class of students with another.
- Avoid encouraging competition among students.
- Avoid giving up or appearing to give up on any student.
- Avoid telling a student how much better he or she could be.
- Avoid using qualifying statements, such as "I like what you did, but . . . " or "It's about time."

■ Get to Know Your Students as People

For classes to move forward smoothly and efficiently, they should fit the learners' cultural backgrounds, learning styles, learning capacities, developmental needs, and interests. To make the learning meaningful and long lasting, build curriculum around students' interests, capacities, perceptions, and perspectives. Therefore, you need to know your students well enough to be able to provide learning experiences that they will find interesting, relevant, valuable, intrinsically motivating, challenging, and rewarding. Knowing your students is as important as knowing your subject, and maybe more important. Eminent Swiss psychologist Carl Jung summed it up this way, ". . . An understanding heart is everything in a teacher, and cannot be esteemed highly enough. One looks back with appreciation to the brilliant teachers, but with gratitude to those who touched our human feelings. The curriculum is so much necessary raw material, but warmth is the vital element for the growing plant and for the soul of the child."[20] The following paragraphs describe a number of things you can do to get to know your students as people.

Quickly learn and use student names Like everyone else, students appreciate being recognized and addressed by name. Not only do you need to learn your students' names, but it is important that classmates know each others' names as well. Quickly learning and using your students' names is an important motivating strategy and will help you with your classroom management. You may need to work hard at quickly learning the names of the students in your classes, but it is worth the extra effort. Be sure to take extra care to learn the proper spelling and pronunciation of non-English first and surnames. Avoid renaming students of Asian descent, other minority groups, or non-native English speakers with common Anglo names unless that is their preference.

One technique for learning names quickly is to use a seating chart. Laminate the seating chart onto a neon-colored (it gives students a visual focus) clipboard that you can carry in class with you. Many teachers prefer to assign permanent seats and then make seating charts from which they can unobtrusively check the roll while students are doing seatwork.

It is usually best to get your students into the lesson before taking roll and before doing other housekeeping chores. Ways of assigning student seating are discussed later in this module (see the section, The First Day).

Digital photography makes it easy for you to create visual likenesses of each of your students that can be labeled with their names, and frequently viewed. Addressing students by name every time you speak to them can also help you to learn and remember their names. Another helpful way to learn students' names is to return papers yourself by calling their names and then handing the papers to them, paying careful attention to look at each student and make mental notes that may help you to associate the name with the face.

Classroom sharing during the first week of school During the first week of school many teachers take some time each day to have students present information about themselves and/or about the day's assignment. This is time well spent. It helps students feel valued and comfortable and builds a sense of community. Perhaps you can select five or six students each day to answer questions, such as "What name would you like to be called by?" "Where did you attend school last year?" "Tell us about your hobbies and other interests." or "What interested you about last night's reading, or yesterday's lesson?" Some students are reluctant to talk off the cuff, or in front of a large group. In order for intro-

verted students, non-native English speakers, or others who might appreciate a "heads up" to have time to prepare their answers, you might provide a list of questions for students to take home the night before and reflect upon. You might also consider having your students share information of this sort with each other in groups of three or four, while you visit each group in turn.

Still another approach is the "me-in-a-bag" activity. With this, each student is to bring to school a paper bag (limit the size) that contains items brought from home that represent that person. The student then is given time in class to share the items brought, explaining how each item represents that student.

How the student answers such questions or participates in such activities can be as revealing about the student as is the information (or the lack thereof) that the student does share. From the sharing, you sometimes get clues about additional information you would like to obtain about the student.

Observe students in the classroom—develop and practice your withitness During learning activities the effective teacher is constantly moving around the classroom and is alert to the individual behavior (non-verbal and verbal) of each student in the class, whether the student is on task or daydreaming and perhaps thinking about other things. Be cautious, however; just because a person is gazing out the window does not mean that the student is not thinking about the learning task. Group work is a particularly good time to observe students and get to know more about each one's skills and interests.

Observations of and conversations with students outside the classroom Another way to learn more about students is by observing them outside class: at school athletic events, at dances, at performing arts events, at lunchtime (finding it an excellent time to get to know their students as well as to provide informal guidance, some teachers open their classrooms at noon for a brown-bag lunch with any student who wishes to come), during advisory or homeroom, in the hallways, and at club meetings. Observations outside the classroom can give information about student personalities, friendships, interests, and potentials. For instance, you may find that a student who seems phlegmatic, lackadaisical, or uninterested in your classroom is a real fireball on the playing field or at some other student gathering.

Conferences and interviews with students Conferences with students, and sometimes with family members as well, afford yet another opportunity to show that you are genuinely interested in each student as a person and as a student. Some teachers choose to make brief telephone calls to each and every student's parents and/or guardians during the first couple of weeks of school to introduce themselves, review their expectations, and share their concern for the child's success in their classroom. This initial communication lays the groundwork for positive problem solving, should the need arise in the future. By being proactive, you can establish allies early on.

Some teachers and teaching teams plan a series of conferences during the first few weeks in which, individually or in small groups of three or four students, students are interviewed by the teacher or by the teaching team. Block scheduling is especially conducive to teacher-parent-student conferences. Such conferences and interviews are managed by using open-ended questions. The teacher indicates by the questions, by listening, and by nonjudgmental and empathic responses (i.e., being able to put her- or himself in the shoes of the student, thereby understanding where the student is coming from) a genuine interest in the students. Keep in mind, however, that students who feel they have been betrayed by prior adult associations may at first be distrustful of your sincerity. In such instances, don't force it. Be patient, but do not hesitate to take advantage of the opportunity afforded by talking with individual students outside of class time. Investing a few minutes of time in a positive conversation with a student, during which you indicate a genuine interest in that student, can pay real dividends when it comes to that student's interest and learning in your classroom.

Student writing and questionnaires Much can be learned about students by what they write (or draw). It is important to encourage writing in your classroom, and to read everything that students write (except for personal journals) and ask for clarification when needed. The journals and portfolios discussed in Module 9 are useful for this purpose.

Some teachers use open-ended interest-discovering and autobiographical questionnaires. Student responses to questionnaires can provide ideas about how to tailor assignments to individual students. However, you must assure students that their answers are optional and that you are not invading their right to privacy.

In an interest-discovering questionnaire, students are asked to answer questions such as "When you read for fun or pleasure, what do you usually read?" "What are your favorite movies, videos, or TV shows?" "Who are your favorite music video performers?" "Athletes?" "Describe your favorite hobby or other nonschool related activity." "What are your favorite sport activities to participate in and to watch?"

In an autobiographical questionnaire, students are asked to answer questions such as "Where were you born?" "What do you plan to do following high school?" "Do you have a job?" "If so, what is it?" "Do you like it?" "How do you like to spend your leisure time?" "Do you like to read?" "What do you like to read?" "Do you have a favorite hobby; what is it?" Many teachers model the process by beginning with reading to the students their own autobiographical answers to the questions.

Cumulative record, discussions with colleagues, and experiential backgrounds The cumulative record for each student is held in the school office, and it contains information recorded from year to year by teachers and other school professionals. The information covers the student's academic background, standardized test scores, and extracurricular activities. However, the Family Educational Rights and Privacy Act (FERPA) of 1974, and its subsequent amendments and local policies, may forbid your reviewing the record, except perhaps in collaboration with an administrator or counselor when you have a legitimate educational purpose for doing so. Although you must use discretion before arriving at any conclusion about information contained in the cumulative record, the record may afford information for getting to know a particular student better. Remember though, a student's past is history and should not be held against that student, but used as a means for understanding a student's experiences and current perceptions. Start fresh with your students; everyone deserves a second chance.

To better understand a student, it is sometimes helpful to talk with the student's other teachers, advisor, or counselor, to learn of their perceptions and experiences with the student. As discussed in Module 1, one of the advantages of schools that use looping or that are divided into "houses," or both, is that teachers and students get to know one another better.

Another way of getting to know your students is to spend time in the neighborhoods in which they live. Observe and listen, finding and noting things that you can use as examples or as learning activities.

■ PREPARATION PROVIDES CONFIDENCE AND SUCCESS

For successful classroom management, beginning the school term well may make all the difference in the world. Remember that you have only one opportunity to make a first and lasting impression. Therefore, you should appear at the first class meeting (and every class meeting thereafter) as well-prepared and confident as possible.

Perhaps in the beginning you will feel nervous and apprehensive, but being ready and well-prepared will help you at least to appear to be confident. It is likely that every beginning teacher is to some degree nervous and apprehensive; the secret is to not appear to be nervous. Being well-prepared provides the confidence necessary to cloud feelings of nervousness. A slow under-the-breath counting to 10 at the start can be helpful, too. Then, if you proceed in a businesslike, matter-of-fact way, the impetus of your well-prepared beginning will, most likely, cause the day, week, and year to proceed as desired.

■ Effective Organization and Administration of Activities and Materials

Taking time for preemptive classroom management is time well spent. In a well-managed classroom student movement about the classroom is routinized, controlled, and purposeful to the learning activities. Reflecting on a room arrangement that will help support your instructional activities, organize supplies and materials, and provide flexibility will limit distractions, off-task behavior, and chaotic transitions. In a well-managed classroom students know what to do, have the materials needed to do it well, and stay on-task while doing it. The classroom atmosphere is supportive; the assignments and procedures for doing them are clear; the materials of instruction are current, interesting, and readily available; and the classroom proceedings are businesslike. At all times, the teacher is in control of events, rather than controlled by them, seeing that students are spending their time on appropriate tasks. Some teachers are so masterful that they appear to be laid back naturals when it comes to classroom management, but make no mistake, they have these systems in place. For your teaching to be effective, you must perfect skills in managing the classroom.

■ Natural Interruptions and Disruptions to Routine

As you plan and prepare to implement your management system, you must also be aware of your own moods and high-stress days and anticipate that your own tolerance levels may vary some. Middle school and high school students, too, are susceptible to personal problems that can be the sources of high stress. As you come to know your students well, you will be able to ascertain when certain students are under an inordinate amount of stress and anxiety.

You must understand that classroom routines may be interrupted occasionally for perfectly natural reasons, especially on certain days and at certain times during the school year. Other more serious incidents may disrupt your plans as well. Carrying out business as usual after the 9/11 tragedy, a student suicide, a school shooting, or other devastating circumstances is not realistic. Sometimes you need to put your lesson plan aside and let students go through a grieving process.

Even under normal circumstances, students will not have the same motivation and energy level on each and every day, nor will you. Energy level also varies throughout the school day. Your anticipation of, and thoughtful and careful planning for, the preactive phase of instruction—periods of high or low energy levels—will preserve your own mental health. Depending on a number of factors, periods of high energy levels might include (a) the beginning of each school day; (b) before a field trip, a holiday, or a school event—such as a dance, homecoming, picture day, or a school assembly; (c) the day of a holiday; (d) the day following a holiday; (e) grade report day; (f) immediately before or/and after lunch; (g) on a minimum day or the day a substitute teacher is present; and (h) toward the end of each school day, toward the end of school each Friday afternoon, and toward the end of the school term or year.

Although there may be no hard evidence, many experienced teachers will tell you that particularly troublesome days for classroom control are those days when there is a strong north wind or a full moon. One teacher jokingly (we suspect) said that on days when there are both a strong north wind and a full moon, she calls in sick.

How should you prepare for these so-called high energy days? There are probably no specific guidelines that will work for all teachers in all situations in each instance from the list. However, these are days to which you need to pay extra attention during your planning, days that students could possibly be restless and more difficult to control, days when you might need to be especially forceful and consistent in your enforcement of procedures, or even compassionate and more tolerant than usual. Plan instructional activities that might be more readily accepted by the students. Preferred activity times (PATs) that serve as skill drills or reviews for tests make learning fun.[21] In no instance is it our intent to imply that learning ceases and play time takes over. What little instructional time is available to a teacher during a school year is too precious for that ever to happen.

■ CLASSROOM PROCEDURES AND GUIDELINES FOR ACCEPTABLE BEHAVIOR

It is impossible to overemphasize the importance of getting the school term off to a good beginning, so let's start this section by discussing how that is done.

■ Designing Your Room Arrangement

Before classes begin, it is important for you to set up your classroom in such a way as to support learning. How you choose to arrange your classroom will be a reflection of your teaching style. Do not leave your classroom arrangement up to the discretion of the custodial staff. It may be convenient to have desks placed in rows for cleaning purposes, but this layout is not conducive to interactive, hands-on collaborative group activities.[22] Eliminate barriers and be sure to leave yourself ample room in the aisles for easy student access. Think about the various small-group and whole class activities you would like to have your students engage in. Also verify that all students can see the board, overhead projector screen, or other necessary equipment from their seats.

In addition to placing the furniture strategically, and using the space you have in an efficient manner, you also want to remove barriers and eliminate congestion in high traffic areas so that you and the students can move freely and easily throughout the classroom when appropriate. You need to arrange your room so that you and your students are comfortable, they can all see you, and you can monitor their work.

Teaching materials and classroom supplies should be stored so that they are easily accessed. When deciding where to put things, you have to keep in mind what your preferred teaching style is and the kinds of activities you will ask your students to engage in.[23] You will spend a lot of time in your classroom, so make it a cheerful place!

■ Starting the School Term Well

Students size you up in the first three minutes of your first encounter. In addition to exuding confidence, there are three important keys to getting the school term off to a good beginning. First, be prepared and be fair. Preparation for the first day of school should include establishing and reviewing your classroom procedures and basic expectations for the students' behavior while they are under your supervision. The procedures and expectations must be consistent with school policy and seem reasonable to your students, and in enforcing them, you must be a fair and consistent professional. However, being coldly consistent is not the same as being fair and professional. Students need structure, but just like good parenting, good classroom facilitation requires flexibility.

As a teacher, you are a professional who deals in matters of human relations and who must exercise professional judgment. You are not a robot, nor are your students. Human beings differ from one another, and seemingly similar situations can vary substantially because the people involved are different. Consequently, your response, or lack of response, to each of two separate but quite similar situations may differ. To be most effective, learning must be enjoyable for students; it cannot be enjoyable when a teacher consistently acts like a marine drill sergeant. If a student breaks a rule, rather than assuming why, or seeming to not care why, or overreacting to the infraction, find out why before deciding your response. See, for example, Classroom Vignette: Late Homework Paper from an At-Risk Student in Module 7.

Second, in preparing your classroom management system, remember that too many rules and detailed procedures at the beginning can be overwhelming. To avoid confusion, it is best at first to present only the minimum number of procedural expectations necessary for an orderly start to the school term. By the time students are in middle school grades, unless they are recent newcomers to this country, they have likely been exposed to the general rules of expected behavior, although great variation in the expectations and enforcement of said expectations may

have existed. Some of your students' prior teachers may not always have been consistent or even fair about applying these expectations. For middle school teachers who are members of a teaching team, a unified approach to classroom expectations may be presented to the students.

Although there are similarities in expectations, expectations change from teacher to teacher, from school to school, and from year to year. For some high school students, it may prove difficult to change classes every 50 minutes and be confronted with different expectations. To make it even more challenging, some secondary teachers do not believe in writing classroom rules or guidelines out and posting them in their classroom, whereas some use one simple word, "respect," or the phrase, "the Golden Rule," because they expect high school students to be well acquainted with the norms for acceptable behavior.[24] Above all, teach your students to be responsible for their behavior.

However, by establishing and sticking to a few explained general expectations (see discussion that follows in the section, The First Day) and to those that may be specific to your subject area, you can leave yourself some room for judgments and maneuvering.

Third, consequences for not following established procedures must be reasonable, clearly understood, and fairly applied. The procedures should be quite specific so that students know exactly what is expected and what is not and what the consequences are when procedures are not followed.

■ Procedures Rather Than Rules; Consequences Rather Than Punishment

To encourage a constructive and supportive classroom environment, we encourage you and your students to practice thinking in terms of procedures (or standards and guidelines)[25] rather than rules, and of consequences rather than punishment. The rationale is this: To many people, the term *rules* has a more negative connotation than does the term *procedures*. When working with a cohort of students, some rules are necessary, but some people feel that using the term *guidelines* has a more positive ring to it. For example, a classroom rule might be that when one person is talking we do not interrupt that person until he or she is finished. When that rule is broken, rather than reminding students of the rule, the emphasis can be changed to a procedure simply by reminding the students, "What is our guideline (or standard expectation) when someone is talking?"

Although some people will disagree, we concur with the contention that thinking in terms of and talking about procedures and consequences are more likely to contribute to a positive classroom atmosphere than using the terms *rules* and *punishment*. Of course, some argue that by the time students are in middle school and high school, you might as well tell it like it is. Especially if your group of students is linguistically and culturally mixed, you will need to be as direct and clear as possible to avoid sending confusing or mixed signals. After considering what experienced others have to say, the final decision is only one of many that you must make and that will be influenced by your own thinking and situation. It might be a decision made in collaboration with members of your teaching team. It is, however, important that expectations are communicated clearly to the students and followed consistently by you and other members of your teaching team.

It is important to get student cooperation, so you want them to have buy in. From time to time, it may be effective to remind middle school students to apply the rules. For instance, you might ask them to reflect on and describe what a good listener acts like, looks like, participates like, and so forth, before a whole class group discussion where you expect students to raise their hands and wait to be called on before speaking and/or to respond to their classmates' statements. You might decide to have your secondary students involved in the determination of appropriate classroom rules. If you have in mind what you would like as classroom guidelines ahead of time, you could guide students to include your ideas, and/or you can reserve final veto power if you dislike any of their suggestions.

Once you have decided your initial expectations or created your expectations to include your students' input, you are ready to explain them to your students and to begin rehearsing a few of the procedures on the very first day of class. You will want to do this in a positive way. Students work best in a positive atmosphere, when teacher expectations are clear to them; when procedures are stated in positive terms, are clearly understood and agreed upon, and have become routine; and when consequences for behavior that is inappropriate are reasonable, clearly understood, and fairly applied.

■ The First Day

On the first day you will want to cover certain major points of common interest to you and your students. The following paragraphs offer guidelines and suggestions for meeting your students the first time.

Greeting the students and first activity Welcome your students with a smile as they arrive, and then conduct the entire class with a friendly but businesslike demeanor. This means that you are not frowning, nor off in a corner of the room doing something else as students arrive. As you greet the students at the classroom door, tell them to take a seat and start on the first activity at their desk. This ensures that students have something to do immediately upon arriving to your classroom. And starting the learning immediately upon arrival should be the routine every day thereafter.

That first activity might be a questionnaire each student completes. This is a good time to instruct students on the expected standard for heading their papers. After giving instructions on how papers are to be handed in, rehearse the procedure by collecting this first paper. Or you may ask students to provide answers to a few discipline and personal questions on the back of a 3×5 card that you use to take attendance throughout the semester/year.

Student seating One option for student seating is to have student names on the first activity paper and placed at student seats when students arrive at that first class meeting. That allows you to have a seating chart ready on the first day, from which you can quickly take attendance and learn student names. Another option, not exclusive of the first, is to tell students that by the end of the week each should be in a permanent seat (either assigned by you or self-selected), from which you will make a seating chart that will help you to learn their names quickly and take attendance efficiently each day. It is important that students know that you will move them if they have chosen seat assignments that do not support their learning. Let them know, too, that from time to time you will redo the seating arrangement (if that is true). For small classes a seating chart is probably unnecessary.

Information about the class After the first assignment has been completed, discussed, and collected, explain to students what the class is about; in other words, what they will be learning and how they will learn it (covering study habits and your expectations regarding the quantity and quality of their work). This is a time you may choose to get student input into the course content in order to give students an opportunity for some empowerment. Although it is not common practice, some secondary teachers put this information in a course syllabus (see the sample in Module 5), give each student a copy, and review it with them, specifically discussing the teacher's expectations about how books will be used; about student notebooks, journals, portfolios, and assignments; about what students need to furnish; and about the location of resources in the classroom, school media center, and elsewhere.

Classroom procedures and endorsed behavior Now discuss in a positive way your expectations regarding classroom behavior, procedures, and routines (discussed next). Students work best when teacher expectations are well understood, with established routines. In the beginning it is important that there be no more procedures than necessary to get the class moving effectively for daily operation. Five or fewer expectations should be enough, such as:

- Arrive promptly with needed materials and stay on-task until excused by the teacher (the teacher, not a bell, excuses students).
- Demonstrate respect for the rights, the person, and the property of others.

- Remain seated and listen attentively when someone else is talking.

- Use appropriate and nonoffensive language.

- Work on anchor assignments whenever you have time in class. (We will discuss anchor assignments, any ongoing assignment such as portfolio organization, journal writing, or project work, in Module 5.)

Too many procedural expectations at first can be restricting and even confusing to students. As said earlier, most students already know these things, so you shouldn't have to spend much time on the topic except for those items specific to your course, such as the nature of the anchor assignment, and apparel and safety expectations for laboratory courses, shop and art classes, and physical education. Be patient with yourself on this, for finding and applying the proper level of control for a given group of students is one of the skills that you will develop and refine from experience.

Although many schools traditionally have posted in the halls and in the classrooms a list of prohibited behaviors, exemplary schools tend to focus on the positive, on endorsed attitudes and behaviors. Displaying a list of "do nots" does not encourage a positive school or classroom atmosphere; a list of "dos" does. For example, at Constellation Community Middle School (Long Beach, CA), all students receive regular daily reminders when, after reciting the Pledge of Allegiance, they recite the school's five core principles: (1) Anything that hurts another person is wrong. (2) We are each other's keepers. (3) I am responsible for my own actions. (4) I take pride in myself. (5) Leave it better than when you found it.[26]

■ Establishing Classroom Expectations, Procedures, and Consequences

When establishing classroom behavior expectations and procedures, remember this point: The learning time needs to run efficiently (i.e., with no "dead spots," or times when students have nothing to do), smoothly (i.e., routine procedures are established and transitions between activities are smooth), and with minimum distraction. As discussed in the preceding section, when stating your expectations for student classroom behavior, try to do so in a positive manner, emphasizing procedures, desired attitudes, and behaviors and stressing what students should do rather than what they should not do. Respect for the teacher, for themselves, for fellow classmates, for school property, for the process, and so forth, should be emphasized.

■ What Students Need to Understand from the Start

As you prepare the guidelines, standards, and expectations for classroom behavior, you (and, if relevant, your teaching team) need to consider some of the specifics about what students need to understand from the start. These specific points, then, should be reviewed and rehearsed with the students, sometimes several times, during the first week of school and then followed consistently throughout the school term.

Important and specific things that students need to know from the start will vary considerably depending on whether you are working with sixth graders in a middle school or high school seniors and whether you are teaching an English class or a shop class. Generally, though, each of the following paragraphs describes things that all students need to understand from the beginning.

Signaling the teacher for attention and help At the start of the school term, most teachers who are effective classroom managers expect students to raise their hands until the teacher acknowledges (usually by a nonverbal gesture, such as eye contact and a nod) that the student's hand has been seen. With that acknowledgment, the recommended procedure is that the student should lower his or her hand and return to work.

There are a number of important reasons for expecting students to raise their hands before speaking. Two are that it allows you to (a) control the noise and confusion level and (b) be proactive in deciding who speaks. The latter is important if you are to be in control of classroom events, rather than controlled by them, and if you are to manage a classroom with equality, with equal attention to individuals regardless of their gender, ethnicity, proximity to the teacher, or any other personal characteristic. We are not talking about students having to raise their hands before talking with their peers during group work; we are talking about not allowing students to shout across the room to get your attention and boisterously talk out freely during instruction.

Another important reason for expecting students to raise their hands and be recognized before speaking is to discourage impulsive outbursts and to grow intellectually. An instructional responsibility shared by all teachers is to help students develop intelligent behaviors (discussed in Module 6). Learning to control impulsivity is one of the intelligent behaviors. Teaching youth to control their impulsivity is a highly important responsibility that, in our opinion, is too often neglected by too many teachers (and by too many parents).

Entering and leaving the classroom From the time that the class is scheduled to begin until it officially ends, teachers who are effective classroom managers expect students to be at their learning stations and attentive to the teacher or the learning activity until excused by the teacher. For example, students should not be allowed to begin meandering toward the classroom exit in anticipation of the passing bell or the designated passing time. Otherwise, their meandering toward the door will begin earlier and earlier each day and the teacher will increasingly lose control. Besides, it is a waste of a very valuable and very limited resource—instructional time. As mentioned earlier, PATs can be used as a productive alternative when students become restless, or when students complete an activity earlier than anticipated.

Maintaining, obtaining, and using materials for learning and items of personal use Students need to know where, when, and how to store, retrieve, and care for items such as their coats, backpacks, books, pencils, and medicines; how to get papers and materials; and when to use the classroom pencil sharpener and wastebasket. Classroom control is easiest to maintain when (a) items that students need for class activities and for their personal use are neatly and safely arranged (for example, backpacks stored under tables or chairs rather than in aisles) and located in places that require minimum foot traffic, (b) there are established procedures that students clearly expect and understand, (c) there is the least amount of student off-task time, and (d) students do not have to line up for anything. Therefore, you will want to plan the room arrangement, equipment and materials storage, preparation of equipment and materials, and transitions between activities to avoid needless delays, confusion, and safety hazards. Remember this well: Problems in classroom control will most certainly occur whenever some or all students have nothing to do, even if only briefly.

Leaving class for a personal matter Normally, most students of middle school and high school age should be able to get of a drink of water or go to the bathroom between classes, if necessary; however, sometimes they do not or, for medical reasons or during long block classes, cannot. Reinforce the notion that they should do those things before coming into your classroom or during the scheduled times, but be flexible enough for the occasional student who has an immediate need. Whenever permitting a student to leave class for a personal reason, follow established school procedures, which may for reasons of security mean that students can only leave the room in pairs and with a hall pass or when accompanied by an adult, such as a campus security person.

Reacting to a visitor or an intercom announcement Unfortunately, class interruptions do occur, and in some schools they occur far too often and for reasons that are not as important as interrupting a teacher and students' learning would imply. For an important reason the principal, a vice-principal, or some other person from the school's office may interrupt the class to see the teacher or a student or to make an announcement to the entire class. Students need to understand what behavior is expected of them during those interruptions. When there is a visitor to the class, the expected procedure should be for students to continue their learning task unless directed otherwise by you. To learn more about class interruptions, do Exercise 3.1 now.

EXERCISE 3.1

■ Observing a Classroom for Frequency of External Interruptions

Instructions: It is disconcerting to know how often teachers and students in some school classrooms are interrupted by announcements from the intercom, a phone call, or a visitor at the door. After all, no one would even consider interrupting a surgeon during the most climactic moments of an open-heart operation, nor a defense attorney at the climax of her summation. But it seems far too often that teachers are interrupted just at the moment they have their students at a critical point in a lesson. Once lost because of an interruption, student attention and that teachable moment are difficult to recapture.

Arrange to visit a school classroom and observe for classroom interruptions created from outside the classroom.

School administrators and office personnel must sometimes be reminded that the most important thing going on in the school is that which teachers have been hired to do—teach. The act of teaching must not be frivolously interrupted. In our opinion, except for absolutely critical reasons, teachers should never be interrupted after the first five minutes of a class period and before the last five minutes. That policy should be established and rigidly adhered to. Otherwise, after many years of being a student, the lesson learned is that the least important thing going on at the school is that which is going on in the classroom. No wonder, then, that it is so difficult for teachers in some schools to gain student attention and respect. That respect must be shown starting from the school's central office. Because the turnaround and refocus must somehow begin now, for our effort toward that end we have added this exercise to this book.

(continued)

1. School and class visited: _____

2. Time (start and end of class period): _____

3. Interruptions (tally for each interruption) _____

   intercom: _____

   phone: _____

   visitor at door: _____

   emergency drill: _____

   other (specify): _____

4. Total number of interruptions: _____

5. My conclusion: _____

6. Share and compare your results and conclusion with your classmates. _____

To access this exercise online, go to the Companion Website at **www.prenhall.com/kellough.**

When late to class or leaving early You must abide by school policies on early dismissals and late arrivals. Make your own procedures routine so students clearly understand what they are to do if they must leave your class early (e.g., for a medical appointment) or when they arrive late. Procedures in your classroom, and indeed throughout the school, should be such that late arriving and early dismissal students do not have to disturb you or other teachers or the learning in progress.

When students are allowed to interrupt the learning in progress because the teacher has not established such procedures, and these interruptions happen repeatedly and regularly, the covert message conveyed by the hidden curriculum, at least in that classroom if not in the entire school, is that instruction is relatively low on the list of priorities. Do not let this happen!

Consequences for inappropriate behavior Most teachers who are effective classroom managers routinize their procedures for handling inappropriate behavior and en-

sure that the students understand the consequences for inappropriate behavior. The consequences are posted in the classroom and, depending on the school, may be similar to the five-step model shown in Figure 3.1.

Whether offenses subsequent to the first one are those that occur on the same day or within a designated period of time, such as one week, is one of the many decisions that must be made by a teacher or by members of a teaching team, department, or the entire faculty, with administrative approval.

Emergency drills (practice) or real emergencies Students need to clearly understand what to do, where to go, and how to behave in emergency conditions, such as those that might occur because of a fire, storm, earthquake, or a disruptive campus intruder. Students must be expected to behave during practice drills as well as in real emergencies.

To further your understanding of classroom management and to begin the development of your own management system, do Exercises 3.2 and 3.3.

First offense results in a direct but reasonably unobtrusive (often nonverbal) reminder from the teacher to the student.

Second offense results in a private but direct verbal warning.

Third offense results in a time-out in an isolation area (but one with adult supervision) followed by a private teacher-student (or teacher-student-parent) conference.

Fourth offense results in a suspension from class until there is a student-parent-teacher (and perhaps counselor) conference.

Fifth offense results in a referral to the vice-principal or principal or counselor, sometimes followed by a limited or permanent suspension from that class or a total expulsion from school.

FIGURE 3.1 ● *Sample Consequences for Inappropriate Behavior*

EXERCISE 3.2

■ Teachers' Behavior Management Systems

Instructions: The purpose of this exercise is to interview two teachers, one from a middle or junior high and the other from a high school, to discover how they manage their classrooms. Use the outline format that follows, conduct your interviews, and then share the results with your classmates, perhaps in small groups.

1. Teacher interviewed:

2. Date: 4. School:

3. Grade level: 5. Subject(s):

6. Please describe your classroom management system. Specifically, I would like to know your procedures for the following:
    a. How are students to signal that they want your attention and help?
    b. How do you call on students during question and discussion sessions?
    c. How and when are students to enter and exit the classroom?
    d. How are students to obtain the materials for instruction?
    e. How are students to store their personal items?
    f. What are the procedures for students going to the drinking fountain or bathroom?
    g. What are the procedures during class interruptions?
    h. What are the procedures for tardies or early dismissals?
    i. What are the procedures for turning in homework?

7. Describe your expectations for classroom behavior and the consequences for misbehavior.

    In discussion with classmates following the interviews, consider the following:

    Many modern teachers advocate the use of a highly structured classroom, and then, as appropriate over time during the school year, they share more of the responsibility with the students. Did you find this to be the case with the majority of teachers interviewed? Was it more or less the case in middle schools, junior highs, or high schools? Was it more or less the case with any particular subject areas?

 To access this exercise online, go to the Companion Website at **www.prenhall.com/kellough.**

EXERCISE 3.3

■ Beginning the Development of My Classroom Management System

Instructions: The purpose of this exercise is to begin preparation of the management system that you will explain to your students during the first day or week of school. Answer the questions that follow and share those answers with your peers for their feedback. Then make changes as appropriate. (Upon completion of this module, you may want to revisit this exercise to make adjustments to your management plan, as you will from time to time throughout your professional career.)

1. My teaching subject area and anticipated grade level:

(continued)

2. Attention to procedures. Use a statement to explain your procedural expectation for each of the following:
   a. How are students to signal that they want your attention and help?
   b. How do you call on students during question and discussion sessions?
   c. How and when are students to enter and exit the classroom?
   d. How are students to obtain the materials for instruction?
   e. How are students to store their personal items?
   f. What are the procedures for students going to the drinking fountain or bathroom?
   g. What are the procedures during class interruptions?
   h. What are the procedures for tardies or early dismissal?
   i. What are the procedures for turning in homework?

3. List of student behavior expectations that I will present to my class (no more than five):

   Rule 1:

   Rule 2:

   Rule 3:

   Rule 4:

   Rule 5:

4. Explanation of consequences for broken rules:

5. How procedures, rules, or consequences may vary (if at all) according to the grade level taught or according to any other criteria, such as in team teaching:

 To access this exercise online, go to the Companion Website at **www.prenhall.com/kellough.**

■ USING POSITIVE REWARDS

As you probably learned in a psychology course, reinforcement theory contends that a person's gratification derived from receiving a reward strengthens the tendency for that person to continue to act in a certain way, while the lack of a reward (or the promise of a reward) weakens the tendency to act that way. For example, according to the theory, if students are promised a reward of preferred activity time (PAT) on Friday if they work well all week long, then the students are likely to work toward that reward, thus improving their standards of learning. Preferred activity time is your bargaining chip. You should be happy to award students PAT, because while they are having fun, they will be learning content. Some educators argue that (a) once the extrinsic reinforcement (i.e., the reward from outside the learner) has been removed, the desired behavior tends to diminish; and that (b) rather than *extrinsic* sources of reinforcement, focus should be on increasing the student's inter-

nal sense of accomplishment, an *intrinsic* reward. Perhaps, for the daily work of a teacher in a classroom of many diverse individuals, the practical reality is somewhere in-between. After all, the reality of classroom teaching is less than ideal, and all activities cannot be intrinsically rewarding. Further, for many young people intrinsic rewards are often too remote to be effective.

The promise of extrinsic rewards is not always necessary or beneficial. Students generally will work harder to learn something because they want to learn it (i.e., it is intrinsically motivating) than they will merely to earn PAT, points, grades, candy, or some other form of reward (called extrinsic motivator). In addition, regarding the promise of PAT on Friday, many young people are so preoccupied with "now" that, for them, the promise on Monday of preferred activity time on Friday probably will have little desired effect on their behavior on Monday. To them, Friday seems to be a long way off from Monday.

Activities that are interesting and intrinsically rewarding are not further served by the addition of extrinsic rewards. This is especially true when working with students who are already highly motivated to learn. Adding extrinsic incentives to learning activities that are already highly motivating tends to reduce student motivation. For most students, the use of extrinsic motivators should be minimal and is probably most useful in skills learning, where there is likely to be a lot of repetition and the potential for boredom. If students are working diligently on a highly motivating student-initiated project of study, extrinsic rewards are not necessary and could even have negative effects.

■ MANAGING CLASS MEETINGS

The guidelines for the first meeting with your students hold true for every meeting thereafter. When it is time for the class period to begin, you should start the learning activities at once, with no delay. By beginning your class meeting without delay you discourage the kind of fooling around and time wasting that might otherwise occur. To minimize problems with classroom control, you must practice this from the very first day of your teaching career.

[Note: At the beginning of your student teaching, you may need to follow the opening procedures already established by your cooperating teacher. If your cooperating teacher's procedures for classroom management are largely ineffective, it is important for you to remember that you are a guest in that classroom. If you have a good working relationship established with your cooperating teacher, you may try talking directly to him/her and making suggestions. If the lines of communication are strained, chalk this up as a learning experience. Remember, sometimes we learn more about teaching by observing what we do not want to do in our classrooms than by having someone model stellar behavior. In a worst case scenario, you should talk with your university supervisor about a different placement.]

Once class has begun, the pace of activities should be lively enough to keep students alert and busy, without dead time, but not so fast as to discourage or lose some students. The effective teacher runs a businesslike classroom; at no time does any student sit or stand around with nothing to do. To maintain a smooth and brisk pace and to lessen distractions and prevent dead time, consider the guidelines that follow.

■ Opening Activities

Although many schools no longer use a bell system for the beginning and ending of every class period, many teachers still refer to the initial class activity as the bell ac-

tivity. More frequently, perhaps, it is referred to as the warm-up activity or opener.

At the beginning of each class, in order to take attendance and to attend to other routine administrative matters, most teachers expect the students to be in their assigned seats. You should greet the students warmly and start their learning quickly. (Unless you really want responses, it perhaps is best to avoid greeting students with a rhetorical question such as "How was your weekend?" If you are teaching in a school where you must monitor attendance at the beginning of each class meeting and are not yet comfortable with your overlapping skill, an effective management procedure is to have the overhead projector on each day when students arrive in class, with the day's agenda and immediate assignment or warm-up activity clearly written on a transparency and displayed on the screen, which then is referred to after your greeting. Once administrative matters are completed (usually in a matter of a minute or two), the day's regular lesson should begin, which could mean that students will move to other stations within the classroom.

When there are no announcements or other administrative matters to cover, you should try to begin the day's first lesson immediately. Then, within a few minutes after the students have begun their lesson activities, take attendance. Some teachers recommend beginning the day's lesson immediately while giving a reliable classroom aide or student assistant the responsibility of taking attendance and dealing with other routine administrative tasks. However, when another person performs the daily attendance routines, it remains your responsibility to check and sign the relevant attendance forms. Perhaps the best routine, one that requires your practice and overlapping skill, is to do both simultaneously—take attendance while starting a learning activity. Whichever the case, once the class period has begun, routines and lesson activities should move forward briskly and steadily until the official end of the class period, or, in the case of extended class periods or blocks, until a scheduled break.

Warm-up activities include any variety of things, such as a specific topic or question each student responds to by writing in his or her journal or the same topic or question that pairs (dyads) of students discuss and write about in their journals. Other activities include a problem to be solved by each student or student pair, the exchange and discussion of a homework assignment, the completion of the write-up of a laboratory activity, and the writing of individual or student dyad responses to textbook questions.

Now do Exercise 3.4 to learn further how experienced teachers open their class meetings.

EXERCISE **3.4**

■ Observation and Analysis of How Teachers Start Class Meetings

Instructions: Select three teachers, all of the same subject and grade level, to observe how they begin their class meetings. Observe only the first five minutes of each class. After collecting this data, share, compile, and discuss the results as follows.

Grade level and subject discipline I observed: _____

1. Make a check next to each of the following observations that you made, and for each teacher place a number (1, 2, 3, etc.) next to the things that teacher did first, second, third, etc., during that initial five minutes from the time students begin entering the classroom until after the official clock start of class (i.e., when class was supposed to begin).

	[√]	Teacher 1	Teacher 2	Teacher 3
Greeting the students	____	____	____	____
Warm and friendly?	____	____	____	____
Giving an assignment (i.e., a warm-up activity)	____	____	____	____
Taking attendance	____	____	____	____
Talking with another adult	____	____	____	____
Talking with a classroom aide	____	____	____	____
Talking with one or a few students	____	____	____	____
Readying teaching materials or equipment	____	____	____	____
Working at desk	____	____	____	____
Handing out student papers or materials	____	____	____	____
Other (specify)	____	____	____	____

2. For these three teachers, was there a common beginning observed?

3. Compile your results with those of your classmates. Write the results here.

4. Compare the results of observations for all subjects and middle and secondary school grade levels. What are the similarities and differences?

5. Are there any conclusions you can reach as a class about teachers of particular grade levels and disciplines and how they spent the first five minutes with their students?

 To access this exercise online, go to the Companion Website at **www.prenhall.com/kellough.**

■ Smooth Implementation of the Lesson

Lessons should move forward briskly and purposefully, with natural transitions from one lesson activity to the next and with each activity starting and ending conclusively, especially when using direct (teacher-centered) instruction. As a beginning teacher, it will take time to develop finesse in your application of this guideline; during your student-teaching experience, your cooperating teacher and college or university supervisor will understand that it takes time and will help you develop and hone your skill in the application of this principle. Transitions (discussed in the section that follows), in particular, are a most troublesome time for many beginning teachers. Transitions are less troublesome when planned carefully during the preactive phase of instruction and written into the lesson plan.

When giving verbal instructions to students, do so succinctly, without talking too long and giving so much detail that students begin to get restless and bored. Children are quickly bored with long-winded verbal instructions from a teacher. To address the linguistic needs of the English Language Learners as well as the preferences of the visual learners in your class, you may consider displaying directions on the board or on an overhead.

Once students are busy at their learning tasks, avoid interrupting them with additional verbal instructions, statements, or announcements that get them off-task and could as easily be written on the board or overhead transparency; also avoid interventions that could be communicated to a student privately without disturbing the rest of the class. Many students are easily distracted; do not be the cause of their distractions.

With whole-class instruction, before starting a new activity, be sure that the present activity is satisfactorily completed by most students. Students who finish early can work on an anchor or transitional activity. End each activity conclusively before beginning a new activity, and with a relevant and carefully prepared transition, bridge the new activity with the previous one so students understand the connection. Helping students understand connections is a continuing focus and theme for the classroom teacher.

With your skill in withitness, you will carefully and continuously monitor all students during the entire class period. If one or two students become inattentive and begin to behave inappropriately, quietly (i.e., using indirect or nonobtrusive intervention) redirect their attention without interrupting the rest of the class.

To help in the prevention of dead time and management problems, especially when using multiple learning tasks and indirect (student-centered) instruction, you will want to establish and rehearse the students in the use of anchor or transitional activities, which are ongoing, relevant tasks that students automatically move to whenever they have completed their individual or small-group classroom learning activities. Examples of an anchor activity would be working on their portfolio or writing in their journal.

■ Transitions: A Difficult Skill for Beginning Teachers

Transitions are the moments in lessons between activities or topics, that is, times of change. It will probably take you a while to sharpen the skill of smooth transitions. Planning and consistency are important in mastering this important skill. With a dependable schedule and consistent routines, transitions usually occur efficiently and automatically, without disruption. Still, it is probable that for classroom teachers the greatest number of discipline problems occur during times of transitions, especially when students must wait for the next activity. To avoid problems during transitions, eliminate wait time by thinking and planning ahead. During the preactive phase of instruction, plan your transitions and write them into your lesson plan.

Transitions in lessons are of two types, and at times, both are used. The first is achieved by the teacher's connecting one activity to the next so that students understand the relationship between the two activities. That is a lesson transition. The second type of transition occurs when some students have finished a learning activity but must wait for others to catch up before starting the next. This we call a transitional or, as we will discuss in Module 5, an anchor activity. The transitional (or anchor) activity is one intended to keep all students academically occupied, allowing no time where students have nothing to do but wait. A common example occurs during testing when some students have finished the test while others have not. The effective teacher plans a transitional activity and gives instructions or reminders for that activity or for an ongoing anchor activity before students begin the test.

Teachers who are most effective are those who, during the preactive phase of instruction, plan and rehearse nearly every move they and the students will make, thinking ahead to anticipate and avoid problems in classroom control. Transitions are planned and students are prepared for them by using clearly established transition routines. While in transition and waiting for the start of the next activity, students engage in these transitional activities. You can plan a variety of transitional activities relevant and appropriate to the topics being studied, although not necessarily related to the next activity of that particular day's lesson. Transitional activities may include any number of meaningful activities such as journal writing, worksheet activity, lab reports, portfolio work, homework, project work, and even work on an assignment for another class.

As a beginning teacher, it will take time to develop finesse in your application of these guidelines for effective lesson management. Well aware of that fact, your cooperating teacher and college or university supervisor will be patient and help you develop and sharpen your skills during your student-teaching experience.

■ STUDENT MISBEHAVIOR

Student behavior that is inappropriate in the classroom can range from minor acts to very serious ones. Sometimes the causes of student misbehavior are the result of problems that originate outside the classroom and spill over into it. Others are simply misbehaviors that result from the fact that whenever 30 or so young people are grouped together for a period of time mischief is likely to result. Still others are the result of something the teacher did or did not do. Read on attentively to the guidelines and suggestions that follow in the remaining pages of this module.

■ Categories of Student Misbehavior

Described next, in order of increasing seriousness, are categories of student misbehavior that classroom teachers sometimes have to contend with.

Transient nondisruptive behavior This least-serious category includes these common and usually nondisruptive behaviors: fooling around, chatting with a neighbor, and momentarily being off-task. Fortunately, in most instances, this type of behavior is transient, and sometimes it might even be best if you pretend for a moment or so not to be aware of it.[27] If it persists, all it may take to get the student back on-task is an unobtrusive (silent and private) redirection. Examples of silent and private redirection techniques include a stare or a stare accompanied by a frown (when eye contact with the student is made) or moving to stand next to the student. If this doesn't work, then go to the second-level intervention by quickly name-dropping (calling the student by name but without making an issue of it). If this doesn't work, go to a third-level intervention by calling on the student by name and reminding the student of the correct procedure or of what the student is supposed to be doing.

Avoid asking an off-task student any question such as a content question, "Bob, what are the end-products of photosynthesis?" When you know full well the student is not paying attention; or an inquiry, "Bob, why are you doing that?" Avoid also making a threat such as "Bob, if you don't turn around and get to work I will send you outside." It is important not to make "mountains out of molehills," or you could cause more problems than you would resolve. Maintain students' focus on the lesson rather than the off-task behavior.

Examples of trivial nondisruptive behaviors that you need not worry about unless they become disruptive are emotionally excited student behavior because the student is really "into the lesson"; brief whispering during a lesson; or short periods of inattentiveness, perhaps accompanied by visual wandering or daydreaming. Teacher responses to student behavior and enforcement of procedures such as raising hands and being recognized before speaking will naturally vary depending on the particular subject, size of the class, lesson activity, and maturity of the students.

In addition, there is sometimes a tendency among beginning teachers, especially when they have a problem with students being disruptive, to assume that the entire class of students is being unruly; in fact, more often it is only one, two, or maybe three students. When this is so, you want to avoid saying to the entire class of students anything that implies that you perceive them all as being unruly. That false accusation will only serve to alienate the majority of the students who are being attentive to the learning task.

Class disruptions This category includes talking out of turn, walking about the room without permission, and persistent clowning, all of which students know are behaviors that are unacceptable in the classroom. In handling such misbehaviors, it is important that you explain their consequences to students, and then, following your stated procedures, promptly and consistently deal with the violations. Too many beginning

teachers (and veteran teachers, too) tend to ignore these class disruptions (seemingly in hope that, if not recognized, they will discontinue). You must not ignore minor infractions of this type, for if you do, they most likely will escalate beyond your worst expectations. It is important to take care of discipline before instruction. Without displaying any anger (otherwise students are winning the battle for control), simply and quickly enforce your consequences and keep the focus on the lesson, not on the inappropriate behavior. In other words, maintain your control of classroom events, rather than become controlled by them. Or, putting it another way, with respect to classroom management, be proactive rather than reactive.

Defiance, back talk, cheating, lying, and stealing When a student refuses to do what you say, the student's defiance may be worthy of temporary or permanent removal from the class. Depending upon your judgment of the seriousness of the act of defiance, you may simply give the student a time-out or you may suspend the student from class until there has been a conference about the situation, perhaps involving the teacher, members of your teaching team, the student, the student's parent or guardian, and a school official.

Back talk may come in the form of insults and/or profanity. Students may insult you by commenting on your personal hygiene, your grooming, your dress, or any number of other topics. Profanity, consisting of vulgar or inappropriate language or swearing, is about who is in control (i.e., who has the power). Teachers need to remember that when these power struggles are taking place, silence is the key to success. Do not escalate the situation by responding in kind. Frederic Jones sums it up this way, "It takes one fool to start Back Talk, but it takes two fools to make a conversation out of it."[28]

Any cheating, lying, and stealing may be an isolated act, and the student may only need a one-on-one talk to find out what precipitated the incident and what might be done to prevent it from ever happening again. A student who habitually exhibits any of these behaviors may need to be referred to a specialist. Whenever you have reason to suspect immoral behavior, you should discuss your concerns with members of your teaching team and a school counselor or psychologist.

Violence Today's teachers are sometimes confronted with major problems of misbehavior that have ramifications beyond the classroom or that begin elsewhere and spill over into the classroom. If this happens, you may need assistance and should not hesitate to ask for it. As a teacher, you must stay alert. In the words of Johnson and Johnson:

> Teaching is different from what it used to be. Fifty years ago, the main disciplinary problems were running in halls, talking out of turn, and chewing gum. Today's transgressions include

physical and verbal violence, incivility, and in some schools, drug abuse, robbery, assault, and murder. The result is that many teachers spend an inordinate amount of time and energy managing classroom conflicts. When students poorly manage their conflicts with each other and with faculty, aggression results. Such behavior is usually punished with detentions, suspensions, and expulsions. As violence increases, pressure for safe and orderly schools increases. Schools are struggling with what to do.[29]

Today's schools are adopting a variety of types of schoolwide and classroom instructional programs designed to reduce or eliminate violent, aggressive student behaviors. Educators are being encouraged to enhance their ability to spot signs of trouble by increasing their efforts at establishing caring, responsive, and supportive relationships with students.[30]

■ There Are Success Stories

There are success stories; examples are described in the following pargraphs.

After instituting nontraditional flexible scheduling (discussed in Module 1), it is not uncommon for schools to report an improved school climate with significant improvement in student attitudes, behavior, attendance, and academic success.[31]

After instituting looping (keeping students with the same teacher for multiple years) and creating a focus on character development, Kennedy Middle School (Eugene, OR) reports higher student achievement and improved student behavior.[32]

A diet high in saturated fat and refined sugar has been proven to negatively impact the health and behavior of our students. In his film *Super Size Me*, Morgan Spurlock documents what happens to him as a result of eating McDonald's food three times a day for 30 days. Some people think that Spurlock's experiment is an unfair attack on the fast-food industry in this country, but the connection between fast-food menus and obesity in our youth is undeniable.

Does diet negatively impact student behavior as well? Spurlock investigated school lunch programs and questioned if eliminating junk food could reduce discipline problems. His documentary highlighted an alternative high school in the Midwest that instituted a healthy lunch program. The at-risk students attending Appleton Central Alternative High School in Appleton, Wisconsin, were offered wholesome breakfasts and lunches with a lot of healthy choices including fresh fruit and salads, cooked meats, and whole grain breads. By instituting these dietary changes the school reported a remarkable decline in behavioral problems. Since the program's inception in 1997, Principal LuAnn Coenen has reported a decline in the number of dropouts, an elimination of truant behavior, a decrease in drug use and suicide, an improvement in grades, and overall better behavior among the students. "Suddenly, the revolving discipline plans, metal detectors, security officers, and all the other tactics schools currently use to deal with rowdy students were no longer needed. . . . The improvement in student behavior is obvious to all. Teachers report fewer daily discipline issues and classroom disruptions."[33]

When teachers, counselors, students, parents, and community representatives work together, it is not uncommon for a school to report improved student attendance and a decline in the dropout rate. A successful effort at helping students make a connection with the value and goals of school has been through school and business partnerships. A special form of partnership called mentoring has had success with at-risk students as they become more receptive to schooling. The mentoring component of the partnership movement is a one-on-one commitment by community volunteers to improve the self-esteem, attitudes, and attendance of youngsters. Around the country there are a number of successful mentoring programs.[34]

Successful strategies include incorporating modern technology, making classes more student-centered, altogether eliminating the lower curriculum track and raising expectation standards for all students, and linking the school with parents and community representatives. By providing newsletters and other correspondence in Spanish and/or other languages spoken in the homes of the students, and hiring administrative staff and teachers who are bilingual, more parents will feel comfortable about becoming involved. Time and again schools report that using these combined strategies results in a decline in suspensions and an increase in student attendance and academic success, with a decrease in the rate of student dropout and failure. The school becomes a positive force in enhancing students' lives and in improving their academic achievement and their desire to come to and remain in school.[35]

■ Teacher Response to Student Misbehavior: Direct and Indirect Intervention

The goal in responding to student misbehavior is to intervene and redirect the student's focus, and to do so successfully with the least amount of classroom disturbance. Typically, teachers respond to student classroom misbehaviors in one of three ways: hostile, assertive, or nonassertive. Hostile and nonassertive responses should be avoided. Unlike a hostile response, an assertive response is not abusive or derogatory to the student. Unlike a nonassertive response, an assertive response is a timely and clear communication to the student about what the teacher wants and an indication that the teacher is prepared to back that want with action.[36]

Too often, teachers intervene with verbal commands—direct intervention—when nonverbal gesturing such as eye contact, proximity, gesturing (e.g., finger to the lips or raised hand), and body language—indirect and unobtrusive intervention strategies—are less disruptive and often more effective in redirecting a misbehaving student. Although the offense might be identical, the teacher's intervention for one student might have to be direct, while for another student indirect intervention is enough to stop the misbehavior.

Order of behavior intervention strategies To redirect a student's attention, your usual first effort should be indirect (nonverbal) intervention (e.g., proximity, eye contact, gesturing, body posture, silence). Your second effort could be the simplest (that is, the most private) direct (verbal) intervention (e.g., "David, please follow procedures"). Your third effort, one that closely follows the second in time interval (i.e., within the same class period), should follow your rules and procedures as outlined in your management system, which might mean a time-out or detention and a phone call to the student's parent or guardian (in private, of course). Normally, such a third effort is not necessary. A fourth effort, still rarer, is to suspend the student from class (and/or school) for some period of time until decisions about the future of that student in school are made by school officials in consultation with the student, the parents or guardians, and other professionals such as the school psychologist.

Direct intervention should be reserved for repetitive and serious misbehavior. When using direct intervention, you should give a direct statement, either reminding the student of what he or she is supposed to be doing or telling the student what to do. You should avoid asking a rhetorical question such as, "David, why are you doing that?" When giving students directions about what they are supposed to be doing, you may be asked by a student, "Why do we have to do this?" To that question, you may give a brief academic answer, but do not become defensive or make threats. And rather than spending an inordinate amount of time on the misbehavior, try to focus the student's attention on a desired behavior.

One reason that direct intervention should be held in reserve is because by interrupting the lesson to verbally intervene, you are doing exactly what the student who is being reprimanded was doing—interrupting the lesson. Not only is that improper modeling, but it can create a host of management problems beyond your wildest nightmares. Another reason for saving direct intervention is that, when used too often, direct intervention loses it effectiveness.

TEACHER-CAUSED STUDENT MISBEHAVIOR: SCENARIOS FOR REVIEW

As a classroom teacher, one of your major responsibilities is to model appropriate behavior and not to contribute to or cause problems in the classroom. Some student misbehaviors and problems in classroom control are caused or escalated by the teacher. (Yes, you may unwittingly contribute to your students' misbehavior!) In some cases, problems can be prevented or easily rectified if the teacher behaves or acts differently.

In addition to sometimes ignoring minor inappropriate behaviors, you should also avoid using negative methods of procedures enforcement and ineffective forms of punishment, such as exemplified by the following scenarios. You and your classmates might decide to treat these scenarios as case studies for small groups to consider and then discuss before the whole class.

- *Capricious.* Because of her arbitrary and inconsistent enforcement of classroom rules, Fran Fickle, a ninth-grade English teacher, has lost respect and trust of her students as well as control of her language arts classes. Students are constantly testing Fran to see what they can get away with.

- *Extra assignments.* When students in Margaret Malopropros's seventh-grade reading class misbehave, she habitually assigns extra reading and written work as punishment, even for the most minor offenses. This behavior has simply reinforced the view of many of her students that school is drudgery, so they no longer look forward to her classes, and behavior problems in her class have steadily increased since the beginning of the school year.

- *Embarrassment.* When eighth-grade social studies teacher Denise Degradini was having difficulty controlling the behavior of one of her students, she got on the classroom phone, called the student's parent, and, while the entire class of 33 students could hear the conversation, told the parent about her child's behavior in class and how she was going to have to give the student a referral if the student's behavior did not improve. From that one act Denise lost all respect from her students. Class academic achievement grades plummeted for the rest of the year.

- *Group punishment.* Because Fred Flock has not developed his withitness and overlapping skills, he has developed the unfortunate habit of punishing the entire group for every instance of misbehavior. Yesterday, for example, because some students were noisy during a video presentation, he gave the entire class an unannounced quiz on the content of the film. Not only has he lost the respect of the students, but students are hostile toward him, and his problems with classroom control are steadily growing worse.

■ *Harsh and humiliating punishment.* Vince Van Pelt, a high school physical education teacher, has lost control of his classes and the respect of his students. His thrashing, whipping, tongue-lashing, and use of humiliation are ineffective and indicative of his loss of control. Parents have complained and one is suing him. The district has given Mr. Van Pelt official notice of the nonrenewal of his contract.

■ *Loud talk.* The noisiest person in Steve Shrill's high school English class is Mr. Shrill. His constant and mistaken efforts to talk over the classes have led to his own yelling and screaming, to complaints from neighboring teachers about the noise in his classes, and to a reprimand from the principal.

■ *Lowered marks.* Eunice Erudite, an eighth-grade language arts/social studies core teacher, has a policy of writing a student's name on the board each time the person is reprimanded for misbehavior. Then, when a student has accumulated five marks on the board, she lowers his or her academic grade by one letter. As a result of her not separating their academic and social behaviors, her students are not doing as well as they were at the start of the year. Parents and students have complained about this policy to the administration, arguing that the grades Ms. Erudite is giving do not reflect the students' academic progress or abilities.

■ *Nagging.* Paul Peck's continual and unnecessary scolding and criticizing of students upsets the recipient students and arouses resentment from their peers. His nagging resolves nothing, and, like a snowball building in size as it rolls down the hill, causes Mr. Peck, a ninth-grade social studies teacher, more and more problems in the classroom.

■ *Negative direct intervention.* In the seventh-grade humanities block class, Joshua swears more and more frequently and with graphic and startling language. Other students are beginning to behave similarly. Rather than giving Joshua alternative ways of expressing his feelings, Polly Premio, one team teacher, verbally reprimands Joshua each time this happens and threatens to call his parents about it. Ms. Premio doesn't realize that by giving her attention to Joshua's swearing she is rewarding, reinforcing, and causing the increase in Joshua's unacceptable behavior.

■ *Negative touch control.* When Ezzard, an eighth-grade bully, pushes and shoves other students out of his way for no apparent reason other than to physically manipulate them, his teacher, Tony Trenchant, grabs Ezzard and yanks him into his seat. What "roughneck" Tony the teacher doesn't realize is that he is using the very behavior (physical force) that he is trying to stop Ezzard from using. This simply confuses students and teaches them (especially Ezzard) that the use of physical force is okay if you are bigger or older than the recipient of that force. In this situation, unfortunately, hostility begets hostility.

■ *Overreact.* Randall, a tenth-grade student, was reading a magazine when his English teacher, Harriet Harshmore, grabbed it from Randall's hands, called it pornographic, ripped out the offending pages, and tossed them into a waste basket. The magazine was *National Geographic*, and the pornographic article was on evolution and included drawings of unclothed humans. Harriet was later reprimanded by the school superintendent who said that although he supported her right to put a stop to what she considered a class disruption, Ms. Harshmore had crossed the line when she damaged the magazine. The magazine, apparently a rare collector's issue, had been brought from Randall's home at his teacher's encouragement to bring reading material from home.

■ *Physical punishment.* Mr. Fit, a ninth-grade geography teacher, punishes students by making them go outside and run around the school track when they misbehave in his class. Last week, Sebastian, a student whom he told to go out and run four laps for "mouthing off in class," collapsed and died while running. Mr. Fit has been placed on paid leave and is being used for negligence by Sebastian's parents.

■ *Premature judgments and actions.* Because of Kathy Kwik's impulsiveness, she does not think clearly before acting, and more than once she has reprimanded the wrong student. Because of her hasty and faulty judgments, students have lost respect for her. For them, her French I class has become pure drudgery.

■ *Taped mouths.* Miss Ductless taped the mouths of 20 of her sixth-grade students in order to keep them quiet. Later in the school day several of the students went to the school nurse complaining of allergic reactions caused by the duct tape. Until a full investigation is made, Miss Ductless has been relieved of her teaching duties.

■ *Threats and ultimatums.* Threats and ultimatums from ninth-grade math teacher Bonnie Badger are known to be empty; because she does not follow through, her credibility with the students has been lost. Like wildfire, the word has spread around—"We can do whatever we want in old Badger's class."

- *Too hesitant.* Because Tim Timideo is too hesitant and slow to intervene when students get off-task, his classes have increasingly gotten further and further out of his control, and it is still early in the school year. As a result, neighbor teachers are complaining about the noise from his classroom and Tim has been writing more and more referrals.

- *Writing as punishment.* Because they were "too noisy," high school biology teacher Steve Scribe punished his class of 28 students by making each one hand-copy 10 pages from encyclopedias. When they submitted this assignment, he tore up the pages in front of the class and said, "Now, I hope you have learned your lesson and from now on will be quiet." Upon hearing about this, all six teachers of the school's English department signed and filed a complaint with the principal about Mr. Scribe's use of writing as punishment.

■ PREVENTING A SHIP FROM SINKING IS MUCH EASIER THAN SAVING A SINKING ONE: MISTAKES TO AVOID

During your beginning years of teaching, no one, including you, should expect you to be perfect. You should, however, be aware of common mistakes teachers make that often are the causes of student inattention and misbehavior. Many classroom control problems are teacher-caused and preventable. In this section, you will find descriptions of mistakes commonly made by beginning (and even experienced) teachers. To have a most successful beginning to your career, you will want to sharpen your skills to avoid these mistakes, which requires both knowledge of the potential errors and a reflection upon one's own behaviors in relation to the errors.

1. *Inadequately attending to long-range and daily planning.* A teacher who inadequately plans ahead is heading for trouble. Inadequate long-term and sketchy daily planning is a precursor to ineffective teaching and, eventually, to teaching failure. Students are motivated best by teachers who clearly are working hard and intelligently for them. Plan, plan, plan; there is no such thing as overplanning.

2. *Emphasizing the negative.* Too many warnings to students for their inappropriate behavior—and too little recognition for their positive behaviors—do not help to establish the positive climate needed for the most effective learning to occur. Reminding students of procedures is more positive and will bring you quicker success than reprimanding them

when they do not follow procedures. Remember, there is no reality, only perception. Some describe the glass as half-empty where others see the same glass as half-full. Keep a positive attitude.

Too often, teachers try to control students with negative language, such as "There should be no talking," "No gum or candy in class or else you will receive detention," and "No getting out of your seats without my permission." Teachers sometimes allow students, too, to use negative language on each other, such as "Shut up!" Negative language does not help instill a positive classroom climate. To encourage a positive atmosphere, use concise, positive language. Tell students precisely what they are supposed to do rather than what they are not supposed to do. Disallow the use of disrespectful and negative language in your classroom.

3. *Not requiring students to raise hands and be acknowledged before responding.* While ineffective teachers often are ones who are controlled by class events, competent teachers are those who are in control of class events. You cannot be in control of events and your interactions with students if you allow students to shout out their comments, responses, and questions whenever they feel like it. The most successful beginning teacher is one who quickly establishes his or her control of classroom events.

In addition, indulging their natural impulsivity does not help students to grow intellectually. When students develop impulse control, they think before acting. Students can be taught to think before acting or shouting out an answer. One of several reasons that teachers should insist on a show of student hands before a student is acknowledged to speak is to discourage students from the impulsive, disruptive, and irritating behavior of shouting out in class.[37]

4. *Allowing students' hands to be raised too long.* When students have their hands raised for long periods before you recognize them and attend to their questions or responses, you are providing them with time to fool around. Although you don't have to call on every student as soon as he or she raises a hand, you should acknowledge him or her quickly, such as with a nod or a wave of your hand, so the student can lower his or her hand and return to work. Then you should get to the student as quickly as possible. The students should clearly understand these procedures, and you should practice them consistently.

5. *Spending too much time with one student or one group and not monitoring the entire class.* Spending too much time with any one student or a small group of students is, in effect, ignoring the rest of the students. As a novice teacher you cannot afford to ignore the rest of the class, even for a moment.

6. *Beginning a new activity before gaining the students' attention.* A teacher who consistently fails to insist that students follow procedures and who does not wait until all students are in compliance before starting a new activity is destined for major problems in classroom control. You must estabish and maintain classroom procedures. Starting an activity before all students are in compliance is, in effect, telling the students that they don't have to follow expected procedures. You cannot afford to tell students one thing and then do another. In the classroom, your actions will always speak louder than your words.

7. *Pacing teacher talk and learning activities too fast.* Pacing instructional activities is one of the more difficult skills for beginning teachers to master. Students need time to disengage mentally and physically from one activity before engaging in the next. You must remember that this takes more time for a room of 25 or so students than it does for just one person, you. This is a reason that transitions, as discussed in Module 4, need to be scheduled and written into your lesson plan.

8. *Using a voice level that is always either too loud or too soft.* A teacher's voice that is too loud day after day can become irritating to some students, just as one that cannot be heard or understood can become frustrating.

9. *Assigning a journal entry without giving the topic careful thought.* If the question or topic about which students are supposed to write is ambiguous or obviously hurriedly prepared—without your having given thought to how students will interpret and respond to it—students will judge that the task is busywork (e.g., something to keep them busy while you take attendance). If they do it at all, it will be with a great deal of commotion and much less enthusiasm than were they writing on a topic that had meaning to them.

10. *Standing too long in one place.* Most of the time in the classroom, you should be mobile, schmoozing, "working the crowd."

11. *Sitting while teaching.* As a middle or secondary school teacher, unless you are physically unable to stand, in most situations there is no time to sit while teaching. It is difficult to monitor the class while seated. You cannot afford to appear that casual.

12. *Being too serious and no fun.* No doubt, good teaching is serious business. But students are motivated by and respond best to teachers who obviously enjoy working with students and helping them learn.

13. *Falling into a rut by using the same teaching strategy or combination of strategies day after day.* A teacher in such a rut is likely to become boring to students. Because of the multitude of differences, students are motivated by and respond best to a variety of well-planned and meaningful learning activities.

14. *Inadequately using silence (wait time) after asking a content question.* When expected to think deeply about a question, students need time to do it. A teacher who consistently gives insufficient time to students to think is teaching only superficially, at the lowest cognitive level, and is destined to have problems in student motivation and classroom control.

15. *Poorly or inefficiently using instructional tools.* The ineffective use of teaching tools such as books, the overhead projector, writing board, and computer says to students that you are not a competent teacher. Would you want an auto mechanic who did not know how to use the tools of her trade to service your automobile? Would you want a brain surgeon who did not know how to use the tools of her trade to remove your tumor? Working with adolescents in a classroom is no less important. Like a competent automobile mechanic or a competent surgeon, a competent teacher selects and effectively uses the best tools available for the job. If you plan on integrating technology into a lesson, always be sure to have a backup plan in case things do not go as planned.

16. *Ineffectively using facial expressions and body language.* As said earlier, your gestures and body language communicate more to students than your words do. For example, one teacher didn't understand why his class of seventh graders would not respond to his repeated expression of "I need your attention." In one 15-minute segment, he used that expression eight times. Studying videotape of that class period helped him understand the problem. His dress was very casual, and he stood most of the time with his right hand in his pocket. At 5 foot 8 inches, with a slight build, a rather deadpan facial expression, and an unexpressive voice, he was not a commanding presence in the classroom. After seeing himself on tape, he returned to the class wearing a tie, and he began using his hands, face, and body more expressively. Rather than saying, "I need your attention," he waited in silence for the students to become attentive. It worked.

17. *Relying too much on teacher talk for classroom control.* Beginning teachers have a tendency to rely too much on teacher talk. Too much teacher talk can be deadly. Unable to discern between the important and the unimportant verbiage, students will quickly tune a teacher out.

Some teachers rely too much on verbal interaction and too little on nonverbal intervention techniques. Verbally reprimanding a student for his or her interruptions of class activities is reinforcing the very behavior you are trying to stop. In addition, verbally reprimanding a student in front of his or her peers can backfire on you. Instead, develop your indirect, silent intervention techniques such as eye contact, mobility, frown, silence, body stance, and proximity.

18. *Inefficiently using teacher time.* During the preactive phase of your instruction (the planning phase), think carefully about what you are going to be doing every minute, and then plan for the most efficient and therefore the most productive use of your time in the classroom. Consider the following example. During a brainstorming session a teacher is recording student contributions on a large sheet of butcher paper that has been taped to the wall. She solicits student responses, acknowledges those responses, holds and manipulates the writing pen, walks to the wall, and writes on the paper. Each of those actions requires decisions and movements that consume precious instructional time and that can distract her from her students. An effective alternative should be to have a reliable student helper do the writing while the teacher handles the solicitation and acknowledgment of student contributions. That way she has fewer decisions and fewer actions to distract her. And she does not lose eye contact and proximity with the classroom of students.

19. *Talking to and interacting with only half the class.* While leading a class discussion, there is a tendency among some beginning teachers to favor (by their eye contact and verbal interaction) only 40 to 65% of the students, sometimes completely ignoring the others for an entire class period. Knowing that they are being ignored, those students will, in time, become uninterested and perhaps unruly. Remember to spread your interactions and eye contact throughout the entire class. Students who are eager to participate make the teacher's job easy. It is important to remember, though, that some students' learning styles are different and they may need more encouragement, a "heads-up," longer wait time, and so forth, in order to participate.

20. *Collecting and returning student papers before assigning students something to do.* If, while turning in papers or waiting for their return, students have nothing else to do, they get restless and inattentive. Students should have something to do while papers are being collected or returned.

21. *Interrupting while students are on-task.* It is not easy to get an entire class of students on-task. Once they are on-task, you do not want to be the distracter. Try to give all instructions before students begin their work. The detailed instructions should be written in your lesson plan; that way you are sure not to forget anything. Once on-task, if there is an important point you wish to make, write it on the board. If you want to return papers while students are working, do it in a way and at a time that is least likely to interrupt them from their learning task.

22. *Using "Shhh" as a means of quieting students.* When you do that, you simply sound like a balloon with a slow leak. The sound should be deleted from your professional vocabulary.

23. *Using poor body positioning.* Develop your skill of withitness by always positioning your body so you can continue to visually monitor the entire class even while talking to and working with one student or a small group. Avoid turning your back to even a portion of the class.

24. *Settling for less when you should be trying for more—not getting the most from student responses.* The most successful schools are those with teachers who expect and get the most from all students. Don't hurry a class discussion; "milk" student responses for all you can, especially when discussing a topic that students are obviously interested in. Ask a student for clarification or reasons for his or her response. Ask for verification. Have another student paraphrase what a student said. Pump students for deeper thought and meaning. Too often, the teacher will ask a question, get an abbreviated (often a one word and low cognitive level) response from a student, and then move on to another subject. Instead, follow up a student's response to your question with a sequence of questions, prompting and cueing to elevate the student's thinking to higher levels.

25. *Using threats.* Avoid making threats of any kind. One teacher, for example, told her class that if they continued with their inappropriate talking (as if the entire classroom of students was talking inappropriately), they would lose their break time. She should have had that consequence as part of the understood procedures and consequences and then taken away the break time for some students if warranted.

26. *Avoid punishing the entire class for the misbehavior of a few.* Although the rationale behind such action is clear (i.e., to get group pressure working for you), often the result is the opposite. Students who have been behaving well are alienated from the teacher because they feel they have been punished unfairly for the misbehavior of others. Those students expect the teacher to be able to handle the misbehaving students without punishing those who are not misbehaving, and they are right!

27. *Using global praise.* Global praise is pretty useless. An example is: "Class, your rough drafts were really wonderful." This is hollow and says nothing—simply another instance of useless verbiage from the teacher. Instead, be specific—tell what it was about their drafts that made them so wonderful. As an-

other example, after a student's oral response to the class, rather than simply saying "Very good," tell the student what was so good about the response.

28. *Using color meaninglessly.* The use of color on transparencies and the writing board is nice but will shortly lose its effectiveness unless the colors have meaning. If, for example, everything in the classroom is color-coded and students understand the meaning of the code, then use of color can serve as an important mnemonic to student learning.

29. *Verbally reprimanding a student from across the room.* This is yet another example of a needless interruption of all students. In addition, because of peer pressure (students tend to support one another) it increases the "you versus them" syndrome. Reprimand when necessary, but do it quietly and as privately as possible.

30. *Interacting with only a chosen few students rather than spreading interactions around to all.* As a beginning teacher, especially, it is easy to fall into a habit of interacting with only a few students, especially those who are vocal and who have significant contributions. Your job, however, is to teach all the students. To do that, you must be proactive, not reactive, in your interactions.

31. *Not intervening quickly enough during inappropriate student behavior.* When allowed to continue, inappropriate student behavior only gets worse, not better. It will not go away by itself. It's best to nip it in the bud quickly and resolutely. A teacher who ignores inappropriate behavior, even briefly, is in effect approving it. In turn, that approval reinforces the continuation and escalation of inappropriate behaviors.

32. *Not learning and using student names.* To expedite your success, you should quickly learn and use students' names. A teacher who does not know or use names when addressing students is, in effect, viewed by the students as impersonal and uncaring.

33. *Reading student papers only for correct (or incorrect) answers and not for process and student thinking.* Reading student papers only for correct responses reinforces the false notion that the process of arriving at answers or solutions is unimportant and that alternative solutions or answers are impossible or unimportant. In effect, it negates the importance of the individual and the very nature and purpose of learning.

34. *Not putting time plans on the board for students.* Yelling out how much time is left for an activity interrupts student thinking and implies that their thinking is unimportant. Avoid interrupting students once they are on-task. Show respect for their on-task behavior. In this instance, write on the board before the activity begins how much time is

allowed for it. Write the time it is to end. If during the activity a decision is made to change the end time, then write the changed time on the board.

35. *Asking global questions that nobody likely will answer.* Examples are "Does everyone understand?" and "Are there any questions?" and "How do you all feel about . . . ?" It is a brave young soul who in the presence of peers is willing to admit ignorance. It is a waste of precious instructional time to ask such questions. If you truly want to check for student understanding or opinions, then do a spot check: Ask specific questions, allow think-time, and then call on individuals.

36. *Failing to do frequent comprehension checks (every few minutes during most direct instruction situations) to see if students are understanding.* Too often teachers simply plow through a big chunk of the lesson, or the entire lesson, assuming that students are understanding it. Or, in the worst case scenario, teachers rush through a lesson without even caring if students are getting it. Students are quick to recognize teachers who really don't care.

37. *Using poorly worded ambiguous questions.* Key questions you will ask during a lesson should be planned and written into your lesson plan. Refine and make precise the questions by asking them to yourself or a friend, and try to predict how students will respond to particular questions.

38. *Trying to talk over student noise.* This simply tells students that their making noise while you are talking is acceptable behavior. When this happens, everyone, teacher included, usually gets increasingly louder during the class period. All that you will accomplish when trying to talk over a high student noise level is a sore throat by the end of the school day and, over a longer period of time, the potential for nodules on your vocal cords.

39. *Wanting to be liked by students.* Forget it. If you are a teacher, then teach. Respect is earned as a result of your effective teaching. Being liked may come later.

40. *Permitting students to be inattentive to an educationally useful media presentation.* This usually happens because the teacher has failed to give the students a written handout of questions or guidelines for what they should acquire from the program. Sometimes students need an additional focus. Furthermore, a media presentation is usually audio and visual. To reinforce student learning, add the kinesthetic, such as the writing required when a handout of questions is used. This provides minds-on and hands-on activities that enhance learning.

41. *Starting in stutters.* A stutter start is when the teacher begins an activity, is distracted, begins again, is distracted again, tries again to start, and so on. During stutter starts, students become increasingly restless

and inattentive, and sometimes even amused by the teacher's futility, making the final start almost impossible for the teacher to achieve. Avoid stutter starts. Begin an activity clearly and decisively. This is best done when lesson plans are prepared thoughtfully and in detail.

42. *Introducing too many topics simultaneously.* It is important that you not overload students' capacity to engage mentally by introducing different topics simultaneously. For example, during the first ten minutes of class a teacher started by introducing a warm-up activity, which was a journal write with instructions clearly presented on the overhead; the teacher also verbally explained the activity, although she could have simply pointed to the screen, thereby nonverbally instructing students to begin work on the activity (without disrupting the thinking of those who had already begun). One minute later, the teacher was telling students about their quarter grades and how later in the period they would learn more about those grades. Then she returned to the warm-up activity, explaining it a second time (a third time if one counts the detailed explanation already on the screen). Next she reminded students of the new tardy rules (thereby introducing a third topic). At this time, however, most of the students were still thinking and talking about what she had said about quarter grades, few were working on the warm-up activity, and hardly any were listening to the teacher talking about the new tardy rules. There was a lot of commotion among the students. The teacher had tried to focus student attention on too many topics at once, thus accomplishing little and losing control of the class in the process.

43. *Failing to give students a pleasant greeting on a Monday or following a holiday or to remind them to have a pleasant weekend or holiday.* Students are likely to perceive such a teacher as uncaring or impersonal.

44. *Sounding egocentric.* Whether you are or are not egocentric, you want to avoid appearing so. Sometimes the distinction is subtle, although apparent, such as when a teacher says, "What I am going to do now is . . . " rather than "What we are going to do now is . . . " If you want to strive for group cohesiveness—a sense of "we-ness"—then teach not as if you are the leader and your students are the followers, but rather in a manner that empowers your students in their learning.

45. *Taking too much time to give verbal instructions for an activity.* Students become impatient and restless during long verbal instructions from the teacher. It is better to give brief instructions (two or three minutes should do it) and get the students started on the task. For more complicated activities, teach

three or four students the instructions and then have those students do workshops with five or six students in each workshop group. This frees you to monitor the progress of each group.

46. *Taking too much time for an activity.* No matter what the activity, during your planning think carefully about how much time students can effectively attend to it. A general rule for most classes (age level and other factors will dictate variation) is when only one or two learning modalities are involved (e.g., auditory and visual), the activity should not extend beyond about 15 minutes; when more than two modalities are engaged (e.g., add tactile or kinesthetic), then the activity might extend longer, say for 20 or 30 minutes.

47. *Being uptight and anxious.* Consciously or subconsciously, students are quick to detect a teacher who is afraid that events will not go well. And it's like a contagious disease—if you are uptight and anxious, your students will likely become the same. To prevent such emotions, at least to the extent they damage your teaching and your students' learning, you must prepare lessons carefully, thoughtfully, and thoroughly. Unless there is something personal going on in your life that is making you anxious, you are more likely to be in control and confident in the classroom when you have lessons that are well-prepared. How do you know if your lesson is well-prepared? You will know! It's when you develop a written lesson plan that you are truly excited about and looking forward to implementing, and then before doing so, you review it one more time.

If you have a personal problem going on in your life that is distracting and making you anxious (and occasionally most of us do), you need to concentrate on ensuring that your anger, hostility, fear, or other negative emotions do not adversely affect your teaching and your interactions with students. Regardless of your personal problems your classes of students will face you each day expecting to be taught reading, mathematics, history, science, physical education, or whatever it is you are supposed to be helping them to learn.

48. *Using a one-size-fits-all technique; failing to apply the best of what is known about how young people learn.* Too many teachers unrealistically seem to expect success having all 33 students doing the same thing at the same time rather than having several alternative activities simultaneously occurring in the classroom, called multilevel teaching or multitasking. For example, a student who is not responding well (i.e., being inattentive and disruptive) to a class discussion might behave better if given the choice of moving to a quiet reading center in the classroom or to a learning center to work alone. If after trying an alternative activity, the student continues to be

disruptive, then you may have to try still another alternative activity. You may have to send the student to another supervised location out of the classroom, to a place previously arranged by you, until you have time after class or after school to talk with the student about the problem.

49. *Overusing punishment for classroom misbehavior—jumping to the final step without trying alternatives.* Teachers sometimes mistakenly either ignore inappropriate student behavior (see number 31) or skip steps for intervention, resorting too quickly to punishment. They immediately send the misbehaving student outside to stand in the hall (not a wise choice because the student is not supervised) or too quickly assign detention (usually an ineffective form of punishment). In-between steps to consider include the use of alternative activities in the classroom (as in number 48).

50. *Being inconcise and inconsistent.* Perhaps one of the most frequent causes of problems in classroom control for beginning teachers is when they fail to say what they mean or mean what they say. A teacher who gives only vague instructions or who is inconsistent in his or her behavior confuses students (e.g., does not enforce his or her own classroom procedural expectations). A teacher's job is not to confuse students.

You have heard and will repeatedly hear how important it is to be consistent. Students who believe that rules are unfairly and inconsistently enforced are usually the ones who are most likely to misbehave.[38]

Now direct your attention to other specific instances of teacher behaviors, some of which reinforce or cause student misbehavior, by completing Exercises 3.5 and 3.6.

EXERCISE 3.5

■ Applying Measures of Control

Instructions: The purpose of this exercise is for you to determine when you might use each of the various options available when there is a student behavior problem in your classroom. For each of the following, as specifically as possible identify both a situation in which you would and one in which you would not use that measure. Then share your responses with those of others in your class.

1. Eye contact and hand signal to the student.

   Would:

   Would not:

2. Send student immediately to the office of the vice-principal.

   Would:

   Would not:

3. Ignore the student.

   Would:

   Would not:

4. Assign the student to detention.

   Would:

   Would not:

5. Send a note home to parent or guardian about the student's misbehavior.

   Would:

   Would not:

(continued)

6. Touch a student on the shoulder.

   Would:

   Would not:

7. Provide candy as rewards.

   Would:

   Would not:

8. Provide a time-out from academic time.

   Would:

   Would not:

9. Verbally redirect the student's attention.

   Would:

   Would not:

10. Use a verbal reprimand.

    Would:

    Would not:

 To access this exercise online, go to the Companion Website at **www.prenhall.com/kellough.**

EXERCISE **3.6**

■ Selecting Measures of Control

Instructions: The purpose of this exercise is to provide situations to help you in determining which measures of control you would apply in similar situations. For each of the following, write what you would do in that situation. Then share your responses with your classmates.

1. A student reveals a long knife and threatens to cut you.

2. During a test a student appears to be copying answers from a neighboring student's answer sheet.

3. Although you have asked a student to take his seat, he refuses.

4. While talking with a small group of students, you observe two students on the opposite side of the room tossing paper airplanes at each other.

5. During small-group work one student seems to be aimlessly wandering around the room.

6. Although chewing gum is against your classroom rules, at the start of the class period you observe a student chewing what appears to be gum.

7. During band rehearsal you (as band director) observe a student about to stuff a scarf down the saxophone of another student.

(continued)

8. During the viewing of a film, two students on the side of the room opposite you are quietly whispering.

9. At the start of the period, while a student is about to take his seat, a boy pulls the chair from beneath him. He falls to the floor.

10. Suddenly, for no apparent reason, a student gets up and leaves the room.

 To access this exercise online, go to the Companion Website at **www.prenhall.com/kellough.**

■ SUMMARY

Students are more likely to learn when they feel that the learning is important or worth the time. In this module we described factors important for learning to occur. As a classroom teacher you should not be expected to solve all the societal woes that can spill over into the classroom. Yet as a professional you have certain responsibilities, including to prepare thoughtfully and thoroughly for your classes; to manage and control your classes; and to be able to diagnose, prescribe, and remedy those learning difficulties, disturbances, and minor misbehaviors that are the norm for classrooms and for the age group with which you are working. If you follow the guidelines provided in this book, you will be well on your way to developing a teaching style and management system that, for the most part, should provide teaching that runs smoothly and effectively, without serious problems.

It is important to select strategies most appropriate to your teaching plans and that complement your management system. Modules that follow in Part 3 present guidelines for doing that.

■ MODULE 3 **POSTTEST**

Multiple Choice

1. If your class of students is getting too noisy, you can try any of the following except
   a. remaining quiet until the class is quiet.
   b. changing the lesson strategy to a distinctly different activity.
   c. holding your hand in the air, thereby nonverbally asking for quiet.
   d. talking louder or, if necessary, yelling over their noise, asking them to be quiet.

2. The least recommended of the following, although sometimes necessary for the teacher's intervention of student misbehavior, is the use of
   a. eye contact.
   b. physical contact.
   c. a voice command.
   d. teacher proximity to the offending student.

3. Effective classroom management should rely on
   a. calm and silence.
   b. fear and subordination.
   c. orderliness and control.
   d. warning and punishment.

4. An important rule of thumb about the establishment of classroom behavior rules is that
   a. established rules are not necessary.
   b. the more established rules the better.
   c. only the minimum number of rules necessary should be established.
   d. a list of 12 rules is the minimum required to cover basic behaviors.

(continued)

5. Which one of the following is a true statement about behavior problems in the middle school and secondary school classroom?
   a. Students are unruly by nature.
   b. Most student misbehavior is preventable.
   c. Administrators do not adequately support teachers.
   d. The occasional use of corporal punishment is absolutely necessary to maintain classroom control.

6. When assigning a written paper, which one of the following is a desired verbal command?
   a. Don't plagiarize your assignment.
   b. I will know if you have copied someone else's paper.
   c. Please try to use your own ideas, and credit others whenever you do use theirs.
   d. If you try to turn in your first writing draft without rewriting, I guarantee you will get a poor grade.

7. Withitness and overlapping are
   a. skills used by teachers for supervising student behavior.
   b. natural consequences in dealing with disruptive classroom behavior.
   c. teacher strategies especially necessary for working in multicultural classrooms.
   d. techniques for integrating mild and moderately disabled students into the regular education classroom.

8. While showing the class of students a video, you are best advised to
   a. use that time to grade papers.
   b. go to the faculty room to relax.
   c. stand at the rear of the classroom and watch the movie.
   d. stand at the rear of the classroom and monitor student behavior.

9. Efficient classroom management is synonymous with
   a. routinizing clerical tasks.
   b. controlling student behavior.
   c. not allowing any nonsense from students.
   d. running a businesslike classroom where students are under self-control and work diligently at their learning tasks free from distractions.

10. A usually effective safeguard against disruptive classroom behavior is
   a. a well-prepared lesson.
   b. a supportive school principal.
   c. the threat of corporal punishment.
   d. a teacher who is physically intimidating to the students.

Short Explanation

1. Identify at least four guidelines for using positive reinforcement for a student's appropriate behavior.
2. Explain why it is important to prevent behavior problems before they occur. Describe at least five preventive steps you will take to minimize your classroom management problems.
3. It has been said that too many teachers attempt to resolve problems with individual students within the regular class period. Describe options for what you can do outside of regular class time if you have a problem with the classroom behavior of a student.
4. Explain the rationale for the phrase "catch them being good."
5. Why do you suppose many learning psychologists (e.g., Montessori and Piaget) oppose the teacher's use of extrinsic reinforcement for managing student behavior in the classroom?
6. Explain how and why your classroom management procedures and expectations might differ depending upon the students and the learning activities.
7. Explain the difference between reprimanding a student for his or her inappropriate classroom behavior and reminding the student of classroom procedures. Give examples of when you might use each.
8. Explain why stopping instruction to verbally reprimand a student for his or her inappropriate behavior is an inappropriate (although occasionally necessary) teacher behavior.
9. Is it better to be very strict with students at first and then relax once your control has been established, or to be relaxed at first and then tighten the reins later if students misbehave? Explain your answer.
10. Explain what you would do if two errant student behaviors occurred simultaneously in different locations in your classroom.

(continued)

Essay

1. Some experts say that 90% of control problems in the classroom are teacher caused. Do you agree or disagree? Explain why or why not.

2. Some supervisors of student teachers prefer that the student teacher never conduct a class while seated. Is it ever appropriate for a (nondisabled) teacher to be seated while teaching? Explain why it is or is not.

3. It has been said that students are more likely to learn when they feel that the learning is important or worth the time. Explain how a teacher in your subject field can make that happen, that is, students feeling that the learning is important and worth their time.

4. It is not uncommon to find that a particular student achieves well and behaves well in one teacher's class but not in another's. What explanations can there be for such a difference in a student's behavior and achievement?

5. From your current observations and fieldwork related to this teacher preparation program, clearly identify one specific example of educational practice that seems contradictory to exemplary practice or theory presented in this module. Present your explanation for the discrepancy.

 To access this posttest and the answers online, go to the Companion Website at www.prenhall.com/kellough.

■ SUGGESTED READINGS

Alcock, M. W. (1998). Repecharge, reflection, and brain processing: Personality influence in the classroom. *NASSP Bulletin, 82*(598), 56–62.

Ben-Avie, M. (1998). Secondary education: The school development program at work in three high schools. *Journal of Education for Students Placed At Risk (JESPAR), 3*(1), 53–70.

Bodine, R. J., & Crawford, D. K. (1998). *The handbook of conflict resolution education: A guide to building quality programs in schools.* San Francisco: Jossey-Bass.

Brophy, J., & Alleman, J. (1998). Classroom management in a social studies learning community. *Social Education, 62*(1), 56–58.

Curwin, R. L., & Mendler, A. N. (1999). *As tough as necessary: Countering aggression, violence, and hostility in schools.* Alexandria, VA: Association for Supervision and Curriculum Development.

Fogarty, R. (1998). The intelligence-friendly classroom. *Phi Delta Kappan, 79*(9), 655–657.

Foster-Harrison, E. S., & Adams-Bullock, A. (1998). *Creating an inviting classroom environment.* Fastback 422. Bloomington, IN: Phi Delta Kappa Educational Foundation.

Freiberg, H. J. (Ed.). (1999). *Beyond behaviorism: Changing the classroom management paradigm.* Needham Heights, MA: Allyn & Bacon.

Hansen, J. M., & Childs, J. (1998). Creating a school where people like to be. *Educational Leadership, 56*(1), 14–17.

Hardin, C. J., & Harris, E. A. (2000). *Managing classroom crises.* Fastback 465. Bloomington, IN: Phi Delta Kappa Educational Foundation.

Hardy, L. (1999). A cold climate. *American School Board Journal, 186*(9), 31–33.

Hassenpflug, A. (1999). Courts and peer sexual harassment by middle school students. *Middle School Journal, 31*(2), 49–56.

Jensen, E. (1998). How threats and stress affect learning. In E. Jensen, *Teaching with the Brain in Mind* (Chap. 6).

Alexandria, VA: Association for Supervision and Curriculum Development.

Kovalik, S., & Olsen, K. D. (1998). How emotions run us, our students, and our classrooms. *NASSP Bulletin, 82*(598), 29–37.

Landau, B. M., & Gathercoal, P. (2000). Creating peaceful classrooms: Judicious discipline and class meetings. *Phi Delta Kappan, 81*(6), 450–452, 454.

Marshall, M. (1998). *Fostering social responsibility.* Fastback 428. Bloomington, IN: Phi Delta Kappa Educational Foundation.

McEwan, B. (2000). *The art of classroom management: Effective practices for building equitable learning communities.* Upper Saddle River, NJ: Merrill/Prentice Hall.

Nissman, B. S. (2000). *Teacher-tested classroom management strategies.* Upper Saddle River, NJ: Merrill/Prentice Hall.

Petrie, G., et al. (1998). Nonverbal cues: The key to classroom management. *Principal, 77*(3), 34–36.

Rea, D., Millican, K. P., & Watson, S. W. (2000). The serious benefits of fun in the classroom. *Middle School Journal, 31*(4), 23–28.

Sesno, A. H. (1998). *97 savvy secrets for protecting self and school: A practical guide for today's teachers and administrators.* Thousand Oaks, CA: Corwin Press.

Sprenger, M. (1999). *Learning & memory: The brain in action.* Alexandria, VA: Association for Supervision and Curriculum Development.

Tauber, R. T. (1998). *Good or bad, what teachers expect from students they generally get!* ERIC Digest 426985 98. Washington, DC: ERIC Clearinghouse on Teaching and Teacher Education.

Tomal, D. R. (1999). *Discipline by negotiation: Methods for managing student behavior.* Lancaster, PA: Technomic.

Tomlinson, C. A. (1999). *The differentiated classroom* (Chap. 4). Alexandria, VA: Association for Supervision and Curriculum Development.

■ ENDNOTES

[1]H. Ginott, *Teacher and Child: A Book for Parents and Teachers* (New York: Simon & Schuster, 1994), pp. 15–16.

[2]See B. McEwan, *The Art of Classroom Management: Effective Practices for Building Equitable Learning Communities.* (Upper Saddle River, NJ: Merrill, Prentice Hall, Inc., 2000).

[3]See V. Jones and L. Jones, *Comprehensive Classroom Management: Creating Communities of Support and Solving Problems* (7th edition) (Boston, MA: Pearson, 2004).

[4]J. L. T. Jones, *Positive Classroom Discipline: Instructor's Guide* (Santa Cruz, CA: Fredric H. Jones & Associates, Inc., 1994).

[5]See V. Jones and L. Jones, *Comprehensive Classroom Management: Creating Communities of Support and Solving Problems,* (7th edition) (Boston, MA: Pearson, 2004), Chapter 1.

[6]See, for example, D. E. Matus, Humanism and Effective Urban Secondary Classroom Management, *Clearing House 72*(5), 305–307 (May/June 1999).

[7]I. A. Hyman and J. D'Allessandro, Oversimplifying the Discipline Problem, *Education Week 3*(29), 24 (April 11, 1984).

[8]See B. F. Skinner, *The Technology of Teaching* (New York: Appleton-Century-Crofts, 1968); and *Beyond Freedom and Dignity* (New York: Knopf, 1971).

[9]See L. Canter and M. Canter, *Assertive Discipline: Positive Behavior Management for Today's Schools,* rev. ed. (Santa Monica, CA: Lee Canter & Associates, 1992).

[10]See R. Dreikurs and P. Cassel, *Discipline Without Tears* (New York: Hawthorne Books, 1972); and R. Dreikurs, B. B. Grunwald, and F. C. Pepper, *Maintaining Sanity in the Classroom: Classroom Management Techniques* (2nd ed.) (New York: Harper & Row, 1982).

[11]L. Albert, *A Teacher's Guide to Cooperative Discipline: How to Manage Your Classroom and Promote Self-Esteem* (Circle Pines, MN: American Guidance Service, 1989, revised 1996).

[12]J. Nelsen, Positive Discipline (2nd ed.) (New York: Ballantine Books, 1987); and J. Nelsen, L. Lott, and H. S. Glenn, *Positive Discipline in the Classroom: How to Effectively Use Class Meetings and Other Positive Discipline Strategies* (Rocklin, CA: Prima Publishing, 1993).

[13]See, for example, W. Glasser, A New Look at School Failure and School Success, *Phi Delta Kappan 78*(8), 597–602 (April 1997).

[14]See W. Glasser, *Reality Therapy: A New Approach to Psychiatry* (New York: Harper & Row, 1965); *Schools Without Failure* (New York: Harper & Row, 1969); *Control Theory in the Classroom* (New York: Harper & Row, 1986); *The Quality School* (New York: Harper & Row, 1990); and *The Quality School Teacher* (New York: HarperPerennial, 1993).

[15]See H. G. Ginott, *Teacher and Child* (New York: Macmillan, 1971).

[16]T. Gordon, *Discipline That Works: Promoting Self-Discipline in Children* (New York: Penguin, 1989).

[17]F. Jones, *Positive Classroom Discipline* (New York: McGrawHill, 1987); and F. Jones, *Positive Classroom Instruction* (New York: McGraw-Hill, 1987).

[18]J. S. Kounin, *Discipline and Group Management in Classrooms* (New York: Holt, Rinehart and Winston, 1977).

[19]For guidelines for holding class meetings, see B. M. Landau and P. Gathercoal, Creating Peaceful Classrooms: Judicious Discipline and Class Meetings, *Phi Delta Kappan 81*(6), 450–452, 454 (February 2000).

[20]Jung, C. *The Development of Personality.* (New York: Pantheon, 1964), p. 144.

[21]J. L. T. Jones, *Positive Classroom Discipline: Instructor's Guide* (Santa Cruz, CA: Fredric H. Jones & Associates, Inc., 1994), Chapter 1.

[22]Ibid., Chapter 8.

[23]E. T. Emmer, C. M., Evertson, B. S. Clements, and M. E. Worsham, *Classroom Management for Secondary Teachers* (4th ed.) (Boston: Allyn & Bacon, 1997).

[24]Ibid., Chapter 4.

[25]See J. A. Queen et al., *Responsible Classroom Management for Teachers and Students* (Upper Saddle River, NJ: Merrill/Prentice Hall, 1997), especially Standards and Guidelines versus Rules and Replacing Rules with Standards, pp. 110 and 111–112 (respectively).

[26]D. Harrington-Lueker, Emotional Intelligence, *High Strides 9*(4), 1 (March/April 1997).

[27]See, for example, T. L. Good and J. E. Brophy, *Looking in Classrooms* (8th ed.) (New York: Addison-Wesley/Longman, 2000), p. 165.

[28]J. L. T. Jones, *Positive Classroom Discipline: Instructor's Guide* (Santa Cruz, CA: Fredric H. Jones & Associates, Inc., 1994), p. 87.

[29]D. W. Johnson and R. T. Johnson, *Reducing School Violence Through Conflict Resolution* (Alexandria, VA: Association for Supervision and Curriculum Development, 1995), p. 1.

[30]J. Cohen, The First 'R': Reflective Capacities, *Educational Leadership 57*(1), 70–75 (September 1999).

[31]See examples in Southern Regional Education Board, *1995 Outstanding Practices* (Atlanta, GA: Southern Regional Education Board, 1995).

[32]See "National Schools of Character Awards," on The Character Education Partnership Web site [online January 30, 2000] **http://www.character.org/schools/index.cgi?detail:schools**.

[33]See the Education Reporter, Number 207, The Newspaper of Education Rights, April 2003. **http://www.eagleforum.org/educate/2003/apr03/WI-High-School.shtml**.

[34]S. G. Weinberger, *How to Start a Student Mentor Program,* Fastback 333 (Bloomington, IN: Phi Delta Kappa Educational Foundation, 1992), p. 8.

[35]See, for example, D. K. Schnitzer and M. J. Caprio, Academy Rewards, *Educational Leadership 57*(1), 48 (September 1999).

[36]C. H. Edwards, *Classroom Discipline and Management* (2nd ed.) (Upper Saddle River, NJ: Prentice Hall, 1997), pp. 71–72.

[37]For further reading about the relation between impulse control and intelligence, see D. Goleman, *Emotional Intelligence: Why It Can Matter More Than IQ* (New York: Bantam Books, 1995); and D. Harrington-Lueker, Emotional Intelligence, *High Strides 9*(4), 1, 4–5 (March/April 1997).

[38]D. T. Gordon, Rising to the Discipline Challenge, *Harvard Education Letter 15*(5), 3 (September/October 1999).

Selecting Content and Preparing Objectives

Module 4 Overview

Now that you know how to set up a classroom management system, your classroom is organized, and your guidelines and procedures have been established, it is time to focus on what you are going to teach. We begin this module by emphasizing the importance of planning. Then we will take you through the process of selecting content for a course and preparing the specific learning outcomes expected as students learn that content. From that content outline and the related and specific learning outcomes, a teacher prepares units and daily lessons (discussed in Module 5).

Although planning is a critical skill for a teacher, a well-developed plan will not guarantee the success of a lesson or unit or even the overall effectiveness of a course. But the lack of a well-developed plan will almost certainly result in poor teaching. Like a good map, a good plan helps you reach your destination with more confidence and with fewer wrong turns.

Specific Objectives

At the completion of this module, you should be able to:

- Explain the relationship of planning to the preactive and reflective thought-processing phases of instruction.
- Explain the primary focus of national curriculum standards for your subject field.
- Explain the value and limitations of student textbooks for your subject field.
- Identify the value of collaborative planning.
- Demonstrate an ability to plan the long-range sequence of content for teaching in your subject field.
- Write concise and measurable cognitive, affective, and psychomotor instructional objectives.

Introduction

Planning the instruction constitutes a large part of a teacher's job. The teacher is responsible for planning at three levels: (a) courses for a semester or academic year, (b) units of instruction, and (c) lessons. Throughout your career, you will be engaged almost continually in planning at each of these three levels. Planning for instruction is a steady and cyclical process that involves the preactive and reflective thought-processing phases (discussed in Module 1). The importance of mastering the process at the very beginning of your career cannot be overemphasized.

"If your plan is for one year,
plant rice;
If your plan is for ten years,
plant trees;
If your plan is for a hundred years;
educate children."

—Confucius

Let us begin the discussion by clarifying a few relevant terms. A **course** can be defined as a complete sequence of instruction that presents a major division of a subject matter or discipline. Courses are laid out for a year, a semester, a quarter, or, in the case of minicourses or intensive courses, a few weeks. Each course is composed of units. A **unit** is a major subdivision of a course, comprising planned instruction about some central theme, topic, issue, or problem for a period of several days to several weeks. Units that take much longer than 3 weeks (with the exception of interdisciplinary units) tend to lose their effectiveness as recognizable units of instruction. Each unit is composed of lessons. A **lesson** is a subdivision of a unit, usually taught in a single class period or, on occasion, for two or three successive periods.

The heart of good planning is decision making. For every plan, you must decide what your goals and objectives are, what specific subject matter should be taught, what materials of instruction are available and appropriate, and what methods and techniques should be employed to accomplish the objectives. Making these decisions can be complicated because there are so many choices. Therefore, you must be knowledgeable about the principles that are the foundation for effective course, unit, and lesson planning. That the principles of all levels of educational planning are much the same makes mastering the necessary skills easier than you might think.

■ REASONS FOR PLANNING THOUGHTFULLY AND THOROUGHLY

Thoughtful and thorough planning is vital for effective teaching to occur. Such planning helps produce well-organized classes and a purposeful classroom atmosphere, and also reduces the likelihood of problems in classroom control. A teacher who has not planned or who has underprepared will have more problems than imaginable. While planning, you should keep in mind these two goals: (a) select strategies that keep students physically and mentally on-task and that ensure student learning and (b) do not waste anyone's time.

Careful planning has several other benefits as well. Planning well helps guarantee that you know the subject, for in planning you will more likely become a master of the material and the methods to teach it. No one can know everything about a discipline, but careful planning can save you from fumbling through half-digested, poorly understood content and making errors along the way. Thoughtful planning is likely to make your classes livelier, more interesting, more accurate, and more relevant, and thus make your teaching more successful.

Another important reason for careful planning is to ensure program coherence. Periodic lesson plans constitute an integral part of a larger plan, represented by course goals and objectives. The students' learning experiences should be thoughtfully planned in sequence and then orchestrated by a teacher who understands the rationale for their respective positions in the curriculum—not precluding, of course, an occasional diversion from planned activities.

Unless your course stands alone, following nothing and leading to nothing (which is unlikely), there are prerequisites to what you want your students to learn, and there are learning objectives to follow that build upon this learning. Good planning addresses both the *scope* (breadth and depth of the content coverage) and the *sequence* (what comes before and what follows) of the content.

Another important reason for careful planning is that the diversity of students in today's schools demands that the teacher addresses those individual differences—such as diverse cultural experiences, different learning styles and capacities, and various levels of proficiency in the use of English. Still another reason for planning is to ensure program continuation. In case a substitute teacher is needed or other members of the teaching team must fill in, the program continues without you.

Careful and thoughtful planning is important, too, for teacher self-assessment. After an activity, a lesson, or a unit, as well as at the end of a semester and the school year, you will assess what was done and the effect it had on student achievement (the reflective phase of instruction, discussed in Module 1).

Finally, supervisors and administrators expect you to plan well. Your plans represent a criterion recognized and evaluated by administrators—the experienced know that inadequate attention to planning usually results in incompetent teaching.

■ COMPONENTS OF INSTRUCTIONAL PLANNING

Eight components should be evident in a complete instructional plan:

1. *Statement of philosophy.* This is a general statement about why the plan is important and how students will learn its content.

2. *Needs assessment.* The wording of the statement of philosophy should demonstrate an appreciation for the cultural diversity of the school context, with a corresponding perception of the needs of society, the community, and the learners, and of the functions served by the school. The statement of philosophy and needs assessment should be consistent with the school's mission or philosophy statement.

3. *Aims, goals, and objectives.* The plan's stated aims, goals, and objectives should be consistent with the school's mission or philosophy statement. Aims, goals, and objectives are discussed in this module.

4. *Sequence.* The sequence of a plan refers to its relationship to the preceding and subsequent curricula.

A presentation of the sequence, or the *vertical artic-ulation,* shows the plan's relationship to the learn-ing that preceded and the learning that follows, from kindergarten through twelfth grade (in some instances, to the learning that follows high school graduation, such as in tech-prep high schools where the curriculum is articulated with that of a neigh-boring postsecondary vocational school).

5. *Integration.* The integration component concerns the plan's connection with other curricula and cocurricular activities across the grade level. For example, the language arts curriculum at a middle school may be closely integrated with that school's social studies curriculum; or, at a high school, several of the humanities courses may be integrated. The integration component is also re-ferred to as the *horizontal articulation* of a plan. "Writing across the curriculum," as used in many schools, is an example of both vertical and hori-zontal integration.

6. *Sequentially planned learning activities.* This is the presentation of the organized and sequential units and lessons, which must be appropriate for the sub-ject and grade level and for the age and diversity of the students. Preparing an instructional plan is the topic of Module 5.

7. *Resources needed.* This is a listing of resources, such as books, speakers, field trips, and media. Resources are integrated throughout Modules 6, 7, and 8.

8. *Assessment strategies.* These strategies, which must be consistent with the objectives, include procedures for diagnosing what students know or think they know prior to the instruction (preassessment), as well as the evaluation of student achievement during (formative assessment) and at completion of the instruction (summative assessment). Assessment is the topic of Module 9.

■ PLANNING A COURSE

When planning a course, you must decide exactly what is to be accomplished in that time period for which students take the course, whether for an academic year, a semester, or some shorter time period. Plan-ning ahead what it is that you want students to learn and then designing instructional activities that will fa-cilitate their learning those things is *outcome-based ed-ucation.* Planning ahead, designing activities to accomplish those goals and objectives, and then as-sessing student achievement against those goals and objectives is called *criterion-referenced education.* An education that is outcome-based should also be one that is criterion-referenced, and vice versa. To plan what is to be accomplished, you should (a) review school and other public documents for mandates and guidelines; (b) probe, analyze, and translate your own convictions, knowledge, and skills into behaviors that foster the intellectual development of your students; and (c) talk with colleagues and learn about their expectations.

■ Documents That Provide Guidance for Content Selection

Curriculum publications of your state department of ed-ucation, district subject matter standards and courses of study, school-adopted printed and nonprinted materi-als, and resource units are all valuable sources you will use in planning the school year. Your college or univer-sity library may have some of these documents. Others may be obtained from cooperating teachers or adminis-trative personnel at local schools and sites on the Inter-net. For sample Internet sites, see Figure 4.1. Many of these documents are generated through the process of state accreditation.

General and multiple disciplines
- <http://www.mcrel.org>.
- <http://www.enc.org/reform/fworks/index.htm>.

Discipline-specific national standards
- **Economics** <http://www.ncee.org>.
- **English/reading** <http://www.ncte.org>.
  ISTE: International Society for Technology in Education <http://www.iste.org>.
- **Mathematics** <http://www.nctm.org>.
  NASPE <http://www.aahperd.org/naspe/template.cfm?template=main.html>.
- **Psychology** <http://www.apa.org/ed/>.
- **Science** <http://www.nsta.org>.
  Social studies: National council for the Social studies <http://www.ncss.org/>.

Standards state by state, discipline by discipline
- <http://www.statestandards.com>.

FIGURE 4.1 ● Sample Internet Resources on National and State Curriculum Standards and Frameworks

To receive *accreditation* (which is usually renewed every three to six years), a high school is reviewed by an accreditation team. Prior to the team's visit, the school prepares self-study reports, for which each department reviews and updates the curriculum guides that provide information about the objectives and content of each course and program offered. In some states, middle schools and junior high schools also are accredited by state or regional agencies. In other states, those schools can volunteer to be reviewed for improvement. The accreditation process, which can be expensive, is paid for with school or district funds.

■ National Curriculum Standards

Curriculum standards are a definition of what students should know (content) and be able to do (process and performance). At the national level, curriculum standards did not exist in the United States until they were developed and released for mathematics education in 1989. Shortly after the release of the mathematics standards, support for national goals in education was endorsed by the National Governors Association, and the National Council on Education Standards and Testing recommended that in addition to those for mathematics, national standards for subject matter content in K–12 education be developed for the arts, civics/social studies, English/language arts/reading, geography, history, and science. Initial funding for the development of national standards was provided by the U.S. Department of Education. In 1994 the U.S. Congress passed the *Goals 2000: Educate America Act,* amended in 1996 with an Appropriations Act, encouraging states to set standards (see Table 1.2 in Module 1). Long before, however, as was done for mathematics by the National Council for Teachers of Mathematics, national organizations devoted to various disciplines were already articulating standards.

The national standards represent the best thinking by expert panels, including teachers from the field, about what are the essential elements of a basic core of subject knowledge that all students should acquire. They serve not as national mandates but rather as voluntary guidelines to encourage curriculum development to promote higher student achievement. State and local curriculum developers decide the extent to which the standards are used. Strongly influenced by the national standards, nearly all 50 states have completed or are presently developing state standards for the various disciplines.

By 1992, for example, most states, usually through state curriculum frameworks, were following the 1989 standards for mathematics education to guide what and how mathematics is taught and how student progress is assessed. The essence of many of those recommendations—a hands-on, inquiry-oriented, performance-based approach to learning less but learning it better—can also be found in the standards that were subsequently developed for other disciplines.

Standards by content area The following paragraphs describe standards development for content areas of the K–12 curriculum. Although the date when the standards were first published is listed below, standards are revised on a regular basis. Consult the various disciplines for specific updates. Many of the standards are available on the Internet (see Figure 4.1).

Arts (visual and performing). Developed jointly by the American Alliance for Theater and Education, the National Art Education Association, the National Dance Association, and the Music Educators National Conference, the National Standards for Arts Education were published in 1994.

Economics. Developed by the National Council on Economic Education, standards for the study of economics were published in 1997.

English/language arts/reading. Developed jointly by the International Reading Association, the National Council of Teachers of English, and the University of Illinois Center for the Study of Reading, standards for English education were published in 1996.

Foreign languages. Standards for Foreign Language Learning: Preparing for the 21st Century was published by the American Council on the Teaching of Foreign Languages (ACTFL) in 1996.[1]

Geography. Developed jointly by the Association of American Geographers, the National Council for Geographic Education, and the National Geographic Society, standards for geography education were published in 1994.[2]

Health. Developed by the Joint Committee for National School Health Education Standards, *National Health Education Standards: Achieving Health Literacy* was published in 1995.[3]

History/civics/social studies. The Center for Civic Education and the National Center for Social Studies developed standards for civics and government, and the National Center for History in the Schools developed the standards for history, all of which were published in 1994.

Mathematics. In 1989, the National Council of Teachers of Mathematics (NCTM) published *Curriculum and Evaluation Standards for School Mathematics.* Revised standards were developed and released in 2000. See the NCTM mathematics site in Figure 4.1.

Physical education. In 1995, the National Association of Sport and Physical Education (NASPE) published *Moving Into the Future: National Standards for Physical Education.*

Psychology. In 1999, the American Psychological Association released voluntary national standards for what students should be taught in high school psychology courses.

Science. In 1995, with input from the American Association for the Advancement of Science and the National Science Teachers Association, the National Research Council's National Committee on Science Education Standards and Assessment published the standards for science education.

Technology. With initial funding from the National Science Foundation and the National Aeronautics and Space Administration, and in collaboration with the International Technology Education Association, National Educational Technology Standards (NETS) are being developed. For an update see the technology site designation in Figure 4.1.

Supplements to the national standards are available from the Bureau of Indian Affairs for the arts (dance, music, theater, and visual), civics and government, geography, health, language arts, mathematics, science, and social studies.[4] The *American Indian Supplements* may be used by Indian nations as guides in their preparation of tribally specific local standards. They are also useful to school districts serving American Indian children in adapting state standards to be more culturally relevant to their communities.

Proceed now to Exercises 4.1, 4.2, and 4.3, through which you will explore national standards and state and local curriculum documents.

EXERCISE 4.1

■ Examining National Curriculum Standards

Instructions: The purpose of this exercise is to become familiar with the national curriculum standards for various subjects of the K–12 curriculum. Using the addresses of sources provided in the preceding section. National Curriculum Standards, and other sources, such as professional journals, review the standards for your subject or subjects. Use the following questions as a guideline for small- or large-group class discussions. Following small-group, subject-area discussion, share the developments in each field with the rest of the class.

Subject area _____

1. Name of the standards document reviewed

2. Year of document publication

3. Developed by

4. Precise K–12 goals specified by the new standards

5. Are the standards specific as to subject-matter content for each grade level? Explain.

6. Do the standards offer specific strategies for instruction? Describe.

7. Do the standards offer suggestions for teaching children who are culturally and linguistically diverse and/or who are students with special needs? Describe.

8. Do the standards offer suggestions or guidelines for dealing with controversial topics?

9. Do the standards offer suggestions for specific resources? Describe.

10. Do the standards refer to assessment? Describe.

11. In summary, compared with what has been taught and how it has been taught in this field, what is new with the standards?

12. Is there anything else about the standards you would like to discuss in your group?

 To access this exercise online, go to the Companion Website at **www.prenhall.com/kellough.**

EXERCISE **4.2**

■ Examining State Curriculum Documents

Instructions: The purpose of this exercise is to become familiar with curriculum documents published by your state department of education. You must determine if that department publishes a curriculum framework for various subjects taught in schools. State frameworks provide valuable information about both content and process, and teachers need to be aware of these documents. You may want to duplicate this form so you can use it to evaluate several documents. After examining documents that interest you, use the following questions as a guideline for small- or large-group class discussions.

1. Are there state curriculum documents available to teachers for your state? If so, describe them and explain how they can be obtained.

   Title of document:

   Source:

   Most recent year of publication:

   Other pertinent information:

2. Examine how closely the document follows the eight components presented in this module. Are any components omitted? Are there additional components? Specifically, check for these components:

		Yes	No
2.1	Statement of philosophy?	_____	_____
2.2	Evidence of a needs assessment?	_____	_____
2.3	Aims, goals, and objectives?	_____	_____
2.4	Schemes for vertical articulation (sequence)?	_____	_____
2.5	Schemes for horizontal articulation (scope)?	_____	_____
2.6	Recommended instructional prcedures?	_____	_____
2.7	Recommended resources?	_____	_____
2.8	Assessment strategies?	_____	_____
	Other:		

3. Are the documents specific as to subject-matter content for each grade level? Describe evidence of both vertical and horizontal articulation schemes.

4. Do the documents offer specific strategies for instruction? If yes, describe.

5. Do the documents offer suggestions and resources for working with culturally and linguistically diverse students, for students with special needs, and for students who are intellectually gifted and talented? Describe.

6. Do the documents offer suggestions or guidelines for dealing with controversial topics? If so, describe.

7. Do the documents distinguish between what shall be taught (mandated) and what can be taught (permissible)?

8. Do the documents offer suggestions for specific resources?

9. Do the documents refer to assessment strategies? Describe.

10. Is there anything else about the documents you would like to discuss in your group?

 To access this exercise online, go to the Companion Website at **www.prenhall.com/kellough.**

EXERCISE 4.3

■ Examining Local Curriculum Documents

Instructions: The purpose of this exercise is to become familiar with curriculum documents prepared by local school districts. A primary resource for what to teach is referred to as a *curriculum guide,* or *course of study,* which normally is developed by teachers of a school or district. Samples may be available in your university library or in a local school district resource center. Or perhaps you could borrow them from teachers you visit. Obtain samples from a variety of sources and then examine them using the format of this exercise. (You may duplicate this form for each document examined.) An analysis of several documents will give you a good picture of expectations. If possible, compare documents from several schools, districts, and states.

Title of document:

District or school:

Date of document:

1. Examine how closely the documents follow the eight components. Does the document contain the following components?

		Yes	No
1.1	Statement of philosophy?	_____	_____
1.2	Evidence of a needs assessment?	_____	_____
1.3	Aims, goals, and objectives?	_____	_____
1.4	Schemes for vertical articulation (sequence)?	_____	_____
1.5	Schemes for horizontal articulation (scope)?	_____	_____
1.6	Recommended instructional procedures?	_____	_____
1.7	Recommended resources?	_____	_____
1.8	Assessment strategies?	_____	_____

2. Does the document list expected learning outcomes? If so, describe what they are.

3. Does the document contain detailed unit plans? If so, describe them by answering the following questions:
   3.1 Do they contain initiating activities (how to begin a unit)?
   3.2 Do they contain specific learning activities?
   3.3 Do they contain suggested enrichment activities (as for gifted and talented students)?
   3.4 Do they contain culminating activities (activities that bring a unit to a climax)?
   3.5 Do they contain assessment procedures (for determining student achievement)?
   3.6 Do they contain activities for learners with special needs? or for learners who are different in other respects?

4. Does it provide bibliographic entries for
   ■ The teacher?
   ■ The students?

5. Does it list audiovisual and other materials needed?

6. Does the document clearly help you understand what the teacher is expected to teach?

7. Are there questions not answered by your examination of this document? If so, list them for class discussion.

 To access this exercise online, go to the Companion Website at **www.prenhall.com/kellough.**

STUDENT TEXTBOOKS

For several reasons—the recognition of the diversity of learning styles, capacities, and modalities of students; the increasing cost of textbooks; and the availability of non-printed materials—textbook appearance, content, and use have changed considerably in recent years and will likely continue to change in the years to come.

School districts periodically adopt new textbooks (usually every five to eight years). If you are a student teacher or a first-year teacher, this will most likely mean that someone will say to you, "Here are the textbooks you will be using."

Even if you are handed a textbook that your school or district has adopted, you can still make additions and modifications to your curriculum choices. The suggestions listed here will help you select supporting textbooks and materials for your classes that provide realistic and balanced portrayals of females, various racial and ethnic groups, people with disabilities, English Language Learners, and other traditionally mis- or underrepresented groups.

After you have some teaching experience under your belt you may be asked to serve on a textbook selection committee. Textbook selection plays a key role in promoting an unbiased curriculum. Therefore, it is important that you view textbooks with discerning eyes. There are some specific types of bias you want to avoid and some basic guidelines you can follow when contemplating textbook adoption. Sadker and Sadker highlight seven forms of textbook bias that you should be on the lookout for and avoid: *invisibility* (excluding certain groups altogether), *stereotyping* (portraying all members of certain groups in a limited role or negative light), *imbalance and selectivity* (presenting only one perspective), *unreality* (omitting unpleasant truths), *fragmentation and isolation* (not integrating information about certain groups or including that information as an "add-on"), *linguistic bias* (selecting language with negative connotations to describe certain groups), and *cosmetic bias* (making minimal surface changes to appear to address diversity).[5]

Broad guidelines for selecting a student textbook and support materials that are free of bias include the following: the textbook preface should make reference to diversity and/or multiculturalism; the concepts, historical events, and issues should be presented from a variety of perspectives; and there should be diversity among the contributing authors.[6] In addition, verify that the teacher's edition provides lesson adaptations and accommodations for students with special needs, English Language Learners, gifted and talented students, and so forth. Make sure the commitment to diversity is replicated in all supporting materials as well.

Benefit of Student Textbooks to Student Learning

It is unlikely that anyone could rationally argue that textbooks are of no benefit to student learning. Textbooks can provide (a) an organization of basic or important content for the students, (b) a basis for deciding content emphasis, (c) previously tested activities and suggestions for learning, (d) information about other readings and resources to enhance student learning, and (e) a foundation for building higher-order thinking activities (e.g., inquiry discussions and student research) that help develop critical thinking skills. The textbook, however, should not be the "be all and end all" of the instructional experiences.

Problems with Reliance on a Single Textbook

The student textbook is only one of many teaching tools and not the ultimate word. Of the many ways in which you may use textbooks for student learning, the least acceptable is to show a complete dependence on a single book and require students simply to memorize material from it. This is the lowest level of learning; furthermore, it implies that you are unaware of other significant printed and nonprinted resources and have nothing more to contribute to student learning.

Another potential problem brought about by reliance upon a single textbook is that because textbook publishers prepare books for use in a larger market—that is, for national or statewide use—a state- and district-adopted book may not adequately address issues of special interest and importance to the community in which you teach.[7] That is one reason why some teachers and schools provide supplementary printed and nonprinted resources.

Still another problem brought about by reliance upon a single source is that the adopted textbook may not be at the appropriate reading level for many students. For example, in a recent study of the readability of high school chemistry textbooks, 80% of the books were found to have reading levels beyond high school. In other words, most high school students would not be able to read and comprehend the majority of books adopted for use in teaching high school chemistry.[8] In today's heterogeneous classrooms, the level of student reading can vary by as much as two-thirds of the chronological age of the students. This means that if the chronological age is 12 years (typical for seventh graders) then the reading-level range would be 8 years—that is, the class may have some students reading at only the third grade level while others have eleventh-grade level reading ability.

Examine student textbooks and teacher's editions of those books by doing Exercise 4.4.

EXERCISE **4.4**

■ Examining Student Textbooks and Teachers' Editions

Instructions: The purpose of this exercise is to become familiar with textbooks that you may be using in your teaching. Student textbooks are usually accompanied by a teacher's edition that contains specific objectives, teaching techniques, learning activities, assessment instruments, test items, and suggested resources. Your university library, local schools, and cooperating teachers are sources for locating and borrowing these enhanced textbooks. For your subject field of interest, select a textbook that is accompanied by a teacher's edition and examine the contents of both using the following format. If there are no standard textbooks available for your teaching field (such as might be the case for art, home economics, industrial arts, music, and physical education), then select a field in which there is a possibility you might teach. Beginning teachers are often assigned to teach in more than one field—sometimes, unfortunately, in fields for which they are untrained or have only minimal training. After completion of this exercise, share the book and your analysis of it with your classmates.

Title of book:

Author(s):

Publisher:

Date of most recent publication:

1. Analyze the teacher's edition for the following elements.

	Yes	No
a. Are its goals consistent with the goals of local and state curriculum documents?	_____	_____
b. Are there specific objectives for each lesson?	_____	_____
c. Does the book have scope and sequence charts for teacher reference?	_____	_____
d. Are the units and lessons sequentially developed, with suggested time allotments?	_____	_____
e. Are there any suggested provisions for individual differences?	_____	_____
for reading levels?	_____	_____
for students with special needs?	_____	_____
for students who are gifted and talented?	_____	_____
for students who have limited proficiency in English?	_____	_____
f. Does it recommend specific techniques and strategies?	_____	_____
g. Does it have listings of suggested aids, materials, and resources?	_____	_____
h. Are there suggestions for extension activities (to extend the lessons beyond the usual topic or time)?	_____	_____
i. Does the book have specific guidelines for assessment of student learning?	_____	_____

2. Analyze the student textbook for the following elements.

	Yes	No
a. Does it treat the content with adequate depth?	_____	_____
b. Does it treat ethnic minorities and women fairly?*	_____	_____
c. Is the format attractive?	_____	_____
d. Does the book have good quality binding with suitable type size?	_____	_____
e. Are illustrations and visuals attractive and useful?	_____	_____
f. Is the reading clear and understandable for the students?	_____	_____

(continued)

3. Would you like to use this textbook? Give reasons why or why not.

*For a detailed procedure that is more specific to subject areas, see Carl A. Grant and Cristine E. Sleeter, *Turning on Learning: Five Approaches for Multicultural Teaching Plans for Race, Class, Gender, and Disability* (Upper Saddle River, NJ: Prentice Hall, 1989), pp. 104–109.

 To access this exercise online, go to the Companion Website at **www.prenhall.com/kellough.**

■ Guidelines for Textbook Use

Generally speaking, students benefit by having their own copies of a textbook in the current edition. However, because of budget constraints, this may not always be possible. The book may be outdated, or quantities may be limited. When the latter is the case, students may not be allowed to take the books home or perhaps may only occasionally do so. In other classrooms, there may be no textbook at all. Yet still, in some classrooms, there are two sets of the textbook, one set that remains for use in the classroom and another set that is assigned to students to take home to use for home studying. With that arrangement, students do not have to carry around heavy books in their backpacks. The following general guidelines apply to using the textbook as a learning tool.

Progressing through a textbook from the front cover to the back in one school term is not necessarily an indicator of good teaching. The textbook is one resource; to enhance their learning, students should be encouraged to use a variety of resources. Encourage students to search for additional sources to update the content of the textbook. This is especially important in certain disciplines such as science and social sciences, where the amount of new information is growing rapidly and students may have textbooks that are several years old. The library and the Internet should be researched by students for the latest information on certain subjects. Keep supplementary reading materials for student use in the classroom. School and community librarians and resource specialists usually are delighted to cooperate with teachers in the selection and provision of such resources.

Individualize the learning for students of various reading abilities. Consider differentiated reading and workbook assignments in the textbook and several supplementary sources (see multitext and multireadings approaches, a topic that follows). Except to make life simpler for the teacher, there is no advantage in all students working out of the same book and exercises. Some students benefit from the drill, practice, and reinforcement afforded by workbooks that accompany textbooks, but this is not true for all students, nor do all benefit from the same activity. In fact, the traditional workbook may eventually become extinct, as it is replaced by the modern technology afforded by computer software and laser discs. As the cost of hardware and software programs becomes more realistic for schools, the use of computers by individual students is also becoming more common. Computers and other interactive media provide students with a psychologically safer learning environment in which they have greater control over the pace of the instruction, can repeat instruction if necessary, and can ask for clarification without the fear of having to do so publicly.

Several methods have been invented by teachers to help students develop their higher-level thinking skills and their comprehension of expository material. Some of these methods are:

- *K-W-L method.* Students recall what they already know (K) about a topic, determine what they want to learn (W), and later assess what they have learned (L).

- *POSSE method. Predict* ideas, *organize* ideas, *search* for structure, *summarize* main ideas, and *evaluate* understanding.

- *PQRST method. Preview, question, read, state* the main idea, and *test* yourself by answering the questions you posed earlier.

- *RAP method. Read* paragraphs, *ask* questions about what was read, and *put* in your own words.

- *SQ3R method. Survey* the chapter, ask *questions* about what was read, *read, recite,* and *review.*

- *SQ4R method. Survey* the chapter, ask *questions* about what was read, *read* to answer the questions, *recite* the answers, *record* important items from the chapter into their notebooks, then *review* it all.

- *SRQ2R method (survey, read, question, recite, review).* Use **reciprocal teaching** where students are taught and practice the reading skills of summarizing, questioning, clarifying, and predicting.[9]

Just because something is in print, or on the Internet, does not guarantee its accuracy or truth. Textbooks and Web pages are often riddled with typographical errors, half truths, omissions, and inaccuracies. Encourage students to be alert for errors in the textbook, both in content and printing—perhaps by giving them some sort of credit reward, such as points, when they bring an error to your attention. This helps students develop the skills of critical reading, critical thinking, and healthy skepticism. For example, a history book is reported to have stated that the first person to lead a group through the length of the Grand Canyon was John Wesley Powell. Critically thinking students quickly made the point that perhaps Powell was only the first white person to do this, but Native Americans had traveled the length of the Grand Canyon for centuries.[10]

■ Introducing the Textbook

Students seldom know how to use their texts efficiently and effectively. Therefore, on the first day before they begin to read, you might introduce students to the textbook in a lesson in which you and they discuss these elements of the text:

1. *Title page.* What information does it give? When was the book written? Has it been revised? Who is the publisher? Where was it published? Do these indicate any likelihood of bias?

2. *Preface.* What does the author claim he or she intended to do? What was his or her purpose?

3. *Table of contents.* How much weight is given to various topics? How can we use the information contained in the table of contents to help study the text?

4. *List of maps, charts, and illustrations.* What is the importance of these devices? How can one use them to aid study? Choose examples of each—maps, charts, tables, graphs, illustrations—and have students find essential information in them.

5. *Appendix.* What does appendix mean? What is it for?

6. *Index.* Use drill exercises to give students practice in using the index. These can be made into games or contests.

7. *Glossary.* What is a glossary? Why is it included? Use exercises that call for looking up words and then using them in sentences.

8. *Study aids at the ends of chapters.* How can study questions be used? Which are thought questions? Which are fact questions?

9. *Chapter headings, section headings, paragraph leads, introductory overviews, preliminary questions, and summaries.* What are the purposes of each of these? Use exercises that call for getting meaning from aids such as these without reading the entire text.

■ MULTITEXT AND MULTIREADINGS APPROACHES

Expressing dissatisfaction with the single-textbook approach to teaching, some teachers have substituted a multitext strategy, in which they use one set of books for one topic and another set for another topic. This strategy provides some flexibility, although it really is only a series of single texts.

Other teachers—usually the more knowledgeable and proficient—use a strategy that incorporates many readings for a topic during the same unit. This multireading strategy gives the students a certain amount of choice in what they read. The various readings allow for differences in reading ability and interest level. By using a study guide, all the students can be directed toward specific concepts and information, but they do not have to all read the same selections. To implement this type of multireading approach: (a) select your instructional objectives; (b) solicit the help of your school librarian—generally, school librarians are quite willing to help you put a list of readings together; (c) select a number of readings that throw light on your objectives, being sure there are several readings for each objective to provide variation in students' reading levels and interests as you make your selections; (d) build a study guide that directs the students toward the objectives, and suggest readings appropriate to each objective; (e) let the students select what they will read to meet the provisions of the guide.

■ OTHER PRINTED MATERIALS

Besides the student textbook and maybe an accompanying workbook, a vast array of other printed materials is available for use in teaching—and many materials are available without cost. Printed materials include books, workbooks, pamphlets, magazines, brochures, newspapers, professional journals, periodicals, and duplicated materials. When thinking about what materials to use, be alert for (a) appropriateness of the material in both content and in reading level; (b) articles in newspapers, magazines, and periodicals related to the content that your students will be studying or to the skills they will be learning; (c) assorted workbooks that emphasize thinking and problem solving rather than rote memorization; with an assortment of workbooks you can have students working on similar but different assignments depending upon their interests and abilities—an example of multilevel teaching; (d) pamphlets, brochures, and other duplicated materials that students can read for specific information and viewpoints about particular topics; and (e) relatively inexpensive paperback books that would both provide multiple book readings for your class and make it possible for students to read primary sources.

For free and inexpensive printed materials look for sources in your college, university, or public library, or in the resource center at a local school district, sources such as those listed in Figure 4.2. Additionally, teachers obtain free and inexpensive teaching materials through connections on the Internet. When considering using materials that you have obtained free or inexpensively,

- Civil Aeronautics Administration, *Sources of Free and Low-Cost Materials.* Washington, DC: U.S. Department of Commerce.
- Educators Progress Service, Inc., *Educator's Guide to Free Materials; Educator's Guide to Free Teaching Aids.* 214 Center Street, Randolph, WI 53956, phone (414) 326-3126.
- *Freebies: The Magazine with Something for Nothing.* PO Box 5025, Carpinteria, CA 93014-5025.
- Freebies editors. *Freebies for Teachers.* Los Angeles: Lowell House, 1994.
- *A Guide to Print and Nonprint Materials Available from Organizations, Industry, Governmental Agencies and Specialized Publishers.* New York: Neal Schuman.
- *Video Placement Worldwide (VPW).* Source of free sponsored educational videos and print materials on Internet at <http://www.vpw.com>.
- Best freeware and shareware at <http://wwwl.zdnet.com/pccomp/1001dl/html/1001.html>.
- Professional periodicals and journals.
- *Catalog of Audiovisual Materials: A Guide to Government Sources* (ED 198 822). Arlington, VA: ERIC Documents Reproduction Service.
- *Educator's Guide to Free Audio and Video Materials; Educator's Guide to Free Films; Educator's Guide to Free Filmstrips; Guide to Free Computer Materials; Educator's Guide to Free Science Materials,* Educator's Progress Service, Inc., 214 Center Street, Randolph, WI 53956 (414) 326-3126.
- *Video Placement Worldwide (VPW).* Source of free sponsored educational videos on the Internet at <http://www.vpw.com>.

FIGURE 4.2 ● Resources for Free and Inexpensive Printed Materials

you will want to ensure that the materials are appropriate for use with the age group with whom you work, and that they are free of bias or an unwanted message.[11]

THE FUTURE FOR SCHOOL TEXTBOOKS

Within the span of your professional career, you likely will take part in a revolution in the design of school textbooks. Already some school districts and states allow teachers in certain disciplines (where the technology is available) to choose between traditional student textbooks and interactive media programs.

One prediction is that with the revolution in microcomputer-chip technology, student textbooks may soon take on a whole new appearance. That will produce dramatic changes in the importance and use of student texts, as well as new problems for the teacher, some of which are predictable. Student texts may become credit card size, increasing the chance of students' losing their books. On the positive side, the classroom teacher will probably have available a variety of textbooks to better address the variety of reading levels, interests, learning styles, and abilities of individual students. Distribution and maintenance of reading materials could create an even greater demand on the teacher's time. Regardless, dramatic and exciting changes have begun to occur in a teaching tool that previously had not changed much throughout the history of education in the United States. As an electronic multimedia tool, the textbook of the 21st century may be an interactive device that offers text, sound, and video and allows for worldwide communication.

COLLABORATIVE PLANNING

As noted, the textbook is only one resource for determining content to be studied. Your students and teaching colleagues are resources, too. Although you will do much of your instructional planning alone, many teachers also do a considerable amount of shared planning in instructional teams, both at the department level and between departments, and involve their students in phases of the planning as well.

By integrating teachers, we can integrate the curriculum. In middle schools and high schools across the country, teachers are working collaboratively in teams to produce interdisciplinary theme-based units. In an effort to make learning more relevant to students' lives, educators at the middle and secondary levels are taking advantage of natural connections between the disciplines. In Module 5 we will discuss planning for integrated teaching in detail.

■ Team Planning

In some schools, teachers plan together in teams (as discussed in Module 1). Planning procedures are much the same as recommended previously in this module, the difference being that the team members might split the planning responsibilities. Coming back together to share their individual planning, the team members work cooperatively to develop a final plan. Team planning works best when members of the team share a common planning time that is a minimum of four hours a week and that is separate from their individual preparation periods.

Teacher-Student Collaboration in Planning

Many teachers today encourage students to participate in the planning of some phase of the learning activities, units, and courses. Such participation tends to give students a proprietary interest in the activities, thereby increasing their motivation. In addition, sharing with them the instructional accountability is more likely to ensure student achievement in learning. What students have contributed to the plan often seems more relevant to them than what others have planned for them. And students like to see their own plans succeed. Thus, teacher-student collaboration in planning can be a very effective motivational tool.

PREPARING FOR THE YEAR

You have reviewed the rationale and the components for instructional planning and examined state and local curriculum documents and student reading materials. While doing so you undoubtedly have reflected on your own biases regarding content you believe should be included in a subject at a particular grade level. Now it is time to obtain practical experience in long-range planning.

Some educators believe that writing objectives (learning targets) should be the first step in preparing to teach. It is our contention that a more logical first step is to prepare a sequential general major topic outline. The second step is then to detail the outline, that is, to add second- and third-level headings. Then, the third step is to write the instructional objectives from your detailed outline—the final focus of this module. Once you have decided the content and objectives, you are ready to create the subdivisions known as units of instruction and then prepare those units with their daily lessons (the topics of Module 5).

For most beginning teachers, topic outlines and instructional objectives are presented in the course of study or the teacher's edition of the student textbook, with the expectation that these will be used in teaching. Yet someone had to have written those outlines and objectives, and that someone was one or several teachers. As a teacher candidate, you should know how it is done, for someday you will be concentrating on it in earnest.

For now, then, the next step is for you to experience preparing a year-long (or, in some instances, a semester-long) content outline for a subject and grade level that you intend to teach. Please be cautioned that beginning teachers often have unrealistic expectations about the amount of content that teenagers can study, comprehend, and learn over a given period of time. Reviewing school and other public documents and talking with experienced teachers in your local schools can be very helpful in developing a realistic selection and sequencing of content, as well as the time frame for teaching that content. Keeping that caution in mind and recognizing the fact that during implementation you may very possibly make adjustments to the original content outline, now work on preparing a content outline by doing Exercise 4.5.

EXERCISE **4.5**

■ Preparing a Content Outline

Instructions: The purpose of this exercise is for you to organize your ideas about subject content and the sequencing of content. Unless instructed otherwise by your instructor, you should select the subject (e.g., algebra I, biology, English, U.S. history) and the grade level (7–12).

With *three levels of headings* (see the example that follows), prepare a sequential topic outline (on a separate piece of paper as space is not provided here) for a subject and grade level you intend to teach. Identify the subject by title, and clearly state the grade level. This outline is of topic content only and does not need to include student activities associated with the learning of that content (i.e., do not include experiments, assignments, or assessment strategies).

For example, for the study of earth science, three levels of headings might include

    I.   The Earth's surface
        A. Violent changes in Earth's surface
            1. Earthquakes
            2. Volcanoes
        B. Earth's land surface
            1. Rocks

and so forth.

(continued)

If the study of earth science was just one unit for a grade level's study of the broader area of science, then three levels of headings for that study might include

I.   Earth science
   A. The Earth's surface
      1. Violent changes in Earth's surface

and so forth.

Share your completed outline to obtain feedback from your colleagues and university instructor. Because content outlines are never to be carved into stone, make adjustments to your outline when and as appropriate.

Here are some content outline evaluation guidelines:

- Does the outline follow a logical sequence, with each topic logically leading to the next?
- Does the content assume prerequisite knowledge or skills that the students are likely to have?
- Is the content inclusive and to an appropriate depth?
- Does the content consider individual student differences?
- Does the content allow for interdisciplinary studies?
- Are there serious content omissions?
- Is there content that is of questionable value for this level of instruction?

Save this completed exercise for later when you are working on Exercise 4.7.

 To access this exercise online, go to the Companion Website at **www.prenhall.com/kellough.**

■ PREPARING FOR AND DEALING WITH CONTROVERSY

Controversial content and issues abound in teaching, especially in certain disciplines: For example, in English/language arts, over the use of certain books (see Exercise 4.6B); in social studies, over values and moral issues; in science, over biological evolution; in health, over lifestyle choices. As a general rule, if you have concern that a particular topic or activity might create controversy, it probably will. During your teaching career, you undoubtedly will have to make decisions about how you will handle such matters. When selecting content that might be controversial, consider the paragraphs that follow as guidelines.

Maintain a perspective with respect to your own goal, which is at the moment to obtain your teaching credential, then a teaching job, and then tenure. Student teaching is not a good time to become involved in controversy. If you communicate closely with your cooperating teacher and your college or university supervisor, you should be able to prevent any major problems dealing with controversial issues.

Sometimes, during normal discussion in the classroom, a controversial subject will emerge spontaneously, catching the teacher off guard. If this happens, think before saying anything. You may wish to postpone further discussion until you have had opportunity to talk over the issue with members of your teaching team or your supervisors. Controversial topics can seem to arise from nowhere for any teacher, and this is perfectly normal. Young people are in the process of developing their moral and value systems, and they need and want to know how adults feel about issues that are important to them, particularly those adults they hold in esteem—their teachers. Students need to discuss issues that are important to society, and there is absolutely nothing wrong with dealing with those issues as long as certain guidelines are followed.

First, students should learn about all sides of an issue. Controversial issues are open-ended and should be treated as such. They do not have right answers or correct solutions. If they did, there would be no controversy. (As used in this book, an *issue* differs from a *problem* in that a problem generally has a solution, whereas an issue has many opinions and several alternative solutions.) Therefore, the focus should be on process as well as on content. A major goal is to show students how to deal with controversy and to mediate wise decisions on the basis of carefully considered information. Another goal is to help students learn how to disagree without being disagreeable—how to resolve conflict. To that end students need to learn the difference between conflicts that are destructive and those that can be constructive; in other words, to see that conflict (disagreement) can be healthy and have positive value. A third goal, of course, is to help students learn about the content of an issue so, when necessary, they can make decisions based on knowledge, not on ignorance.

Second, as with all lesson plans, one that deals with a topic that could lead to controversy should be well thought out ahead of time. Potential problem areas and resources must be carefully considered and prepared for in advance. Problems for the teacher are most likely to occur when the plan has been poorly thought out.

Third, at some point all persons directly involved in an issue have a right to input: Students, parents and guardians, community representatives, and other faculty. This does not mean, for example, that people outside of the public school have the right to censor a teacher's lesson plan, but it does mean that parents or guardians and students should have the right *without penalty* not to participate and to select an alternate activity. Most school districts have written policies that deal with challenges to instructional materials. As a beginning teacher, you should become aware of policies of your school district. In addition, professional associations such as the NCTE, NCSS, and NSTA have published guidelines for dealing with controversial topics, materials, and issues.

Fourth, we see nothing wrong with students knowing a teacher's opinion about an issue as long as it is clear that the students may disagree without reprisal or academic penalty. However, it is probably best for a teacher to wait and give her or his opinion only after the students have had full opportunity to study and report on facts and opinions from other sources. Sometimes it is helpful to assist students in separating facts from opinions on a particular issue being studied by setting up on the overhead or writing board a fact-opinion tab... stated at the top and then two parallel co... facts, the other for related opinions.

A characteristic that has made this country ...t is the freedom granted by the First Amendment ...r all its people to speak out on issues. This freedom should not be excluded from public school classrooms. Teachers and students should be encouraged to express their opinions about the great issues of today, to study the issues, to suspend judgment while collecting data, and then to form and accept each other's reasoned opinions. We must understand the difference between teaching truth, values, and morals, and teaching about truth, values, and morals. (Aspects of character education are presented in both Module 2 and later in this module.)

As a public school teacher there are limits to your academic freedom, much greater than are the limits on a university professor. You must understand this fact. The primary difference is that the students with whom you will be working are not yet adults (unlike postsecondary students); they must be protected from dogma and allowed the freedom to learn and to develop their values and opinions, free from coercion from those who have power and control over their learning. You should also keep in mind that cultural differences may arise in classroom discussions or activities. It is important to be respectful of all opinions, expect all students to act with integrity, and not let differences be divisive.

Now that you have read our opinion and suggested guidelines, what do you think about this topic, which should be important to you as a teacher? For the development and expression of your opinion, please proceed to Exercises 4.6A and 4.6B.

EXERCISE **4.6A**

■ Dealing with Controversial Content and Issues

Instructions: The purpose of this exercise is for you to discover controversial content and issues that you may face as a teacher and to consider what you can and will do about them. After completing this exercise, share it with members of your class.

1. After studying current periodicals and talking with colleagues in the schools you visit, list two potentially controversial topics that you are likely to encounter as a teacher. (Two examples are given for you.)

Issue	*Source*
Use of chimpanzees for medical research	*National Geographic, March 1992*
Human cloning	*Time, March 1997*

2. Take one of these issues, and identify opposing arguments and current resources.

3. Identify your own position on this issue.

4. How well can you accept students (and parents or guardians) who assume the opposite position?

5. Share the preceding with other teacher candidates. Note comments that you find helpful or enlightening.

 To access this exercise online, go to the Companion Website at **www.prenhall.com/kellough.**

EXERCISE **4.6B**

■ Censorship: Books That Are Sometimes Challenged

Instructions: Continuing with the topic introduced in Exercise 4.6A, this exercise concentrates on certain books that, although frequently used in teaching, are sometimes challenged by members of some communities. Book censorship becomes a concern when literature is the base for integrated teaching because there may be attempts to censor books and curricular materials in the schools. Books that have been challenged include:

The Adventures of Huckleberry Finn (Mark Twain)

Annie on My Mind (Nancy Garden)

The Arizona Kid (Ron Koertge)

The Catcher in the Rye (J. D. Salinger)

The Chocolate War (Robert Cormier)

Christine (Stephen King)

The Clan of the Cave Bear (Jean Auel)

The Color Purple (Alice Walker)

(continued)

A Day No Pigs Would Die (Robert Newton Peck)

Diary of a Young Girl (Anne Frank)

Fallen Angels (Walter Dean Myers)

Flowers in the Attic (V. C. Andrews)

Forever (Judy Blume)

Go Ask Alice (Anonymous)

The Great Santini (Pat Conroy)

Grendel (John Gardner)

The Handmaid's Tale (Margaret Atwood)

I Am the Cheese (Robert Cormier)

I Know Why the Caged Bird Sings (Maya Angelou)

Lord of the Flies (William Golding)

Of Mice and Men (John Steinbeck)

The Outsiders (S. E. Hinton)

Romeo and Juliet (William Shakespeare)

Running Loose (Chris Crutcher)

Scary Stories to Tell in the Dark (Alvin Schwartz)

Tarzan of the Apes (Edgar Rice Burroughs)

Review one of these books and explain how it might be challenged for censorship and how you would respond to the challenge. We leave the organization of this exercise for your class to decide; we recommend that you assign small groups to review certain books, then report to the entire class so that all the books on the list have been addressed.

_____
_____
_____

_____

 To access this exercise online, go to the Companion Website at **www.prenhall.com/kellough.**

■ AIMS, GOALS, AND OBJECTIVES: A CLARIFICATION

Now that you have examined content typically taught in the grades 7 through 12 curriculum and have experienced preparing a tentative content outline for a subject that you intend to teach for that content learning, it is time for you to learn to write specific learning targets for that content learning. Such learning targets are called *instructional objectives.* They are statements describing what the student will be able to do upon completion of the instructional experience. Whereas some authors distinguish between instructional objectives (hence referring to objectives that are not behavior specific) and behavioral or performance objectives (objectives that are behavior specific), the terms are used here as if they are synonymous to emphasize the importance of writing instructional objectives in terms that are measurable.

As a teacher, you frequently will encounter the compound structure that reads "goals and objectives," as you likely found in the curriculum documents that you reviewed earlier in this module. A distinction needs to be understood. The easiest way to understand the difference between the words *goals* and *objectives* is to look at your intent.

Goals are ideas that you intend to reach, that is, ideals that you would like to accomplish. Goals may be stated as teacher goals, or collaboratively, as team goals. Ideally, in both, the goal is the same. If, for example, the goal is to improve students' knowledge of how a democratic legislative body works, it could be stated as follows:

"To help students improve their knowledge of how a democratic legislative body works"—Teacher or course goal

Educational goals are general statements of intent and are prepared early in course planning. (*Note:* Some writers use the phrase "general goals and objectives," but that is incorrect usage. Goals are general; objectives are specific.) Goals are useful when planned collaboratively with students and/or when shared with students as advance mental organizers—for instance, to establish a mind-set. The students then know what to expect and will begin to prepare mentally to learn it. From the goals, objectives are prepared. **Objectives** are not intentions. They are the actual behaviors teachers intend to cause students to display. In short, objectives are what students do.

The most general educational objectives are often called aims; the objectives of schools, curricula, and courses are called goals; the objectives of units and lessons are called instructional objectives. **Aims** are more general than goals, and goals are more general than objectives. Instructional objectives are quite specific. Aims, goals, and objectives represent the targets, from general to specific statements of learning expectations, to which curriculum and instruction are designed and aimed.

■ INSTRUCTIONAL OBJECTIVES AND THEIR RELATIONSHIP TO CURRICULUM AND ASSESSMENT

As implied in the preceding paragraphs, goals guide the instructional methods; objectives drive student performance. Assessment of student achievement in learning should be an assessment of that performance. An assessment procedure that matches the instructional objectives is sometimes referred to as assessment that is aligned or authentic (discussed in Module 9). When objectives, instruction, and assessment match the stated goals, we have what is referred to as an aligned curriculum.

Goals are general statements, usually not even complete sentences and often beginning with the infinitive *to,* that identify what the teacher intends the students to learn. Objectives, stated in performance terms, are specific actions and should be written as complete sentences that include the verb *will* to indicate what each student is expected to be able to do as a result of the instructional experience. When writing instructional objectives for their unit and lesson plans, some beginning teachers err by stating what they intend to do rather than what the anticipated student performance is. The value of stating learning objectives in terms of student performance is well documented by research.[12]

While instructional goals may not always be quantifiable (that is, readily measurable), instructional objectives should be measurable. Furthermore, those objectives then become the essence of what is measured for in instruments designed to assess student learning; they are the learning targets. Consider the examples shown in Figure 4.3.

■ Learning Targets and Goal Indicators

The main purpose for writing objectives in performance terms is to be able to assess with precision whether the instruction has resulted in the desired behavior. In many school districts the educational goals are established as learning targets, competencies that the students are expected to achieve. These goals are then divided into performance objectives, sometimes referred to as *goal indicators.* Instruction is designed to teach toward those objectives. When students perform the competencies called for by these objectives, their education is considered successful. This is known variously as *results-driven, criterion-referenced, competency-based, performance-based,* or *outcome-based* education. Expecting students to achieve

Goals
1. To acquire knowledge about the physical geography of South America.
2. To develop an appreciation for music.
3. To develop an enjoyment for reading.

Objectives
1. On a map the student will identify specific mountain ranges of South America.
2. The student will identify ten different musical instruments by listening to a tape recording of the Boston Pops Symphony Orchestra and identifying which instrument is being played at specified times as determined by the teacher.
3. The student will read two books, three short stories, and five newspaper articles at home within a two-month period. The student will maintain a daily written log of these activities.

FIGURE 4.3 ● Examples of Goals and Objectives

one set of competencies before moving on to the next set is called **mastery learning.** The success of the student achievement, teacher performance, and the school may each be assessed according to these criteria.

■ Overt and Covert Performance Outcomes

Assessment is not difficult to accomplish when the desired performance is **overt behavior,** that is, behavior that can be observed directly. Each of the sample objectives of the preceding section is an example of an overt objective. Assessment is more difficult to accomplish when the desired behavior is a **covert behavior,** that is, when it is not directly observable. Although certainly no less important, behaviors that call for *appreciation, discovery,* or *understanding,* for example, are not directly observable because they occur within a person. Since covert behavior cannot be observed directly, the only way to tell whether the objective has been achieved is to observe behavior that may be indicative of that achievement. The objective, then, is written in overt language, and evaluators can only assume or trust that the observed behavior is, in fact, reasonably close to being indicative of the expected learning outcome.

Furthermore, when assessing whether an objective has been achieved—that learning has occurred—the assessment device must be consistent with the desired learning outcome. Otherwise, the assessment is not aligned; it is invalid. When the measuring device and the learning objective are compatible, we say that the assessment is authentic. For example, a person's competency to teach specific skills in mathematics to high school sophomores is best (i.e., with highest reliability) measured by directly observing that person *doing that* very thing—teaching specific skills in mathematics to high school sophomores. Using a standardized paper-and-pencil test of multiple-choice items to determine a person's ability to teach specific mathematical skills to high school sophomores is not authentic assessment.

■ Balance of Behaviorism and Constructivism

While behaviorists assume a definition of learning that deals only with changes in overt behavior, constructivists hold that learning entails the construction or reshaping of mental schemata and that mental processes mediate learning. Thus, people who adhere to constructivism or cognitivism are concerned with both overt and covert behaviors.[13] Does this mean that you must be one or the other, a behaviorist or a constructivist? Probably not. For now, the point is that when writing instructional objectives, you should write most or all of your basic expectations (minimal competency expectations) in overt terms (the topic of the next section). However, you cannot be expected to foresee all learning that occurs nor to translate all that is learned into performance terms—most certainly not before it occurs.

■ Teaching Toward Multiple Objectives, Understandings, and Appreciations

Any effort to write all learning objectives in behavioral terms neglects, in effect, the individual learner for whom it purports to be concerned. Such an approach does not allow for diversity among learners. *Learning that is most meaningful to students is not so neatly or easily predicted or isolated.* Rather than teaching one objective at a time, much of the time you should direct your teaching toward the simultaneous learning of multiple objectives, understandings, and appreciations. However, when you assess for learning, assessment is cleaner when objectives are assessed one at a time. More on this matter of objectives and their use in teaching and learning follows later in this module. Let's now review how objectives are prepared.

PREPARING INSTRUCTIONAL OBJECTIVES

When preparing instructional objectives, you must ask yourself, "How is the student to demonstrate that the objective has been reached?" The objective must include an action that demonstrates that the objective has been achieved. Inherited from behaviorism, this portion of the objective is sometimes called the *anticipated measurable performance.*

The ABCDs of Writing Objectives

When completely written, an instructional objective has four key components. To aid your understanding and remembering, you can refer to these as the ABCDs of writing behavioral objectives.

One component is the *audience.* The A of the ABCDs refers to the students for whom the objective is intended. To address this, sometimes teachers begin their objectives with the phrase "The student will be able to . . . , " or, to personalize the objective, "You will be able to . . . ." (*Note:* To conserve space and to eliminate useless language, in examples that follow we eliminate use of "be able to," and write simply "The student will. . . ." For brevity writers of objectives sometimes use the abbreviation "TSWBAT . . ." for "The student will be able to . . . ".)

The second key component is the expected *behavior,* the B of the ABCDs. This second component represents the important learning target. The expected behavior (or performance) should be written with verbs that are mea-surable—that is, with action verbs—so that it is directly observable that the objective, or target, has been reached. As discussed in the preceding section, some verbs are too vague, ambiguous, and not clearly measurable. When writing objectives, you should avoid verbs that are not clearly measurable, covert verbs such as *appreciate, comprehend,* and *understand* (see Figure 4.4). For the three examples given earlier, for Objectives 1 and 2 the behaviors (action or overt verbs) are *will identify,* and for Objective 3, the behaviors are *will read* and *maintain.*

Now, to test and to further your understanding, do Exercise 4.7, Recognizing Verbs That Are Acceptable for Overt Behaviors.

Most of the time, when writing objectives for your unit and lesson plans, you will not bother yourself with including the next two components. However, as you will learn, they are important for the assessment of learning.

The third ingredient is the *conditions,* the C of the ABCDs, the setting in which the behavior will be demonstrated by the student and observed by the teacher. Conditions are forever changing; although the learning target should be clearly recognizable long before the actual instruction occurs, the conditions may not. Thus, conditions are not often included in the objectives teachers write. For the first sample objective, the conditions are "on a map." For the second sample objective, the conditions are "by listening to a tape recording of the Boston Pops Symphony Orchestra" and "specified times as determined by the teacher." For the third sample, the conditions are "at home within a two-month period."

appreciate	familiarize	learn
believe	grasp	like
comprehend	indicate	realize
enjoy	know	understand

FIGURE 4.4 ● Verbs to Avoid When Writing Overt Objectives

EXERCISE 4.7

Recognizing Verbs That Are Acceptable for Overt Objectives— A Self-Check Exercise

Instructions: The purpose of this exercise is to check your recognition of verbs that are suitable for use in overt behavioral objectives. From the list of verbs below, circle those that *should not* be used in overt objectives—that is, those verbs that describe covert behaviors that are not directly observable and measurable. Check your answers against the answer key that follows. Discuss any problems with the exercise with your classmates and instructor.

1. apply
2. appreciate
3. believe
4. combine

5. comprehend
6. compute
7. create
8. define

9. demonstrate
10. describe
11. design
12. diagram

(continued)

13. enjoy	19. indicate	25. predict
14. explain	20. infer	26. realize
15. familiarize	21. know	27. select
16. grasp*	22. learn	28. solve
17. identify	23. name	29. state
18. illustrate	24. outline	30. understand

 To access this exercise online, go to the Companion Website at **www.prenhall.com/kellough.**

Answer Key for Exercise 4.7

1. The following verbs should be circled: 2, 3, 5, 13, 15, 16, 21, 22, 26, 30. If you missed more than a couple, then you need to read the previous sections again and discuss your errors with your classmates and instructor.

*NOTE: Words in English often have multiple meanings. For example, *grasp* as listed here could mean "to take hold," or it could mean "to comprehend." For the former it would be an acceptable verb for use in overt objectives; for the latter it would not.

The fourth ingredient, which again is not always included in objectives written by teachers, is the *degree* (or level) of expected performance—the D of the ABCDs. This is the ingredient that allows for the assessment of student learning. When mastery learning is expected, the level of expected performance is usually omitted (because it is understood). In teaching for mastery learning, the performance-level expectation is 100%. In reality, however, the performance level will most likely be between 85 and 95%, particularly when working with a group of students rather than with an individual student. The 5 to 15% difference allows for human error, as can occur when using written and oral communication. Like conditions, standards will vary depending on the situation and purpose and thus are not normally included in the unit and lessons that teachers prepare. Now, to reinforce your comprehension, do Exercise 4.8.

EXERCISE 4.8

Recognizing the Parts of Criterion-Referenced Behavioral Objectives—A Self-Check Exercise

Instructions: The purpose of this exercise is to practice your skill in recognizing the four components of a behavioral objective. In the following two objectives, identify the parts of the objectives by underlining once the *audience,* twice the *behavior,* three times the *conditions,* and four times the *performance level* (degree or standard of performance). Check against the answer key that follows; discuss any problems with your classmates and instructor.

1. You will write a 500-word account of the battle between the forces of Gondor and its allies against those of Mordor and its allies, as related in *The Lord of the Rings,* completely from memory. This account will be accurate in all basic details and include all the important incidents of the battle.

2. Given an interurban bus schedule, at the end of the lesson the student will be able to read the schedule well enough to determine at what time buses are scheduled to leave randomly selected points, with at least 90% accuracy.

 To access this exercise online, go to the Companion Website at **www.prenhall.com/kellough.**

Answer Key for Exercise 4.8

	Objective 1	Objective 2
Audience	you	the student
Behavior	will write a 500-word account of the battle between the forces of Gondor and its allies against those of Mordor and its allies	will be able to read the schedule
Conditions	completely from memory	given an interurban bus schedule
Performance level	this account will be accurate in all basic details and include all the important incidents of the battle	well enough to determine (and) with at least 90% accuracy

Performance level is used to assess student achievement, and sometimes it is used to evaluate the effectiveness of the teaching. Student grades might be based on performance levels; evaluation of teacher effectiveness might be based on the level of student performance. Now, with Exercise 4.9, try your skill at recognizing measurable objectives.

EXERCISE 4.9

■ Recognizing Objectives That Are Measurable—
A Self-Check Exercise

Instructions: The purpose of this exercise is to assess your skill in recognizing measurable objectives—those stated in behavioral terms. Place a check before each of the following that is a student-centered behavioral objective or a learning objective that is clearly measurable. Although the audience, conditions, and degree of the ABCD structure may be absent, ask yourself, "As stated, is it a student-centered and measurable objective?" If it is, then place a check in the blank. An answer key follows. After checking your answers, discuss any problems with your classmates and instructor.

_____ 1. The students will understand that the basic issue that resulted in secession was the extension of slavery.

_____ 2. Digestion is the chemical change of foods into particles that can be absorbed.

_____ 3. To explain what an acid is and what an acid's properties are.

_____ 4. Introduction to vector qualities and their use.

_____ 5. The students will be able to convert Celsius temperatures to Fahrenheit temperatures.

_____ 6. The students will understand that vibrating bodies provide the source of all sounds and sound waves.

_____ 7. At the end of the lesson, with at least 90% accuracy, the students will be able to read a bus schedule well enough to determine at what time buses are scheduled to arrive and leave at designated stations.

_____ 8. Given a number of quadratic equations with one unknown, the students will be able to solve the equations correctly in 80% of the cases.

_____ 9. The students will appreciate the problems faced by those who have emigrated from Southeast Asia to the United States.

_____ 10. A study of the external features and internal organs of the frog through video films of dissections.

(continued)

_____ 11. To discuss the reasons why the field of philosophy was well developed by the ancient Greeks.

_____ 12. Animals' physical adaptation to their environments.

 To access this exercise online, go to the Companion Website at **www.prenhall.com/kellough.**

Answer Key for Exercise 4.9

1. This is a behavioral objective. Although another verb might be more appropriate (e.g., *recognize*), understanding is a kind of behavior. In this case, understanding that slavery was the basic issue that brought about secession is the terminal behavior the teacher expects of the students.

2. This is not a behavioral objective. Rather, it is a description of a concept and does not describe an expected terminal behavior.

3. This is not a behavioral objective. It describes teacher behavior rather than student terminal behavior. It is more a teaching procedure than an objective.

4. This is not a behavioral objective—or even an objective of any type. It is a topic or title.

5. This is a behavioral objective. It describes clearly what the students will be able to do as a result of the instruction; it describes their expected terminal behavior.

6. This is a behavioral objective. The objective is rather broad, and another verb might have been more useful. Understanding is a kind of terminal behavior, but the objective might have been more measurable had the teacher used a verb other than *understanding*. A better formulation would have been: "The students will be able to recall that . . . " or "The students will be able to demonstrate that . . . ".

7. This is a behavioral objective. It is specific and very clear about the teacher's expectation of student behavior at completion of the lesson.

8. This is a clearly written behavioral objective.

9. This is a behavioral objective. Although the terminal behavior described is vague and general, it is nevertheless a terminal behavior. Perhaps a clearer formulation would have been: "The students will demonstrate an appreciation of the problems faced by those who have emigrated from Southeast Asia to the United States by recalling the many problems the people faced before, during, and following that emigration."

10. This is not a behavioral objective. It describes no behavior of any kind. It is the title of a topic with a mention of methods.

11. This is not a behavioral objective. It is not an objective at all, but rather a description of the teaching procedure to be used.

12. This is not a behavioral objective. Again, this is a title of a topic. It describes no behavior and no objective.

CLASSIFYING INSTRUCTIONAL OBJECTIVES

When planning instructional objectives, it is useful to consider the three domains of learning objectives:

Cognitive domain involves mental operations from the lowest level of the simple recall of information to complex, high-level evaluative processes.

Affective domain involves feelings, attitudes, and values and ranges from the lower levels of acquisition to the highest level of internalization and action.

Psychomotor domain ranges from the simple manipulation of materials to the communication of ideas, and finally to the highest level of creative performance.

The Domains of Learning and the Developmental Needs of Youth

Educators attempt to design learning experiences to meet the following areas of developmental needs of youth: intellectual, physical, emotional/psychological, and moral/ethical. As a teacher, you must include objectives that address learning within each of these categories of needs. While the intellectual needs are primarily within the cognitive domain and the physical are within the psychomotor, the other needs mostly are within the affective domain.

Too frequently, teachers focus on the cognitive domain while assuming that the psychomotor and affective will take care of themselves. Many experts argue that teachers should do just the opposite: That when the affective is directly attended to, the psychomotor and cognitive naturally develop. In any case, you should plan your teaching so your students are guided from the lowest to highest levels of operation within each of the three domains, separately or simultaneuolsy. The three developmental hierarchies are discussed next to guide your understanding of each of the five areas of needs. Notice the illustrative verbs within each hierarchy. These verbs help you fashion your objectives when you are developing unit plans and lesson plans. (To see how goals and objectives are fit into one lesson plan, see Figure 5.8, Module 5, Multiple-Day, Project-Centered, Interdisciplinary, and Transcultural Lesson Using Worldwide Communication via the Internet.) Caution must be urged, however, for there can be considerable overlap among the levels at which some action verbs may appropriately be used. For example, the verb *identifies* is appropriate in each of the following objectives at different levels (identified in parentheses) within the cognitive domain:

- The student will identify the correct definition of the term *osmosis*. (knowledge)
- The student will identify examples of the principle of osmosis. (comprehension)
- The student will identify the osmotic effect when a cell is immersed into a hypotonic solution. (application)
- The student will identify the osmotic effect on turgor pressure when the cell is placed in a hypotonic solution. (analysis)

Cognitive domain hierarchy In a widely accepted taxonomy of objectives, Bloom and his associates arranged cognitive objectives into classifications according to the complexity of the skills and abilities they embodied.[14] The result was a ladder ranging from the simplest to the most complex intellectual processes. Within each domain, prerequisite to a student's ability to function at one particular level of the hierarchy is the ability to function at the preceding level or levels. In other words, when a student is functioning at the third level of the cognitive domain, that student is automatically also functioning at the first and second levels. Rather than an orderly progression from simple to complex mental operations as illustrated by Bloom's Taxonomy, other researchers prefer an organization of cognitive abilities that ranges from simple information storage and retrieval, through a higher level of discrimination and concept attainment, to the highest cognitive ability to recognize and solve problems.[15]

The six major categories (or levels) in Bloom's Taxonomy of cognitive objectives are (a) *knowledge*—recognizing and recalling information;

(b) *comprehension*—understanding the meaning of information; (c) *application*—using information; (d) *analysis*—dissecting information into its component parts to comprehend the relationships; (e) *synthesis*—putting components together to generate new ideas; and (f) *evaluation*—judging the worth of an idea, notion, theory, thesis, proposition, information, or opinion. In this taxonomy, the top four categories or levels—application, analysis, synthesis, and evaluation—represent what are called *higher-order cognitive thinking skills*.[16]

Although space does not allow elaboration here, Bloom's Taxonomy includes various subcategories within each of these six major categories. It is probably less important that an objective be absolutely classified than it is for a teacher to be cognizant of hierarchies of thinking and doing and to understand the importance of attending to student intellectual behavior from lower to higher levels of operation in all three domains. Discussion of each of Bloom's six categories follows.

Knowledge. The basic element in Bloom's Taxonomy concerns the acquisition of knowledge, that is, the ability to recognize and recall information. (As discussed in Module 7, this is similar to the *input level* of thinking and questioning.) Although this is the lowest of the six categories, the information to be learned may not itself be of a low level. In fact, it may be of an extremely high level. Bloom includes here knowledge of principles, generalizations, theories, structures, and methodology, as well as knowledge of facts and ways of dealing with facts.

Action verbs appropriate for this category include *choose, complete, cite, define, describe, identify, indicate, list, locate, match, name, outline, recall, recognize, select,* and *state.*

The following are examples of objectives at the knowledge level. Note especially the verb (in italics) used in each example:

- From memory, the student *will recall* the letters in the English alphabet that are vowels.
- The student *will list* the organelles found in animal cell cytoplasm.
- The student *will identify* the major parts of speech in the sentence.
- The student *will name* the positions of players on a soccer team.

The remaining five categories of Bloom's Taxonomy of the cognitive domain deal with the use of knowledge. They encompass the educational objectives aimed at developing cognitive skills and abilities, including comprehension, application, analysis, synthesis, and evaluation of knowledge.

Comprehension. Comprehension includes the ability to translate, explain, or interpret knowledge and to extrapolate from it to address new situations. Action verbs appropriate for this category include *change, classify, convert, defend, describe, discuss, estimate, expand, explain, generalize, infer, interpret, paraphrase, predict, recognize, retell, summarize,* and *translate.*

Examples of objectives in this category are:

- From a sentence, the student *will recognize* the letters that are vowels in the English alphabet.

- The student *will describe* each of the organelles found in animal cell cytoplasm.

- The student *will recognize* the major parts of speech in the sentence.

- The student *will recognize* the positions of players on a soccer team.

Application.   Once learners understand information, they should be able to apply it. Action verbs in this category of operation include *apply, calculate, demonstrate, develop, discover, exhibit, modify, operate, participate, perform, plan, predict, relate, show, simulate, solve,* and *use.* Examples of objectives in this category are:

- The student *will use* in a sentence a word that contains at least two vowels.

- The student *will predict* the organelles found in plant cell cytoplasm.

- The student *will demonstrate* in a complete sentence each of the major parts of speech.

- The student *will relate* how the positions of players on a soccer team depend upon each other.

Analysis.   This category includes objectives that require learners to use the skills of analysis. Action verbs appropriate for this category include *analyze, arrange, break down, categorize, classify, compare, contrast, debate, deduce, diagram, differentiate, discover, discriminate, group, identify, illustrate, infer, inquire, organize, outline, relate, separate,* and *subdivide.* Examples of objectives in this category include:

- From a list of words, the student *will differentiate* those that contain vowels from those that do not.

- Under the microscope, the student *will identify* the organelles found in animal cell cytoplasm.

- The student *will analyze* a paragraph for misuse of major parts of speech.

- The student *will illustrate* on the writing board the different positions of players on a soccer team.

Synthesis.   This category includes objectives that involve such skills as designing a plan, proposing a set of operations, and deriving a series of abstract relations. Action verbs appropriate for this category include *arrange, assemble, categorize, classify, combine, compile, compose, constitute, create, design, develop, devise, document, ex-*

plain, *formulate, generate, hypothesize, imagine, invent, modify, organize, originate, plan, predict, produce, rearrange, reconstruct, revise, rewrite, summarize, synthesize, tell, transmit,* and *write.* Examples of objectives in this category are:

- From a list of words, the student *will rearrange* them into several lists according to the vowels contained in each.

- The student *will devise* a classification scheme of the organelles found in animal cell and plant cell cytoplasm according to their functions.

- The student *will write* a paragraph that correctly uses each of the major parts of speech.

- The student *will illustrate* on the chalkboard an offensive plan that uses the different positions of players on a soccer team.

Evaluation.   This, the highest category of Bloom's Cognitive Taxonomy, includes offering opinions and making value judgments. Action verbs appropriate for this category include *appraise, argue, assess, choose, compare, conclude, consider, contrast, criticize, decide, discriminate, estimate, evaluate, explain, interpret, judge, justify, predict, rank, rate, recommend, relate, revise, standardize, support,* and *validate.* Examples of objectives in this category are:

- The student *will listen* to and evaluate other students' identifications of vowels from sentences written on the board.

- While observing living cytoplasm under the microscope, the student *will justify* his or her interpretation that certain structures are specific organelles of a plant or animal cell.

- The student *will evaluate* a paragraph written by another student for the proper use of major parts of speech.

- The student *will interpret* the reasons for an opposing team's offensive use of the different positions of players on a soccer team.

Affective domain hierarchy Krathwohl, Bloom, and Masia developed a useful taxonomy of the affective domain.[17] The following are their major levels (or categories), from least internalized to most internalized: (a) *receiving*—being aware of the affective stimulus and beginning to have favorable feelings toward it; (b) *responding*—taking an interest in the stimulus and viewing it favorably; (c) *valuing*—showing a tentative belief in the value of the affective stimulus and becoming committed to it; (d) *organizing*—placing values into a system of dominant and supporting values; and (e) *internalizing*—demonstrating consistent beliefs and behavior that have become a way of life. Although there is considerable overlap from one category to another within the affective domain, these categories do give a basis by which to judge the quality of objectives and the nature of learning within this area. A discussion of each of the five categories follows.

Receiving. At this level, which is the least internalized, the learner exhibits willingness to give attention to particular phenomena or stimuli, and the teacher is able to arouse, sustain, and direct that attention. Action verbs appropriate for this category include *ask, choose, describe, differentiate, distinguish, hold, identify, locate, name, point to, recall, recognize, reply, select,* and *use.* Examples of objectives in this category are:

■ The student *demonstrates sensitivity* to the property, beliefs, and concerns of others.

■ The student *listens attentively* to the ideas of others.

■ The student *pays attention* to the directions for enrichment activities.

Responding. At this level, learners respond to the stimulus they have received. They may do so because of some external pressure, or because they find the stimulus interesting, or because responding gives them satisfaction. Action verbs appropriate for this category include *answer, applaud, approve, assist, command, comply, discuss, greet, help, label, perform, play, practice, present, read, recite, report, select, spend (leisure time in), tell,* and *write.* Examples of objectives at this level are:

■ The student *reads* for enrichment.

■ The student *discusses* what others have said.

■ The student *cooperates* with others during group activities.

Valuing. Objectives at the valuing level deal with learner's beliefs, attitudes, and appreciations. The simplest objectives concern the acceptance of beliefs and values; the higher ones involve learning to prefer certain values and to finally become committed to them. Action verbs appropriate for this level include *argue, assist, complete, describe, differentiate, explain, follow, form, initiate, invite, join, justify, propose, protest, read, report, select, share, study, support,* and *work.* Examples of objectives in this category include:

■ The student *protests* against racial or ethnic discrimination.

■ The student *synthesizes* a position on biological evolution.

■ The student *argues* a position against abortion or pro-choice for women.

Organizing. This fourth level in the affective domain concerns the building of a personal value system. Here the learner is conceptualizing and arranging values into a system that recognizes their relative importance. Action verbs appropriate for this level include *adhere, alter, arrange, balance, combine, compare, defend, define, discuss, explain, form, generalize, identify, integrate, modify,*

order, organize, prepare, relate, and *synthesize.* Examples of objectives in this category are:

■ The student *forms judgments* concerning proper behavior in the workplace.

■ The student *integrates* into a personal work ethic.

■ The student *defends* the important values of a particular subculture.

Internalizing. This is the last and highest category within the affective domain, at which the learner's behaviors have become consistent with his or her beliefs. Action verbs appropriate for this level include *act, complete, display, influence, listen, modify, perform, practice, propose, qualify, question, revise, serve, solve,* and *verify.* Examples of objectives in this category are:

■ The student's behavior *displays* a well-defined and ethical code of conduct.

■ The student *practices* accurate verbal and nonverbal communication.

■ The student *performs* independently.

Psychomotor domain hierarchy Whereas identification and classification within the cognitive and affective domains are generally agreed upon, there is less agreement on the classification within the psychomotor domain. Originally, the goal of this domain was simply to develop and categorize proficiency in skills, particularly those dealing with gross and fine muscle control. The classification of the domain presented here follows this lead, but includes at its highest level the most creative and inventive behaviors, thus coordinating skills and knowledge from all three domains. Consequently, the objectives are in a hierarchy ranging from simple gross locomotor control to the most creative and complex, requiring originality and fine locomotor control—for example, from simply turning on a computer to designing a software program. From Harrow we offer the following taxonomy of the psychomotor domain: (a) *moving,* (b) *manipulating,* (c) *communicating,* and (d) *creating.*[18]

Moving. This level involves gross motor coordination. Action verbs appropriate for this level include *adjust, carry, clean, grasp, jump, locate, obtain,* and *walk.* Sample objectives for this category are:

■ The student *will jump* a rope 10 times without missing.

■ The student *will correctly grasp* the putter.

■ The student *will carry* the microscope to the desk correctly.

Manipulating. This level involves fine motor coordination. Action verbs appropriate for this level include *assemble, build, calibrate, connect, play, thread,* and *turn.* Sample objectives for this category are:

- The student *will assemble* a kite.
- The student *will play* the C-scale on the clarinet.
- The student *will turn* the fine adjustment until the microscope is in focus.

Communicating. This level involves the communication of ideas and feelings. Action verbs appropriate for this level include *analyze, ask, describe, draw, explain,* and *write.* Sample objectives for this category are:

- By *asking* appropriate questions the student will demonstrate active listening skills.
- The student *will draw* what he or she observes on a slide through the microscope.
- The student *will describe* his or her feelings about the cloning of humans.

Creating. Creating is the highest level of this domain and of all domains and represents the student's coordination of thinking, learning, and behaving in all three domains. Action verbs appropriate for this level include *create, design,* and *invent.* Sample objectives for this category are:

- The student *will design* a mural.
- The student *will create, choreograph,* and *perform* a dance pattern.
- The student *will invent* and build a kite pattern.

Now, with Exercise 4.10, assess your recognition of performance objectives according to the domain to which they belong. Then, with Exercise 4.11, begin writing your own objectives for use in your teaching.

EXERCISE 4.10

■ Assessing Recognition of Objectives According to Domain— A Self-Check Exercise

Instructions: The purpose of this exercise is to assess your ability to recognize objectives according to their domains. Classify each of the following instructional objectives by writing in the blank space the appropriate letter according to its domain: *C* = cognitive, *A* = affective, *P* = psychomotor. Check your answers with the key at the end; then discuss the results with your classmates and instructor.

_____ 1. The student will continue shooting free throws until the student can successfully complete 80% of the attempts.

_____ 2. The student will identify on a map the mountain ranges of the eastern United States.

_____ 3. The student will summarize the historical development of the Democratic party of the United States.

_____ 4. The student will demonstrate a continuing desire to learn more about using the classroom computer for word processing by volunteering to work at it during free time.

_____ 5. The student will volunteer to tidy up the storage room.

_____ 6. After listening to several recordings, the student will identify the respective composers.

_____ 7. The student will translate a favorite Cambodian poem into English.

_____ 8. The student will accurately calculate the length of the hypotenuse.

_____ 9. The student will indicate an interest in the subject by voluntarily reading additional library books about earthquakes.

_____ 10. The student will write and perform a piano concerto.

 To access this exercise online, go to the Companion Website at **www.prenhall.com/kellough.**

(continued)

Answer Key for Exercise 4.10

| 1. D | 3. C | 5. A | 7. C | 9. A |
| 2. C | 4. A | 6. C | 8. C | 10. D |

EXERCISE **4.11**

■ Preparing My Own Instructional Objectives

Instructions: The purpose of this exercise is to begin the construction of objectives for your own teaching. For a subject content and grade level of your choice (perhaps from your content outline, Exercise 4.5), prepare 10 specific objectives. (Audience, conditions, and performance level are not necessary unless requested by your course instructor.) Exchange completed exercises with your classmates; then discuss and make changes where necessary.

Subject field: Grade level:

1. Cognitive knowledge:

2. Cognitive comprehension:

3. Cognitive application:

4. Cognitive analysis:

5. Cognitive synthesis:

6. Cognitive evaluation:

7. Affective (low level):

8. Affective (highest level):

9. Psychomotor (low level):

10. Psychomotor (highest level):

 To access this exercise online, go to the Companion Website at **www.prenhall.com/kellough.**

■ USING THE TAXONOMIES

Theoretically, the taxonomies are constructed so that students achieve each lower level before being ready to move to the higher levels. But, because categories and behaviors overlap, as they should, this theory does not always hold in practice. Furthermore, as explained by others, feelings and thoughts are inextricably interconnected; they cannot be neatly separated, as the taxonomies would imply.[19]

The taxonomies are important in that they emphasize the various levels to which instruction must aspire. For learning to be worthwhile, you must formulate and teach to objectives from the higher levels of the taxonomies as well as from the lower ones. Student think-

Results-based education helps produce people who are lifelong learners, who are effective communicators, who have high self-esteem, and are:

Problem solvers
- are able to solve problems in their academic and personal lives.
- demonstrate higher-level analytical thinking skills when they evaluate or make decisions.
- are able to set personal and career goals.
- can use knowledge, not just display it.
- are innovative thinkers.

Self-directed learners
- are independent workers.
- can read, comprehend, and interact with text.
- have self-respect with an accurate view of themselves and their abilities.

Quality producers
- can communicate effectively in a variety of situations (oral, aesthetic/artistic, nonverbal).
- are able to use their knowledge to create intelligent, artistic products that reflect originality.
- have high standards.

Collaborative workers
- are able to work interdependently.
- show respect for others and their points of view.
- have their own values and moral conduct.
- have an appreciation of cultural diversity.

Community Contributors
- have an awareness of civic, individual, national, and international responsibilities.
- have an understanding of basic health issues.
- have an appreciation of diversity.

FIGURE 4.5 ● Sample School District-Expected Learning Outcome Standards

ing and behaving must be moved from the lowest to the highest levels of thinking and behavior. When it is all said and done, it is, perhaps, the highest level of the psychomotor domain (creating) to which we aspire.

In using the taxonomies, remember that the point is to formulate the best objectives for the job to be done. In schools that use outcome-based education (known also as *results-driven education*) models, those models describe levels of mastery standards (rubrics) for each outcome. The taxonomies provide the mechanism for ensuring that you do not spend a disproportionate amount of time on facts and other low-level learning, and can be of tremendous help where teachers are expected to correlate learning activities to one of the school's or district's outcome standards (see Figure 4.5).

Preparing objectives is essential to the preparation of good items for the assessment of student learning. Clearly communicating your performance expectations to students and then specifically assessing student learning against those expectations makes the teaching most efficient and effective, and it makes the assessment of the learning closer to being authentic. This does not mean to imply that you will always write performance objectives for everything taught, nor will you always be able to accurately measure what students

have learned. As said earlier, learning that is meaningful to students is not as easily compartmentalized as the taxonomies of educational objectives would intimate.

■ Observing for Connected (Meaningful) Learning: Logs, Portfolios, and Journals

In learning that is most important and that has the most meaning to students, the domains are inextricably interconnected. Consequently, when assessing for student learning, both during instruction (**formative assessment**) and at the conclusion of the instruction (**summative assessment**), you must look for those connections.

Ways of looking for connected learning include (a) maintain a teacher's (or team's) log with daily or nearly daily entries about the progress of each student, (b) have students maintain personal learning journals in which they reflect on and respond to their learning, and (c) have students assemble individual learning portfolios that document students' thinking, work, and learning experiences.

Dated and chronologically organized items that students place in their portfolios can include notes and communications; awards; brainstorming records; photos of bulletin board contributions and of charts, posters, displays, and models made by the student; records of peer coaching; visual maps; learning contract; record of debate contributions; demonstrations or presentations; mnemonics created by the student; peer evaluations; reading record; other contributions made to the class or to the team; record of service work; and test and grade records.

Student journals and portfolios are discussed further in Module 9.

■ Character Education

Related especially to the affective domain, although not exclusive of the cognitive and psychomotor domains, is an interest in the development of students' values, especially those of honesty, kindness, respect, and responsibility, an interest in what is sometimes called **character education** (see also Module 2). For example, Wynne and Ryan state that "transmitting character, academics, and discipline—essentially, 'traditional' moral values—to pupils is a vital educational responsibility."[20] Thus, if one agrees with that interpretation, then the teaching of moral values is the transmission of character, academics, and discipline and clearly implies learning that transcends the three domains of learning presented in this module. Stimulated by a perceived need to reduce student antisocial behaviors (such as drug abuse and violence) and to produce more respectful and responsible citizens, with a primary focus on the affective domain, many schools are developing curricula in character education and instruction in conflict resolution. The ultimate goal of those efforts is to develop in students values that lead to responsible citizenship and moral action. Specific techniques and resources on character education are presented in Module 2.

■ LEARNING THAT IS NOT IMMEDIATELY OBSERVABLE

Unlike behaviorists, constructivists do not limit the definition of learning to that which is observable behavior. You shouldn't either. Bits and pieces of new information are stored in short-term memory, where the new information is "rehearsed" until ready to be stored in long-term memory. If the information is not rehearsed, it eventually fades from short-term memory. If it is rehearsed and made meaningful through connections with other stored knowledge, then this new knowledge is transferred to and stored in long-term memory, either by building existing schemata or by forming new schemata. As a teacher, your responsibility is to provide learning experiences that will result in the creation of new schemata as well as the modification of existing schemata.

To be an effective teacher, the challenge is to use performance-based criteria, but simultaneously use a teaching style that encourages the development of intrinsic sources of student motivation, which allows, provides, and encourages coincidental learning—learning that goes beyond what might be considered predictable, immediately measurable, and representative of minimal expectations.

■ SUMMARY

As you reviewed curriculum documents and student textbooks, you probably found most of them well-organized and useful. In your comparison and analyses of courses of study and the teacher's editions of student textbooks, you probably discovered that some are accompanied by sequentially designed resource units from which the teacher can select and build specific teaching units. A resource unit usually consists of an extensive list of objectives, a large number and variety of activities, suggested materials, and extensive bibliographies for teacher and students, from which the teacher will select those that best suit his or her needs to build an actual teaching unit.

As you also may have discovered, some courses of study contain actual teaching units that have been prepared by teachers of that particular school district. An important question often asked by beginning teachers, as well as by student teachers, is this: How closely must I follow the school's curriculum guide or course of study? You need the answer before you begin teaching. To obtain that answer, you need to talk with teachers and administrators of that particular school.

In conclusion, your final decisions about what content to teach are guided by all of the following: (a) articles in professional journals; (b) discussions with other teachers; (c) local courses of study and state curriculum documents; (d) the differences, interests, and abilities of your students; and (e) your own personal convictions, knowledge, and skills.

After discovering what you will teach comes the process of preparing the plans. The next module guides you through the planning process. Although teachers' textbook editions and other curriculum documents make the process easier, they should never substitute for your own specific planning.

In attempting to blend the best of behaviorism and constructivism, many teachers do not bother to try to write specific objectives for all the learning activities in their teaching plans. Clearly, though, when teachers do prepare specific objectives (by writing them or borrowing from other sources) and teach toward those objectives, student learning is better.

Most school districts require teachers to use objectives that are specifically stated. There is no question that clearly written instructional objectives are worth the time, especially when the teacher teaches toward those objectives and evaluates students' progress and learning against them—that is called *performance-based teaching* or *outcome-based* or *criterion-referenced assessment*. It is not imperative that you write all the instructional objectives that you will need. In fact, many of them are usually already available in textbooks and other curriculum documents.

As a teacher, you should plan specifically what you intend your students to learn, convey your expectations to your students, and then assess their learning against that specificity. There is a danger inherent in such performance-based or criterion-referenced teaching, however. Because it tends toward high objectivity, it could become too objective and thus have negative consequences. The danger is this: If students are treated as objects, then the relationship between teacher and student is impersonal and counterproductive to real learning. Highly specific and impersonal teaching can be discouraging to serendipity, creativity, and the excitement for real discovery and meaningful learning. It can also have a negative impact on the development of students' self-esteem.

Performance-based instruction works well when teaching toward mastery of basic skills, but mastery learning often assumes that there is some foreseeable endpoint to learning—an assumption that is obviously erroneous. With performance-based instruction, the source of student motivation tends to be mostly extrinsic. Teacher expectations, grades, society, and peer pressures are examples of extrinsic sources that drive student performance. To be an effective teacher, you must use performance-based criteria but simultaneously use a teaching style that encourages the development of intrinsic sources of student motivation. Your teaching style must allow for, provide for, and encourage coincidental learning—learning that goes beyond the predictable and immediately measurable and that represents minimal expectations. Part 3 is designed to assist you in meeting that challenge.

Now, with your content outline (Exercise 4.5) and instructional objectives (Exercise 4.11) in hand, you are ready to prepare detailed instructional plans, discussed in the next module.

■ MODULE 4 **POSTTEST**

Multiple Choice

1. Which one of the following is least likely to be an appropriate source of content for what you are expected to teach in middle or secondary schools?
   a. public school curriculum documents
   b. the common expectations of your colleagues
   c. your own convictions, knowledge, and skills in the subject
   d. lecture notes from your college or university courses in your academic major

2. When developing your curriculum, you need to consult
   a. a variety of textbooks, courses of study, and other public documents.
   b. your own convictions.
   c. colleagues.
   d. all of the above.

3. Statements that describe what the student will be able to do upon completion of an instructional experience are called
   a. course goals.
   b. instructor goals.
   c. covert objectives.
   d. performance objectives.

4. When writing performance objectives, which of the following is the only acceptable verb?
   a. know
   b. write
   c. appreciate
   d. understand

5. Which one of the following sets of verbs describes behaviors at the highest cognitive level?
   a. match, list, define
   b. show, predict, use
   c. rank, assess, argue
   d. describe, infer, explain

(continued)

6. Development of character, acceptable values, and ethics is at the highest level of which domain?
   a. affective
   b. cognitive
   c. psychomotor
   d. none of the above

7. The purpose of the taxonomies, according to this module, is to establish
   a. proper learning activities.
   b. levels to which learning should aspire.
   c. standards for curriculum improvement.
   d. standards for assessment of student learning.

8. Which one of the following statements is unconditionally true?
   a. High schools are periodically evaluated for accreditation.
   b. Secondary schools are periodically evaluated for accreditation.
   c. Junior high schools are periodically evaluated for accreditation.
   d. All public schools are periodically evaluated for regional or state accreditation.

9. The adoption of a good textbook does not mean that students will automatically learn, but it does ensure that the students have the advantage afforded by
   a. practice.
   b. feedback.
   c. organization.
   d. expert opinion.

10. Which one of the following terms does not mean the same as the others?
    a. performance-based education
    b. competency-based education
    c. results-driven education
    d. mastery learning

Short Explanation

1. When you have prepared a course topic outline, how will you know if the content of that outline is appropriate content for the subject and grade level for which the outline is intended?
2. Explain the relationship of planning to the preactive and reflective thought-processing phases of instruction.
3. Explain the intent of having national standards for each core subject taught in public schools. Who prepared these standards in your field? For your subject field, what are some of the major features that distinguish the standards from traditional teaching of that subject?
4. Explain how a textbook can be helpful to a student's learning in your discipline. How might reliance on a single textbook be a hindrance to student learning?
5. Contrast the psychomotor and affective domains of learning.
6. Describe the PQRST method of textbook learning.
7. Compare and contrast behaviorist and constructivist approaches to learning.
8. Give an example of a covert learning objective from your teaching field and describe how you would decide whether a student had reached the objective.
9. Identify one controversial issue in your subject field and explain why it is controversial.
10. Identify the three levels of planning for which a classroom teacher is responsible.

Essay

1. It is sometimes said that teaching less can be better. Think back to your own schooling. What do you really remember? Do you remember lectures and worksheets, or do you remember projects, your presentations, the lengthy research you did, and your extra effort for artwork to accompany your presentation? Maybe you remember a compliment by a teacher or a pat on the back by peers. Most likely you do not remember the massive amount of content that was covered. Write a one-page essay expressing and defending your agreement or disagreement with the original statement of this paragraph.
2. Do you believe that your students should have input in the planning of a course? Explain why or why not.

(continued)

3. Describe the meaning of the term *quality education* as it relates to your teaching field.

4. From your current observations and fieldwork as related to this teacher preparation program, clearly identify one specific example of educational practice that seems contradictory to exemplary practice or theory as presented in this module. Present your explanation for the discrepancy.

5. Describe any prior concepts you held that changed as a result of your experiences with this module. Describe the changes.

 To access this posttest and the answers online, go to the Companion Website at **www.prenhall.com/kellough.**

■ SUGGESTED READINGS

Baker, J. C., & Martin, F. G. (1998). *A neural network guide to teaching.* Fastback 431. Bloomington, IN: Phi Delta Kappa Educational Foundation.

Battista, M. T. (1999). The mathematical miseducation of America's youth. *Phi Delta Kappan, 80*(6), 425–433.

Burns, P. C., & Roe, B. D. (1999). *Informal reading inventory: Preprimer to twelfth grade* (5th ed.). Wilmington, MA: Houghton-Mifflin.

Cossey, R. (1999). Are California's math standards up to the challenge? *Phi Delta Kappan, 80*(6), 441–443.

Daniel, M. F., & Bergman-Drewe, S. (1998). Higher-order thinking, philosophy, and teacher education in physical education. *Quest, 50*(1), 33–58.

Glatthorn, A. A., & Jailall, J. (2000). Curriculum for the new millennium. In R. S. Brandt (Ed.), *Education in a new era* (Chap. 5, pp. 97–121). Alexandria, VA: ASCD Yearbook, Association for Supervision and Curriculum Development.

Hynd, C. R. (1999). Teaching students to think critically using multiple texts in history. *Journal of Adolescent & Adult Literacy, 42*(6), 428–436.

Jenkinson, A. (1999). *Reading, writing, and speaking about contemporary issues. Lesson plans for teachers of English and social studies.* Bloomington, IN: EDINFO Press.

Lambert, L. T. (2000). The new physical education. *Educational Leadership, 57*(6), 34–38.

Lerner, L. S. (1998). *State science standards: An appraisal of science standards in 36 states.* Washington, DC: Thomas B. Fordham Foundation.

Martin, B. L., & Briggs, L. J. (1986). *The affective and cognitive domains.* Englewood Cliffs, NJ: Educational Technology Publications.

Ohanian, S. (2000). Goals 2000: What's in a name? *Phi Delta Kappan, 81*(5), 344–355.

Reys, B., et al. (1999). Mathematics curricula based on rigorous national standards: What, why, and how? *Phi Delta Kappan, 80*(6), 454–456.

Ryan, K., & Boblin, K. (1999). *Building character in schools.* San Francisco: Jossey-Bass.

Saxe, D. W. (1998). *State history standards: An appraisal of history standards in 37 states and the District of Columbia.* Washington, DC: Thomas B. Fordham Foundation.

Schmoker, M., & Marzano, R. J. (1999). Realizing the promise of standards-based education. *Educational Leadership, 56*(6), 17–21.

Schoen, H. L., et al. (1999). Issues and options in the math wars. *Phi Delta Kappan, 80*(6), 444–453.

Smagorinsky, P. (1999). Standards revisited: The importance of being there. *English Journal, 88*(4), 82–88.

Tchudi, S., & Mitchell, D. (1999). *Exploring and teaching the English language arts* (4th ed.). New York: Addison-Wesley Longman.

Victor, E., & Kellough, R. D. (2000). *Science for the elementary and middle school* (9th ed.). Upper Saddle River, NJ: Prentice Hall.

Wiggins, G., & McTighe, J. (1998). *Understanding by design.* Alexandria, VA: Association for Supervision and Curriculum Development.

Zabaluk, B. L., & Samuels, S. J. (1988). *Readability: Its past, present, and Future.* Newark, DE: International Reading Association.

■ ENDNOTES

[1]Contact ACTFL, Six Executive Plaza, Yonkers, NY 10701-6801.

[2]Contact National Geographic Society, PO Box 1640, Washington, DC 20013-1640.

[3]Contact the American Alliance for Health, Physical Education, Recreation and Dance (AAHPRD), 1900 Association Drive, Reston, VA 22091.

[4]Bureau of Indian Affairs, 1849 C St., NW, Washington, DC 20240–0001, phone: 202–208–3710; Web site at **http://www.doi. gov/bureau-indian-affairs.html.**

[5]M. P. Sadker and D. M. Sadker, *Teachers, Schools, and Society* (7th edition) (Boston, MA: McGraw Hill, 2005), pp. 260–261.

[6]J. V. D. Diller and J. Moule, *Cultural Competence: A Primer for Educators* (Belmont, CA: Thomson Wadsworth, 2005), pp. 165–166.

[7]At least 24 states use statewide textbook adoption committees to review books and to then provide local districts with lists of recommended titles from which to choose.

[8]L. Chavkin, Readability and Reading Ease Revisited: State-Adopted Science Textbooks, *Clearing House 70*(3), 151–154 (January-February 1997).

[9]Source of K-W-L: D. M. Ogle, K-W-L: A Teaching Model That Develops Active Reading of Expository Text, *Reading Teacher 39*(6), 564–570 (February 1986). Source of POSSE: C. S. Englert and T. V. Mariage, Making Students Partners in the Comprehension Process: Organizing the Reading "POSSE," *Learning Disability Quarterly 14*(1), 23–138 (September 1991). Source of PQRST: E. B. Kelly, *Memory Enhancement for Educators*, Fastback 365 (Bloomington, IN: Phi Delta Kappa Educational Foundation, 1994), p. 18. Source of RAP: J. B. Schumaker et al., *The Paraphrasing Strategy* (Lawrence, KS: Edge Enterprises, 1984). Source of SQ3R: F. P. Robinson, Effective Study (rev. ed.) (New York: Harper & Brothers, 1961). The original source of SQ4R is unknown. For SRQ2R, see M. L. Walker, Help for the "Fourth-Grade Slum"—SRQ2R Plus Instruction in Text Structure or Main Idea, *Reading Horizons 36*(1), 38–58 (1995). About reciprocal teaching, see C. J. Carter, Why Reciprocal Teaching? *Educational Leadership 54*(6), 64–68 (March 1997), and T. L. Good and J. E. Brophy, *Looking in Classrooms* (8th ed.) (New York: Addison Wesley Longman, 2000), pp. 431–432.

[10]R. Reinhold, Class Struggle, *The New York Times Magazine*, September 29, 1991, 46.

[11]The National Education Association (NEA) published guidelines for teachers to consider before using commercial materials. For a free copy of the guidelines contact NEA Communications, 1201 16th Street, NW, Washington, DC 20036; phone: (202) 822-7200.

[12]See, for example, J. C. Baker and F. G. Martin, *A Neural Network Guide to Teaching*, Fastback 431 (Bloomington, IN: Phi Delta Kappa Educational Foundation, 1998); and T. L. Good and J. E. Brophy, *Looking in Classrooms* (8th ed.) (New York: Addison-Wesley/Longman, 2000), pp. 252–253.

[13]See, for example, the many articles in "The Constructivist Classroom," the November 1999 theme issue of *Educational Leadership*, Volume 57, number 3; D. R. Geelan, Epistemological Anarchy and the Many Forms of Constructivism, *Science and Education 6*(1–2), 15–28 (January 1997); and R. DeLay, Forming Knowledge: Constructivist Learning and Experiential Education, *Journal of Experiential Education 19*(2), 76–81 (August/September 1996).

[14]B. S. Bloom (Ed.), *Taxonomy of Educational Objectives, Book 1, Cognitive Domain* (White Plains, NY: Longman, 1984).

[15]See R. M. Gagne, L. J. Briggs, and W. W. Wager, *Principles of Instructional Design* (4th ed.) (New York: Holt, Rinehart & Winston, 1994).

[16]Compare Bloom's higher-order cognitive thinking skills with R. H. Ennis's A Taxonomy of Critical Thinking Dispositions and Abilities, and Qellmalz's Developing Reasoning Skills, both in J. B. Barron and R. J. Sternberg (Eds.), *Teaching Thinking Skills: Theory and Practice* (New York: W. H. Freeman, 1987); and with Marzano's "complex thinking strategies" in R. J. Marzano, *A Different Kind of Classroom: Teaching with Dimensions of Learning* (Alexandria, VA: Association for Supervision and Curriculum Development, 1992).

[17]D. R. Krathwohl, B. S. Bloom, and B. B. Masia, *Taxonomy of Educational Goals*, Handbook 2, Affective Domain (New York: David McKay, 1964).

[18]A. J. Harrow, *Taxonomy of the Psychomotor Domain* (New York: Longman, 1977). A similar taxonomy for the psychomotor domain is that of E. J. Simpson, *The Classification of Educational Objectives in the Psychomotor Domain. The Psychomotor Domain: Volume 3* (Washington, DC: Gryphon House, 1972).

[19]R. N. Caine and G. Caine, *Education on the Edge of Possibility* (Alexandria, VA: Association for Supervision and Curriculum Development, 1997), pp. 104–105.

[20]E. A. Wynne and K. Ryan, *Reclaiming Our Schools: A Handbook on Teaching Character, Academics, and Discipline* (Upper Saddle River, NJ: Prentice Hall, 1993) p. 3.

Preparing an Instructional Plan

Module 5 Overview

Having prepared a topic content outline (Exercise 4.5) and related instructional objectives (Exercise 4.11), you have begun development of an instructional plan. This module is designed to acquaint you with the basic components and procedures necessary for developing effective units and lessons. It includes both examples and suggestions that should prove helpful. Ultimately, however, you as the teacher will have to adapt, alter, and adjust these suggestions to meet the needs of your own particular groups of students. You will have to develop a lesson-plan style that is comfortable for you, usable in your teaching, and effective in facilitating student learning.

The teacher's edition of the student textbook and other resource materials will expedite your planning but should not substitute for it. You must know how to create a good instructional plan. In this module you will learn how it is done. With that knowledge you will develop an instructional plan with daily lessons (see Exercise 5.6A).

Specific Objectives

At the completion of this module, you should be able to:

- Describe why curriculum mapping is effective, and prepare a curriculum map for your discipline.

- Prepare a teaching unit complete with daily lesson plans, demonstrating an understanding of the basic components of a lesson plan.

- Differentiate among preassessment, formative assessment, and summative assessment and describe how each is used.

- Explain the characteristics, usefulness, and general procedures for developing an interdisciplinary thematic unit of instruction.

- Explain the concept of planning as a continual process.

- Explain the place and role of each of the four decision-making and thought-processing phases in unit planning and unit implementation.

Introduction

Seldom, if ever, can a teacher enter a classroom of students unprepared or underprepared and yet teach effectively. Spur-of-the-moment teaching rarely results in forceful, meaningful, logically presented lessons from which students develop a clear understanding of knowledge, skills, or concepts. Such lessons require careful thought and preparation. The teacher must decide which aspects of the subject should be the focus of each lesson, how a topic

> *"This important work of several decades ago, as well as much of what has since been in the forefront of educational thought, stresses the importance of teachers finding ways to make subject matter relevant to students, to involve students in setting their own goals, to vary the ways of learning to use approaches that employ all of the senses, and to be sure that there are opportunities for relating the knowledge to experiences or actually using it."[1]*
>
> —John I. Goodlad

should be adapted to a particular group of students, how a lesson should build upon preceding lessons, and how a lesson should prepare students for lessons to come. Without careful attention to these matters, lessons tend to be dull, drifting aimlessly toward no good purpose. Here we will discuss the lesson writing process and various types of units.

■ PLANNING FOR INSTRUCTION: A THREE-LEVEL AND SEVEN-STEP PROCESS

As introduced at the beginning of Module 4, complete planning for instruction occurs at three levels—the semester or year, the units, and the daily lessons. There are seven steps in the planning process. This section identifies and describes each of those steps. Some of the planning guidelines that follow have previously been addressed and are included here to show you where they fit in the seven-step planning procedure.

The seven steps of instructional planning involve:

1. *Course, grade level, and school goals.* Consider and understand your curriculum goals and their relationship to the mission and goals of the school. Your course does not exist in isolation but is an integral part of the total school curriculum.

2. *Expectations.* Consider topics and skills that you are expected to teach, such as those found in the course of study (Module 4).

3. *Academic year, semester, or trimester plan.* Think about the goals that you want the students to reach months from now. Working from your tentative topic outline and with the school calendar in hand, you will begin by deciding how much time should be devoted to each topic (or unit), penciling those times onto the outline. (Unless you are doing your planning at a computer, we suggest pencil because you will probably modify these many times.)

4. *Course schedule.* This schedule becomes a part of the course syllabus that you can present to students at the start of the school year. However, the schedule must remain flexible to allow for the unexpected, such as the cancellation or interruption of a class meeting or the extended study of a particular topic.

5. *Plans for each class meeting.* Working from the calendar plan or the course schedule, you are now ready to prepare plans for each class meeting, keeping in mind the abilities and interests of your students while making decisions about appropriate strategies and learning experiences. (Strategies are the focus of Part 3.) The preparation of daily plans takes considerable time and continues throughout the year as you arrange and prepare instructional notes, demonstrations, discussion topics and questions, and classroom exercises, as well as arrange for guest speakers, audiovisual materials and media equipment, field trips, and tools for the assessment of student learning. Because the content of each class meeting is often determined by the accomplishments of, and your reflections upon, the preceding one, your lessons are never "set in concrete" but need continual revisiting and assessment by you.

6. *Instructional objectives.* Once you have the finalized schedule, and as you prepare the daily plans, you will complete your preparation of the instructional objectives (begun in Exercise 4.11). These instructional objectives are critical for proper development of the next and final step.

7. *Assessment.* The final step is to decide how to assess student achievement. Included in this component are your decisions about how you will accomplish diagnostic or **preassessment** (assessment of what students know or think they know at the start of a new unit of study or a new topic), *formative assessment* (ongoing assessment during a unit of study on what the students are learning), and *summative assessment* (assessment of learning at the conclusion of a unit of study on what the students learned). Also included in the assessment component are your decisions about assignments and the grading procedures (discussed in Module 9).

You will proceed through these steps as you develop your first instructional plan. Before we get into that, consider the nature of the course syllabus.

■ THE SYLLABUS

A syllabus is a written statement of information about the workings of a particular class or course. As a student in postsecondary education, you have seen a variety of syllabi written by professors, each with their individual ideas about what general and specific logistic information is most important for students to know about a course. Not all public school teachers use a course syllabus, at least as described and illustrated here, but for reasons we will explore in this discussion, we believe they should at least cover this information with their students even if they do not distribute a syllabus to their classes. Related to that belief are several questions that are answered next: Why should teachers prepare a syllabus? What purpose does it fulfill? How do I develop one? Can students have input into its contents and participate in its development? Where do I start? What information should be included? How rigidly should it be followed?

■ Use and Development of a Syllabus

The syllabus contains information about the class or course, which is usually presented to students on the first day or during the first week of school. (See the sample shown in Figure 5.1.) The syllabus may be developed

English 8   **Room 23, Mrs. Biletnikoff**

Course Description

English 8 is a course designed to provide instruction in the areas of reading, analyzing, and writing about literature, while using texts that support the History 8 coursework. Essay writing, especially descriptive writing, is emphasized. In addition to intensive vocabulary study, students will be writing on a daily basis. Also, the students will read one million words of outside texts, in addition to their assigned reading. The readings for English 8 are an eclectic mix. The novels that the class will be reading this semester are *April Morning, The Giver,* and *The Diary of Anne Frank.*

Materials Required

Students are required to bring pen, pencil, and paper to class each day. Journal binder should be a two-pocket, three-prong paper binder. The school provides the vocabulary text and all literary texts.

Goals

- To understand and recognize the various aspects of literature: Character, setting, plot, point of view, and theme.
- To increase vocabulary, preparing students for more advanced writing.
- To develop and enhance students' descriptive writing and organizational skills.
- To increase oral and listening skills.

Objectives

- Students will participate in projects, class discussions, journal writing, quizzes, essay writing, and tests that are designed to help them grasp the concepts of plot, setting, character, theme, and other literary devices. Through these activities students will demonstrate improvement in their writing and oral/listening skills.
- Students will participate in class activities such as sustained silent reading (SSR), read aloud, and project development to help in their learning of the material.

Assignments

There are weekly vocabulary quizzes. There is also weekly vocabulary homework. Throughout the course, students will be writing journal entries, quickwrites, and essays. All completed and graded work is returned to the corresponding class file. Students are free to check the file before or after class.

Assessment Criteria

- Students will complete weekly vocabulary quizzes.
- Quizzes are administered when the teacher needs to check the students' progress.
- Test dates will be announced in class and class time is used for test preparation.
- Class participation accounts for 15% of the student's grade, therefore absences and tardiness can negatively affect this assessment component.
- Group work is graded, therefore lack of participation can negatively affect the student's grade.

Method of Evaluation

Evaluation is done through oral and written quizzes and tests. Additionally, students are evaluated on class participation, assignments, projects, and class discussions. All grades are based on a point system.

Papers, quizzes and tests	= 50% of total points
Homework	= 20% of total points
Journals	= 15% of total points
Group work and class participation	= 15% of total points

Grading Scale

90–100% of total points	= A
80–89%	= B
70–79%	= C
50–69%	= D
<50%	= F

Grades are posted (by codes, not names) biweekly

FIGURE 5.1 ● Sample Course Syllabus

SOURCE: Courtesy of Angela Biletnikoff

(continued)

Classroom Citizenship Behavior and Consequences for Inappropriate Behavior

Students are expected to be prompt, prepared, polite, productive, and positive (the 5Ps).

Students may earn five points per day by observing the 5Ps guidelines. Students may forfeit their citizenship points by excessive bathroom requests, tardiness, or leaving class without an approved excuse.

Consequences for inappropriate behavior:

> 1st infraction = verbal warning
> 2d infraction = 15 minutes at time-out and a phone call to parent or guardian
> 3d infraction = referral to OR and a call home
> 4th infraction = administrative referral and possible suspension
> *Note:* Any step in the above process may be skipped at the teacher's discretion.

Attendance

Regular attendance is crucial for success. It enables the student to understand assignments and take advantage of the guidance provided by the teacher and others. In addition, the students will receive immediate feedback regarding their progress. If a student needs to leave early or enter late, please make arrangements with the teacher beforehand if possible.

Tardiness

Students are tardy when they are not in their seats when the tardy bell rings. Any student who elects to leave the classroom for any reason takes a tardy for that period. Tardiness affects citizenship as well as the privilege to participate in extracurricular activities before and after school.

Bathroom Privileges

Students are allowed two bathroom passes per quarter. Each pass is redeemed at the time of use. If the student does not use the two passes for the quarter, the student receives five extra points per pass with a total of ten points possible towards their citizenship grade. If a student chooses to use the bathroom beyond the two-pass limit, then that student forfeits the citizenship points (five) for the day.

Make-Up

Students may make up assignments one day after returning from an excused absence. All other work is accepted at the teacher's discretion.

Extra Credit Work

There is no extra credit work in this class.

Instructional Schedule for English 8, Fall Semester

> Unit I   Introduction to the short story (two weeks)
>   Vocabulary, journal, SSR, and outside readings begin
> Unit II   *April Morning* (four–five weeks)
> Unit III *The Giver* (four–five weeks)
> Unit IV   *The Diary of Anne Frank* (four–five weeks)

FIGURE 5.1 *continued* ● Sample Course Syllabus

SOURCE: Courtesy of Angela Biletnikoff

completely by you or in collaboration with colleagues. As you shall learn, it also can be developed collaboratively with students. However it is developed, the syllabus should be designed so that it helps establish a rapport among students, parents or guardians, and the teacher; helps students feel at ease by providing an understanding of what is expected of them; and helps them to organize, conceptualize, and synthesize their learning experiences.

The syllabus should provide a reference, helping eliminate misunderstandings and misconceptions about the nature of the class—its rules, expectations, procedures, requirements, and other policies. The syllabus should also serve as a plan to be followed by you and the students, and it should serve as a resource for substitute teachers and (when relevant) members of a teaching team. When teaming, each team member should have a copy of every

other member's syllabus. In essence, the syllabus stands as documentation for what is taking place in the classroom for those outside the classroom (i.e., parents or guardians, administrators, other teachers, and students). For access by parents and other interested persons, some teachers include at least portions of their course syllabus, such as homework assignment specifications and due dates, with the school's Web site on the Internet.

Usually the syllabus, at least portions of it, is prepared by the teacher long before the first class meeting. If you maintain a syllabus template on your computer, then it is a simple task to customize it for each group of students you teach. You may find that it is more useful if students participate in the development of the syllabus, thereby empowering the students with a sense of ownership of the syllabus and a commitment to its contents. By having input into the workings of a course and

Step 1

Sometime during the first few days of the course, arrange students in heterogeneous groups (mixed abilities) of three or four members to brainstorm the development of their syllabus.

Step 2

Instruct each group to spend five minutes listing everything they can think of that they would like to know about the course. Tell the class that group *recorders* must be chosen to write their lists of ideas on paper and then, when directed to do so, to transfer the lists to the writing board or to sheets of butcher paper to be hung in the classroom for all to see (or on overhead transparencies—a transparency sheet and pen are made available to each group). Tell them that each group should select a group *spokesperson* who will address the class, explaining the group's list. Each group could also appoint a *materials manager* whose job is to see that the group has the necessary materials (e.g., pen, paper, transparency, chalk), and a *task master* whose job is to keep the group on-task and to report to the teacher when each task is completed.

Step 3

After five minutes, have the recorders prepare their lists. When using transparencies or butcher paper, the lists can be prepared simultaneously while recorders remain with their groups. If using the writing board, then recorders, one at a time, write their lists on areas of the board that you have designated for each group's list.

Step 4

Have the spokesperson of each group explain the group's list. As this is being done, you should make a master list. If transparencies or butcher paper are being used, rather than the writing board, you can ask for them as backup to the master list you have made.

Step 5

After all spokespersons have explained their lists, you ask the class collectively for additional input. "Can anyone think of anything else that should be added?"

Step 6

You now take the master list and design a course syllabus, being careful to address each question and to include items of importance that students may have omitted. However, your guidance during the preceding five steps should ensure that all bases have been covered.

Step 7

At the next class meeting, give each student a copy of the final syllabus. Discuss its content. (Duplicate copies to distribute to colleagues, especially those on your teaching team, interested administrators, and parents and guardians at back-to-school night.)

FIGURE 5.2 ● Steps for Involving Students in the Development of Their Course Syllabus

knowing that their opinions count, students will take more interest in what they are doing and learning. This has been demonstrated, for example, at East Paulding High School (Dallas, GA) where students in applied communications participate in developing the course syllabus by choosing literature selections, preparing study guides, creating project assignments, and devising assessment criteria.[2] Figure 5.2 shows steps you can use as a collaborative learning experience in which students spend time during the first (or an early) class meeting brainstorming the content of their syllabus.

▣ Content of a Syllabus

The syllabus should be concise, matter-of-fact, uncomplicated, and brief—perhaps no more than two pages—and should include the following information:

- *Descriptive information about the course.* This includes the teacher's name, course title, class period and days of class meetings, beginning and ending times, and room number.

- *Importance of the course.* This information should describe the course, cite how students will profit from it, and tell whether the course is a required course and (if relevant) from which program in the curriculum: A core curriculum course, a co-curriculum course, an exploratory or elective course, a vocational course, an advanced placement course, or some other arrangement.

- *Goals and objectives.* Include the major goals and a few of the major objectives.

- *Materials required.* Explain what materials are needed—such as a textbook, notebook, binder, portfolio, supplementary readings, safety goggles—and specify which are supplied by the school, which must be supplied by each student, and what materials must be available each day.

- *Types of assignments.* These should be clearly explained in as much detail as possible this early in the school term. There should be a statement of your estimate of time required (if any) for homework each night. There should also be a statement about where daily assignments will be posted in the classroom (the same place each day), the procedures for completing and turning in assignments, and (if relevant) procedures for making corrections to assignments already turned in (see information on second opportunities in the next paragraph). Include your policy regarding late work. Also, parents will want to know your expectations of them regarding helping their children with assignments. (Homework is discussed in Module 7.)

- *Attendance expectations.* Explain how attendance is related to grades and to promotion (if relevant) as well as the procedure for making up missed work. Typical school policy allows that for an excused absence, missed work can be completed without penalty if done within a reasonable period of time after the student returns to school. To strongly encourage regular attendance, the policy of Talent Development secondary schools is that a student automatically fails a course when the student accumulates five or more absences per quarter. However, to encourage students, the policy also includes recovery strategies. For example, each absence can be nullified if the student accumulates five consecutive days of perfect attendance. Policy also provides students with second opportunities for success on assignments, although at some cost so as to encourage a strong first effort.[3]

■ *Assessment and marking/grading procedures.* Explain the assessment procedures and the procedures for determining marks or grades. Will there be quizzes, tests, homework, projects, and group work? What will be their formats, coverage, and weights in the procedure for determining grades? For group work, how will the contributions and learning of individual students be evaluated?

■ *Other information specific to the course.* Field trips, special privileges, computer work, parental expectations, homework hotline, and classroom procedures and expectations (discussed in Module 3) should be included here. To affirm that your policies as indicated in the first draft of your syllabus are not counter to any existing school policies, if you are a beginning teacher or are new to the school, you probably should share your first draft of the syllabus with members of your team or the department chairperson for their feedback. Now do Exercises 5.1 and 5.2.

EXERCISE **5.1**

■ Content of a Course Syllabus

Instructions: The purpose of this exercise is to begin your thinking about preparing a syllabus for use in your teaching. From the following list of items that might appear on a course syllabus, identify (by circling) all those you would include in your own course syllabus. And, for each, explain why you would or would not include that item. Then share the syllabus with your classmates. After sharing, you might want to make revisions in your own list.

1. Name of teacher (my name):

2. Course title (and/or grade level):

3. Room number:

4. Beginning and ending times:

5. Time when students could schedule a conference with teacher:

6. Course description:

7. Course philosophy or rationale (underline which):

8. Instructional format (such as lecture-discussion, student-centered learning groups, or laboratory-centered):

(continued)

9. Absence policy:

10. Tardy policy:

11. Classroom procedures and rules for behavior:

12. Goals of course:

13. Objectives of course:

14. Policy about plagiarism:

15. Name of textbook and other supplementary materials:

16. Policy about use and care of textbook and other reading materials:

17. Materials to be supplied by student:

18. Assignments:

19. Policy about homework assignments (due dates, format, late assignments, weights for grades):

20. Course relationship to advisor-advisee program, core, cocurricular, exploratories, or some other aspect of the school curriculum:

21. Grading procedure:

22. Study skills:

23. Themes to be studied:

24. Field trips and other special activities:

25. Group work policies and types:

26. Other members of the teaching team and their roles:

27. Tentative daily schedule:

28. Other (specify):

29. Other (specify):

30. Other (specify):

To access this exercise online, go to the Companion Website at **www.prenhall.com/kellough.**

EXERCISE **5.2**

■ Preparing a Course Syllabus—An Exercise in Collaborative Thinking

Instructions: The purpose of this exercise is to prepare (in a group) a syllabus for a course that you intend to teach. Using your results from Exercise 5.1, work in groups of three or four members to develop one syllabus for a course you and other group members may someday teach. Each group should produce one course syllabus that represents that group's collaborative thinking; the finished product should be duplicated and shared with the entire class. Discuss within your group the pros and cons of having student input into the course syllabus (see Figure 5.1). Share the results of that discussion with the entire class.

 To access this exercise online, go to the Companion Website at **www.prenhall.com/kellough.**

■ THE INSTRUCTIONAL UNIT

The *instructional unit* is a major subdivision of a course (for one course there are several to many units of instruction) and is comprised of instruction planned around a central theme, topic, issue, or problem. Organizing the entire year's content into units makes the teaching process more manageable than when no plan or only random choices are made by a teacher.

The instructional unit, whether an interdisciplinary thematic unit (known also as an *integrated unit*), or a stand-alone standard subject unit, is not unlike a chapter in a book, an act or scene in a play, or a phase of work when undertaking a project such as building a house. Breaking down information or actions into component parts and then grouping the related parts makes sense out of learning and doing. The unit brings a sense of cohesiveness and structure to student learning and avoids the piecemeal approach that might otherwise unfold. You can learn to articulate lessons within, between, and among unit plans and focus on important elements while not ignoring tangential information of importance. Students remember chunks of information, especially when those chunks are related to specific units.

■ Types of Instructional Units

Although the steps for developing any type of instructional unit are essentially the same, units can be organized in a number of ways, basically differentiated and described as follows.

Conventional unit A conventional unit (known also as a standard unit) consists of a series of lessons centered on a topic, theme, major concept, or block of subject matter. In a standard unit each lesson builds on the previous lesson by contributing additional subject matter, providing further illustrations, and supplying more practice or other added instruction, all of which are aimed at bringing about mastery of the knowledge and skills on which the unit is centered.

Integrated unit When a conventional unit is centered on a theme, such as "transportation," then the unit may be referred to as a **thematic unit.** When, by design, the thematic unit integrates disciplines, such as one that combines the learning of science and mathematics or history/social studies and English/language arts, or all four of the core disciplines, then it is called an **integrated** (or **interdisciplinary**) **thematic unit.**

Self-instructional unit A self-instructional unit (known also as a *modular unit*) is a unit of instruction that is designed for individualized or modularized self-instruction. Such a unit is designed for independent, individual study; because it covers much less content than the units previously described, it can generally be completed in a much shorter time, usually an hour or less. The unit consists of instruction, references, self-check exercises, problems, and all other information and materials that a student needs to independently carry out the unit of work. Consequently, students can work on the units individually at their own speed, and different students can be working on different units at the same time. Students who successfully finish a modular unit can move on to another unit of work without waiting for the other students to catch up. Such units are essential ingredients of continuous-progress (multiage or nongraded) programs. Self-instructional units are useful in courses taught via distance education (see Module 8). And, finally, whether for purposes of remediation, enrichment, or make-up, self-instructional units work especially well when done at and in conjunction with a learning center. (Learning centers are discussed further in Module 6.)

Contract unit A contract unit is an individualized unit of instruction for which a student agrees (contracts) to carry out certain activities. Some contract units have a variable-letter-grade agreement built into them. For example, the contract may contain specified information such as the following:

- For an A grade, you must complete activities 1–5 plus satisfactorily complete six of the optional related activities and receive no less than a B on the posttest.

- For a grade of B, you must complete activities 1–5 plus satisfactorily complete four of the optional related activities and receive a grade of no less than B on the posttest.

- For a grade of C, you must complete activities 1–5, receive at least a C on the posttest, and satisfactorily complete two optional related activities.

- To pass with a D grade, you must complete activities 1–5 and pass the posttest.

Planning and Developing Any Unit of Instruction

For the several types of unit plans—a conventional unit, a contract unit, a self-instructional unit, and an interdisciplinary thematic unit—steps in planning and developing the unit are the same and are described in the following paragraphs.

1. *Select a suitable theme, topic, issue, or problem.* These may be already laid out in your course of study or textbook or already have been agreed to by members of the teaching team. However, many schools change their themes or add new ones from year to year.

2. *Select the goals of the unit and prepare the overview.* The goals are written as an overview or rationale, covering what the unit is about and what the students are to learn. In planning the goals, you should (a) become as familiar as possible with the topic and materials used; (b) consult curriculum documents, such as courses of study, state frameworks, and resource units, for ideas; (c) decide the content and procedures (i.e., what the students should learn about the topic and how); (d) write the rationale or overview, where you summarize what you expect the students will learn about the topic; and (e) be sure your goals are congruent with those of the course or grade-level program.

3. *Select suitable instructional objectives.* In doing this, you should (a) include understandings, skills, attitudes, appreciations, and ideals; (b) be specific, avoiding vagueness and generalizations; (c) write the objectives in performance terms; and (d) be as certain as possible that the objectives will contribute to the major learning described in the overview.

4. *Detail the instructional procedures.* These procedures include the subject content and the learning activities, established as a series of lessons. Proceed with the following steps in your initial planning of the instructional procedures.

   a. By referring to curriculum documents, resource units, and colleagues as resources, gather ideas for learning activities that might be suitable for the unit.

   b. Check the learning activities to make sure that they will actually contribute to the learning designated in your objectives, discarding ideas that do not.

   c. Make sure that the learning activities are feasible. Can you afford the time, effort, or expense? Do you have the necessary materials and equipment? If not, can they be obtained? Are the activities suited to the intellectual and maturity levels of your students?

   d. Check available resources to be certain that they support the content and learning activities.

   e. Decide how to introduce the unit. Provide *introductory activities* that will arouse student interest; inform students of what the unit is about; help you learn about your students— their interests, their abilities, and their experiences and present knowledge of the topic; provide transitions that bridge this topic with that which students have already learned; and involve the students in the planning.

   f. Plan *developmental activities* that will sustain student interest, provide for individual student differences, promote the learning as cited in the specific objectives, and promote a project.

   g. Plan *culminating activities* that will summarize what has been learned, bring together loose ends, apply what has been learned to new situations, provide students with an opportunity to demonstrate their learning, and provide transfer to the unit that follows.

5. *Make lesson plan modifications to meet the needs of all of your students.* When planning your unit and its components, the daily lessons and specific activities, be sure to consider the accommodations you will make for the learners with special needs. Vary instructional strategies and consider students' learning modalities, learning styles, and learning capacities as well as the suggested guidelines discussed in Module 2.

6. *Plan for preassessment and assessment of student learning.* Preassess what students already know or think they know. Assessment of student progress in achievement of the learning objectives (formative evaluation) should permeate the entire unit (that is, as often as possible, assessment should be a daily component of lessons). Plan to gather information in several ways, including informal observations,

checklist observations of student performance and their portfolios, and paper-and-pencil tests. As discussed in Module 9, assessment must be congruent with the instructional objectives.

7. *Provide for the materials and tools of instruction.* The unit cannot function without materials. Therefore, you must plan long before the unit begins for media equipment and materials, references, reading materials, reproduced materials, and community resources. Librarians and media center personnel are usually more than willing to assist in finding appropriate materials to support a unit of instruction.

Unit Format, Inclusive Elements, and Time Duration

Follow the seven steps previously noted to develop any type of unit. In addition, two general points should be made. First, although there is no single best format for a teaching unit, there are minimum inclusions. Particular formats may be best for specific disciplines or grade levels, topics, and types of activities. During your student teaching, your college or university program for teacher preparation and/or your cooperating teacher(s) may have a format that you will be expected to follow. Regardless of the format, the following elements should be evident in any unit plan: (a) identification of grade level, subject, topic, and time duration of the unit; (b) statement of rationale and general goals for the unit; (c) major objectives of the unit; (d) materials and resources needed; (e) lesson plans; (f) assessment strategies; and (g) a statement of how the unit will attend to variations in students' reading levels, experiential and cultural backgrounds, and special needs.

Second, there is no set time duration for a unit plan, although for specific units curriculum guides will recommend certain time spans. Units may extend for a minimum of several days or, as in the case of some interdisciplinary thematic units, for several weeks to an entire school year. However, be aware that when conventional units last more than two or three weeks they tend to lose the character of clearly identifiable units. For any unit of instruction, the exact time duration will be dictated by several factors, including the topic, problem, or theme; the age, interests, and maturity of the students; and the scope of the learning activities.

CURRICULUM INTEGRATION

In recent years, it has become apparent to many teachers that to be most effective in teaching important understandings to the diversity of students in today's classrooms, much of the learning in each discipline can be made more effective and longer lasting when that learning is integrated with the whole curriculum and made meaningful to the lives of the students, rather than when simply taught as an unrelated and separate discipline at the same time each day.

In an exercise Heidi Hayes Jacobs refers to as *curriculum mapping*, middle and high school teachers start the process of designing integrated curriculum by listing out what they each teach in their disciplines in a calendar year. Hayes Jacobs refers to this plan as the road map of their year, with each month corresponding to a signpost on the road map. Instead of having teachers list what they are required, expected, and hope to teach, she has teachers focus on what they actually cover in order to brainstorm opportunities for integrating the curriculum. According to Hayes Jacobs, integrating curriculum is really about integrating teachers. Discipline isolation can be avoided if we teach teachers to look for obvious connections among their content areas. It requires space and time for teachers to plan together. As a result, students become engaged, empowered learners who take responsibility for their learning.[4]

Procedural and Conceptual Knowledge

It is also quite clear that if learning is defined only as being the accumulation of bits and pieces of information, then we already know how that is learned and how to teach it. However, the accumulation of pieces of information (which is called *declarative knowledge*) is at the lowest end of a spectrum of types of learning and leads to what is sometimes referred to as *procedural knowledge* (which is knowing how to do something). For higher levels of thinking and for learning that is most meaningful and longest lasting, that is, knowing when to use declarative and procedural knowledge, referred to as conceptual knowledge, the results of research support the use of (a) a curriculum where disciplines are integrated, and (b) instructional techniques that involve the learners in social interactive learning, such as cooperative learning, peer tutoring, and cross-age teaching.[5]

The Spectrum of Integrated Curriculum

When learning about **integrated curriculum,** it is easy to be confused by the plethora of terms that are used, such as *thematic instruction, multidisciplinary teaching, integrated studies, interdisciplinary curriculum, interdisciplinary thematic instruction*, and *integrated curriculum*. In essence, regardless of which of these terms is being used, the reference is to the same thing.

Before going further, because it is not always easy to tell where curriculum leaves off and instruction begins, let's assume for now that, for the sake of better understanding the meaning of *integrated curriculum*, there is no difference between what is **curriculum** and what is **instruction.** In other words, for the intent of this discussion, there is no relevant difference between the two terms. Whether we use the term *integrated curriculum* or the term *integrated instruction*, we are referring to the same thing.

Definition of Integrated Curriculum

Integrated curriculum (or any of its synonyms mentioned in the preceding discussion) refers to both a way of teaching and a way of planning and organizing the instructional program so that the discrete disciplines of subject matter are related to one another in a design that (a) matches the developmental needs of the learners and (b) helps to connect their learning in ways that are meaningful to their current and past experiences. In that respect, integrated curriculum is the antithesis of traditional, isolated subject matter-oriented teaching and curriculum designations.

Integrated Curricula Past and Present

The reason for the variety of terminology is, in part, because the concept of integrated curriculum is not new. It has had a roller-coaster ride throughout most of the history of education in the United States. Therefore, over time, efforts to integrate student learning have had varying labels.

Without reviewing that history, suffice to say that prior to now, in some form or another, the most recent popularity stems from the late 1950s, with some of the discovery-oriented, student-centered projects supported by the National Science Foundation. Some of these are *Elementary School Science* (ESS), a hands-on and integrated science program for grades K–6; *Man: A Course of Study* (MACOS), a hands-on, anthropology-based program for fifth graders; and *Environmental Studies* (name later changed to *ESSENCE*), an interdisciplinary program for use in all grades, K–12, regardless of subject-matter orientation. The popularity of integrated curriculum also stems from the "middle school movement," which began in the 1960s (discussed in Module 1), and from the "whole-language movement" in language arts, which began in the 1980s.

Current interest in the development and implementation of integrated curriculum and instruction has risen from at least three sources: (a) the success at curriculum integration that has been enjoyed by many schools, (b) the literature-based movement in reading and language arts, and (c) recent research in cognitive science and neuroscience about how children learn.

An integrated curriculum approach may not necessarily be the best approach for every school or the best tactic for every student's learning, nor is it necessarily the manner by which every teacher should or must always plan and teach. As evidenced by practice, the truth of this statement becomes obvious.

Levels of Curriculum Integration

In attempts to connect students' learning with their experiences, efforts fall at various places on a spectrum or continuum, from the least integrated instruction (level 1) to the most integrated (level 5), as illustrated in Figure 5.3.[6]

It is not our intent that this illustration be interpreted as going from worst-case scenario (far left) to best-case scenario (far right), although some experts may interpret it in exactly that way. It is meant solely to illustrate how efforts to integrate fall on a continuum of sophistication and complexity. The paragraphs that follow describe each level of the continuum.

Level 1 Level 1 is the traditional organization of curriculum and classroom instruction, where teachers plan and arrange the subject-specific scope and sequence in the format of topic outlines, much as you did for Exercise 4.5. If there is an attempt to help students connect their learning and their experiences, then it is up to individual classroom teachers to do it. A student who moves during the school day from classroom to classroom, teacher to teacher, subject to subject, from one topic to another, is likely learning in a level 1 instructional environment. A topic in science, for example, might be earthquakes. A related topic in social studies might be the social consequences of natural disasters. These two topics may or may not be studied by a student at the same time.

Least Integrated Level 1	Level 2	Level 3	Level 4	Most Integrated Level 5
Subject-specific topic outline	Subject-specific	Multidisciplinary	Interdisciplinary thematic	Integrated thematic
No student collaboration in planning	Minimal student input	Some student input	Considerable student input in selecting themes and in planning	Maximum student and teacher collaboration
Teacher solo	Solo or teams	Solo or teams	Solo or teams	Solo or teams

Student input into decision making is low.   Student input into Student input into decision making is high.   decision making is very high.

FIGURE 5.3 ● Levels of Curriculum Integration

Level 2 If the same students are learning English/language arts, social studies/history, mathematics, or science through a thematic approach rather than a topic outline, then they are learning at level 2. At this level, themes for one discipline are not necessarily planned and coordinated to correspond to or integrate with themes of another or to be taught simultaneously. The difference between what is a topic and what is a theme is not always clear. For example, earthquakes and social consequences of natural disasters are topics, whereas natural disasters could be the theme or umbrella under which these two topics could fall. At this level, the students may have some input into the decision making involved in planning themes and content.

Level 3 When the same students are learning two or more of their core subjects (English/language arts, social studies/history, mathematics, and science) around a common theme, such as the theme *natural disasters*, from one or more teachers, they are then learning at level 3 integration. At this level, teachers agree on a common theme, then they *separately* deal with that theme in their individual subject areas, usually at the same time during the school year. Therefore, what the student is learning from a teacher in one class is related to and co-ordinated with what the student is concurrently learning in another or several other classes. Some authors may refer to levels 2 or 3 as *coordinated curriculum*. At level 3, students may have some input into the decision making involved in selecting and planning themes and content.

Level 4 When teachers and students do collaborate on a common theme and its content and when discipline boundaries begin to disappear as teachers teach about this common theme, either solo or as an interdisciplinary teaching team (as discussed in Module 1), level 4 integration is achieved.

Level 5 When teachers and their students have collaborated on a common theme and its content, when discipline boundaries are truly blurred during instruction,

and when teachers of several grade levels and/or of various subjects teach toward student understanding of aspects of the common theme, then this is level 5, an integrated thematic approach.

■ Procedure for Planning and Developing an Interdisciplinary Thematic Unit

The seven steps outlined earlier in this module are essential for planning any type of teaching unit, including the interdisciplinary unit, which is made of smaller subject-specific units. The primary responsibility for the development of interdisciplinary thematic units can depend on a single teacher or upon the cooperation of several teachers representing several disciplines. Remember, as discussed in Module 1, this interdisciplinary team may meet daily during a common planning time. Flexible scheduling allows for instructional blocks so that team members can have such common time, and unit lessons likewise can be less constrained by time.

A teaching team may develop from one to four interdisciplinary thematic units a year. Over time, then, a team will have several units that are available for implementation. However, the most effective units are often those that are the most current or the most meaningful to students. This means that ever-changing global, national, and local topics provide a veritable smorgasbord from which to choose, and teaching teams must constantly update old units and develop new and exciting ones.

One teaching team's unit should not conflict with another's at the same or another grade level. If a school has two or more teams at the same grade level that involve the same disciplines, for example, the teams may want to develop units on different themes and share their products. As another example, a ninth-grade team must guard against developing a unit quite similar to one that the students had earlier or will have later at another grade level. Open lines of communication within, between, and among teams and schools are critical to the success of thematic teaching.

Because developing interdisciplinary thematic units is an essential task for many of today's teachers, teacher candidates should learn this process now. One other point needs to be made: An interdisciplinary thematic unit can be prepared and taught by one teacher, but more often it is prepared and taught by a team of teachers. When the latter is the case, the instructional strategy is referred to as *interdisciplinary thematic team teaching*. A thematic unit may be designed by the core curriculum teachers, or a teaching team might consist of fewer than four disciplines, for example, just math and science or English and history or an academic discipline and a vocational class or some other combination of subjects. Here are a few recent examples:

- *Elk Grove High School (Elk Grove, CA).* Teachers of English and history work together with all second-semester sophomore students on a project with an Elizabethan theme as the central focus.

- *Manatee High School (Bradenton, FL).* Students from mathematics and vocational business studies worked together on a backyard swimming pool project; students from a computer-assisted drafting class and an honors geometry class actually designed and built a nine-hole miniature golf course; and students from marketing classes and foreign language classes worked together to examine international laws and customs.

- *North Penn High School (Lansdale, PA).* Students in child development, mathematics, and manufacturing classes combined their efforts to design and produce equipment for the school's child development program playground, including a 40-foot-long simulated train consisting of a locomotive and four cars. All students submitted papers for their English classes about the project.

- *Tolsia High School (Fort Gay, WV).* Students from English and vocational classes worked together at designing and building a scale-model medieval town complete with castles.

- *Waialua High School (Waialua, HI).* Students from applied technology, mathematics, art, and English classes combine knowledge and skills to build and race electric cars and make presentations on the construction and design of their cars.

The following steps are used to develop an interdisciplinary thematic unit.

1. *Agree on the nature or source of the unit.* Team members should view the interdisciplinary approach as a collective effort in which all members (and other faculty) can participate if appropriate. Write what you want the students to receive from interdisciplinary instruction. Troubleshoot possible stumbling blocks.

2. *Discuss subject-specific frameworks, goals, and objectives; curriculum guidelines; textbooks and supplemental materials; and units already in place for the school year.* Focus on what you must teach, and explain the scope and sequence of the teaching so all team members understand the constraints and limitations.

3. *Choose a topic and develop a timeline.* From the information provided by each subject-specialist teacher in step 2, start listing possible topics that can be drawn from within the existing course outlines. Give-and-take is essential here, as some topics will fit certain subjects better than others. The chief goal is to find a topic that can be adapted to each subject without detracting from the educational plan already in place. This may require choosing and merging content from two or more other units previously planned. The theme is then drawn from the topic. When considering a theme, you should ask these questions:

   a. Is the theme within the realm of understanding and experience of the teacher involved?

   b. Will the theme interest all members of the team?

   c. Do we have sufficient materials and resources to supply information we might need?

   d. Does the theme lend itself to active learning experiences?

   e. Can this theme lead to a unit that is of the proper duration, not too short and not too long?

   f. Is the theme helpful, worthwhile, and pertinent to the course objectives?

   g. Will the theme be of interest to students, and will it motivate them to do their best?

   h. Is the theme novel enough so that teachers can share in the excitement of the learning?

4. *Establish two timelines.* The first is for the team only and is to ensure that the deadlines for specific work required in developing the unit will be met by each member. The second timeline is for both students and teachers and shows how long the unit will be, when it will start, and in which classes it will be taught.

5. *Develop the scope and sequence for content and instruction.* To develop the unit, follow the six steps for planning and developing a unit of instruction outlined earlier in this module. This should be done by each team member as well as by the group during common planning time so members can coordinate dates and activities in logical sequence and depth. This is an organic process and will generate both ideas and anxiety. Under the guidance of the team leader, members should strive to keep this anxiety at a level conducive to learning, experimenting, and arriving at group consensus.

6. *Share goals and objectives.* Each team member should have a copy of the goals and objectives of every other team member. This helps to refine the unit and lesson plans and to prevent unnecessary overlap and confusion.

7. *Give the unit a name.* The unit has been fashioned and is held together by the theme you have chosen. Giving the theme a name and using that name tells the students that this unit of study is integrated, important, and meaningful to both school and life.

8. *Share subject-specific units, lesson plans, and printed and nonprinted materials.* Exchange the finalized unit to obtain one another's comments and suggestions. Keep a copy of each teacher's unit(s) as a resource, and see if you could present a lesson using it as your basis (some modification may be necessary).

9. *Field test the unit.* Beginning at the scheduled time and date, present the lessons. Team members may trade classes from time to time. Team teaching may take place when two or more classes can be combined for instruction (if a classroom space large enough is available), such as is possible with block scheduling.

10. *Evaluate and perhaps adjust and revise the unit.* Team members should discuss their successes and failures during their common planning time and determine what needs to be changed and how and when that should be done to make the unit successful. Adjustments can be made along the way (formative assessments), and revisions for future use can be made after the unit (summative assessment).

The preceding steps are not absolutes and should be viewed only as guides. Differing teaching teams and levels of teacher experience and knowledge make the strict adherence to any plan less productive than the use of group-generated plans. For instance, some teachers have found that the last point under step 3 could state exactly the opposite; they recommend that the topic for an interdisciplinary unit should be one that a teacher or a teaching team already knows well. In practice, the process that works well—one that results in meaningful learning for the students and in their positive feelings about themselves, about learning, and about school—is the appropriate process.

Now do Exercises 5.3 and 5.4.

EXERCISE 5.3

■ Generating Ideas for Interdisciplinary Units

Instructions: The purpose of this exercise is to use brainstorming to generate a list of potential topics suitable as interdisciplinary units. Divide your class into groups of three to five. Each group is to decide the grade or age level for which their ideas will be generated. If the group chooses, cooperative learning can be used; group members are then assigned roles such as facilitator, recorder, reporter, monitor of thinking processes, on-task monitor, and so on. Each group is to generate as many topics as possible. One member of each group should record all ideas. Reserve discussion of ideas until no further topics are generated. Lists can be shared with the entire class.

Grade-level interest of the group:

1. Existing subject-area content units (as the group knows them to be or as they are predicted to exist):

2. Current topics of
    a. Global interest:
    b. National interest:
    c. Statewide interest:
    d. Local interest:
    e. Interest to the school:
    f. Interest to students of this age:

 To access this exercise online, go to the Companion Website at **www.prenhall.com/kellough.**

EXERCISE **5.4**

Instructions: The purpose of this exercise is to practice weaving interdisciplinary themes into our curricula. In groups of three or four, choose one idea that was generated during Exercise 5.3 and derive a list of suggestions about how that theme could be woven into the curricula of various classes, programs, and activities, as indicated below. It is possible that not all areas listed are relevant to the grade level to which your group is addressing its work. Cooperative learning can be used, with appropriate roles assigned to group members. One person in the group should be the recorder. Upon completion, share your group's work (the process and product of which will be much like that of an actual interdisciplinary teaching team) with the class. Copies should be made available to those who want them.

Unit theme:

1. In core classes
    a. English:

    b. Social studies:

    c. Mathematics:

    d. Science:

    e. Reading:

    f. Physical education:

    g. Art:

    h. Music:

2. In cocurricular programs and activities
    a. Electives:

    b. Clubs:

    c. School functions:

    d. Assemblies:

    e. Intramurals:

    f. Study skills:

3. In exploratories:

4. In homerooms:

5. Explain how multicultural components could be incorporated into the unit.

6. As individuals and as a group, how productive was this exercise?

 To access this exercise online, go to the Companion Website at **www.prenhall.com/kellough.**

■ LESSON PLANNING: RATIONALE AND ASSUMPTIONS

As described at the beginning of this module, step 5 of the seven steps of instructional planning is the preparation for class meetings. The process of designing a lesson is important in learning to provide the most efficient use of valuable and limited instructional time and the most effective learning for the students to meet the unit goals.

Notice the title of this section does not refer to the "*daily* lesson plan," but rather to the "lesson plan." The focus is on how to prepare a lesson plan, which may or may not be a daily plan. In some instances, a lesson plan may extend for more than one class period or days, perhaps two or three. In other instances, the lesson plan is in fact a daily plan and may run for an entire class period. In block scheduling, one lesson plan may run for part of, or for an entire 2-hour block of, time. See the section The Problem of Time later in this module.

Effective teachers are always planning for their classes. For the long range, they plan the scope and sequence and develop content. Within this long-range planning, they develop units, and within units they design the activities to be used and the assessments of learning to be done. They familiarize themselves with books, materials, media, and innovations in their fields of interest. Yet, despite all this planning activity, the lesson plan remains pivotal to the planning process. Consider now the rationale, description, and guidelines for writing detailed lesson plans.

■ Rationale for Preparing Written Lesson Plans

Carefully prepared and written lesson plans show everyone— first and foremost your students, then your colleagues, your administrator, and, if you are a student teacher, your college or university supervisor—that you are a committed professional. Sometimes, beginning teachers are concerned with being seen by their students using a written plan in class, thinking it may suggest that the teacher has not mastered the material. On the contrary, a lesson plan is tangible evidence that you are working at your job and demonstrates respect for the students, yourself, and the profession. A written lesson plan shows that preactive thinking and planning have taken place. There is absolutely no excuse for appearing before a class without evidence of being prepared.

Written and detailed lesson plans provide an important sense of security, which is especially useful to a beginning teacher. Like a rudder of a ship, it helps keep you on course. Without it, you are likely to drift aimlessly. Sometimes a disturbance in the classroom can distract from the lesson, causing the teacher to forget an important part of the lesson. A written and detailed lesson plan provides a road map to guide you and help keep you on track.

Written lesson plans help you to be or become a reflective decision maker. Without a written plan, it is difficult or impossible to analyze how something might have been planned or implemented differently after the lesson has been taught. Written lesson plans serve as resources for the next time you teach the same or a similar lesson and are useful for teacher self-evaluation as well as the evaluation of student learning and of the curriculum.

Written lesson plans help you organize material and search for loopholes, loose ends, or incomplete content. Careful and thorough planning during the preactive phase of instruction includes anticipation of how the lesson activities will develop as the lesson is being taught. During this anticipation you will actually visualize yourself in the classroom teaching your students, using that visualization to anticipate possible problems.

Written plans provide evidence for administrators that specific content was taught. This is especially important in states where teachers are judged on how well their students perform on standardized tests.

Written plans help other members of the teaching team understand what you are doing and how you are doing it. This is especially important when implementing an interdisciplinary thematic unit. *Written lesson plans also provide substitute teachers with a guide to follow if you are absent.*

The preceding reasons clearly express the need to write detailed lesson plans. The list is not exhaustive, however, and you may discover additional reasons why written lesson plans are crucial to effective teaching. In summary, two points must be made: (a) lesson planning is an important and ongoing process; and (b) teachers must take time to plan, reflect, write, test, evaluate, and rewrite their plans to reach optimal performance.

■ Assumptions About Lesson Planning

Not all teachers need elaborate written plans for every lesson. Sometimes effective and skilled veteran teachers need only a sketchy outline. Sometimes they may not need written plans at all. Veteran teachers who have taught the topic many times in the past may need only the presence of a class of students to stimulate a pattern of presentation that has often been successful (though frequent use of old patterns may lead one into the rut of unimaginative and uninspiring teaching).

Considering the diversity among middle school and secondary school teachers, their instructional styles, their students, and what research studies indicate, certain assumptions about lesson planning can be made.

1. Although not all teachers need elaborate written plans for all lessons, all effective teachers do have clearly defined goals and objectives in mind and a planned pattern of instruction for every lesson, whether that plan is written out or not.

2. Beginning teachers need to prepare detailed written lesson plans. Failing to prepare is preparing to fail.

3. Some subject-matter fields, topics, or learning activities require more detailed planning than others.

4. The depth of knowledge a teacher has about a subject or topic influences the amount of planning necessary for the lessons.

5. The skill a teacher has in remaining calm and in following a trend of thought in the presence of distraction will influence the amount of detail necessary when planning activities and writing the lesson plan.

6. A plan is more likely to be carefully and thoughtfully plotted when it is written out.

7. The diversity of students within today's public school classroom necessitates careful and thoughtful consideration about individualizing the instruction; these considerations are best implemented when they have been thoughtfully written into lesson plans.

8. There is no particular pattern or format that all teachers need to follow when writing out plans. Some teacher-preparation programs have agreed on certain lesson-plan formats for their teacher candidates; you need to know if this is the case for your program.

In summary, well-written lesson plans provide many advantages. They give a teacher an agenda or outline to follow in teaching a lesson, they give a substitute teacher a basis for presenting appropriate lessons to a class—thereby retaining lesson continuity in the regular teacher's absence—and they are certainly very useful when a teacher is planning to use the same lesson again in the future. Lesson plans provide the teacher with something to fall back on in case of a memory lapse, an interruption, or some distraction such as a call from the office or a fire drill. In addition, using a written plan demonstrates to students that you care and are working for them. Above all, lesson plans provide beginning teachers security because, with a carefully prepared plan, a beginner can walk into a classroom with confidence and professional pride gained from having developed a sensible framework for that day's instruction.

Thus, as a beginning teacher, you should make considerably detailed lesson plans. Naturally, this will require a great deal of work for at least the first year or two, but the reward of knowing that you have prepared and presented effective lessons will compensate for that effort.

■ A Continual Process

Lesson planning is a continual process even for experienced teachers, for there is always a need to keep materials and plans current and relevant. Because no two classes of students are ever identical, today's lesson plan will need to be tailored to the peculiar needs of each classroom of students. Moreover, because the content of instruction and learning will change as each distinct group of students with their own needs and interests give input, new thematic units are developed, new developments occur, or new theories are introduced, your objectives and the objectives of the students, school, and teaching faculty will change.

For these reasons, lesson plans should be in a constant state of revision. Once the basic framework is developed, however, the task of updating and modifying becomes minimal. If your plans are maintained on a computer, making changes from time to time is even easier.

■ Well Planned but Open to Last-Minute Change

The lesson plan should provide a tentative outline of the time period given for the lesson but should always remain flexible. A carefully worked out plan may have to be set aside because of the unpredictable, serendipitous effect of a "teachable moment" (see the following vignette) or because of unforeseen circumstances, such as a delayed school bus, an impromptu school assembly program, an emergency drill, or the cancellation of school due to inclement weather conditions. Student teachers often are appalled at the frequency of interruptions during a school day and of disruptions to their lesson planning that occur. A daily lesson planned to cover six aspects of a given topic may end with only three of the points having been considered. Although far more frequent than necessary in too many schools, these occurrences are natural in a school setting and the teacher and the plans must be flexible enough to accommodate this reality.

Although you may have your lesson plans completed for several consecutive lessons, as can be inferred by the

---

CLASSROOM VIGNETTE
A Teachable Moment

Casey was teaching an eighth-grade humanities block, a two-hour block course that integrates student learning in social studies, reading, and language arts. On this particular day while Casey and her students were discussing the topic of Manifest Destiny, a student raised his hand and, when acknowledged by Casey, asked, "Why aren't we [the United States] still adding states? [that is, taking more territory into the United States]". Casey immediately replied with "There aren't any more states to add." By responding too quickly, Casey missed one of those "teachable moments," moments when the teacher has the students thinking and asking questions. What could Casey have done? When was Hawaii added as a state? Why hasn't Puerto Rico become a state? Guam? and so forth. Aren't those possibilities? Why *aren't* more states or territories being added? What are the political and social ramifications today and how do they differ from those of the 1800s?

LESSON PLAN

Descriptive Course Data

Instructor: Michelle Yendrey   *Course:* Western Civilizations   *Period:* 1

Grade level: 9   *Unit:* History of Religion   *Topic:* Persecution of Christians

Objectives

Upon completion of this lesson students will be able to:

1. make connections between persecutions today and persecutions that occurred approximately 2000 years ago.
2. describe the main teachings of Christianity and how the position of Christianity within the Roman Empire changed over time.
3. share ideas in a positive and productive manner.

Instructional Components

Activity 1 (Anticipatory Set: 10 minutes). Write on overhead: You have until 8:40 (5 minutes) to write a defense to one of the following statements. (Remember, there are no right or wrong answers. Support your position to the best of your ability.)

- The recent hate crimes in our city can be related to our current unit on the history of religion.
- The recent hate crimes in our city cannot be related to our current unit on the history of religion.

Activity 2 (3–5 minutes). Students will be asked, by a show of hands, how many chose statement A and how many chose statement B. Some reasons for each will be shared orally and then all papers collected.

Activity 3 (3–5 minutes). Return papers of previous assignment. Give students new seat assignments for the activity that follows, and have them assume their new seats.

Activity 4 (15 minutes). The students are now arranged into seven groups. Each group will write a paragraph using the concepts from certain assigned words (for their definition sheets of Section 3 of Chapter 7, "Christianity spread through the empire") to answer the essay question(s) at the end of the definition sheet.

Each group will select a:

task master to keep members of the group on-task.

recorder to write things down.

spokesperson to present the results.

timekeeper to keep the group alert so task is completed on time.

In addition, some groups will have a

source master to look up or ask about any questions that arise.

Activity 5 (15–20 minutes). Each group's spokesperson will come to the front of the classroom and present the group's result for Activity 4.

Alternate Activity (Plan B: 5–10 minutes). Should the activities run more quickly than anticipated, the students will take out their "Religion Comparison Sheets." Using Chapter 2, Section 2, "Jews worshipped a single God," and Chapter 7, Section 3 definition sheets, with the teacher's direction, the students will fill in the boxes for "similar" and "different" with regard to Christianity and Judaism.

Second Alternate Activity (Plan C: 25–30 minutes). In the unlikely event that timing is really off, each student will be given a blank grid and assigned 10 vocabulary words from the definition sheets. Students will be directed to create a crossword puzzle using the definitions as clues and the words as answers. After 15–20 minutes, the crosswords will be collected and distributed to different students to solve. If not completed in class, students will finish and hand them in later along with their essays, for a few points of extra credit. Students will be required to write their names in the appropriate spaces marked "Created By" and "Solved By."

Activity 6 (7–10 minutes). Collect the overhead sheets and pens. Hand out the take-home essay test. Explain and take questions about exactly what is expected from the essay. (This is their first take-home test.)

Materials and Equipment Needed

Overhead projector and transparency sheets (7) and transparency markers (7); 36 copies of the essay question plus directions; 36 copies of the blank grid sheets.

Assessment, Reflection, and Plans for Revision

FIGURE 5.4 ● Lesson Plan Sample with Alternative Activities

SOURCE: Courtesy of Michelle Yendrey

DAILY LESSON PLAN BOOK

Grade _____   Lesson _____   Teacher _____

Date	Content	Materials	Procedure	Evaluation
Monday				
Tuesday				
Wednesday				
Thursday				
Friday				

FIGURE 5.5 ● Daily Lesson Plan Book

vignette involving Casey and her students, what actually transpires during the implementation of today's lesson may necessitate late adjustments to the lesson you have planned for tomorrow.

The Problem of Time

A lesson plan should provide enough materials and activities to consume the entire class period or time allotted. As mentioned earlier, it should be well understood that, in your planning for teaching, you need to plan for every minute of every class period. The lesson plan, then, is more than a plan for a lesson to be taught; it is a plan that accounts for the entire class period or time that you and your students are together in the classroom. Because planning is a skill that takes years of experience to master, especially when teaching a block of time that may extend for 90 or more minutes and that involves more than one discipline and perhaps more than one teacher, as a beginning teacher you should overplan rather than run the risk of having too few activities to occupy the time the students are in your classroom. One way of ensuring that you overplan is to include "if time remains" activities in your lesson plan (see Figure 5.4).

When a lesson plan does not provide sufficient activity to occupy the entire class period or time that the students are available for the lesson, a beginning teacher often loses control of the class as behavior problems mount. Thus, it is best to prepare more than you likely can accomplish in a given period of time. This is not to imply that you should involve the students in meaningless busy work. Students can be very perceptive when it comes to a teacher who has finished the plan and is attempting to bluff through the minutes that remain before dismissal.

If you ever do get caught short—as most teachers do at one time or another—one way to avoid embarrassment is to have students work on what is referred to as an *anchor assignment* (or transitional activity). This is an ongoing assignment, and students understand that whenever they have spare time in class they should be working on it. Example anchor activities include a re-

view of material that has been covered that day or in the past several days, allowing students to work on homework, journal writing, portfolio organization, and long-term project work. Regardless of how you handle time remaining, it works best when you plan for it and write that aspect into your lesson plan and when the procedures for doing it are well understood by the students.

A Caution About "The Daily Planning Book"

A distinction needs to be made between actual lesson plans and the book for daily planning that many schools require teachers to maintain and even submit to their supervisors a week in advance. Items that a teacher writes in the boxes in a daily planning book (see Figure 5.5) most assuredly are not lesson plans; rather, the pages are a layout by which the teacher writes into the boxes to show what lessons will be taught during the day, week, month, or term. Usually the book provides only a small lined box for time periods for each day of the week. These books are useful for outlining the topics, activities, and assignments projected for the week or term, and supervisors sometimes use them to check the adequacy of teachers' course plans. However, they are too sketchy to be called lesson plans.

CONSTRUCTING A LESSON PLAN: FORMAT, COMPONENTS, AND SAMPLES

Although it is true that each teacher develops a personal system of lesson planning—the system that works best for that teacher in her or his unique situation—a beginning teacher needs a more substantial framework from which to work. For that, this section provides a *preferred* lesson plan format (Figure 5.6). Review the preferred format and samples, and unless your program of teacher preparation insists otherwise, use it with your own modifications until you find or develop a better model.

LESSON PLAN

1. Descriptive Data

Teacher _____ Class _____ Date _____ Grade level _____

Room number _____ Period _____ Unit _____

Lesson number _____ and Topic _____

2. Goals and Objectives

Instructional Goals:

Specific Objectives:

   Cognitive:

   Affective:

   Psychomotor:

3. Rationale

4. Procedure (Procedure with time plan, modeling examples, transitions, guided practice experiences, etc.)

Content:

_____ minutes. Activity 1 (set introduction):

_____ minutes. Activity 2:

_____ minutes. Activity 3 (the exact number of activities in the procedures will vary):

_____ minutes. Final Activity (lesson conclusion or closure):

If time remains:

FIGURE 5.6 ● Preferred Lesson Plan Format with Nine Components

SOURCE: Adapted from Linfield College Education Depatment Lesson Plan

(continued)

5. Assignments and Reminders of Assignments

Special notes and reminders to myself:

6. Materials and Equipment Needed

Audiovisual:

Other:

7. Accommodations for Students with Special Needs. (Specifically describe what you plan to do to ensure the success of each and every one of your students who is identified as having special needs.)

8. Assessment of Student Learning

Assessment of student learning tied directly to instructional objectives.

9. Reflection Evaluation (Discuss the relative success or failure of your lesson)

Reflective thoughts about lesson:

Suggestions for revision:

FIGURE 5.6 *continued* ● Preferred Lesson Plan Format with Nine Components
SOURCE: Adapted from Linfield College Education Department Lesson Plan

■ For Guidance, Reflection, and Reference

While student teaching and during your first few years as a beginning teacher, your lesson plans should be printed from a computer, or, if that isn't possible, then written out in an intelligible style. If you have a spelling problem, then we suggest that you use a spell check and print your plans from the computer. There is good reason to question teachers who say they have no need for a written plan because they have their lessons planned in their heads. The hours and periods in a school day range from several to many, as are the numbers of students in each class. When multiplied by the number of school days in a week, a semester, or a year, the task of keeping so many things in one's head becomes mind-boggling. Few persons could effectively do that. Until you have considerable experience behind you, you will need to prepare and maintain detailed lesson plans for guidance, reflection, and reference.

■ BASIC ELEMENTS OF A LESSON PLAN

A written lesson plan should contain the following basic elements: (a) descriptive data, (b) goals and objectives, (c) rationale, (d) procedure, (e) assignments and assignment reminders, (f) materials and equipment, (g) accommodations for students with special needs, (h) a section for assessment of student learning, and (i) reflection on the lesson, and ideas for lesson revision. These nine components need not be present in every written lesson plan, nor must they be presented in any particular order. They are neither inclusive nor exclusive; therefore, you might choose to include additional components or subsections.

Several sample lesson plans are included in this module so you can examine a variety of styles. Contributions are from seasoned professionals, teacher educators, and student teachers. Figure 5.6 illustrates a format that includes several of the previously mentioned components and sample subsections of those components. Additionally, Figure 5.7 illustrates a unit plan for a science class

UNIT PLAN SAMPLE WITH A DAILY LESSON

Course *Science*

Teacher _____ **Duration of Unit** *Ten days*

Unit Title What's the Matter? **Grade Level** *Grades 7–12*

Purpose of the Unit

This unit is designed to develop students' understanding of the concept of matter. At the completion of the unit, students should have a clearer understanding of matter and its properties, of the basic units of matter, and of the source of matter.

Rationale of the Unit

This unit topic is important for building a foundation of knowledge for subsequent courses in science. This can increase students' chances of success in those courses and thereby improve their self-confidence and self-esteem. A basic understanding of matter and its properties is important because of daily decisions that affect the manipulation of matter. It is more likely that students will make correct and safe decisions when they understand what matter is, how it changes form, and how its properties determine its use.

Goals of the Unit

The goals of this unit are for students to

1. Understand that all matter is made of atoms.
2. Understand that matter stays constant and that it is neither created nor destroyed.
3. Develop certain basic physical science laboratory skills.
4. Develop a positive attitude about physical science.
5. Look forward to taking other science courses.
6. Understand how science is relevant to their daily lives.

Instructional Objectives of the Unit

Upon completion of this unit of study, students should be able to

1. List at least 10 examples of matter.
2. List the four states of matter, with one example of each.
3. Calculate the density of an object when given its mass and volume.
4. Describe the properties of solids, liquids, and gases.
5. Demonstrate an understanding that matter is made of elements and that elements are made of atoms.
6. Identify and explain one way that knowledge of matter is important to their daily lives.
7. Demonstrate increased self-confidence in pursuing laboratory investigations in physical science.
8. Demonstrate skill in communicating within the cooperative learning group.
9. Demonstrate skill in working with the triple-beam balance.

Unit Overview

Throughout this unit, students will be developing a concept map of matter. Information for the map will be derived from laboratory work, class discussions, lectures, student readings, and research. The overall instructional model is that of concept attainment. Important to this is an assessment of students' concepts about matter at the beginning of the unit. The preassessment and the continuing assessment of their concepts will center on the following:

1. What is matter and what are its properties? Students will develop the concept of matter by discovering the properties that all matter contains (that is, it has mass and takes up space).
2. Students will continue to build upon their understanding of the concept of matter by organizing matter into its four major states (that is, solid, liquid, gas, plasma). The concept development will be used to define the attributes of each state of matter, and students will gather information by participating in laboratory activities and class discussions:
3. What are some of the physical properties of matter that make certain kinds of matter unique? Students will experiment with properties of matter such as elasticity, brittleness, and density. Laboratory activities will allow students to contribute their observations and information to the further development of their concept of matter. Density activities enable students to practice their lab and math skills.
4. What are the basic units of matter, and where did matter come from? Students will continue to develop their concept of matter by working on this understanding of mixtures, compounds, elements, and atoms.

FIGURE 5.7 ● Sample of a Unit Plan with One Daily Lesson for Lab Science

SOURCE: Courtesy of Will Hightower

(continued)

Assessment of Student Achievement

For this unit, assessment of student achievement will be both formative and summative. Formative evaluation will be done daily by checklists of student behavior, knowledge, and skills. Summative evaluation will be based on the following criteria:

1. Student participation as evidenced by completion of daily homework, class work, laboratory activities, and class discussions, and by the information on the student behavior checklists.
2. Weekly quizzes on content.
3. Unit test.

....

Lesson Number _____   **Duration of Lesson** _1–2 hours_ _____

Unit Title _What's the Matter?_ _____   **Teacher** _____

Lesson Title _Mission Impossible_ _____   **Lesson Topic** _Density of Solids_ _____

Objectives of the Lesson

Upon completion of this lesson, the students should be able to

1. Determine the density of a solid cube.
2. Based on data gathered in class, develop their own definition of density.
3. Prepare and interpret graphs of data.
4. Communicate the results of their experiments to others in the class.

Materials Needed

1. Two large boxes of cereal and two snack-size boxes of the same cereal.
2. Four brownies (two whole and two cut in halves).
3. Four sandboxes (two large plastic boxes and two small boxes, each filled with sand).
4. Two triple-beam balances.
5. Several rulers.
6. Six handheld calculators.
7. Eighteen colored pencils (six sets with three different colors per set).
8. Copies of lab instructions (one copy for each student).

Instructional Procedure with Approximate Timeline

ANTICIPATORY SET (10–15 MINUTES)

Begin class by brainstorming to find what students already know about density. Place the word on the board or overhead, and ask students if they have heard of it. Write down their definitions and examples. Hold up a large box of cereal in one hand and the snack-size box in the other. Ask students which is more dense. Allow them time to explain their responses. Then tell them that by the end of this lesson they will know the answer to the question and that they will develop their own definition of density.

LABORATORY INVESTIGATION (30–60 MINUTES)

Students are divided into teams of four students of mixed abilities. Each member has a role:

1. *Measure master:* In charge of the group's ruler and ruler measurements.
2. *Mass master:* In charge of the group's weighings.
3. *Engineer:* In charge of the group's calculator and calculations.
4. *Graph master:* In charge of plotting the group's data on the graph paper.

Each team has 8 minutes before switching stations. Each team completes three stations and then meets to make their graphs and to discuss results.

Station 1: Cereal Box Density. Students calculate the density of a large and a small box of cereal to determine if a larger and heavier object is more dense. The masses versus the volumes of the two boxes are plotted on graph paper using one of the pencil colors.

FIGURE 5.7 *continued* ● Sample of a Unit Plan with One Daily Lesson for Lab Science

SOURCE: Courtesy of Will Hightower

(continued)

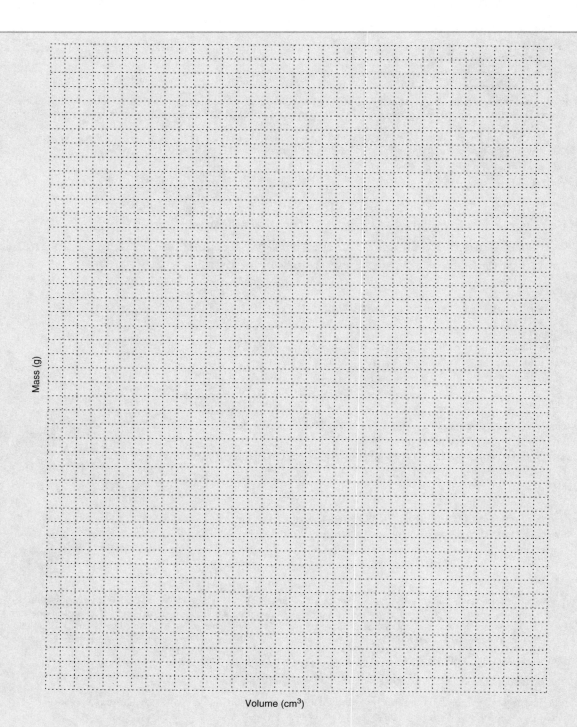

Instructions

1. The density of any object is determined by dividing its mass by its volume. Density in grams is divided by volume in cubic centimeters. Example: 20 g/10 cm^3 = 2 g/cm^3.

2. Measure the volume of the small cereal box (length × width × height), and use the balance to determine its mass in grams. The engineer can do the calculations on the calculator. The graph master should graph the results of each trial and connect two points with a straight line.

3. Repeat the procedure using the large box of cereal.

4. The engineer computes the density of both cereal boxes with the calculator and records the results on the proper blank below the graph.

FIGURE 5.7 *continued* ● Sample of a Unit Plan with One Daily Lesson for Lab Science

SOURCE: Courtesy of Will Hightower

(continued)

a. Density of large box of cereal _____

b. Density of small box of cereal _____

c. Density of large brownie _____

d. Density of small brownie _____

e. Density of large sandbox _____

f. Density of small sandbox _____

Station 2: Brownie Density. Students calculate the density of a full-size brownie and a half-size brownie. Results are plotted on the same graph as in Station 1, but with the second color.

Instructions

1. The density of any object is determined by dividing its mass by its volume. Density in grams is divided by volume in cubic centimeters. Example: 20 g/10 cm^3 = 2 g/cm^3.
2. Measure the volume of a small brownie (length × width × height), and use the balance to determine its mass in grams. The engineer can do the calculations on the calculator. The graph master should graph the results of each trial and connect two points with a straight line.
3. Repeat the procedure using the large brownie.
4. The engineer computes the density of both brownies and records the result on the proper blank.

Station 3: Sandbox Density. Students calculate the density of a large and a small box filled with sand. Results are plotted on the graph, but with the third color.

Instructions

1. The density of any object is determined by dividing its mass by its volume. Density in grams is divided by volume in cubic centimeters. Example: 20 g/10 cm^3 = 2 g/cm^3.
2. Measure the volume of the small sandbox (length × width × height), and use the balance to determine its mass in grams. The engineer can do the calculations on the calculator. The graph master should graph the results of each trial and connect two points with a straight line.
3. Repeat the procedure using the large sandbox.
4. The engineer computes the density of both boxes and records the results on the proper blank.

Lab Worksheet. Teams return to their seats to do the graphing, analyze the results, and answer the following questions from their lab sheets:

1. Is a larger, heavier object more dense than its smaller counterpart? Explain your evidence.
2. What is your definition of density?
3. Which is more dense, a pound of feathers or a pound of gold? Explain your answer.

LESSON CLOSURE (10 MINUTES OR MORE)
When all teams are finished, teams should display their graphs, and share and discuss the results.

Concepts

1. Density is one of the properties of matter.
2. Mass and volume are related.
3. Density is determined by dividing mass by volume.

Extension Activities

1. Use a density graph to calculate the mass and volume of a smaller brownie.
2. Explore the story of Archimedes and the king's crown.

Evaluation, Reflection, and Revision of Lesson

Upon completion of this lesson and of the unit, revision in this lesson may be made on the basis of teacher observations and student achievement.

FIGURE 5.7 *continued* ● Sample of a Unit Plan with One Daily Lesson for Lab Science

SOURCE: Courtesy of Will Hightower

with a sample one-day lesson plan for an investigatory activity. Figure 5.8 displays a mathematics lesson from a student teacher's unit plan on Algebra Tiles that incorporates many of the developmentally appropriate learning activities discussed in this book. Figures 5.9 and 5.10 are also examples from student teachers' unit plans in U.S. history and language arts, respectively. Figure 5.11 is an exemplary interdisciplinary lesson integrating the use of a variety of technologies. Following are descriptions of the major components of the preferred format. Look for examples of each of the components described in the various lesson plans included here. How do they compare?

■ Descriptive Data

A lesson plan's descriptive data include demographic and logistical information that identifies details about the class. Anyone reading this information should be able to identify when and where the class meets, who is teaching it, and what is being taught. Although as the teacher you know this information, someone else may not. Members of the teaching team, administrators, and substitute teachers (and, if you are the student teacher, your university supervisor and cooperating teacher) appreciate this information. Most teachers discover which items of descriptive data are most beneficial in their situation and develop their own identifiers. Remember this: The mark of a well-prepared, clearly written lesson plan is the ease with which someone else (such as another member of your teaching team or a substitute teacher) could implement it. The descriptive data include:

1. Name of course or class. These serve as headings for the plan and facilitate orderly filing of plans.
2. Name of the unit. Inclusion of this facilitates the orderly control of the hundreds of lesson plans a teacher constructs.
3. Topic to be considered within the unit. This is also useful for control and identification.

■ Goals and Objectives

The goals are general statements of intended accomplishments from that lesson. Teachers and students need to know what the lesson is designed to accomplish. In clear, understandable language, the general goal statement provides that information. Because the goals are also included in the unit plan, sometimes a teacher may include only the objectives in the daily lesson plan. The instructional objectives state what you want your students to be able to do as a result of the experiences that you provide.

Setting the learning objectives A crucial step in the development of any lesson plan is setting the objectives. It is at this point that many lessons go wrong and where many beginning teachers have problems.

A common error and how to avoid it. Teachers sometimes confuse *learning activity* (*how* the students will

learn it) with the *learning objective* (*what* the student will learn as a result of the learning activity). For example, teachers sometimes mistakenly list what they intend to do—such as "lecture on photosynthesis" or "lead a discussion on the causes of the Civil War"—and fail to focus on just what the learning objectives in these activities truly are—that is, what the students will be able to do (performance) as a result of the instructional activity. Or, rather than specifying what the student will be able to do as a result of the learning activities, the teacher mistakenly writes what the students will do in class (the learning activity)—such as, "In pairs the students will do the 10 problems on page 72"—as if that were the learning objective.

When you approach this step in your lesson planning, to avoid error ask yourself, "What should students learn *as a result* of the activities of this lesson?" Your answer to that question is your objective! Objectives of the lesson are included as specific statements of performance expectations, detailing precisely what students will be able to do as a result of the instructional activities.

No need to include all domains and hierarchies in every lesson Not all three domains (cognitive, affective, and psychomotor) are necessarily represented in every lesson plan. As a matter of fact, any given lesson plan may be directed to only one or two, or a few, specific objectives. Over the course of a unit of instruction, however, all domains, and most if not all levels within each, should be addressed.

■ Rationale

The rationale is an explanation of why the lesson is important and why the instructional methods chosen will achieve the objectives. Parents, students, teachers, administrators, and others have the right to know why specific content is being taught and why the methods employed are being used. Prepare yourself well by setting a goal for yourself of always being prepared with intelligent answers to those two questions. Teachers become reflective decision makers when they challenge themselves to think about *what* (the content) they are teaching, *how* (the learning activities) they are teaching it, and *why* (the rationale) it must be taught.

■ Procedure

The **procedure** consists of the instructional activities for a scheduled period of time. The substance of the lesson—the information to be presented, obtained, and learned—is the content. Appropriate information is selected to meet the learning objectives, the level of competence of the students, and the grade level or course requirements. To be sure your lesson actually covers what it should, you should write down exactly what minimum content you intend to cover. This material may be placed in a separate

LINFIELD COLLEGE

Education Department

Student ID Number:	Time/Period: 11:06–12:16/3rd	Date: March 18, 2004
Lesson/Unit Title: Algebra Tiles Activity	Subject: Algebra 1C	Grade Level: 10–12

Instructional Objectives:

(State what you want your students to be able to do as a result of the experiences that you provide. These objectives should represent a variety of cognitive levels, and each one should be tied to one or more specific instructional strategies and assessments in your plan.)

1. Select appropriate Algebra Tiles to use for activities (Knowledge).
2. Build models to represent factorization of polynomials (Application/Psychomotor).
3. Construct and test Algebra Tiles representation of factored polynomials for accuracy (Synthesis/Psychomotor).

Terms or Vocabulary:

Algebra Tiles

Learning Materials or Aids:

Overhead, overhead manipulatives (Algebra Tiles), student-made Algebra Tiles, two algebra activity recording sheets

Adaptations:

(Specifically describe what you plan to do to ensure the success of each and every one of your students who is identified as having special needs.)

In order to ensure success for each of my students, I will continue practicing the techniques that I currently employ in the classroom. One of these strategies is to always give a verbal and visual representation of the information being presented. I also frequently check for understanding and encourage students to ask questions or share comments. I have asked all of my students to choose a seat in the class where they feel that they can be the most successful, and I trust that they have done so. If any seating arrangements are disruptive to students' success, I will move that student to a location in which I feel he or she can be more productive in class.

I have two students with Individualized Education Plans (IEPs) in this class, only one of which has a specification for mathematics. This particular student has an annual goal of solving equations with one unknown as well as maintaining his current skills and performance level. He shows excellent progress and maintenance in these areas every day. On top of my frequent checks for understanding, I will ask him personally after each lesson if he has any questions on what was covered and how he would evaluate his progress and success/failure on his previous night's homework. For my other student with an IEP, I implement all of the above mentioned strategies and do a daily one-on-one check for understanding and comprehension.

I also have one student who is an English language learner (ELL). My cooperating teacher and I have set up a situation for him where he may leave class during work time and go get help from one of the English as a second language (ESL) teachers.

Instructional Strategies:

(Describe the instructional experiences that you will provide for your students.)

- Class will begin with a brief greeting and some disciplinary tasks that need to be addressed such as appropriate behavior in class, using time well, and the job of both the students and myself.
- After our greeting, students will be asked to work on their warm-up activity that covers last night's homework.
- I will go over all of the problems on the warm-up activity on the board and/or overhead in order to clarify anything that the students may still be stuck on.
- After the warm-up activity is complete, I will ask students to pair up by sliding their desks next to the person in the row across from them. They will be instructed to compare their homework answers and come to an agreement on any problems that either student missed (about how to solve the problem correctly).
- I will answer any questions that the students still have on their homework before moving on to the Algebra Tiles activity.
- Students are expected to have their Algebra Tiles ready for use in class. If they do not they will be provided with problems from the textbook to work on while the rest of the class works on their Algebra Tiles activity.
- I will do an introduction to Algebra Tiles and explain to the students that they will understand better once they begin working with them, which is why I have two activity sheets for them to complete. By the end of these activities, my hope is that the majority of my students feel comfortable factoring with Algebra Tiles.

FIGURE 5.8 ● Sample Mathematics Lesson Plan

SOURCE: Prepared by Jordanne Nevin During Her Student Teaching

(continued)

- As a class we will work through Activity 1 and Activity 3 in the textbook. I will then ask students to work silently on the first Algebra Tiles activity sheet.
- Students will be given time to work on their own. Once students start to finish their first nine problems, I will do some teaching with my overhead manipulatives geared toward the introduction to our next lesson.

Assessment:

(Specifically describe how you will know if each of your objectives has been met during this lesson.)

Assessment of objectives 1–3 will take place during the Algebra Tiles activity, as well as when I collect the activity sheets at the beginning of the next lesson, to monitor students' understanding.

Closure:

(Describe how you will effectively conclude your lesson.)

Students will be dismissed with a quick rundown of their behavior, and a reminder about their homework assignment. They are expected to finish the two Algebra Tiles activity sheets, and read Section 9.3 in their textbook.

Reflection/Evaluation:

(Discuss the relative success or failure of your lesson.)

Excellent day! After putting so much effort into yesterday's lesson and having it be mediocre, I was feeling down and knew that today needed to begin with a new strategy and a sterner attitude on my part. In order to ensure success in today's lesson, I started with a check of how my students felt about their homework. At least half of the class got halfway through the assignment, but thought it was very difficult, while many others told me that they didn't even try because it was too hard. Hearing those comments reassured me that a talk about expectations was needed. I spent about 5 minutes explaining to my students that I expect them to take responsibility for their learning. I am available to help them at many times during the day and I am more than willing to make time for any student. But they need to take the initiative to ask for help. During this discussion I also made it clear that I want all of my students to be communicating with each other during class, but at the appropriate times and about appropriate material. I also made sure to note how wonderful their questions are and urged them to continue asking them, but prompted them to use their textbook, notes, and classmates as resources before me. My students understood my concerns for them and seemed satisfied with my expectations.

I asked the students to attempt all of the problems on their warm-up activity to the best of their ability. After giving ample time to finish the six warm-up problems, I explained that I would not collect last night's homework because I wanted everyone to feel confident enough to move ahead. I asked my students to take notes as I went over the warm-up problems on the overhead. By the time I finished the first two, at least five students had had an "ah ha" moment, and everything began to click. I was especially excited when one of my students who had failed last trimester came in with every problem on his homework attempted. He told me that he really understood it after the warm-up problems, which made me very happy. The student who made this comment was the same student I spoke with after the pretest. I am very proud of his accomplishments so far. He has had his homework complete every day this first week. Since he earned only 40% of his homework points last trimester this is a major feat. I made sure to catch him before he left class today and let him know that I appreciated his effort and am very glad that he has chosen to take the Internet course on top of this class because I enjoy having him in class.

Although many students seemed to understand the material better as we worked through it, I did have to continue to remind them to take notes and participate so they could remember what we were learning for future lessons and tests.

The next portion of class was our introduction to Algebra Tiles. I did not get to spend enough time on this for the students to really understand the concept of Algebra Tiles. If they are resourceful tonight and use their textbook to assist in their understanding, I'm sure they will be successful. If they are, however (which is more likely), we may spend a bit more time than planned tomorrow learning about how Algebra Tiles work and how to use them for particular sections of the book.

Another huge success today was during lunch, which is right after I teach this class. One of my female students came in for help about 5 minutes after lunch started. She is a new student to the school and is still adapting to the environment. I asked if she was adjusting, and she said no, trying to hide that she was crying. I don't know exactly why she was so upset, but I think that part of it was her frustration with the material in class. She was struggling quite a bit and seemed to be feeling left behind. She did not understand the Algebra Tiles activity sheets, so I got my overhead manipulatives and sat down in the desk next to hers to start working through the activity sheets I had given for homework. She seemed to feel more comfortable as I explained to her that I had never used Algebra Tiles before this week and we were learning how to use them together. We did a few problems and then talked about how the examples in the book can really help with comprehension as long as we are willing to read all the way through them and not just look at the pictures. She stayed in my room for the rest of lunch working with the overhead manipulatives to finish her activity sheets. She was back to her cheerful demeanor by the end of lunch and thanked me for my help.

I believe that my students are beginning to understand why I am asking them to learn how to factor using Algebra Tiles and appreciate how willing and excited I am to help them. What makes me so happy about today is that I got through these lessons and reached many of my students after being stern with them at the beginning of class and requiring more attention and participation from them. My next big task is to somehow plan a lesson allowing students time to work with each other so that I can meet individually with a few of my students with issues. I have one boy who sleeps every day, or just doesn't work. I would like to talk with him about what we can do as a team to meet his needs some time in the next few days. I have been feeling overwhelmed with a full class load, new students, a work sample, and curriculum, not to mention my life outside of the classroom. I am certain, however, that I will become more comfortable with my workload in the next few weeks.

FIGURE 5.8 *continued* ● Sample Mathematics Lesson Plan

SOURCE: Prepared by Jordanne Nevin During Her Student Teaching

LINFIELD COLLEGE

Education Department   Lesson Plan

Student ID Number:	Time/Period: 1 day (70 mn)	Date: Thursday, November 22
Lesson Title: FDR and the New Deal	Subject: U.S. History	Grade Level: 9

Instructional Objectives:

TSWBAT: Describe how FDR attempted to lift the country out of the Depression
Evaluate the programs of the New Deal
Compare and contrast FDR's response to the Depression with that of Hoover's

Terms or Vocabulary:

New Deal, Fireside Chat, ABC Programs

Learning Materials or Aids:

Film - *The Century*, recording of one of FDR's fireside chats, textbook, assorted research materials

Adaptations:

The teacher will give Students #10 and #17 frequent reminders to stay on-task. If the distractions become too frequent the students will be asked to move to a seat which will not offer as many distractions.

Instructional Strategies:

1. The teacher will begin class by instructing the students to answer the question "What qualities make a great leader?" in their journals. Once the students are finished the teacher will ask for volunteers to share their ideas with the class.
2. Following the discussion the teacher will explain that today the class will be learning about one of America's great leaders, FDR. The teacher will then share some biographical information on FDR and briefly explain the way in which the American public viewed him as the President.
3. A clip of the film will be shown which explains the impact FDR's presidency had on the people of the 1930s and what he tried to do to restore the country's strength.
4. The teacher will play a portion of one of FDR's fireside chats in order for the students to hear firsthand the charismatic, soothing nature of the programs.
5. The teacher will briefly describe FDR's New Deal and the effect it had on America.
6. The students will be instructed to arrange themselves into groups of two or three. Each group will be given an ABC Program to research. The class will be given roughly 15 minutes to research their program.
7. While the rest of the class takes notes, each of the groups will present to the class the information they found on their ABC Program.
8. The teacher will conclude class with a discussion comparing and contrasting the presidencies of Herbert Hoover and FDR.

Assessment:

The class will take a quiz on the information presented by each group, which the teacher will create after listening to the presentations. For homework, the students will write a short essay comparing FDR's policies with those of Hoover's.

Closure:

Refer to Instructional Strategy #8. Also, for homework the students will create a (profile of a) character living during the Depression. They are to write a letter to FDR asking for help as the character that they have created. The letters should be on material that shows the personality of their character. For example, a fisherman living on the coast would write his letter on a seashell.

Reflection/Evaluation:

This lesson went fairly well. The main problem was lack of time. The entire lesson felt rushed, and I am unsure if some of the important points were stressed upon as much as they probably should have been. Perhaps if this lesson took place over 2 days or the research was created into a larger project, the students would get the "aha" impact of the information.

FIGURE 5.9 ● Sample U.S. History Lesson Plan

SOURCE: Prepared by Jonee Silva During His Student Teaching

(continued)

The New Deal

Relief

1933

Federal Emergency
Relief Administration

PWA, Public Works
Administration
- construction jobs

CWA, Civil Works
Administration
- jobless people, 1933–34-4 mil
people

CCC, Civilian
Conservation Corps
- 18–25 yrs old
- $30 pay, $22 went to
families

TVA, Tennessee Valley
Authority

AAA, Agricultural
Adjustment Act
- paid farmers not to
produce crops

NRA, National
Recovery
Administration

1935
WPA, Works Progress
Administration
- built hospitals, schools

Recovery

1933

NIRA, National
Industrial Recovery Act

1935

Social Security
- 1st to get Ida May
Nfiller, $22.40

Soil Conservation Act
- reduced acreage of
some crops

Rural Electrification Act
- gave electricity to
farms

1938

Minimum Wage
- 25 cents

Reform

1933

FDIC, Federal Deposit
Contribution Act

NIRA, National
Industrial Relations Act
- the right to join unions

1934

SEC, Security Exchange
Commission
1935

Wagner Act-
established 40-hour
work week

Revenue Act
- tax on wealthier
corporations

Truth Securities Act

FIGURE 5.9 *continued* ● Sample U.S. History Lesson Plan

SOURCE: Prepared by Jonee Silva During His Student Teaching

section or combined with the procedure section. Be sure that your information is written down, as it's important to be able to refer to it quickly and easily when you need to.

If, for instance, you intend to conduct the lesson using discussion, you should write out the key discussion questions. Or, if you are going to introduce new material using a 10-minute lecture, then you need to outline the content of that lecture. The word *outline* is not used casually—you need not have pages of notes to sift through, nor should you ever read declarative statements to your students. You should be familiar enough with the content so that an outline (in as much detail as you believe necessary) will be sufficient to carry on the lesson, as in the following example of a content outline:

Causes of Civil War
   a. Primary causes
      1. Economics
      2. Abolitionist pressure
      3. Slavery
      4. etc.
   b. Secondary causes
      1. North-South friction
      2. Southern economic dependence
      3. etc.

The procedure or procedures to be used, sometimes referred to as the *instructional components*, make up the

LINFIELD COLLEGE

Education Department | Lesson Plan 5

Student ID Number:	Time/Period: Period 1	Date: Friday, April 9
Lesson Title: Coming to Terms	Subject: Language Arts	Grade/level: 9th grade

Instructional Objectives:

Students will be able to. . .

1. Define and explain idioms
2. Demonstrate a literal comprehension of the text

Terms or Vocabulary:

Idiom

Learning Materials or Aids:

Textbook, discussion questions, idiom worksheet, idioms with context clues, idiom overhead, white sheet of paper, colored pencils

Adaptations:

Teacher will photocopy a section of the text for students with reading disabilities to practice before class with a specialist.

Instructional Strategies:

Teacher begins the class with the journal topic, "What is one activity that you find difficult to do? How do you feel when you have to do this activity?" Teacher gives the students five minutes to complete their entries and then complete D.O.L. Teacher gives a mini-lesson on idioms and has examples of idioms on the overhead. Students volunteer to guess what they think these idioms mean. Next, teacher explains the fun idiom assignment. Students break into partners and get an idiom and white sheet of paper from the teacher. Students are instructed to draw a literal representation of their idiom. After students have completed their drawings, they present their idiom to the class. Partners should read their idiom to the class, explain their picture, read their context clues, and use that information to guess the meaning of the idiom. Introduce the story, *On Being Bright, Seventeen and Unable to Read,* and have students pay close attention to idioms used throughout the story. Explain that the main character of the story is dyslexic and tell about how the education system dealt with dyslexic students when this story was written. Have the students read pages 137–138 and pass out discussion questions and the idioms worksheet. Have students break into small groups to complete the two worksheets.

Assessment:

1. Teacher will assess the idiom worksheet.
2. Teacher will assess the discussion questions.

Closure:

Ask students how they think dyslexia would affect them not only in school but also in their pastimes.

Do they feel any connection with the main character in the story?

Reflection/Evaluation:

I thought the students remained engaged and actively involved in this entire lesson. The students immediately began their daily procedures of journal writing and D.O.L. I was surprised that many of the students were unfamiliar with the idioms I chose for the mini-lesson, and thought that the context clues helped them gain clear understanding of each idiom. The students seemed to enjoy working with a partner on their idiom and many drew very detailed illustrations. The students listened attentively while the pairs presented and applauded after each group. To make the audience more involved and gather positive feedback from the class, I could have the audience try to guess the idioms. For instance, I could have each pair model Hangman and draw lines illustrating the number of words in the idiom. These activities also helped ELL students who were unfamiliar with many common idioms in the English language. The students' enthusiasm for this activity was also apparent by the large number of students working in groups to complete the extra credit assignment on idioms.

FIGURE 5.10 ● Sample Language Arts Lesson Plan

SOURCE: Prepared by Melissa Balmer During Her Student Teaching

(continued)

Idiom: A group of words that says one thing but means another.

1. **Beat around the bush**

"Quit **beating around the bush!** If you don't want to go with me, just tell me!"

Definition: **To evade an issue; avoid giving a direct answer.**

2. **Bite off more than one can chew**

I'm really behind with my project. Can you help me? I'm afraid I **bit off more than I could chew!**"

Definition: **To take responsibility for more than one can manage.**

3. **Don't count your chickens before they've hatched**

A: "I'm sure that I'm going to win a lot of money in Las Vegas."
B: "**Don't count your chickens before they've hatched!**"

Definition: **Don't assume that something will happen until it *has* happened.**

4. **Wet behind the ears**

"Don't include Fred as part of the bargaining team. He's just started working here and is still too **wet behind the ears.**"

Definition: **To be inexperienced and naive.**

5. **Make a mountain out of a molehill**

"Calm down. There's really nothing to worry about. You're **making a mountain out of a molehill.**"

Definition: **To make something seem more important than it is.**

Fun Idiom Assignment
Objective: To draw and explain an idiom
Each person should. . .

1. Choose a partner
2. Draw the literal meaning of an idiom
3. Present the idiom to the class

   During their presentation partners should. . .
   A. State their idiom
   B. Explain their drawings
   C. Read their context clues
   D. Guess, using the context clues, the real meaning of their idiom

FIGURE 5.10 *continued* ● Sample Language Arts Lesson Plan
SOURCE: Prepared by Melissa Balmer During Her Student Teaching

procedure component of the lesson plan. It is the section that outlines what you and your students will do during the lesson. Appropriate instructional activities are chosen to meet the objectives, to match the students' learning styles and special needs, and to ensure that all students have an equal opportunity to learn. Ordinarily, you should plan this section of your lesson as an organized entity having a beginning (an introduction or set), a middle, and an end (called the **closure**) to be completed during the lesson. This structure is not always needed, because some lessons are simply parts of units or long-term plans and merely carry on activities spelled out in those long-term plans. Still, most lessons need to include in the procedure: (a) an *introduction,* the process used to prepare the students mentally for the lesson, sometimes referred to as the set, or initiating activity; (b) *lesson development,* the detailing of activities that occur between the beginning and the end of the lesson, including the transitions that connect activities; (c) *plans for practice,* sometimes referred to as the follow-up—that is, ways that you intend on having students interact in the classroom (such as individual practice, in dyads, or small groups) while receiving guidance or coaching from each other and from you; (d) the *lesson conclusion* (or closure), the planned process of bringing the lesson to an end, thereby providing students with a sense of completeness and, with effective teaching, accomplishment and comprehension by helping students to synthesize the information learned from the lesson; (e) a *timetable* that serves simply as a planning and implementation guide; (f) a *plan* for what to do if you finish the lesson and time remains; and (g) *assignments,* that is, what students are instructed to do as follow-up to the lesson, either as homework or as in-class work, thus providing

Surviving the Donner Party: A Learning Cycle

Exploration
Materials per group:

Donner Party lists on Excel spreadsheet (see Resources below)

Calculators

Scratch paper

Procedure:

Distribute the calculators and scratch paper and have the groups analyze the data. They will be looking for patterns in the data such as:

1. Who lived?
2. Who died?
3. When in the year did they die?
4. Did the age or gender of a person play a role in survival?

Allow enough time for the students to explore the data, discover the patterns, and create charts and graphs in Excel. Some patterns are not as obvious as others; allow a minimum of 30 minutes for an average class.

Explanation
Materials per group of two or three:

Ideally, a computer projector should be used to project the Excel charts and graphs. If that is not possible, have the students transfer the graphs to chart paper or overhead transparencies.

Blank overhead acetate or large piece of chart paper

Overhead pens or markers

Procedure:

Have students compile their data and present their findings to the class.

The question to be answered through the analysis of the data is:

What factors led to survival?

Sample statistics derived from the raw data:

- Of the 81 people who made it to the mountain camps, 47 were male and 34 were female.
- In the mountain camps, 27 males (57%) and 9 females (26%) died.
- Mean age of the survivors was 17 yrs; of those who died, 25 yrs.
- Median age of survivors was 14 yrs; of those who died, 25 yrs.
- Of those 5 years old and under—7 lived, 12 died.
- Of those between ages 6 and 15—20 lived and 3 died.
- Of those between ages 16 and 30—13 lived and 15 died.
- Of those older than 30—6 lived and 10 died.
- Of 19 adult males *without families*, 3 died on the trail, 13 died in the mountains (or 84% perished).
- Of those with a family affiliation, 62% survived.

Many factors led to the survival of people in this pioneer group. Two-thirds of the males died while only one-third of the females died. Those with family affiliation survived; only three traveling alone did. The very young and the elderly did not survive regardless of gender or family affiliation.

Expansion
Example from Geography:

Analysis of the demographic data can be developed in many ways; for example, you may wish to explore the biology behind the demise/survival of individuals or the role of family affiliation in survival. One question that certainly arises is: Where were these people trapped and how did they become trapped?

Materials per group:

A blank map of the United States west of the Mississippi River

A map of the western United States showing geographic features

A topographic map of the Sierra Nevada Mountains near Truckee, CA and Donner Pass (available at http://www.topozone.com).

Photographs/video showing east and west sides of the Sierra Nevada OR *The Donner Party*, a documentary made by Ric Burns for The American Experience, PBS (very useful but may be too intense for sensitive viewers).

FIGURE 5.11 ● *Model Lesson Plan Integrating Technology*

SOURCE: Courtesy of Dr. Melanie A. Reap, Winona University

(continued)

(Note: Most maps of the westward expansion show the Donner Party route. Hard copies of topographic maps are available from most state land-grant university libraries, the United States Geological Survey, or from specialty map stores.)

Provide the students a list of points to plot on their blank map so that they trace the pioneer party's route. Pay close attention to the location of Hasting's Cut-off, the Wasatch Mountains, the Great Salt Lake, The Great Basin Desert, the Humboldt and Truckee rivers, the Ruby Mountains, and the pass through the Sierra Nevada Mountains near present day Truckee Lake and Donner Lake.

After plotting the route, have the students analyze the topographic maps of the Sierra Nevada Mountains. Compare photos (or watch video) of the east and west sides of the mountains and the mountains in the four seasons (emphasize snow amounts). Alternatively, if it is fall or winter, students could download current snow conditions at Truckee, California, by going to http://www.weather.com.

Snowfall in the Sierra Nevada Mountains is very high due to the uplift of moisture-laden air from the Pacific, which condenses and falls as rain or snow. Most moisture falls on the mountains and very little falls east of the Sierras. The area beyond the mountains (Great Basin Desert) is called a rain shadow.

The Donner Party got to the pass late in the season (October) because they took Hasting's Cut-off. As they tried to go over the pass, it began to snow. They had no road and became bogged down in the heavy snow. They had to remain in the mountains until help arrived in March.

Resources
- A list of Donner Party members that gives the names, family association, age, sex, rescue status, and final condition (lived/died) can be found at the Web sites listed. One of the best lists is from the article *Surviving the Donner Party* by Jared Diamond in the March 1992 issue of *Discover* magazine. You may also contact Dr. Melanie A. Reap at mreap@winona.edu.
- Useful Web sites:
  http://www.utahcrossroads.org/DonnerParty/
  http://members.aol.com/danmrosen/donner/index.htm
  http://raiboy.tripod.com/Donner/index.html
  http://www.spartacus.schoolnet.co.uk/WWdonnerP.htm
  http://www.topozone.com
  http://www.weather.com
- Selected Bibliography:
  Diamond, Jared. (March 1992). *Living through the Donner Party. Discover*, 100–107.
  Hastings, L. W. (originally published in 1845, reprint by Applewood Books). *The emigrants' guide to Oregon and California*. Bedford, MA: Applewood Books.
  King, Joseph A. (1992). *Winter of entrapment: A new look at the Donner Party*. Lafayette, CA: K&K Publications.
  Mullen, Jr., F. (1977). *The Donner Party chronicles*. Carson City, NV: Nevada Humanities Commission.
  Murphy, Virginia Reed. (1980 edition). *Across the plains in the Donner Party: A personal narrative of the overland trip to California, 1846–47*. Golden, CO: Outbooks.

FIGURE 5.11 *continued* ● Model Lesson Plan Integrating Technology

SOURCE: Courtesy of Dr. Melanie A. Reap, Winona University

students an opportunity to practice and enhance what is being learned. Let's now consider some of those elements in detail.

Introduction to the lesson Like any good performance, a lesson needs an effective beginning. In many respects the introduction sets the tone for the rest of the lesson by alerting the students that the business of learning is to begin. The introduction should be an attention-getter. If it is exciting, interesting, or innovative, it can create a favorable mood for the lesson. In any case, a thoughtful introduction serves as a solid indicator that you are well prepared. Although it is difficult to develop an exciting introduction to every lesson taught each day, many options are available by which to spice up the launching of a lesson. You might, for instance, begin the lesson by briefly reviewing the previous lesson, thereby helping students connect the learning. Another possibility is to review vocabulary words from previous lessons and to introduce

new ones. Still another possibility is to use the key point of the day's lesson as an introduction and then again as the conclusion. Sometimes teachers begin a lesson by demonstrating a discrepant event (i.e., an event that is contrary to what one might expect), sometimes referred to as a "hook." Yet another possibility is to begin the lesson with a writing activity on some controversial aspect of the ensuing lesson. Sample introductions might include

- *For English, study of interpretations.* As students enter the classroom, the state song, "I Love You, California," is playing softly in the background. After a warm greeting, the teacher begins by showing on the overhead the state seal and asks "Does anyone know what this is?"

- *For U.S. history, study of westward expansion.* The teacher asks "Who has lived somewhere else other than (*name of your state*)?" After students show hands and answer, the teacher asks individuals why they moved to (*name of your state*). The teacher then asks students to recall why the first European settlers came to the United States, then moves into the next activity.

- *For science, study of the science process skill of predicting.* The teacher fills a glass to the brim with colored water (colored so it is more visible) and asks students, in dyads (pairs), to predict how many pennies can be added to the glass before any water spills over its rim.

- *For western civilizations, the study of history of religion (the lesson plan shown in Figure 5.4).* You have 5 minutes to write an argument in support of or against the following statement: The recent hate crimes in our nation can be related to what we are learning about the history of religion.

In short, you can use the introduction of the lesson to review past learning, tie the new lesson to the previous lesson, introduce new material, point out the objectives of the new lesson, help students connect their learning with other disciplines or with real life, or—by showing what will be learned and why the learning is important—induce in students some motivation and a mind-set favorable to the new lesson.

Lesson development The developmental activities make up the bulk of the plan and are the specifics by which you intend to achieve your lesson objectives. They include activities that present information, demonstrate skills, provide reinforcement of previously learned material, and provide other opportunities to develop understanding and skill. Furthermore, by actions and words, during lesson development the teacher models the behaviors expected of the students. Students need such modeling. By effective modeling, the teacher can exemplify the anticipated learning outcomes. Activities of this section of the lesson plan should be described in some detail so that (a) you will know exactly what it is you plan to do and (b) during the intensity of the class meeting you do not forget important details and content. For this reason you should consider, for example, noting answers (if known) to questions you intend to ask and solutions (if known) to problems you intend to have students solve.

Lesson conclusion Having a concise closure to the lesson is as important as having a strong introduction. The concluding activity should summarize and bind together what has ensued in the developmental stage and should reinforce the principal points of the lesson. Ways to accomplish these ends include: (a) restate or outline the key points of the lesson; (b) have students devise one-sentence summaries; and (c) provide answers that represent a review, but have the students create the questions. Sometimes the closure is not only a review of what was learned but also the summarizing of a question left unanswered that signals a change in your plan of activities for the next day. In other words, it becomes a transitional closure.

Timetable Estimating the time factors in any lesson can be very difficult, especially for a new teacher. A good procedure is to gauge the amount of time needed for each learning activity and note that alongside the activity and strategy in your plan, as shown in the preferred sample lesson plan format. However, placing too much faith in your time estimate may be foolish; an estimate is more for your guidance during the preactive phase of instruction than for anything else. Beginning teachers frequently find that their planned discussions and presentations do not last as long as was expected. To avoid being embarrassed by running out of material, try to make sure you have planned enough meaningful work to consume the entire class period. (See the section The Problem of Time, discussed earlier in this module.) Another important reason for including a time plan in your lesson is to give information to students about how much time they have for a particular activity, such as a quiz or a group activity. Students appreciate that sort of thoughtfulness on the part of the teacher.

Assignments

When an assignment is to be given, it should be noted in your lesson plan. The time to present an assignment to the students is optional, but it should never be yelled as an afterthought as the students are exiting the classroom at the end of the period. Whether they are to be begun and completed during class time or done out of school, assignments should be written on the writing board, in a special place on the bulletin board, in each student's assignment log maintained in a binder, on a handout, or in some combination of these. Be sure that assignment specifications are perfectly clear to all students. Many teachers give assignments to their students on a weekly or other periodic basis. When given on a periodic basis, rather than daily, assignments should still show in your daily lesson plans in order to remind yourself to remind students of them.

Once assignment specifications and due dates are given, it is a good idea not to make major modifications to them, and it is especially important not to change assignment specifications several days after an assignment has been given. Last-minute changes in assignment specifications can be very frustrating to students who have already begun or completed the assignment; it shows little respect to those students. (See also Learning from Assignments and Homework in Module 7.)

Assignment versus procedure Understand the difference between assignments and procedures. An assignment tells students *what* is to be done, while procedures explain *how* to do it. Although an assignment may include procedures, spelling out procedures alone is not the same thing as giving an academic assignment. When students are given an assignment, they need to understand the reasons for doing it and have some notion of ways the assignment might be done.

Benefits of coached practice Allowing time in class for students to begin work on homework assignments and long-term projects is highly recommended; it provides an opportunity for the teacher to offer personalized attention to students. Being able to coach students is the reason for using in-class time to begin assignments. The benefits of *coached practice* include being able to (a) monitor student work so a student doesn't go too far in a wrong direction, (b) help students develop their metacognitive skills (that is, to reflect on their thinking), (c) assess the progress of individual students, (d) provide for peer tutoring, and (e) discover or create a "teachable moment." For the latter, for example, while observing and monitoring student practice the teacher might discover a commonly shared student misconception. The teacher then stops and discusses that issue in an attempt to clarify the misconception, or the teacher may collaboratively, with students, plan a subsequent lesson focusing on the common misconception.

Special notes and reminders In their lesson plan format many teachers have a regular place for special notes and reminders concerning such things as announcements to be made, school programs, long-term assignment due dates, and individual work for certain students. This section should be able to be quickly referenced.

Materials and Equipment to Be Used

Materials of instruction include books, media, handouts, and other supplies necessary to accomplish the lesson objectives. You must be *certain* that the proper and necessary materials and equipment are available for the lesson; to be certain requires planning. Teachers who, for one reason or another, have to busy themselves during class looking for materials or equipment that should have been readied before class began are likely to experience classroom control problems.

Accommodations for Students with Special Needs

For every student in your class who has an Individualized Education Plan (IEP) you need to specifically describe what you plan to do to ensure his/her success. By consulting the guidelines provided in Module 2, you can describe the steps you will take to accommodate that student.

Assessment

Details of how you will assess how well students are learning (formative assessment) and how well they have learned (summative assessment) should be included in your lesson plan. This does not mean to imply that both types of assessment will be in every daily plan. Comprehension checks for formative assessment can be in the form of questions you ask and that the students ask during the lesson (in the procedural section), as well as various kinds of checklists.

For summative assessment, teachers typically use review questions at the end of a lesson (as a closure) or the beginning of the next lesson (as a review or transfer introduction), in independent practice or summary activities at the completion of a lesson, and in tests.

Reflection and Revision

In most modern lesson plan formats, there is a section reserved for the teacher to make notes or reflective comments about the lesson. Reflections about the lesson are useful for you and for those who are supervising you if you are a student teacher or a teacher being mentored or considered for tenure. Sample reflective questions you might ask yourself are shown in Figure 5.12.

Writing, and later reading, your reflections can not only provide ideas that may be useful if you plan to use the lesson again at some later date, but can offer catharsis, easing the tension caused from teaching. To continue working effectively at a challenging task (that is, to prevent intellectual **downshifting,** or reverting to earlier learned, lower cognitive level behaviors) requires significant amounts of reflection. After you have reviewed the sample lesson plan formats, proceed to Exercise 5.5, where you will analyze a lesson that failed; then, as instructed by your course instructor, do Exercises 5.6A, 5.6B, and 5.7.

- What is my overall feeling about today's lesson—good, fair, or bad? What made me feel this way?
- Did students seem to enjoy the lesson? What makes me think so?
- Did the objectives seem to be met? What evidence do I have?
- What aspects of the lesson went well? What makes me believe so?
- Were I to repeat the lesson, what changes might I make? Why?
- Which students seemed to do well? Which ones should I give more attention to? Why and how?
- To what extent was this lesson personalized according to student learning styles, abilities, interests, talents, and needs? Could I do more in this regard? Why or why not?
- Did the students seem to have sufficient time to think and apply? Why or why not?
- Would I have been proud had the school superintendent been present to observe this lesson? Why or why not?

FIGURE 5.12 ● Questions for Lesson Self-Reflection

EXERCISE **5.5**

■ Analysis of a Lesson That Failed

Instructions: The planning and structure of a lesson are often predictors of the success of its implementation. The purpose of this exercise is to read the following synopsis of the implementation of a lesson, answer the discussion questions individually, and use your responses as a basis for class discussion in small groups about the lesson.

The Setting: Ninth-grade Life Science class; 1:12–2:07 P.M., spring semester

Synopsis of Events

1:12	Bell rings.
1:12–1:21	Teacher directs students to read from their texts, while he or she takes attendance.
1:21–1:31	Teacher distributes a handout to each student; students are to label the parts of a flower shown on the handout.
1:31–1:37	Silent reading and labeling of the handout.
1:37–1:39	Teacher verbally gives instructions for working on a real flower (e.g., by comparing it with the drawing on the handout). Students may use microscope if they want.
1:39–1:45	Teacher walks around room, giving each student a real flower.
1:45–2:05	Chaos erupts. There is much confusion, with students wandering around, throwing flower parts at each other. Teacher begins writing referrals and sends two students to the office for misbehavior. Teacher is flustered, directs students to spend remainder of period quietly reading from their texts. Two more referrals are written.
2:05–2:07	A few students begin meandering toward the exit.
2:07	End of period (much to the delight of the teacher).

Questions for Class Discussion

1. Do you think the teacher had a lesson plan? If so, what (if any) were its good points? Its problems?

2. If you believed that the teacher had a lesson plan, do you believe that it was written and detailed? Explain your response. What is your evidence?

3. How might the lesson have been prepared and implemented to avoid the chaos?

4. Was the format of the lesson traditional? Explain.

5. Have you experienced a class such as this? Explain.

6. Which teacher behaviors were probable causes of much of the chaos? (*Hint:* See in Module 6, "The Learning Experiences Ladder.")

7. What teacher behaviors could have prevented the chaos and made the lesson more effective?

8. Within the 55-minute class period, students were expected to operate rather high on the Learning Experiences Ladder (see Module 6). Consider this analysis: 9 minutes of silent reading; 10 minutes of listening; 6 minutes of silent reading and labeling; 2 minutes of listening; 6 minutes of action (the only direct experience); and an

(continued)

additional 22 minutes of silent reading. In all, there were approximately 49 minutes (89% of the class time) of abstract verbal and visual symbolization. Is this a problem?

9. What have you learned from this exercise?

 To access this exercise online, go to the Companion Website at **www.prenhall.com/kellough.**

EXERCISE 5.6A

■ Preparing a Lesson Plan

Instructions: Use the model lesson format or an alternative format that is approved by your instructor to prepare a _____ minute lesson plan (length to be decided in your class) for a grade and course of your choice. After completing your lesson plan, evaluate it yourself, modify it, and then have your modified version evaluated by at least three peers, using Exercise 5.6B for the evaluation, before turning it in for your instructor's evaluation. This exercise may be connected with Exercise 5.7.

 To access this exercise online, go to the Companion Website at **www.prenhall.com/kellough.**

EXERCISE 5.6B

■ Self- and Peer-Assessment of My Lesson Plan

Instructions: You may duplicate blank copies of this form for evaluation of the lesson you developed for Exercise 5.6A. Have your lesson plan evaluated by two of your peers and yourself. For each of the items below, evaluators should check either "yes" or "no," and write instructive comments. Compare the results of your self-evaluation with the other evaluations.

	No	Yes	Comments
1. Are descriptive data adequately provided?	_____	_____	_____
2. Are the goals clearly stated?	_____	_____	_____
3. Are the objectives specific and measurable?	_____	_____	_____
4. Are objectives correctly classified?	_____	_____	_____
5. Are objectives only low-order or is higher-order thinking expected?	_____	_____	_____
6. Is the rationale clear and justifiable?	_____	_____	_____
7. Is the plan's content appropriate?	_____	_____	_____
8. Is the content likely to contribute to achievement of the objectives?	_____	_____	_____
9. Given the time frame and other logistical considerations, is the plan workable?	_____	_____	_____
10. Will the opening (set) likely engage the students?	_____	_____	_____
11. Is there a preassessment strategy?	_____	_____	_____

(continued)

	No	Yes	Comments
12. Is there a proper mix of learning activities for the time frame of the lesson?	_____	_____	_____
13. Are the activities developmentally appropriate for the intended students?	_____	_____	_____
14. Are transitions planned?	_____	_____	_____
15. If relevant, are key questions written out and key ideas noted in the plan?	_____	_____	_____
16. Does the plan indicate how coached practice will be provided for each student?	_____	_____	_____
17. Is adequate closure provided in the plan?	_____	_____	_____
18. Are materials and equipment needed identified and are they appropriate?	_____	_____	_____
19. Is there a planned formative assessment, formal or informal?	_____	_____	_____
20. Is there a planned summative assessment?	_____	_____	_____
21. Is the lesson coordinated in any way with other aspects of the curriculum?	_____	_____	_____
22. Is the lesson likely to provide a sense of meaning for the students by helping bridge their learning?	_____	_____	_____
23. Is an adequate amount of time allotted to address the information presented?	_____	_____	_____
24. Is a thoughtfully prepared and relevant student assignment planned?	_____	_____	_____
25. Could a substitute who is knowledgeable follow the plan?	_____	_____	_____

Additional comments:

 To access this exercise online, go to the Companion Website at **www.prenhall.com/kellough.**

EXERCISE 5.7

■ Preparing an Instructional Unit

Instructions: The purpose of this exercise is threefold: (1) to give you experience in preparing an instructional unit, (2) to assist you in preparing an instructional unit that you can use in your teaching, and (3) to start your collection of instructional units that you may be able to use in your teaching. This is an assignment that will take several hours to complete, and you will need to read ahead in the book. Our advice, therefore, is that the assignment be started early, with a due date much later in the course. Your course instructor may have specific guidelines for your completion of this exercise; what follows is the essence of what you are to do.

First, divide your class into two teams, each with a different assignment pertaining to this exercise. The units completed by these teams are to be shared with all members of the class for feedback and later use.

(continued)

■ TEAM 1

Members of this team, individually, will develop standard teaching units, perhaps with different grade levels in mind. (You will need to be knowledgeable about material in Modules 6–9.) Using a format that is practical, individuals on this team will each develop a minimum 2-week unit for a particular grade level. Regardless of format chosen, each unit plan should include the following elements:

1. Identification of (a) grade level, (b) subject, (c) topic, and (d) time duration.

2. Statement of rationale and general goals.

3. Separate list of instructional objectives for each daily lesson. Wherever possible, the unit should include objectives from all three domains—cognitive, affective, and psychomotor.

4. List of the materials and resources needed and where they can be obtained (if you have that information). These should also be listed for each daily lesson.

5. Each of the daily lessons (see Exercise 4.6A).

6. List all items that will be used to assess student learning *during* and at *completion* of the unit of study.

7. Statement of how the unit will attend to variations in students' reading levels, socioethnic backgrounds, and special needs.

■ TEAM 2

In collaboration, members of this team will develop interdisciplinary thematic units. (*Note:* Completed ITUs can be seen in the publication by Roberts and Kellough listed at the end of this module.) Depending upon the number of students in your class, Team 2 may actually be comprised of several teams, with each one developing an ITU. Each team should be composed of no less than two members (e.g., a math specialist and a science specialist) and no more than four (e.g., social studies, language arts/reading, mathematics, and science).

 To access this exercise online, go to the Companion Website at **www.prenhall.com/kellough**.

■ SUMMARY

Developing units of instruction that integrate student learning and that provide a sense of meaning for the students requires coordination throughout the curriculum—which is defined here as consisting of all the planned experiences students encounter while at school. Hence, for students, learning is a process of discovering how information, knowledge, and ideas are interrelated—learning to make sense out of self, school, and life. Molding chunks of information into units and units into daily lessons helps students process and make sense out of knowledge. Having developed your first unit of instruction, you are on your way to becoming a competent planner of instruction. There is no single best way to organize a daily plan, no "one-size-fits all" lesson plan format, no foolproof formula that will guarantee a teacher an effective lesson. With experience and the increased competence that comes from reflecting on that experience, you will develop your own style, your own methods of implementing that style, and your own formula for preparing a lesson plan. Like a map, your lesson plan charts the course, places markers along the trails, pinpoints danger areas, highlights areas of interest and importance along the way, and ultimately brings the traveler to the successful completion of the objective.

The best-prepared units and lessons, though, will go untaught or only poorly implemented if presented in a poorly managed classroom. Refer to Module 3 to review, how to provide a supportive classroom environment—to effectively manage the classroom for the most efficient instruction and student achievement.

■ MODULE 5 **POSTTEST**

Multiple Choice

1. The written document explaining the workings of a class, given to students during the first few days of the school year, is the
   a. syllabus.
   b. textbook.
   c. course of study.
   d. curriculum guide.

2. The major reason for instructional planning is to
   a. provide curriculum continuity.
   b. prepare for students who are different from you.
   c. have lesson plans available for a substitute teacher.
   d. design student experiences that are concrete learning experiences.

3. Which follows a unit of instruction as an assessment of student learning of that unit?
   a. preassessment
   b. formative evaluation
   c. summative evaluation
   d. diagnostic assessment

4. When the teacher monitors student work during a lesson by using guided practice and questioning, and when the teacher assigns independent practice at the completion of the lesson, that teacher is
   a. shifting interaction.
   b. implementing an orientation set.
   c. checking for student comprehension.
   d. assessing student achievement for grading purposes.

5. The lesson plan format that works best is
   a. the one required by the university supervisor.
   b. the format that the teacher can most effectively implement.
   c. the lesson plan that includes details of all seven common steps.
   d. different for a middle school teacher than it is for a secondary school teacher.

6. All else considered equal, which one of the following transitions in learning activities is probably best during the same instructional period?
   a. teacher talk to student discussion
   b. teacher talk to student investigation
   c. cooperative learning to student oral reports
   d. video presentation to a 35-mm slide presentation

7. Which one of the following is a false statement?
   a. There is no set time duration for a unit of study.
   b. Summative assessment occurs throughout a unit of study.
   c. Culminating activities for a unit of study are those that bring together what has been learned.
   d. There is no single best format for a teaching unit that works best for all subject fields and/or all grade levels.

8. A complete and planned sequence of instruction that presents a major division of a subject or a discipline is called
   a. an instructional unit.
   b. a resource unit.
   c. a syllabus.
   d. a course.

9. The teacher's completion of the reflection and revision components of any lesson plan occurs during the _____ phase of decision making and instruction.
   a. preactive
   b. reflective
   c. projective
   d. interactive

(continued)

10. Which one of the following terms is least likely to be referring to the same thing as the others?
    a. aligned curriculum
    b. thematic instruction
    c. integrated curriculum
    d. multidisciplinary instruction

Short Explanation

1. Explain the concept of unit and lesson planning and where and how it fits in a curriculum built around a block schedule with classes that are sometimes integrated disciplines and that are each perhaps up to 150 minutes long.

2. Explain three reasons why a beginning teacher needs to prepare detailed lesson and unit plans, even when the textbook program you are using provides them.

3. Describe a situation during instruction when, if ever, you can or should divert from the written plan.

4. Explain the importance of preassessment of student learning. When do you do a preassessment? How can it be done? What is done with the information obtained?

5. Explain why lesson planning is or should be a continual process.

6. Explain why supervisors of student teachers expect student teachers to plan and prepare their classroom management systems in writing and to do very detailed and written unit and lesson planning.

7. Explain the concept of a student-negotiated curriculum. Is it used today in middle school and secondary school teaching? Why or why not? Would you use it? Why or why not?

8. Explain the importance of the idea that all teachers are teachers of reading, writing, studying, and thinking. Do you agree or disagree with the statement? Why?

9. Describe specific considerations you should give to student safety when preparing unit and lesson plans, especially in your subject field.

10. Define and describe each of the various levels of curriculum integration.

Essay

1. Describe three different types of activities that could be used to introduce a unit of instruction for a particular grade level in your subject field.

2. Explain the importance of organizing instruction into units. Is there ever a time when you might not do so? Explain.

3. Describe the advantages and disadvantages of interdisciplinary thematic instruction for a teacher of your subject field and grade-level interest.

4. From your current observations and fieldwork related to this teacher preparation program, clearly identify one specific example of educational practice that seems contradictory to exemplary practice or theory presented in this module. Present your explanation for the discrepancy.

5. Describe any prior concepts you held that changed as a result of your experiences with this module. Describe the changes.

 To access this posttest and the answers online, go to the Companion Website at **www.prenhall.com/kellough.**

■ SUGGESTED READINGS

Bottoms, G., & Phillips, I. (1998). How to design challenging vocational courses. *Techniques: Making Educational and Career Connections, 73*(4), 27–29.

Butchart, R. E., & McEwan, B. (Eds.). (1998). *Classroom discipline in American schools: Problems and possibilities for democratic education.* Albany, NY: State University of New York Press.

Cunningham, B., & Omolayole, O. (1998). An assessment-oriented syllabus model for business courses. *Journal of Education for Business, 73*(4), 234–240.

Jenkins, K. D., & Jenkins, D. M. (1998). Integrating curriculum in a total quality school. *Middle School Journal, 29*(4), 14–27.

Johnson, A. (1999). Fiber meets fibonacci; The shape of things to come. *Mathematics Teaching in the Middle School, 4*(4), 256–262.

Kirkwood, T. F. (1999). Integrating an interdisciplinary unit in middle school: A school-university partnership. *Clearing House, 72*(3), 160–163.

Marshall, M. (1998). Fostering social responsibility and handling disruptive social behavior. *NASSP Bulletin, 82*(596), 31–39.

Powell, R., et al. (1998). Toward an integrative multicultural learning environment. *Middle School Journal, 29*(4), 3–13.

Richburg, R. W., & Nelson, B. J. (1998). Integrating content standards and higher-order thinking: A geography lesson plan. *Social Studies, 89*(2), 85–90.

Roberts, P. L., & Kellough, R. D. (2000). *A guide for developing an interdisciplinary thematic unit* (2nd ed.). Upper Saddle River, NJ: Merrill/Prentice Hall.

Roblyer, M. D. (1999). *Integrating technology across the curriculum: A database of strategies and lesson plans.* Upper Saddle River, NJ: Merrill/Prentice Hall.

Rubink, W. L., & Taube, S. R. (1999). Mathematical connections from biology: "Killer" bees come to life in the classroom. *Mathematics Teaching in the Middle School, 4*(6), 350–356.

Shiman, D. (1999). Human rights and foreign policy: A lesson plan. *Social Education, 63*(1), 58–60.

Totten, S. (1998). Using reader-response theory to study poetry about the holocaust with high school students. *Social Studies, 89*(1), 30–34.

Usnick, V., & McCarthy, J. (1998). Turning adolescents onto mathematics through literature. *Middle School Journal, 29*(4), 50–54.

■ ENDNOTES

[1] J. Goodlad, *A Place Called School: Prospects for the future* (New York: McGraw Hill, 1984), p. 231.

[2] Southern Regional Educational Board, *1995 Outstanding Practices* (Atlanta, GA: Author, 1995), p. 8.

[3] V. LaPoint et al., *Report 1: The Talent Development High School—Essential Components* [Online]. Available (Downloaded June 19, 1998): **http://www. csos.jhu.edu/crespar/CRESPAR%20Reports/report01entire.html.**, p. 6.

[4] See *Integrating the Curriculum* with Heidi Hayes Jacobs. (1998). The Video Journal of Education. Salt Lake City, UT. 1-800-572-1153. ISBN#1-58740-016-2.

[5] See, for example, the articles in the theme issue of *Educational Leadership 49*(2) (October 1994).

[6] The section entitled, "The Spectrum of Integrated Curriculum," was first developed in 1996 by Richard D. Kellough and has appeared since then in similar form in several Prentice-Hall publications authored or coauthored by Kellough.

Selecting and Implementing Instructional Strategies

Part 3 Overview

As discussed in Part 1 and Part 2, what goes on in each classroom should be consistent with the reality of the world outside the classroom. Today's theory of effective instruction urges teachers to give recognition to the various skills needed to function as a human being, a worker, a citizen, a consumer, and a parent. Teachers must help students to develop a more sophisticated awareness of the uses of knowledge, as well as to become concerned not only with knowing *about* but also with knowing *how*.

Building a repertoire of instructional strategies will prepare you to effectively meet the complex needs of all of your students. The three modules in Part 3 will assist in your decision making about when each approach is most appropriate and will provide guidelines for their use. The modules in Part 3 facilitate your selection and implementation of particular instructional strategies by:

- Reviewing important principles of instruction and learning by comparing student-centered and teacher-centered instruction.
- Providing an important rule for planning and selecting learning activities.
- Providing skill development in the use of questioning.
- Providing guidelines for teaching thinking skills.
- Providing descriptions of problem-solving, inquiry, and discovery methods.
- Providing guidelines for using teacher talk strategies.
- Providing guidelines for your use of discussion, demonstrations, the textbook, recitation, review, projects, group work, written work, assignments, and homework, as well as other strategies.
- Providing guidelines for ensuring equality in the classroom.
- Providing guidelines for selecting and using printed and display materials, teaching materials, audiovisual and media sources, as well as community resources, speakers, and field trips.

> *When teaching a group of students of mixed learning capacities, mixed modality strengths, mixed language proficiencies, and mixed cultural backgrounds, the integration of learning modalities is a must. A teacher who uses only one style of teaching for all students in the same classroom setting, day after day, is shortchanging the achievement of students who could learn better if another way of teaching were used.*
>
> —Joseph F. Callahan,
> Leonard H. Clark
> and
> Richard D. Kellogh
> (7th Edition)

Student-Centered Instructional Strategies

Module 6 Overview

By now you are probably well aware that the education profession, like other disciplines, contains its own special jargon, which can be confusing. The use of the terms *direct teaching* (or its synonym, **direct instruction**), and its antonym, **direct experience**, is an example of how confusing the jargon can be. The term **direct teaching** (or *direct instruction, expository teaching,* or *teacher-centered instruction*) can also have a variety of definitions, depending on who is defining it. For this book, you should keep this distinction in mind: Do not confuse the term *direct instruction* with the term *direct experience*. The two terms indicate two separate (though not incompatible) instructional modes. The dichotomy of pedagogical opposites shown in Figure 6.1 provides a useful visual distinction of the opposites. While terms in one column are similar if not synonymous, they are near or exact opposites of those across in the other column.

Rather than focusing your attention on the selection of a particular model of teaching, our preference is to emphasize the importance of an eclectic approach where you will select the best instructional strategy from various models. For example, there will be times when you want to use a direct, teacher-centered instructional strategy, perhaps by using a minilecture or a demonstration. There will also be more times when you will want to use an indirect, student-centered or social-interactive instructional strategy, such as the use of cooperative learning and other small-group activities. And perhaps there will be even more times when you will be doing both simultaneously, for example, when working with a teacher-centered approach with one small group of students, perhaps giving them direct instruction, while in another area of the classroom another group or several groups of students are working on their project study (a student-centered approach).

In this module we present and discuss a number of teaching strategies that all have two common elements: (a) social interaction and (b) problem solving. These strategies require that students interact with one another and draw conclusions, learn concepts, and form generalizations through induction, deduction, and observation or through application of principles. The premises underlying these strategies are that a person learns to think by thinking and sharing his or her thoughts with others and that knowledge gained through active learning and self-discovery is more meaningful, permanent, and transferable than knowledge gained through rote memorization and expository techniques.

Delivery mode of instruction	vs.	Access mode of instruction
Didactic instruction	vs.	Facilitative teaching
Direct instruction	vs.	Indirect instruction
Direct teaching	vs.	Direct experiencing
Expository teaching	vs.	Discovery learning
Teacher-centered instruction	vs.	Student-centered instruction

FIGURE 6.1 ● Pedagogical Opposites

Specific Objectives

At the completion of this module, you should be able to:

- Demonstrate an understanding of the advantages and disadvantages of direct and indirect instructional strategies and of when each type is likely to be most appropriate; and demonstrate how and why in one class period you would combine direct and indirect instructional strategies.

- Give examples in your subject field of learning experiences from each of these categories, and when, why, and how you would use each category: verbal, visual, vicarious, simulated, and direct.

- Describe situations in your subject field when you would use each of the following: dyad teaching, learning center, small-group learning, and Cooperative Learning Groups.

- Differentiate as well as discuss the relationships among problem solving, inquiry, and discovery.

- Demonstrate an understanding of ways that teaching your subject field can help students develop their thinking skills.

- Demonstrate knowledge of how to encourage student writing while teaching your subject.

Introduction

Teachers are urged to accept the principle that learning is an active process. They are told that the goals of education encompass not only the acquisition of knowledge but also the guidance of every person to her or his fullest potential. Such guidance involves development of a multitude of skills, including those needed for critical thinking, independent inquiry and problem solving, and active participation in group endeavors.

Group activity is a part of life—in the circles of family and friends as well as in the work, civic, religious, economic, governmental, and social recreational realms. At one time or another, everyone is involved in activities with others, either as a participant or an observer. These activities include those at the workplace, legislative committees, collective negotiations in business and labor, radio and television talk shows, round-table discussions, religious and club activities, various symposia and panels, and town hall meetings. Group participatory skills are learned skills, not innate ones. The school has a role to play in the development of those skills, both by encouraging awareness and analysis and by experiential approaches. Therefore, teachers need to add to their repertoire of strategies a variety of techniques that provide students with opportunities to interact with one another. Here we will select a mode of instruction and highlight the strengths and weaknesses of student-centered instructional strategies.

■ PRINCIPLES OF CLASSROOM INSTRUCTION AND LEARNING: A SYNOPSIS

A student does not learn to write by learning to recognize grammatical constructions of sentences. Neither does a person learn to play soccer solely by listening to a lecture on soccer. Learning is superficial unless the instructional methods and learning activities are (a) developmentally appropriate for the learners and (b) intellectually appropriate for the understanding, skills, and attitudes desired. Memorizing, for instance, is not the same as understanding. Yet far too often, memorization seems all that is expected of students in many classrooms. The result is low-level learning, a mere verbalism or regurgitation of information. That is not intellectually appropriate and it is not teaching, but just the orchestration of short-term memory exercises. A mental model of learning that assumes that a brain is capable of doing only one thing at a time is invidiously incorrect.[2]

When selecting the mode of instruction, you should bear in mind the following six basic principles of classroom instruction and learning.

1. To a great degree, it is the mode of instruction that determines what is learned.

2. Students must be actively involved in their own learning and in the assessment of their learning.

3. You must hold high expectations for the learning of each student (although not necessarily identical

expectations for every student), and not waiver from those expectations.

4. Students need constant, steady, understandable, positive, and reliable feedback about their learning.

5. Students should be engaged in both independent study and cooperative learning and give and receive individualized instruction.

6. No matter what content area you are prepared to teach, you are also a teacher of reading, writing, thinking, and study skills.

Conceptual knowledge refers to the understanding of relationships, whereas *procedural knowledge* entails the recording in memory of the meanings of symbols, rules, and procedures needed in order to accomplish tasks. Unless it is connected in meaningful ways to the formation of conceptual knowledge, the accumulation of memorized procedural knowledge is fragmented, ill fated, and will be remembered for only a brief time.

To help students establish conceptual knowledge, learning, for them, must be meaningful. To help make learning meaningful for your students, you should use direct and real experiences as often as practical and possible. Vicarious experiences are sometimes necessary to provide students with otherwise unattainable knowledge; however, direct experiences that engage all the students' senses and all their learning modalities are more powerful. Students learn to write by writing and by receiving coaching and feedback about their progress in writing. They learn to play soccer by playing soccer and by receiving coaching and feedback about their developing skills and knowledge in playing the game. They learn these things best when they are actively (hands-on) and mentally (minds-on) engaged in doing them. This is real learning, learning that is meaningful; it is *authentic learning*.

■ Culturally Sensitive Pedagogy

In **culturally sensitive pedagogy** the cultural beliefs, traditions, values, and mores of the students and their families are reflected in all aspects of the teaching/learning process. To promote culturally sensitive pedagogy, teachers learn special strategies to align the school and home environments, use culturally relevant materials, support all learning modalities, employ classroom management techniques that are culturally acceptable, and have students engage in higher-order thinking and problem-solving skills that directly apply to their real-life experiences. This student-centered curricular approach helps *all* students meet the content standards in academically challenging content courses.[3]

■ Direct vs. Indirect Instructional Modes: Strengths and Weaknesses of Each

When selecting an instructional strategy, there are two distinct choices (modes): Should you deliver informa-

tion to students directly or should you provide students with access to information? (Refer to the comparison of pedagogical opposites in Figure 6.1.)

The *delivery mode* (known also as the *didactic, expository,* or *traditional style*) is designed to deliver information. Knowledge is passed on from those who know (the teachers, with the aid of textbooks) to those who do not (the students). Within the delivery mode, traditional and time-honored strategies are textbook reading, the lecture (formal teacher talk), questioning, and teacher-centered or teacher-planned discussions.

With the *access mode,* instead of direct delivery of information and direct control over what is learned, you provide students with access to information by working *with* the students. In collaboration with the students, experiences are designed that help students build their existing schemata and obtain new knowledge and skills. Within the access mode, important instructional strategies include cooperative learning, inquiry, and investigative student-centered project learning, each of which most certainly will use questioning, although the questions more frequently will come from the students than from you, the textbook, or some other source extrinsic to the student. Discussions and lectures on particular topics also may be involved. But when used in the access mode, discussions and lectures occur during or after (rather than preceding) direct, hands-on learning by the students. In other words, rather than preceding student inquiry, discussions and lectures *result from* student inquiry, and then may be followed by further student investigation.

You are probably more experienced with the delivery mode. To be most effective as a classroom teacher, however, you must become knowledgeable and skillful in using access strategies. For young learners, strategies within the access mode clearly facilitate their positive learning and acquisition of conceptual knowledge and help build their self-esteem.

You should appropriately select and effectively use strategies from both modes, but with a strong favoring of access strategies. Thus, from your study of this and the next module, you will become knowledgeable about specific techniques so you can make intelligent decisions about choosing the best strategy for particular goals and objectives for your subject and the interests, needs, and maturity level of your own unique group of students.

Figures 6.2 and 6.3 provide an overview of the specific strengths and weaknesses of each mode. By comparing those figures you can see that the strengths and weaknesses of one mode are nearly mirror opposites of the other. As noted earlier, although as a teacher you should be skillful in the use of strategies from both modes, for the most developmentally appropriate teaching for most groups of learners you should concentrate more on using strategies from the access mode. Strategies within that mode are more student-centered, hands-on, and concrete; students interact with one another and are actually, or are closer to, doing what they are learning to do—that

---

Delivery Mode

Strengths
- Much content can be covered within a short span of time, usually by formal teacher talk, which then may be followed by an experiential activity.
- The teacher is in control of what content is covered.
- The teacher is in control of time allotted to specific content coverage.
- Strategies within the delivery mode are consistent with competency-based instruction.
- Student achievement of specific content is predictable and manageable.

Potential weaknesses
- The sources of student motivation are mostly extrinsic.
- Students have little control over the pacing of their learning.
- Students make few important decisions about their learning.
- There may be little opportunity for divergent or creative thinking.
- Student self-esteem may be inadequately served.

FIGURE 6.2 ● Delivery Mode: Its Strengths and Weaknesses

Access Mode

Strengths
- Students learn content, and in more depth.
- The sources of student motivation are more likely intrinsic.
- Students make important decisions about their own learning.
- Students have more control over the pacing of their learning.
- Students develop a sense of personal self-worth.

Potential weaknesses
- Content coverage may be more limited.
- Strategies are time-consuming.
- The teacher has less control over content and time.
- The specific results of student learning are less predictable.
- The teacher may have less control over class procedures.

FIGURE 6.3 ● Access Mode: Its Strengths and Weaknesses

---

is, the learning is likely more authentic. Learning that occurs from the use of that mode is longer lasting, that is, it fixes into long-term memory. And, as the students interact with one another and with their learning, they develop a sense of "can do," which enhances their self-esteem.

■ SELECTING LEARNING ACTIVITIES

Returning to our soccer example, can you imagine a soccer coach teaching students the skills and knowledge needed to play soccer but without ever letting them play the game? Can you imagine a science teacher instructing students on how to read a thermometer without ever letting them actually read a real thermometer? Can you imagine a geography teacher teaching students how to read a map without ever letting them put their eyes and hands on a real map? Can you imagine a piano teacher teaching a student to play piano without ever allowing the student to touch a real keyboard? Unfortunately, still

today, too many teachers do almost those exact things—they try to teach students to do something without letting the students practice doing it.

In planning and selecting appropriate learning activities, an important rule to remember is to select activities that are as close to the real thing as possible, that is, have them learn through direct experiencing. When students are involved in direct experiences, they are using more of their sensory input channels, their learning modalities (i.e., auditory, visual, tactile, kinesthetic). And when all the senses are engaged, learning is more integrated, and is most effective, meaningful, and longest lasting. This "learning by doing" is *authentic learning*—or, as often referred to, **hands-on/minds-on learning.**

■ The Learning Experiences Ladder

Figure 6.4 depicts what is called the *Learning Experiences Ladder,* a visual depiction of a range of the kinds of

FIGURE 6.4 ● The Learning Experiences Ladder

SOURCE: Earlier versions of this concept were Charles F. Hoban, Sr., et al., *Visualizing the Curriculum* (New York: Dryden, 1937), p. 39; Jerome S. Bruner, *Toward a Theory of Instruction* (Cambridge: Harvard University Press, 1966), p. 49; Edgar Dale, *Audio-Visual Methods in Teaching* (New York: Holt, Rinehart & Winston, 1969), p. 108; and Eugene C. Kim and Richard D. Kellough, *A Resource Guide for Secondary School Teaching*, 2nd ed. (Upper Saddle River, NJ: Prentice Hall, 1978), p. 136.

ABSTRACT ↑

Verbal Experiences
Teacher talk, written words; engaging only one sense; using the most abstract symbolization; students physically inactive. *Examples:* (a) Listening to the teacher talk about tide pools. (b) Listening to a student report about the Grand Canyon. (c) Listening to a guest speaker talk about how the state legislature functions.

Visual Experiences
Still pictures, diagrams, charts; engaging only one sense; typically symbolic; students physically inactive. *Examples:* (a) Viewing slide photographs of tide pools. (b) Viewing drawings and photographs of the Grand Canyon. (c) Listening to a guest speaker talk about the state legislature and show slides of it in action.

Vicarious Experiences
Laser videodisc programs; computer programs; video programs; engaging more than one sense; learner indirectly "doing"; may be some limited physical activity. *Examples:* (a) Interacting with a computer program about wave action and life in tide pools. (b) Viewing and listening to a video program about the Grand Canyon. (c) Taking a field trip to observe the state legislature in action.

Simulated Experiences
Role-playing; experimenting; simulations; mock-up; working models; all or nearly all senses engaged; activity often integrating disciplines; closest to the real thing. *Examples:* (a) Building a classroom working model of a tide pool. (b) Building a classroom working model of the Grand Canyon. (c) Designing a classroom role-play simulation patterned after the operating procedure of the state legislature.

Direct Experiences
Learner actually doing what is being learned; true inquiry; all senses engaged; usually integrates disciplines; the real thing. *Examples:* (a) Visiting and experiencing a tide pool. (b) Visiting and experiencing the Grand Canyon. (c) Designing an elected representative body to oversee the operation of the school-within-the-school program and patterned after the state legislative assembly.

CONCRETE ↓

learning experiences from which a teacher may select. Hands-on/minds-on learning is at the bottom of the ladder. At the top are abstract experiences, where the learner is exposed only to symbolization (i.e., letters and numbers) and uses only one or two senses (auditory or visual). The teacher lectures while the students sit, watch, and hear. Visual and verbal symbolic experiences, although impossible to avoid when teaching, are less effective in ensuring that planned and meaningful learning occurs. This is especially so with learners who have special needs, learners who are culturally different, and English Language Learners. Thus, when planning learning experiences and selecting instructional materials, you are advised to select activities that engage the students in the most direct experiences possible.

As can be inferred from the Learning Experiences Ladder, when teaching about tide pools (the first example for each step), the most effective mode is to take the students to a tide pool (direct experience), where students can use all their senses (see, hear, touch, smell, and perhaps even taste if not polluted with toxins) to experience the tide pool. If a field trip to a tide pool is not possible, students could experience a tide pool through a multimedia presentation or virtual reality adventure via the Internet. The least effective mode is for the teacher to merely talk about the tide pool (verbal experience, the most abstract and symbolic experience), engaging only one sense—auditory.

Of course, for various reasons—such as time, matters of safety, lack of resources, geographic location of your school—you may not be able to take your students to a tide pool. You cannot always use the most direct experience, so sometimes you must select an experience higher on the ladder. Self-discovery teaching is not always appropriate. Sometimes it is more appropriate to build upon what others have discovered and learned. Although learners do not need to reinvent the wheel, the most effective and longest-lasting learning is that which engages most or all of their senses. On the Learning Experiences Ladder, those are the experiences that fall within the bottom three categories—direct, simulated, and vicarious. This is true with adult learners, primary grade children, or students of any age group in-between.

Direct, Simulated, and Vicarious Experiences Help Connect Student Learning

Another value of direct, simulated, and vicarious experiences is that they tend to be interdisciplinary; that is, they blur or bridge subject-content boundaries. That makes those experiences especially useful for teachers who want to help students connect the learning of one discipline with that of others and to bridge what is being learned with their own life experiences. Direct, simulated, and vicarious experiences are more like real life. That means that the learning resulting from those experiences is authentic.

Many resources can provide ideas for instructional activities. Figure 6.5 provides addresses for Internet sources for the various disciplines. Now do Exercises 6.1 and 6.2.

EXERCISE 6.1

A Reflection on My Past Involvement with Student-Centered Instructional Activities

Instructions: The purpose of this exercise is for you to reflect on your past involvement in participatory activities and then to share those thoughts with your classmates. To that end, this exercise contains a list of such activities.

1. For each activity write *F* if you are *f*amiliar with it, *E* if you have observed it *e*ffectively used by a teacher, and *L* if as a student it was an activity that you *l*iked. You may use any one, two, or all three of the letter codes in your response to each activity.

   _____ Brainstorming
   _____ Buzz session
   _____ Case study
   _____ Committee
   _____ Cooperative learning
   _____ Debate
   _____ Discovery
   _____ Discussion, whole-class
   _____ Field trip
   _____ Fishbowl
   _____ Forum

   _____ Inquiry
   _____ Jury trial
   _____ Learning activity center
   _____ Panel discussion
   _____ Project or independent study
   _____ Role-playing
   _____ Roundtable discussion
   _____ Simulation
   _____ Sociodrama
   _____ Symposium

2. Share your marks and experiences with your classmates in small groups of three or four per group.

3. As you study this module, try to engage in various group activities with your classmates. Assume the various roles discussed. Keep records of involvement and interaction. Perhaps ask someone to serve each time as observer to help you analyze the process and its effectiveness. As you gain knowledge and experience about these various student-centered activities, consider how you might use them in your own teaching.

 To access this exercise online, go to the Companion Website at **www.prenhall.com/kellough.**

All Subjects, Lessons, Units, and Project Ideas
- **Global Schoolhouse** <http://www.gsh.org>.
- **Intercultural E-Mail Classroom Connections** <http://www.iecc.org/>.
- **PBS Teacher Source** <http://www.pbs.org/teachersource>.
- **Teachers Helping Teachers** <http://www.pacific.net/~mandel/index.html>.
- **Teachers Net Lesson Bank** <http://teachers.net/lessons>.
- **The Library in the Sky** <http://www.nwrel.org/sky>.

Arts
- **American Alliance for Theatre & Education** <http://www.aate.com/>.
- **Association of Theatre Movement Educators** <http://www.asu.edu/cfa/atme/>.
- **Crayola Creativity Center** <http://www.crayola.com>.
- **Dance links** <http://www.SapphireSwan.com/dance/>.
- **Music Education Resource Links** <http://www.isd77.k12.mn.us/resources/staffpages/shirk/k12.music.html>.
- **World Wide Arts Resources** <http://wwar.com/>.

Environmental Issues
- **North American Association for Environmental Education** <http://www.naaee.org>.
- **World Bank** <http://www.worldbank.org/depweb>.

Social Studies/History
- **Albert Shanker Institute** <http://www.shankerinstitute.org>.
- **American Women's History** <http://frank.mtsu.edu/~kmiddlet/history/women.html>.
- **Best of hHistory Web sites** <http://www.besthistorysites.net>.
- **Choices Program** <http://www.choices.edu/index.cfm>.
- **Civics Online** <http://civics-online.org>.
- **Facing History and Ourselves** <http://facinghistory.org>.
- **FedWorld** <http://www.fedworld.gov>.
- **Historical Text Archive** <http://historicaltextarchive.com>.
- **History Net** <http://www.thehistorynet.com>.
- **Houghton Mifflin Social Studies Center** <http://www.eduplace.com/ss/>.
- **Links to lesson plans, unit plans, thematic units, and resources** <http://www.csun.edu/~hcedu013/index.html>.
- **Mexico Online** <http://www.mexonline.com>.
- **National Council for the Social Studies** <http://www.socialstudies.org>.
- **Scrolls from the Dead Sea** <http://sunsite.unc.edu/expo/deadsea.scrolls.exhibit/intro.html>.
- **Social Science Resources** <http://www.nde.state.ne.us/SS/ss.html>.
- **U.S. History, From Revolution to Reconstruction** <http://grid.let.rug.nl/~welling/usa/usa.html>.

Language and Literacy
- **Language and Literacy** <http://www.uis.edu/~cook/langlit/index.html>.
- **Language links** <http://polyglot.lss.wisc.edu/lss/lang/langlink.html>.
- **National Clearinghouse for English Language Acquisition & Language Instruction Education Programs** <http://www.ncela.gwu.edu>.
- **Second language learning** <http://www.sdkrashen.com>.

Mathematics
- **Fun Mathematics Lessons** <http://www.math.rice.edu/~lanius/Lessons>.
- **Math Activities** <http://www.k111.k12.il.us/king/math.htm>.
- **Math Archives** <http://archives.math.utk.edu>.
- **Math for Elementary Teachers** <http://www.mtlakes.org/ww/tech/webtools/math.htm>.
- **Math Forum** <http://forum.swarthmore.edu/>.
- **Mathematics Lesson Plans K–12** <http://www.coled.org/cur/math.html#math3>.
- **MathSource (Wolfram)** <http://mathsource.wri.com>.
- **Mega Mathematics** <http://www.c3.lanl.gov/mega-math>.
- **PlaneMath** <http://www.planemath.com>.
- **Show-Me Project** <http://www.showmecenter.missouri.edu>.

FIGURE 6.5 ● Internet Sites for Teaching Ideas for Various Disciplines

(continued)

Science

- **Columbia Education Center K–12 lesson plan collection** <http://www.col-ed.org/cur/science.html#scil>.
- **Dive and Discover** <http://www.divediscover.whoi.edu>.
- **Electronic Zoo** <http://netvet.wustl.edu/e-zoo.htm>.
- **Mandel's collection** <http://www.pacificnet.net/~mandel/Science.html>.
- **Stanford Solar Center** <http://solar-center.stanford.edu>.
- **Windows to the Universe** <http://www.windows.umich.edu >.

FIGURE 6.5 *continued* ● Internet Sites for Teaching Ideas for Various Disciplines

---

EXERCISE **6.2**

■ Recalling My Own Learning Experiences in School

Instructions: The purpose of this exercise is to recall and share learning experiences from your own school days. You should reflect upon those with respect to their relationship to the Learning Experiences Ladder and the discussion of the access and delivery modes of instruction.

1. Recall one vivid learning experience from each level of your schooling and identify its position on the Learning Experiences Ladder (Figure 6.4).

   Secondary school experience:

   Position on ladder:

   College experience:

   Position on ladder:

2. Share with classmates in small groups. After sharing your experiences with others of your group, what, if anything, can your group conclude? Write those conclusions here and then share them with the entire class.

 To access this exercise online, go to the Companion Website at **www.prenhall.com/kellough.**

■ THE TOTAL CLASS AS A GROUP ENTERPRISE

To start your thinking about the processes of participation and group interaction, it may be helpful to view the whole class as a group. In efforts to provide experiences for learners, teachers sometimes overlook the opportunity to make sessions with the total class more interactive.

Consider for a moment the major characteristics of the traditional—and prevalent—teacher-centered, recitation-type strategy: Teacher-led and teacher-dominated sessions; questions of a relatively superficial, information-seeking nature; repeating or restating (reciting) what has previously been learned, studied, read, or memorized; the "hearing" of lessons to detect right and wrong answers; checking to see if students have done their work; a one-to-one relationship between the questioner and hearer and between teller and answerer; and all decision making in the hands of the teacher regarding purpose, content, process, and participation.

A flowchart of participation in such a session would probably reveal a significant number of tallies for the teacher, with a smaller number distributed over a relatively small number of students who were selected by the teacher to participate. The major mode of operation would tend to be a question and an answer, with an occasional comment about the accuracy or character of student responses. There also might be the occasional lecture or minilecture. Figure 6.6 is a diagram showing the flow of interaction found in a typical recitation. Note

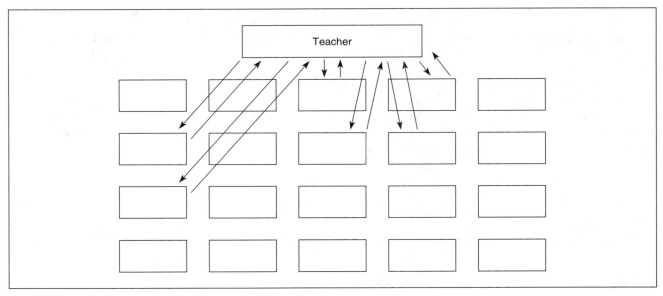

FIGURE 6.6 ● Diagram of a Traditional Recitation-Type Strategy

that the interaction is between the teacher and individual students only. There is no cross flow between student and student.

In contrast, consider the possibilities inherent in the concept of a total-class activity, viewed as genuine discussion with student interactive participation. The focus is not on hearing lessons but on inquiry and discovery. Figure 6.7 is a diagram showing the flow of interaction in a whole-class discussion. In that class, students have been arranged in an open square. Arrows pointing to the center of the square indicate that the person is speaking to the group as a whole. Arrows pointing to individuals indicate the person the speaker is addressing. Note that the conversation includes much cross talk between student and student and much talk addressed to the group as a whole. The teacher's role in the discussion is that of facilitator.

In contrast to the traditional strategy, an interactive, whole-class discussion is characterized by probing exploration of ideas, concepts, and issues; building upon student responses in a developmental flow; interaction among class members; shifting leadership among participants; questioning, sharing, differing, and conjecturing on the part of all; student participation in decision making; and hypothesizing and problem solving.

The essential difference between the two types of classrooms is that the first (the teacher-centered discussion) is based on the view that knowledge consists of a series of correct answers, with students as more-or-less passive participants, whereas the second is based on the view that knowledge is the product of creative inquiry through social interaction, with the students as active participants in that inquiry. Only through genuine student involvement and interaction can the contributions

and thinking of each participant be seen as being welcomed and accepted. And only with such interaction can hypotheses be tested, views expressed and analyzed, questions raised, controversies examined, and insights developed, along with other desirable cognitive and affective processes and outcomes.

A whole-class discussion (discussed further in Module 7) is not the only strategy you have at your disposal to promote interactive learning. Many other strategies will provide the opportunity for students to participate interactively in the learning process. For our purposes here, the tactics and strategies are broadly classified into four categories: (a) dyad groups; (b) Cooperative Learning Groups; (c) the relatively formal, planned, short-term, presentation-type technique; and (d) those group strategies that involve more student interaction and work of a long-term nature (e.g., projects) with varied purposes, including the analysis of the group process itself.

■ LEARNING IN PAIRS

It is sometimes advantageous to pair students (dyads) for learning. Four types of dyads are described as follows.

■ Peer Tutoring, Mentoring, and Cross-Age Coaching

Peer tutoring, mentoring, or peer-assisted learning (PAL) is a strategy whereby one classmate tutors another. It is useful, for example, when one student helps another who is an English Language Learner or when a

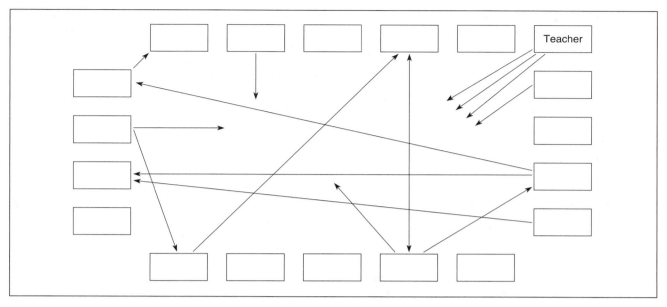

FIGURE 6.7 ● Diagram of an Interactive, Whole-Class Discussion

student skilled in math helps another who is less skilled. It has been demonstrated repeatedly that peer tutoring is a significant strategy for promoting active learning.[4] Furthermore, peer tutoring increases the academic achievement not only for those receiving tutoring but of those students doing the tutoring.[5]

Cross-age **coaching** is a strategy where one student is coached by another from a different, and usually higher, grade level. This is similar to peer tutoring, except that the coach is from a different age level than the student being coached.[6] Many middle schools and high schools have service learning projects that involve students mentoring younger elementary school children. Sometimes students from nearby colleges and universities mentor local middle school and high school students.

■ Paired Team Learning

Paired team learning is a strategy whereby students study and learn in teams of two. Students identified as gifted work and learn especially well when paired. Specific uses for paired team learning include drill partners, book report pairs, homework partners,[7] and project assignment pairs.

■ Think-Pair-Share

Think-pair-share is a strategy where students, in pairs, examine a new concept or topic about to be studied. After the students of each dyad discuss what they already know or think they know about the concept, they present their perceptions to the whole group. This technique is useful for discovering student's **misconceptions,**

also called **naïve theories,** about a topic. Introducing a writing step, the modification called *think-write-pair-share,* is when the dyad thinks and writes their ideas or conclusions before sharing with the larger group.

■ The Learning Center

Another significantly beneficial way of pairing students for instruction is by using the **Learning Center (LC).** An LC is a special station located in the classroom where one student (or two, if student interaction is necessary or preferred at the center) can quietly work and learn more about a special topic or improve specific skills at his or her own pace. All materials needed are provided at that station, including clear instructions for operation of the center. Whereas the LC used to be thought of as being effective in elementary or self-contained classrooms, now, with block scheduling and longer class periods, the LC has special relevance for all teachers, regardless of grade level. Familiar examples are the personal computer station and the reading center.

The value of Learning Centers as instructional devices undoubtedly lies in the following facts. LCs can provide instructional diversity. While working at a center, the student is giving time and quality attention to the learning task (learning toward mastery) and is likely to be engaging her most effective learning modality or integrating several modalities or all of them. To adapt instruction to students' personal needs and preferences, it is possible to design a learning environment that includes several learning centers, each of which uses a different medium and modality or focuses on a special aspect of the curriculum. Students then rotate through the various learning centers according to their needs and preferences.

Learning Centers are of three types. In the *direct-learning center,* performance expectations for cognitive learning are quite specific and the focus is on mastery of content. In the *open-learning center,* the goal is to provide opportunity for exploration, enrichment, motivation, and creative discovery. In the *skill center,* as in a direct-learning center, performance expectations are quite specific but the focus is on the development of a particular skill or process.

Although in all instances the primary reason for using a Learning Center is to personalize—that is, to provide collections of materials and activities adjusted to the various readiness levels, interests, and learning profiles of students—there are additional reasons. These are to provide (a) a mechanism for learning that crosses discipline boundaries; (b) a special place for a student with special needs; (c) opportunities for creative work, enrichment experiences, and multisensory experiences; and (d) opportunity to learn from learning packages that use special equipment or media of which only one or a limited supply may be available for use in your classroom (e.g., science materials, a microscope, a computer, or a laser videodisc player, or some combination of these).

To construct an LC you should follow these guidelines. The center should be designed with a theme in mind, preferably one that integrates the students' learning by providing activities that cross discipline boundaries. Decide the purpose of the center and give the center a name, such as "the center for the study of wetlands," "walking tour of Florence," "traveling to Quebec City," "structure and function," "patterns in nature," "the United Nations," "patterns of discrimination," "editing a video," "the center for worldwide communication," and so on. The purpose of the center should be clearly understood by the students. Centers should always be used for educational purposes, *never* for punishment.

The center should be designed to be attractive, purposeful, and uncluttered and should be identified with an attractive sign. Learning Centers should be activity-oriented (i.e., dependent on the students' manipulation of materials, not just paper-and-pencil tasks).

Topics for the center should be related to the instructional program—for review and reinforcement, remediation, or enrichment. The center should be self-directing (i.e., specific instructional objectives and procedures for using the center should be clearly posted and understandable to the student users). An audio- or videocassette or a computer program is sometimes used for this purpose. The center should also be self-correcting (i.e., student users should be able to tell by the way they have completed the task whether or not they have done it correctly and have learned).

The center should contain a variety of activities geared to the varying abilities and interest levels of the students. A choice of two or more activities at a center is one way to provide for this.

Materials to be used at the center should be maintained at the center, with descriptions for use provided to the students. Materials should be safe for student use, and the center should be easily supervised by you or another adult. Some centers may become more or less permanent centers, that is, remain for the school term or longer, whereas other centers may change according to what is being studied at the time.

■ LEARNING IN SMALL GROUPS

Small groups are those involving three to eight students, in either a teacher- or a student-directed setting. Using small groups for instruction, including the Cooperative Learning Group, enhances the opportunities for students to assume greater control over their own learning, sometimes referred to as *empowerment.*

■ Purposes for Using Small Groups

Small groups can be formed to serve a number of purposes. They might be useful for a specific learning activity (e.g., reciprocal reading groups, where students take turns asking questions, summarizing, making predictions about, and clarifying a story), or they might be formed to complete an activity that requires materials that are of short supply (to complete a science experiment or a project), only lasting as long as the project does. Teachers have various rationales for assigning students to groups. Groups can be formed by grouping students according to (a) personality type (e.g., sometimes a teacher may want to team less-assertive students together in order to give them the opportunity for greater management of their own learning), (b) social pattern (e.g., sometimes it may be necessary to break up a group of rowdy friends, or it may be desirable to broaden the association among students), (c) common interest, (d) learning styles (e.g., forming groups of either mixed styles or of styles in common), or (e) their abilities in a particular skill or their knowledge in a particular area. One specific type of small-group instruction is the Cooperative Learning Group.

■ COOPERATIVE LEARNING

Lev Vygotsky (1896–1934) studied the importance of a learner's social interactions in learning situations. Vygotsky argued that learning is most effective when learners cooperate with one another in a supportive learning environment under the careful guidance of a teacher. Cooperative learning, group problem solving, problem-based learning, and cross-age tutoring are instructional strategies used by teachers that have grown in popularity as a result of research evolving from the work of Vygotsky.

■ The Cooperative Learning Group (CLG)

The *Cooperative Learning Group* is a **heterogeneous group** (i.e., mixed according to one or more criteria, such as ability or skill level, ethnicity, learning style, learning capacity, gender, and language proficiency) consisting of three to six students who work together in a teacher- or student-directed setting, emphasizing support for one another. Oftentimes, a CLG consists of five students of mixed ability, learning styles, gender, and ethnicity, with each member of the group assuming a particular role.

The theory and use of cooperative learning The theory of **cooperative learning** is that when small groups of students of mixed backgrounds and capabilities work together toward a common goal, members of the group increase their friendship and respect for one another. As a consequence, each individual's self-esteem is enhanced, students are more motivated to participate in higher-order thinking, and academic achievement is accomplished.[8]

There are several techniques for using cooperative learning. Of special interest to teachers are general methods of cooperative learning, such as "student team-achievement division" (STAD), where the teacher presents a lesson, students work together in teams to help each other learn the material, individuals take quizzes, and team rewards are earned based on the individual scores on the quizzes; "teams-games-tournaments" (TGT), where tournaments (rather than quizzes) are held in which students compete against others of similar academic achievements and then winners contribute toward their team's score; and group investigations.[9] Yet the primary purpose of each is for the groups to learn—which means, of course, that individuals within a group must learn. Group achievement in learning, then, is dependent upon the learning of individuals within the group. Rather than competing for rewards for achievement, members of the group cooperate with one another by helping one another learn, so that the group reward will be a good one.

Roles within the Cooperative Learning Group It is advisable to assign roles (specific functions) to each member of the CLG. (The lesson plan shown in the unit plan of Figure 5.7, Module 5, shows the use of a CLG activity using assigned roles for a lesson in lab science.) These roles should be rotated, either during the activity or from one time to the next. Although titles may vary, five typical roles are:

- *Group facilitator*—role is to lead the group by soliciting everyone's input and facilitating the group discussion.
- *Recorder*—role is to record all group activities and processes, and perhaps to periodically assess how the group is doing. Either the recorder or group facilitator may report the group process and accomplishments to the teacher and/or to the entire class.

- *Task master*—role is to see that all members carry out their respective roles, to keep the group on-task, and to make sure the group completes the task at hand within the time frame allotted.
- *Materials manager*—role is to obtain, maintain, and return materials needed for the group to function.
- *Thinking monitor*—role is to identify and record the sequence and processes of the group's thinking. This role encourages metacognition and the development of thinking skills.

It is important that students understand and perform their individual roles, and that each member of the CLG performs her or his tasks as expected. No student should be allowed to ride on the coattails of the group. To give significance to and to reinforce the importance of each role and to be able to readily recognize the role any student is serving during a CLG activity, one teacher made a trip to an office supplier and had permanent badges made for the various CLG roles. During CLGs, then, each student attaches the appropriate badge to her or his clothing.

What students and the teacher do when using Cooperative Learning Groups Actually, for learning by CLGs to take place, each member of the CLG must understand and assume two roles or responsibilities—the role he or she is assigned as a member of the group, and that of seeing that all others in the group are performing their roles. Sometimes this requires interpersonal skills that students have yet to learn or to learn well. This is where the teacher must assume some responsibility, too. Simply placing students into CLGs and expecting each member and each group to function and to learn the expected outcomes may not work. In other words, skills of cooperation must be taught, and if all your students have not yet learned the skills of cooperation, then you will have to teach them. This doesn't mean that if a group is not functioning you immediately break up the group and reassign members to new groups. Part of group learning is learning the process of how to work out conflict. A group may require your assistance to work out a conflict. With your guidance the group should be able to discover what the problem is that is causing the conflict, then identify some options and mediate at least a temporary solution. If a particular skill is needed, then with your guidance students can identify and learn that skill.

When to use Cooperative Learning Groups CLGs can be used for problem solving, investigations, opinion surveys, experiments, review, project work, test making, or almost any other instructional purpose. Just as you would for small-group work in general, you can use CLGs for most any purpose at any time; but as with any other type of instructional strategy, it should not be overused.

Outcomes of using Cooperative Learning Groups When the process is well-planned and managed, the outcomes of cooperative learning include (a) improved communication and relationships of acceptance among students of differences; (b) quality learning with fewer off-task behaviors; (c) improved ability to perform four key thinking strategies—problem solving, decision making, critical thinking, and creative thinking—and (d) increased academic achievement. In the words of Good and Brophy, "Cooperative learning arrangements promote friendships and prosocial interaction among students who differ in achievement, sex, race, or ethnicity, and they promote the acceptance of mainstreamed handicapped students by their nonhandicapped classmates. Cooperative methods also frequently have positive effects, and rarely have negative effects, on affective outcomes such as self-esteem, academic self-confidence, liking for the class, liking and feeling liked by classmates, and various measures of empathy and social cooperation."[10]

Cooperative group learning, assessment, and grading
Normally, the CLG is rewarded on the basis of group achievement, though individual members within the group can later be rewarded for individual contributions. Because of peer pressure, when using CLGs you must be cautious about using group grading.[11] Some teachers give bonus points to all members of a group to add to their individual scores when everyone in the group has reached preset criteria. In establishing preset standards, the standards can be different for individuals within a group, depending on each member's ability and past performance. It is important that each member of a group feel rewarded and successful. Often students' complaints of CLG experiences center on unfair grading. Hold students individually responsible while promoting group accountability. For determination of students' report card grades, measure individual student achievement later through individual results on tests and other sources of data.

■ Why Some Teachers Have Difficulty Using CLGs

Sometimes, teachers have difficulty when they think they are using CLGs, and they either give up trying to use the strategy or simply tell students to divide into groups for an activity and call it cooperative learning.[12] As emphasized earlier, for the strategy to work, each student must be given training and have acquired basic skills in interaction and group processing and must realize that individual achievement rests with that of their group. And, as true for any other strategy, the use of CLGs must not be overused—teachers must vary their strategies.

For the use of CLGs to work well, advanced planning and effective management are a must. Students must be instructed in the necessary skills for group learning. Each student must be assigned a responsible role within the group and be held accountable for fulfilling that responsibility. And, when a CLG activity is in process, groups must be continually monitored by the teacher for possible breakdown of this process within a group. In other words, while students are working in groups the teacher must exercise his or her skills of *withitness*. When a potential breakdown is noticed, the teacher quickly intervenes to help the group get back on track.

■ TEACHING THINKING FOR INTELLIGENT BEHAVIOR

Thinking can be thought of as the mental process by which a person makes sense out of experience.[13] Teachers should help students develop their thinking skills. In teaching for thinking, we are interested not only in what students know but also in how students behave when they don't know. Gathering evidence of the performance and growth of intelligent behavior requires observing students as they try to solve the day-to-day academic and real-life problems they encounter. By collecting anecdotes and examples of written, oral, and visual expressions, we can see students' increasingly voluntary and spontaneous performance of intelligent behaviors.

■ Characteristics of Intelligent Behavior

Characteristics of intelligent behavior that you should model, teach, and observe developing in your students, as identified by Costa,[14] are described in the following paragraphs.

Perseverance Perseverance is making a continual steady effort and sticking to a task until it is accomplished. Consider the following examples.

- Nearly single-handedly and against formidable odds, Clara Barton persevered to form the American Red Cross in 1882.

- Refusing to be intimidated by the chemical industry, powerful politicians, and the media, Rachel Carson was persistent in her pursuit to educate society about the ill effects of pesticides on humans and the natural world and refused to accept the premise that damage to nature was the inevitable cost of technological and scientific progress. Her book *Silent Spring*, published in 1963, was the seed for the beginning of the development of today's more responsible ecological attitude.

- Because of childhood diseases, Wilma Rudolf, at the age of 10, could not walk without the aid of leg braces. Just 10 years later at the age of 20, she was declared to be the fastest running woman in the world, having won three gold medals in the 1960 World Olympics.

Decreasing impulsivity When students develop impulse control, they think before acting. Impulsive behavior can worsen conflict and inhibit effective problem solving.[15] Students can be taught to think before shouting out an answer, before beginning a project or task, and before arriving at conclusions with insufficient data. One of several reasons that teachers should usually insist on a show of hands before a student is acknowledged to respond or ask a question is to help students develop control over the impulsive behavior of shouting out in class.[16]

Listening to others with understanding and empathy Some psychologists believe that the ability to listen to others, to empathize with and to understand their point of view, is one of the highest forms of intelligent behavior. Empathic behavior is considered an important skill for conflict resolution. Piaget refers to this behavior as *overcoming egocentrism*. In class meetings, brainstorming sessions, think tanks, town meetings, advisory councils, board meetings, and legislative bodies, people from various walks of life convene to share their thinking, to explore their ideas, and to broaden their perspectives by listening to the ideas and reactions of others.

Cooperative thinking-social intelligence Humans are social beings. Real-world problem solving has become so complex that seldom can any person go it alone. Not all students come to school knowing how to work effectively in groups. They may exhibit competitiveness, narrow-mindedness, egocentrism, ethnocentrism, or criticism of others' values, emotions, and beliefs. Listening, consensus seeking, giving up an idea to work on someone else's, empathy, compassion, group leadership, cooperative learning, knowing how to support group efforts, and altruism are behaviors indicative of intelligent human beings, and they can be learned by students at school and in the classroom.

Flexibility in thinking Sometimes referred to as *lateral thinking*, flexibility in thinking is the ability to approach a problem from a new angle—using a novel approach. With modeling by the teacher, students can develop this behavior as they learn to consider alternative points of view and to deal with several sources of information simultaneously.

Metacognition Learning to plan, monitor, assess, and reflect on one's own thinking, known as **metacognition,** is another characteristic of intelligent behavior. Cooperative Learning Groups, journals, portfolio conferences, self-assessment, and thinking aloud in dyads are strategies that can be used to help students develop this intelligent behavior. Thinking aloud is good modeling for your students, helping them to develop their own cognitive skills of thinking, learning, and reasoning.[17]

Striving for accuracy and precision Teachers can observe students growing in this behavior when students take time to check over their work, review the procedures, refuse to draw conclusions with only limited data, and use concise and descriptive language.

Sense of humor The positive effects of humor on the body's physiological functions are well established: A drop in the pulse rate, an increase of oxygen in the blood, the activation of antibodies that fight against harmful microorganisms and the release of gamma interferon, a hormone that fights viruses and regulates cell growth. Humor liberates creativity and provides high-level thinking skills, such as anticipation, finding novel relationships, and visual imagery. The acquisition of a sense of humor follows a developmental sequence similar to that described by Piaget[18] and Kohlberg.[19] Initially, young children may find humor in all the wrong things—human frailty, ethnic jokes, sacrilegious riddles, or ribald profanities. Later, creative children thrive on finding incongruity and will demonstrate a whimsical frame of mind during problem solving.

Questioning and problem posing Young people are usually full of questions and, unless discouraged, they do ask them. We want students to be alert to, and recognize discrepancies and phenomena in, their environment and to freely inquire about their causes. In exemplary educational programs, students are encouraged to ask questions (see Module 7) and then from those questions develop a problem-solving strategy to investigate their questions.

Drawing on knowledge and applying it to new situations A major goal of formal education is for students to apply school-learned knowledge to real-life situations. To develop skills in drawing on past knowledge and applying that knowledge to new situations, students must be given an opportunity to practice doing that very thing. Problem recognition, problem solving, and project-based learning are ways of providing that opportunity.

Taking risks Students should be encouraged to venture forth and explore their ideas. Teachers should model this behavior and can provide opportunities for students to develop this intelligent behavior by using techniques such as **brainstorming,** exploratory investigations, projects, and cooperative learning.

Using all the senses As discussed early in this module, as often as is appropriate and feasible, students should be encouraged to use and develop all their sensory input channels for learning (i.e., verbal, visual, tactile, and kinesthetic).

Ingenuity + originality + insightfulness = creativity All students must be encouraged to do, and be discouraged from saying "I can't." Students must be taught in such a way as to encourage intrinsic motivation rather than reliance on extrinsic sources. Teachers need to offer criticism in such a way that the student understands that the criticism is constructive and not a criticism of self. In exemplary programs, students learn the value of feedback.

Wonderment + inquisitiveness + curiosity + the enjoyment of problem solving = a sense of efficacy as a thinker Young children express wonderment, an expression that should never be stifled. Through effective teaching, adolescents can recapture that sense of wonderment as they are guided by an effective teacher into a feeling of "I can," and an expression of "I enjoy."

We should strive to help our own students develop these characteristics of intelligent behavior. Now, let's review additional research findings that offer important considerations in the facilitation of student learning and intelligent behavior.

Direct Teaching for Thinking and Intelligent Behavior

The curriculum of any school includes the development of skills that are used in thinking. Because the academic achievement of students increases when they are taught thinking skills directly, many researchers and educators concur that direct instruction should be given to all students on how to think and behave intelligently.[20]

Research Imperatives for the Teaching of Thinking

Four research perspectives have influenced the direct teaching of thinking. The *cognitive view of intelligence* asserts that intellectual ability is not fixed but can be developed. The *constructivist approach to learning* maintains that learners actively and independently construct knowledge by creating and coordinating relationships in their mental repertoire. The *social psychology view of classroom experience* focuses on the learner as an individual who is a member of various peer groups and a society. The *perspective of information processing* deals with the acquisition, elaboration, and management of information.[21]

Direct Teaching of Skills Used in Thinking

Rather than assuming that students have developed thinking skills (such as *classifying, comparing, concluding, generalizing, inferring,* and others—see Figure 6.9), teachers should devote classroom time to teaching them directly. When teaching a thinking skill directly, the subject content becomes the vehicle for thinking. For example, a social studies lesson can teach students how to distinguish fact and opinion; a language arts lesson instructs students how to compare and analyze; and a science lesson can teach students how to set up a problem for their inquiry.

■ INQUIRY TEACHING AND DISCOVERY LEARNING

Inquiry teaching and **discovery learning** are both useful tools for learning and for teaching thinking skills. Intrinsic to the effectiveness of both inquiry and discovery is the assumption that students would rather actively seek knowledge than receive it through traditional expository (i.e., information delivery) methods such as lectures, demonstrations, and textbook reading. Although inquiry and discovery are important teaching tools, there is sometimes confusion about exactly what inquiry teaching is and how it differs from discovery learning. The distinction should become clear as you study the following descriptions of these two important tools for teaching and learning.

Problem Solving

Perhaps a major reason why inquiry and discovery are sometimes confused is that, in both, students are actively engaged in problem solving. Problem solving is *the ability to define or describe a problem, determine the desired outcome, select possible solutions, choose strategies, test trial solutions, evaluate outcomes, and revise these steps where necessary.*[22]

Inquiry vs. Discovery

Problem solving is *not* a teaching strategy but a higher-order intellectual behavior that facilitates learning. What a teacher can and should do is provide opportunities for students to identify and tentatively solve problems. Experiences in inquiry and discovery can provide those opportunities. With the processes involved in inquiry and discovery, teachers can help students develop the skills necessary for effective problem solving. Two major differences between discovery and inquiry are (a) who identifies the problem and (b) the percentage of decisions that are made by the students. Table 6.1 shows three levels of inquiry, each level defined according to what the student does and decides.

It should be evident from Table 6.1 that what is called *Level I inquiry* is actually traditional, didactic, "cookbook" teaching, where both the problem and the process for resolving it are defined for the student. The student then works through the process to its inevitable resolution. If the process is well designed, the result is inevitable because the student discovers what was intended by the

TABLE 6.1 Levels of Inquiry			
	Level I (Not True Inquiry)	**Level II**	**Level III**
Problem identification	Identified by teacher or textbook	Identified by teacher or textbook	Identified by student
Process of solving problem	Decided by teacher or textbook	Decided by student	Decided by student
Identification of tentative solution to problem	Resolved by student	Resolved by student	Resolved by student

program's designers. This level is also called *guided inquiry* or *discovery* because the students are carefully guided through the investigation to (the predictable) discovery.

Level I is in reality a strategy within the *delivery mode*, the advantages of which were described earlier in this module. Because Level I inquiry is highly manageable and the learning outcome is predictable, it is probably best for teaching basic concepts and principles. Students who never experience learning beyond Level I are missing an opportunity to engage their highest mental opera-

tions, and they seldom (or never) get to experience more motivating, real-life problem solving. Furthermore, those students may come away with the false notion that problem solving is a linear process, which it is not. As illustrated in Figure 6.8, true inquiry is cyclical rather than linear. For that reason, Level I is *not* true inquiry because it is a linear process. Real-world problem solving is a cyclical rather than a linear process. One enters the cycle whenever a discrepancy or problem is observed and recognized, and that can occur at any point in the cycle.

REAL-LIFE SCENARIO
Problem Solving and Decision Making in the Real World Is an Integrated and Interdisciplinary Inquiry Activity[23]

On any given day or specified time period, teacher and students can look at a problem or subject of study from the point of view of many separate disciplines. Such an interdisciplinary approach to some degree has been adopted not only by educators but by other professionals as well. It is *the* mode of meaningful learning and real-life problem solving.

For example, consider the fact-finding and decision-making approach of public officials in the State of Colorado when confronted with the task of making decisions about projects proposed for watersheds in their state. While gathering information, the officials brought in Dave Rosgen, a state hydrologist. Rosgen led the officials into the field to demonstrate specific ways by which he helped control erosion and rehabilitate damaged streams. He look the officials to Wolf Creek, where they donned high waders. Rosgen led the group down the creek to examine various features of that complex natural stream. He pointed out evidence of the

creek's past meanders, patterns that he had incorporated into his rehabilitation projects. In addition to listening to this scientist's point of view, the public officials listened to other experts to consider related economic and political issues, before making final decisions about projects that had been proposed for watersheds in that state.

During interdisciplinary thematic units, students study a topic and its underlying ideas as well as related knowledge from various disciplines on an ongoing basis. The teacher, sometimes with the help of students and other teachers and adults, introduces experiences designed to elicit specific ideas and skills from various disciplines, just as Rosgen introduced information from hydrology to develop literacy skills through the unit. For instance, the teacher might stimulate communication skills through creative writing and other projects. Throughout the unit, the students are guided in exploring ideas related to different disciplines, to integrate their knowledge.

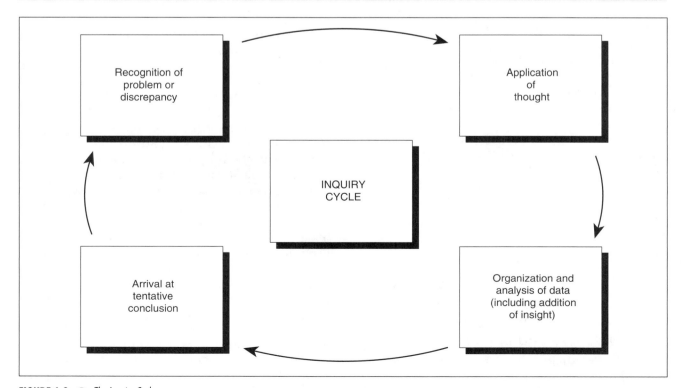

FIGURE 6.8 ● The Inquiry Cycle

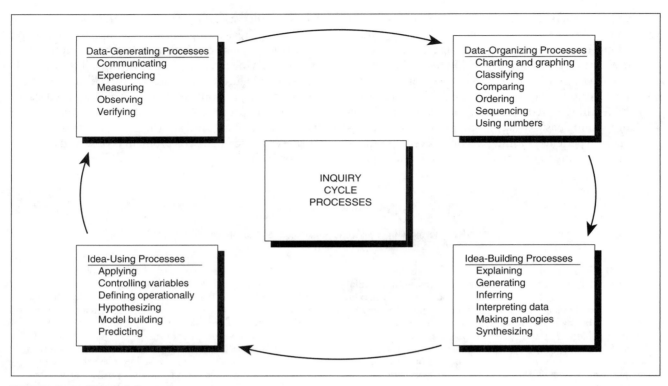

FIGURE 6.9 ● Inquiry Cycle Processes

■ True Inquiry

By the time students are in middle and secondary school, they should be provided experiences for true inquiry that begins with *Level II,* where students actually decide and design processes for their inquiry. In true inquiry there is an emphasis on the tentative nature of conclusions, which makes the activity more like real-life problem solving where decisions are always subject to revision if and when new data so prescribe.

At *Level III* inquiry students recognize and identify the problem as well as decide the processes for resolving it and reach conclusions. In *project-centered teaching,* students are usually engaged at this level of inquiry. By the time students are in middle grades and certainly by the time they are in secondary school, Level III inquiry should be a major strategy for instruction. However, it is not easy; like most good teaching practices it is a lot of work, but the intrinsic rewards make the effort worthwhile. As exclaimed by one teacher using interdisciplinary thematic instruction with student-centered inquiry, "I've never worked harder in my life, but I've never had this much fun, either."

■ The Critical Thinking Skills of Discovery and Inquiry

In true inquiry, students generate ideas and then design ways to test those ideas. The various processes used represent the many critical thinking skills. Some of those skills are concerned with generating and organizing data; others are concerned with building and using ideas. Figure 6.9 provides four main categories of these thinking processes and illustrates the place of each within the inquiry cycle.

Some processes in the cycle are discovery processes, and others are inquiry processes. Inquiry processes include the more complex mental operations (including all of those in the idea-using category). Project-centered teaching provides an avenue for inquiry processes, as does problem-centered teaching.

Inquiry learning is a higher-level mental operation that introduces the concept of the discrepant event, something that establishes cognitive disequilibrium (using the element of surprise to challenge students' prior notions) to help students develop skills in observing and being alert for discrepancies. Such a strategy provides opportunities for students to investigate their own ideas about explanations.[24] Inquiry, like discovery, depends upon skill in problem solving; the difference between the two is in the amount of decision-making responsibility given to students. Experiences afforded by inquiry help students understand the importance of suspending judgment and also the tentativeness of answers and solutions. With those understandings, students eventually are better able to deal with life's ambiguities. When students are not provided these important educational experiences, their education is incomplete.

One of the most effective ways of stimulating inquiry is to use materials that provoke students' interest. These ma-

Presentation of the Problem. In groups of three or four, students receive the following information.

Background. You (your group is considered as one person) are one of 120 passengers on the ship, the *Prince Charles.* You left England 12 weeks ago. You have experienced many hardships, including a stormy passage, limited rations, sickness, cold and damp weather, and hot, foul air below deck. Ten of your fellow immigrants to the New World, including three children, have died and been buried at sea. You are now anchored at an uncertain place, off the coast of the New World, which your captain believes to be somewhere north of the Virginia Grants. Seas are so rough and food so scarce that you and your fellow passengers have decided to settle here. A landing party has returned with a map they made of the area. You, as one of the elders, must decide at once where the settlement is to be located. The tradesmen want to settle along the river, which is deep, even though this seems to be the season of low water levels. Within ten months they expect deep-water ships from England with more colonists and merchants. Those within your group who are farmers say they must have fertile, workable land. The officer in charge of the landing party reported seeing a group of armed natives who fled when approached. He feels the settlement must be located so that it can be defended from the natives and from the sea.

Directions, step one: You (your group) are to select a site on the attached map which you feel is best suited for a colony. Your site must satisfy the different factions aboard the ship. A number of possible sites are already marked on the map (letters *A–G*). You may select one of these locations or use them as reference points to show the location of your colony. When your group has selected its site, list and explain the reasons for your choice. When each group has arrived at its tentative decision, these will be shared with the whole class.

Directions, step two: After each group has made its presentation and argument, a class debate is held about where the colony should be located.

Notes to teacher: For the debate, have a large map drawn on the writing board or on an overhead transparency, where each group's mark can be made for all to see and discuss. After each group has presented its argument for its location and against the others, we suggest that you then mark on the large map the two, three, or more hypothetical locations (assuming that, as a class,

there yet is no single favorite location). Then take a straw vote of the students, allowing each to vote on his or her own, independently rather than as members of groups. At this time you can terminate the activity by saying that if the majority of students favor one location, then that, in fact, is the solution to the problem—that is, the colony is located wherever the majority of class members believe it should be. No sooner will that statement be made by you than someone will ask, "Are we correct?" or "What is the right answer?" They will ask such questions because, as students in school, they are used to solving problems that have right answers (Level I inquiry teaching). In real-world problems, however, there are no "right" answers, though some answers may seem better than others. It is the process of problem solving that is important. You want your students to develop confidence in their ability to solve problems and understand the tentativeness of "answers" to real-life problems.

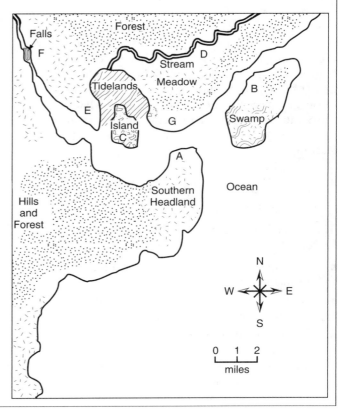

FIGURE 6.10 ● Locating a Colony: A Level II Inquiry

SOURCE: Adapted by Permission from Unpublished Material Provided by Jennifer Devine and Dennis Devine

terials should be presented in a nonthreatening, noncompetitive context, so students think and hypothesize freely. The teacher's role is to encourage students to form as many hypotheses as possible and then support their hypotheses with reasons. After the students suggest several ideas, the teacher should begin to move on to higher-order, more abstract questions that involve the development of generalizations and evaluations. True inquiry problems have a

special advantage in that they can be used with almost any group of students. Members of a group approach the problem as an adventure in thinking and apply it to whatever background they can muster. Background experience may enrich a student's approach to the problem, but is not crucial to the use or understanding of the evidence presented to him or her. Figure 6.10 is a Level II inquiry about locating a colony. As a class, do the inquiry now.

■ PROJECT-CENTERED LEARNING: GUIDING LEARNING FROM INDEPENDENT AND GROUP INVESTIGATIONS, PAPERS, AND ORAL REPORTS

For the most meaningful student learning to occur, **independent study,** individual writing, student-centered projects, and oral reports should be major features of your instruction. There will be times when the students are interested in an in-depth inquiry of a topic and will want to pursue a particular topic for study. This undertaking of a learning project can be flexible: An individual student, a team of two, a small group, or the entire class can do the investigation. The *project* is a relatively long-term investigative study from which students produce something called the *culminating presentation.* It is a way for students to apply what they are learning. The culminating presentation is a final presentation that usually includes an oral and written report accompanied by a hands-on item of some kind (e.g., a display, play or skit, book, song or poem, multimedia presentation, diorama, poster, map, chart, and so on). Some high schools have adopted what they call the Senior Project, which is required for graduation,[25] as a culminating experience and exhibition of student learning.

■ Values and Purposes of Project-Centered Learning

The values and purposes of encouraging project-centered learning are to:

- Develop individual skills in cooperation and social-interaction.
- Develop student skills in writing, communication, and higher-level thinking and doing.
- Foster student engagement and independent learning and thinking skills.
- Optimize personal meaning of the learning to each student by considering, valuing, and accommodating individual interests, learning styles, learning capacities, and life experiences.
- Provide opportunity for each student to become especially knowledgeable and experienced in one area of subject content or in one process skill, thus adding to the student's knowledge and experience base and sense of importance and self-worth.
- Provide opportunity for students to become intrinsically motivated to learn because they are working on topics of personal meaning, with outcomes and even timelines that are relatively open-ended.

- Provide opportunity for students to make decisions about their own learning and to develop their skills in managing time and materials.
- Provide opportunity for students to make some sort of a real contribution.

As has been demonstrated time and again, when students choose their own projects, integrating knowledge as the need arises, motivation and learning follow naturally.[26]

Guidelines for guiding students in project-centered learning In collaboration with the teacher, students select a topic for the project. What you can do is to stimulate ideas and provide sample model studies. You can stimulate ideas by providing lists of things students might do; by mentioning each time an idea comes up in class that this would be a good idea for an independent, small-group, or class project; by having former students tell about their projects; by showing the results of other students' projects; by suggesting Internet resources and readings that are likely to give students ideas; and by using class discussions to brainstorm ideas.

Sometimes a teacher will write the general problem or topic in the center of a graphic web and ask the students to brainstorm some questions, which will lead to ways for students to investigate, draw sketches, construct models, record findings, predict items, compare and contrast, and discuss understandings. In essence, brainstorming such as this is the technique often used by teachers in collaboration with students for the selection of an interdisciplinary thematic unit of study.

Allow students to individually choose whether they will work alone, in pairs, or in small groups. If they choose to work in groups, then help them delineate job descriptions for each member of the group. For project work, groups of four or fewer students usually work better than groups of more than four. Even if the project is one the whole class is pursuing, the project should be broken down into parts with individuals or small groups of students undertaking independent study of these parts.

You can keep track of the students' progress by reviewing weekly updates of their work. Set deadlines with the groups. Meet with groups daily to discuss any questions or problems they have. Based on their investigations, the students will prepare and present their findings in culminating presentations.

Provide coaching and guidance. Work with each student or student team in topic selection, as well as in the processes of written and oral reporting. Allow students to develop their own procedures, but guide their preparation of work outlines and preliminary drafts, giving them constructive feedback and encouragement along the way. Aid students in their identification of potential resources and in the techniques of research. Your coordination with the library and other resource centers is central to the success of project-centered teaching. Frequent drafts and progress reports from the students are a must. With each of these stages, provide students with constructive feedback and encouragement. Provide written guidelines and negotiate timelines for the outlines, drafts, and the completed project.

Promote sharing. Insist that students share both the progress and the results of their study with the rest of the class. The value of this type of instructional strategy comes not only from individual contributions but also from the learning that results from the experience and the communication of that experience with others.

Without careful planning, and unless students are given steady guidance, project-based teaching can be a frustrating experience, for both the teacher and the students, not to mention a beginning teacher who is inexperienced in such an undertaking. Students should choose and do projects because they want to and because the project seems meaningful. Therefore, students with guidance from you should decide *what* project to do and *how* to do it. Your role is to advise and guide students so they experience success. There must be a balance between structure and opportunities for student choices and decision making. Without frequent reports on progress by the student and guidance and reinforcement from the teacher, a student can get frustrated and quickly lose interest in the project.

Writing should be a required component of project-centered learning Provide options but insist that writing be a part of each student's work. Research examining the links among writing, thinking, and learning has helped emphasize the importance of writing. Writing is a complex intellectual behavior and process that helps the learner create and record his or her understanding—that is, construct meaning. So, insist that writing be a part of the student's work (see section that follows).

When teachers use project-centered teaching, a paper and an oral presentation are usually automatically required of all students. It is recommended that you use the *I-Search paper* instead of the traditional research paper. Using the I-Search paper method, under your careful guidance, the student (a) lists things that she would like to know, and from the list selects one that becomes the research topic; (b) conducts the study while maintaining a log of activities and findings, which, in fact, becomes a process journal; (c) prepares a booklet that presents the student's findings and that consists of paragraphs and visual representations; (d) prepares a summary of the findings including the significance of the study and the student's personal feelings; and (e) shares the project as a final oral report with the teacher and classmates.

Assess the final product The final product of the project, including papers, oral reports, and presentations, should be graded. The method of determining the grade should be clear to students from the beginning, as well as the weight of the project grade toward the term grade. Provide students with clear descriptions (**rubrics**) of how evaluation and grading will be done. **Evaluation** should include meeting deadlines for drafts and progress reports. The final grade for the study should be based on four criteria: (a) how well it was organized, including meeting draft deadlines; (b) the quality and quantity of both content and procedural knowledge gained from the experience; (c) the quality of the students' sharing of that learning experience with the rest of the class; and (d) the quality of the students' final written or oral report.

■ WRITING ACROSS THE CURRICULUM

Because writing is a discrete representation of thinking, every teacher should consider himself or herself to be a teacher of writing. In exemplary schools, student writing is encouraged in all subjects across the curriculum.

■ Kinds of Writing

A student should experience a variety of kinds of writing rather than the same form, class after class, year after year. Perhaps most important is that writing should be emphasized as a process that illustrates one's thinking, rather than solely as a product completed as an assignment. Writing and thinking develop best when a student experiences during any school day various forms of writing to express his or her ideas, such as the following.

Analysis. Speculation about effects; the writer conjectures about the causes and effects of a specific event.

Autobiographical incident. The writer narrates a specific event in his or her life and states or implies the significance of the event.

Evaluation. The writer presents a judgment on the worth of an item—book, movie, art work, consumer product—and supports this with reasons and evidence.

Eyewitness account. The writer tells about a person, group, or event that was objectively observed from the outside.

Firsthand biographical sketch. Through incident and description, the writer characterizes a person he or she knows well.

Problem solving. The writer describes and analyzes a specific problem and then proposes and argues for a solution.

Report of information. The writer collects data from observation and research and chooses material that best represents a phenomenon or concept.

Story. Using dialogue and description, the writer shows conflict between characters or between a character and the environment.

- **International Reading Association,** 800 Barksdale Road, Newark, DE 19711.
- **R. J. Maxwell,** *Writing Across the Curriculum in Middle and High Schools* (Des Moines, IA: Allyn & Bacon, 1996).
- **National Center for the Study of Writing and Literature (NCSWL),** School of Education, University of California— Berkeley, Berkeley, CA 94720. [Having completed its mission the NCSWL no longer functions as an independent entity; its publications may be obtained from the NWP headquarters.]
- **National Council of Teachers of English,** 1111 Kenyon Road, Urbana, IL 61801 <http://www.ncte.org>.
- **National Writing Project** at <http://www.writingproject.org/>.
- **D. K. Pugalee,** Connecting Writing to the Mathematics Curriculum, *Mathematics Teacher 90*(4), 308–310 (April 1997).
- **Whole Language Umbrella,** Unit 6–846, Marion Street, Winnipeg, Manitoba, Canada R2JOK4.
- **Writing to Learn,** Council for Basic Education, 725 15th Street, NW, Washington, DC 20005.

FIGURE 6.11 ● Resources for Writing Across the Curriculum

■ Student Journals

Many teachers across the curriculum have their students maintain journals in which the students keep a log of their activities, findings, and thoughts (i.e., *process journals*, as previously discussed) and write their thoughts about what it is they are studying (*response journals*). Actually, two types of response journals are commonly used: *Dialogue journals* and reading-response journals. Dialogue journals are used for students to write anything that is on their minds, usually on the right side of a page, while peers, teachers, and parents or guardians respond on the left side of a page, thereby "talking with" the journal writer. Response journals are used for students to write (and perhaps draw—a "visual learning log") their reactions to what is being studied.

■ Purpose and Assessment of Student Journal Writing

Normally, academic journals are not personal diaries with the writer's recollection of daily events and thoughts about the events. Rather, the purpose of journal writing is to encourage students to write, to think about their writing, to record their creative thoughts about *what they are learning*, and to share their written thoughts with an audience—all of which help in the development of their thinking skills, in their learning, and in their development as writers. Students are encouraged to write about experiences, both in school and out, that are related to the topics being studied. They should be encouraged to record their feelings about what and how they are learning.

Journal writing provides practice in expression and should not be graded by the teacher. Negative comments and evaluations from the teacher will discourage creative and spontaneous expression by students. Teachers should read the journal writing and then offer constructive and positive feedback; but teachers should avoid negative comments or grading the jour-

nals. For grading purposes, most teachers simply record whether or not a student does, in fact, maintain the required journal.

The National Council of Teachers of English (NCTE) has developed guidelines for journal writing. Your school English/language arts department may have a copy of these guidelines, or you can contact NCTE directly or via the Internet. Resources on writing across the curriculum are shown in Figure 6.11.

■ LEARNING BY EDUCATIONAL GAMES

Educational games include a wide variety of learning activities, such as simulations, role-play and socio-drama activities, mind games, board games, computer games, and sporting games, all of which provide valuable learning experiences for participants. That is, they are experiences that tend to involve several senses and several learning modalities, tend to engage higher-order thinking skills, and tend to be quite effective as learning tools.

Of all the arts, drama involves the learner-participant most fully—intellectually, emotionally, physically, verbally, and socially. Interactive drama, which is role-playing, a simplified form of drama, is a method by which students can become involved with literature. Studies show that comprehension increases and students are highly motivated to read if they are involved in analyzing and actively responding to the characters, plot, and setting of the story being read.

Simulations, a more complex form of drama, serve many of the developmental needs of young people. They provide for interaction with peers and allow students of differences to work together on a common project. They engage students in physical activity and give them an opportunity to try out different roles, which help them to better understand themselves. Role-play simulations can provide concrete experiences that help students to understand complex concepts and issues, and they provide

- J. Bassett, The Pullman Strike of 1894, *OAH Magazine of History 11*(2), 34–41 (Winter 1997).
- D. Bogan and D. Wood, Simulating Sun, Moon, and Earth Patterns, *Science Scope 21*(2), 46, 48 (October 1997).
- J. Collom, Illot-Mollo and Other Games, *Teachers & Writers 30*(5), 12–13 (May/June 1999). Instructions for two word games useful in secondary writing classrooms.
- C. Collyer, Winter Secrets: An Instant Lesson Plan, *Pathways: The Ontario Journal of Outdoor Education 9*(2), 18–20 (April 1997). Instructions for two games about predator-prey relationships.
- S. A. Farin, Acting Atoms, *Science Scope 21*(3), 46 (November/December 1997).
- J. Gorman, Strategy Games: Treasures From Ancient Times, *Mathematics Teaching in the Middle School 3*(2), 110–116 (October 1997). Presents several games for integrating history and mathematics.
- S. Hightshoe, Sifting Through the Sands of Time: A Simulated Archaeological Special Feature, *Social Studies and the Young Learner 9*(3), 28–30 (January/February 1997).
- M. J. Howle, Play-Party Games in the Modern Classroom, *Music Educators Journal 83*(5), 24–28 (March 1997). Introduces games that were popular on the 19th-century American frontier.
- T. Levy, The Amistad Incident: A Classroom Reenactment, *Social Education 59*(5), 303–308 (September 1995).
- T. M. McCann, A Pioneer Simulation for Writing and for the Study of Literature, *English Journal 85*(3), 62–67 (March 1996).
- H. Morris, Universal Games From A to Z, *Mathematics in School 26*(4), 35–40 (September 1997). See also F. Tapson, Mathematical Games, pp. 2–6 of same issue.
- K. D. Owens et al., Playing to Learn: Science Games in the Classroom, *Science Scope 20*(5), 31–33 (February 1997).
- R. J. Quinn and L. R. Wiest, Exploring Probability Through an Evens-Odds Dice Game, *Mathematics Teaching in the Middle School 4*(6), 358–362 (March 1999).
- J. V. Vort, Our Town's Planning Commission Meeting, *Journal of Geography 96*(4), 183–190 (July/August 1997).

FIGURE 6.12 ● Sample Professional Journals with Educational Games and Simulations

opportunities for exploring values and developing skill in decision making.

Educational games can play an integral role in interdisciplinary teaching and serve as valuable resources for enriching the effectiveness of students' learning. As with any other instructional strategy, the use of games should follow a clear educational purpose, have a careful plan, and be congruent with the instructional objectives.

■ Purposes of Educational Games

Games can be powerful tools for teaching and learning. A game can have one to several of the following purposes: (a) add variety and change of pace, (b) assess student learning, (c) enhance student self-esteem, (d) motivate students, (e) offer a break from the usual rigors of learning, (f) provide learning about real-life issues through simulation and role-playing, (g) provide learning through tactile and kinesthetic modalities, (h) provide problem-solving situations and experiences, (i) provide skill development and motivation through computer usage, (j) provide skill development in inductive thinking, (k) provide skill development in verbal communication and debate, (l) reinforce convergent thinking, (m) review and reinforce subject matter learning, (n) encourage learning through peer interaction, (o) stimulate critical thinking, (p) stimulate deductive thinking, (q) stimulate divergent and creative thinking, and (r) teach both content and process.

■ Sources of Educational Games

Sources for useful educational games include professional journals (see Figure 6.12) and the Internet.

■ INTEGRATING STRATEGIES FOR INTEGRATED LEARNING

In today's exemplary classrooms, instructional strategies are combined to establish the most effective teaching-learning experience. For example, in an integrated middle school language-arts program, teachers are interested in their students' speaking, reading, listening, thinking, study, and writing skills. These skills (and not textbooks) form a holistic process that is the primary aspect of integrated language arts.

In the area of speaking skills, oral discourse (discussion) in the classroom has a growing research base that promotes methods of teaching and learning through oral language. These methods include cooperative learning, instructional scaffolding, and inquiry teaching.

In cooperative learning groups, students discuss and use language for learning that benefits both their content learning and skills in social interaction. Working in heterogeneous groups, students participate in their own learning and can extend their knowledge base and cultural awareness with students of different backgrounds. When students share information and ideas, they are completing difficult learning tasks, using divergent thinking and decision making, and developing their understanding of concepts. As issues are presented and responses are challenged, student thinking is clarified. Students assume the responsibility for planning within the group and for carrying out their assignments. When needed, the teacher models an activity with one group in front of the class, and when integrated with student questions, the modeling can become inquiry teaching. Activities can include:

- *Brainstorming.* Members generate ideas related to a key word and record them. Clustering or chunking, mapping, and the Venn diagram (all discussed in the following text) are variations of brainstorming.

- *Chunking or clustering.* Groups of students apply mental organizers by clustering information into chunks for easier manipulation and remembering.

- *Memory strategies.* The teacher and students model the use of acronyms, mnemonics, rhymes, or clustering of information into categories to promote learning. Sometimes, such as in memorizing one's social security number, one must learn information by rote, that is, without any connection to any prior knowledge. To do that, it is helpful to break the information to be learned into smaller chunks, such as dividing the eight-digit social security number into smaller chunks of information (with, in this instance, each chunk separated by a hyphen). Learning by rote is also easier if one can connect that which is to be memorized to some prior knowledge. Strategies such as these are used to bridge the gap between rote learning and meaningful learning and are known as mnemonics. Mnemonic devices include acronyms, rap, music, and peg systems. Sample mnemonics are:

  - The notes on a treble staff are FACE for the space notes and Empty Garbage Before Dad Flips (EGBDF) for the line notes. The notes on the bass staff are All Cows Eat Granola Bars (ACEGB) or Grizzly Bears Don't Fly Airplanes (GBDFA).

  - The order of the planets from the Sun are My Very Educated Mother Just Served Us Nine Pizzas (Mercury, Venus, Earth, Mars, Jupiter, Saturn, Uranus, Neptune, and Pluto—although, in reality, Pluto and Neptune alternate in this order because of their elliptical orbits).

  - The names of the Great Lakes: HOMES for Huron, Ontario, Michigan, Erie, and Superior.

  - Visual mnemonics are useful too, such as remembering that Italy is shaped in the form of a boot.

- *Comparing and contrasting.* Similarities and differences between items are found and recorded.

- *Visual tools.* A variety of terms describing the visual tools useful for learning have been invented terms (some of which are synonymous) such as

brainstorming web, mindmapping web, spider map, cluster, concept map™, cognitive map, semantic map, Venn diagram, visual scaffold, and graphic organizer. Visual tools are separated into three categories, according to purpose: (a) *brainstorming tools* (such as mind mapping, webbing, and clustering) for developing one's knowledge and creativity; (b) *task-specific organizers* (such as life-cycle diagrams used in biology, decision trees used in mathematics, and text structures in reading); and (c) *thinking process maps* (such as concept mapping™) for encouraging cognitive development across disciplines.[27] It is the latter about which we are interested here.

Based on Ausubel's theory of meaningful learning,[28] thinking process mapping has been found useful for helping students change their prior notions—their misconceptions, sometimes referred to as *naïve views*. It can help students in their ability to organize and represent their thoughts, as well as to connect new knowledge to their past experiences and precepts.[29] Simply put, *concepts* can be thought of as classifications that attempt to organize the world of objects and events into a smaller number of categories. In everyday usage, the term *concept* means "idea," as when someone says, "My concept of love is not the same as yours." Concepts embody a meaning that develops in complexity with experience and learning over time. For example, the concept of love that is held by a second grader is unlikely to be as complex as that held by a ninth grader. Thinking process mapping is a graphical way of demonstrating the relationships among concepts.

Typically, a thinking process map refers to a visual or graphic representation of concepts with bridges (connections) that show relationships. Figure 6.13 shows a partially complete thinking process map in social studies, where students have made connections of concept relationships related to fruit farming and marketing. The general procedure for thinking process mapping is to have the students: (a) identify important concepts in materials being studied, often by circling them; (b) rank order the concepts from the most general to the most specific; and (c) arrange the concepts on a sheet of paper, connect related ideas with lines, and define the connections between the related ideas.

Other activities include:

- *Inferring.* For instance, students assume the roles of people (real or fictional) and infer their motives, personalities, and thoughts.

- *Outlining.* Each group completes an outline that contains some of the main ideas but with subtopics omitted.

- *Paraphrasing.* In a brief summary, each student restates a short selection of what was read or heard.

- *Reciprocal teaching.* In classroom dialogue, students take turns at generating questions, summarizing, clarifying, and predicting.[30]

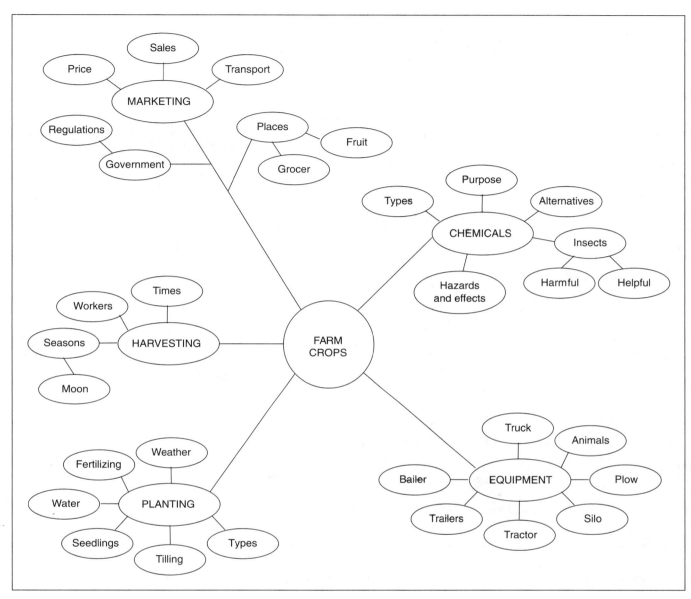

FIGURE 6.13 ● Sample Partially Completed Thinking Process Map

- *Study strategies.* Important strategies that should be taught explicitly include vocabulary expansion, reading and interpreting graphic information, locating resources, using advance organizers, adjusting one's reading rate, and skimming, scanning, and study reading.[31]

- *Textbook study strategies.* Students use the SQ4R or related study strategies (see Module 4).

- *Vee mapping.* This road map is completed by students as they learn, showing the route they follow from prior knowledge to new and future knowledge.

- *Venn diagramming.* This is a technique for comparing two concepts or, for example, two stories, to show similarities and differences. Using stories as an example, a student is asked to draw two circles that intersect and to mark the circles one and two and the area where they intersect three. In circle one, the student lists characteristics of one story, and in circle two she or he lists the characteristics of the second story. In the area of the intersection, marked three, the student lists characteristics common to both stories.

- *Visual learning log (VLL).* This is another kind of road map completed by students showing the route they follow from prior knowledge to new and future knowledge, except that the VLL consists of pictograms (free-form drawings) that each student makes and that are maintained in a journal. Now, to further explore inquiry teaching and integrated learning, do Exercise 6.3.

EXERCISE **6.3**

■ A Study of Inquiry and Strategy Integration

Instructions: The purpose of this exercise is to experience a Level II inquiry, to analyze the Locating a Colony inquiry (Figure 6.10) and the preceding discussion about integrating strategies, and to synthesize that information for use in your own teaching. We suggest that you first answer the questions of this exercise and then share your answers with others in your discipline (in groups of about four). Finally, share your group's collective responses with the entire class.

1. My subject field:

2. a. How I could use the Locating a Colony inquiry in my subject field (for what purpose, goals, or objectives):

    b. Content in my subject field that students might be expected to learn from doing the Locating a Colony inquiry:

3. How I could involve my students in cooperative learning while doing the Locating a Colony inquiry:

4. How brainstorming could be used while doing the Locating a Colony inquiry:

5. How clustering could be used while doing the Locating a Colony inquiry:

6. How thinking process mapping could be used while doing the Locating a Colony inquiry:

7. How comparing and contrasting could be used while doing the Locating a Colony inquiry:

8. How outlining could be used while doing the Locating a Colony inquiry:

9. How paraphrasing could be used while doing the Locating a Colony inquiry:

10. How summarizing could be used while doing the Locating a Colony inquiry:

11. How memory strategies could be used while doing the Locating a Colony inquiry:

12. How inferring could be used while doing the Locating a Colony inquiry:

13. What other skills could be taught while doing the Locating a Colony inquiry? For each, briefly describe how.

 To access this exercise online, go to the Companion Website at **www.prenhall.com/kellough**.

■ SUMMARY

You have learned about the importance of learning modalities, active learning, and instructional modes, as well as about the importance of providing an accepting and supportive learning environment. You have learned important principles of teaching and learning.

This module has initiated the development of a repertoire of teaching strategies necessary for you to become an effective teacher. As you know, many students can be quite peer-conscious, have relatively short attention spans, and prefer active learning experiences that engage many of their senses. Most are intensely curious about things of interest to them. Cooperative learning, independent study, and teaching strategies that emphasize shared inquiry and discovery within a psychologically safe environment encourage the most positive aspects of thinking and learning. Central to your strategy selection should be those strategies that encourage students to become independent thinkers and skilled learners who can help in the planning, structuring, regulating, and assessing of their own learning and learning activities.

In this module we presented and discussed a number of teaching strategies that all have two common elements: social interaction and problem solving. These teaching strategies require students to interact with one another and to draw conclusions, learn concepts, and form generalizations through induction, deduction, and observation, or through application of principles. The premises underlying these methods are (a) that a person learns to think by thinking and sharing his or her thoughts with others, thereby obtaining feedback and doing further thinking; and (b) that knowledge gained through active learning and self-discovery is more meaningful, permanent, and transferable than knowledge obtained through expository techniques.

The strategies that have been presented in this module are not easy to implement. Using them effectively and without classroom control problems requires conviction and careful preparation. Even then, there may need to be a period of trial and error before you perfect your skills in their implementation. Yet techniques that use cooperative learning, problem solving, and discovery are important teaching tools. They are absolutely worth the effort, time, and potential frustrations that can occur for the beginning teacher who deviates from the traditional, teacher-centered strategies. Such expository methods of instruction are presented in Module 7.

■ MODULE 6 POSTTEST

Multiple Choice

1. Which one of the following is least like the others?
   a. student-centered teaching
   b. direct learning experience
   c. expository teaching
   d. indirect instruction

2. If you are a physical education instructor and you want your students to learn how to shoot a free throw in basketball, with all else being equal, the best teaching technique would be to
   a. lecture to the class about how to shoot a free throw.
   b. have cooperative learning groups discuss how to shoot a free throw.
   c. have a guest speaker discuss with the students how to shoot free throws.
   d. demonstrate to the students how to shoot a free throw and follow that with guided practice shooting free throws.

3. Which one of the following includes learning modalities that tend to rely more on abstract symbolization?
   a. visual and auditory
   b. tactile and auditory
   c. tactile and kinesthetic
   d. kinesthetic and visual

4. If a high school government class takes a field trip to observe the state legislature in session, for the students this is
   a. an abstract verbal experience.
   b. a concrete visual experience.
   c. a simulated experience.
   d. a direct experience.

5. To promote student inquiry, which one of the following is least useful?
   a. the use of dogmatism
   b. an open classroom environment
   c. encouraging guessing and intuitive thinking
   d. encouraging skepticism and the suspension of judgment

6. Except for personal writing, student journals should be _____ by the teacher.
   a. read
   b. read and critiqued
   c. read, critiqued, and evaluated
   d. read, critiqued, evaluated, and graded

(continued)

7. A major value in using role-playing learning activities lies in
   a. promoting the creative instincts of students.
   b. enhancing the acting skills of talented students.
   c. permitting ego gratification on the part of some students.
   d. deepening insights/understandings about the issues and personalities involved.

8. Which one of the following is not a guideline for using cooperative group learning?
   a. Group grading should be avoided.
   b. Preset standards for achievement should be the same for all students within a group.
   c. Competition for rewards and grades between students within a group should be avoided.
   d. Group achievement may be recognized by awarding bonus points to all students within a group.

9. Personalized instruction is when an individual student's learning needs, abilities, and attitudes determine the instructional
   a. pacing.
   b. content.
   c. sequence.
   d. all of the above.

10. Which pair of terms represents the highest level of mental activity?
    a. communicating, experiencing
    b. comparing, classifying
    c. explaining, inferring
    d. applying, hypothesizing

Short Explanation

1. Explain when and why vicarious student learning experiences are appropriate.
2. Describe the steps to critical thinking and problem solving. Describe a situation in your own teaching where you would engage your students in critical thinking and problem solving.
3. Explain the concept of hands-on, minds-on learning.
4. Explain the advantages and disadvantages of project-centered teaching and learning in your subject field.
5. Explain the rationale for using cooperative learning groups in teaching. Do you believe that the use of cooperative learning groups enhances or impedes the learning of students who are identified as being academically gifted and talented? Explain your answer and reason for it.
6. Identify and describe three guidelines for making student-centered projects an effective learning strategy.
7. Contrast the three levels of inquiry.
8. Identify 10 basic thinking skills.
9. Identify three ways that you could help students develop their reading, writing, thinking, and studying skills while they are learning your discipline.
10. Distinguish between discovery and inquiry. Explain how they are different and how they are similar.

Essay

1. Explain why you agree or disagree with the statement: Every teacher should emphasize skill development in reading, writing, thinking, and studying.
2. Do you accept the view that achievement in school learning is the product of creative inquiry through social interaction with the students as active participants in that inquiry? Explain why you do or do not agree.
3. From your current observations and fieldwork related to this teacher preparation program, clearly identify one specific example of educational practice that seems contradictory to exemplary practice or theory presented in this module. Present your explanation for the discrepancy.
4. Is problem solving a teaching strategy or a way of thinking? Explain.
5. Describe any prior concepts you held that changed as a result of the experiences of this module. Describe the changes.

 To access this posttest and the answers online, go to the Companion Website at **www.prenhall.com/ kellough.**

■ SUGGESTED READINGS

Abdal-Haqq, I. (1998). *Constructivism in teacher education: Considerations for those who would link practice to theory.* ERIC Digest 426986 98. Washington, DC: ERIC Clearinghouse on Teaching and Teacher Education.

Abdullah, M. H. (1998). *Problem-based learning in language instruction: A constructivist model.* Eric Digest 423550 98. Bloomington, IN: ERIC Clearinghouse on Reading, English, and Communication.

Barker, M. (2000). Student-centered seismology activities. *Science Scope, 23*(4), 12–17.

Bevevino, M. M., Dengel, J., & Adams, K. (1999). Constructivist theory in the classroom: Internalizing concepts through inquiry learning. *Clearing House, 72*(5), 275–278.

Bockler, D. (1998). Let's play doctor: Medical rounds in ancient Greece. *American Biology Teacher, 60*(2), 106–111.

Boerman-Cornell, W. (1999). The five humors. *English Journal, 88*(4), 66–69.

Boston, J. A. (1998a). Unequal resources: A group simulation. *Social Studies Review, 37*(2), 33–37.

Boston, J. A. (1998b). Using simulations. *Social Studies Review, 37*(2), 31–32.

Bower, B., & Lobdell, J. (1998). History alive! Six powerful constructivist strategies. *Social Education, 62*(1), 50–53.

Brandt, R., & Perkins, D. N. (2000). The evolving science of learning. In R. S. Brandt (Ed.), *Education in a new era* (Chap. 7, pp. 159–184). Alexandria, VA: ASCD Yearbook, Association for Supervision and Curriculum Development.

Callison, D. (1999). Inquiry. *School Library Media Activities Monthly, 15*(6), 38–42.

Clemens-Walatka, B. (1998). Amusement park inquiry. *Science Teacher, 65*(1), 20–23.

Cohen, E. G. (1998). Making cooperative learning equitable. *Educational Leadership, 56*(1), 18–21.

Collom, J. (1999). Illot-Mollo and other games. *Teachers & Writers, 30*(5), 12–13.

Como, R. M., & O'Connor, J. S. (1998). History on trial: The case of Columbus. *OAH Magazine of History, 12*(2), 45–48.

Crocco, M. S. (1998). Putting the actors back on stage: Oral history in the secondary school classroom. *Social Studies, 89*(1), 19–24.

Fastback 445. Bloomington, IN: Phi Delta Kappa Educational Foundation.

Finkel, L., et al. (1998). Freshwater ecology. *Science Teacher, 65*(5), 42–43.

Ford, B. (1998). Critically evaluating scientific claims in the popular press. *American Biology Teacher, 60*(3), 174–180.

Ford, R. H. (1998). A transpiration experiment requiring critical thinking skills. *American Biology Teacher, 60*(1), 46–49.

Foshay, J. D. (1999). *Project-based multimedia instruction.*

Gabriel, A. E. (1999). Brain-based learning: The scent of the trail. *Clearing House, 72*(5), 288–290.

Gorman, M. E., et al. (1998). Turning students into inventors: Active learning modules for secondary students. *Phi Delta Kappan, 79*(7), 530–537.

Hannel, G. I., & Hannel, L. (1998). The seven steps to critical thinking: A practical application of critical thinking skills. *NASSP Bulletin, 82*(598), 87–93.

Harmelink, K. (1998). Learning the write way. *Science Teacher, 65*(1), 36–38.

Haroutunian-Gordon, S. (1998). A study of reflective thinking: Patterns in interpretive discussion. *Educational Theory, 48*(1), 33–58.

Harris, B., Kohlmeier, K., & Kiel, R. D. (1999). *Crime scene investigation.* Englewood, CO: Teacher Ideas Press.

Holloway, J. H. (1999). Improving the reading skills of adolescents. *Educational Leadership, 57*(2), 80–81.

Holt, P. W. (1998). The Oregon trail: Wyoming students construct a CD-ROM. *Social Education, 62*(1), 41–45.

Hynd, C. R. (1999). Teaching students to think critically using multiple texts in history. *Journal of Adolescent & Adult Literacy, 42*(6), 428–436.

Jacobs, G. M., et al. (1998). Cooperative learning and second-language teaching: Frequently-asked questions. *Mosaic, 5*(2), 13–16.

Kaldhusdal, T., Wood, S., & Truesdale, J. (1998). Virtualville votes: An interdisciplinary project. *Multimedia Schools, 5*(1), 30–35.

Lach, M., & Loverude, M. (1998). An active introduction to evolution. *American Biology Teacher, 60*(2), 132–136.

Leinhardt, G., Stainton, C., & Bausmith, J. M. (1998). Constructing maps collaboratively. *Journal of Geography, 97*(1), 19–30.

Martino-Brewster, G. (1999). Reversing the negative. *Voices From the Middle, 6*(3), 11–14.

Marzano, R. J. (2000). 20th century advances in instruction. In R. S. Brandt (Ed.), *Education in a new era* (Chap. 4, pp. 67–95). Alexandria, VA: ASCD Yearbook, Association for Supervision and Curriculum Development.

McMahon, M. (1999). Are we having fun yet? Humor in the English class. *English Journal, 88*(4), 70–72.

Murphey, C. E. (1998). Using the five themes of geography to explore a school site. *Social Studies Review, 37*(2), 49–52.

Ngeow, K. Y. (1998). *Enhancing student thinking through collaborative learning.* ERIC Digest 422586. Bloomington, IN: ERIC Clearinghouse on Reading, English, and Communication.

Nilsen, A. P., & Nilsen, D. L. F. (1999). The straw man meets his match: Six arguments for studying humor in English classes. *English Journal, 88*(4), 34–42.

Novak, J. D. (1998). *Learning, creating, and using knowledge: Concept maps as facilitative tools in schools and corporations.* Mahwah, NJ: Lawrence Erlbaum.

Oden, D. (1998). Constructing a prehistoric adventure. *Science Teacher, 65*(4), 38–41.

O'Reilly, K. (1998). What would you do? Constructing decision-making guidelines through historical problems. *Social Education, 62*(1), 46–49.

Quinn, R. J., & Wiest, L. R. (1999). Exploring probability through an evens-odds dice game. *Mathematics Teaching in the Middle School, 4*(6), 358–362.

Randall, V. (1999). Cooperative learning: Abused and overused? *Gifted Child Today Magazine, 22*(2), 14–16.

Reid, L., & Golub, J. N. (Eds.). (1999). *Reflective activities: Helping students connect with texts. Classroom practices in teaching English* (Vol. 30). Urbana, IL: National Council of Teachers of English.

Ruggieri, C. A. (1999). Laugh and learn: Using humor to teach tragedy. *English Journal, 88*(4), 53–58.

Schlenker, R. M., Cullen, D., & Schlenker, K. R. (1999). Using acid-base reagent problems as a high school science research activity. *Science Activities, 35*(4), 19–23.

Schug, T. (1998). Teaching DNA fingerprinting using a hands-on simulation. *American Biology Teacher, 60*(1), 38–41.

Shanker, J. L., & Edwall, E. E. (1998). *Locating and correcting reading difficulties* (7th ed.). Upper Saddle River, NJ: Merrill/Prentice Hall.

Starnes, B. A. (1999). *The Foxfire approach to teaching and learning: John Dewey, experiential learning, and the core*

practices. ERIC Digest 426826 99. Charleston, WV: ERIC Clearinghouse on Rural Education and Small Schools.

Stephens, E. C., & Brown, J. E. (2000). *A handbook of content literacy strategies: 75 practical reading and writing ideas.* Norwood, MA: Christopher-Gordon.

Stroka, S. R. (2000). Education is not a laughing matter! Or is it? *Middle Ground, 3*(4), 32–34.

Tomlinson, C. A. (1999). *The differentiated classroom.* Alexandria, VA: Association for Supervision and Curriculum Development.

Townsend, J. S. (1998). Silent voices: What happens to quiet students during classroom discussions? *English Journal, 87*(2), 72–80.

Zinn, B., Gnut, S., & Kafkafi, U. (1999). First-rate crops from second-rate water: Classroom activities model a real-world problem. *Science Activities, 35*(4), 27–30.

■ ENDNOTES

[1] C. G. Jung, *The Development of Personality* (New York: Patheon, 1964), p. 144.

[2] See, for example, E. Jensen, *Teaching with the Brain in Mind* (Alexandria, VA: Association for Supervision and Curriculum Development, 1998); and J. C. Baker and F. G. Martin, *A Neural Network Guide to Teaching,* Fastback 431 (Bloomington, IN: Phi Delta Kappa Educational Foundation, 1998).

[3] See D. Gollnick and P. Chinn, *Multicultural Education in a Pluralistic Society* (Upper Saddle River, NJ: Merrill/Prentice Hall, 2002); M. B. Ginsberg and R. J. Wlodkowski, *Creating Highly Motivating Classrooms for All Students: A Schoolwide Approach to Powerful Teaching with Diverse Learners* (San Francisco, CA: Jossey-Bass, 2000); J. P. Comer and N. M. Haynes, *Summary of School Development Program Effects: The Family Is Critical to Student Achievement* (New Haven, CT: Yale ChildStudy Center, 1992); G. Ladson-Billings, But That's Just Good Teaching! The Case for Culturally Relevant Pedagogy. *Theory Into Practice, 34*(3), 159–165 (1995).

[4] See, for example, E. S. Foster-Harrison, *Peer Tutoring for K–12 Success,* Fastback 415 (Bloomington, IN: Phi Delta Kappa Educational Foundation, 1997).

[5] A. W. Longwill and H. L. Kleinert, The Unexpected Benefits of High School Peer Tutoring, *Teaching Exceptional Children 30*(4), 60–65 (March/April 1998).

[6] See, for example, T. G. Jones et al., Show-and-Tell Physics, *Science Teacher 63*(8), 24–27 (November 1996).

[7] See, for example, C. Kaplan, Homework Partners, *Mathematics Teaching in the Middle School 2*(3), 168–169 (January 1997).

[8] See, for example, R. E. Slavin, Cooperative Learning in Middle and Secondary Schools, *Clearing House 69*(4), 200–204 (March/April 1996).

[9] For details about these CLG strategies and others, see R. E. Slavin, *Student Team Learning: A Practical Guide for Cooperative Learning* (3rd ed.) (Washington, DC: National Education Association, 1991); and E. Coelho, Learning Together in the Multicultural Classroom (Portsmouth, NH: Heinemann, 1994).

[10] T. L. Good and J. E. Brophy, *Looking in Classrooms* (8th ed.) (New York: Addison Wesley Longman, 2000), p. 291.

[11] See S. Kagan, Group Grades Miss the Mark, *Educational Leadership 52*(8), 68–71 (May 1995); and D. W. Johnson and R. T. Johnson, The Role of Cooperative Learning in Assessing and Communicating Student Learning, in T. R. Guskey (Ed.), *Communicating Student Learning,* Chap.

4, ASCD Yearbook (Alexandria, VA: Association for Supervision and Curriculum Development, 1996).

[12] See, for example, C. A. Tomlinson et al., Use of Cooperative Learning at the Middle Level: Insights From a National Survey, *Research in Middle Level Education Quarterly 20*(4), 37–55 (Summer 1997).

[13] B. K. Beyer, *Practical Strategies for the Teaching of Thinking* (Boston: Allyn & Bacon, 1987).

[14] A. L., Costa, *The School as a Home for the Mind* (Palatine, IL: Skylight Publishing 1991), pp. 20–31. See also Armstrong's 12 qualities of genius—curiosity, playfulness, imagination, creativity, wonderment, wisdom, inventiveness, vitality, sensitivity, flexibility, humor, and joy— in T. Armstrong, *Awakening Genius in the Classroom* (Alexandria, VA: Association for Supervision and Curriculum Development, 1998), pp. 2–15; and Project Zero's 7 dispositions for good thinking—the disposition (a) to be broad and adventurous; (b) toward wondering, problem finding, and investigating; (c) to build explanations and understandings; (d) to make plans and be strategic; (e) to be intellectually careful; (f) to seek and evaluate reasons; and (g) to be metacognitive—at **http://pzweb.harvard.edu/HPZpages/PatThk.html**

[15] See, for example, M. Goos and P. Galbraith, Do It This Way! Metacognitive Strategies in Collaborative Mathematics Problem Solving, *Educational Studies in Mathematics 30*(3), 229–260 (April 1996).

[16] For further reading about the relation of impulse control to intelligence, see D. Goleman, *Emotional Intelligence: Why It Can Matter More Than IQ* (New York: Bantam Books, 1995); and D. Harrington-Lueker, Emotional Intelligence, *High Strides 9*(4), 1, 4–5 (March/April 1997).

[17] See, for example, J. W. Astington, Theory of Mind Goes to School, *Educational Leadership 56*(3), 46–48 (November 1998); and K. D. Wood and C. P. Fisher, Building Assets in the Classroom Through Creative Response, *Middle School Journal 31*(4), 57–60 (March 2000).

[18] J. Piaget, The Psychology of Intelligence (Totowa, NJ: Littlefield Adams, 1972).

[19] I. Kohlberg, *The Meaning and Measurement of Moral Development* (Worcester, MA: Clark University Press, 1981).

[20] See, for example, A. Whimbey, Test Results From Teaching Thinking, in A. L. Costa (Ed.), *Developing Minds: A Resource Book for Teaching Thinking* (Alexandria, VA: Association for Supervision and Curriculum Development, 1985), pp. 269–271.

[21] B. Z. Presseisen, *Implementing Thinking in the School's Curriculum,* unpublished paper presented at the Third Annual Meeting of the

International Association for Cognitive Education, Riverside, CA, on February 9, 1992.

[22]A. L. Costa (Ed.), *Developing Minds: A Resource for Teaching Thinking* (Alexandria, VA: Association for Supervision and Curriculum Development, 1985), p. 312.

[23]From P. L. Roberts and R. D. Kellough, *A Guide for Developing Thematic Units (2nd ed.)* (Upper Saddle River, NJ: Merrill/Prentice Hall, 2000), pp. 147–148. Adapted with permission.

[24]See, for example, E. L. Wright and G. Govindarajan, Discrepant Event Demonstrations, *Science Teacher 62*(1), 24–28 (January 1995); T. O'Brien et al., Baker's Dozen of Discrepantly Dense Demos, *Science Scope 18*(2), 35–38 (October 1994); and C. Ruck et al., Using Discrepant Events to Inspire Writing, *Science Activities 28*(2), 27–30 (Summer 1991).

[25]See, for example, A. O'Grady, Information Literacy Skills and the Senior Project, *Educational Leadership 57*(2), 61–62 (October 1999).

[26]See, for example, M. Tassinari, Hands-On Projects Take Students Beyond the Book, *Social Studies Review 34*(3), 16–20 (Spring 1996).

[27]D. Hyerle, *Visual Tools for Constructing Knowledge* (Alexandria, VA: Association for Supervision and Curriculum Development, 1996).

[28]D. P. Ausubel, *The Psychology of Meaningful Learning* (New York: Grune & Stratton, 1963).

[29]About thinking process mapping, see J. D. Novak, Concept Maps and Vee Diagrams: Two Metacognitive Tools to Facilitate Meaningful Learning, *Instructional Science 19*(1), 29–52 (1990); J. D. Novak and B. D. Gowin, *Learning How to Learn* (Cambridge, England: Cambridge University Press, 1984); and E. Plotnick, *Concept Mapping: A Graphical System for Understanding the Relationship Between Concepts,* ED407938 (Syracuse, NY: ERIC Clearinghouse on Information and Technology, 1997).

[30]See C. J. Carter, Why Reciprocal Teaching? *Educational Leadership 54*(6), 64–68 (March 1997).

[31]J. S. Choate and T. A. Rakes, *Inclusive Instruction for Struggling Readers,* Fastback 434 (Bloomington, IN: Phi Delta Kappa Educational Foundation, 1998).

Teacher-Centered Instructional Strategies

Module 7 Overview

In this module we consider teaching methods that are basically expository in nature, such as lecturing, whole-class discussion and recitation, questioning, and demonstrating. All of these methods are largely or usually teacher-centered; their basic purpose is to deliver information to students. Although strategies presented in this module are somewhat easier to implement than student-centered strategies because classroom control is more easily managed, they are no less difficult to master. As a consequence, there are, perhaps, more boring classes taught by ineffective teachers using teacher-centered approaches than there are by ineffective teachers using student-centered approaches.

To use teacher-centered instructional strategies effectively, it is advisable for you to do two things: (a) become skilled in their use and (b) either mix them with strategies that are more student-centered or make the strategies themselves more student-centered. To help you in these tasks, the guidelines for using teacher-centered instructional strategies have been prepared to make such strategies more student-centered.

In addition, we discuss the importance of ensuring equality in the classroom, present guidelines for the use of assignments and homework, and discuss the significance of students memorizing and reviewing material that is being studied.

Specific Objectives

At the completion of this module, you should be able to:

- Demonstrate your knowledge and skill in using teacher talk and questioning as instructional strategies.
- Describe techniques for using student recitations and classroom demonstrations effectively.
- Demonstrate your understanding of using homework and assignments for meaningful learning.
- Demonstrate your awareness of the importance of equality in the classroom and ways of ensuring it.
- Demonstrate your awareness of the importance of student questioning to learning.
- Demonstrate your knowledge of guidelines for using memorizing and reviews.

Introduction

Consider again the potential strengths and weaknesses of teacher-centered instruction, as presented in Figure 6.2 of Module 6. The strengths include (a) much content can be covered within a short span of time, (b) the teacher has great control over the content covered and the time allotted, and (c) student achievement of specific content is predictable and manageable. The weaknesses include (a) the sources of student motivation are mostly extrinsic, (b) students have little control over pacing and make few important decisions about their learning, (c) opportunity for divergent or creative thinking is lacking, and (d) student self-esteem may be inadequately served. Here we will cover teacher talk, demonstrations, recitations, questioning, leading classroom discussions, and using homework and assignments in-depth.

■ TEACHER TALK: FORMAL AND INFORMAL

Teacher talk encompasses both lecturing *to* students and talking *with* students. A lecture is considered formal teacher talk, whereas a discussion with students is considered informal teacher talk.

■ Cautions in Using Teacher Talk

Whether your talk is formal or informal, there are certain cautions that you need to keep in mind. Perhaps the most important is that of *talking too much.* If a teacher talks too much, the significance of the teacher's words may be lost because some students will tune the teacher out.

Another caution is to avoid *talking too fast.* Students can hear faster than they can understand what they hear. It is a good idea to remind yourself to talk slowly and to check frequently for student comprehension of what you are talking about. By *frequent checks for comprehension,* we mean on the average at least one check per minute. Checks for comprehension can be in the form of questions you ask and those the students ask during the lesson as well as various kinds of checklists.

It is also important to remember that students respond to sensory input (auditory in this instance) at different rates. Because of this, you will need to pause to let words sink in, and you will need to pause during transitions from one point or activity to the next.

A third caution is to be sure you are *being heard and understood.* Sometimes teachers talk in too low a pitch or use words that are not understood by many of the students, or both. You should vary the pitch of your voice, and you should stop and help students with their understanding of vocabulary that may be new to them. Remember, as discussed in Part 1, if you have students in your class who are English Language Learners, then you need to help them learn what is essentially two new vocabularies—the vocabulary of the English language in general and the vocabulary that is unique to the subject you teach.

A fourth caution is to remember that just *because students have heard something before does not necessarily mean that they understand it or have learned it.* From our earlier discussions of learning experiences (such as the Learning Experiences Ladder in Module 6), remember that although verbal communication is an important form of communication, because of its reliance on the use of abstract symbolization it is not a very *reliable* form of communication. Teacher talk relies on words and on skill in listening, a skill that is not mastered by many adolescents (or for that matter, even many adults). Therefore, to ensure student understanding, it is good to reinforce your teacher talk with either direct or simulated learning experiences.

Related to that is yet another caution—*to resist believing that students have attained a skill or have learned something that was taught previously by you or by another teacher.* During any discussion (formal or informal), rather than assuming that your students know something, you should ensure they know it. For example, if the discussion and a student activity involve a particular thinking skill, then you will want to make sure that students know how to use that skill (thinking skills are discussed later in this module).

Still another problem is *talking in a humdrum monotone.* Students need teachers whose voices exude enthusiasm and excitement (although not to be overdone) about the subject and about teaching and learning. Such enthusiasm and excitement for learning are infectious. A voice that demonstrates enthusiasm for teaching and learning is more likely to motivate students to learn.

Keep these cautions in mind as you study the general principles and specific guidelines for the productive and effective use of teacher talk.

■ Teacher Talk: General Guidelines

Certain general guidelines should be followed whether your talk is formal or informal. First, *begin the talk with an advance organizer.* **Advance organizers** are introductions that mentally prepare students for a study by helping them make connections with material already learned or experienced—a *comparative organizer*—or by providing students with a conceptual arrangement of what is to be learned—an *expository organizer.*[2] The value of using advance organizers is well documented by research.[3] An advance organizer can be a brief introduction or statement about the main idea you intend to convey and how it is related to other aspects of the students' learning (an expository organizer), or it can be a presentation of a discrepancy to arouse curiosity (a comparative organizer, in this instance causing students to compare what they have observed with what they already knew or thought they knew). Preparing an organizer helps you plan and organize the sequence of ideas, and its presentation helps students organize their own learning and become motivated about it. An advance organizer can also make their learning meaningful by providing important connections between what they already know and what is being learned.

Second, *your talk should be planned so that it has a beginning and an end, with a logical order between.* During your talk, you should reinforce your words with visuals (discussed in the specific guidelines that follow). These visuals may include writing unfamiliar terms on the board (helping students learn new vocabulary), visual organizers, and prepared graphs, charts, photographs, and various audiovisuals.

Third, *pacing is important.* Your talk should move briskly, but not too fast. The ability to pace the instruction is a difficult skill for many beginning teachers (the tendency among many beginning teachers is to talk too fast and too much), but one that will improve with experience. Until you have honed your skill in pacing lessons you probably will need to constantly remind yourself during lessons to slow down and provide silent pauses (allowing for **think-time**) and frequent checks for student comprehension. Specifically, your talk should:

- Be brisk, though not too fast, with occasional slowdowns to change the pace and to check for student comprehension. Allow students time to think, ask questions, and make notes.
- Have a time plan. A talk planned for 10 minutes, if interesting to students, will probably take longer. If not interesting to them, it will probably take less time.
- Always plan with careful consideration of the characteristics of the students. For example, if you have a fairly high percentage of English language learners or students with special needs, then your teacher talk may be less brisk, sprinkled with even more visuals and repeated statements and frequent checks for student comprehension.

Fourth, *encourage student participation.* Their active participation enhances their learning. This encouragement can be planned as questions that you ask, time allowed for students to comment and ask questions, or some sort of a visual and conceptual outline that students complete during the talk.

Fifth, *plan a clear ending (closure).* Be sure your talk has a clear ending, followed by another activity (during the same or next class period) that will help secure the learning. As for all lessons, you want to strive for planning a clear and mesmerizing beginning, an involving lesson body, and a firm and meaningful ending.

■ Teacher Talk: Specific Guidelines

Specific guidelines for using teacher talk are presented in the following paragraphs.

Understand the various purposes for using teacher talk Teacher talk, formal or informal, can be useful to discuss the progress of a unit of study, explain an inquiry, introduce a unit of study, present a problem, promote student inquiry or critical thinking, provide a transition from one unit of study to the next, provide information otherwise unobtainable to students, share the teacher's experiences, share the teacher's thinking, summarize a problem, summarize a unit of study, and teach a thinking skill by modeling that skill.

Clarify the objectives of the talk Your talk should center around one idea. The learning objectives, which should not be too numerous for one talk, should be clearly understood by the students.

Choose between informal and formal talk Although an occasional formal cutting edge lecture may be appropriate for some classes, spontaneous interactive informal talks of 5 to 12 minutes are preferred. You should never give long lectures with no teacher-student interaction. Remember, though, a formal period-long noninteractive lecture, common in some college teaching, is developmentally inappropriate when teaching most groups of young adolescent learners. (Some experts believe that its appropriateness is questionable for most learning even at the college level.)

Remember also, today's youth are of the "media," or "light," generation; they are accustomed to video interactions and "commercial breaks." For many lessons, especially those that are teacher-centered, after about 10 minutes student attention is likely to begin to stray. For that eventuality you need elements planned to recapture student attention. These planned elements can include: (a) analogies to help connect the topic to students' experiences; (b) verbal cues, such as voice inflections; (c) pauses to allow information to sink in; (d) humor; (e) visual cues, such as the use of slides, overhead transparencies, charts, board drawings, excerpts from videodiscs, real objects (realia), or body gestures; and (f) sensory cues, such as eye contact and proximity.

Vary strategies and activities frequently Perhaps the most useful strategy for recapturing student attention is changing to an entirely different strategy or learning modality. For example, from teacher talk (a teacher-centered strategy) you would change to a student activity (a student-centered strategy). Notice that changing

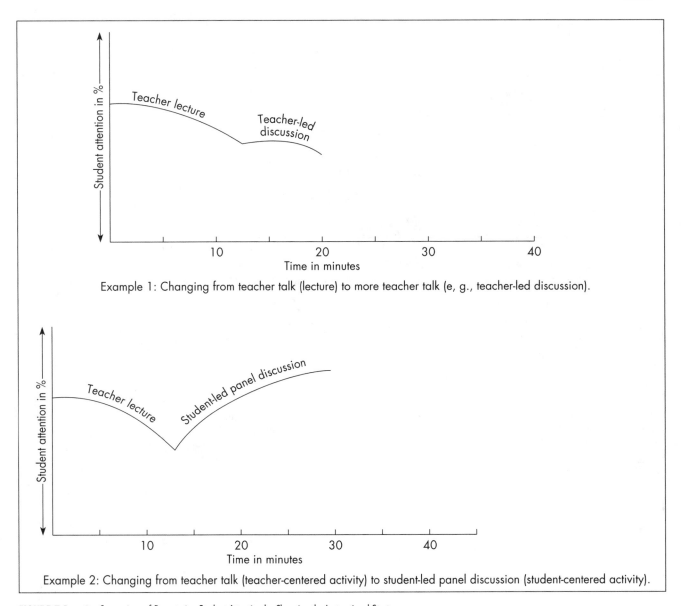

Example 1: Changing from teacher talk (lecture) to more teacher talk (e, g., teacher-led discussion).

Example 2: Changing from teacher talk (teacher-centered activity) to student-led panel discussion (student-centered activity).

FIGURE 7.1a ● Comparison of Recapturing Student Attention by Changing the Instructional Strategy

from a lecture (mostly teacher talk) to a teacher-led discussion (mostly more teacher talk) would not be changing to an entirely different modality. Figures 7.1a and b provide a comparison of different changes.

As a generalization, when using teacher-centered direct instruction, with most classes you will want to change the learning activities about every 10 to 15 minutes. (That is one reason that in the sample preferred lesson plan format shown in Figure 5.6 of Module 5, you find space for at least four activities, including the introduction and closure.) This means that in a 60-minute time block, for example, you should probably plan three or four *sequenced* learning activities, with some that are teacher-centered and many others that

are more student-centered. In a 90-minute block, plan five or six learning activities. In exemplary classrooms teachers often have several activities concurrently being performed by individuals, dyads, and small groups of students (that is, using multitasking or multilevel instruction).

Prepare and use notes as a guide for your talk
Planning your talk and preparing notes to be used during formal and informal teacher talk is important—just as important as implementing the talk with visuals. There is absolutely nothing wrong with using notes during your teaching. As you move around the room your notes can be carried on a clipboard, perhaps a brightly

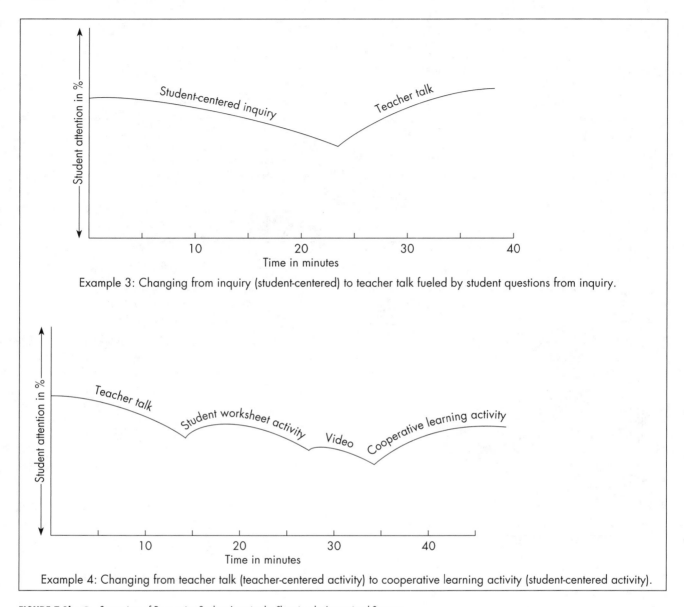

Example 3: Changing from inquiry (student-centered) to teacher talk fueled by student questions from inquiry.

Example 4: Changing from teacher talk (teacher-centered activity) to cooperative learning activity (student-centered activity).

FIGURE 7.1b ● Comparison of Recapturing Student Attention by Changing the Instructional Strategy

colored one that gives students a visual focus. Your notes for a formal talk can first be prepared in narrative form; for class use, though, they should be reduced to an outline form. *Talks to students should always be from an outline, never read from prose.*

In your outline, use color coding with abbreviated visual cues to yourself. You will eventually develop your own coding system; whatever coding system you use, keep it simple lest you forget what the codes are for. Consider these examples of coding: Where transition of ideas occurs and you want to allow silent moments for ideas to sink in, mark *P* for *pause,* *T* for a *transition,* and *S* for moments of *silence;* where a slide or other visual aid will be used, mark *AV* for *audiovisual;* where you intend to stop and ask a question, mark *TQ* for *teacher question,*

and mark *SQ* or? where you want to stop and allow time for *student questions;* where you plan to have a discussion, mark *D;* or mark *SG* where you plan *small-group* work and *L* where you plan to switch to a *laboratory investigation;* for *reviews* and *comprehension checks,* mark *R* and *CS.*

Share your note organization with your students. Prepare a guided lecture and provide students with a skeletal outline so they can add information as you lecture. This will help the students take notes and decide what kinds of things they should write down. Use colored chalk or writing pens to outline and highlight your talk; suggest to your students that they use colored pencils for note-taking, so their notes can be color-coded to match your writing board (or overhead projector) notes.

Rehearse your talk Rehearsing your planned talk is important. Using your lesson plan as your guide, rehearse your talk using a camcorder or an audio recorder. Including a time plan for each subtopic allows you to gauge your timing during implementation of the talk.

Avoid racing through the talk solely to complete it by a certain time It is more important that students understand some of what you say than that you cover it all and they understand none of it. If you do not finish, continue it later.

Augment your talk with multisensory stimulation and allow for think-time Your presentation should not overly rely on verbal communication. When using visuals, such as video excerpts or overhead transparencies, do not think that you must be constantly talking; after clearly explaining the purpose of a visual, give students time to look at it, think about it, and ask questions about it. The visual is new to the students, so give them sufficient time to take it in.

Carefully plan the content of your talk The content of your talk should supplement and enhance what is found in the student textbook rather than simply rehash content from the textbook. Students may never read their book if you tell them in an interesting and condensed fashion everything that they need to know from it.

Monitor your delivery Your voice should be pleasant and interesting to listen to rather than a steady, boring monotone or a constantly shrieking, irritating, high pitch. However, it is good to show enthusiasm for what you are talking about while teaching and learning. Occasionally you should use dramatic voice inflections to emphasize important points and meaningful body language to give students a visual focus.

As is always the case when teaching, *avoid standing in the same spot for long periods of time.* Even during direct instruction, you need to monitor student behavior. Use proximity as a means of keeping students on-task.

View the vocabulary of the talk as an opportunity to help students with their word morphology The students should easily understand words you use, though you should still model professionalism and help students develop their vocabulary—both the special vocabulary of your subject field and the more general vocabulary of the English language. During your lesson planning, predict when you are likely to use a word that is new to most students, and plan to stop to ask a student to help explain its meaning and perhaps demonstrate its derivation. Help students with word meaning. This helps students with their remembering. Remember, regardless of subject or grade level, *all teachers are language arts teachers.* Knowledge of word morphology is an important component of skilled reading and includes the ability to generate new words from prefixes, roots, and suffixes. For some students, nearly every subject in the curriculum is challenging. That is certainly true for some English Language Learners, for whom teacher talk, especially formal teacher talk, should be used sparingly, if at all. Every teacher has the responsibility of helping students learn how to learn, and that includes helping students develop their word comprehension skills, reading skills, thinking and memory skills, and their motivation for learning.

For example, if introducing to students the word *hermaphrodite,* the science teacher has the opportunity to teach a bit of Greek mythology in the process of helping the students understand that important biology term, through showing students the origin of the word's two roots (Hermes, or Mercury, the messenger of the gods; and Aphrodite, or Venus, Goddess of love and beauty). Taking time to teach a bit of Greek mythology affords the science teacher an opportunity to cross disciplines and captures the interest of a few more students.

Give thoughtful and intelligent consideration to student diversity During the preactive phase of planning, while preparing your talk, consider students in your classroom who are culturally and linguistically different and those who have special needs. Personalize the talk for them by choosing your vocabulary carefully and appropriately, speaking slowly and methodically, repeating often, paraphrasing, and planning meaningful analogies and examples as well as relevant audio and visual displays.

Use familiar examples and analogies to help students make relevant connections (bridges) Although this sometimes takes a great deal of creative thinking as well as action during the preactive planning phase, it is important that you attempt to connect the talk with ideas and events with which the students are already familiar. The most effective talk is one that makes frequent and meaningful connections between what students already know and what they are learning, which bridges what they are learning with what they have experienced in their lives. Of course, this means you need to "know" your students. (See section of Module 3 titled, "Get to Know the Students as People.")

Establish eye contact frequently Your primary eye contact should be with your students—always! That important point cannot be overemphasized. Only momentarily should you look at your notes, your visuals, the projection screen, the writing board, and other adults or objects in the classroom. You can learn to establish eye contact with each student about once a minute. To "establish" eye contact means that you hold the eye contact with that particular person for several seconds; the student is aware that you are looking at him or her.

Frequent eye contact can have two major benefits. First, as you read a student's body posture and facial expressions, you gain clues about that student's attentiveness and comprehension. Second, eye contact helps to establish rapport between you and a student. Be alert, though, for students who are from cultures where eye contact is infrequent or unwanted and could have negative consequences. In other words, don't force it!

Frequent eye contact is easier when using an overhead projector than when using the writing board. When using a writing board, you have to turn at least partially away from your audience, and you may also have to pace back and forth from the board to the students in order to retain that important proximity to them. Remember our discussions about "overlapping" (Module 3) as an important teaching skill? Well, this is one of those times when its importance really comes into play. While lecturing on a topic you must remain aware and attentive to everything that is happening in the classroom (that is, to student behavior as well as to the content of your lecture).

DEMONSTRATION

Most students like demonstrations because the demonstrator is actively engaged in a learning activity rather than merely verbalizing about it. Demonstrations can be used by any teacher in any subject and for a variety of purposes. The teacher demonstrates role-playing in preparation for a social studies simulation. A teacher demonstrates the steps in solving a mathematics problem. A language arts/English teacher demonstrates clustering to students ready for a creative writing assignment. A science teacher demonstrates the effect of combining an acid and a base to form saltwater. The physical education teacher demonstrates the proper way to serve in volleyball.

Purposes of Demonstrations

A demonstration can be designed to serve any of the following purposes: To assist in recognizing a solution to an existing problem; to bring an unusual closure to a lesson or unit of study; to demonstrate a thinking skill; to model a skill used in conflict resolution; to establish problem recognition; to give students an opportunity for vicarious participation in active learning; to illustrate a particular point of content; to introduce a lesson or unit of study in a way that grabs the students' attention;

to reduce potential safety hazards (where the teacher demonstrates with materials that are too dangerous for students to handle); to review; to save time and resources (as opposed to the entire class doing that which is being demonstrated); and to set up a discrepancy recognition.

Guidelines for Using Demonstrations

When planning a demonstration, consider the following guidelines.

Decide what is the most effective way to conduct the demonstration, such as, for example, as a verbal or a silent demonstration; by a student or by the teacher; by the teacher with a student helper; to the entire class or to small groups; or by some combination of these such as first by the teacher followed then by a repeat of the demonstration by a student or a succession of students.

Be sure that the demonstration is visible to all students. Practice with the materials and procedure before demonstrating to the students. During your practice, try to prepare for anything that could go wrong during the real demonstration; if you don't, as Murphy's Law says, anything that can go wrong probably will. Then, if something does go wrong during the live demonstration, use that as an opportunity for a teachable moment—engage the students in trying to understand what went wrong, or if that isn't feasible, then go to Plan B (see Module 8).

Consider your pacing of the demonstration, allowing for enough student wait-see and think-time. At the start of the demonstration, explain its purpose and the learning objectives. Remember this adage: Tell them what you are going to do, show them, and then tell them what they saw. As with any lesson, plan your closure and allow time for questions and discussion. During the demonstration, as in other types of teacher talk, use frequent stops to check for student understanding.

Safety is key, so be sure that the demonstration table and area are free of unnecessary objects that could distract, be in the way, or pose a safety hazard. With potentially hazardous demonstrations, such as might occur in physical education, science, or vocational classes, you should first decide whether the demonstration is really that important and necessary. If your answer is "yes," then be sure to *model* proper safety precautions: Wear safety goggles, have fire-safety equipment at hand, and position a protective shield between the demonstration table and nearby students. To review the components of the lecture, do Exercise 7.1.

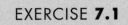

EXERCISE 7.1

■ The Lecture—Summary Review and Practice

Instructions: The purpose of this exercise is to provide a summary review to check your comprehension of this important, often used, and frequently misused teaching strategy. Answer each of the following questions and then share your responses with your classmates.

1. How does the lecture differ from informal teacher talk?

2. Although sometimes a useful technique, lecturing should be used sparingly in high school classes and even less in junior high and middle school classes. Why is it not as useful as some other strategies?

3. Specifically, when might you use a formal lecture?

4. What can a lecturer do to arouse and maintain interest in the lecture?

5. While planning a lecture, what principles should be kept in mind?

6. Identify at least five things you can do to make a lecture successful.

7. Thinking back to the classes given by the best lecturer in your college experience, what did that professor do that made his or her lectures better than average?

8. Thinking of a lecture or informal talk given by one of your current professors or colleagues, what aids did the lecturer use to spice up the lecture? What devices might have been used that were not? If you were the lecturer, would you have done it differently? If so, explain how.

9. For a specific grade level, prepare a major behavioral objective for a topic in your field. Identify the major points that you would try to make and how you would try to get those points across in a lecture designed to support that major objective.

   Field: Grade level: Topic:

   Major objective:

   Major points:

   Method of achieving:

   Estimate of amount of time needed to present this lecture:

10. Now, implement the lecture of the previous item (number 9) to a group of your peers and obtain their feedback, using the criteria of item 8 for that feedback. If the equipment is available, you may wish to videotape your lecture so you can watch it and evaluate it yourself. Upon completion of implementing the lecture and obtaining evaluative feedback about it, prepare a self-evaluation of the lecture, again using the criteria of item 8. Share this self-evaluation with your course instructor.

  To access this exercise online, go to the Companion Website at **www.prenhall.com/kellough.**

■ QUESTIONING

A strategy of fundamental importance to any mode of instruction is questioning. You will use questioning for so many purposes that you must be skilled in its use to teach effectively.

■ Purposes for Using Questioning

You will adapt the type and form of each question to the purpose for which it is asked. The purposes that questions can serve can be separated into five main categories, as follows.

1. *Make polite requests.* An example is, "José, would you please turn out the lights so we can show the slides?" Although they probably should avoid doing so, teachers sometimes also use rhetorical questions for the purpose of regaining student attention and maintaining classroom control, like, "José, would you please attend to your work?" Rhetorical questions can sometimes backfire on the teacher. In this case, for example, José might say "No"; then the teacher would have a problem that could perhaps have been avoided had the teacher at first been more direct and simply told José to attend to his work, rather than asking him if he would.

2. *To review and remind students of classroom procedures.* For example, if students continue to talk when they shouldn't, you can stop the lesson and ask, "Class, I think we need to review the procedure for listening when someone else is talking. Who can tell me, what is the procedure that we agreed upon?"

3. *To gather information.* Examples are: "How many of you have finished the assignment?" or, to find out whether a student knows something, "Louise, can you please tell us the difference between a synonym and antonym?"

4. *To discover student knowledge, interests, or experiences.* Examples might be: "How many of you think you know the process by which water in our city is made potable?" or "How many of you have visited the local water treatment plant?"

5. *To guide student thinking and learning.* It is this category of questioning that is the focus here. In teaching, questions in this category are used to:

   - ■ *Develop appreciation.* For example, "Do you now understand the ecological relationship among that particular root fungus, voles, and the survival of the large conifers of the forests of the Pacific Northwest?"

   - ■ *Develop student thinking.* For example, "What do you suppose the effects on the ecology are when standing water is sprayed with an

insecticide that is designed to kill all mosquito larvae?"

   - ■ *Diagnose learning difficulty.* For example, "What part of the formula don't you understand, Sarah?"

   - ■ *Emphasize major points.* For example, "If humans have never been to the sun, how do we know what it is made of?"

   - ■ *Encourage students.* For example, "OK, so you didn't remember the formula for glucose. What really impressed me in your essay is what you did understand about photosynthesis."

   - ■ *Establish rapport.* For example, "We have a problem here, but I think we can solve it if we put our heads together. What do you think ought to be our first step?"

   - ■ *Evaluate learning.* For example, "John, what is the effect when two rough surfaces are rubbed together?"

   - ■ *Give practice in expression.* For example, "Yvonne, would you please share with us the examples of impressionism that you found?"

   - ■ *Help students in their own metacognition.* For example, "Yes, something did go wrong in the experiment. Do you still think your original hypothesis is correct? If not, then where was the error in your thinking? Or if you still think your hypothesis is correct, then where might the error have been in the design of your experiment? How might we find out?"

   - ■ *Help students interpret materials.* For example, "Something seems to be wrong with this compass. How do you suppose we can find out what is wrong with it?"

   - ■ *Help students organize materials.* For example, "If you really want to carry out your proposed experiment, then we are going to need certain materials. We are going to have to deal with some strategic questions here, such as, what do you think we will need, where can we find those things, who will be responsible for getting them, and how will we store and arrange them once we are ready to start the investigation?"

   - ■ *Provide drill and practice.* For example, "Team A has prepared some questions that they would like to use as practice questions for our unit exam, and they are suggesting that we use them to play the game of Jeopardy on Friday. Is everyone in agreement with their idea?"

   - ■ *Provide review.* For example, "Today, in your groups, you are going to study the unit review questions I have prepared. After each group has studied and prepared its answers to these

written questions, your group will pick another group and ask them your set of review questions. Each group has a different set of questions. Members of Team A will keep score, and the group that has the highest score from this review session will receive free pizza at tomorrow's lunch. Ready?"

- *Show agreement or disagreement.* For example, "Some scientists fear that the Antarctic ice shelf is breaking up and melting and that this will cause worldwide flooding. With evidence that you have collected from recent articles and what you have found searching the Internet, do you agree with this conclusion? Explain why or why not."

- *Show relationships such as cause and effect.* For example, "What do you suppose would be the global effect if just one inch of the total Antarctic ice shelf were to rather suddenly melt?"

- *Build the curriculum.* It is the students' questions that provide the basis for the learning that occurs in an effective program that is inquiry based and project centered, as was discussed in Module 6. We return to this category of students' questions later in this discussion of questioning.

■ Questions to Avoid Asking

While it is important to avoid asking rhetorical questions, that is, questions for which you do not want a response, you should also avoid asking questions that call for little or no student thinking, such as those that can be answered with a simple yes or no or some other sort of alternative response. Unless followed up with questions calling for clarification, questions that call for simple responses such as yes or no have little or no diagnostic value; they encourage guessing and inappropriate student responses that can cause classroom control problems for the teacher.

It is even more important to avoid using questions that embarrass a student, punish a student, or in any way deny the student's dignity. Questions that embarrass or punish tend to damage the student's developing self-esteem and serve no meaningful academic or instructional purpose. Questioning is an important instructional tool that should be used by the teacher only for academic reasons. Although it is not always possible to predict when a student might be embarrassed by a question, a teacher should *never* deliberately ask questions for the purpose of embarrassment or punishment. In other words, avoid asking a student a content question when you know full well that the student was not paying attention and/or does not know the answer.

■ Types of Questions: A Glossary

Let us now define, describe, and provide examples for each of the kinds of questions that you will use in teaching. This will be followed by a discussion about a special technique called *Socratic questioning.* Following that, your attention is focused on the *levels* of questions.

Clarifying question The clarifying question is used to gain more information from a student to help the teacher better understand a student's ideas, feelings, and thought processes. Often, asking a student to elaborate on an initial response will lead the student to think more deeply, restructure his or her thinking, and while doing so, discover a fallacy in the original response. Examples of clarifying questions are "What I hear you saying is that you would rather work alone than in your group. Is that correct?" "So, Patrick, you think the poem is a sad one, is that right?" Research has shown a strong positive correlation between student learning and development of metacognitive skills (that is, their thinking about thinking) and the teacher's use of questions that ask for clarification.[4] In addition, by seeking clarification, you are likely to be demonstrating an interest in the student and her or his thinking.

Convergent-thinking question Convergent thinking questions, also called *narrow questions,* are low-order thinking questions that have a single correct answer (such as recall questions, discussed further in the next section). Examples of convergent questions are "How would you classify the word spelled *c-l-o-s-e,* as a homophone or homograph?" "If the radius of a circle is 20 meters, what is its circumference?" "What is the name of what is considered to be the first battle of the Civil War?" When using questions of this type, try to come back with follow-up questions when possible so the student answering can demonstrate thinking beyond rote memory.

Cueing question If you ask a question to which, after sufficient **wait time,** no students respond or to which their inadequate responses indicate they need more information, then you can ask a question that cues the answer or response you are seeking.[5] In essence, you are going backward in your questioning sequence to cue the students. For example, to introduce a lesson on the study of prefixes, a teacher asks her students, "How many legs each do crayfish, lobsters, and shrimp have?" If no one accurately responds, she might then cue the answer with the following information and question, "The class to which those animals belong is class Decapoda. Does that give you a clue about the number of legs they have?" If that clue is not enough and after allowing sufficient time for students to think (longer than 2 seconds), she might ask, "What is a decathlon?" "What is the decimal system?" "What is a decimeter?" "What is a decibel?" "What is a decade?" "What is the Decalogue?" and so on.

Divergent-thinking question Divergent-thinking questions (also known as *broad, reflective,* or *thought questions*) are *open-ended* (i.e., usually having no singularly correct answer) higher-order thinking questions (requiring analysis, synthesis, or evaluation), which require students to think creatively, to leave the comfortable confines of the known and reach out into the unknown. Examples of questions that require divergent thinking are "What measures could be taken to reduce crime in our neighborhood?" and "What measures could be taken to improve the post-lunchtime trash problem on our campus?"

Evaluative question Whether convergent or divergent, some questions require students to place a value on something or to take a stance on some issue; these are referred to as evaluative questions. If the teacher and the students all agree on certain premises, then the evaluative question would also be a convergent question. If original assumptions differ, then the response to the evaluative question would be more subjective, and therefore that evaluative question would be divergent. Examples of evaluative questions are "Should the United States allow clear-cutting in its national forests?" and "Should women have the right as individuals to choose whether or not to have abortions?" and "Is it an impeachable offense?"

Focus question This category includes any question that is designed to focus student thinking. For example, the first question of the preceding paragraph is a focus question when the teacher asking it is attempting to focus student attention on the economic issues involved in clear-cutting.

Probing question Similar to a clarifying question, the probing question requires student thinking to go beyond superficial first-answer or single-word responses. Examples of probing questions are "Why, Antoine, do you think that every citizen should have the right to have a gun?"

■ Socratic Questioning

In the fifth century B.C.E., Socrates, the great Athenian teacher, used the art of questioning so successfully that to this day we still hear of the Socratic method.[6] What, exactly, is the Socratic method? Socrates' strategy was to ask his students a series of leading questions that gradually snarled them up to the point where they had to look carefully at their own ideas and to think rigorously for themselves. Today that strategy is referred to as the Socratic approach or method.

Socratic discussions were informal dialogues where Socrates sometimes had to go to considerable lengths to ignite his students' intrinsic interest; their response was natural and spontaneous. In his dialogues, Socrates tried to aid students in developing ideas. He did not impose his own notions on the students. Rather, he encouraged them to develop their own conclusions and draw their own inferences. Of course, Socrates may have had preconceived notions about what the final learning should be and carefully aimed his questions so that the students would arrive at the desired conclusions. Still, his questions were open-ended, causing divergent rather than convergent thinking. The students were free to go mentally wherever the facts and their thinking led them.

Throughout history, teachers have tried to adapt the Socratic method to the classroom. In some situations, they have been quite successful in using it as a major mode of instruction. However, we must remember that Socrates used this method in the context of a one-to-one relationship between the student and himself. Some teachers have adapted it for whole-class direct instruction by asking questions first of one student and then of another, moving slowly about the class. This technique may work, but it is difficult because the essence of the Socratic technique is to build question on question in a logical fashion so that each question leads the student a step further toward the understanding sought. When you spread the questions around the classroom, you may find it difficult to build up the desired sequence and to keep all the students involved in the discussion. Sometimes you may be able to use the Socratic method by directing all the questions at one student—at least for several minutes—while the other students look on and listen in. That is how Socrates did it. When the topic is interesting enough, this technique can be quite successful and even exciting, but in the long run, the Socratic method works best when the teacher is working in one-on-one coaching situations or with small groups of students, rather than in whole-class direct instruction.

In using Socratic questioning the focus is on the questions, not answers, and thinking is valued as the quintessential activity.[7] In essence, to conduct Socratic questioning with the student or class, identify a problem (either student- or teacher-posed) and then ask the students a series of probing questions designed to cause them to examine critically the problem and potential solutions to it. The main thrust of the questioning and the key questions must be planned in advance so that the questioning will proceed logically. It is the Socratic method that you will be using in a micro peer-teaching exercise later in this module (Exercise 7.6).

■ Levels of Cognitive Questions and Student Thinking

The questions you pose are cues to your students to the level of thinking expected of them, ranging from the lowest level of mental operation, requiring simple recall of knowledge (convergent thinking), to the highest, requiring divergent thought and application of that thought. It is important that you are aware of the levels of thinking and that you understand the importance of attending to student thinking from low to higher levels of operation. What one student may view as a matter of simple recall of information, for another student may *require* a higher-order mental activity, such as figuring something out by deduction.

You should structure and sequence your questions (and assist students in developing their own skill in structuring and sequencing their questions) in a way that is designed to guide students to higher levels of thinking. For example, when students respond to questions in complete sentences that provide supportive evidence for their ideas, it is fairly safe to assume that their thinking is at a higher level than were the response an imprecise and nondescriptive single-word answer.

To help your understanding, three levels of questioning and thinking are described next.[8] You may recognize the similarity between these three levels of questions and the six levels of thinking from Bloom's Taxonomy of cognitive objectives (Module 4). For your daily use of questioning, though, it is just as useful but more practical to think and behave in terms of these three levels, rather than Bloom's six.

1. *Lowest level (the data input phase): Gathering and recalling information.* At this level questions are designed to solicit from students concepts, information, feelings, or experiences that were gained in the past and stored in memory. Sample key words and desired behaviors are: *complete, count, define, describe, identify, list, match, name, observe, recall, recite,* and *select.*

   Thinking involves receiving data through the senses, followed by the processing of those data. Inputting without processing is brain-dysfunctional. Information that is not processed is stored only in short-term memory.

2. *Intermediate level (the data processing phase): Processing information.* At this level questions are designed to draw relationships of cause and effect, to synthesize, analyze, summarize, compare, contrast, or classify data. Sample key words and desired behaviors are: *analyze, classify, compare, contrast, distinguish, explain, group, infer, make an analogy, organize, plan,* and *synthesize.*

   Thinking and questioning that involve processing of information can be conscious or unconscious. When students observe the teacher thinking aloud, and when they are urged to think aloud, to think about their thinking, and to analyze it as it occurs, they are in the process of developing their intellectual skills.

   At the processing level, this internal analysis of new data may challenge a learner's preconceptions (and misconceptions) about a phenomenon. The learner's brain will naturally resist this challenge to existing beliefs. The greater the mental challenge, the greater will be the brain's effort to draw upon data already in stor-

age. With increasing data, the mind will gradually examine existing concepts and ultimately, as necessary, develop new mental concepts.

If there is a match between new input and existing mental concepts, no problem exists. Piaget called this process *assimilation.*[9] If, however, in processing new data there is no match with existing mental concepts, then the situation is what Piaget called **cognitive disequilibrium.** The brain does not like this disequilibrium and will drive the learner to search for an explanation for the discrepancy. Piaget called this process *accommodation.* However, although learning is enhanced by challenge, in situations that are threatening the brain is less flexible in accommodating new ideas. As discussed in Module 3, that is why each student must feel welcomed in the classroom, and the classroom environment must be perceived by the learner as challenging but nonthreatening—what is referred to as an environment of *relaxed alertness.*[10]

3. *Highest level (the data output phase): Applying and evaluating in new situations.* Questions at the highest level encourage learners to think intuitively, creatively, and hypothetically; to use their imagination; to expose a value system; or to make a judgment. Sample key words and desired behaviors are: *apply a principle, build a model, evaluate, extrapolate, forecast, generalize, hypothesize, imagine, judge, predict,* and *speculate.*

You must use questions at the level best suited for the purpose, use questions of a variety of different levels, and structure questions in a way intended to move student thinking to higher levels. When teachers use higher-level questions, their students tend to score higher on tests of critical thinking and on standardized tests of achievement.[11]

When questioning students about reading material in particular, consider using the **question-answer relationship (QAR) strategy.** QAR involves asking a question and, if a student is unable to respond, providing one of three types of cues. The cues are related to the level of thinking required. "Right there" is used for questions for the lowest level, that is, in which the answer can be found explicitly stated in the sentence or paragraph. "Search and think" means the answer is not directly stated and therefore must be inferred. "On your own" is used for highest level critical thinking questions for which the answers are neither explicit nor inferred in the text.[12]

With the use of questions as a strategy to move student thinking to higher levels, the teacher is facilitating the students' intellectual development. Developing your skill in using questioning requires attention to detail and practice. The following guidelines will provide that detail and some practice. But first, do Exercise 7.2 to check your understanding of the levels of questions.

EXERCISE 7.2

■ Identifying the Cognitive Levels of Questions— A Self-Check Exercise

Instructions: The purpose of this exercise is to test your understanding and recognition of the levels of questions. Mark each of the following questions with a:

- *1*, if it is at the lowest level—gathering and recalling data.
- *2*, if it requires the student to process data.
- *3*, if it is at the highest level of mental operation, requiring the student to apply or to evaluate data in a new situation.

Check your answers against the answer key that follows. Resolve problems by discussing them with your instructor and classmates.

_____ 1. John, do you agree with Maria?

_____ 2. How does the repetition in *Bolero* affect you?

_____ 3. Do you believe that argument will hold up in the case of Swaziland?

_____ 4. What must I multiply by in order to clear the fractions in this equation?

_____ 5. Did O. Henry's trick ending make the story more interesting?

_____ 6. How would you end the story?

_____ 7. Who came out of the door, the lady or the tiger?

_____ 8. How do the natural resources of the United States compare with those of China?

_____ 9. If you were setting up the defense of the colonies, where would you put the forts?

_____ 10. In view of all the information we have, do you believe the union's sending out seventy thousand letters asking voters to defeat the six assemblymen was justified?

_____ 11. What difference has an equal rights amendment made?

_____ 12. Who was Otto Jespersen?

_____ 13. Should a teacher be entitled to unemployment benefits during the summer months when school is not in session?

_____ 14. What would you do in this situation if you were governor?

_____ 15. What would have happened if Washington had decided to attack New Brunswick rather than Quebec?

_____ 16. What would happen if you used H_2SO_4 instead of HCl?

_____ 17. How would you set up the equation?

_____ 18. Why did you like this poem better than the previous one?

_____ 19. Which type of cell, animal or plant, has a cell wall?

_____ 20. When $2N - 10 = 0$, what does N equal?

 To access this exercise online, go to the Companion Website at **www.prenhall.com/kellough.**

Answer Key for Exercise 7.2

5. 3 (evaluate)	10. 3 (evaluate)	15. 3 (hypothesize)	20. 2 (apply)
4. 1 (recall)	9. 3 (hypothesize)	14. 3 (design)	19. 1 (recall)
3. 3 (evaluate)	8. 2 (compare)	13. 3 (judge)	18. 3 (evaluate)
2. 3 (evaluate)	7. 1 (recall)	12. 1 (recall)	17. 2 (explain)
1. 2 (analyze, compare)	6. 3 (design)	11. 3 (generalize)	16. 3 (predict)

■ Guidelines for Using Questioning

As emphasized many times in several ways throughout this book, your goals are to help your students learn how to solve problems, to make decisions and value judgments, to think creatively and critically, and to feel good about themselves, their schools, and their learning—rather than simply to fill their minds with bits and pieces of information that will likely last only a brief time in the students' short-term memory. How you construe your questions and how you carry out your questioning strategy is important to the realization of these goals.

Preparing questions When preparing questions, consider the following guidelines.

Key cognitive questions should be planned, thoughtfully worded, and written into your lesson plan. Thoughtful preparation helps to ensure that questions are clear and specific, not ambiguous; that the vocabulary is appropriate; and that each question matches its purpose. Incorporate questions into your lessons as instructional devices, welcomed pauses, attention grabbers, and as checks for student comprehension. Thoughtful teachers even plan questions that they intend to ask specific students, targeting questions to the readiness level, interest, or learning profile of a student.

Match questions with their target purposes. Carefully planned questions allow them to be sequenced and worded to match the levels of cognitive thinking expected of students. To help students in developing their thinking skills, you need to demonstrate how to do this by using terminology that is specific and that provides students with examples of experiences supporting the meanings of the cognitive words. You should demonstrate this every day so students learn the cognitive terminology. As stated by Brooks and Brooks, "Framing tasks around cognitive activities such as analysis, interpretation, and prediction—and explicitly using those terms with students—fosters the construction of new understandings."[13] See the three examples in Figure 7.2.

Implementing questioning Careful preparation of questions is one part of the skill of questioning. Implementation is the other part. Here are guidelines for effective implementation.

Ask your well-worded question before calling on a student for a response. A common error made is when the teacher first calls on a student and then asks a question, such as, "Sean, would you please tell us what you believe the author meant by the title 'We Are One'?" Although probably not intended by the teacher, as soon as the teacher called on Sean, that signaled to the rest of the class that they were released from having to think about the question. The preferred strategy is to phrase the question, allow time for all students to think, and then call on Sean and other students for their interpretations of the author's meaning of the title.

Avoid bombarding students with too much teacher talk. Sometimes teachers talk too much. This could be especially true for teachers who are nervous, as might be the case for many during their initial weeks of student teaching. Knowing the guidelines presented here will help you avoid that syndrome. Remind yourself to be quiet after you ask a question that you have carefully formulated. Sometimes, due to lack of confidence, and especially when a question hasn't been carefully thought out during the preactive phase of instruction, the teacher asks the question and then, with a slight change in wording, asks it again, or asks several questions, one after another. This is called "shotgun questioning," and it only confuses students, allowing too little time for them to think.

After asking a question, provide students with adequate time to think. The pause after asking a question is called wait time (or think-time). Because they know the subject better than the students know it and have given prior thought to the subject, too many teachers, after asking a question, fail to allow students sufficient time to think, especially for questions that require processing of information and higher-order thinking. In addition, by the time they have reached the middle school grades, students have learned pretty well how to play the "game"—that is, they know that if they remain silent long enough the teacher will probably answer his or her own question. After asking a well-worded question you should remain quiet for a while, allowing students time to think and to respond. If you wait long enough, they usually will.

As researchers have verified since the original and now classic wait-time studies of M. B. Rowe in 1974, increasing wait time to at least two seconds often leads to longer and higher-quality student responses and participation by a

Instead of	Say
"How else might it be done?"	"How could you *apply* . . . ?"
"Are you going to get quiet?"	"If we are going to hear what Joan has to say, what do you need to do?"
"How do you know that is so?"	"What evidence do you have?"

FIGURE 7.2 ● Examples of Questions Converted to Appropriate Cognitive Terminology

greater number of students.[14] After asking a question, how long should you wait before you do something? You should wait at least 2 seconds, and as many as 5 seconds. Stop reading now and look at your watch or a clock to get a feeling for how long 2 seconds is. Then, observe how long 5 seconds is. Because most of us are not used to silence in the classroom, 2 seconds of silence can seem quite long, while 5 seconds may seem eternal. If, for some reason, students have not responded after a period of 2 to 5 seconds of wait time, then you can ask the question again (but don't reword an already carefully worded question, or else students are likely to think it is a new question). Pause for several seconds; then, if you still haven't received a response, you can call on a student, then another, if necessary, after sufficient wait time. Soon you will get a response that can be built upon. Avoid answering your own question!

Now do Exercise 7.3 to further your understanding about the art of questioning and the importance of student think-time.

Practice gender equity. To practice gender equity while using questioning, here are four rules to follow. (a) Avoid going to a boy to bail out a girl who fails to answer a question, and (b) avoid going to a boy to improve upon a girl's answer. For the first, without seeming to badger, try to give the female student clues until she can answer with success. For the second, hold and demonstrate high expectations for all students. (c) Allow equal wait time regardless of student gender. (d) Call on males and females equally.

EXERCISE 7.3 ■ Think-Time and the Art of Questioning—An In-Class Exercise

Instructions: The purpose of this exercise is to further your understanding of the art and power of questioning, of the importance of well-worded questions with well-prepared and clear instructions, and of allowing students time to think.

1. Role-play simulation: From your class ask for three volunteers. One volunteer will read the lines of Estella, a second will read the one line of student, while the third volunteer uses a stop watch to direct Estella and the student to speak their lines at the designated times. The rest of your class can pretend to be students in Estella's English class.

   1:00: Estella: "Think of a man whom you admire, perhaps a father figure, and write a three-sentence paragraph describing that person." Students begin their writing.

   1:00:05: Estella: "Only three sentences about someone you look up to. It might be your father, uncle, anyone."

   1:00:07: Student: "Does it have to be about a man?" *Estella:* "No, it can be a man or a woman, but someone you truly admire."

   1:01: Estella works the rows, seeing that students are on-task.

   1:01:10: Estella: "Three sentences are all you need to write."

   1:01:15: Estella: "Think of someone you really look up to, and write three sentences in a paragraph that describes that person."

   1:01:30: Estella: "Someone you would like to be like."

   1:02: Estella continues walking around helping students who are having difficulty. All students are on-task.

   1:04: Estella: "Now I want you to exchange papers with the person behind or beside you, read that person's description of the person they admire, and describe a setting that you see their person in. Write a paragraph that describes that setting."

   1:04:–1:05: Students exchange papers; teacher walks around seeing that everyone has received another student's paper.

   1:05: Estella: "Where do you see that person being? Below the paragraph I want you to write a new paragraph describing where you see this person, perhaps in an easy chair watching a ball game, or on a porch, in a car, in the kitchen cooking."

   1:05:10: Estella: "Describe a scene you see this person in."

   1:05:15: Estella: "After you read the description I want you to create a setting for the person described."

(continued)

1:05:18: Students seem confused either about what they are reading (e.g., asking the writer what a word is or means) or what they are supposed to do.

1:05:19: Estella: "Anything is fine. Use your imagination to describe the setting."

1:05:22: Estella: "Describe a setting for this person."

1:09: Estella: "Now I want you to exchange papers with yet someone else, and after reading the previous two paragraphs written by two other students, write a third paragraph describing a problem you think this admired person has."

2. After the role-play simulation, hold a whole-class or small-group discussion and use the following as a springboard for your discussion: Describe what you believe are the good points and weak points of this portion of Estella's lesson and her implementation of it.

 To access this exercise online, go to the Companion Website at **www.prenhall.com/kellough.**

Practice calling on all students. Related to Rule (d) of the preceding paragraph, you must call on not just the bright or the slow, not just the boys or the girls, not only those in the front or middle of the room, but all of the students. To do these things takes concentrated effort on your part, but it is important. To ensure that students are called on equally, some teachers hold in hand laminated copies of their seating charts, perhaps on bright neon-colored clipboards (gives students a visual focus), and, with a wax pencil or water-soluble marker, make a mark next to the name of the student each time he or she is called on. With the seating chart laminated, and using erasable markers, the marks can be erased later and the seating chart used over and over. Additional suggestions for practicing equity follow later in this module.

Give the same minimum amount of wait time (think-time) to all students. This, too, will require concentrated effort on your part, but is important to do. A teacher who waits for less time when calling on a slow student or students of one gender is showing bias toward or lack of confidence in certain students, both of which are detrimental when a teacher is striving to establish for all students a positive, equal, and safe environment for classroom learning. Show confidence in all students, and never discriminate by expecting less or more from some than from others. Although some students may take longer to respond, it is not necessarily because they are not thinking or have less ability. There may be cultural differences to think about, in that some cultures simply allow more wait time than others do. The important point here is to individualize to allow students who need more time to have it. Variation in wait time allowed should not be used to single out some students and to lead to lower expectations but rather to allow for higher expectations.

Require students to raise their hands and be called on. When you ask questions, instead of allowing students to randomly shout out their answers, require students to raise their hands and to be called on before responding. Establish that procedure at the beginning of the school year and stick with it. This helps to ensure that you call on all students equally, fairly distributing your interactions with the students, and that girls are not interacted with less because boys tend to be more boisterous. Even in same-gender classrooms, some students tend to be more vocal while others are less so and, when allowed by the instructor, tend to monopolize and control the flow of the verbal interactions. Every teacher has the responsibility to guarantee a nonbiased classroom and an equal distribution of interaction time in the classroom. Another important reason for this advice is to aid students in learning to control their impulsivity. Controlling one's impulsivity is one of the characteristics of intelligent behavior presented in the previous module.

Actively involve as many students as possible in the questioning-answering discussion session. The traditional method of the teacher asking a question and then calling on a student to respond is essentially a one-on-one interaction. Many students, those not called on, are likely to view that as their opportunity to disengage in the lesson at hand. Even though you call on one student you want the other students not to mentally disengage. There are many effective ways to keep all engaged. Consider the following.

To keep all students mentally engaged, before calling on anyone you can have all students write their answers to the question. You will want to call on students who are sitting quietly and have not raised their hands as well as those who have, but avoid badgering or humiliating an unwilling participant. When a student has no response, you might suggest he or she think about it.

Then come back to the student to ensure he or she eventually understands or has an answer to the original question.

By dividing a single question into several parts, the number of students involved can be increased. For example, "What are the causes of the Civil War? Who can give one reason?" followed then by "Who can give another?" Or, you can involve several students in answering a single question. For example, ask one student for an answer to a question such as, "What was the first battle of the Civil War?", a second to read the text aloud to verify the student's answer, and sometimes a third to explore the reason or thinking that makes it the accepted answer.

Carefully gauge your responses to students' responses to your questions. The way you respond to students' answers influences their subsequent participation. Responses by the teacher that encourage student participation include probing for elaboration, discussing student answers, requesting justification, asking how answers were arrived at, and providing positive reinforcement.[15]

Use strong praise sparingly. If you want students to think divergently and creatively, you should be stingy with the use of strong praise to student responses. Strong praise from a teacher tends to terminate divergent and creative thinking.

One of your goals is to help students find **intrinsic** sources for **motivation,** that is, an inner drive of intent or desire that causes them to want to learn. Use of strong praise tends to build conformity, causing students to depend upon outside forces—that is, the giver of praise—for their worth rather than upon themselves. An example of a strong praise response is "That's right! Very good." In brainstorming sessions, the teacher could generate a great deal of expression of high-level thought.

■ Questions from Students: The Question-Driven Classroom

Student questions can and should be used as springboards for further questioning, discussions, and investigations. Indeed, in a constructivist learning environment, student questions often drive content. Students should be encouraged to ask questions that challenge the textbook, the process, or other persons' statements, and they should be encouraged to seek the supporting evidence behind a statement.

Being able to ask questions may be more important than having right answers. Knowledge is derived from asking questions. Being able to recognize problems and to formulate questions is a skill and the key to problem solving and critical thinking skill development. You have a responsibility to encourage students to formulate questions and to help them word their questions in such

a way that tentative answers can be sought. That is the process necessary to build a base of knowledge that can be drawn upon whenever necessary to link, interpret, and explain new information in new situations.

Questioning: the cornerstone of critical thinking, real-world problem solving, and meaningful learning With real-world problem solving, there are usually no absolute right answers. Rather than answers being correct, some are better than others. The student needs to learn how to (a) recognize the problem, (b) formulate a question about that problem (e.g., Should I date this person or not? Should I take this job or not? To which colleges should I apply? Should I study Spanish or not?), (c) collect data, and (d) arrive at a temporarily acceptable answer to the problem, while realizing that at some later time new data may dictate a review of the former conclusion. For example, if an astronomer believes she has discovered a new planetary system, there is no textbook or teacher or any other outside authoritative source to which she may refer in order to inquire if she is correct. Rather, on the basis of her self-confidence in identifying problems, asking questions, collecting enough data, and arriving at a tentative conclusion based on those data, she assumes that for now her conclusion is safe.

Encourage students to ask questions about content and process. As emphasized in the book *Tried and True*, question asking often indicates that the inquirer is curious, puzzled, and uncertain; it is a sign of being engaged in thinking about a topic. And, yet, in too many classrooms too few students ask questions.[16] Students should be encouraged to ask questions. From students, there is no such thing as a dumb question. Sometimes students, like everyone else, ask questions that could just as easily have been looked up or are irrelevant or show lack of thought or sensitivity. Those questions can consume precious class time. For a teacher, they can be frustrating. A teacher may too quickly and mistakenly brush off that type of question with sarcasm, while assuming that the student is too lazy to look up an answer. In such instances, you are advised to think before responding and to respond kindly and professionally, although in the busy life of a classroom teacher that may not always be so easy to remember to do. However, be assured that there is a reason for a student's question. Perhaps the student is signaling a need for recognition or simply demanding attention.

As mentioned in Module 1, in large schools, it is sometimes easy for a student to feel alone and insignificant (although this seems less the case with schools that use a "house" plan, or where one cadre of teachers remains with the same cohort of students for 2 or more years[17]). When a student makes an effort to interact with you, that can be a positive sign, so gauge carefully your responses to those efforts. If a student's question is really off track, off the wall, out of order, and out of context with the content of the lesson, consider using this response: "That is an interesting question and I would very much like to talk with you more about it. Could we meet at lunchtime or before or after school or at some other time that is mutually convenient?"

Avoid bluffing an answer to a question for which you do not have an answer. Nothing will cause you to lose credibility with students faster than faking an answer.

There is nothing wrong with admitting that you do not know. It helps students realize that you are human. It helps them maintain an adequate self-esteem, realizing that they are okay. What is important is that you know where and how to find possible answers and that you help students develop that same knowledge and those same skills.

Now, to reinforce your comprehension, do Exercises 7.4, 7.5, and 7.6.

EXERCISE 7.4

■ An Analysis of the Quality of Questions—A Self-Check Exercise

Instructions: The purpose of this exercise is to practice your skill in analyzing questions. Evaluate each of the following questions by checking the Poor, Fair, or Good column for each question. Use the following code in the right column to indicate your reasons why.

A = Calls for no answer and is a pseudoquestion.

B = Asks for recall but little or no thinking.

C = Challenging, stimulating, or discussion-provoking type of question that calls for high-level thinking, including reasoning and problem solving.

Upon completion, check your responses against the answer key and discuss any problems with your classmates and instructor.

Questions	Poor	Fair	Good	Why?
1. In what region are major earthquakes located?				
2. According to the theory of isostasy, how would you describe our mountainous regions?				
3. What mineral will react with HCl to produce CO_2?				
4. What kind of rock is highly resistant to weathering?				
5. Will the continents look different in the future? Why?				
6. Who can describe what a continental shelf is?				
7. What caused the Industrial Revolution?				
8. What political scandal involved President Harding?				
9. This is a parallelogram, isn't it?				
10. Wouldn't you agree that the base angles of an isosceles triangle are congruent?				
11. In trying to determine the proof of this exercise, what would you suggest we examine at the outset?				
12. What conclusion can be drawn concerning the points of intersection of two graphs?				
13. Why is pure water a poor conductor of electricity?				
14. How do fossils help explain the theory of plate tectonics?				
15. If Macbeth had told you about his encounter with the apparitions, what advice would you have offered?				
16. Who said, "If it were done when 'tis done, then 'twere well it were done quickly"?				

(continued)

Questions	Poor	Fair	Good	Why?
17. In the poem "The Sick Rose," what do you think Blake means by "the invisible worm"?				
18. Should teachers censor the books that students read?				
19. Explain the phrase "ontogeny recapitulates phylogeny."				
20. Name the 10 life functions.				
21. What living thing can live without air?				
22. What is chlorophyll?				
23. Explain the difference between RNA and DNA.				
24. Who developed the periodic table based on the fact that elements are functions of their atomic weight?				
25. Johnny, why aren't you in your seat?				

 To access this exercise online, go to the Companion Website at **www.prenhall.com/kellough.**

Answer Key for Exercise 7.4

25. P, A	20. F, B	15. G, C	10. P, A	5. G, C
24. F, B	19. G, C	14. G, C	9. P, A	4. F, B
23. G, C	18. G, C	13. F, B	8. F, B	3. F, B
22. F, B	17. G, C	12. G, C	7. G, C	2. G, C
21. F, B	16. F, B	11. G, C	6. P, A	1. F, B

EXERCISE 7.5

■ Observing the Cognitive Levels of Classroom Verbal Interaction

Instructions: The purpose of this exercise is to develop your skill in recognizing the levels of classroom questions. Arrange to visit a middle school or secondary school classroom. Tally each time you hear a question (or statement) from the teacher that causes students to gather or recall information, to process information, or to apply or evaluate data. In the left-hand column you may want to write in additional key words to assist your memory. After your observation, compare and discuss the results of this exercise with your classmates.

School and class visited:

Date of observation:

Level	Tallies of Level of Question or Statement
1. Recall level (key words: *complete, count, define, describe,* and so on)	1.

(continued)

Level	Tallies of Level of Question or Statement
2. Processing level (key words: *analyze, classify, compare,* and so on)	2.
3. Application level (key words: *apply, build, evaluate,* and so on)	3.

 To access this exercise online, go to the Companion Website at **www.prenhall.com/kellough.**

EXERCISE **7.6**

■ A Cooperative Learning Exercise in the Use of Questioning—Micro Peer-Teaching II

Instructions: The purpose of this exercise is to practice preparing and asking questions that are designed to lead student thinking from the lowest level to the highest. Before class, prepare a five-minute lesson for posing questions that will guide the learner from lowest to highest levels of thinking. Teaching will be one-on-one, in groups of four, with each member of the group assuming a particular role—teacher, student, judge, or recorder. Each of the four members of your group will assume each of those roles once for five minutes. (If there are only three members in a group, the roles of judge and recorder can be combined during each 5-minute lesson; or if there are five members in the group, one member can sit out each round or two can work together as judges.) Each member of the group should have his or her own tally sheet.

■ SUGGESTED LESSON TOPICS

- Teaching styles
- Characteristics of youngsters of a particular age
- Learning styles of students
- Evaluation of learning achievement
- A skill or hobby
- Teaching competencies
- A particular teaching strategy
- Student teaching and what it will really be like

  Each of your group members should keep the following role descriptions in mind:

- *Teacher (sender).* Pose recall (input), processing, and application (output) questions related to one of the topics above or to any topic you choose.

(continued)

- *Student (receiver).* Respond to the questions of the teacher.
- *Judge.* Identify the level of each question or statement used by the teacher *and* the level of the student's response.
- *Recorder.* Tally the number of questions or statements used by the teacher (S = sender) at each level, as indicated by the judge; also tally the level of student responses (R = receiver). Record any problems encountered by your group.

TALLY SHEET

	Minute		Input	Processing	Output
Sender _____	1	S			
Receiver _____		R			
	2	S			
		R			
	3	S			
		R			
	4	S			
		R			
	5	S			
		R			

TALLY SHEET

	Minute		Input	Processing	Output
Sender _____	1	S			
Receiver _____		R			
	2	S			
		R			
	3	S			
		R			
	4	S			
		R			
	5	S			
		R			

 To access this exercise online, go to the Companion Website at **www.prenhall.com/kellough.**

■ WHOLE-CLASS DISCUSSION

Whole-class discussion, usually directed by the teacher, is a frequently used teaching technique. On this topic you should consider yourself an expert. Having been a stu-dent in formal learning for at least 15 years, you are un-doubtedly knowledgeable about the advantages and dis-advantages of whole-class discussions. Therefore, explore your knowledge and experiences by responding to Exer-cise 7.7A. Then do Exercise 7.7B, where guidelines for the use of the whole-class discussion will be generated.

EXERCISE 7.7A

■ Whole-Class Discussion as a Teaching Strategy: Building Upon What I Already Know

Instructions: Answer the following questions, and then share your responses with your class, perhaps in discussion groups organized by subject field or grade level.

1. Your grade-level interest or subject field:

2. For what reasons would you hold a whole-class discussion?

3. Assuming that your classroom has movable seats, how would you arrange them?

4. What would you do if the seats were not movable?

5. What rules would you establish before starting the discussion?

6. Should student participation be forced? Why or why not? If so, how?

7. How would you discourage a few students from dominating the discussion?

8. What preparation should the students and the teacher be expected to make before beginning the discussion?

9. How would you handle digression from the topic?

10. Should students be discussion leaders? Why or why not? If so, what training, if any, should they receive, and how?

11. What teacher roles are options during a class discussion?

12. When is each of these roles most appropriate?

13. When, if ever, is it appropriate to hold a class meeting for discussing class procedures, not subject matter?

14. Can brainstorming be a form of whole-class discussion? Why or why not?

15. What follow-up activities would be appropriate after a whole-class discussion? On what basis would you decide to use each?

16. What sorts of activities should precede a class discussion?

17. Should a discussion be given a set length? Why or why not? If so, how long? How is the length to be decided?

(continued)

18. Should students be graded for their participation in class discussion? Why or why not? If so, how? On what basis? By whom?

19. For effective discussions, 10 to 12 feet is the maximum recommended distance between participants. During a teacher-led discussion, what can a teacher do to keep within this limit?

20. Are there any pitfalls or other points of importance that a teacher should be aware of when planning and implementing a whole-class discussion? If so, explain them and how to guard against them.

 To access this exercise online, go to the Companion Website at **www.prenhall.com/kellough.**

EXERCISE **7.7B**

■ Generating Guidelines for Using Whole-Class Discussions

Instructions: Share your responses to Exercise 7.7A with your classmates. Then individually answer the first two questions below. Next, as a group, use all three questions to guide you as you generate a list of five general guidelines for the use of whole-class discussion as a strategy in teaching. Share your group's guidelines with the entire class. Then, as a class, derive a final list of general guidelines.

1. How effective was your small-group discussion in sharing Exercise 7.7A?

2. What allowed for or inhibited the effectiveness of that small-group discussion?

3. How effective is this small-group discussion? Why?

General guidelines generated from small-group discussion:

1.

2.

3.

4.

5.

General guidelines: final list derived from whole-class discussion:

 To access this exercise online, go to the Companion Website at **www.prenhall.com/kellough.**

■ Recitation

The old-fashioned recitation method continues to be used, although it is perhaps less in vogue today. Theoretically, it should be one of the easiest to conduct, for essentially it consists of only three steps: (a) the teacher assigns students something to study, (b) the students study it, and (c) the teacher asks the students (in a whole-class situation ordinarily) about what they have studied in order to see if they have understood it.

The method has merit. Because of its long history, it is reasonably well understood and accepted by students.

The question-and-answer technique both provides reinforcement for what has been learned and gives students feedback about accuracy. The expectation of having to face questions in class has motivational value as well. Finally, recitation provides opportunities for students to learn from each other.

If practiced too frequently, though, the recitation method has more faults than merits. Too much of the questioning, for example, is of simple recall. When poorly used, the method tends to yield only superficial understanding, and may even discourage the development of higher mental processes, including attitudes, appreciations, ideals, and skills. When used by an unskilled teacher, recitation tends to be boring and to create an unfriendly, anti-intellectual class atmosphere. To liven recitations up, focus them on interesting and thought-provoking questions.

Open-text recitation The open-textbook recitation is a discussion in which the students may consult their books and other materials to back up their arguments and justify their opinions. The procedure for conducting an open-text recitation is basically the same as that outlined in the previous section. The teacher first makes a study assignment that includes suggestions and questions designed to encourage students to think and draw inferences about what they are to read and study. Then the recitation is focused on open-ended, thought-provoking questions of the Socratic, divergent, or evaluative type. Lower-order recall and convergent questions should be used as well, but ordinarily they do not play as important a role as do broader, open-ended questions. As the recitation proceeds, the teacher encourages students both to challenge and respond to others' statements and to express their own interpretations, inferences, and conclusions. At any time the students are free to consult their texts, notes, or other materials to support their arguments. Finally, someone, the teacher or a student, provides a summary. In many instances, no final decisions or arguments are necessary or desirable—the summary simply cites the positions and arguments taken. At other times, the facts of the case and the nature of the subject matter may require a definite conclusion.

This technique has many advantages. It frees the class from overemphasis on simple recall of facts and opens it up to higher levels of thinking. It helps students realize that facts are means to ends such as concepts, ideas, understandings, and the ability to think critically. It gives students practice in checking and documenting. In the best of circumstances, it shows them the importance of getting the facts straight, of listening to and respecting the opinions of others, and of suspending judgments until sufficient data are in. All in all, this is an excellent means of helping students to use and develop their higher mental faculties, because the basic technique is to use broad divergent and evaluative questions and to bounce follow-up questions around the class until the group begins to discuss the questions freely.

EQUALITY IN THE CLASSROOM

Especially when conducting direct whole-group discussions, it is easy for a teacher to fall into the trap of interacting with only "the stars," or only those in the front of the room or on one side, or only the loudest and most assertive. You must exercise caution and avoid falling into that trap. To ensure a psychologically safe and effective environment for learning for every student in your classroom, you must attend to all students and try to involve all of them equally in all class activities. You must avoid any biased expectations about certain students, and you must avoid discriminating against students according to their gender or some other personal characteristic.

Title IX: Student Rights

You probably already know that as a result of legislation that occurred more than a quarter century ago—federal law Title IX of the education amendments of 1972, P.L. 92-318—a teacher is prohibited from discriminating against students on the basis of their gender. In all aspects of school, male and female students must be treated the same. This means, for example, that a teacher must not pit males against females in a quiz game—or for any other activity or reason. Further, no teacher, student, administrator, or other school employee should make sexual advances toward a student (i.e., touching or speaking in a sexual manner). Students should be informed by their schools of their rights under Title IX, and they should be encouraged to report any suspected violations of their rights to the school principal, Title IX officer, or other designated person. Many schools provide students with a publication of their rights as students. Each school or district should have a clearly delineated statement of steps to follow in the process of protecting students' rights.

Still, today, research identifies the unintentional tendency of teachers of *both* sexes to discriminate on the basis of gender. For example, teachers, along with the rest of society, tend to have lower expectations for girls than for boys in mathematics and science. They tend to call on and encourage boys more than girls. They often let boys interrupt girls but praise girls for being polite and waiting their turn. Avoiding such discrimination may take special effort on your part, no matter how aware of the problem you may be. Some researchers believe the problem is so insidious that separate courses about it are needed in teacher training.[18]

You must not discriminate against students on any basis for any reason! To guarantee equity in interaction with students, many teachers have found it helpful to ask someone secretly to tally classroom interactions between the teacher and students during a class discussion. After an analysis of the results, the teacher arrives at decisions about his or her own attending and facilitating behaviors. Such an analysis is the purpose of Exercise 7.8. You are welcome to make blank copies and share them with your teaching colleagues.

EXERCISE **7.8**

■ Teacher Interaction with Students According to
Student Gender or Other Personal Characteristics

Instructions: The purpose of this exercise is to provide a tool for your analysis of your own interactions with students according to gender. [*Note:* In addition to the gender variable, the exercise can be modified to include responses and their frequencies according to other teacher-student interactions, such as calling on all students equally for responses to your questions, calling on students equally to assist you with classroom helping jobs, chastising students for their inappropriate behavior, or asking questions to assume classroom leadership roles.] To become accustomed to the exercise, you should do a trial run in one of your university classes, then use it during your student teaching and again during your first years of teaching. The exercise can be modified to include (a) the amount of time given for each interaction; (b) the response time given by the teacher according to student gender; and (c) other student characteristics, such as ethnicity.

Prior to class, select a student (this will be you during the trial run recommended above) or an outside observer, such as a colleague, to do the tallying and calculations, as follows. Ask the person to tally secretly the interactions between you and the students by placing a mark after the name of each student (or on the student's position on a seating chart) with whom you have verbal interaction. If a student does the tallying he or she should not be counted in any of the calculations.

Exact time at start _____

Exact time at end _____

Total time in minutes _____

Calculations Before Tallying

  a. Total number of students _____

  b. Number of female students _____

  c. Number of male students _____

  d. Percentage of students who are female _____ (= b divided by a)

  e. Percentage of students who are male _____ (= c divided by a) (Check: d + e should = 100%)

Calculations After Tallying

  f. Total females interacting _____

  g. Total males interacting _____

  h. Percentage of students interacting _____ (f + g divided by a)

  i. Total female tallies _____

  j. Total male tallies _____

  k. Total of all tallies (i + j) _____

  l. Percentage interacting students who are female _____ (i divided by k)

m. Percentage interacting students who are male _____ (j divided by k)

  n. Most tallies for any one male _____

  o. Percentage of class interactions directed to most frequently addressed male _____ (n divided by k)

  p. Most tallies for any one female _____

  q. Percentage of class interactions directed to most frequently addressed female _____ (p divided by k)
    Teacher conclusions:

 To access this exercise online, go to the Companion Website at **www.prenhall.com/kellough**.

■ Ensuring Equity

In addition to the advice given earlier about when using questioning (for example, practice gender equity, call on all students), there are many other ways of ensuring that students are treated fairly in the classroom, including the following:

- Encourage students to demonstrate an appreciation for one another by applauding all individual and group presentations.

- Have and maintain high expectations, although not necessarily identical expectations, for all students.

- Insist on politeness in the classroom. For example, a student can be shown appreciation—such as with a sincere "thank you" or "I appreciate your contribution" or with a genuine smile—for her or his contribution to the learning process.

- Insist that students be allowed to finish what they are saying, without being interrupted by others. Be certain that you model this behavior yourself.

- During whole-class instruction, insist that students raise their hands and be called on by you before they are allowed to speak.

- Keep a stopwatch handy to unobtrusively control the wait time given for each student. Although at first this idea may sound impractical, it works.

- Use a seating chart attached to a clipboard. Next to each student's name, make a tally for each interaction you have with that student. This is a good way to maintain records to reward students for their contributions to class discussion. Again, it is workable at any grade level. The seating chart can be laminated so it can be used day after day simply by erasing the marks of the previous day.

If you haven't already, do Exercise 7.8, through which you will examine a teacher's behavior with students according to gender or other personal characteristics.

■ LEARNING FROM ASSIGNMENTS AND HOMEWORK

An assignment is a statement of *what* the student is to accomplish, or do, and is tied to a specific instructional objective. Assignments, whether completed at home or at school, can ease student learning in many ways, but when poorly planned they can be discouraging to the student. *Homework* is any out-of-class task that a student is assigned as an extension of classroom learning. Like all else that you do as a professional teacher, it is your professional responsibility to think about and plan carefully any and all homework assignments that you give to students, including thinking about how you would feel were you given the assignment and how much out-of-class time you expect the assignment to take.

■ Purposes and Guidelines for Using Assignments and Homework

Purposes for giving homework assignments can be any of the following: To constructively extend the time that students are engaged in learning; to help students develop personal learning; to help students develop their research skills; to help students develop their study skills; to help students organize their learning; to individualize the learning; to involve parents and guardians in their children's' learning; to provide a mechanism by which students receive constructive feedback; to provide students with an opportunity to review and practice what has been learned; to reinforce classroom experiences; and to teach new content. As a general rule, homework assignments should stimulate thinking by arousing a student's curiosity, raising questions for further study, and encouraging and supporting the self-discipline required for independent study.

Plan early and thoughtfully the types of assignments you will give (e.g., daily and long-range; minor and major; in class or at home, or both; individual, paired, or group),[19] and prepare assignment specifications. Assignments must correlate with specific instructional objectives and should never be given as busywork or as punishment. For each assignment, let students know what the objectives are, for example, whether the assignment is to prepare the student for what is to come in class, to practice what has been learned in class, or to extend the learning of class activities.

Use caution in giving assignments that could be controversial or that could pose a hazard to the safety of students. In such cases (especially if you are new to the community), before giving the assignment it is probably a good idea to talk it over with your colleagues, the departmental chair, or an administrator. Also, for a particular assignment, you may need to have parental or guardian permission and even support for students to do it, or be prepared to give an alternate assignment for some students.

Provide differentiated, tiered, or optional assignments—assignment variations given to students or selected by them on the basis of their interests, cultural backgrounds, and learning capacities.[20] Students can select or be assigned different activities to accomplish the same objective, such as read and discuss, or they can participate with others in a more direct learning experience. After their study, as a portion of the assignment, students share what they have learned. This is an example of using multilevel teaching.

Teachers have found it beneficial to prepare individualized study guides with questions to be answered and activities to be done by the student while reading textbook chapters as homework. One advantage of a study guide is that it can make the reading more than a visual experience. A study guide can help to organize student learning by accenting instructional objectives, emphasizing important points to be learned, providing a guide for studying for tests, and encouraging the student to read the homework assignment.

Determine the resources that students will need to complete assignments, and check the availability of these resources. This is important; students can't be expected to use that which is unavailable to them. Many will not use that which is not readily available.

Avoid yelling out assignments as students are leaving your classroom. When giving assignments in class, you should write them on a special place on the writing board or give a copy to each student, or require that each student write the assignment into his or her assignment folder, taking extra care to be sure that assignment specifications are clear to students and that you allow time for students to ask questions about an assignment. In some schools, especially middle schools, it is policy that students use a daily assignment book to record homework and additional reminders. In some cases, the teachers initial the page and parents are to sign it daily or weekly. The belief is that this policy helps students to become organized and responsible for their own learning. Using a daily assignment book also reduces or eliminates the "I didn't know it was due today" excuse. Whatever procedure you use for giving and collecting assignments, it's important that it is consistent throughout the school year.

Students should be given sufficient time to complete their assignments. In other words, avoid announcing an assignment that is due the very next day. As a general rule, all assignments should be given earlier than the day before they are due. Try to avoid changing assignment specifications after they are given. Especially avoid changing them at the last minute. Changing specifications at the last minute can be very frustrating to conscientious students who have already completed the assignment, and it shows little respect for those students.

Allow time in class for students to begin work on homework assignments so you can give them individual attention (guided or coached practice). The opportunity to coach students is the reason for scheduling in-class time for working on assignments. As you have learned, many schools have extended the length of class periods. Extended periods allow more in-class time for teacher guidance on assignments. As said earlier, the benefits of this coached practice include (a) monitoring student work so that a student does not go too far in a wrong direction, (b) helping students reflect on their thinking, (c) assessing the progress of individual students, and (d) discovering or creating a "teachable moment." For example, while monitoring students doing their work, you might discover a commonly shared student misconception. Then, taking advantage of this teachable moment, you may stop and talk about it and attempt to clarify the misconception.

Timely, constructive, and corrective feedback from the teacher on the homework—and grading of homework—increases its positive contributions.[21] If the assignment is important for students to do, then you must give your full and immediate attention to the product of their efforts. Although with varying degrees of scrutiny, read everything that students write. Students are much more willing to do homework when they believe it is useful; when it is treated as an integral part of instruction; when it is read, commented on, and evaluated by the teacher; and when it counts as part of the grade. See the section "How to Avoid Having So Many Papers to Grade That Time for Effective Planning Is Restricted," which follows.

Provide feedback about each student's work, and be positive and constructive in your comments. Always think about the written comments that you make to be relatively certain they will convey your intended message to the student. When writing comments on student papers, consider using a color other than red, such as green or blue. Although to you this may sound unimportant, to many people, red carries a host of negative connotations (e.g., blood, hurt, danger, stop), and students often perceive its use as punitive.

■ GIVING STUDENTS A SECOND CHANCE

Although it is important to encourage high-quality initial efforts by students, sometimes, for a multitude of reasons, a student's first effort is inadequate or is lacking entirely. Perhaps the student is absent from school without legitimate excuse, or the student does poorly on an assignment or fails to turn in an assignment on time or at all. Although accepting late work from students is extra work for the teacher, and although allowing the resubmission of a marked or tentative-graded paper increases the amount of paperwork, we agree with teachers and administrators who believe that it is worthwhile to give students a second chance, who believe in giving students an opportunity for recovery and limited time to make corrections and resubmit an assignment for an improved score.[22] However, out of regard for students who do well from the start and meet due dates, it is probably ill-advised to allow a resubmitted paper or a late paper to receive an A grade.

Students sometimes have legitimate reasons for not completing an assignment by the due date. (Consider the classroom vignette, Late Homework Paper from an At-Risk Student.) It is our opinion that the teacher should listen and exercise professional judgment in each instance. As someone once said, there is nothing democratic about treating unequals as equals. The provision of recovery options seems a sensible and scholastic tactic.

CLASSROOM VIGNETTE
Late Homework Paper from an At-Risk Student

An eleventh-grade student turned in an English class assignment several days late and the paper was accepted by the teacher without penalty although the teacher's policy was that late papers would be severely penalized. During the week that the assignment was due, the student had suffered a miscarriage. In this instance her teacher accepted the paper late sans penalty because the student carried a great deal of psychological baggage and the teacher felt that turning in the paper at all was a positive act; if the paper had not been accepted, or had been accepted only with severe penalty to her grade, then, in the teacher's opinion, the student would have simply quit trying and probably dropped out of school altogether.

■ How to Avoid Having So Many Papers to Grade That Time for Effective Planning Is Restricted

A downfall for some beginning teachers or teachers of certain subjects (language arts, social studies) is that of being buried under mounds of student papers to be read and graded, leaving less and less time for effective planning. To keep this from happening to you, consider the following suggestions. Although we believe in providing second opportunity options and that the teacher should read almost everything that students write, papers can be read with varying degrees of intensity and scrutiny, depending on the purpose of the assignment. For assignments that are designed for learning, understanding, and practice, you can allow students to check them themselves using either self-checking or peer-checking. During the self- or peer-checking, you can walk around the room, monitor the activity, and record whether a student did the assignment or not, or, after the checking, you can collect the papers and do a quick-read and your recording. Besides reducing the amount of paperwork for you, student self- or peer-checking provides other advantages: (a) It allows students to see and understand their errors. (b) It encourages productive peer dialogue. and (c) It helps them develop self-assessment techniques and standards. If the purpose of the assignment is to assess mastery competence, then the papers should be read, marked, and graded only by you.

Warning about using peer-checking Peer-checking can, however, be a problem. During peer-checking of student work, students may spend more time watching the person checking their paper than accurately checking the one given to them. In addition, this strategy does not necessarily allow the student to see or understand his or her mistakes.

The issue of privacy is perhaps an even greater concern. When Student A becomes knowledgeable of the academic success or failure of Student B, Student A, the "checker," could cause emotional or social embarrassment to Student B. Peer-checking of papers perhaps should be done only for editing classmates' drafts of stories or research projects or for making suggestions about content and grammar, but not for assigning a grade or marking answers right or wrong. To protect students' privacy rights, like the public posting of grades, the use of peer-grading for papers also should be avoided. Students may feel harassed and embarrassed, which does not provide a positive and safe learning environment.

■ MEMORIZING AND REVIEWING: UNAVOIDABLE LEARNING STRATEGIES

Sometimes students must memorize things. There is even a time for memorization without much understanding. For example, to learn a language you must first memorize the alphabet. To learn to play the trumpet you must memorize the fingering. To learn mathematics you must first learn the numbering system. In the study of chemistry, you should know the symbols for the common elements. The alphabet, the fingering on the trumpet, numbers, and symbols are all kinds of tools. In mathematics certain assumptions must be memorized before other concepts can be developed. In fact, in all the disciplines, there are basic points that must be memorized before a learner can understand the major concepts.

When teaching through memorizing, the following guidelines will be helpful.

- *Avoid overuse of memorizing.* Be sure there is a purpose for the memorizing and that the students see what that purpose is. Have students memorize only those things that are absolutely essential to memorize.

- *If possible, have students study for meaning before memorizing.* Some things must be memorized, meaningful or not, such as German word order or Greek letters, whose shapes seem arbitrary. These are tools of the trade, and they must be mastered to move on. But it is much easier to memorize those things that have meaning if you understand the meaning. For instance, for someone who does not know Latin it is probably much easier to remember, "There is no accounting for taste" than to remember "*De gustibus non est disputandum.*"

- *Use the recall method, where students study and then try to recall without prompting.*

■ *Encourage the use of mnemonics to aid students in their memorization.* Mnemonics are devices students invent or ones supplied by you. Examples of common mnemonic devices were shown in the section, Integrating Strategies for Integrated Learning, in Module 6.

In any class, frequent reviews are necessary, because memory is aided by use and because understanding is improved by review. In the sciences, for instance, many concepts cannot be fully understood in isolation. Neither can all the scientific terms be fully appreciated until they are seen in the context of later topics. Frequently, notions that were understood only dimly the first time they were studied become much clearer when revisited later while studying other topics.

In conducting reviews, the teacher must be aware both of the character of the students and of the discipline being pursued. In mathematics and in foreign languages, where so much depends upon every link in the great chain, frequent reviews are often necessary. It is profitable to recall almost daily some principles that were previously studied. In disciplines where the parts have less direct connection, such as geography, the reviews may be given at larger intervals, though daily review helps to keep students on their toes.

Here again the techniques of questioning come into play. As far as possible, the review should connect facts to concepts to principles to life's applications, whether in that order or in reverse order or some other combination. Experience in thinking is often more profitable than the knowledge itself.

It is always advantageous to have a general review at the close of any particular study, such as at the end of a unit or of a semester of study. This again enables you to detect any false notions that the students entertained during the study. You now can present the subject as a whole and view one part in the light of another. In human physiology, for instance, much more understanding is gained about the process of growth after a person has studied absorption and secretion. Similarly, the economy of respiration is much clearer when viewed in connection with the circulation of the blood.

A general review can be an enlightening process and is always profitable, with perhaps one exception: When the review is instituted solely as preparation for a written examination. Then, review may degenerate merely into a device for passing the exam. The purpose of reviewing should be to master the subject for its own sake—to unify concepts—but not to be able to talk about it on one special occasion.

In summary, a review is an opportunity for the students to look at a topic again. It is a re-view, a repeat look. It is not the same as drill or practice, though sometimes a teacher can use the same methodology. Review is useful every day as a means for tying the day's lesson to preceding lessons. At this time you can summarize points that should have been made and establish relationships with past and future lessons. End-of-unit and end-of-term reviews are useful, but it is important that reviewing be more frequent than only at the end of a unit or term because frequent reviews are more effective. Besides, end-of-unit and end-of-term reviews tend to become preparations for examinations.

Almost any technique can be used in review sessions, although the common oral quiz in which the teacher goes around the room asking one fact question after another can become pretty boring. If you do use this type of review, use some scheme to mix up the questions to keep students alert. Tactics that you might want to consider are student summaries, quiz games (classroom Jeopardy seems well liked by students and teachers), dramatizations, student-provided test questions, discussion, broad questioning, and application problems. Techniques that require students to use what they should have learned are good because those techniques may not only serve as review but also provide motivation by opening new vistas for students.

Now do Exercise 7.9.

EXERCISE **7.9**

■ Developing a Lesson Using Inquiry Level II, Thinking Skill Development, a Demonstration, or an Interactive Lecture— Micro Peer-Teaching III

Instructions: The purpose of this exercise is to provide the opportunity for you to create a brief lesson (about 20 minutes of instructional time but to be specified by your instructor) designed for a specific grade level and subject and to try it out on your peers for their feedback in an informal (i.e., nongraded) micro peer-teaching demonstration.

Divide your class into four groups. The task of each group's members is to prepare lessons (individually) that fall into one of the four categories: Level II inquiry; thinking level; demonstration; interactive lecture. Schedule class presentations so that each class member has the opportunity to present her or his lesson and to obtain feedback from class members about it. For feedback, class members who are the "teacher's" audience can complete the as-

(continued)

sessment rubric shown after this exercise and give their completed form to the teacher for use in self-assessment. Before your class starts this exercise, you may want to review the scoring rubric and make modifications to it that the class agrees on.

To structure your lesson plan, use one of the sample lesson plan formats presented in Module 4; however, each lesson should be centered around one major theme or concept and be planned for about 20 minutes of instructional time.

Group 1: Develop a Level II inquiry lesson.

Group 2: Develop a lesson designed to raise the level of student thinking.

Group 3: Develop a lesson that involves a demonstration.

Group 4: Develop a lesson that is an interactive lecture.

PEER- AND SELF-ASSESSMENT RUBRIC FOR USE WITH EXERCISE 7.9

For: _____   Group: _____

	1	0.5	0
1. Lesson beginning	effective	less effective	not effective
Comment:			
2. Sequencing	effective	less effective	rambling
Comment:			
3. Pacing of lesson	effective	less effective	too slow/too fast
Comment:			
4. Audience involvement	effective	less effective	none
Comment:			
5. Motivators (e.g., analogies, verbal cues, humor, visual cues, sensory cues)			
	effective	less effective	not apparent
Comment:			
6. Content of lesson	well chosen	interesting	boring or inappropriate
Comment:			
7. Voice of teacher	stimulating	minor problem	major problems
Comment:			
8. Vocabulary used	well chosen	appropriate	inappropriate
Comment:			
9. Eye contact	excellent	average	problems
Comment:			
10. Closure	effective	less effective	unclear/none
Comment:			
Other comments:			

 To access this exercise online, go to the Companion Website at **www.prenhall.com/kellough.**

■ SUMMARY

In this module, you learned guidelines for the use of a number of traditional teaching methods that generally are centered on the teacher and involve a lot of teacher talk. Lectures, questioning, discussions, recitations, and so on, have all stood the test of time, but unless modified to be more student-centered they are less useful today than in the past, because of (a) the diversity of students in our schools and classrooms, (b) what has been learned about how young people learn and construct their knowledge, and (c) rapid technological developments for the enhancement of learning and instruction. The latter is the topic of Module 8.

You are advised to learn well how to use the strategies discussed in this module, however, and to continue to expand your repertoire of methods by developing your understanding and skills in the use of strategies of both modes of acquiring knowledge and skills: The access or student-centered mode and the delivery or teacher-centered mode. Remember, you should strive to be eclectic in your teaching style—use the best of each mode to make the learning personal, interesting, meaningful, and lasting for your students.

To help make the learning personal, interesting, meaningful, and lasting, there are many instructional aids and materials from which you may choose. That is the topic of the next and final module of Part 3.

■ MODULE 7 POSTTEST

Multiple Choice

1. A very general guideline for middle school and secondary school teaching is that
   a. lectures should not be used.
   b. an occasional full-period lecture is okay.
   c. lectures should be no longer than 30 minutes.
   d. lectures should be limited to 10 to 15 minutes.

2. Which type of question would be best as an introduction for a new topic?
   a. a low-order question
   b. a closed question
   c. a question that causes divergent thinking
   d. a question that causes convergent thinking

3. Which one of the following is a false statement?
   a. Key questions to be used should be written in the lesson plan.
   b. The teacher should ensure that all students are given an opportunity to respond to questions.
   c. Questions used by the teacher should be matched with the levels of thinking expected of the students.
   d. After asking a question, you should pause for no longer than 2 seconds before calling upon a student.

4. Questions that cause students to apply a principle to a new situation are
   a. requiring convergent thinking only.
   b. at the lowest level of mental operation.
   c. at the highest level of mental operation.
   d. at the intermediate level of mental operation.

5. Which set of verbs is most likely to require students to use only their short-term memory?
   a. judge, predict
   b. build, evaluate
   c. define, describe
   d. classify, compare

6. Which pair of verbs is asking students to process information?
   a. identify, list
   b. apply, complete
   c. analyze, compare
   d. predict, hypothesize

(continued)

7. Which one of the following is not a teaching strategy but rather an intelligent behavior that can be facilitated by the teacher?
   a. inquiry
   b. recitation
   c. simulation
   d. problem solving

8. During direct instruction, the teacher is advised to establish eye contact with each student about once
   a. every 60 seconds.
   b. every 10 minutes.
   c. a week.
   d. a day.

9. With all other factors equal, which one of the following learning activities is most strongly recommended?
   a. teacher demonstration
   b. teacher-directed whole-class discussion
   c. cooperative learning investigative activity
   d. period-long, noninteractive lecture by the teacher

10. Which one of the following is not a characteristic of intelligent behavior?
    a. dogmatism
    b. persistence
    c. sense of humor
    d. listening with understanding and empathy

Short Explanation

1. Identify and describe five cautions when using teacher talk.
2. Identify ways you can recapture student attention during your use of direct instruction.
3. Explain precautions a teacher needs to consider when going from a student-centered activity to a teacher-centered activity during the same class period.
4. Is hands-on learning necessarily minds-on learning as well? Explain.
5. Identify some of the specific strategies you can use to help students develop their critical-thinking and problem-solving skills in your subject field.
6. Explain the meaning of "establishing eye contact" as it is discussed in this module.
7. Distinguish between role-play and simulation as instructional activities.
8. Give an example of a mnemonic and explain why your example is a mnemonic.
9. Give an example of a demonstration that you would be likely to use for a specific grade level/course (identify) in your subject field. Explain why you would use the demonstration for teaching this content rather than some other strategy.
10. Explain the meaning of metacognition. How would you use metacognition in your teaching?

Essay

1. Which category of instructional strategies—student-centered or teacher-centered—do you believe contributes more to a student's developing self-esteem? Explain why.
2. Describe when, if ever, students should be expected to memorize material in your subject field.
3. Describe specific strategies that you would use to exercise equality in your classroom.
4. From your current observations and fieldwork related to this teacher preparation program, clearly identify one specific example of educational practice that seems contradictory to exemplary practice or theory presented in this module. Present your explanation for the discrepancy.
5. Describe any prior concepts you held that changed as a result of your experiences with this module. Describe the changes.

 To access this posttest and the answers online, go to the Companion Website at **www.prenhall.com/kellough.**

■ SUGGESTED READINGS

Benjamin, B., & Irwin-DeVitis, L. (1998). Censoring girls' choices: Continued gender bias in English language arts classrooms. *English Journal, 87*(2), 64–71.

Cohen, E. G. (1998). Making cooperative learning equitable. *Educational Leadership, 56*(1), 18–21.

Martinello, M. L. (1998). Learning to question for inquiry. *Educational Forum, 62*(2), 164–171.

McClure, L. J. (1999). Wimpy boys and macho girls: Gender equity at the crossroads. *English Journal, 88*(3), 78–82.

Mewborn, D. S. (1999). Creating a gender equitable school environment. *International Journal of Leadership in Education, 2*(2), 103–115.

Paulu, N., & Darby, L. B. (Eds.). (1998). *Helping your students with homework: A guide for teachers.* Washington, DC: U.S. Office of Educational Research and Improvement, U.S. Government Printing Office.

Schank, R. C. (2000). A vision of education for the 21st century. *T.H.E Journal, 27*(6), 42–45.

Sprenger, M. (1999). *Learning & memory: The brain in action.* Alexandria, VA: Association for Supervision and Curriculum Development.

Traver, R. (1998). What is a good guiding question? *Educational Leadership, 55*(6), 70–73.

Vavilis, B., & Vavilis, S. L. (2004). Why are we learning this? What is this stuff good for anyway? The importance of conversation in the classroom, *Phi Delta Kappan, 86*(4), 282–287.

Weinman, J., & Haag, P. (1999). Gender equity in cyberspace. *Educational Leadership, 56*(5), 44–49.

■ ENDNOTES

[1] H. Kohl, Hope and the imagination, *Reading Today's Youth* 4(4), pp. 39–41 (2000).

[2] D. P. Ausubel, *The Psychology of Meaningful Learning* (New York: Addison Wesley Longman, 2000), pp. 252–253.

[3] T. L. Good and J. E. Brophy, *Looking in Classrooms* (8th ed.) (New York: Addison Wesley Longman, 2000), pp. 252–253.

[4] A. L. Costa, *The School as a Home for the Mind* (Palatine, IL: Skylight Publishing, 1991), p. 63.

[5] Studies in wait time began with the classic study of M. B. Rowe, Wait Time and Reward as Instructional Variables, Their Influence on Language, Logic and Fate Control: Part I. Wait Time, *Journal of Research in Science Teaching* 11(2), 81–94 (1974).

[6] See, for example, V. C. Polite and A. H. Adams, *Improving Critical Thinking Through Socratic Seminars,* Spotlight on Student Success, no. 110 (Philadelphia, PA: Mid-Atlantic Laboratory for Student Success, 1996); S. Schoeman, Using the Socratic Method in Secondary Teaching, *NASSP Bulletin* 81(587), 19–21 (March 1997); and M. L. Tanner and L. Casados, Promoting and Studying Discussions in Math Classes, *Journal of Adolescent & Adult Literacy* 41(5), 342–350 (February 1998).

[7] B. R. Brogan and W. A. Brogan, The Socratic Questioner: Teaching and Learning in the Dialogical Classroom, *Educational Forum* 59(3), 288–296 (Spring 1995).

[8] This three-tiered model of thinking has been described variously by others. For example, in E. Eisner's *The Educational Imagination* (Upper Saddle River, NJ: Prentice Hall, 1979), the levels are referred to as *descriptive, interpretive,* and *evaluative.* For a comparison of thinking models, see A. L. Costa, *The School as Home for the Mind,* p. 44.

[9] See, for example, J. Piaget, *The Development of Thought: Elaboration of Cognitive Structures* (New York: Viking, 1977).

[10] R. N. Caine and G. Caine, *Education on the Edge of Possibility* (Alexandria, VA: Association for Supervision and Curriculum Development, 1997), p. 107.

[11] See, for example, B. Newton, Theoretical Basis for Higher Cognitive Questioning—An Avenue to Critical Thinking, *Education* 98(3), 286–290 (March–April 1978); and D. Redfield and E. Rousseau, A Meta-Analysis of Experimental Research on Teacher Questioning Behavior, *Review of Educational Research* 51(2), 237–245 (Summer 1981).

[12] M. E. McIntosh and R. J. Draper, Using the Question-Answer Relationship Strategy to Improve Students' Reading of Mathematics Texts, *Clearing House* 69(3), 154–162 (January/February 1996).

[13] J. G. Brooks and M. G. Brooks, *In Search of Understanding: The Case for Constructivist Classrooms* (Alexandria, VA: Association for Supervision and Curriculum Development, 1993), p. 105.

[14] See M. B. Rowe, Wait-Time and Rewards as Instructional Variables, Their Influence on Language, Logic, and Fate Control: Part One—Wait-Time, *Journal of Research in Science Teaching* 11(2), 81–94 (June 1974); M. B. Rowe, Wait-Time: Slowing Down May Be a Way of Speeding Up, *American Educator* 11(1), 38–47 (Spring 1987); and J. Swift, C. Gooding, and P. Swift, Questions and Wait Time, in J. Dillon (Ed.), *Questioning and Discussion: A Multidisciplinary Study* (Norwood, NJ: Ablex, 1988), pp. 192–212.

[15] J. S. Choate and T. A. Rakes, *Inclusive Instruction for Struggling Readers,* Fastback 434 (Bloomington, IN: Phi Delta Kappa Educational Foundation, 1998), p. 26.

[16] United States Department of Education, *Tried and True: Tested Ideas for Teaching and Learning From the Regional Educational Laboratories* (Washington, DC: Office of Educational Research and Improvement, U.S. Department of Education, 1997), p. 53.

[17] See, for example, M. A. Raywid, Small Schools: A Reform That Works, *Educational Leadership* 55(4), 34–39 (December/January 1997–1998); and M. A. Raywid, *Current Literature on Small Schools,* ED425049 (Charleston, WV: ERIC Clearinghouse on Rural Education and Small Schools, 1999).

[18] See, for example, S. Zaher, Gender and Curriculum in the School Room, *Education Canada* 36(1), 26–29 (Spring 1996); and S. M. Bailey, Shortchanging Girls and Boys, *Educational Leadership* 53(8), 75–79 (May 1996). For information on how to identify equity problems and develop programs to help schools achieve academic excellence for all students, contact EQUITY 2000, 1233 20th St. NW, Washington, DC 20056-2304, phone: (202) 822-5930.

[19] See, for example, C. Kaplan, Homework Partners, *Mathematics Teaching in the Middle School* 2(3), 168–169 (January 1997).

[20] See, for example, M. H. Sullivan and P. V. Sequeira, The Impact of Purposeful Homework on Learning, *Clearing House* 69(6), 346–348 (July/August 1996).

[21] H. J. Walberg, Productive Teaching and Instruction: Assessing the Knowledge Base, *Phi Delta Kappan* 71(6), 472 (February 1990).

[22] To learn how one teacher made "rigid due dates a thing of the past," see the article by Kenan High School (Warsaw, NC) teacher S. H. Benson, Make Mine an A, *Educational Leadership* 57(5), 30–32 (February 2000).

Media, Aids, and Resources

Module 8 Overview

Cognitive tools are important for helping students construct their understandings. You will be pleased to know that there is a large variety of useful and effective educational media, aids, and resources from which to draw as you plan your instructional experiences. However, you could also become overwhelmed by the sheer quantity of different materials available for classroom use: Textbooks, pamphlets, anthologies, encyclopedias, tests, supplementary texts, paperbacks, programmed instructional systems, dictionaries, reference books, classroom periodicals, newspapers, films, records and cassettes, computer software, transparencies, realia, games, filmstrips, audio- and videotapes, slides, globes, manipulatives, CD-ROMs, DVDs, and graphics. You could spend a lot of time reviewing, sorting, selecting, and practicing with these materials and tools. Although nobody can make the job easier for you, information in this module may expedite the process.

Because we have already discussed textbooks (in Module 4), we begin this module with a discussion of other printed resources, visual displays, and the Internet. We end the module with a presentation about using electronic resources.

This module also provides suggestions about where to procure materials for instruction—after all, if you do not have them, you cannot use them. As you peruse this module we remind you again about starting a professional resources file (see Figure 1.4 in Module 1).

Specific Objectives

At the completion of this module, you should be able to:

- Demonstrate an awareness of the variety of materials and resources for use in your teaching.
- Develop a philosophy for integrating technology in your teaching.
- Demonstrate knowledge of copyright laws for using printed and media materials for teaching.
- Demonstrate an understanding about using community resources, speakers, and field trips.
- Demonstrate an awareness of electronic media available for teaching in your subject field, how they can be used, and how and where they can be obtained.
- Demonstrate competency in using standard classroom tools for teaching.

> *"The most extraordinary thing about a really good teacher is that he or she transcends accepted educational methods. Such methods are designed to help average teachers approximate the performance of good teachers."*[1]
>
> —MARGARET MEAD

Introduction

Long ago, when humankind was young and writing had not yet been invented, men and women taught their children by means of very simple tools. Telling children what they should know was an important teaching technique, but there were other teaching and learning methods, too. Children learned to hunt by practicing with spears, by throwing sticks, and by simulating animal hunts. Parents taught geography by maps drawn in the sand and religion by pictures drawn on the walls of caves. Dance and drama portrayed the history, customs, and lore of a group. From the very earliest times, teachers have depended on diverse teaching tools to make their teaching interesting and effective.

Today, teachers still depend on a variety of teaching tools. In some respects, modern teaching tools are much more sophisticated than those of older times. Yet we use our new tools for the same purposes and in much the same ways that our ancestors used theirs: To make things clear, to make instruction real, to spice up the learning process, and to make it possible for students to teach themselves. Teaching would be impossible without some instructional aids. Here we will review a variety of these available tools.

■ PRINTED MATERIALS AND VISUAL DISPLAYS

Historically, of all the materials available for instruction, the printed textbook has had, and still has, the most influence on teaching and learning (discussed in Module 4). Besides the student textbook and perhaps an accompanying workbook, there is a vast array of other printed materials available for use in teaching, many of which are available for free. (See the section, Sources of Free and Inexpensive Printed Materials, that follows.) Printed materials include books, workbooks, pamphlets, magazines, brochures, newspapers, professional journals, periodicals, and duplicated materials including those materials copied from Internet sources.

As mentioned in Module 4, when selecting textbooks, you need to consider the appropriateness of the material in both content and reading level. Other printed materials you may decide to use in your lessons include: (a) current articles from newspapers, magazines, and periodicals related to the content that your students will be studying or to the skills they will be learning; (b) workbooks available from tradebook publishers that emphasize thinking and problem solving rather than rote memorization (With an assortment of workbooks you can have students working on similar but different assignments depending upon their interests and abilities—an example of multilevel teaching.); (c) various pamphlets, brochures, and other duplicated materials that students can read for specific information

and viewpoints about particular topics; and (d) inexpensive paperbacks that would provide multiple book readings for your students. To use these supplemental materials, you need to consult copyright laws.

■ Sources of Free and Inexpensive Printed Materials

For free and inexpensive printed materials, look for sources in your college or university, the public library, or the resource center at a local school district such as those listed in Figure 4.2. Additionally, teachers obtain free and inexpensive teaching materials through connections on the Internet. When considering using materials that you have obtained free or inexpensively, you will want to ensure that the materials are appropriate for use with the age group with which you work and that they are free of bias or an unwanted message. The **National Education Association** (NEA) has published guidelines for teachers to consider before purchasing or using commercial materials; for a free copy contact NEA Communications, 1201 16th Street, NW, Washington, DC 20036; phone (202) 822-7200.

■ The Internet

Originating from a Department of Defense project (called ARPAnet, named after the federal government's Advanced Research Projects Agency) at the University of California, Los Angeles, computer science department in 1969, designed to establish a computer network of military researchers, the federally funded Internet has become an enormous, steadily expanding, worldwide system of connected computer networks. The Internet (also known as the "Information Superhighway," "cyberspace," or just simply the "net") provides literally millions of resources to explore, with thousands more added nearly every day. In 1998, when the sixth edition of this book was published, it was difficult to find published information about the Internet. Today you can surf the Internet and find many sources about how to use it, or walk into most any bookstore and find hundreds of recent titles, most of which give their authors' favorite Web sites. However, new technologies are steadily emerging and the Internet changes every day; some sites and resources disappear or are not kept current, others change their location and undergo reconstruction, and still other new ones appear. Therefore, it would be superfluous for us in this book, which will be around for several years, to get *too* enthused about sites that we personally have viewed and can recommend as teacher resources. Nevertheless, Figures 6.5 and 8.1 list available Internet resources that we found and liked. Other sites have been mentioned throughout this book. Perhaps you have found others that you can share with your classmates (and with us). To that end, now do Exercise 8.1.

- **California Instructional Technology Clearinghouse** <http://clearinghouse.k12.ca.us>.
- **Education World** <http://www.education-world.com/>.
- **Electronic Reference Formats** <http://www.apastyle.org/elecref.html>.
- **Epicenter** <http://www.epicent.com>.
- **ERIC Documents Online** <http://ericir.syr.edu>.
- **Hewlett Packard E-Mail Mentor Program** <http://www.telementor.org>.
- **Interactive Frog Dissection** <http://teach.virginia.edu/go/frog>.
- **Learn the 'Net** <http://www.learnthenet.com>.
- **Map Resources** <http://www.mapresources.com/>.
- **Mathematics Archives** *(www server)* <http://archives.math.utk.edu/>.
- **MLA-Style Citations of Electronic Sources** <http://www.cas.usf.edu/english/walker/mla.html>.
- **National Archives and Records Administration** <http://www.nara.gov>.
- **National Education Association (NEA)** <http://www.nea.org/resources/refs.html>.
- **National Endowment** <http://www.nea.org/>.
- **National Geographic Map Machine** <http://www.nationalgeographic.com>.
- **Resources for Educational Technologists: Center for Educational Technology** <http://www.cet.middlebury.edu/>.
- **School Internet Projects** <http://www.schoolworld.asn.au/projects.html>.
- **School Match** <http://schoolmatch.com>.
- **School Page** <http://www.eyesoftime.com/teacher/index.html>.
- **Science Stuff** <http://www.sciencestuff.com>.
- **Telementoring Young Women in Science, Engineering, and Computing** <http://www.edc.org/CCT/telementoring>.
- **Teacher's Network** <http://www.teachnet.org>. A teacher's exchange.
- **The 21st Century Teacher's Network** <http://www.21ct.org>.
- **United States Copyright Office** <http://lcweb.loc.gov/copyright>.
- **WWW4 Teachers** <http://www.4teachers.org/>.

FIGURE 8.1 ● Internet Sites: Materials and Technology Use

EXERCISE **8.1**

■ Internet Sites of Use to Teachers

Instructions: The purpose of this exercise is to search the Internet for sites that you find interesting and useful, or useless, for teaching and to share those sites with your classmates (and, if you want, with the authors of this book). Make copies of this page for each site visited; then share your results with your classmates.

Web site I investigated: http:// _____

I consider the site   *highly useful   moderately useful   of no use*

Specifically for teachers of (grade level and/or subject field):

Sponsor of site:

Features of interest and usefulness to teachers:

 To access this exercise online, go to the Companion Website at **www.prenhall.com/kellough.**

■ Cautions and Guidelines for Using the Internet

If you have not yet learned to use the Internet, we shall leave the mechanics of that to the many resources available to you, including the experts that can be found among your peers, on your college or university staff, and among members of any public school faculty. The re-

maining pages of this section address the "how" of using the Internet from an academic perspective. Let's begin with the fictitious although feasible Teaching Scenario: Natural Disasters illustrated in the accompanying box.

In the scenario, there is both a desirable aspect and a not-so-desirable aspect. On the positive side, the students used a good technological tool (the Internet) to research a variety of sources, including many primary

TEACHING SCENARIO
Natural Disasters

Let us suppose that the students from your "house" have been working nearly all year on an interdisciplinary thematic unit entitled, "surviving natural disasters." As culmination to their study they "published" a document entitled, *Natural Disaster Preparation and Survival Guide for (name of their community)* and proudly distributed the guide to their parents and members of the community.

Long before preparing the guide, however, the students had to do research. To learn about the history of various kinds of natural disasters that had occurred or might occur locally and about the sorts of preparations a community should take for each kind of disaster, students searched sources on the Internet, such as federal documents, scientific articles, and articles from newspapers from around the world where natural disasters had occurred. They also searched in the local library and the local newspaper's archives to learn of floods, tornadoes, and fires that had occurred during the past 200 years. Much to their surprise, they also learned that their com-

munity is located very near the New Madrid Fault, which did, in fact, experience a serious earthquake in 1811, although none since. As a result of that earthquake, two nearby towns completely disappeared, while the Mississippi River flowed in reverse, changing its course and causing the formation of a new lake in Tennessee.

From published and copyrighted sources, including Web sites, the students found many useful photographs, graphics, and articles, and they included those in whole or in part in their survival guide. They did so without obtaining permission from the original copyright holders or even citing those sources.

You, the other members of your teaching team, and other people were so impressed with the students' work that students were encouraged to offer the document for publication on the school's Web site. In addition, the document was received with so much acclaim that the students decided to sell it in local stores. This would help defray the original cost of duplication and enable them to continue to supply guides.

ones. But when they published their document on the Internet and when they made copies of their guide to be sold, they did so without permission from original copyright holders, and were thus infringing copyright law. Although it would take an attorney to say for sure, with this scenario it is probable that the students, teacher, school, and the school district would be liable. As is true for other documents (such as published photos, graphics, and text), unless there is an explicit statement that materials taken from the Internet are public domain, it is best to assume that they are copyrighted and should not be republished without permission from the original source.

There is a proliferation of information today, from both printed materials and from information on the Internet. You may wonder, except for the obvious reliable sites such as the *New York Times* and the Library of Congress, how can a person determine the validity and currency of a particular piece of information? When searching for useful and reliable information on a particular topic, how can one be protected from wasting valuable time sifting through all the information? People need to know that just because information is found on a printed page or is published on the Internet doesn't necessarily mean that the information is accurate or current. Using a checklist, such as found on the Internet at http://www.infopeople.org/bkmk/select.html, and provided with examples of materials that do and do not meet the criteria of the checklist, students can develop skill in assessing materials and information found on the Internet.

Teaching all students how to access and assess Web sites adds to their repertoire of skills for lifelong learn-

ing. Consider allowing each student or teams of students to become experts on specific sites during particular units of study. It might be useful to start a chronicle of student-recorded log entries about particular Web sites to provide comprehensive long-term data about those sites.

When students use information from the Internet, require that they print copies of sources of citations and materials so you can check for accuracy. These copies may be maintained in their portfolios.

Student work published on the Internet should be considered intellectual material and, as such, is protected from plagiarism by others. Most school districts now post a copyright notice on their home page. Someone at the school usually is assigned to supervise the school Web site to see that district and school policy and legal requirements are observed.

■ Professional Journals and Periodicals

Figure 8.2 lists examples of the many professional periodicals and journals that can provide useful teaching ideas and Web site information, as well as carry information about instructional materials and how to get them. Some of these may be in your university or college library and accessible through Internet sources. Check around for these and other titles of interest to you.

■ The ERIC Information Network

The Educational Resources Information Center (ERIC) system, established by the United States Office of Education, is a widely used network providing access to infor-

The American Biology Teacher	*The Middle School Journal*
American Educational Research Quarterly	*Modern Language Journal*
The American Music Teacher	*Music Educator's Journal*
American Teacher	*NEA Today*
The Art Teacher	*The Negro Educational Review*
The Computing Teacher	*The New Advocate*
The Earth Scientist	*OAH Magazine of History*
Educational Leadership	*Phi Delta Kappan*
English Journal	*Physical Education*
English Language Teaching Journal	*The Physics Teacher*
Hispania	*The Reading Teacher*
The History Teacher	*Reading Today*
Journal of Business Education	*School Arts*
Journal of Chemical Education	*School Library Journal*
Journal of Economic Education	*The School Musician*
Journal of Geography	*School Science and Mathematics*
Journal of Home Economics	*School Shop*
Journal of Learning Disabilities	*Science*
Journal of the National Association of Bilingual	*Science Activities*
Educators	*Science Scope*
Journal of Physical Education and Recreation	*Social Education*
Journal of Reading	*The Science Teacher*
Journal of Teaching in Physical Education	*The Social Studies*
Language Arts	*Social Studies Review*
Language Learning	*Teacher Magazine*
Learning	*TESOL Quarterly*
The Mathematics Teacher	*Theory and Research in Social Education*
Mathematics Teaching in the Middle School	*Voices From the Middle*

FIGURE 8.2 ● Selected Professional Journals and Periodicals of Interest to Middle School and Secondary School Teachers

mation and research in education. Selected clearinghouses and their addresses are shown in Figure 8.3.

■ Copying Printed Materials

Remember that, although on many Web pages there is no notice, the material is still copyrighted. Original material is protected by copyright law; that is just as true for the intellectual property created by a minor as it is for that of an adult.

Although space here prohibits full inclusion of United States legal guidelines, your local school district should be able to provide a copy of current district policies for compliance with copyright laws. District policies should include guidelines for teachers and students in publishing materials on the Internet. If no district guidelines are available, adhere to the guidelines shown in Figure 8.4 when using printed materials.[2]

When preparing to make a copy you must find out whether the law under the category of "permitted use" permits the copying. If not allowed under "permitted use," then you must get written permission to reproduce the material from the holder of the copyright. If the address of the source is not given on the material, addresses

may be obtained from various references, such as *Literary Market Place*, *Audio-Visual Market Place*, and *Ulrich's International Periodical's Directory*.

■ The Classroom Writing Board

As is true for an auto mechanic, a brain surgeon, or any other professional, a teacher needs to know when and how to use the tools of the trade. One of the tools available to almost every classroom teacher is the writing board. In this section you will find guidelines for using this important tool.

Writing boards used to be, and in some schools still are, slate blackboards (slate is a type of metamorphic rock). In today's classroom, however, the writing board is more likely to be either a board made of painted plywood (chalkboard), which, like the blackboard, is also quickly becoming obsolete, to some extent because of the need to be concerned about the dust created from using chalk;[3] or a white or colored (light green and light blue are common) multipurpose dry-erase board on which you write with special marking pens and erase with any soft cloth. In addition to providing a surface upon which you can write and draw, the multipurpose

- **Assessment and Evaluation.** The Catholic University of America, 210 O'Boyle Hall, Washington, DC 20064-4035. <http://ericae2.educ.cua.edu>.
- **Disabilities and Gifted Children.** Council for Exceptional Children (CEC), 1920 Association Drive, Reston, VA 22191-1589. <http://www.ericec.org>.
- **ERIC:** *re-engineering of ERIC system:*
  Links to:
      American Indian and Alaska Native Education
      Mexican American Education
      Migrant Education
      Outdoor Education
      Rural Education
      Small Schools
  see this webpage <http://www.ael.org/page.htm?&index=752&pd=1&pv=x>.
- **Information and Technology.** Center for Science and Technology, Syracuse University, Syracuse, NY 13244-4100. <http://eric.r.syr.edu/ithame>.
- **Languages and Linguistics.** Center for Applied Linguistics, 1118 22nd Street, NW, Washington, DC 20037-1214. <http://www.cal.org/ericcll>.
  Practical Assessment, Research and Evaluation. (formerly ericae) <http://pareonline.net/>.
- **Social Studies/Social Science Education.** Indiana University, Social Studies Development Center, 2805 East 10th Street, Bloomington, IN 47 408-2698. <http://www.indiana.edu/~ssac/eric_chess.html>.

FIGURE 8.3 ● Selected ERIC Addresses

Permitted uses—you may make:
1. Single copies of a(n):
   - chapter of a book.
   - article from a periodical, magazine, or newspaper.
   - short story, short essay, or short poem whether or not from a collected work.
   - chart, graph, diagram, drawing, or cartoon.
   - illustration from a book, magazine, or newspaper.
2. Multiple copies for classroom use (not to exceed one copy per student in a course) of a(n):
   - complete poem if less than 250 words.
   - excerpt from a longer poem, but not to exceed 250 words.
   - complete article, story, or essay of less than 2,500 words.
   - excerpt from a larger printed work not to exceed 10 percent of the whole or 1,000 words.
   - chart, graph, diagram, cartoon, or picture per book or magazine issue.

Prohibited uses—you may *not*:
1. Copy more than one work or two excerpts from a single author during one class term (semester or year).
2. Copy more than three works from a collective work or periodical volume during one class term.
3. Reproduce more than nine sets of multiple copies for distribution to students in one class term.
4. Copy to create or replace or substitute for anthologies or collective works.
5. Copy "consumable" works (e.g., workbooks, standardized tests, or answer sheets).
6. Copy the same work year after year.

FIGURE 8.4 ● Guidelines for Copying Printed Materials that Are Copyrighted
SOURCE: Section 107 of the 1976 Federal Omnibus Copyright Revision Act.

---

board can be used as a projection screen and as a surface to which figures cut from colored transparency film will stick. It may also have a magnetic backing.

Extending the purposes of the multipurpose board correlated with modern technology is an *electronic board* that can transfer information that is written on it to a connected computer monitor, which in turn can save the material as a computer file. The electronic whiteboard uses dry-erase markers and special erasers that have optically encoded sleeves that enable the device to track their position on the board. The data are then converted into a display for the computer monitor, which may then be printed, cut and pasted into other applications, sent as an e-mail or fax message, or networked to other sites.[4]

Use colored chalk or marking pens to highlight your board talk. This is especially helpful for students with learning difficulties. Beginning at the top left of the board, print or write neatly and clearly, with the writing intentionally positioned to indicate content relationships (e.g., causal, oppositional, numerical, comparative, categorical, and so on). Use the writing board to acknowledge acceptance and to record student contributions.

Print instructions for an activity on the board, in addition to giving them orally. Learn to use the board without having to turn your back entirely on students and without blocking their view of the board. When you have a lot of material to put on the board, do it before class and then cover it, or better yet, put the material on transparencies and use the overhead projector rather than the board, or use both.

■ The Classroom Bulletin Board

Bulletin boards also are found in nearly every classroom, although they are sometimes poorly used or not used at all. However, they can be relatively inexpensively transformed into attractive and valuable instructional tools. Among other uses, the bulletin board is a convenient location to post reminders, assignments and schedules, and commercially produced materials, and to celebrate and display model student work and anchor papers.

To plan, design, and prepare bulletin board displays, some teachers use student assistants or committees, giving those students guidance and responsibility for planning, preparing, and maintaining bulletin board displays. When preparing a bulletin board display, keep these guidelines in mind: The display should be simple—emphasizing one main idea, concept, topic, or theme—and captions should be short and concise; illustrations can accent learning topics; verbs can vitalize the captions; phrases can punctuate a student's thoughts; and alliteration can announce anything you wish on the board. Finally, as in all other aspects of the classroom learning environment, remember to ensure that the board display reflects gender, racial, and ethnic equity.

■ The Community as a Resource

One of the richest resources for learning is the local community and the people and places in it. You will want to build your own file of community resources—speakers, sources for free materials, and field trip locations. Your school may already have a community resource file available for your use. However, it may need updating. A community resource file (see Figure 8.5) should contain information about (a) possible field trip locations,

(b) community resource people who could serve as guest speakers or mentors, and (c) local agencies that can provide information and instructional materials.

There are many ways of using community resources, and quite a variety have been demonstrated by the schools specifically mentioned throughout this book (see *Schools* in the index). Here the discussion is limited to two often used, although sometimes abused, instructional tools: (a) guest speakers and (b) out-of-classroom and off-campus excursions, commonly called *field trips*.

■ Guest Speakers

Bringing outside speakers into your classroom can be a valuable educational experience for students, but not automatically so. In essence, guest speakers can be classified within a spectrum of four types, two of which should not be considered. (a) Ideally, a speaker is both informative and inspiring. (b) A speaker may be inspiring but with nothing substantive to offer, except for the possible diversion it might offer from the usual rigors of classroom work. (c) The speaker might be informative but boring to students. (d) At the worst end of this spectrum is the guest speaker who is both boring and uninformative. So, just like any other instructional experience, to make a guest speaking experience most effective takes careful planning on your part. To make sure that the experience is beneficial to student learning, consider the following guidelines.

- If at all possible, meet and talk with the guest speaker in advance to inform him or her about your students and your expectations for the presentation, as well as to gauge how motivational and informative he or she might be. If you believe the speaker might be informative but boring, then perhaps you can help structure the presentation in some way to make it a bit more inspiring. For example, stop the speaker every few minutes and involve the students in questions and discussions of points made.

- Prepare students in advance with key points of information that you expect them to obtain.

- Guide students in preparing questions to ask the speaker. Focus on things the students want to find out, and information you want them to inquire about.

- Follow up the presentation with a thank-you letter to the guest speaker and perhaps further questions that developed during class discussions subsequent to the speaker's presentation.

■ Field Trips

What is the most memorable field trip that you were ever on as a student? What made it memorable? You may want to discuss these questions and others like them with your students.

Airport	Highway patrol station
Apiary	Historical sites and monuments
Aquarium	Industrial plant
Archeological site	Legislature session
Art gallery	Levee and water reservoir
Assembly plant	Library and archive
Bakery	Mass transit authority
Bird and wildlife sanctuary	Military installation
Book publisher	Mine
Bookstore	Museum
Broadcasting and TV station	Native American Indian reservation
Building being razed	Newspaper plant
Building under construction	Observatory
Canal lock	Oil refinery
Cemetery	Park
Chemical plant	Poetry reading
City or county planning commission	Police station
Courthouse	Post office and package delivery company
Dairy	Recycling center
Dam and floodplain	Retail store
Dock and harbor	Sanitation department
Factory	Sawmill or lumber company
Farm	Shopping mall
Fire department	Shoreline (stream, lake, wetland, ocean)
Fish hatchery	Telecommunications center
Flea market	Town meeting
Foreign embassy	Universities and colleges
Forest and forest preserve	Utility company
Freeway under construction	Warehouse
Gas company	Water reservoir and treatment plant
Geological site	Wildlife park and preserve
Health department and hospital	Weather bureau and storm center
Highway construction site	Zoo

FIGURE 8.5 ● Community Resources for Speakers, Materials, and Field Trips

Today's schools often have very limited funds for the transportation and liability costs for field trips. In some cases, there are no funds at all. At times, parent-teacher groups, businesses, and civic organizations help by providing financial resources so that students get valuable first-hand experiences that field trips so often can offer.

To prepare for and implement a successful field trip, there are three important stages of planning—before, during, and after—and critical decisions to be made at each stage. Consider the following guidelines.

Before the field trip When the field trip is your idea (and not the students'), discuss the idea with your teaching team, principal, or department chair (especially when transportation will be needed) *before* mentioning the idea to your students. There is no cause served by getting students excited about a trip before you know if it is feasible.

Once you have obtained the necessary, but tentative, approval from school officials, take the trip yourself (or with team members), if possible. A previsit allows you to determine how to make the field trip most productive. For this previsit you might consider taking a couple of your students along for their ideas and help. If a previsit is not possible, you still will need to arrange for travel directions; arrival and departure times; parking; briefing by the host, if there is one; storage of students' personal items, such as coats and lunches; provisions for eating and restrooms; and fees, if any.

If there are fees involved, inquire about reduced costs for large groups or possible grants to waive admissions fees for school groups. If you need to pay the admissions fees, you need to talk with your administration about who will cover the fees. If the trip is worth taking, the school should cover the costs. If that is not possible, perhaps students can plan a fund-raising activity or financial assistance can be obtained from some other source. If this does not work, you might consider an alternative that does not involve costs.

Arrange for official permission from the school administration. This usually requires a form for requesting, planning, and reporting field trips. After permission has been obtained, you can discuss the field trip with your students and arrange for permissions from their parents or guardians. Although the permission form should include a statement that the parent or guardian absolves the teacher and the school from liability should an accident occur, it *does not* lessen the teacher's and the school's responsibilities should there be negligence by a teacher, driver, or chaperone.

Arrange for students to be excused from their other classes while on the field trip. Using an information form prepared and signed by you and perhaps by the principal, the students should then assume responsibility for notifying their other teachers of the planned absence from classes and for assuring them that whatever work is missed will be made up. In addition, you will need to make arrangements for your own teaching duties to be covered. In some schools, teachers cooperate by filling in for those who will be gone. In other schools, substitute teachers are hired. Sometimes teachers have to hire their own substitute.

Arrange for whatever transportation is needed. Your principal, or the principal's designee, will help you with the details. In many schools, someone else is responsible for arranging transportation. In any case, the use of private automobiles is ill advised, because you and the school could be liable for the acts of the drivers.

Arrange for the collection of money that is needed for fees. If there are out-of-pocket costs to be paid by students, this information needs to be included on the permission form. No students should ever be excluded from the field trip because of a lack of money. Try to anticipate problems; hopefully the school or some organization can pay for the trip so that fees need not be collected from students and therefore potential problems of this sort are avoided.

Plan details for student safety and the monitoring of their safety from departure to return. A first-aid kit and a system of student control, such as a buddy system whereby students must remain paired throughout the trip, should be included. The pairs sometimes are given numbers that are recorded and kept by the teacher and the chaperones, and then checked at departure time, periodically during the trip, at the time of return, and again upon return. Use adult chaperones. As a very general rule, there should be one adult chaperone for every 10 students. Some districts have a policy regarding this. While on a field trip, at all times all students should be under the direct supervision of an adult.

Establish and discuss, to the extent you believe necessary, the rules of behavior your students should follow, including details of the trip, its purpose, directions, what they should wear and bring, academic expectations of them (for example, consider giving each student a study guide), and follow-up activities. In addition, information about what to do if anything should go awry, for example, if a student is late for the departure or return, loses a personal possession along the way, gets lost, is injured, becomes sick, or misbehaves, should be covered.

Because a field trip is supposed to promote learning, the learning expectations need to be clearly defined and the students given an explanation of how and where they may encounter the learning experience. Before the field trip, students should be asked questions such as, "What do we already know about _____?" "What do we want to find out about _____?" "How can we find out?" and then, with their assistance, an appropriate guide can be prepared for the students to use during the field trip. To further ensure learning and individual student responsibility for that learning, you may want to assign different roles and responsibilities to students, just as would be done in cooperative learning, ensuring that each student has a role with responsibility. One role you may assign would be to record the field trip experience.

During the field trip If your field trip has been carefully planned according to the preceding guidelines, it should be a valuable and safe experience for all. En route, while at the trip location, and on the return to school, you and the adult chaperones should monitor student behavior and learning just as you do in the classroom.

After the field trip Plan the follow-up activities. As with any other lesson plan, the field trip lesson is complete only when there is both a proper introduction and a well-planned closure. All sorts of follow-up activities can be planned as an educational wrap-up to this educational experience. For example, a bulletin board committee can plan and prepare an attractive display summarizing the trip. Students can write about their experiences in their journals or as papers. Small groups can give oral reports to the class about what they did and learned. Their reports can then serve as springboards for further class discussion, and perhaps further investigations. Finally, for future planning, all who were involved should contribute to an assessment of the experience.

■ MEDIA TOOLS

Media tools are teaching tools that depend upon electricity to project light and sound and to focus images on screens, including projectors of various sorts, computers, CD-ROMs, DVDs, sound recorders, and video recorders. The aim here is *not* to provide instruction on how to operate modern equipment but to help you develop a philosophy for using it and to provide strategies for using media tools in your teaching. Consequently, to conserve space in this book, we devote no attention to traditional AV equipment, such as 16 mm film, opaque, and slide projectors, but we do cover the overhead projector, document camera, and writing board.

It is important to remember that the role of media tools is to aid student learning, not to teach for you. You must still select the objectives, orchestrate the instructional plan, assess the results, and follow up the lessons, just as you have learned to do with various other instructional strategies. If you use media tools prudently, your teaching and students' learning will benefit.

When Equipment Malfunctions: Troubleshooting

When using media equipment, it is nearly always best to set up the equipment and have it ready to go before students arrive, thereby avoiding problems in classroom management that can occur when there is a delay because the equipment is not ready. Like any other competent professional, a competent teacher is ready when the work is to begin. Of course, delays may be unavoidable when equipment breaks down or if a videotape breaks. Remember Murphy's law, which says if anything can go wrong, it will? It is particularly relevant when using audiovisual equipment. You want to be prepared for such emergencies. Effectively planning for and responding to this eventuality is a part of your system of movement management and takes place during the preactive stage of your planning (see Module 1). That preparation includes consideration of a number of factors.

When equipment malfunctions, three principles should be kept in mind: (a) You want to avoid dead time in the classroom, (b) You want to avoid causing permanent damage to equipment, and (c) You want to avoid losing content continuity of a lesson. So, what do you do when equipment breaks down? Again, the answer is: Be prepared for the eventuality.

If a projector bulb goes out, quickly insert another. That means you should have an extra bulb on hand. If a tape breaks, you can do a quick temporary splice with cellophane tape, which should be readily available. If you must do a temporary splice, do it on the film or videotape that has already run through the machine rather than on the end yet to go through, so as not to mess up the machine or the film. Then, after class or after school, follow up so the tape can be permanently repaired before its next use.

If, while teaching, a computer program freezes or aborts on the screen, or if a fuse blows or for some other reason you lose power and you feel that there is going to be too much dead time before the equipment is working again, that is the time to go to an alternate lesson plan. You have probably heard the expression "go to Plan B." It is a useful phrase; what it means is that without missing a beat in the lesson, to accomplish the same instructional objective or another objective, you immediately and smoothly switch to an alternate

learning activity. For you, the beginning teacher, it does not mean that you must plan two lessons for every one, but that when planning a lesson that uses media equipment, you should plan in your lesson an alternative activity, just in case. Then, you move your students into the planned alternative activity quickly and smoothly.

The Overhead Projector

In addition to a writing board and a bulletin board, nearly every classroom is equipped with an overhead projector. The overhead projector is a versatile, effective, and reliable teaching tool. Except for the bulb burning out, not much else can go wrong with an overhead projector. There is no film to break nor program to crash.

The overhead projector projects light through transparent objects. A properly functioning overhead projector usually works quite well in a fully lit room. Truly portable overhead projectors are available that can be carried easily from place to place in their compact cases.

Other types of overhead projectors include rear-projection systems that allow the teacher to stand off to the side rather than between students and the screen, and overhead video projectors that use video cameras to send images that are projected by television monitors. Some schools use overhead video camera technology that focuses on an object, pages of a book, or a demonstration, while sending a clear image to a video monitor with a screen large enough for an entire class to clearly see.

In some respects, the overhead projector is more practical than the writing board, particularly for a beginning teacher who is nervous. Using the overhead projector rather than the writing board can help avoid tension by decreasing the need to pace back and forth to the board. And by using an overhead projector rather than a writing board, you can maintain both eye contact and physical proximity with students, both of which are important for maintaining classroom control.

Guidelines for using the overhead projector As with any projector, find the best place in your classroom to put it. If there is no classroom projection screen, you can hang white paper or a sheet, use a white multipurpose board, or use a white or near-white wall.

Have you ever attended a presentation by someone who was not using an overhead projector properly? It can be frustrating to members of an audience when the image is too small, out of focus, partially off the screen, or partially blocked from view by the presenter. To use this teaching tool in a professional manner:

- *Turn on the projector (the switch is probably on the front), and place it so that the projected white light covers the entire screen and hits the screen at a 90-degree angle, then focus the image to be projected.*

- *Face the students while using the projector.* The fact that you do not lose eye contact with your students is a major advantage of using the overhead projector rather than a writing board. What you write as you face your students will show up perfectly (unless out of focus or off the screen).

- *Lay the pencil directly on the transparency with the tip of the pencil pointing to the detail being emphasized* rather than using your finger to point to the detail or pointing to the screen (thereby turning away from your students).

- *To lessen distraction, turn the overhead projector off during long pauses, group discussions, or when you want the students to shift attention back to you.*

To preserve the life of the projector's bulb, it is best not to move the projector until the bulb has cooled. In addition, bulbs will last longer if you avoid touching them with your fingers.

For writing on overhead projector transparencies, ordinary felt-tip pens are not satisfactory. Select a transparency-marking pen available at an office supply store. The ink of these pens is water-soluble, so keep the palm of your hand from resting on the transparency or you will have ink smudges on your transparency and on your hand. Non-water-soluble pens—permanent markers—can be used, but the transparency must be cleaned with an alcohol solvent (ditto fluid works but, for safety, be sure there is proper ventilation) or a plastic eraser. When using a cleaning solvent, you can clean and dry with paper toweling or a soft rag. To highlight the writing on a transparency and to organize student learning, use pens in a variety of colors. Transparency pens tend to dry out quickly, and they are relatively expensive, so the caps must be taken on and off frequently, which is something of a nuisance when working with several colors. Practice writing on a transparency, and also practice making overlays. You can use an acetate transparency roll or single sheets of flat transparencies. Flat sheets of transparency come in different colors—clear, red, blue, yellow, and green—which can be useful in making overlays.

Some teachers prepare lesson outlines in advance on transparencies, which allows more careful preparation of the transparencies and means that they are then ready for reuse at another time. Some teachers use an opaque material, such as a 3 × 5 notecard, to block out prewritten material and then uncover it at the moment it is being discussed. For preparation of permanent transparencies, you will probably want to use permanent marker pens, rather than those that are water soluble and easily smudged. Heavy paper frames are available for permanent transparencies; marginal notes can be written on the frames. Personal computers with laser printers and thermal processing (copy) machines, probably located in the teacher's workroom or in the school's main office, can be used to make permanent transparencies.

There are certain guidelines you should keep in mind when preparing text transparencies in your word processing program. First, select an easy-to-read font (Helvetica or other sans serif typefaces work best). Do not use type smaller than you can comfortably read by placing your transparency on the floor and reading it from a standing position (approximately 18 point). Do not overcrowd the page; instead, select key points to highlight.

Other transparent objects can be shown on an overhead projector, such as transparent rulers, protractors, and Petri dishes for science activities. Even opaque objects can be used if you simply want to show silhouette, as you might in math and art activities. Calculators, too, are available specifically for use on the overhead projector, as is a screen that fits onto the platform and is circuited to a computer so that whatever is displayed on the computer monitor is also projected onto the classroom screen.

Commercial transparencies are available from a variety of school supply houses. For sources, check the catalogs available in your school office or at the audiovisual and resources centers in your school district. Publishers also often supply supplemental transparencies with the teacher's edition of the textbook.

The overhead projector can also be used for tracing transparent charts or drawings into larger drawings on paper or on the writing board. The image projected onto the screen can be made smaller or larger by moving the projector closer or farther away, respectively, and then traced when you have the size you want. Also, an overhead projector (or a filmstrip projector) can be used as a light source (spotlight) to highlight demonstrations by you or your students.

The Document Camera

Although much more expensive than overhead projectors, document cameras are becoming popular in classrooms across the country. Document cameras are very versatile classroom presentation tools. They are portable, lightweight and easy to use. Used in conjunction with a projection system, you can project 3-D objects, slides, and other microscopic objects in addition to displaying text. You can also zoom in on objects.

Multimedia Program

A **multimedia program** is a collection of teaching and learning materials involving more than one type of medium and organized around a single theme or topic. The types of media involved vary from rather simple kits—perhaps including videotapes, games, activity cards, student worksheets, and manuals of instructions for the teacher—to sophisticated packages involving building-level site-licensed computer software, student handbooks, reproducible activity worksheets, classroom wall hangings, and online subscriptions to telecommunication

TABLE 8.1	Selected Multimedia Programs with Sources	
Title	**Source (Computer: D = DOS, M = Macintosh, W = Windows)**	**Phone/Internet**
Age of Discovery	Society for Visual Education (M,W)	(800-829-1900)
Atlas of the Ancient World	Maris Multimedia (M,W)	(415-492-2819); www.maris.com
Battles of the World	SoftKey Multimedia (M,W)	(510-792-2101)
Chronicle of the 20th Century	DK Multimedia (M,W)	(212-213-4800); www.dk.com
Civilization II	Spectrum HoloByte, Inc. (W)	(510-522-3584); www.holobyte.com
Culture & Technology	Learning Team, The (M)	(800-793-8326); www.learningteam.org
Decisions, Decisions 5.0	Tom Snyder Productions (M,W)	(800-342-0236); www.teachtsp.com
Discovering America	Lawrence Productions (M,W)	(800-421-4157); www.lpi.com
Exploring Ancient Cities	Sumeria, Inc. (M,W)	(415-904-0800)
Go West!	Steck-Vaughn (M,W)	(800-531-5015); www.steck-vaughn.com
Greatest Moments of Our Time	E.M.M.E. Interactive (M,W)	(800-959-5260); www.cdaccess.com/html/publish/emme.htm
History CD-ROMs	CLEARVUE/eav (M,W)	(800-253-2788); www.clearvue.com
Ideas That Changed the World	Integrated Communications & Entertainment	(416-868-6423)
IDIOM History	Pro Quest Company	(734-761-9700); www.proguestcompany.com
Multicultural CD	UXL (D,M)	(800-877-4253); www.galegroup.com/uxl
Oregon Trail II	Learning Company, The (M,W)	(800-685-6322); www.broderbund.com/welcome.asp
Paths to Freedom	Encyclopaedia Britannica (M)	(800-554-9862); www.britannica.com
Robert E. Lee: Civil War General	Sierra On-Line (W)	(800-853-7788); www.sierra.com
Social Science 2000	Decision Development Corp. (M,W)	(800-835-4332); www.ddc2000.com
The American Journals CD	K-12 Micromedia Publishing (M)	(201-529-4500); www.k12mmp.com
The Balkan Odyssey	Chelsea House Publishers (M,W)	(800-848-2665); www.chelseahouse.com
The Voyages of the Mimi	Sunburst Communications (M,W)	(800-321-7511); www.SUNBURST.com
Time Travel to the 18th Century	Folkus Atlantic (M,W)	(800-780-8266); www.folkus.com
World History Interactive Library	Thynx (M,W)	(609-514-1600)
World War II	Flag Tower Multimedia (W)	(617-338-8720)

networks. Some kits are designed for teacher use, others by individuals or small groups of students; yet many more are designed for the collaborative use of students and teachers. Teachers sometimes incorporate multimedia programs with learning activity centers.

Many multimedia programs are available on CD-ROM; they are designed principally as reference resources for students and teachers but include other aspects as well. One example is National Geographic's *Mammals: A Multimedia Encyclopedia,* which provides a lesson-planning guide, facts on more than 200 animals, 700 still-color photos, range maps, animal vocalizations, full-motion movie clips, an animal classification game, a glossary, and a printing capability. A brief sample selection of additional multimedia programs is shown in Table 8.1.

■ Television, Videos, and Videodiscs

Everyone knows that television, videos, and videodiscs represent a powerful medium. Their use as teaching aids, however, may present scheduling, curriculum, and physical problems that some school systems are yet unable to handle adequately.

Television For purposes of professional discussion, television programming can be divided into three categories: instructional television, educational television, and general commercial television. Instructional television refers to programs specifically designed as classroom instruction. Educational television refers to programs of cable television and of public broadcasting designed to educate in general, but not aimed at classroom instruction. Commercial television programs include the entertainment and public service programs of the television networks and local stations.

Watch for announcements for special educational programs in professional journals. And, of course, television program listings can be obtained from your local commercial, educational, or cable companies or by writing directly to network stations. Some networks sponsor Internet Web sites. For those, see http://www.flnet.com/~tw/media/televisn.htm.

Videos Combined with a television monitor, the VCR (videocassette recorder) is one of the most popular and frequently used tools in today's classroom. Videotaped programs can do nearly everything that the former 16 mm films could do. In addition, the VCR, combined with a video camera, makes it possible to record students

- **A.D.A.M Software, Inc.,** 1600 River Edge Parkway, Suite 800, Atlanta, GA 30328, 800-755-2326, ext. 3018. <http://www.adam.com>.
- **Agency for Instructional Technology,** Box A, Bloomington, IN 47 402-0120, 800-457-4509. <http://www.ait.net>.
- **Broderbund Software,** 500 Redwood Boulevard, Novato, CA 94948, 800-474-8840. <http://www.broderbund.com>.
- **CLEARVUE/eav,** 6465 N. Avondale Avenue, Chicago, IL 60631, 800-253-2788. <http://www.CLEARVUE.com>.
- **D & H Distributing Co.,** 2525 N. 7th Street, Harrisburg, PA 17110, 717-255-7841. <http://www.dandh.com>.
- **DK Publishing & Multimedia,** 95 Madison Avenue, New York, NY 10016, 212-213-4800. <http://www.dk.com>.
- **Educational Activities, Inc.,** 1937 Grand Avenue, Baldwin, NY 11510, 800-645-3739. <http://www.edact.com>.
- **EME Corp.,** 10 Central Parkway, Station 312, Stuart, FL 34995, 800-848-2050. <http://www.emescience.com>.
- **Environmental Media Corp.,** 1102 11th Street, Port Royal, SC 29935, 800-368-3382. <http://www.envmedia.com>.
- **Fisher Science Education,** 485 S. Frontage Road, Burr Ridge, IL 60521, 800-955-1177. <http://www.fisheredu.com>.
- **Harcourt School Publishers,** 6277 Sea Harbor Drive, Orlando, FL 32887, 800-346-8648. <http://www.harcourt.com>.
- **Higher-Order Thinking Co.,** 1733 N.E. Patterson Drive, Lee's Summit, MO 64086, 816-524-2701.
- **IBM Global Education,** 4111 Northside Parkway, Atlanta, GA 30301-2150, 800-426-4968. <http://www.solutions.ibm.com/k12>.
- **Mindscape,** 88 Rowland Way, Novato, CA 94945, 800-231-3088. <http://www.mindscape.com>.
- **Modern School Supplies,** P.O. Box 958, Hartford, CT 06143, 800-243-2329. <http://www.modernss.com>.
- **NASCO-Modesto,** 4825 Stoddard Road, P.O. Box 3837, Modesto, CA 95352-3827, 800-558-9595. <http://www.nascofa.com>.
- **Pitsco, Inc.,** 915 East Jefferson Street, Pittsburg, KS 66762, 800-835-0686. <http://www.pitsco.com>.
- **Sargent, Welch/VWR Scientific Products,** P.O. Box 5229, Buffalo Grove, IL 60089-5229, 800-SAR-GENT. <http://www.SargentWelch.com>.
- **Schoolmasters Science,** 745 State Circle, P.O. Box 1941, Ann Arbor, MI 48106, 800-521-2832. <http://www.schoolmasters.com>.
- **Science Kit and Boreal Laboratories,** 777 East Park Drive, Tonawanda, NY 14150, 800-828-7777. <http://www.sciencekit.com>.
- **Sunburst Communications,** 101 Castleton Street, Pleasantville, NY 10570, 800-321-7511. <http://www.sunburst.com>.
- **SVE & Churchill Media,** 6677 N. Northwest Highway, Chicago, IL 60631, 800-829-1900. <http://www.SVEmedia.com>.
- **Tom Snyder Productions,** 80 Coolidge Hill Road, Watertown, MA 02472-5003, 800-342-0236. <http://www.tomsnyder.com>.
- **Troll School & Library L.L.C.,** 100 Corporate Drive, Mahwah, NJ 07430, 800-979-8765. <http://www.troll.com>.
- **Videodiscovery,** 1700 Westlake Ave., N., Station 600, Seattle, WA 98109-3012, 800-548-3472. <http://www.videodiscovery.com> .

FIGURE 8.6 ● Selected Resources for Videotapes, Computer Software, CD-ROMs, and Interactive Multimedia

during activities, practice, projects, and demonstrations as well as yourself when teaching. It gives students a marvelous opportunity to self-assess as they see and hear themselves in action.

Entire course packages, as well as supplements, are now available on videocassettes or on computer discs. The schools where you student teach and where you eventually are employed may have a collection of such programs. Some teachers make their own. You can also look for resources in the curriculum library in your education department, at your college or university library, or at the school district's resource center.

Carefully selected programs, tapes, discs, films, and slides enhance student learning. For example, videodiscs and CD-ROMs offer quick and efficient accessibility of thousands of visuals, thus providing an appreciated boost to teachers of students with limited language proficiency.

With the use of frame control, students can observe phenomena, in detail, that previous students only read about.

Check school supply catalogs and Internet resources for additional titles and sources for videodiscs. Generally, companies that sell computer software and CD-ROMs also sell videodiscs. Figure 8.6 provides sample addresses from which you may obtain catalogs of information.

■ COMPUTERS AND COMPUTER-BASED INSTRUCTIONAL TOOLS

As a middle school or secondary school classroom teacher, you must be **computer literate**—you must understand and be able to use computers as well as you can read and write. The computer can be valuable to you in several ways. For example, the computer can help you manage the instruction by obtaining information, storing and preparing test materials, maintaining attendance and grade records, and preparing programs to aid in the academic development of individual students. This category of computer uses is referred to as **computer-managed instruction (CMI).**

The computer can also be used for instruction by employing various instructional software programs, and it can be used to teach about computers and to help students develop their metacognitive skills as well as their skills in computer use.[5] When the computer is used to assist students in their learning, it is called **computer-assisted instruction (CAI)** or *computer-assisted learning (CAL).* There are several computer programs to help English Language Learners improve their written and communication skills, as well as comprehensive core curriculum packages to provide self-paced alternatives for students with special needs.

The Placement and Use of Computers: The Online Classroom

How you use the computer for instruction and learning is determined by several factors, including your knowledge of and skills in its use, the number of computers that you have available for instructional use, where computers are placed in the school, the software that is available, printer availability, and the telecommunications capabilities (that is, wiring and phone lines, modems, and servers).

Schools continue to purchase or to lease computers and to upgrade their telecommunications capabilities. Regarding computer placement and equipment and technological support available, here are some possible scenarios and how classroom teachers work within each.

Scenario 1. With the assistance of a computer lab and the lab technician, computers are integrated into the whole curriculum. In collaboration with members of interdisciplinary teaching teams, in a computer lab students use computers, software, and Internet sources as tools to build their knowledge, to write stories with word processors, to illustrate diagrams with paint utilities, to create interactive reports with hypermedia, and to graph data they have gathered using spreadsheets.

Scenario 2. In some schools, students take a computer class as an elective or exploratory course. Students in your classes who are simultaneously enrolled in such a course may be given special computer assignments by you that they can then share with the rest of the class.

Scenario 3. Some classrooms have a computer connected to a large-screen video monitor. The teacher or a student works the computer, and the entire class can see the monitor screen. As they view the screen, students can verbally respond to and interact with what is happening on the computer.

Scenario 4. You may be fortunate to have one or more computers in your classroom for all or a part of the school year, especially ones with Internet connections and CD-ROM playing capabilities; an overhead projector; and a LCD (liquid crystal display) projection system. Coupled with the overhead projector, the LCD projection system allows you to project onto your large wall screen (and TV monitor at the same time) any image from computer software or a videodisc. With this system, all students can see and verbally interact with the multimedia instruction.

Scenario 5. Many classrooms have at least one computer with telecommunications capability, and some have many. When this is the case in your classroom, then you most likely will have one or two students working at the computer station while others are doing other learning activities (**multilevel teaching**). Computers can be an integral part of a learning center and an important aid in your overall effort to personalize the instruction within your classroom.

Selecting Computer Software

When selecting software programs, you and your colleagues need, of course, to choose those that are compatible with your brand of computer(s) and with your instructional objectives.

Programs are continually being developed and enhanced to meet the new and more powerful computers being made available. (Videodiscs, computer software, and CD-ROMs are usually available from the same companies, addresses of which are listed in Figure 8.7.) For

---

- *CD-ROM Finder,* 5th ed., by J. Shelton, Ed. (Medford, NJ: Learned Information, 1993).
- *CD-ROM for Librarians and Educators: A Book to Over 300 Instructional Programs,* by B. H. Sorrow and B. S. Lumpkin (Jefferson, NC: McFarland, 1993).
- *CD-ROMs in Print,* Meckler Publishing, 11 Ferry Lane West, Westport, CT 06880.
- *The Directory of Video, Computer, and Audio-Visual Products,* published annually by the International Communications Industries Association, Fairfax, VA.
- Educational Software Institute catalog, 4213 South 94th Street, Omaha, NE 68127 (800-955-5570).

FIGURE 8.7 ● Resources of Information About CD-ROM Titles

evaluating computer software programs and testing them for their compatibility with your instructional objectives, there are usually forms available from the local school district or from the state department of education, as well as from professional associations.

▪ The CD-ROM

Computers have as many as three types of storage disks—floppy disks of various storage capacities, the hard disk, and the **CD-ROM,** which is an abbreviation for "compact disc—read only memory." Use of a CD-ROM disc requires a computer and a CD-ROM drive. Newer computers may have built-in CD-ROM drives, while others may be connected to one. As with floppy and hard disks, CD-ROMs are used for storing characters in a digital format, while images on a videodisc are stored in an analog format. The CD-ROM is capable of storing some 20,000 images or the equivalent of approximately 250,000 pages of text—the capacity of 1,520 360K floppy disks or eight 70MB hard disks—and therefore is ideal for storing large amounts of information such as dictionaries, encyclopedias, and general reference works full of graphic images that you can copy and modify.

The same material is used for both CD-ROM discs and videodiscs, but the videodisc platter is 12 inches across, while the CD-ROM disc is just 4.5 inches across. Newer CD-ROM discs include video segments, just like those of videodiscs. Any information stored on a CD-ROM disc or a videodisc can be found and retrieved within a few seconds. CD-ROMs are available from the distributors of videodiscs and will likely ultimately replace videodiscs, or both the CD-ROM and videodisc may be replaced by even more advanced technology, such as the **DVD (digital versatile disk or digital video disc).**

Having superior sound and visual performance, the DVD may replace CDs, VCR tapes, and computer CD-ROMs. Although in appearance it resembles the CD-ROM, the DVD can store nearly 17 gigabytes of information, provide a faster retrieval of data, and can be made interactive.

▪ Sources of Free and Inexpensive Audiovisual Materials

For free and inexpensive audiovisual materials, check Internet sources as well as your college or university library for sources listed in Figure 8.8.

▪ Using Copyrighted Video, Computer, and Multimedia Programs

You must be knowledgeable about the laws on the use of copyrighted videos and computer software materials. Although space here prohibits full inclusion of U.S. legal guidelines, your local school district undoubtedly can provide you with a copy of current district policies to ensure your compliance with all copyright laws. As was discussed earlier in the discussion about the use of printed materials that are copyrighted, when preparing to make any copy you must find out whether the copying is permitted by law under the category of "permitted use." If not allowed under "permitted use," then you must get written permission to reproduce the material from the holder of the copyright. Figures 8.9 and 8.10 present guidelines for the copying of videotapes and of computer software.

Usually, when purchasing CD-ROMs and other multimedia software packages intended for schools' use, you are also paying for a license to modify and use its contents for instructional purposes. However, not all CD-ROMs include copyright permission, so always check the copyright notice on any disc you purchase and use. Whenever in doubt, don't use it until you have asked your district media specialists about copyrights or have obtained necessary permissions from the original source.

As yet, there are no guidelines for fair use of films, filmstrips, slides, and multimedia programs. A general rule of thumb for use of any copyrighted material is to treat the work of others as you would want your own material treated were it protected by a copyright (see Figure 8.11).

- Best freeware and shareware at <http://wwwl.zdnet.com/pccomp/1001dl/html/1001.html>.
- Professional periodicals and journals.
- *Catalog of Audiovisual Materials: A Guide to Government Sources,* ED 198 822 (Arlington, VA: ERIC Documents Reproduction Service).
- Educator's Progress Service, Inc., 214 Center Street, Randolph, WI 53956 (414-326-3126): *Educator's Guide to Free Audio and Video Materials; Educator's Guide to Free Films; Educator's Guide to Free Filmstrips; Guide to Free Computer Materials; Educator's Guide to Free Science Materials.*
- *Video Placement Worldwide (VPW).* Source of free sponsored educational videos on the Internet at <http://www.vpw.com>.

FIGURE 8.8 ● Resources for Free and Inexpensive Audiovisual Materials

Permitted uses—you may:

1. Request your media center or audiovisual coordinator to record a program for you if you cannot or if you lack the equipment.
2. Keep a video-recorded copy of a broadcast (including cable transmission) for 45 calendar days, after which the program must be erased.
3. Use the program in class once during the first 10 school days of the 45 calendar days, and a second time if instruction needs to be reinforced.
4. Have professional staff view the program several times for evaluation purposes during the full 45-day period.
5. Make a few copies to meet legitimate needs, but these copies must be erased when the original video recording is erased.
6. Use only a part of the program if instructional needs warrant.
7. Enter into a licensing agreement with the copyright holder to continue use of the program.

Prohibited uses—you may *not*:

1. Video record premium cable services such as HBO without expressed permission.
2. Alter the original content of the program.
3. Exclude the copyright notice on the program.
4. Video record before a request for use is granted—the request to record must come from an instructor.
5. Keep the program, and any copies, after 45 days.

FIGURE 8.9 ● Copyright Law for Off-Air Videotaping

SOURCE. From *Instructional Media and Technologies for Learning* (6th ed., p. 389), by Robert Heinich, Michael Molenda, James D. Russell, and Sharon E. Smaldino, 1999, by Merrill/Prentice Hall. Upper Saddle River, NJ: Merrill/Prentice Hall. Reprinted with permission.

Permitted uses—you may:

1. Make a single backup or archival copy of the computer program.
2. Adapt the computer program to another language if the program is unavailable in the target language.
3. Add features to make better use of the computer program.

Prohibited uses—you may *not*:

1. Make multiple copies.
2. Make replacement copies from an archival or backup copy.
3. Make copies of copyrighted programs to be sold, leased, loaned, transmitted, or given away.

FIGURE 8.10 ● Copyright Law for Use of Computer Software

SOURCE: Congressional Amendment to the 1976 Copyright Act, December 1980.

1. For portions of copyrighted works used in your own multimedia production for use in teaching, follow normal copyright guidelines (e.g., the limitations on the amount of material used, whether it be motion media, text, music, illustrations, photographs, or computer software).
2. You may display your own multimedia work, using copyrighted works, to other teachers, such as in workshops. However, you may *not* make copies to give to colleagues without obtaining permission from copyright holders.
3. You may use your own multimedia production for instruction over an electronic network (e.g., distance learning) provided there are limits to access and to the number of students enrolled. You may *not* distribute such work over any electronic network without expressed permission from copyright holders.
4. You must obtain permissions from copyright holders before using any copyrighted materials in educational multimedia productions for commercial reproduction and distribution or before replicating more than one copy, distributing copies to others, or using copies outside your own classroom.

FIGURE 8.11 ● Fair Use Guidelines for Using Multimedia Programs

DISTANCE LEARNING

Distance learning (or distance education) is the popular term for describing any instructional situation in which the learner is separated in time or space from the point of instruction. Although telecommunications technologies have provided courses (e.g., by mail correspondence) and workshops (e.g., by video) for industry training, medical organizations, and higher education for many years, recent developments have created a renewed interest in distance learning. In fact, Roger Schank at Northwestern University's Institute for the Learning Sciences predicts that learning and instruction over the Internet will be the driving force for educational changes in the 21st century, with an accompanying change in the role of the classroom teacher from less of a deliverer of instruction to more of a facilitator of learning both by providing individual tutoring and by helping students work together in groups.[6]

With the technology of distance learning, students in small rural schools can receive instruction in courses that, because of limited local resources, might otherwise have been unavailable to them; via the Internet all students can interact in real time with people from around the world.

The National Distance Learning Center (NDLC) is a centralized electronic information source for distance learning programs and resources for K–12 education as well as for adult learning and higher education. Access to the database is via the Internet at telnet://ndlc@ndlc. occ.uky.edu. Additional resources on distance learning may be found at http://ericec.org/faq/disted-x.htm.

SUMMARY

You have learned of the variety of tools available to supplement your instruction. When used wisely, these tools will help you reach more of your students more of the time. As you know, teachers must meet the needs of diverse students, including many who are linguistically and culturally different. The material selected and presented in this module should be of help in doing that. The future will undoubtedly continue bringing technological innovations that will be even more helpful—compact discs, computers, and telecommunications equipment have only marked the beginning of a revolution for teaching. New instructional delivery systems made possible by microcomputers and multimedia workstations will likely fundamentally alter what had become the traditional role of the classroom teacher during the 20th century.

You should remain alert to current and developing technologies for your teaching. Digital videodiscs (DVDs), CD-ROMs interfaced with computers (i.e., the use of multimedia), and telecommunications offer exciting technologies for learning. New instructional technologies are advancing at an increasingly rapid rate. You and your colleagues must maintain vigilance over new developments by constantly looking for those that will not only help make student learning meaningful and interesting, and your teaching effective, but that are cost effective as well.

MODULE 8 POSTTEST

Multiple Choice

1. As an overhead projector is positioned farther away from the screen, the image becomes
   a. larger and less brilliant.
   b. larger and more brilliant.
   c. smaller and less brilliant.
   d. smaller and more brilliant.

2. The use of laser videodiscs and CD-ROMs interfaced with computers for instructional purposes is called
   a. distance learning.
   b. instruction with multimedia.
   c. computer-managed instruction.
   d. competency-based instruction.

3. While showing your classroom of students a video, you should
   a. go to the faculty room and relax.
   b. sit at your desk and correct papers.
   c. stand behind the students and monitor student behavior.
   d. stand in the front of the room and monitor student behavior.

(continued)

4. When using copyrighted materials for instruction, which one of the following is an infringement of copyright law?
   a. making a single copy of an entire chapter from a book
   b. making a single copy of an entire magazine article
   c. making a single copy of a picture from a book
   d. making a single copy of an audio recording

5. The legal rights that apply to an original, created work—such as a photograph, poem, or work of art—are referred to as
   a. patent.
   b. fair use.
   c. copyright.
   d. trademark.

6. The fair use provision of copyright law permits teachers, under certain circumstances, to
   a. include a copyrighted work in a course packet for several years.
   b. make several copies of a purchased software program for in-class use.
   c. use a limited excerpt of a copyrighted work for classroom instruction.
   d. duplicate a portion of a copyrighted work for distribution to colleagues.

7. During the preactive phase of instruction that involves media, it is important to plan carefully so that if the equipment breaks down
   a. you can quickly pick up the lesson with no loss of content continuity.
   b. you do not do anything to cause permanent damage to the equipment.
   c. there is no dead time for the students.
   d. all of the above

8. _____ is a national network devoted exclusively as a clearinghouse for providing access to information and research in education.
   a. ERIC
   b. CD-ROM
   c. ARPAnet
   d. Internet

9. Which one is a true statement?
   a. Guest speakers are usually informative and inspiring for the students, and therefore no preparation of the students beforehand is necessary.
   b. When you have an informative but noninspiring guest speaker, there is nothing you can do except delight when the speaker is finished.
   c. Using a guest speaker should be carefully planned, just as you would any other type of lesson.
   d. None of the above are true.

10. Which one of the following is a false statement?
    a. You may make one copy of your multimedia production to give to a colleague.
    b. You may display your own multimedia production that uses copyrighted materials to other teachers.
    c. Following copyright guidelines, you may use portions of copyrighted works in your own multimedia creation.
    d. You may distribute your own multimedia creation over any electronic network but only if you have received express permission from holders of copyrighted material that you have used in the production.

Short Explanation

1. Describe how the use of audiovisual materials helps to reinforce student learning.
2. It has been said that the overhead projector can be one of the teacher's best friends. Explain what this means.
3. Explain how your effective use of the writing board can help students see relationships among verbal concepts or information.
4. Describe what you should look for when deciding whether material that you have obtained free or inexpensively is suitable for use in your teaching.
5. Explain why you agree or disagree that any material obtained free is okay to use in teaching.
6. Describe any planning precautions you should take when preparing to use media tools for instruction.

(continued)

7. Explain various ways that you could use the overhead projector in teaching your subject.

8. Explain ways you might use the Internet in your teaching.

9. Describe what you would do if a student misbehaves while on a field trip at some location distant from the campus.

10. Explain why you would or would not use bulletin boards in your classroom.

Essay

1. Describe your knowledge, observations, and feelings about the use of multimedia and telecommunications for teaching. What more would you like to know about the use of multimedia and telecommunications for teaching? Describe how you might learn more about these things.

2. The local school board is concerned about copyright law and how it relates to instruction. You have been asked to make a presentation on the topic to the board. Prepare a summary of your presentation.

3. What do you predict will be the nature of the student textbook in the year 2025?

4. From your current observations and fieldwork related to this teacher preparation program, clearly identify one specific example of educational practice that seems contradictory to exemplary practice or theory presented in this module. Present your explanation for the discrepancy.

5. Describe any prior concepts you held that changed as a result of the experiences of this module. Describe the changes.

 To access this posttest and the answers online, go to the Companion Website at www.prenhall.com/kellough.

■ SUGGESTED READINGS

Abdullah, M. H. (1998). *Guidelines for evaluating web sites.* ERIC Digest 426440 98. Bloomington, IN: ERIC Clearinghouse on Reading, English, and Communications.

Barron, A. E., & Ivers, K. S. (1998). *The Internet and instruction: Activities and ideas* (2nd ed.). Englewood, CO: Libraries Unlimited.

Block, C. C., & Dellamura, R. J. (December 2000/January 2001). Better book buddies. *The Reading Teacher, 54*(4), 364–370.

Boyle, A. (2005). A formula for successful technology integration must include curriculum, *MultiMedia & Internet @ Schools, 12*(1), 30–33.

Callister, T. A., Jr., & Burbules, N. C. (2004). Just give it to me straight: A case against filtering the Internet, *Phi Delta Kappan, 85*(9), 649–655.

Churma, M. (1999). *A guide to integrating technology standards into the curriculum.* Upper Saddle River, NJ: Merrill/Prentice Hall.

Clyde, L. A. (2004). Electronic whiteboards, *Teacher Librarian, 32*(2), 43–45.

Cotton, E. G. (1998). *The online classroom: Teaching with the Internet* (3rd ed.). Bloomington, IN: EDINFO Press.

Curchy, C., & Kyker, K. (1998). *Educator's survival guide to TV production equipment and setup.* Englewood, CO: Libraries Unlimited.

Donlevy, J. G., & Donlevy, T. R. (1999). wNetSchool. *International Journal of Instructional Media, 26*(1), 9–10.

Ertmer, P. A., Hruskocy, C., & Woods, D. M. (2000). *Education on the Internet.* Upper Saddle River, NJ: Merrill/Prentice Hall.

Foshay, J. D. (1999). *Project-based multimedia instruction.* Fastback 445. Bloomington, IN: Phi Delta Kappa Educational Foundation.

Gorski, P. C. (2004). Multicultural education and progressive pedagogy in the online information age, *Multicultural Perspectives, 6*(4), 37–48.

Harris, J. (1998). *Design tools for the Internet-supported classroom.* Alexandria, VA: Association for Supervision and Curriculum Development.

Heide, A., & Stillborne, L. (1999). *The teacher's complete & easy guide to the Internet* (2nd ed.). New York: Teachers College Press.

Jonassen, D. H., Peck, K. L., & Wilson, B. G. (1999). *Learning with technology: A constructivist perspective.* Upper Saddle River, NJ: Merrill/Prentice Hall.

Kahn, J. (1998). *Ideas and strategies for the one-computer classroom.* Eugene, OR: International Society for Technology in Education.

Leu, D. J., Jr., Leu, D. D., & Leu, K. R. (1999). *Teaching with the Internet: Lessons from the classroom.* Norwood, MA: Christopher-Gordon.

McCullen, C. (1999a). Copyright issues in a digital world. *Middle Ground, 3*(2), 7–9, 52.

McCullen, C. (1999b). The hows and whys of conducting desktop teleconferences. *Middle Ground, 2*(3), 7–8.

Means, B. (2000). Technology in America's schools: Before and after Y2K. In R. S. Brandt (Ed.), *Education in a new era* (Chap. 8, pp. 185–210). Alexandria, VA: ASCD Yearbook, Association for Supervision and Curriculum Development.

Newby, T. J., Stepich, D. A., Lehman, J. D., & Russell, J. D. (2000). *Instructional technology for teaching and learning* (2nd ed.). Upper Saddle River, NJ: Merrill/Prentice Hall.

Pinhey, L. A. (1998). *Global education: Internet resources.* ERIC Digest 417124. Bloomington, IN: ERIC Clearinghouse for Social Studies/Social Science Education.

Rekrut, M. D. (1999). Using the Internet in classroom instruction: A primer for teachers. *Journal of Adolescent & Adult Literacy, 42*(7), 546–557.

Renard, L. (1999/2000). Cut and paste 101: Plagiarism and the net. *Educational Leadership, 57*(4), 38–42.

Roblyer, M. D. (1999). *Integrating technology across the curriculum: A database of strategies and lesson plans.* Upper Saddle River, NJ: Merrill/Prentice Hall.

Roblyer, M. D., & Edwards, J. (2000). *Integrating educational technology into teaching* (2nd ed.). Upper Saddle River, NJ: Merrill/Prentice Hall.

Ruthven, K. (2005). Incorporating Internet resources into classroom practice: pedagogical perspectives and strategies of secondary-school subject teachers, *Computers & Education,* 44(1), pages: 1-eoa.

Tally, B., & Burns, M. (2000). Mining for gold in a mountain of online resources. *Harvard Education Letter, 16*(2), 6–7.

Tapscott, D. (1999). Educating the net generation. *Educational Leadership, 56*(5), 6–11.

Teicher, J. (1999). An action plan for smart Internet use. *Educational Leadership, 56*(5), 70–74.

Weinman, J., & Haag, P. (1999). Gender equity in cyberspace. *Educational Leadership, 56*(5), 44–49.

■ ENDNOTES

[1] M. Mead, What Has Happened to the Generation Gap? *Redbook 139,* p. 70+ (September 1972).

[2] See also the *Copyright and Fair Use* Web site of Stanford University at **http://fairuse.stanford.edu/**.

[3] See M. M. Mullan, Modern Classrooms See Chalkboards Left in the Dust, *Education Week 19*(17), 6 (January 12, 2000).

[4] Sources of electronic whiteboards include MicroTouch, Tewksbury, MA (800-642-7686); Numonics, Montgomeryville, PA (215-362-2766); Smart Technologies, Calgary, AB, Canada (403-245-0333); SoftBoard, Portland, OR (888-763-8262); and TEGRITY, San Jose, CA (408-369-5150).

[5] See, for example, X. Bornas et al., Preventing Impulsivity in the Classroom: How Computers Can Help Teachers, *Computers in the Schools 13*(1–2), 27–40 (1997).

[6] R. C. Schank, A Vision of Education for the 21st Century, *T.H.E. Journal 27*(6), 43–45 (January 2000).

Assessment of Teaching and Learning

Part 4 Overview

While preceding parts of this text address the why (Part 1), what (Part 2), and how (Part 3) of teaching, Part 4 focuses on the fourth and final component—the how well, or the assessment, component. Together, these four components are the essentials of effective instruction.

Teaching and learning are reciprocal processes that depend on and affect one another. Thus, the assessment component deals with how well the students are learning and how well the teacher is teaching. Assessment is an integral part of an ongoing process in the educational arena. When gaps between anticipated results and student achievement exist, efforts are made to eliminate those factors that seem to be limiting the educational output or to improve the situation in some other way. Thus, educational progress occurs.

To learn effectively, students need to know how they are doing. Similarly, to be an effective teacher, you must be informed about what the student knows, feels, and can do so that you can help the student build on her or his skills, knowledge, and attitudes. In short, assessment provides a key for both effective teaching and learning.

The two modules of Part 4 assist you with:

- Sample rubrics and other tools for assessing student achievement.
- Methods of grading and reporting student achievement.
- Means of preparing and administering instruments for assessment.
- Self-assessment through micro-teaching and other methods of assessing teacher performance.
- Knowledge about professional field experiences.
- Guidelines for meeting with parents and guardians.
- Guidelines for continued professional development.
- Guidelines for obtaining a teaching job.

Although best practices in assessment continue to evolve, one point that is clear is that various techniques of assessment must be used to determine how the student works, what the student is learning, and what the student can produce as a result of that learning.

—JOSEPH F. CALLAHAN,
LEONARD H. CLARK, AND
RICHARD D. KELLOUGH
(7TH EDITION)

Assessing and Reporting Student Achievement

Module 9 Overview

This module discusses grading and reporting of student achievement, two responsibilities that can consume much of a teacher's valuable time. Grading is time-consuming and frustrating for many teachers. What should be graded? Should grades represent student growth, level of achievement in a group, effort, attitude, general behavior, or a combination of these? What should determine grades—homework, tests, projects, class participation and group work, or some combination of these? And, what should be their relative weights? These are just a few of the questions that plague teachers, parents, and, indeed the profession.

When teachers are aware of alternative systems, they may be able to develop assessment and reporting processes that are fair and effective for all students in a variety of situations. After beginning with assessment, the final focus in this module considers today's principles and practices in grading and reporting student achievement.

Specific Objectives

At the completion of this module, you should be able to:

- Demonstrate an understanding of the importance of assessment in teaching and learning.
- Explain the value of, and give an example of, a performance assessment that could be used in a particular grade level and discipline.
- Explain how rubrics, checklists, portfolios, and journals are used in the assessment of student learning.
- Differentiate among diagnostic assessment, authentic assessment, summative assessment, and formative assessment, with examples of when and how each can be used.
- Describe the importance of self-assessment in teaching and learning.
- Describe the importance of and manner by which parents can be involved in the education of their children.

Introduction

The importance of continuous assessment mandates that you know various principles and techniques of assessment. Here we explain and demonstrate how to construct and use assessment instruments. We will define terms related to assessment, suggest procedures to use in the construction of assessment items, point out the advantages and disadvantages of different types of assessment items and procedures, and explain the construction and use of alternative assessment devices.

Still today, in too many schools, the grade progress report and final report card are about the only communication between the school and the student's home. Unless the teacher and the school have clearly determined what grades represent and unless such understanding is periodically reviewed with each set of new parents or guardians, these reports may create unrest and dissatisfaction on the parts of parents, guardians, and students, and thereby prove to be alienating devices. The grading system and reporting scheme, then, instead of informing parents and guardians, may separate even further the home and the school, which do have a common concern—the intellectual, physical, social, and psychological development of the student.

The development of the student encompasses growth in the cognitive, affective, and psychomotor domains. Traditional objective paper-and-pencil tests provide only a portion of the data needed to indicate student progress in those domains. As experts have done in the past, many experts today also question the traditional sources of data and encourage the search for, development of, and use of alternative means to assess more authentically the students' development of thinking and higher-level learning. Although best practices in assessment continue to evolve, one point that is clear is that various techniques of assessment must be used to determine how the student works, what the student is learning, and what the student can produce as a result of that learning. As a teacher, you must develop a repertoire of means of assessing learner behavior and academic progress.

Although grades have been a part of school for about 100 years, it is clear to many experts that the conventional report card with grades falls short of being a developmentally appropriate procedure for reporting the academic performance or progress of learners. Some schools are experimenting with other ways of reporting student achievement in learning, but the use of letter grades in middle schools and secondary schools is still firmly entrenched. Parents, students, colleges, and employers have come to expect grades as evaluations. Some critics suggest that the emphasis in schools is on getting a high grade rather than on learning, arguing that, as traditionally measured, the two do not necessarily go hand in hand. Today's interest is (or should be) more on what the student can do (performance testing) as a result of learning than merely on what the student can recall (memory testing) from the experience.

In addition, there have been complaints about subjectivity and unfair practices in testing. As a result of these concerns, a variety of systems of assessment and reporting has evolved, is still evolving, and will likely continue to evolve throughout your professional career. We will define key terms, and discuss different types of assessment, design test items, and report grades.

■ PURPOSES AND PRINCIPLES OF ASSESSMENT

Assessment of achievement in student learning is designed to serve several purposes. These are:

1. *To assist in student learning.* This is the purpose usually first thought of when speaking of assessment, and it is the principal topic of this module. For the classroom teacher it is (or should be) the most important purpose.

2. *To identify students' strengths and weaknesses.* Identification and assessment of students' strengths and weaknesses are necessary for two reasons: To structure and restructure the learning activities and to restructure the curriculum. Concerning the first, for example, data on student strengths and weaknesses in content and process skills are important in planning activities appropriate for both skill development and intellectual development. This is **diagnostic assessment** (known also as *preassessment*). For the second, data on student strengths and weaknesses in content and skills are useful for making appropriate modifications to the curriculum.

3. *To assess the effectiveness of a particular instructional strategy.* It is important for you to know how well a particular strategy helped accomplish a particular goal or objective. Competent teachers continually reflect on and evaluate their strategy choices, using a number of sources: Student achievement as measured by assessment instruments, their own intuition, informal feedback given by the students, and, sometimes, informal feedback given by colleagues, such as members of a teaching team or mentor teachers. (Mentor teachers are discussed in Module 10.)

4. *To assess and improve the effectiveness of curriculum programs.* Components of the curriculum are continually assessed by committees composed of teachers and administrators, and sometimes parents, students, and other members of the school and community. The assessment is done while students are learning (i.e., formative assessment) and after the learning has taken place (summative assessment).

5. *To assess and improve teaching effectiveness.* To improve student learning, teachers are periodically evaluated on the basis of (a) their commitment to working with students at a particular level; (b) their ability to cope with students at a particular age, developmental, or grade level; and (c) their mastery of

appropriate instructional techniques articulated throughout this book.

6. *To provide data that assist in decision making about a student's future.* Assessment of student achievement is important in guiding decision making about course and program placement, promotion, school transfer, class standing, eligibility for honors and scholarships, and career planning.

7. *To provide data in order to communicate with parents and guardians and to involve them in their children's learning.* Parents, communities, and school boards all share in accountability for the effectiveness of children's learning. Today's schools are reaching out more than ever before and engaging parents, guardians, and the community in their children's education. All teachers play an important role in the process of communicating with, reaching out to, and involving parents and the community.

Because the welfare and, indeed, the future of so many people depend on the outcomes of assessment, it is impossible to overemphasize its importance. For a learning endeavor to be successful, the learner must have answers to basic questions: Where am I going? Where am I now? How do I get where I am going? How will I know when I get there? Am I on the right track for getting there? These questions are integral to a good program of assessment. Of course, in the process of teaching and learning, the answers may be ever changing, and the teacher and students continue to assess and adjust plans as appropriate and necessary. The **exemplary school** is in a mode of continuous change and progress.

The following principles, based on the preceding questions, guide the assessment program and are reflected in the discussions in this module.

- Teachers need to know if they are meeting their instructional objectives.

- Students need to know how well they are doing.

- Assessment is a reciprocal process, which includes assessment of teacher performance as well as student achievement.

- The program of assessment should aid teaching effectiveness and contribute to the intellectual and psychological growth of children.

- Evidence and input data for knowing how well the teacher and students are doing should come from a variety of sources and types of data-collecting devices.

- Assessment is a continuous process. The selection and implementation of plans and activities require continual monitoring and assessment to check on progress and to change or adopt strategies to promote desired behavior.

- **Reflection** and self-assessment are important components of any successful assessment program. Reflection and self-assessment are important if students are to develop the skills necessary for them to assume increasingly greater ownership of their own learning.

- A teacher's responsibility is to facilitate student learning and to assess student progress in that learning, and for that, the teacher is, or should be, held accountable.

TERMS USED IN ASSESSMENT

When discussing the assessment component of teaching and learning, it is easy to be confused by the terminology. The following clarification of terms is offered to aid your reading and comprehension.

Assessment and Evaluation

Assessment is the process of finding out what students are learning, and it is a relatively neutral process. In contrast, **evaluation** is making sense of what was uncovered, a subjective process.

Measurement and Assessment

Measurement refers to quantifiable data about specific behaviors. Tests and the statistical procedures used to analyze the results are examples. Measurement is a descriptive and objective process; that is, it is relatively free from human value judgments.

Assessment includes objective data from measurement but also other types of information, some of which are more subjective, such as information from anecdotal records and teacher observations and ratings of student performance. In addition to the use of objective data (data from measurement), assessment also includes arriving at value judgments made on the basis of subjective information.

An example of the use of these terms is as follows. A teacher may share the information that Jerilee Jackson received a score in the 90th percentile on the eighth-grade statewide achievement test in reading (a statement of measurement) but may add that "according to my assessment of her work in my language-arts class, she has not performed to her potential" (a statement of assessment).

Validity and Reliability

The degree to which a measuring instrument actually measures that which it is intended to measure is the instrument's **validity.** For example, when we ask if an instrument (such as a performance assessment instrument) has validity, key questions concerning that instrument are:

- Does the instrument adequately sample the intended content?
- Does it measure the cognitive, affective, and psychomotor knowledge and skills that are important to the unit of content being tested?
- Does it sample all the instructional objectives of that unit?

The accuracy with which a technique consistently measures that which it does measure is its **reliability.** If, for example, you know that you weigh 115 pounds, and a scale consistently records 115 pounds when you stand on it, then that scale has reliability. However, if the same scale consistently records 100 pounds when you stand on it, we can still say the scale has reliability. By this example, then, it should be clear to you that an instrument could be reliable (it produces similar results when used again and again) although not necessarily valid. In this second instance, the scale is not measuring what it is supposed to measure, so although it is reliable, it is not valid. Although a technique might be reliable but not valid, a technique must have reliability before it can have validity. The greater the number of test items or situations on a particular content objective, the higher the reliability. The higher the reliability, the more consistency there will be in students' scores measuring their understanding of that particular objective.

■ Authentic Assessment: Advantages and Disadvantages

When assessing for student achievement, it is important that you use procedures that are compatible with the instructional objectives. This is referred to as **authentic assessment.** Other terms used for *authentic* assessment are *accurate, active, aligned, alternative,* and *direct.* Although performance assessment is sometimes used, **performance assessment** refers to the type of student response being assessed, whereas *authentic* assessment refers to the assessment situation. Although not all performance assessments are authentic, assessments that are authentic are most assuredly performance assessments.

Consider this example: "If students have been actively involved in classifying objects using multiple characteristics, it sends them a confusing message if they are then required to take a paper-and-pencil test that asks them to 'define classification' or recite a memorized list of characteristics of good classifications schemes."[2] An authentic assessment technique would be a performance item that actually involves the students in classifying objects. In other words, to obtain an accurate assessment of a student's learning, the teacher uses a performance-based assessment procedure, that is, a procedure that requires students to produce rather than to select a response.

Advantages claimed for the use of authentic assessment include (a) the direct (also known as performance-based, criterion-referenced, or outcome-based) measurement of what students should know and can do and (b) an emphasis on higher-order thinking. However, disadvantages of authentic assessment include a higher cost, difficulty in making results consistent and usable, and problems with validity, reliability, and comparability.

Unfortunately, a teacher may never see a particular student again after a given school semester or year is over, and the effects that teacher has had on a student's values and attitudes may never be observed by that teacher at all. In schools where groups or teams of teachers remain with the same cohort of students—as in the house concept and looping programs discussed in Module 1—those teachers often do have the opportunity to observe the positive changes in their students' values and attitudes.

■ Diagnostic, Formative, and Summative Assessment

Assessing a student's achievement is a three-stage process, involving:

1. *Diagnostic assessment* (sometimes called *preassessment*)—the assessment of the student's knowledge and skills before the new instruction;
2. *Formative assessment*—the assessment of learning during the instruction; and
3. *Summative assessment*—the assessment of learning after the instruction, ultimately represented by the student's final term, semester, or year's achievement grade.

Grades or marks shown on unit tests, progress reports, deficiency notices, and interim reports are examples of formative evaluation reports. However, an end-of-chapter test or a unit test is summative when the test represents the absolute end of the student's learning of material for that instructional unit.

■ ASSESSING STUDENT LEARNING: THREE AVENUES

Three general avenues are available for assessing a student's achievement in learning. You can assess:

1. What the student *says*—for example, the quantity and quality of a student's contributions to class discussions;
2. What the student *does*—for example, a student's performance (e.g., the amount and quality of a student's participation in the learning activities); and
3. What the student *writes*—for example, as shown by items in the student's portfolio (e.g., homework assignments, checklists, project work, and written tests).

Student _____	Course _____	School _____
Observer _____	Date _____	Period _____

Objective for Time Period	Desired Behavior	What Student Did, Said, or Wrote

Teacher's (Observer's) Comments:

FIGURE 9.1 ● Evaluating and Recording Student Verbal and Nonverbal Behaviors: Sample Form

In a diverse classroom, an eclectic approach to assessment that includes the different stages and avenues highlighted here will allow students to demonstrate their comprehension of covered material and to improve in areas they find challenging.

■ Importance and Weight of Each Avenue

Although your own situation and personal philosophy will dictate the levels of importance and weight you give to each avenue of assessment, you should have a strong rationale if you value and weigh the three avenues for assessment differently than one-third each.

■ Assessing What a Student Says and Does

When evaluating what a student says, you should listen to the student's oral reports, questions, responses, and interactions with others, and observe the student's attentiveness, involvement in class activities, creativeness, and responses to challenges. Notice that we say you should *listen* and *observe*. While listening to what the student is saying, you should also be observing the student's nonverbal behaviors. For this you can use narrative observation forms (see Figure 9.1), observations with checklists and scoring rubrics (see sample checklists in Figures 9.2, 9.4, and 9.5, and sample scoring rubrics in Figures 9.2, 9.3, 9.10, and 9.11), and periodic conferences with the student.

With each technique used, you must proceed from your awareness of anticipated learning outcomes (the instructional objectives), and you must assess a student's progress toward meeting those objectives, referred to as **criterion-referenced assessment.**

Observation form Figure 9.1 illustrates a sample generic form for recording and evaluating teacher observations of a student's verbal and nonverbal behaviors. With modern technology, such as is afforded, for example, by the software program *Learner Profile*™, a teacher can record observations electronically anywhere at any time.[3]

Checklist versus scoring rubric As you can see from the sample rubric and sample checklist shown in Figure 9.2, there is little difference between what a checklist is and what a rubric is. The difference is that rubrics show the degrees for the desired characteristics while checklists usually show only the desired characteristics. The checklist could easily be made into a scoring rubric and the rubric could easily be made into a checklist.

Guidelines for assessing what a student says and does When assessing a student's verbal and nonverbal behaviors you should:

1. Maintain an anecdotal record (teacher's log) book or folder, with a separate section in it for your records of each student.
2. List the desirable behaviors for a specific activity.
3. Check the list against the specific instructional objectives.
4. Record your observations as quickly as possible following your observation. Audio or video recordings, and, of course, computer software programs, can help you maintain records and check the accuracy of your memory; but if this is inconvenient, you should spend time during school, immediately after school, or later that evening recording your observations while they are still fresh in your memory.
5. Record your professional judgment about the student's progress toward the desired behavior, but

Sample rubric for assessing a student's skill in listening:

Score Point 3—Strong listener
- responds immediately to oral directions
- focuses on speaker
- maintains appropriate attention span
- listens to what others are saying
- is interactive

Score Point 2—Capable listener
- follows oral directions
- usually attentive to speaker and to discussions
- listens to others without interrupting

Score Point 1—Developing listener
- has difficulty following directions
- relies on repetition
- often inattentive
- has short attention span
- often interrupts the speaker

Sample checklist for assessing a student's skill in map work:

Check each item if the map comes up to standard in this particular category.

_____ 1. Accuracy

_____ 2. Neatness

_____ 3. Attention to details

FIGURE 9.2 ● Checklist and Rubric Compared

think it through before transferring it to a permanent record.

6. Write comments that are reminders to yourself, such as, "Discuss observation with the student," "Check validity of observation by further testing," "Discuss observations with student's mentor" (e.g., an adult representative from the community), and "Discuss observations with other teachers on the teaching team."

■ Assessing What a Student Writes

When assessing what a student writes, you can use worksheets, written homework and papers, student journal writing, student writing projects, student portfolios, and tests (all discussed later in this module). In many schools, portfolios, worksheets, and homework assignments are the tools usually used for the formative evaluation of each student's achievement. Tests, too, should be a part of this assessment, but tests are also used for summative evaluation at the end of a unit and for diagnostic purposes.

Your summative evaluation of a student's achievement and any other final judgment made by you about a student can have an impact upon the psychological and intellectual development of that student. Non-native-English speakers may be sensitive to criticism of their language progress. You want to help these students improve, but you do not want them to feel that anything

short of a native-like command of the English language is acceptable. Focus on the message and avoid correcting every grammatical, pronunciation, or vocabulary error he/she makes while participating in class discussions or doing a formal presentation. Later in the section, we will pay special attention to this matter in Recording Teacher Observations and Judgments.

Guidelines for assessing student writing Use the following guidelines when assessing what a student writes. *Student writing assignments, test items, and scoring rubrics* (see Figure 9.3) *should be criterion-referenced*, that is, they should correlate and be compatible with specific instructional objectives. Regardless of the avenue chosen and their relative weights given by you, you must evaluate against the instructional objectives. Any given objective may be checked by using more than one method and by using more than one instrument. Subjectivity, inherent in the assessment process, may be reduced as you check for validity, comparing results of one measuring strategy against those of another.

Read nearly everything a student writes (except, of course, for personal writing in a student's journal). If it is important for the student to do the work, then it is equally important that you give your professional attention to the product of the student's efforts. Of course, papers can be read with varying degrees of intensity and scrutiny, depending on the purpose of the assignment.

Score Point 4—correct purpose, mode, audience; effective elaboration; consistent organization; clear sense of order and completeness; fluent

Score Point 3—correct purpose, mode, audience; moderately well elaborated; organized but possible brief digressions; clear, effective language

Score Point 2—correct purpose, mode, audience; some elaboration; some specific details; gaps in organization; limited language control

Score Point 1—attempts to address audience; brief, vague, unelaborated; wanders off topic; lack of language control; little or no organization; wrong purpose and mode

---

FIGURE 9.3 ● Sample Scoring Rubric for Assessing Student Writing

SOURCE: Texas Education Agency, *Writing Inservice Guide for English Language Arts and TAAS* (Austin, TX: Author, 1993)

Provide written or verbal comments about the student's work, and be positive in those comments. Rather than just writing "good" on a student's paper, briefly state what it was about it that made it good. Rather than simply saying or pointing out that the student didn't do it right, tell or show the student what is acceptable and how to achieve it. For reinforcement, use positive comments and encouragement as frequently as possible. Think before writing a comment on a student's paper, asking yourself how you think the student (or a parent or guardian) will interpret and react to the comment and if that is a correct interpretation or reaction to your intended meaning.

When assessing written work completed by English Language Learners (ELLs), provide separate feedback on the mechanics (spelling, punctuation, grammar) of the paper and the content. Avoid writing evaluative comments or grades in student journals.[4] Student journals are for encouraging students to write, to think about their thinking, and to record their creative thoughts. In journal writing, students should be encouraged to write about their experiences in and out of school and especially about their experiences related to what is being learned. They should be encouraged to write their feelings about what is being learned and about how they are learning it. Writing in journals gives them practice in expressing themselves in written form and in connecting their learning, and should provide nonthreatening freedom to do it. Avoid correcting spelling or grammar or making value statements. Comments and evaluations from teachers might discourage creative and spontaneous expression. You can write simple empathic comments such as "Thank you for sharing your thoughts," or "I think I understand what makes you feel that way."

When reading student journals, talk individually with students to seek clarification about their expressions. Student journals are useful to the teacher (of any subject) in understanding the student's thought processes and writing skills (diagnostic assessment) and should not be graded. For grading purposes, teachers may simply record whether the student is maintaining a journal and, perhaps, an assessment regarding the quantity of writing in it, but no judgment should be made about the quality.

When reviewing student portfolios, discuss with students individually the progress in their learning as shown by the materials in their portfolios. As with student journals, the portfolio should not be graded or compared in any way with those of other students. Its purpose is for student self-assessment and to show progress in learning. For this to happen, students should keep in their portfolios all or major samples of papers related to the course. (Student portfolios are discussed later.)

■ Assessment for Affective and Psychomotor Domain Learning

While assessment of cognitive domain learning lends itself to traditional written tests of achievement, the assessment of learning within the affective and psychomotor domains is best suited by the use of performance checklists where student behaviors can be observed in action. However, many educators today are encouraging the use of alternative assessment procedures (i.e., alternatives to traditional paper-and-pencil written testing). After all, in learning that is most important and that has the most meaning to students, the domains are inextricably interconnected. Learning that is meaningful to students is not as easily compartmentalized as the taxonomies of educational objectives would imply. Alternative assessment strategies include the use of projects, portfolios, skits, papers, oral presentations, and performance tests.

■ STUDENT INVOLVEMENT IN ASSESSMENT

Students' continuous self-assessment should be planned as an important component of the assessment program. If students are to progress in their understanding of their own thinking (metacognition) and in their intellectual development, then they must receive instruction and guidance in how to become more responsible for their own learning. During that empowerment process they learn to think better of themselves and of their individual capabilities. Achieving this self-understanding and improved self-esteem requires the experiences afforded by successes, along with guidance in self-understanding and self-assessment.

To meet these goals, teachers provide opportunities for students to think about what they are learning, about how they are learning it, and about how far they have progressed. Specifically, to engage students in the assessment process you can provide opportunities for the students to identify learning targets that are especially valued by the students; to help in the design of assessment devices for the units of study; to evaluate the tests that are furnished by the textbook publisher in terms of how well they match learning targets identified by you and the students; and to help interpret assessment results. To aid in the interpretation of results students can maintain portfolios of their work, using rating scales or checklists periodically to self-assess their progress.

Using Student Portfolios

Portfolios are used by teachers as a means of instruction and by teachers and students as one means of assessing student learning. Although there is little research evidence to support or to refute the claim, educators believe that the instructional value comes from the process of the student's assembling and maintaining a personal portfolio. During that creative process the student is expected to self-reflect and to think critically about what has and is being learned and assume some responsibility for his or her own learning.

Student portfolios fall into three general categories, and the purpose in a given situation may transcend some combination of all three. The categories are (a) *selected works portfolio*, in which students maintain samples of their work as prompted by the teacher; (b) *longitudinal or growth portfolio*, which is oriented toward outcome-driven goals and includes samples of student work from the beginning and end of the school term (or thematic unit of study) to exemplify achievement toward the goals; and (c) *passport or career portfolio*, which contains samples of student work that will enable the student to transition, such as from one school grade level to the next.

Student portfolios should be well-organized and, depending on the purpose (or category), should contain assignment sheets, class worksheets, the results of homework, project binders, forms for student self-assessment

and reflection on their work, and other class materials thought important by the students and teacher.[5] As a model of a real-life portfolio, you can share your personal career portfolio with your students (see Module 10).

Portfolio assessment: knowing and dealing with its limitations Although **portfolio assessment** has gained momentum in recent years as an alternative to traditional methods of evaluating student progress, establishing standards has been difficult. Research on the use of portfolios for assessment indicates that validity and reliability of teacher evaluation are often quite low. In addition, portfolio assessment is not always practical for use by every teacher. For example, if you are the sole art teacher at a middle school and are responsible for teaching art to every one of the 700 students in the school, you are unlikely to have the time or storage capacity for 700 portfolios. For your assessment of student learning, the use of checklists, rubrics, and student self-assessment may be more practical.

Before using portfolios as an alternative to traditional testing, you are advised to carefully consider and clearly understand the reasons for doing it and its practicality in your situation. Then decide carefully portfolio content, establish rubrics or expectation standards, anticipate grading problems, and consider and prepare for parent reactions.

While emphasizing the criteria for assessment, rating scales and checklists provide students with means of expressing their feelings and give the teacher still another source of input data for use in assessment. To provide students with reinforcement and guidance to improve their learning and development, teachers can meet with individual students to discuss their self-assessments. Such conferences should provide students with understandable and achievable short-term goals as well as help them develop and maintain an adequate self-esteem.[6]

Although almost any instrument used for assessing student work can be used for student self-assessment, in some cases it might be better to construct specific instruments with the student's understanding of the instrument in mind. Student self-assessment and self-reflection should be done on a regular and continuing basis so periodic comparisons can be made by the student. You will need to help students learn how to analyze these comparisons. Comparisons should provide a student with information previously not recognized about his or her own progress and growth.

Using Checklists

One of the items that can be maintained by students in their portfolios is a series of checklists. Checklist items

Checklist: Oral Report Assessment

Student _____   Date _____

Teacher _____   Time _____

Did the student:	Yes	No	Comments
1. Speak so that everyone could hear?	_____	_____	_____
2. Finish sentences?	_____	_____	_____
3. Seem comfortable in front of the group?	_____	_____	_____
4. Give a good introduction?	_____	_____	_____
5. Seem well informed about the topic?	_____	_____	_____
6. Explain ideas clearly?	_____	_____	_____
7. Stay on the topic?	_____	_____	_____
8. Give a good conclusion?	_____	_____	_____
9. Use effective visuals to make the presentation interesting?	_____	_____	_____
10. Give good answers to questions from the audience?	_____	_____	_____

FIGURE 9.4 ● Sample Checklist: Assessing a Student's Oral Report

can be used easily by a student to compare with previous self-assessments. Items on the checklist will vary depending on your purpose, subject, and grade level. (See sample forms, Figures 9.4 and 9.5.) Open-ended questions allow the student to provide additional information as well as to do some expressive writing. After a student has demonstrated each of the skills satisfactorily, a check is made next to the student's name, either by the teacher alone or in conference with the student.

Guidelines for using portfolios for assessment Here are general guidelines for using student portfolios in the assessment of learning.

■ Contents of the portfolio should reflect course aims and objectives.

■ Students should date everything that goes into their portfolios.

■ Determine what materials should be kept in the portfolio and announce clearly (post schedule in room) when, how, and by what criteria portfolios will be reviewed by you.

■ Give responsibility for maintenance of the portfolios to the students.

■ Portfolios should be kept in the classroom.

■ The portfolio should not be graded or compared in any way with those of other students. Its purpose is for student self-assessment and for showing progress in learning. For this to happen, students should keep in their portfolio all papers, or major papers, related to the course. For grading purposes, you can simply record whether or not the portfolio was maintained and, by checklist, whether all materials are in the portfolio that are supposed to be.

■ MAINTAINING RECORDS OF STUDENT ACHIEVEMENT

You must maintain well-organized and complete records of student achievement. You may do this on an electronic record book or in a written record book. At the very least, the record book should include attendance records and all records of scores on tests, homework, projects, and other assignments.

Daily interactions and events occur in the classroom that may provide informative data about a student's intellectual and psychological development. Maintaining a dated log of your observations of these interactions and events can provide important information that might otherwise be forgotten. At the end of a unit and again at the conclusion of a grading term, you will want to review your records. During the course of the school year, your anecdotal records (and those of other members of your teaching team) will provide important information about the development of each student and ideas for attention to be given to individual students.

■ Recording Teacher Observations and Judgments

You must think carefully about any written comments that you intend to make about a student. Teenagers can be quite sensitive to what others say about them, and most particularly to comments made about them by a teacher.

Additionally, we have seen anecdotal comments in students' permanent records that said more about the teachers who made the comments than about the recipient students. Comments that have been carelessly,

Checklist: Interdisciplinary Thematic Unit Learning

Student _____   Date _____

Teacher _____   Time _____

Did the student:	Yes	No	Comments/Evidence
1. Identify theme, topic, main idea of the unit	_____	_____	_____
2. Identify contributions of others to the theme	_____	_____	_____
3. Identify problems related to the unit of study	_____	_____	_____
4. Develop skills in:	_____	_____	_____
Applying knowledge	_____	_____	_____
Assuming responsibility	_____	_____	_____
Classifying	_____	_____	_____
Categorizing	_____	_____	_____
Decision making	_____	_____	_____
Discussing	_____	_____	_____
Gathering resources	_____	_____	_____
Impulse control	_____	_____	_____
Inquiry	_____	_____	_____
Justifying choices	_____	_____	_____
Listening to others	_____	_____	_____
Locating information	_____	_____	_____
Metacognition	_____	_____	_____
Ordering	_____	_____	_____
Organizing information	_____	_____	_____
Problem recognition/identification	_____	_____	_____
Problem solving	_____	_____	_____
Reading text	_____	_____	_____
Reading maps and globes	_____	_____	_____
Reasoning	_____	_____	_____
Reflecting	_____	_____	_____
Reporting to others	_____	_____	_____
Self-assessing	_____	_____	_____
Sharing	_____	_____	_____
Studying	_____	_____	_____
Summarizing	_____	_____	_____
Thinking	_____	_____	_____
Using resources	_____	_____	_____
Working with others	_____	_____	_____
Working independently	_____	_____	_____
(Others unique to the unit)	_____	_____	_____

Additional teacher and student comments:

FIGURE 9.5 ● Sample Checklist: Student Learning Assessment for Use with Interdisciplinary Thematic Instruction

hurriedly, and thoughtlessly made can be detrimental to a student's welfare and progress in school. Teacher comments must be professional; that is, they must be diagnostically useful to the continued intellectual and psychological development of the student. This is true for any comment you make or write, whether on a student's paper, on the student's permanent school record, or on a message sent to the student's home.

As an example, consider the following unprofessional comment observed in one student's permanent record. A teacher wrote, "John is lazy." Describing John as *lazy* could be done by anyone; it is nonproductive, and it is certainly not a professional diagnosis. How many times do you suppose John needs to receive such negative descriptions of his behavior before he begins to believe that he is just that—lazy—and as a result, to act that way even more often? Written comments like that can also be damaging because they may be read by the teacher who next has John in class and may lead that teacher to simply perpetuate the same expectation of John. To say that John is lazy merely describes behavior as judged by the teacher who wrote the comment. More important, and more professional, would be for the teacher to try to analyze *why* John is behaving that way, then to *prescribe* activities that are likely to motivate John to assume more constructive charge of his own learning behavior.

For students' continued intellectual and psychological development, your comments should be useful, productive, analytical, diagnostic, and prescriptive. The professional teacher makes diagnoses and prepares descriptions; a professional teacher does not label students as *lazy, vulgar, slow, stupid, difficult,* or *dumb.* The professional teacher sees the behavior of a student as being goal-directed. Perhaps *lazy* John found that particular behavioral pattern won him attention. John's goal, then, was attention (don't we all need attention?), and John assumed negative, perhaps even self-destructive, behavioral patterns to reach that goal. The professional task of any teacher is to facilitate the learner's understanding (perception) of a goal, and help the student identify acceptable behaviors positively designed to reach that goal.

GRADING AND MARKING STUDENT ACHIEVEMENT

If conditions were ideal (which they are not), and if teachers did their job perfectly well (which many of us do not), and if students all worked up to their academic potential, then all students would receive top marks (the ultimate in mastery or quality learning), and there would be less of a need here to talk about grading and marking. Mastery learning implies that some endpoint of learning is attainable; however, there probably isn't an endpoint. In any case, because conditions for teaching are never ideal and we teachers are mere humans, let us continue

with the topic of grading, which is undoubtedly of special interest to you, your students, their parents or guardians, and school counselors, administrators and school boards, potential employers, providers of scholarships, and college admissions officers.

The term *achievement*, used frequently throughout this book, means accomplishment, but is it accomplishment of the instructional objectives against preset standards, or is it simply accomplishment? Most teachers probably choose the former, where the teacher subjectively establishes a standard that must be met in order for a student to receive a certain grade for an assignment, project, test, quarter, semester, or course. Achievement, then, is decided by degrees of accomplishment.

Preset **standards** are usually expressed in percentages (degrees of accomplishment) needed for marks or ABC grades. If no student achieves the standard required for an A grade, for example, then no student receives an A. However, if all students meet the preset standard for the A grade, then all receive A's. Determining student grades on the basis of preset standards is referred to as *criterion-referenced grading*.

Criterion-Referenced Versus Norm-Referenced Grading

While criterion-referenced (or competency-based) grading is based on preset standards, **norm-referenced** grading measures the relative accomplishment of individuals in the group (e.g., one classroom of high school chemistry students) or in a larger group (e.g., all students enrolled in high school chemistry) by comparing and ranking students, and is commonly known as *grading on a curve.* Because it encourages competition and discourages cooperative learning, *norm-referenced grading is not recommended* for the determination of student grades. Norm-referenced grading is educationally dysfunctional. For your personal interest, after several years of teaching, you can produce frequency-distribution studies of grades you have given over a period of time, but *do not* give students grades that are based on a curve. The idea that grading and reporting should always be done in reference to learning criteria and never on a curve is well supported by research studies and authorities on the matter.[7] Grades for student achievement should be tied to performance levels and determined on the basis of each student's achievement toward preset standards.

In criterion-referenced grading, the aim is to communicate information about an individual student's progress in knowledge and work skills in comparison to that student's previous attainment or in the pursuit of an absolute, such as content mastery. Criterion-referenced grading is featured in programs that focus on personalized (individualized) education.

Criterion-referenced grading is based on the level at which each student meets the specified objectives (standards) for the course or grade level. The objectives must be clearly stated to represent important student learning outcomes. This approach implies that effective teaching and learning result in high grades (A's) or marks for most students. In fact, when a mastery concept is used, the student must accomplish the objectives before being allowed to proceed to the next learning task. The philosophy of teachers who favor criterion-referenced procedures recognizes individual potential. Such teachers accept the challenge of finding teaching strategies to help students progress from where they are to the next designated level. Instead of wondering how Juanita compares with Sally, the comparison is between what Juanita could do yesterday and what she can do today and how well these performances compare to the preset standard.

Most school systems use some sort of combination of both norm-referenced and criterion-referenced data usage. Sometimes both kinds of information are useful. For example, a report card for a student in the eighth grade might indicate how that student is meeting certain criteria, such as an A grade for addition of fractions. Another entry might show that this mastery is expected, however, in the sixth grade. Both criterion- and norm-referenced data may be communicated to the parents or guardians and the student. Appropriate procedures should be used: A criterion-referenced approach to show whether or not the student can accomplish the task, and if so, to what degree; and a norm-referenced approach to show how well that student performs compared to the larger group to which the student belongs. The latter is important data for college admissions officers and for committees that appropriate academic scholarships.

Determining Grades

Final grades have significant impacts upon the futures of students. When determining achievement grades for student performance, you must make several important and professional decisions. Although in a few schools, and for certain classes or assignments, only marks such as *E*, *S*, and *I* or "pass/no pass" are used, percentages of accomplishment and letter grades are used for most courses taught in middle and secondary schools.[8]

Guidelines for determining grades For determining student grades, consider the guidelines presented in the following paragraphs.

At the start of the school term, explain your grading policies *first to yourself,* then to your students and to their parents or guardians at back-to-school night, or by a written explanation that is sent home, or both. Share sample scoring and grading rubrics with students and parents. In fact, engaging students with you in the collaborative development of rubrics can be a potent bene-

fit to *instruction.*[9] In addition, include your grading policy when you cover your course syllabus.

When converting your interpretation of a student's accomplishments to a letter grade, be as objective as possible. For the selection of criteria for ABC grades, select a percentage standard, such as 92% for an A, 85% for a B, 75% for a C, and 65% for a D. Cutoff percentages used are your decision, although the district, school, program area, or department may have established guidelines that you are expected to follow.

For the determination of students' final grades, many teachers use a point system, where things that students write, say, and do are given points (but not journals or portfolios, except perhaps simply for whether the student does one or not); then the possible point total is the factor for determining grades. For example, if 92% is the cutoff for an A and 500 points are possible, then any student with 460 points or more $(500 \times .92)$ has achieved an A. Likewise, for a test or any other assignment, if the value is 100 points, the cutoff for an A is 92 $(100 \times .92)$. With a point system and preset standards, the teacher and students, at any time during the grading period, always know the current points possible and can easily calculate a student's current grade standing. Report grades frequently to students—weekly if possible, but no fewer than two times during a given semester. Then, as far as a current grade is concerned, students always know where they stand in the course.

It is important to remember that a grade of zero has a negative effect on student effort, motivation, and grade averages, especially when using a point system for grading. These negative effects caused by a zero grade can be offset by providing options such as the elimination of one low grade, second-effort rewards, and recovery (see Module 7).

Build your grading policy around degrees of accomplishment rather than failure and when students proceed from one accomplishment to the next. This *continuous promotion* is not necessarily the promotion of the student from one grade level to the next, but promotion within the classroom.

Remember that *assessment* and *grading* are not synonymous. As you learned earlier, assessment implies the collection of information from a variety of sources, including measurement techniques and subjective observations. These data, then, become the basis for arriving at a final grade, which in effect is a final value judgment. Grades are one aspect of evaluation and are intended to communicate educational progress to students and to their parents or guardians. To be valid as an indicator of that progress, data for determining a student's final grade must come from a variety of sources.

Decide beforehand your policy about make-up work. Students will be absent and will miss assignments and tests, so it is best that your policies about late assignments and missed tests be clearly communicated to students and to their parents or guardians. For make-up work, please consider the following.

Homework assignments As discussed earlier (in Module 7), we recommend that after due dates have been negotiated or set for assignments no credit or reduced credit be given for work that is turned in late. Sometimes, however, a student has legitimate reasons why he or she could not get an assignment done by the due date, and the teacher must exercise a professional judgment in each instance. Although it is important that teachers have rules and procedures—and that they consistently apply those—the teacher is a professional who must consider all aspects of a student's situation and, after doing so, show compassion, caring, and understanding of the human situation. (Refer to the section, Giving Students a Second Chance, in Module 7.)

Tests If students are absent when tests are given, you have several options. Some teachers allow students to miss or discount one test per grading period. Another technique is to allow each student to substitute a written homework assignment or project for one missed test. Still another option is to give the absent student the choice of either taking a make-up test or having the next test count double. When make-up tests are given, they should be taken within a week of the regular test unless there is a compelling reason (e.g., medical or family problem) why this cannot happen.

Sometimes students miss a testing period, not because of being absent from school but because of involvement in other school activities. In those instances, the student may be able to arrange to come into and take the test during another of your class periods, or your prep period, on that day or the next. If a student is absent during performance testing, the logistics and possible diminished reliability of having to readminister the test for one student may necessitate giving the student an alternate paper-and-pencil test or some other option.

Quizzes Many teachers give frequent and brief quizzes as often as every day. As opposed to tests (see next section), quizzes are usually brief (perhaps taking only 5 minutes of class time) and intended to reinforce the importance of frequent study and review. (However, quizzes should be prepared using the same care and precision as presented in the guidelines that follow in the sections for testing and preparation of assessment items.) When quizzes are given at frequent intervals, no single quiz should count very much toward the student's final grade. Therefore, you will probably want to avoid having to schedule and give make-up quizzes for students who were absent during a quiz period. The following are reasonable options for administering make-up quizzes and are presented here in order of our preference, the first item being our first choice. (a) Give a certain number of quizzes during a grading period, say 10, but allow a student to discount a few quiz scores, say 2 of the 10, thereby allowing the student to discount a low score or a missed quiz or both due to absence. (b) Count the next quiz double for a student who missed one due to absence. About the only problem with this option is when a student misses several quizzes. If that happens, (c) count the unit test a certain and relative percentage greater for any student who missed a quiz during that unit. By the way, we see absolutely no educational value in giving "pop" or unannounced quizzes that are graded and recorded.

■ TESTING FOR ACHIEVEMENT

One source of information used for determining grades is data obtained from testing for student achievement. There are two kinds of tests, those that are standardized and those that are not.

■ Standardized and Nonstandardized Tests

Standardized tests are those that have been constructed and published by commercial testing bureaus and used by states and districts to determine and compare student achievement, principally in the core subjects. Standardized norm-referenced tests are best for diagnostic purposes and should not be used for determining student grades. Space in this book does not allow a consideration of standardized achievement testing. Rather, our focus is on nonstandardized tests that are designed by you, the classroom teacher, for your own unique group of students.

Textbook publisher's tests, test item pools, and standardized tests are available from a variety of sources. However, those materials were not prepared for your students. Because schools, teachers, and students are different, most of the time you will be designing or collaboratively participating in designing and preparing tests for your own purposes for your distinct group of students.

Competent planning, preparing, administering, and scoring of tests is an important professional skill. You may want to refer to the guidelines that follow while you are student teaching, and again, occasionally, during your initial years as an employed teacher.

■ Purposes for Testing

Tests can be designed for several purposes, and a variety of kinds of tests and alternate test items will keep your testing program interesting, useful, and reliable. As a college student, you are probably most experienced with testing that measures achievement, but you will use tests for other reasons as well. Tests are also used to assess and aid in curriculum development; help determine teaching effectiveness; help students develop positive attitudes, appreciations, and values; help students increase their understanding and retention of facts, principles, skills, and concepts; motivate students; provide diagnostic information for planning for individualization of the instruction; provide review and drill to enhance teaching and learning; and serve as informational data for students and parents.

■ Frequency of Testing

First of all, assessment for student learning should be continual; that is, it should be going on every minute of every class day. For grading or marking purposes, it is difficult to generalize about how often to formally test for student achievement, but we believe that testing should be cumulative and frequent. By *cumulative*, we mean that each assessment should assess the student's understanding of previously learned material as well as for the current unit of study—that is, it should assess connected learning. By *frequent*, we mean as often as once a week for classes that meet for an hour or so each day. Advantages of assessment that is cumulative include the review, reinforcement, and articulation of old material with the most recent. Advantages of frequent assessment include a reduction in student anxiety over tests and an increase in the validity of the summative assessment.

■ Test Construction

After determining the reasons for which you are designing and administering a test, you need to identify the specific instructional objectives the test is being designed to measure. (As you learned in Module 4, your written instructional objectives are specific so that you can write assessment items to measure against those objectives, and that is criterion-referenced assessment.) So, the first step in test construction is identification of the purpose(s) for the test. The second step is to identify the objectives to be measured, and the third step is to prepare the test items. The best time to prepare draft items is after you have prepared your instructional objectives— while the objectives are fresh in your mind, which means before the lessons are taught. After a lesson is taught you will then want to rework your first draft of the test items to make any modifications based on the instruction that occurred.

■ Administering Tests

For many students, test taking can be a time of high anxiety. Middle school and secondary school students demonstrate test anxiety in various ways. Just before and during testing some are quiet and thoughtful, while others are noisy and disruptive. To more accurately measure student achievement you will want to take steps to reduce their anxiety. To control or reduce student anxieties, consider the following discussion as guidelines for administering tests.

Since many people respond best to a familiar routine, plan your formative assessment program so tests are given at regular intervals and administered at the same time and in the same way. In some secondary schools in particular, days of the week are assigned to departments for administering major tests. For example, Tuesdays might be assigned for language arts and mathematics testing, while Wednesday is the day for social studies and science testing.

Avoid tests that are too long and that will take too much time. Sometimes beginning teachers have unreasonable expectations of young people about their attention spans during testing. Frequent testing with frequent sampling of student knowledge is preferred over infrequent and long tests that attempt to cover everything.

Attend to creature comforts. Try to arrange the classroom so it is well ventilated, the temperature is comfortable, and, when giving paper-and-pencil tests individually, the seats are well spaced. If spacing is a problem, then consider group testing or using alternate forms of the test, where students seated adjacent to one another have different forms of the same test (for example, multiple choice answer alternatives are arranged in different order).

Before distributing the test, explain to students what they are to do when finished, such as quietly beginning an assignment or an anchor activity (see Module 5), because not all of the students will finish at the same time. It is unreasonable to expect most students to just sit quietly after finishing a test; they need something to do.

When ready to test, don't drag it out. Distribute tests quickly and efficiently. Once testing has begun, avoid interrupting the students. Items or announcements of important information can be written on the board, or if unrelated to the test, held until all students are finished with the test. Stay in the room and visually monitor the students. If the test is not going to take an entire class period (for class periods of 50 or more minutes, most shouldn't) and it's a major test, then administer it at the beginning of the period, if possible, unless you are planning a test review just prior to it (although that seems rather late to conduct a meaningful review).

■ Controlling Cheating

Cheating does occur. In a recent national survey of teachers, 90% of the teachers claimed that cheating by students was a problem.[10] There are steps you can take to discourage cheating in your classroom or to reduce the opportunity and pressure that cause students to cheat on tests. Consider the following.

Preventing cheating Space students or, as mentioned before, use alternate forms of the test. Another technique used by some teachers, especially those of middle schools and where students sit at tables rather than at individual desks, is to use space dividers. Space dividers can be made by attaching three approximately 8×10 inch rectangular sections of cardboard. The divider is placed in front of the student, making it impossible for neighboring students to see over. Dividers can be made from cardboard boxes or heavy folders of various sorts. It could be a project at the beginning of the year for each student to design and make his or her own space divider, which is then stored in the classroom for use on test days. Students enjoy being allowed to personalize their dividers.

Frequent testing and not allowing a single test to count too much toward a term grade reduce test anxiety and the pressure that can cause cheating, as well as increase student learning by "stimulating greater effort and providing intermittent feedback" to the student.[11] Prepare test questions that are clear and not ambiguous, thereby reducing student frustration that is caused by a question or instructions that students do not understand. Avoid giving tests that will take too much time. During long tests, some students get discouraged and restless; that is a time when classroom management problems can occur.

By their sheer nature, performance tests can cause pressure on students and can also provide greater opportunity for cheating. When administering performance tests to an entire class, it is best to have several monitors, such as members of your teaching team. If that isn't possible, consider testing groups of students, such as Cooperative Learning Groups, rather than individuals. Evaluation of test performance, then, would be based on group rather than individual achievement.

Consider using open-text and open-notebook tests or allowing each student to prepare a page of notes to use during the test. Allowing students to use their books and notes not only reduces anxiety but also helps them with the organization of information and the retention of what has been learned.

Stopping cheating The preceding paragraphs provide hints to prevent student cheating. If you suspect cheating is occurring, move and stand in the area of the suspected student. That will usually stop it.

Dealing with cheating When you suspect cheating has occurred, you are faced with a dilemma. Unless your suspicion is backed by solid proof, you are advised to forget it, but keep a close watch on the student the next time to prevent cheating from happening. Your job is not to catch students being dishonest but to discourage dishonesty. If you have absolute proof that a student has cheated, then you are obligated to proceed with school policy on student cheating, which may call for a session with the counselor or the student and the student's parent or guardian, perhaps an automatic *F* grade on the test, and even a temporary suspension from class.

TABLE 9.1	Approximate Time to Allow for Testing as Determined by the Types of Items*
Type of Test Item	**Time Needed Per Item**
Matching	1 minute per matching item
Multiple-choice	1 minute
Completion	1 minute
Completion drawing	2–3 minutes
Arrangement	2–3 minutes
Identification	2–3 minutes
Short explanation	2–3 minutes
Essay and performance	10 or more minutes

*Students with special needs and English Language Learners may need more time per item

Determining the Time Needed to Take a Test

Again, avoid giving tests that are too long and that will take too much time. Preparing and administering good tests is a skill that you will develop over time. In the meantime, it is best to test frequently and to use tests that sample student achievement rather than try for a comprehensive measure of that achievement.

Some students take more time on the same test than do others. You want to avoid giving too much time, or problems in classroom management will result. However you don't want to cut short the time needed by students who can do well but need more time to think and to write. As a very general guide, use the table of time needed for different types of test items (Table 9.1). This is only a guide for determining the approximate amount of time to allow students to complete a test. For example, for a test made up of 10 multiple-choice items, five arrangement items, and two short-explanation items, you would want to plan for about 30 minutes for students to complete the test.

PREPARING ASSESSMENT ITEMS

Preparing and writing good assessment items is yet another professional skill, and to become proficient at it takes study, time, practice, and reflection. Because of the importance of an assessment program, please assume this professional charge seriously and responsibly. Although poorly prepared items take no time at all to construct, they will cause you more trouble than you can ever imagine. As a professional you should take time to study different types of assessment items that can be used and how best to write them, and then practice writing them. Remember, when preparing assessment items, ensure that they match and sufficiently cover the instructional objectives. In addition, you should prepare each item carefully enough to be reasonably confident that each item will be understood by the student in the manner that you anticipate its being understood. With the diversity of students in today's school classroom, especially with respect to their proficiency in oral and written English language and students with special needs, this is an especially important point. Finally, after administering a test you must take time to analyze the results and reflect on the value of each item before ever using that item again.

General Guidelines for Preparing for Assessment

Consider the following six general guidelines when preparing for assessment. (a) Include several kinds of items and assessment instruments (see 12 types that follow). (b) Ensure that content coverage is complete (i.e., that all objectives are being measured). (c) Ensure that each item is reliable—that is, that it measures the intended objective. One way to check item reliability is to have more than one item measuring for the same objective. (d) Ensure that each item is clear and unambiguous to all students. (e) Plan each item to be difficult enough for the poorly prepared student but easy enough for the student who is well prepared. (f) Because it is time-consuming to write good assessment items, you are advised to maintain a bank of items, with each item coded according to its matching instructional objective, its domain of learning (cognitive, affective, or psychomotor), (perhaps) its level within the hierarchy of a particular domain, and whether it requires thinking that is recall, processing, or application. Computer software programs are available for this. Ready-made test item banks are available on computer disks and accompany many programs or textbooks. If you use them, be certain that the items were well written and match your course objectives. When preparing items for your test bank, use your creative thinking and best writing skills—prepare items that match your objectives, put them aside, think about them, then work them over again.

Every test that you administer to your students should represent your best professional effort—void of spelling and grammar errors. A quickly and poorly prepared test can cause you more grief than you can imagine. One that is obviously hurriedly prepared and wrought with spelling and grammar errors will quickly be frowned upon by discerning parents or guardians.

Classification of Assessment Items

Assessment items and assessment instruments (such as entire tests) can be classified as verbal (oral or written words), visual (pictures and diagrams), and manipulative or performance (handling of materials and equipment; performing). Written verbal items are the ones that have traditionally been most frequently used in test-

ing. However, visual items and visual tests are useful, for example, when working with students who lack fluency with the written word or when testing students who are English Language Learners.

Performance items and tests are useful when measuring for psychomotor skill development. Common examples are performance testing of a student's ability to carry a microscope or hold a jumping rope in place (gross motor skill) or to focus a microscope or to jump rope (fine motor skill). Performance testing also can and should be a part of a wider testing program that includes testing for higher-level thinking skills and knowledge, as, for example, when a student or small group of students is given the problem of creating from discarded materials a habitat for an imaginary animal and then display, write about, and orally present their product to the rest of the class.

For the past decade or so, and as noted often throughout this book, educators have taken a rekindled interest in this last described form of performance testing as a means of assessing learning that is closer to measuring for the real thing—that is, authentic. In a program for teacher preparation, **micro peer-teaching** and the **student teaching** experience are examples of performance assessment, that is, assessment practices used to assess the teacher candidate's ability to teach (to perform). It seems axiomatic that assessment of student teaching is a more authentic assessment of a candidate's ability to teach than would be a written (paper-and-pencil test) or verbal (oral test) form of assessment. Although less direct and perhaps less reliable than a check-list observation and analysis of a student teacher actually teaching, an observation of a student teacher's analysis of a videorecorded episode (that is, with pictures) of another teacher's performance would be another way of more authentically assessing a teacher's ability to teach than would be a paper-and-pencil response item test.

Performance Testing Can Be Expensive and Time-Intensive

Performance testing is usually more expensive and time-consuming than is verbal testing, which in turn is more time-demanding and expensive than is written testing. However, a good program of assessment will use alternate forms of assessment and not rely solely on one form (such as written) and one type of written item (such as multiple choice) so that all students have ample opportunities to demonstrate their learning.

The type of test and items that you use depend upon your purpose and objectives. Carefully consider the alternatives within that framework. To provide validity checks and to account for the individual differences of students, a good assessment program should include items from all three types. That is what writers of articles

CONTENT	BEHAVIORS								TOTAL
Social Studies Grade 8	Cognitive						Affective	Psycho-motor	
Ancient Greece	Knowl-edge	Compre-hension	Appli-cation	Analysis	Synthesis	Evalu-ation			
I. Vocabulary Development		2 (1,2)	1 (2)						3
II. Concepts		2	2 (3,4)						4
III. Applications	1	1 (5)	1 (5)	1 (5)	1 (5)	1 (5)			6
IV. Problem-solving			1 (6)		1 (6)				2
TOTAL	1	5	5	1	2	1			15

FIGURE 9.6 ● Table of Specifications I

CONTENT	BEHAVIORS							TOTAL
	Cognitive			Affective		Psychomotor		
	Input	Processing	Application	Low	High	Low	High	
I.								
II.								
III.								
IV.								
TOTAL								

FIGURE 9.7 ● Table of Specifications II

in professional journals are referring to when they talk about **alternative assessment.** They are encouraging the use of multiple assessment items, as opposed to the traditional heavy reliance on objective items such as multiple-choice questions.

■ Attaining Content Validity

To ensure that your test measures what is supposed to be measured, you can construct a table of specifications. A two-way grid indicates behavior in one dimension and content in the other (see Figures 9.6 and 9.7).

In this grid, behavior relates to the three domains: cognitive, affective, and psychomotor. In Figure 9.6, the cognitive domain is divided, according to Bloom's Taxonomy (Module 4), into six categories: Knowledge or simple recall, comprehension, application, analysis, synthesis (often involving an original product in oral or written form), and evaluation. The specifications table of Figure 9.6 does not specify levels within the affective and psychomotor domains.

To use a table of specifications, the teacher examining objectives for the unit decides what emphasis should be given to the behavior and to the content. For instance, if vocabulary development is a concern for this eighth-grade study of ancient Greece, then probably 20% of the test on vocabulary would be appropriate, but 50% would be unsuitable. This planning enables the teacher to design a test to fit the situation rather than a haphazard test that does not correspond to the objectives either in content or behavior emphasis. Since knowledge questions are easy to write, tests often fail to go beyond that level even though the objectives state that the student will analyze and evaluate. The sample table of specifications for an eighth-grade social studies unit on ancient Greece indicates a distribution of questions on a test. Since this test is to be an objective test and it is so difficult to write objective items to test affective and psychomotor behaviors, this table of specifications calls for no test items in these areas. If these categories are included in the unit objectives, some other assessment devices must be used to test learning in these domains. The teacher could also show the objectives tested, as indicated within parentheses in Figure 9.6. Then, checking later for inclusion of all objectives is easy.

Some teachers prefer the alternative table shown in Figure 9.7. Rather than differentiating among all six of Bloom's cognitive levels, this table separates cognitive objectives into just three levels: Those that require simple low-level recall of knowledge, those that require information processing, and those that require application of the new knowledge (refer to the section in Module 7, Levels of Cognitive Questions and Student Thinking). In addition, the affective and psychomotor domains each are divided into low- and high-level behaviors. A third alternative, not illustrated here, is a table of specifications that shows all levels of each of the three domains.

■ TYPES OF ASSESSMENT ITEMS: DESCRIPTIONS, EXAMPLES, AND GUIDELINES FOR PREPARING AND USING THEM

This section presents descriptions, advantages and disadvantages, and guidelines for preparing and using 12 types of assessment items. When reading about the advantages and disadvantages of each, you will notice that some types are appropriate for use in direct or performance assessment while others are not.

■ Arrangement

Description. Terms or real objects (**realia**) are to be arranged in a specified order.

Example 1. Arrange the following list of events on a timeline in the order of their occurrence: Maximilian I elected King of Germany; Maximilian I becomes Holy Roman Emperor; Diet of Augsburg establishes Council of Regency, divides Germany into six regions; Charles I of Spain becomes Holy Roman Emperor; Ferdinand I assumes the title of Holy Roman Emperor.

Example 2. The assortment of balls on the table represents the planets in our solar system. (*Note:* The balls are of various sizes, such as marbles, tennis balls, basketballs, and so on, each labeled with a planetary name, with a large sphere in the center labeled the Sun.) Arrange the balls in their proper order around the Sun.

Advantages. This type of item tests for knowledge of sequence and order and is good for review, for starting discussions, and for performance assessment. Example 2 is also an example of a performance test item.

Disadvantages. Scoring could be difficult, so be cautious and meticulous when using this type of item for grading purposes.

Guidelines for use. To enhance reliability, you may need to include instructions asking students to include the rationale for their arrangement, making it a combined arrangement and short-explanation type of assessment and allowing space for explanations on an answer sheet. This item is useful for small, heterogeneous group assessment to allow students to share and learn from their collaborative thinking and reasoning.

■ Completion Drawing

Description. An incomplete drawing is presented and the student is to complete it.

Example 1. Connect the following items with arrow lines to show the stages from introduction of a new bill to it becoming law (items not included here).

Example 2. In the following food web (not included here), draw arrow lines indicating which organisms are consumers and which are producers.

Advantages. This type requires less time than would a complete drawing that might be required in an essay item. Scoring is relatively easy.

Disadvantages. Care needs to be exercised in the instructions so students do not misinterpret the expectation.

Guidelines for use. Use occasionally for diversion, but take care in preparing. This type can be instructive when assessing for student thinking and reasoning as it can measure conceptual knowledge. Consider making the item a combined completion-drawing, short-explanation type by having students include their rationales for the thinking behind their completion drawing. Be sure to allow space for their explanations. This assessment item is useful for small, heterogeneous group assessment to allow students to share and learn from their collaborative thinking and reasoning.

■ Completion Statement

Description. Sometimes called a fill-in-the-blank item, an incomplete sentence is presented and the student is to complete it by filling in the blank space(s).

Example 1. A group of words that have a special meaning, such as "a skeleton in the closet," is called a(n) _____.

Example 2. To test their hypotheses, scientists and social scientists conduct _____.

Advantages. This type is easy to devise, take, and score.

Disadvantages. When using this type, there is a tendency to emphasize rote memory and measure procedural knowledge only. Provision of a word bank of possible answers is sometimes useful, especially with mainstreamed students, to reduce dependency on rote memory. It is difficult to write this type of item to measure for conceptual knowledge and higher levels of cognition. You must be alert for a correct response different from the expected. For example, in Example 2, although the teacher's key has *experiments* as the correct answer, a student might answer the question with *investigations* or *tests* or some other response that is equally valid.

Guidelines for use. Use occasionally for review or for pre-assessment of student knowledge. Avoid using this type of item for grading unless you can write quality items that extend student thinking beyond mere recall. In all instances, avoid copying items verbatim from the student book. As with all types, be sure to provide adequate space for students' answers and large spaces for students with motor control difficulties. Try to use only one blank per item.

■ Correction

Description. This is similar to the completion type except that sentences or paragraphs are complete but with italicized or underlined words that can be changed to make the sentences correct.

Example 1. The work of the TVA was started by building *sandcastles*. A *sandcastle* is a wall built across a *kid* to stop its flow. The *sandcastle* holds back the *football* so the *kids* do not overflow their *backpacks* and cause *tears*.

Example 2. 1, 1, 2, 3, 5, 8, *12*, 21, 34, *87*, 89.

Advantages. Writing this type of assessment item can be fun for the teacher for the purpose of preassessment of student knowledge or for review. Students may enjoy this type, especially when used only occasionally, for the tension relief afforded by the incorrect absurdities. This type can be useful for introducing words with multiple meanings.

Disadvantages. As with the completion type, the correction type tends to measure for low-level recall and rote memory (although this is not necessarily the case in Example 2; if a student is unfamiliar with the Fibonacci number series in mathematics, it would be a relatively high-level question). The underlined incorrect items could be so whimsical that they might cause more classroom disturbance than you want.

Guidelines for use. Use occasionally for diversion and discussion. Try to write items that measure for higher-level cognition. Consider making it a combined correction, short-explanation type. Be sure to allow space for student explanations.

■ Essay

Description. A question or problem is presented, and the student is to compose a response in the form of sustained prose, using the student's own words, phrases, and ideas, within the limits of the question or problem.

Example 1. In the story just read, does the author elaborate the setting in great detail or barely sketch it? Explain your response.

Example 2. A healthy green coleus plant sitting in front of you has been planted in fertile soil and sealed in a glass jar. If we place the jar on the windowsill where it will receive strong sunlight and the temperature inside the jar is maintained between 60 and 80°F, how long do you predict the plant will live? Justify your prediction.

Advantages. This type measures conceptual knowledge and higher mental processes, such as the ability to synthesize material and express ideas in clear and precise written language. It is especially useful in integrated thematic teaching. It provides practice in written expression and can be used in performance assessment, as is the case for Example 2.

Disadvantages. Essay items require a good deal of time to read and score. They tend to provide an unreliable sampling of achievement and are vulnerable to teacher subjectivity and unreliable scoring. Furthermore, they tend to punish the student who writes slowly and laboriously, one who has limited proficiency in the written language but who may have achieved as well as a student who writes faster and is more proficient in the language. Essay items tend to favor students who have fluency with words but whose achievement may not necessarily be better. In addition, unless the students have been given instruction in the meaning of key directive verbs and in how to respond to them, the teacher should not assume that all students understand such verbs (such as *explain* in the first example and *justify* in the second).

Guidelines for using an essay item

1. When preparing an essay-only test, many questions, each requiring a relatively short prose response (see the short-explanation type), are preferable to a smaller number of questions requiring long prose responses. Briefer answers tend to be more precise, and the use of many items provides a more reliable sampling of student achievement. When preparing short prose response questions, be sure to avoid using words verbatim from the student textbook.

2. Allow students adequate test time for a full response.

3. Different qualities of achievement are more likely comparable when all students must answer the same questions, as opposed to providing a list of essay items from which students may select those they answer.

4. After preparing essay items, make a tentative scoring key, and determine the key ideas you expect students to identify and how many points will be allotted to each.

Compare asks for an analysis of similarity and difference, but with a greater emphasis on similarities or likenesses.

Contrast asks more for differences than for similarities.

Criticize asks for the good and bad of an idea or situation.

Define means to express clearly and concisely the meaning of a term, as from a dictionary or in the student's own words.

Diagram means to put quantities or numerical values into the form of a chart, graph, or drawing.

Discuss means to explain or argue, presenting various sides of events, ideas, or situations.

Enumerate means to name or list one after another, which is different from "explain briefly" or "tell in a few words."

Evaluate means to express worth, value, and judgment.

Explain means to describe, with emphasis on cause and effect.

Generalize means to arrive at a valid generalization from provided specific information.

Identify means to state recognizable or identifiable characteristics.

Infer means to forecast what is likely to happen as a result of information provided.

Illustrate means to describe by means of examples, figures, pictures, or diagrams.

Interpret means to describe or explain a given fact, theory, principle, or doctrine within a specific context.

Justify means to show reasons, with an emphasis on correct, positive, and advantageous.

List means just that, to simply name items in a category or to include them in a list, without much description.

Outline means to give a short summary with headings and subheadings.

Prove means to present materials as witnesses, proof, and evidence.

Relate means to tell how specified things are connected or brought into some kind of relationship.

Summarize means to recapitulate the main points without examples or illustrations.

Trace means to follow a history or series of events, step by step, by going backward over the evidence.

FIGURE 9.8 ● Meaning of Key Directive Verbs for Essay Item Responses

5. Students should be informed about the relative test value for each item. Point values, if different for each item, can be listed in the margin of the test next to each item.

6. Inform students of the role of spelling, grammar, and sentence structure in your scoring of their essay items.

7. When reading student essay responses, read all student papers for one item at a time in one sitting, and, while doing that, make notes to yourself; then repeat and, while reading that item again, score each student's paper for that item. Repeat the process for the next item but alter the order of the papers so you are not reading them in the same order by student. While scoring essay responses, keep in mind the nature of the objective being measured, which may or may not include the qualities of handwriting, grammar, spelling, punctuation, and neatness.

8. To nullify the "halo effect" that can occur when you know whose paper you are reading, have students put their name on the back of the paper or use a number code rather than having students put their names on essay papers, so while reading the papers, you are unaware of whose paper is being read.

9. While having some understanding of a concept, many students are not yet facile with written expression, so you must remember to be patient, tolerant, positive, and prescriptive. Mark papers with positive and constructive comments, showing students how they could have explained or responded better.

10. Prior to using an essay question test item, give instruction and practice to students in responding to key directive verbs that will be used (see Figure 9.8).

■ Grouping

Description. Several items are presented, and the student is to select and group those that are in some way related.

Example 1. Separate the following words into two groups (words are not included here); those that are homonyms, place in group A, and those that are not homonyms, place in group B.

Example 2. Circle the figure that is least like the others (showing a wrench, screwdriver, saw, and swing).

Advantages. This type of item tests knowledge of grouping and can be used to measure conceptual knowledge, to gain higher levels of cognition, and to stimulate discussion. As Example 2 shows, it can be similar to a multiple-choice item.

Disadvantages. Remain alert for the student who has an alternative but valid rationale for her or his grouping.

Guidelines for use. To allow for an alternative correct response, consider making the item a combination grouping, short-explanation type, being certain to allow adequate space to encourage student explanations.

■ Identification

Description. Unknown "specimens" are to be identified by name or some other criterion.

Example 1. Identify each of the plant specimens on the table by its common name.

Example 2. Identify by style each of the three poems shown on the screen.

Advantages. Verbalization (i.e., the use of abstract symbolization) is less significant, as the student is working with real materials; identification should be measuring for higher-level learning rather than simple recall. The item can also be written to measure for procedural understanding, such as for the identification of steps for booting up a computer program. This is another useful type of item for authentic and performance assessments.

Disadvantages. Because of a special familiarity with the material, some students may have an advantage over others; to be fair, specimens used should be equally familiar or unfamiliar to all students. This type takes more time than many of the other item types, both for the teacher to prepare and for students to do.

Guidelines for use. Whatever specimens are used, they must be familiar to all or to none of the students, and they must be clear, not confusing (e.g., fuzzy photographs or unclear photocopies, dried and incomplete plant specimens, and garbled music recordings can be confusing and frustrating to try to discern). Consider using dyad or team rather than individual testing.

■ Matching

Description. Students are to match related items from a list of numbered items to a list of lettered choices or in some way to connect those items that are the same or are related. Or, to eliminate paper-and-pencil and make the item more direct, use an item such as, "Of the materials on the table, pair up those that are most alike."

Example 1. In the blank space next to each description in column A (stem or premises column) put the letter of the correct answer from column B (answer or response column).

A (stem column)

___1. Current president of the United States
___2. Most recent past president of the United States
___3. U.S. president during the Persian Gulf War
___4. First president of the United States

B (answer column)
A. Bill Clinton
B. George W. Bush
C. Thomas Jefferson
D. George Washington
E. etc.

Example 2. Match items in column A (stem column) to those in column B (answer column) by drawing lines connecting the matched pairs.

Column A	Column B
ann/enn	conquer
auto	large
min	self
vic/vinc	small
(etc.)	year

Advantages. Matching items can measure for ability to judge relationships and to differentiate between similar facts, ideas, definitions, and concepts. They are easy to score and can test a broad range of content. They reduce guessing, especially if one group (e.g., answer column) contains more items than the other and they are interesting to students and adaptable for performance assessment.

Disadvantages. Although the matching item is adaptable for performance assessment, items are not easily adapted to measuring for higher cognition. Because all parts must be homogeneous, it is possible that clues will be given, thus reducing item validity.

Guidelines for use. The number of items in the response or answer column should exceed the number in the stem column. The number of items in the stem column to be matched should not exceed 10. Less is better. Matching sets should have high homogeneity (i.e., items in both columns or groups should be of the same general category; avoid, for example, mixing dates, events, and names). Answers in the response column should be kept short, to one or two words each, and should be ordered logically, such as alphabetically. If answers from the response column can be used more than once, and that is advised to avoid guessing by elimination, the directions should so state. Be prepared for the student who can legitimately defend an incorrect response.

■ Multiple Choice

Description. This type is similar to the completion item in that statements are presented (the stem), sometimes in incomplete form, but with several options or alternatives requiring recognition or even higher cognitive processes rather than mere recall.

Example 1. Of four cylinders with the following dimensions, the one that would cause the highest-pitched sound would be

   a. 4 inches long and 3 inches in diameter.

   b. 4 inches long and 1 inch in diameter.

   c. 8 inches long and 3 inches in diameter.

   d. 8 inches long and 1 inch in diameter.

Example 2. Which one of the following is a pair of antonyms?

   a. loud—soft

   b. halt—finish

   c. absolve—vindicate

   d. procure—purchase

Advantages. Items can be answered and scored quickly. A wide range of content and higher levels of cognition can be tested in a relatively short time. This type is excellent for all testing purposes—motivation, review, and assessment of learning.

Disadvantages. Unfortunately, because multiple-choice items are relatively easy to write, there is a tendency to write items measuring only for low levels of cognition. Multiple-choice items are excellent for major testing, but it takes care and time to write quality questions that measure higher levels of thinking and learning.

Guidelines for using multiple-choice items

1. If the item is in the form of an incomplete statement, it should be meaningful in itself and imply a direct question rather than merely lead into a collection of unrelated true and false statements.

2. Use a level of language that is easy enough for even the poorest readers and those who are English Language Learners to understand; avoid unnecessary wordiness.

3. If there is much variation in the length of alternatives, arrange the alternatives in order from shortest to longest (i.e., first alternative is the shortest, last alternative is the longest). For single-word alternatives, consistent use of arrangement of alternatives is recommended, such as by length of answer or alphabetically.

4. Arrangement of alternatives should be uniform throughout the test and listed in vertical (column) form rather than in horizontal (paragraph) form.

5. Incorrect responses (distracters) should be plausible and related to the same concept as the correct alternative. Although an occasional humorous distracter may help relieve test anxiety, along with absurd dis-

tracters they should generally be avoided. They offer no measuring value and increase the likelihood of the student *guessing* the correct response.

6. It is not necessary to maintain a fixed number of alternatives for every item, but the use of less than three is not recommended. Although it is not always possible to come up with four or five plausible responses, the use of four or five reduces chance responses and guessing, thereby increasing reliability for the item. If you cannot think of enough plausible distracters, include the item on a test the first time as a completion item. As students respond, wrong answers will provide you with a number of plausible distracters that you can use the next time to make the item a multiple-choice type item.

7. Some students (with special needs) may work better when allowed to circle their selected response rather than writing its letter or number in a blank space.

8. Responses such as "all of these" or "none of these" should be used only when they will contribute more than another plausible distracter. Care must be taken that such responses answer or complete the item. "All of the above" is a poorer alternative than "none of the above" because items that use it as a correct response need to have four or five correct answers; also, if it is the right answer, knowledge of any two of the distracters will cue it.

9. Every item should be grammatically consistent. For example, if the stem is in the form of an incomplete sentence, it should be possible to complete the sentence by attaching any of the alternatives to it.

10. The stem should state a single and specific point.

11. The stem must mean the same thing to every student.

12. The item should be expressed in positive form. A negative form can present a psychological disadvantage to students. Negative items are those that ask what is not characteristic of something or what is the least useful. Discard the item if you cannot express it in positive terminology.

13. The stem must not include clues to the correct alternative. For example, "A four-sided figure whose opposite sides are *parallel* is called _____ ."

   a. an octagon

   b. a parallelogram

   c. a trapezoid

   d. a triangle

Use of the word *parallel* clues the answer.

14. There must be only one correct or best response. However, this is easier said than done (refer to guideline 19).

15. Measuring for understanding of definitions is better tested by furnishing the name or word and requiring choice between alternative definitions than by presenting the definition and requiring choice between alternative words.

16. Avoid using alternatives that include absolute terms such as *never* and *always*.

17. Multiple-choice items need not be entirely verbal. Consider the use of realia, charts, diagrams, videos, and other visuals. This will make the test more interesting, especially to students with low verbal abilities or those who are English Language Learners. Consequently, it will make the assessment more direct.

18. Once you have composed a series of multiple-choice items or a test comprised completely of this item type, tally the position of answers to be sure they are evenly distributed, to avoid the common psychological habit (when there are four alternatives) of having the correct alternative in the third position. In other words, when alternative choices are A, B, C, and D, or 1, 2, 3, and 4, unless the test designer is aware and avoids it, more correct answers will be in the "C" or "3" position than in any other.

19. Consider providing space between test items for students to include their rationales for their response selections, thus making the test a combination multiple-choice and short-explanation item type. This provides for the measurement of higher levels of cognition and encourages writing. It provides for the student who can rationalize an alternative that you had not considered plausible, which is especially possible today with the diversity of cultural experiences represented by students. For example, we recall the story of the math question on a test that asked if a farmer saw eight crows sitting on a fence and shot three of them, how many would be left. Of course, the "correct" response on the answer key was 5. However, one critical-thinking student chose *none* as his response, an answer that was marked "wrong" by the teacher. However, the student was thinking that those crows that weren't shot would be frightened and would all fly away, thus he selected *none* as his answer.

20. While scoring, on a blank copy of the test, for each item tally the incorrect responses. Analyze incorrect responses for each item to discover potential errors in your scoring key. If, for example, many students

select B for an item for which your key says the correct answer is A, you may have made a mistake on your scoring key or in teaching the lesson.

21. Sometimes teachers attempt to discourage cheating by preparing several versions of the multiple-choice exam with the questions in different order. This could be giving one group of students an unfair advantage if the order of their questions is in the same sequence in which the information was originally presented and learned and, for another group of students, the questions are in a random order. To avoid this, questions should be in random order on every version of the exam.

■ Performance

Description. Provided with certain conditions or materials, the student solves a problem or accomplishes some other action.

Example 1. Write a retelling of your favorite fable and create a diorama to go along with it.

Example 2. (As a culminating project for a unit on sound, groups of students were challenged to design and make their own musical instruments.) The performance assessment included:

1. Play your instrument for the class.
2. Show us the part of the instrument that makes the sound.
3. Describe the function of other parts of your instrument.
4. Demonstrate how you change the pitch of the sound.
5. Share with us how you made your instrument.

Example 3. Demonstrate your understanding of diffusion by designing and completing an experiment using only those chemicals and materials located at this learning station.

Example 4. Measure and calculate the square footage of our gymnasium playing floor to the nearest centimeter.

Advantages. Performance test item types come closer to direct measurement (authentic assessment) of certain expected outcomes than do most other types. As has been indicated in discussions of the preceding question types, other types of questions can actually be prepared as performance-type items, that is, where the student actually does what he or she is being tested for.

---

1. Specify the performance objective.
2. Specify the test conditions.
3. Establish the standards or criteria (scoring rubric) for judging the quality of the process and/or product.
4. Prepare directions in writing, outlining the situation, with instructions that the students are to follow.
5. Share the procedure with a colleague for feedback before using it with students.

FIGURE 9.9 ● Procedure for Setting Up a Performance Assessment Situation

Disadvantages. This type can be difficult and time-consuming to administer to a group of students. Maintaining an adequate supply of materials could be a problem. Scoring may tend to be subjective. It could be difficult to give make-up tests to students who were absent.

Guidelines for use. Use your creativity to design and use performance tests, as they tend to measure well the important objectives. To reduce subjectivity in scoring, prepare distinct scoring guidelines (rubrics), as was discussed in scoring essay-type items and as shown, for example, in Figures 9.10 and 9.11. To set up a performance assessment situation, see instructions in Figure 9.9.

■ Short Explanation

Description. The short explanation question is like the essay type but requires a shorter answer.

Example 1. Briefly explain in a paragraph how you would end the story.

Example 2. Briefly explain why organ pipes are made to vary in length.

Advantages. As with the essay type, student understanding is assessed, but this type takes less time for the teacher to read and to score. By using several questions of this

	14–15	12–13	11	1–10
Parenthetical References	All documented correctly. Paper's references document a wide variety of sources cited—at least five from bibliography.	Most documented correctly. Few minor errors. At least three sources from bibliography are cited.	Some documented correctly. Some show no documentation at all. May not correlate to the bibliography.	Few to none are documented. Does not correlate to the bibliography. May be totally absent.
	14–15	**12–13**	**11**	**1–10**
Bibliography and Sources	Strong use of library research. Exceeds minimum of five sources. Bibliography is correctly formatted.	Good use of library research. Exceeds minimum of five sources. Bibliography has few or no errors in format.	Some use of library research. Meets minimum of five sources. Bibliography is present but may be problematic.	Fails to meet minimum standards for library research. Bibliography has major flaws or may be missing.
	14–15	**12–13**	**11**	**1–10**
Mechanics/ Format	Correct format and pagination. Neat title page, near-perfect spelling, punctuation, and grammar.	Mostly correct format and pagination. Neat. Few errors in title page, spelling, punctuation, and grammar.	Errors in format and pagination. Flawed title page. Distracting errors in spelling, punctuation, and grammar.	Incorrect format. Title page is flawed or missing. Many errors in spelling, punctuation, and grammar. Lack of planning is obvious. Paper is difficult to read.
	9–10	**8**	**7**	**1–6**
Thesis	An original and comprehensive thesis that is clear and well thought out. All sections work to support it.	Comprehensive and well-focused thesis, which is clearly stated. All sections work to support it.	Adequate thesis that is understandable but may be neither clear nor focused. It covers the majority of the issues found in the sections.	Inadequate thesis that is disconnected from the research or may be too broad to support. May be convoluted, confusing, or absent.
	18–20	**16–17**	**14–15**	**1–13**
Completeness/ Coherence	Paper reads as a unified whole. There is no repetition of information. All sections are in place, and transitions between them are clearly developed.	Paper reads as a unified whole with no repetition. All sections are in place, but transitions between them are not as smooth.	Paper has required sections. Repetitions may be evident. The paper does not present a unified whole. Transitions are missing or inadequate.	Paper lacks one or more sections and makes no attempt to connect sections as a whole unit. Sections may be grossly repetitive or contradictory.
	23–25	**20–22**	**18–19**	**1–16**
Thinking/Analyzing	Strong understanding of the topic. Knowledge is factually relevant, accurate, and consistent. Solutions show analysis of research discussed in paper.	Good understanding of the topic. Uses main points of information researched. Solutions build on examination of research discussed in paper.	General understanding of topic. Uses research and attempts to add to it; solutions refer to some of the research discussed.	Little understanding of topic. Uses little basic information researched. Minimal examination of the topic. Solutions may be based solely on own opinions, without support.

FIGURE 9.10 ● Sample of a Scoring Rubric for Student Research Paper. Possible score = 100. Scorer marks a relevant square in each of the six categories (the horizontal rows), and the student's score for that category is the number within that square.

SOURCE: Elk Grove School District, Elk Grove, CA. Used with permission.

Professional Presentation	**14–15** Well organized; smooth transitions between sections; all enthusiastically participate and share responsibility.	**12–13** Well organized with transitions, students confer/present ideas; group shows ability to interact; attentive discussion of research.	**11** Shows basic organization; lacks transitions; some interaction; discussion focuses mostly on research.	**1–10** Unorganized, lacks planning; no transitions; reliance on one spokes-person; little interaction; disinterest; too brief.
Engagement of Audience	**14–15** Successfully and actively engages audience in more than one pertinent activity; maintains interest throughout.	**12–13** Engages audience in at least one related activity; maintains attention through most of presentation.	**11** Attempts to engage audience in at least one activity; no attempt to involve *entire* audience. May not relate in significant way.	**1–10** Fails to involve audience; does not maintain audience's attention; no connection with audience. No relationship between activity and topic.
Use of Literature	**18–20** Strong connection between literature and topic; significant, perceptive explanation of literature; pertinent to topic. At least two pieces used.	**16–17** Clear connection between literature and topic; clear explanation; appropriate to topic. Two pieces used.	**14–15** Weak connection to topic; unclear explanation; one genre; one piece used.	**1–13** No connection to topic; no explanation; inappropriate literature; no literature.
Knowledge of Subject	**18–20** Strong understanding of topic; knowledge factually relevant, accurate, and consistent; solution shows analysis of evidence.	**16–17** Good understanding of topic; uses main points of information researched; builds solution on examination of major evidence.	**14–15** Shows general understanding; focuses on one aspect, discusses at least one other idea; uses research, attempts to add to it; solution refers to evidence.	**1–13** Little understanding or comprehension of topic; uses little basic information researched; forms minimal solution; relies solely on own opinions without support.
Use of Media	**18–20** Effectively combines and integrates three distinct forms with one original piece; enhances understanding; offers insight into topic.	**16–17** Combines two forms with one original piece; relates to topic; connection between media and topic is explained.	**14–15** Includes two or three forms but no original piece; media relates to topic. Explanation may be vague or missing.	**1–13** One form; no original piece; connection between media and topic is unclear.
Speaking Skills	**9–10** Clear enunciation; strong projection; vocal variety; eye contact with entire audience; presentation posture; solid focus with no interruptions.	**8** Good enunciation; adequate projection; partial audience eye contact; appropriate posture.	**7** Inconsistent enunciation; low projection with little vocal variety; inconsistent posture.	**1–6** Difficult to understand; inaudible; monotonous; no eye contact; inappropriate posture; interruptions and distractions.

FIGURE 9.11 ● Sample of a Scoring Rubric for Student Project Presentation. Possible score = 100. Scorer marks a relevant square in each of the six categories (the horizontal rows), and the student's score for that category is the number within that square.

SOURCE: Elk Grove School District, Elk Grove, CA. Used with permission.

type, a greater amount of content can be covered than with a lesser number of essay questions. This type of question is good practice for students to learn to express themselves succinctly in writing.

Disadvantages. Some students will have difficulty expressing themselves in a limited fashion or in writing. They need practice, coaching, and time.

Guidelines for use. This type is useful for occasional reviews and quizzes and as an alternative to other types of questions. For scoring, establish a scoring rubric and follow the same guidelines as for the essay-type item.

■ True-False

Description. A statement is presented that students are to judge as being accurate or not.

Example 1. A suffix is any bound morpheme added to the end of a root word. T or F?

Example 2. Christopher Columbus discovered America in 1492. T or F?

Advantages. Many items can be answered in a relatively short time, making broad content coverage possible. Scoring is quick and simple. True-false items are good as discussion starters, for review, and for diagnostic evaluation (preassessment) of what students already know or think they know.

Disadvantages. It is sometimes difficult to write true-false items that are purely true or false or without qualifying them in such a way that clues the answer. In the second sample question, for example, the student may question whether Columbus really did discover America or misunderstand the meaning of *discovering America*. Weren't there people already there when he landed? Where, in fact, did he land? What is meant by *America?* Example 2 is poor also because it tests for more than one idea—Columbus, America, and 1492. Much of the content that most easily lends itself to the true-false type of test item is trivial. Students have a 50% chance of guessing the correct answer, thus giving this item type both *poor validity and poor reliability.* Scoring and grading give no clue about why the student missed an item. Finally, for students who tend to think abstractly, true-false items cause unwanted stress because those students tend to analyze every word, reading much more into the questions than necessary. Consequently, the disadvantages of true-false items far outweigh the advantages; *pure true-false items should not be used for arriving at grades.*

Guidelines for preparing true-false items

1. For preparing a false statement, first write the statement as a true statement, then make it false by changing a word or phrase.
2. Try to avoid using negative statements since they tend to confuse students.
3. A true-false statement should include only one idea.
4. Use close to an equal number of true and false items.
5. Try to avoid using specific determiners (e.g., *always, all,* or *none*), because they usually clue that

the statement is false. Avoid also words that may clue that the statement is true (e.g., *often, probably,* and *sometimes*).

6. Avoid words that may have different meanings for different students.
7. Avoid using verbatim language from the student textbook.
8. Avoid trick items, such as a slight reversal of numbers in a date.
9. Rather than using symbols for the words *true* and *false* (sometimes teachers use symbols such as 1 and 2) which might be confusing, or having students write the letters *T* and *F* (sometimes a student does not write the letters clearly enough for the teacher to be able to distinguish which it is), have students either write out the words *true* and *false* or, better yet, have students simply circle *T* and *F* in the left margin of each item as indicated by the two previous samples.
10. Proofread your items (or have a friend do it) to be sure that sentences are well-constructed and free from typographical errors.
11. To avoid "wrong" answers, caused by variations in thinking, and to make the item more valid and reliable, students should be encouraged to write in their rationale for selecting *true* or *false*, making the item a *modified true-false* item. For example, When a farmer saw 8 crows sitting on the fence surrounding his corn field, he shot 3 of them. Five were left on the fence. T or F? _____

    *Explanation:*_____

Now do Exercise 9.1 to start the development of your skill in writing assessment items. As you work on Exercise 9.1, you may want to correlate it with your previous work on Exercises 3.5 and 4.7.

EXERCISE 9.1

■ Preparing Assessment Items

Instructions: The purpose of this exercise is to practice your skill in preparing the different types of assessment items discussed in the previous section. For use in your own teaching, select one specific instructional objective and write assessment items for it. When completed, share this exercise with your classmates for their feedback.

Objective:

Grade and subject:

1. Arrangement item

2. Completion drawing item

3. Completion statement item

(continued)

4. Correction item

5. Essay item

6. Grouping item

7. Identification item

8. Matching item

9. Multiple-choice item

10. Performance item

11. Short-explanation item

12. *Modified* true-false item

 To access this exercise online, go to the Companion Website at **www.prenhall.com/kellough.**

■ REPORTING STUDENT ACHIEVEMENT

One of your responsibilities as a classroom teacher is to report student progress in achievement to parents or guardians as well as to the school administration for record keeping. In some instances the reporting is of student progress and effort as well as achievement. As described in the discussions that follow, reporting is done in at least two and sometimes more than two ways.

■ The Grade Report

Periodically a grade report (report card) is issued (generally from three to six times a year, depending upon the school, its purpose, and its type of scheduling). Grade reports may be distributed during an advisory period or they may be mailed to the student's home. This grade report represents an achievement grade (formative evaluation). The final report of the semester is the semester grade, and for courses that are only one semester long it also is the final grade (summative evaluation). In essence, the first and sometimes second reports are progress notices, with the semester grade being the one that is transferred to the student's transcript of records.

In addition to the student's academic achievement, you must report the student's social behaviors (classroom conduct) while in your classroom. Whichever reporting form is used, you must separate your assessments of a student's social behaviors from the student's academic achievement. Academic achievement (or accomplishment) is represented by a letter (sometimes a number) grade (*A* through *E* or *F*, or *E*, *S*, and *U*, *P* or *F*, or *1* to *5*,

and sometimes with minuses and pluses), and the social behavior by a *satisfactory* or an *unsatisfactory*, by more specific items, or supplemented by teacher-written or computer-generated comments.

In addition to grading and reporting on subject matter knowledge, some secondary schools are including a broader set of *workplace or life skills* that transcend particular subject areas. For example, Academy High School (Fort Myers, FL) uses a *work ethic checklist* that is part of the senior portfolio in the school's internship preparation program.

In some instances, especially at the middle school level, there may be a location on the reporting form for the teacher to check whether basic grade-level standards have been met in the core subjects.

■ MORE ABOUT PARENTAL INVOLVEMENT AND HOME-SCHOOL CONNECTIONS

Study after study shows that when parents get involved in their child's school and school work, students learn better and earn better grades, and teachers experience more positive feelings about teaching. As a result, many schools increasingly are searching for new and better ways to involve parents. What follows are additional suggestions and resources.

■ Contacting Parents

Although it is not always obligatory, some teachers make a point to contact parents or guardians by telephone or by e-mail, especially when a student has shown a sudden turn for either the worse or the better in academic achievement or in classroom behavior. That initiative and contact by the teacher are usually welcomed by parents and can lead to productive conferences with the teacher. By being proactive and making the first contact, you show concern and you may gain an ally.

Another way of contacting parents is by letter. You may ask for help in translating your letter for culturally and linguistically diverse parents. Contacting a parent by letter gives you time to think and to make clear your thoughts and concerns to that parent and to invite the parent to respond at her or his convenience by letter, by phone, or by arranging to have a conference with you.

Also, most schools have either a computer-link assignment/progress report hotline for parent use, or a progress report form that, upon request by a parent, can be obtained as often as weekly.

■ Meeting Parents

You will meet some of the parents or guardians early in the school year during fall "back-to-school," "meet-the-teacher," or "curriculum" night; throughout the year in individual parent conferences; and later in the year during spring open house. For the beginning teacher, these meetings with parents can be anxious times. But, in fact, it is a time to celebrate your work and to solicit parental support. The following paragraphs provide guidelines to help you with those experiences.[12]

Back-to-school night is the evening early in the school year when parents (and guardians) come to the school and meet their children's teachers. After arriving at the school at a designated time, the parents proceed through a simulation of their child's school day; as a group, they meet each class and each teacher for a few minutes. Later, in the spring, there is an open house where parents may have more time to talk individually with teachers, although the major purpose of the open house is for the school and teachers to celebrate and display the work and progress of the students for that year. Throughout the school year, there will be opportunities for you and parents to meet and talk about their child.

At back-to-school night, parents are anxious to learn as much as they can about their children's teachers. You will meet each group of parents for a brief time, perhaps about 10 minutes. During that meeting you will provide them with a copy of the course syllabus, make some straightforward remarks about yourself, and talk about the course, its requirements, your expectations of the students, and how the parents can support their children's learning.

Although there will be precious little time for questions from the parents, during your introduction the parents will be delighted to learn that you have your program well planned, appreciate their interest and welcome their support, and will communicate with them. The parents and guardians will be pleased to know that

you are "from the school of the three Fs"—that is, that you are firm, friendly, and fair.

Specifically, parents will expect to learn about your curriculum—goals and objectives, any long-term projects, class size, when tests will be given and whether given on a regular basis, and your grading procedures. They will want to know what you expect of them: Will there be homework, and if so, should they help their children with it? How can they contact you? Try to anticipate other questions. Your principal, department chair, or colleagues can be of aid in helping you anticipate and prepare for these questions. Of course, you can never prepare for the question that comes from left field. Just remain calm and avoid being flustered (or at least appear so). Ten minutes will fly by quickly, and parents will be reassured to know you are an in-control person.

■ Parent Conferences

When meeting parents for conferences, you should be as specific as possible when explaining to a parent the progress of that parent's child in your class. Again, express your appreciation for parents' interest. Be helpful to their understanding, and avoid overwhelming the parent with more information than he or she needs. Resist any tendency to talk too much. Allow time for the parent to ask questions. Keep your answers succinct. Never compare one student with another or with the rest of the class. If the parent asks a question for which you do not have an answer, tell the parent you will try to find an answer and will phone the parent as quickly as you can. Then do it. Have students' portfolios and other work with you during the parent conference so you can show examples of what is being discussed. Also, have your grade book on hand, or a computer printout of it, but be prepared to protect from parents the names and records of other students.

Sometimes it is helpful to have a three-way conference, a conference with the parent, the student, and you, or a conference with the parent, the principal or counselor, and several or all of the student's teachers. If, especially as a beginning teacher, you would like the presence of an administrator at a parent-teacher conference as backup, don't be hesitant to arrange that.

Some educators prefer a student-led conference, arguing that "placing students in charge of the conference makes them individually accountable, encourages them to take pride in their work, and encourages student-parent communication about school performance."[13] However, like most innovations in education, the concept of student-led conferences has its limitations—the most important of which perhaps is the matter of time.[14]

When a parent asks how she or he may help in the student's learning, the paragraphs that follow offer suggestions for your consideration. Many schools have made special and successful efforts to link home and school. At some schools, through homework hotlines, parents have

Alliance for Parental Involvement in Education, P.O. Box 59, East Chatham, NY 12060-0059; 518-392-6900.
Center on Families, Communities, Schools & Children's Learning, 3505 N. Charles St., Baltimore, MD 21218; 410-516-8800.
National Coalition for Parent Involvement in Education, Box 39, 1201 16th St., NW, Washington, DC 20036.
National Community Education Association, 3929 Old Lee Highway, Suite 91A, Fairfax, VA 22030-2401; 703-359-8973.
National PTA, 330 North Wabash Ave., Ste. 2100, Chicago, IL60611-3690; 312-670-6782.
Parents for Public Schools, P.O. Box 12807, Jackson, MS 39236-2807; 800-880-1222.

FIGURE 9.12 ● Resources for Developing Home-School Partnerships

phone access to their children's assignment specifications and to their progress in their schoolwork, and parents with a personal computer and a modem have access to tutorial services to assist their children with assignments.

Helping students become critical thinkers is one of the aims of education and one that parents can help with by reinforcing the strategies being used in the classroom. Ways to do this are to ask "what if" questions; think aloud as a model for the student's thinking development; encourage the student's own metacognition by asking questions such as, "How did you arrive at that conclusion?" or "How do you feel about your conclusion now?" and asking these questions about the student's everyday social interactions, topics that are important to the student; ask the student to elaborate on his or her ideas; and accept the fact that the young person may make mistakes but encourage the student to learn from them.

Many resources are available for parents to use at home. The U.S. government, for example, has a variety of free or low-cost booklets available. For information, contact the Consumer Information Center, Department BEST, Pueblo, CO 81009 or the Web site at http://www.pueblo.gsa.gov. Figure 9.12 presents addresses for additional ideas and resources for home-school partnerships.

■ Dealing with an Irate Parent or Guardian

If a parent or guardian is angry or hostile toward you and the school, the paragraphs that follow offer guidelines for dealing with that hostility.

Remain calm in your discussion with the parent, allowing the parent to talk out his or her hostility while you say very little; usually, the less you say the better off you will be. Staying calm shows strength. It is hard to scream at someone who is acting concerned, collected, and reasonable. By controlling your emotions, you will help de-escalate the situation. What you do say must be objective and to the point of the student's work in your classroom. The parent may just need to vent frustrations that might have very little to do with you, the school, or even the student.

Do not allow yourself to be intimidated, put on the defensive, or backed into a verbal corner. If the parent tries to do so by attacking you personally, do not press your defense at this point. Perhaps the parent has made a point that you should take time to consider, and now

is a good time to arrange for another conference with the parent for about a week later. In a follow-up conference, if the parent agrees, you may want to consider bringing in a mediator, such as another member of your teaching team, an administrator, or a school counselor.

You must *not* talk about other students; keep the conversation focused on this parent's child's progress. The parent is *not* your rival; at least, he or she should not be. You both share a concern for the intellectual and psychological well-being of the student. Use your best skills in critical thinking and problem solving by trying to focus the discussion on identifying the problem, defining it, and then arriving at some decision about how mutually to go about solving it. To this end you may need to ask for help from a third party, such as the student's school counselor. If agreed to by the parent, please take that step.

Parents do *not* need to hear about how busy you are, about your personal problems, or about how many other students you are dealing with on a daily basis, unless, of course, a parent asks. Parents expect you to be the capable professional who knows what to do and is doing it.

■ SUMMARY

Whereas preceding parts of this book addressed the *why, what,* and *how* components of teaching, this module has focused your attention on the fourth and final component—the *how well* component—and on the first of two aspects of that component. Assessment is an integral and ongoing factor in the teaching-learning process; consequently, this module has emphasized the importance of your including the following in your teaching performance:

- Collect a body of evidence, using a variety of instruments, to reliably assess students' learning that focuses on their individual development.

- Involve students in the assessment process; keep students informed of their progress. Return tests promptly, review answers to all questions, and respond to inquiries about marks given.

- Consider your assessment and grading procedures carefully, plan them, and explain your policies to the students.

- Make sure to explain any ambiguities that result from the terminology used, and base your assessments on the material that has been taught.

- Strive for objective and impartial assessment as you put your assessment plan into operation.
- Try to minimize arguments about grades, cheating, and teacher subjectivity by involving students in planning, in reinforcing individual student development, and in providing an accepting, stimulating learning environment.
- Maintain accurate and clear records of assessment results so that you will have an adequate supply of data on which to base your judgmental decisions about achievement.

Because teaching and learning work hand-in-hand and because they are reciprocal processes in that one depends on and affects the other, the *how well* component deals with the assessment of both how well the students are learning and how well the teacher is teaching. This module has dealt with the first. In the next and final module of this book, your attention is directed to techniques designed to help you develop your teaching skills and assess that development, a process that will continue throughout your teaching career.

■ MODULE 9 POSTTEST

Multiple Choice

1. A criterion-referenced test is constructed so that
   a. the student will be compared to other students and his or her position in the group will be determined.
   b. the test measures what it is supposed to test or meets the criterion established.
   c. each student will attain a perfect score if the student has mastered the objectives.
   d. the deficiencies of a student are located in a specific area of behavior.

2. Assessment and measurement are defined so that
   a. the terms are synonymous.
   b. assessment includes measurement.
   c. measurement includes assessment.
   d. measurement and assessment are not directly related.

3. The items on a true-false test are least likely to
   a. encourage guessing.
   b. measure complex cognitive behavior.
   c. cover a quantity of material in a short time.
   d. take a reasonable amount of teacher time for constructing and checking.

4. Which teacher comment about scoring essay tests will improve the reliability of the test?
   a. "I can tell how much a student knows by scanning the student's paper."
   b. "I can do a better job of scoring when I don't know whose paper I'm reading."
   c. "I like to read all the student's answers at one time to get an overview of what the student knows."
   d. "The time it takes to separate test papers item by item is time I could use more profitably for other purposes."

5. An effective grading system is least likely to
   a. be limited to academic achievement.
   b. include assessment of a variety of student behaviors.
   c. provide information about the achievement of objectives.
   d. be able to provide criterion- and norm-referenced grades.

6. Students learn best when they are
   a. homogeneously grouped and encouraged to work together on similar tasks.
   b. reminded of their shortcomings so that they are more realistic in setting goals.
   c. accepted as worthy individuals and encouraged to undertake challenging tasks.
   d. heterogeneously grouped and encouraged to work together on similar tasks.

7. A student's final semester grade is an example of
   a. authentic assessment.
   b. formative assessment.
   c. diagnostic assessment.
   d. summative assessment.

(continued)

8. If a major test is going to take an entire class period, then
   a. it should be given at the end of the period.
   b. it should be given at the beginning of the period.
   c. it should be given during the middle of the class period.
   d. students should be allowed to leave class whenever they finish.

9. The degree to which an item or test measures that which it is intended to measure is called its
   a. validity.
   b. reliability.
   c. homogeneity.
   d. central tendency.

10. A limitation to portfolio assessment is
    a. it provides more of an opportunity for bluffing.
    b. it may place too much emphasis on memorizing.
    c. it provides a broad picture of what the student knows and can do.
    d. conclusions drawn from it can be heavily influenced by the evaluator.

Check

A group from the Student Council of Walton High School studied grading systems. Its report to the Advisory Committee included a statement of purpose for grading. Read the following statements, and check those that provide valid reasons for grades.

1. Teachers can control student behavior with grades.
2. Colleges and employers can get information about students.
3. Grades give a student information about his or her progress.
4. Grades replace learning as a motivation for students.
5. Grades encourage continuous evaluation of student learning.

Analyze

Mr. Taylor decided to use a weight system for 6-week grades. The four items selected were class participation, tests, group projects, and assignments. He decided that the most important phase of the learning activities was class participation, which should be half of the grade. The group projects and tests were of equal value, but the assignments were half as important as the tests. Set up a system of weights for Mr. Taylor to use. Put the appropriate number in each blank.

1. Class participation
2. Tests
3. Group projects
4. Assignments

   If the following table of specifications is set up for a unit on short stories in ninth-grade English, indicate the appropriate placement of the tally for each question listed. Put the letter(s) of the correct cells in the blanks. Use the highest cognitive level involved.

5. Ten items listing synonyms to be matched with 10 of 13 words given.
6. What effect on the reader is expected when the author tells the story in the first person?
   a. The reader is an observer of the action.
   b. The reader identifies with the author.
   c. The reader gets a broad insight into the motivation of all characters.
   d. The reader quickly perceives the theme of the story.
7. Compare *The Tell Tale Heart* with *The Fugitive* in regard to
   a. point of view.
   b. setting.
   c. plot.
8. At the end of "Split Cherry Tree," Pa feels that Professor Herbert is a "fine man" because
   a. Professor Herbert had a good education.
   b. Professor Herbert respected the gun Pa carried.

(continued)

   c. Professor Herbert treated Pa as a worthy individual.

   d. Professor Herbert displayed his intelligence to Pa.

9. Select the best story you read, and defend your selection using four criteria for a good short story.

Matching

Match the correct test characteristic (a through h below) with the question asked about the test. Use a term only once.

1. Does the test measure what is supposed to be measured?

2. Can the test be constructed, administered, and scored conveniently?

3. Are the results consistent?

4. Do the test results show the different achievement levels of the students?

5. Are results affected by the student or the scorer?

Completion Statement

List four uses of test results.

1. _____

2. _____

3. _____

4. _____

Short Explanation

1. Other than a paper-and-pencil test, identify three alternative techniques for assessing student learning during or at completion of an instructional unit.

2. When using a point system for determining student grades for a course, is it educationally defensible to give a student a higher grade than that student's points call for? A lower grade? Give a rationale for your answers.

3. Explain the dangers in using true-false and completion-type items to assess student learning and in using the results for grade determination.

4. Explain the concept of authentic assessment. Is it the same as performance assessment? Explain why or why not.

5. Describe any student learning activities or situations that should not be graded but should or could be used for assessment of student learning.

Essay

1. For a course and grade level that you intend to teach, describe the items and their relative weights that you would use for determining course grades. Explain your rationale for the percentage weight distribution.

2. Explain the value and give a specific example of a performance test item that you would use in teaching your subject to middle school or secondary school students.

3. Do you believe that a student's self-esteem is bolstered from a "feel-good" grade inflation system where no students get less than a C and where those who do not excel are still given A's? Explain why you agree or disagree with the idea that being generous to students on their report cards is a way to spur them toward higher achievement.

4. From your current observations and fieldwork related to this teacher preparation program, clearly identify one specific example of educational practice that seems contradictory to exemplary practice or theory presented in this module. Present your explanation for the discrepancy.

5. Describe any prior concepts you held that changed as a result of the experiences of this module. Describe the changes.

 To access this posttest and the answers online, go to the Companion Website at
www.prenhall.com/kellough.

■ SUGGESTED READINGS

Allen, D. (Ed.). (1998). *Assessing student learning: From grading to understanding.* New York: Teachers College Press.

Asp, E. (2000). Assessment in education: Where have we been? Where are we headed? In R. S. Brandt (Ed.), *Education in a New Era* (Chapter 6, pp. 123–157). Alexandria, VA: ASCD Yearbook, Association for Supervision and Curriculum Development.

Birk, L. (2000). Grade inflation: What's really behind all those A's? *Harvard Education Letter, 16*(1), 1–3.

Bishop, J. E., & Fransen, S. (1998). Building community: An alternative assessment. *Phi Delta Kappan, 80*(1), 39–40, 57–58.

Black, P., & Dylan, W. (1998). Inside the black box: Raising standards through classroom assessment. *Phi Delta Kappan, 80*(2), 139–144, 146–148.

Black, P. Harrison, C., Lee, C., Marshall, B., & Wiliam, D. (2004). Working inside the black box: Assessment for learning in the classroom, *Phi Delta Kappan, 86*(1), 9–21.

Bracey, G. W. (2000). *A short guide to standardized testing.* Fastback 459. Bloomingon, IN: Phi Delta Kappa Educational Foundation.

Chase, C. I. (1999). *Contemporary assessment for educators.* New York: Addison-Wesley Longman.

Colby, S. A. (1999). Grading in a standards-based system. *Educational Leadership, 56*(6), 17–21.

Cole, K. A. (1999). Walking around: Getting more from informal assessment. *Mathematics Teaching in the Middle School, 4*(4), 224–227.

Conway, K. D. (1999). Assessing open-ended problems. *Mathematics Teaching in the Middle School, 4*(8), 510–514.

Danielson, C., & Marquez, E. (1998). *A collection of performance tasks and rubrics. High School Mathematics.* New York: Eye on Education.

Doran, R., Chan, F., & Tamir, P. (1998). *Science educator's guide to assessment.* Arlington, VA: National Science Teachers Association.

Gredler, M. E. (1999). *Classroom assessment and learning.* New York: Addison-Wesley Longman.

Gronlund, N. E. (1998). *Assessment of student achievement* (6th ed.). Needham Heights, MA: Allyn & Bacon Longman.

Gustafson, C. (1998). Phone home. *Educational Leadership, 56*(2), 31–32.

Haladyna, T. M. (1997). *Writing test items to evaluate higher order thinking.* Needham Heights, MA: Allyn & Bacon.

Kelly, K. (1999). Retention vs. social promotion: Schools search for alternatives. *The Harvard Education Letter, 15*(1), 1–3.

Marzano, R. J. (2000). *Transforming classroom grading.* Alexandria, VA: Association for Supervision and Curriculum Development.

Mehrens, W. A., Popham, W. J., & Ryan, J. M. (1998). How to prepare students for performance assessments. *Educational Measurement: Issues and Practice, 17*(1), 18–22.

Mitchell, J. P., et al. (1998). Making sense of literacy portfolios: A four-step plan. *Journal of Adolescent & Adult Literacy, 41*(5), 384–386.

Popham, W. J. (1999). *Classroom assessment: What teachers need to know* (2nd ed.). Needham Heights, MA: Allyn & Bacon.

Schurr, S. L. (1998). Teaching, enlightening: A guide to student assessment. *Schools in the Middle, 7*(3), 22–27, 30–31.

Stephens, D., & Story, J. (Eds.). (2000). *Assessment as inquiry: Learning the hypothesis-test process.* Urbana, IL: National Council of Teachers of English.

Stiggins, R. J. (2001). *Student-involved classroom assessment* (3rd ed.). Upper Saddle River, NJ: Merrill/Prentice Hall.

Taggart, G. L., Phifer, S. J., Nixon, J. A., & Wood, M. (Ed.). (1998). *Rubrics: A handbook for construction and use.* Lancaster, PA: Technomic.

Wiggins, G., & McTighe, J. (1998). *Understanding by design.* Alexandria, VA: Association for Supervision and Curriculum Development.

Zmuda, A., & Tomaino, M. (1999). A contract for the high school classroom. *Educational Leadership, 56*(6), 59–61.

■ ENDNOTES

[1] P. Wellstone, High Stakes Tests: A Harsh Agenda for America's Children. Remarks by U.S. Senator Paul D. Wellstone (MN), at Teacher's College, Columbia University, March 31, 2000. http://www.educationrevolution.org/paulwellstone.html.

[2] S. J. Rakow, Assessment: A Driving Force, *Science Scope 15*(6), 3 (March 1992).

[3] For information about Learner Profile™, see Sunburst Technology, at http://www.sunburst.com., or phone 1-800-321-7511.

[4] See, for example, A. Chandler, Is This for a Grade? A Personal Look at Journals, *English Journal 86*(1), 45–49 (January 1997).

[5] Software packages for the development of student electronic portfolios are available, such as Classroom Manager from CTB Macmillan/McGraw-Hill (Monterey, CA), *Electronic Portfolio* from Learning *Quest*

(Corvallis, OR), and Grady Profile from Aurbach and Associates (St. Louis, MO).

[6] For a discussion of the biological importance and educational benefits of positive feedback, student portfolios, and group learning, see R. Sylwester, The Neurobiology of Self-Esteem and Aggression, *Educational Leadership 54*(5), 75–79 (February 1997).

[7] See, for example, T. R. Guskey (Ed.), *Communicating Student Learning* (Alexandria, VA: 1996 Yearbook, Associating for Supervision and Curriculum Development, 1996), pp. 18–19; and R. J. Stiggins, *Student-Centered Classroom Assessment* (2nd ed.) (Upper Saddle River, NJ: Prentice Hall, 1997), pp. 436–437.

[8] For other methods being used to report student achievement, see J. Bailey and J. McTighe, Reporting Achievement at the Secondary

Level: What and How, Chapter 10 in T. R. Guskey, *Communicating Student Learning*, pp. 119–140.

[9]H. G. Andrade, Using Rubrics to Promote Thinking and Learning, *Educational Leadership 57*(5), 13–18 (February 2000).

[10]K. Bushweller, Generation of Cheaters, *American School Board Journal 186*(4), 24–30, 32 (April 1999).

[11]H. J. Walberg, Productive Teaching and Instruction: Assessing the Knowledge Base, *Phi Delta Kappan 71*(6), 472 (February 1990).

[12]For suggestions for "delivering powerful presentations to parents" at back-to-school night, see W. B. Ribas, Tips for Reaching Parents, *Educational Leadership 56*(1), 83–85 (September 1998).

[13]D. W. Johnson and R. T. Johnson, The Role of Cooperative Learning in Assessing and Communicating Student Learning, in T. R. Guskey, *Communicating Student Learning*, p. 43.

[14]For a discussion of the pros and cons of using the student-led conference, and for a conference organizer tool, see J. Bailey and J. McTighe, Reporting Achievement at the Secondary Level: What and How, in T. R. Guskey, *Communicating Student Learning*, pp. 137–139. See also L. Countryman and M. Schroeder, When Students Lead Parent-Teacher Conferences, *Educational Leadership 53*(7), 64–68 (April 1996); and D. G. Hackmann, *Student-Led Conferences at the Middle Level*, ED407171 (Champaign, IL: ERIC Clearinghouse on Elementary and Early Childhood Education, 1997).

Self-Assessment of Teaching and Continued Professional Development

"The older I get, the more I realize the importance of exercising the various dimensions of my body, soul, mind, and heart. Taken together, these aspects give me a sense of wholeness. I want to be a whole human being rather than one who limps on one leg because I don't know how to use all my parts. Intellectual, emotional, and physical activity are not separate entities. Rather, they are dimensions of the same human being."[1]

—ROBERT FULGHUM

Module 10 Overview

Although most of us are not born with innate teaching skills, teaching skills can be learned. Teachers who wish to improve their teaching can do so, and (in addition to this book) there are many resources that can help.

This module addresses the evaluation and development of your effectiveness as a classroom teacher, a process that continues throughout your professional career. Teaching is such an electrifying profession that it is not easy to remain energetic and to stay abreast of changes and trends that result from research and practice. You will need to make a continuous and determined effort to remain an alert and effective teacher.

One way to collect data and to improve your effectiveness is through periodic assessment of your teaching performance, either by an evaluation of your teaching in the real classroom or, if you are in a preservice program of teacher preparation, by a technique called *micro peer-teaching*. The latter is the focus of the final section of this module and is an example of a type of final performance (authentic) assessment for this textbook.

Two terms used throughout this module are **pre-service** and **in-service.** By pre-service we are referring to the teacher in training, that is, to all the professional experiences prior to credentialing (or licensing) and employment as a teacher. In-service refers to the experiences of the credentialed (or licensed) and employed teacher.

Specific Objectives

At the completion of this module, you should be able to:

- Demonstrate your growing teacher competencies.
- Describe the various ways to gain from practical field experiences.
- Demonstrate your awareness of the scope and importance of the student teaching experience.
- Demonstrate your awareness of ways of finding a teaching job.
- Demonstrate knowledge of how to remain an alert and effective classroom teacher throughout your teaching career.

Introduction

In order to prepare you to teach in today's middle and secondary school classrooms, most teacher education programs integrate classroom experience with coursework. It is important that you have ample opportunities to work with middle and secondary students during your teacher preparation program. Classroom observation, aiding, one-on-one or small-group tutoring, team-teaching, and/or solo teaching a lesson or two may all be required components of your professional field experiences. These hands-on classroom experiences will help you to be ready for the demands of student teaching. Practical field experiences can also help undecided students discover if they want to pursue a career in teaching, or help students wavering among grade levels or content areas commit to an age group and/or subject they really want to teach. Here we will describe various practical field experiences you may participate in, tips for finding a teaching position, advice on building a career portfolio, and continued professional development opportunities.

■ PROFESSIONAL DEVELOPMENT THROUGH FIELD EXPERIENCES

Professional field experiences include the portions of your college or university program in which you observe classroom teachers in the act of teaching, participate in conducting classes, teach simulated classes and minilessons, microteach, work with curricula, and teach real classes in the student teaching or internship experience. Field experiences prior to student teaching are called *early field experiences* and begin as early as the junior year of undergraduate preparation or even earlier. Student teaching and internship experiences generally come toward the end of the program. Evidence indicates that more and earlier field experiences result in better prepared teachers.[2]

Internship can sometimes refer simply to student teaching by another name, or it can sometimes refer to a longer or more independent and paid apprenticeship period. In this module, the term *student teaching* refers to both concepts. This module considers observation, participation, and student-teaching experiences that occur in middle and secondary schools.

Unless you are different from most persons preparing to be teachers, your professional field experiences will have the greatest impact of all your college or university experiences. These experiences are real, often exciting, and full of opportunities for creative learning and application of what you have learned and are learning. They provide a milieu in which you can experiment with different styles and strategies and develop skills in the various teaching techniques.

■ Observation

Most programs for teacher preparation provide early field experience opportunities to observe teachers and students in the public schools. Often, a portion of the observation will occur in a middle school, and then in a junior or senior high school, then sometimes in alter-

native schools. Programs may also allow students to observe how other students teach as well as provide demonstration lessons. This variety of observation can give you insights into relations between students and teachers; the various backgrounds of students you will teach; and the effects of different teaching strategies, different instructional materials, and different styles of teaching. The more different styles you observe and analyze, the better your understanding of the potentials of the various approaches will be. Ways to make your observation profitable are presented in the following paragraphs.

- *Concentrate on watching the students in the classrooms.* Note the range of differences in appearance, abilities, and interests that appear in a single class. Note how students react to different teaching approaches. Which teaching techniques and materials excite their interest and which engender boredom? Follow a student's schedule all day long—this is called *shadowing* a student. How does it feel to go through the routine of being a middle or secondary school student today? (It may be quite different from what you remember.) Try to think of ways that you as a teacher could make the classes more enjoyable and profitable.

- *Observe the classroom management techniques the teacher uses.* How does the teacher have the classroom arranged? Are the classroom guidelines or rules posted? What are the expectations of the students? How does the teacher deal with students who are off-task?

- *Observe the ways different teachers handle their classes.* How do they get their classes started? How do they bring their classes to a conclusion? How do they develop the important points? How do they create interest? How do they get students involved in their own learning? How do they provide for differences in students? What techniques for motivation, probing, discovery, inquiry, closure, and reinforcement are used? How do students respond to the various tactics? What procedures are used to establish and maintain classroom control?

- *Observe the classroom environment.* What seems to have created the environment? Does the class seem more teacher-centered or more student-centered? Is the student morale high or low, and what seems to be the cause for the state of the morale?

- *Give particular attention to the manner in which the teachers implement various strategies and the students' responses to each of the strategies.*

- *Observe the ways teachers promote equal educational opportunity.* How are the needs of English Language Learners; students with learning disabilities; students with mental, emotional, or physical challenges; gifted and talented students; and so forth, addressed? Do you notice any gender differences? Are students treated equally? What lesson accommodations does the teacher make?

■ Student Teaching

During student teaching, after a period of observation and participation, the teacher candidate gradually begins to take over some of the classes and other duties that make up a teacher's load, under the supervision of one or more cooperating teachers as well as a college or university supervisor. The experience is expected to develop into a genuine simulation of teaching reality. The cooperating teacher, the professional of record, always retains ultimate responsibility for what happens in the classroom, but the intent is for the student teacher to assume as much responsibility as possible—as though the class were fully his or hers to lead. The legal, instructional, and pedagogical ramifications of this activity are such that only a simulation of reality is possible. However, the greater the effort to approximate the real thing and the greater the sensitivity to the goals of the activity on the part of everyone concerned, the more rewarding the student teaching experience will be. For most teacher candidates, student teaching is the capstone of their teacher preparation program. It can be both exciting and rewarding. It can also be both difficult and trying.

Perhaps the first thing to remember about student teaching is that, like observation and participation, it is intended to be a learning experience. It is in student teaching that the beginning teacher applies the theories and techniques learned in college classes to real teaching situations. Here you will have an opportunity to try out various strategies and techniques so as to begin to build a wide repertoire of teaching skills and to develop an effective, comfortable teaching style. From the beginning, it is important that the students identify you as a teacher. Your dress and professional demeanor will help you to establish your position.

Student teaching is also a time of trial and error. Do not be discouraged if you make mistakes or your lessons do not go well at first. If you were already a skilled teacher, you would not need the practice. Making mistakes is part of the learning process. Use them as a means for improvement. With the help of your cooperating teacher and supervisor, try to analyze your teaching to find what steps to take to do better next time. Perhaps your execution of the strategies and techniques was faulty; perhaps you used a strategy or technique inappropriate for the particular situation. Such errors can be quite easily remedied as you gain experience. Failure to devote enough time to planning adequately, neglect of previewing audiovisual equipment, lack of research on the topic of presentation, and overusing a limited repertoire of instructional strategies are common errors new teachers make and should be avoided.

As you become more skilled in using various strategies and techniques, you will find that all have their uses. Do not be quick to reject a teaching strategy or technique that fails for you. Do not allow yourself to become one of those boring teachers who can teach in only one way. Instead, if a strategy or technique does not work for you, examine the situation to see what went wrong. Then try it again in a new situation after brushing up your technique and correcting your faults.

During your student teaching assignment, you may have multiple sections of the same course (prep) and a lesson may go very differently in one class than it does with another group of students. Teaching multiple sections of the same course provides you with the opportunity to compare and contrast your interactions with your students and reflect on what went well and what you could have done better. By isolating variables and examining the dynamics of the classroom you may uncover interesting information about your teaching style and your students.

Since student teaching is a time for learning and for getting the mistakes out of your system, it is important not to become discouraged. Many student teachers who do miserably for the first weeks blossom into excellent teachers by the end of the student-teaching period. However, if things seem to go well at first, do not become overconfident. Many beginners, too soon satisfied with the seeming success of early classes, become complacent and doom themselves to mediocrity. In any case, examine your classes to see what went well and what went wrong. Then try to correct your faults and capitalize on your strengths.

After your initial anxiety and nervousness wear off, use your student teaching as an opportunity to try out new strategies and techniques. Avoid becoming a clone of the cooperating teacher or a replica of the old-time teacher who gave lectures, heard recitations, and sometimes did very little else. But work out the new approaches and techniques you wish to try with your cooperating teacher before you use them. Usually the cooperating teacher can show you how to get the most out of your new ventures and warn you of pitfalls you might encounter. Things will go more smoothly if you continue with the same strategies and tactics to which the class is accustomed. Students used to a particular style may not readily adapt to innovations. This reluctance is especially bad when the teacher confronts students with quick changes in the length and difficulty of homework assignments or an abrupt switch from prescriptive, didactic methods to discovery and inquiry approaches.

Sometimes the cooperating teacher may think it necessary to veto what seem to you to be your best ideas. Usually there is a sound basis for the veto. It may be, in the cooperating teacher's view, that these ideas will not serve the objectives well, or they may require time, money, or equipment not available to you; violate school policy; or seem unsuited to the age and abilities of the students. Sometimes your ideas may be rejected because they conflict with the cooperating teacher's pedagogical and philosophical beliefs or biases. Whatever the objection, you should accept the decision gracefully and concentrate on procedures the cooperating teacher finds acceptable. After all, you are a temporary guest in the classroom and ultimately the classes and the instruction are the cooperating teacher's responsibility.

Furthermore, you need to become a master of many techniques. If you master the techniques and style your cooperating teacher recommends now, you will have begun to assemble a suitable repertoire of teaching skills. Later, when you are teaching your own classes, you can expand your repertoire by trying out other strategies and styles you find appealing.

Success in student teaching requires more study and preparation than most teacher candidates think possible. To do the job, you must know what you are doing, so pay particular attention to your planning. Carefully review the content of your lessons and units and lay them out step by step. Leave nothing to chance. Check and double-check to be sure you have your facts straight, that your teaching strategies and tactics will yield your objectives, that you have the necessary teaching materials on hand, that you know how to use them, and so on. It is most embarrassing when you find you cannot solve the problems you have given to the students, cannot answer the students' questions, and cannot find the equipment you need or cannot operate the projector. As a rule, you should ask your cooperating teacher to approve your plan before you become committed to it. If the cooperating teacher suggests changes, incorporate them into the plan and try to carry them out.

Often you will be required to design and produce a unit plan during your student teaching assignment. Planning lessons and units for student teaching is no easy task. To become really sure of your subject matter and to think out how to teach it in the short time available during your student teaching is asking a lot of yourself. Therefore, prepare as much as you can before the student-teaching period begins. Try to find out what topics you will be expected to teach, and master the content before you report for your student teaching. Then when you start student teaching you can concentrate on planning and teaching, confident that you have a firm understanding of the content. Many students have botched their student teaching because they had to spend so much time learning the content that they never had time to learn how to teach! Remember that middle and secondary school classes are not replicas of college classes.

Because student teaching is difficult and time demanding, most teacher education institutions strongly recommend or require that student teachers not combine student teaching with other courses or outside work. If you have to work to eat, you must, but very few people are able to both hold down a job and perform creditably in their student teaching. Outside jobs, additional courses, trying to master inadequately learned subject content, and preparing classes are just too much for one ordinary person to do well at the same time. It is true that many successful teachers have moonlighted on outside jobs or on coursework for advanced degrees. It is also true that many undergraduate students have maintained high grades with a full load of college courses and have simultaneously worked full-time in the evenings. But the student-teaching experience is so unique in the many demands that it makes on a student teacher's time that it is virtually impossible for you to perform in a superior fashion if you bog yourself down with outside responsibilities in this crucial early part of your career.

Usually student teaching starts with a few days of observing. This gives you a few days to get ready for teaching. Use this time to become familiar with the classroom situation. Get to know the students. Learn their names. Borrow the teacher's seating chart and study it and the students as the class proceeds. In this way you will learn to associate names with faces and also have some inkling of the sort of persons with whom you will soon be dealing. Learn the classroom routines and other details of classroom management. Familiarize yourself with the types of teaching, activities, and assignments that the class is used to so that you can gradually assume the classroom teaching responsibility without too much disruption. Remember, at first students are likely to resent too much deviation from what they have come to expect.

In your observation of the efforts of your cooperating teacher in the act of teaching, keep in mind the following topics and questions:

- *Objectives.* What were the objectives of the lesson? How did the teacher make the students aware of them? Were the objectives achieved?

- *Administrative duties.* How did the teacher handle taking the roll and reporting attendance? How were tardies handled? How were announcements made? How did the teacher handle other serendipitous events?

- *Homework.* Did the teacher make a homework assignment? At what point in the lesson was the assignment made? How did the assignment relate to the day's work? How was the assignment from the previous day handled? How did the teacher deal with students who failed to submit completed work? How much time did the teacher spend on the assignment for the next day? Did the students appear to understand the assignment?

- *Review.* How much of the period was devoted to review of the previous lesson? Did the teacher make any effort to fit the review into the day's lesson? How did the teacher conduct the review—question and answer, or student summarization of important points?

- *Methods.* What various methods did the teacher use in the day's lesson? Was multilevel instruction used? Did the teacher lecture? For what length of time? How did the teacher shift from one method to the next (**transitions**)? How did the teacher motivate the students to attend? Was any provision made for individual differences and learning styles among the students? Was any provision made for student participation in the lesson? Were the students kept busy during the entire period? Did any classroom management problems arise? How did the teacher handle them?

- *Accommodations.* How did the teacher modify the lesson to address the needs of all of the students?

- *Miscellaneous.* Was the teacher's voice pleasant enough to listen to? Did the teacher have any distracting idiosyncratic habits? Were lighting and ventilation adequate? What system did the teacher use for checking attendance?

- *Evaluation.* How might this lesson have been improved?

■ Guidelines for Behaving Professionally During Field Experiences

When you participate in professional field experiences, you are in a rather delicate position. In a sense, you are neither teacher nor student; yet, in another sense, you are both teacher and student. Many teacher candidates have found this position trying. Therefore, included here are a number of suggestions that may help you to be successful during your field experiences. Although these suggestions apply to observation, participation, and student-teaching experience, they are somewhat geared toward student teaching. These suggestions are conclusions drawn from years of observing and helping student teachers.

In professional field experiences your relationship with your cooperating teacher is critical. You should concentrate on keeping these relationships friendly and professional. Whether you like it or not, student teaching—and to a lesser degree, observation and participation—is a job as well as a learning experience, and the cooperating teacher and college supervisor are your bosses. Ordinarily, you can expect them to be nice bosses who will not only strive to help you in every way they can but will also be tolerant of your mistakes. They are bosses, however, and must be perceived as such.

They will, or should, have pretty high expectations of you. Not only will they expect you to have an adequate command of the subject to be taught, but they will also expect you to have (a) an ability to work with other adults, (b) an ability to reflect on your work and to listen to and accept suggestions, (c) a current understanding of the nature of middle and secondary school learners and learning, (d) a repertoire of teaching skills and a developing competence in using them, and (e) a functional

understanding of the purposes and processes of assessment. Do not disappoint them. You should check yourself in each of these areas. If you believe yourself deficient in any of them, now is the time to bring yourself up to par. Student teaching is too hectic to take time out for learning and collecting what you already should have learned and collected.

Your colleagues in the school will also expect you to be a professional—a beginning professional, but a professional just the same. You will be expected to do your job carefully without carping, criticizing, or complaining. Carry out instructions carefully. Keep to the routines of the school. If next week's lesson plans are due at the department head's office before the beginning of school Friday morning, make sure that they are there. Be prompt with all assignments. Never be late or absent unless previous arrangements have been made. If an emergency arises, phone in. Pay attention to details. Fill out reports, requisitions, and so on, accurately and on time. Be meticulous in the preparation of your unit and lesson plans. Never approach a class unprepared. Be sure you know your content and exactly how you plan to teach it. *Nothing upsets cooperating teachers and university supervisors more than classes that do not go well because the student teacher was not sufficiently prepared.*

Build a reputation for being responsible and dependable by carrying out your assignments faithfully and accurately. Sometimes student teachers fail because they do not fully understand what their responsibilities are or how to carry them out. Study the student teacher's handbook, observe the cooperating teacher, and heed the cooperating teacher's instructions so that you will know just what to do and when and how. If you are uncertain about what to do or how to do it, ask even though it may embarrass you to admit ignorance. It is much better to admit you do not understand than to keep quiet and reveal it.

Be proactive. Evidence of initiative impresses teachers, principals, and college supervisors. Volunteer to do things before you have to be asked. Willingly take on such tasks as reading papers and correcting tests. Take part in cafeteria supervision, extracurricular activities, attendance at PTO meetings, and the like. Participating in such activities will give you experience and expertise in these areas of the teacher's job and will also indicate to your colleagues that you are a professionally minded person who does not shun the nitty-gritty. Develop a close relationship with your college or university supervisor. Keep in frequent (weekly, if not daily) contact with him/her. Once you have started your student teaching, it can be helpful toward establishing a feeling of community, reducing your sense of isolation, and encouraging reflection if you and your college or university supervisor can communicate by e-mail over the Internet.[3]

During your professional field experiences you are a guest of the school in which you are observing, participating, or student teaching. Your place in the school is not a right but a privilege. Behave in a way that will make you and succeeding student teachers welcome. As quickly as you can, adapt yourself to the culture of the school and conform to the mores of the school as they apply to teachers. Do not stand on your rights—as a guest of the school you may not have many—but concentrate on your responsibilities. Try as soon as possible to become a member of the school staff and to set up pleasant relationships with your cooperating teacher and other colleagues. As a student teacher, it helps if you have your own mailbox, too.

Be sure to protect student confidentiality, and refrain from criticizing the school, its administration, or its teachers. Be particularly careful about what you say to teachers and other student teachers. If some things in a situation bother you, seek the advice of your university supervisor before you do anything drastic. If there is to be any friction, let the supervisor absorb the sparks. It is your university supervisor's job to see that your experience runs smoothly and that you get the best practical learning experience possible.

Do not under any circumstances discuss school personnel with the students. Often students tell student teachers how much better they are than their regular teachers. Regardless of how much your ego loves to hear it, do not respond to such bait. Allowing yourself to discuss a teacher's performance and personality with a student is unprofessional and can only lead to trouble.

Professional field experiences, particularly student teaching, throw students and cooperating teachers into a closeness that can be richly rewarding and also extremely difficult. From the point of view of the cooperating teacher, the student-teaching period presents a threat in several ways. Allowing a newcomer to interfere in the smooth running of the class is risky. More than one teacher has had to work extra long hours to repair the damage done to a class by an incompetent student teacher. Teachers who are insecure may find the presence of any other adult in their classes threatening; the presence of a student teacher critically observing the teacher's work can be particularly disturbing. So avoid any appearance of opposing or competing with the cooperating teacher. Consult with him or her before you undertake anything and follow his or her advice and instructions carefully. If you believe the instructions or advice is wrong, your only recourse is to consult with your university supervisor.

Above all, listen to what the cooperating teacher tells you! Teachers (and college supervisors as well) sometimes complain that student teachers do not listen to what they are told. If a student teacher does not listen it is probably because the student teacher is so caught up in his or her personal problems that the student teacher finds it difficult to concentrate on anything else. The student teacher may be too busy justifying his or her own behavior or explaining away what has gone amiss in class to hear someone else's criticism. Although it may require some effort, try to hear what the cooperating teacher has to say and

follow through on the suggestions. Teachers and supervisors find it exasperating when student teachers carry on in unwanted ways in spite of the teacher's long and detailed instructions or explanations of what should be done.

As with any public figure in the community, you can expect that students as well as parents in the community will discuss you and your performance. Know that student teachers are held to the same high standards expected of all school personnel. Before being placed for your student teaching assignment you will probably be asked to complete a character questionnaire or sign a professional conduct document prepared by your state department of education or your teacher education program stating you will uphold high professional standards for ethical behavior. You may also need to be fingerprinted and have a criminal background check run on you before ever entering the classroom.

Once placed in the school, you may hear all sorts of comments from students. Sometimes chance remarks are caught as you walk through the halls or as students are leaving the room. Let them not turn your head, because often these remarks are quite flattering. At the same time, guard against that feeling of depression that usually follows derogatory statements about your efforts or intentions. Whether you are praised or denounced, try to assume an objective attitude and use the comments for the inherent value they may possess. Remind yourself that you cannot always be all things to all people, nor should you even try to be. Your personality, the school regulations, and the classroom procedures will not let you be equally appealing to or effective with all of your students. You must expect that in the process of upholding your standards you will leave an occasional student dissatisfied. Only by keeping your reactions under control will you be able to preserve a positive feeling for your job.

■ Relationships with Students

Your relationships with students may make or break you in your practical field experience, so try to make them as friendly and purposeful as possible. Students like teachers who treat them with respect and whom they can respect. Therefore, treat them courteously and tactfully but at the same time require of them standards of behavior and academic productivity reasonably close to those established by the regular teacher. Show that you have confidence in them and expect them to do well. Let them know you are interested in them and in their activities.

The best way to earn the students' respect is to do a good job of teaching and to treat all students fairly and cordially. Do not, however, become overly friendly. Be friendly, not chummy. Your role is not to be a buddy, but to be a teacher. The students will respect and like you more if you act your age and assume your proper professional role. Seek respect rather than popularity, and above all avoid personal fraternization and inappropriate contact with students. Remember that you are an adult, not a kid.

In her report, "Educator Sexual Misconduct: A Synthesis of Existing Literature," Dr. Charol Shakesaft of Hofstra University claims that the incidence of illegal sexual misconduct in our schools is greater than we are led to believe. Shakesaft conducted a comprehensive literature review that describes educator sexual misconduct in our schools, the common characteristics of offenders, and suggestions for addressing this problem. According to Shakesaft, 9.6% of students in our public school system are victimized by teachers during their school careers.[4] Fortunately most schools adhere to a no tolerance policy where sexual misconduct is concerned. Under no circumstances should you ever engage in inappropriate sexual relationships with your students.

■ FINDING A TEACHING POSITION

As your successful student teaching experience draws to a close, you will embark upon finding your first paid teaching position. You should be encouraged in your goal of finding that first job by the fact that the projected need for new teachers for the next several years is great. The guidelines that follow are provided to help you accomplish your goal.

■ Guidelines for Locating a Teaching Position

To prepare for finding the position you want, you should focus on (a) letters of recommendation from your cooperating teacher(s), your college or university supervisor, and, in some instances, the school principal; (b) your professional preparation as evidenced by your letters of recommendation and other items in your professional portfolio (discussed next); and (c) your job-interviewing skills.

First, consider the recommendations about your teaching. Most colleges and universities have a career center, usually called a *job (or career) placement center*, where there is probably a counselor who can advise you how to open the job placement file that will hold your professional recommendations. This enables prospective personnel directors or district personnel who are expecting to employ new teachers to review your recommendations. Sometimes there are special forms for writing these recommendations. It is your responsibility to request letters of recommendation and, when appropriate, to supply the person writing the recommendation with the blank form and an appropriately addressed stamped envelope. Sometimes the job placement files are confidential, so your recommendations will be mailed directly to the placement office. The confidentiality of recommendations may be optional, and, when possible, you may want to maintain your own copies of letters of recommendation and include them in your professional portfolio.

The letters of recommendation from educators at the school(s) where you did your student teaching should include the following information: The name of the school and district where you did your student teaching; the grade levels and subjects you taught; your proven skills in meeting the needs of diverse students in the classroom; your content mastery; your skills in assessing student learning and in reflecting on your teaching performance and learning from that reflection; and your skills in communicating and interacting with students and adults.

Second, consider your preparation as a teacher. Teachers, as you have learned, represent a myriad of specialties. Hiring personnel will want to know how you see yourself—for example, as a specialist in middle school core, or as a high school music teacher. You may indicate a special interest or skill, such as competency in teaching English as a second language. Or, perhaps, although your teaching field is mathematics, you also are bilingual and have had rich and varied cross-cultural experiences. Have you had rich and varied experiences so that you will feel comfortable when you are hired and placed in the one assignment in which you were least interested? The hiring personnel who consider your application will be interested in your sincerity and will want to see that you are academically and socially impressive.

Last, consider your in-person interview with a district official. Sometimes, you will have several interviews or you will be interviewed simultaneously with other candidates. There may be an initial screening interview by an administrative panel from the district, followed by an interview by a department chairperson, a school principal, or a school team composed of one or more teachers and administrators from the interested school or district. In all interviews, your verbal and nonverbal behaviors will be observed as you respond to various questions, including (a) factual questions about your student teaching or about particular curriculum programs with which you would be expected to work, and (b) hypothetical questions, such as "What would you do if . . . ?" Often these are questions that relate to your philosophy of education, your reasons for wanting to be a teacher, your approach to handling a particular classroom situation, and perhaps specifically your reasons for wanting to teach at this particular school and in this district. Interview guidelines follow later in this section.

■ The Professional Career Portfolio

A way to be proactive in your job search is to create a professional portfolio to be shared with persons who are considering your application for employment. That is the objective of Exercise 10.1.

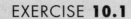

EXERCISE 10.1

■ Development of My Professional Portfolio

Instructions: The purpose of this exercise is to guide you in the creation of a professional portfolio that will be shared with persons who are considering your application for employment as a credentialed teacher.

Because it would be impractical to send a complete portfolio with every application you submit, it is suggested that you have a minimum portfolio (portfolio B) that could be sent with each application in addition to a complete portfolio (portfolio A) that you could make available upon request or that you would take with you to an interview. However it is done, the actual contents of the portfolio will vary depending on the specific job being sought; you will continually add to and delete materials from your portfolio. Suggested categories and subcategories of items to include in your portfolio, listed in the order that they may be best presented in portfolios A and B, are as follows.

1. Table of contents of portfolio (not too lengthy)—portfolio A only.

2. Your professional résumé—both portfolios.

3. Evidence of your language and communication skills (evidence of your use of English and of other languages, including American Sign)—portfolio A. (Also state this information briefly in your letter of application. See the résumé section that follows.)
   a. Your teaching philosophy (written in your own handwriting to demonstrate your handwriting).
   b. Other evidence to support this category.

4. Evidence of teaching skills—portfolio A.
   a. For planning skills, include instructional objectives, a syllabus, and a unit plan. (See Exercise 4.5, 5.2, and 5.7.)
   b. For teaching skills, include a sample lesson plan and a video of your actual teaching.
   c. For assessment skills, include a sample personal assessment and samples of student assessment.

5. Letters of recommendation and other documentation to support your teaching skills—both portfolios.

6. Other (for example, personal interests related to the position for which you are applying)—portfolio A.

 To access this exercise online, go to the Companion Website at **www.prenhall.com/kellough.**

The professional career portfolio is organized to provide clear evidence of your teaching skills and to make you professionally desirable to a hiring committee. A professional portfolio is not simply a collection of your accomplishments randomly tossed into a folder. It is a deliberate, current, and organized collection of your skills, attributes, experiences, and accomplishments. Exercise 10.1 suggests categories and subcategories of items to include in your portfolio, listed in the order that they may be best presented in portfolios A and B.[5]

■ Resources for Locating Teaching Vacancies

To locate teaching vacancies, you can establish contact with any of the following resources.

1. *Academic employment network.* A network employment page on the Internet at http://www.academploy.com/. Contact AEN, 2665 Gray Road, Windham, ME 04062. Phone 800-890-8283. E-mail infoacademploy.com.

2. *College or university placement office.* Establishing a career placement file with your local college or university placement service is an excellent way to begin the process of locating teaching vacancies.

3. *Local school or district personnel office.* You can contact school personnel offices to obtain information about teaching vacancies and sometimes about open job interviews.

4. *County educational agency.* Contact local county offices of education about job openings.

5. *State departments of education.* Some state departments of education maintain information about job openings statewide. (State departments of education Internet addresses appear later.)

6. *Independent schools.* You can contact non-public-supported schools that interest you, either directly or through educational placement services such as:

IES (Independent Educational Services), 20 Nassau Street, Princeton, NJ 08540 (800-257-5102). European Council of Independent Schools, 21B Lavant St., Petersfield, Hampshire, GU32 3EL, England.

7. *Commercial placement agencies.* Nationwide job listings and placement services are available from such agencies as:

Carney, Sandoe & Associates, 136 Boylston Street, Boston, MA 02116 (800-225-7986). National Education Service Center, PO Box 1279, Department NS, Riverton, WY 82501-1279 (307-856-0170). National Teachers Clearinghouse SE, PO Box 267, Boston, MA 02118-0267 (617-267-3204).

8. *Out-of-country teaching opportunities.* Information regarding teaching positions outside the United States can be obtained from:

American Field Services Intercultural Programs, 313 East 43rd St., New York, NY 10017. Department of Defense Dependent Schools, 4040 N. Fairfax Dr., Arlington, VA 22203-1634. European Council of Independent Schools, 21B Lavant St., Petersfield, Hampshire, GU32 3EL, England. International Schools Service, PO Box 5910, Princeton, NJ 08543. Peace Corps, Recruitment Office, 806 Connecticut Ave., NW, Washington, DC 20526. Teachers Overseas Recruitment Centers, National Teacher Placement Bureaus of America, Inc., PO Box 09027, 4190 Pearl Rd., Cleveland, OH 44109. YMCA of the USA, Attn: Teaching in Japan and Taiwan, 101 N. Wacker Dr., Chicago, IL 60606.

9. *Professional educational journals and other publications.* Professional teaching journals (as found in Figure 8.2, Module 8) often run advertisements of teaching vacancies, as do education newspapers such as *Education Week.* These can be found in your college or university library. See also *Education Week*'s site on the Internet at http://www.edweek.org/.

■ State (and Territorial) Sources for Information About Credential Requirements

If you are interested in the credential requirements for other states and U.S. territories, check at the appropriate office of your own college or university teacher prepara-

tion program to see what information is available about requirements for states of interest to you, and whether the credential that you are about to receive has reciprocity with other states. Addresses and contact numbers for information about state credentials are available on the Internet at http://www.ed.gov/Programs/bastmp/SEA.htm.

■ The Professional Résumé

Résumé preparation is the subject of how-to books, computer programs, and commercial services, but a teacher's résumé is specific. Although no one can tell you exactly what résumé will work best for you, a few basic guidelines are especially helpful for the preparation for a teacher's résumé:

- The résumé should be no more than *two pages* in length. If it is any longer, it becomes a life history rather than a professional résumé. If you feel it is necessary to include more information, you may consider printing your resume back-to-back or on an $11'' \times 17''$ sheet that you can fold to the $8\frac{1}{2}'' \times 11''$ format. On the extra space you gain you may decide to include an inspirational quote, a photograph of you teaching, or a photo of your students' work.

- The presentation should be neat and uncluttered.

- Page size should be standard $8\frac{1}{2} \times 11$ inches. Oversized and undersized pages can get lost.

- Stationery color should be white or off-white.

- Do *not* give information such as your age, height, weight, marital status, or the number or names of your children because including personal data may make it appear that you are trying to prejudice members of the hiring committee, which is simply unprofessional.

- Sentences should be clear and concise; avoid educational jargon, awkward phrases, abbreviations, or unfamiliar words. No personal pronouns should be included and verbs should be in the past tense.

- Organize the information carefully, in this order: Your name, address, and telephone number, followed by your education, professional experience, credential status, location of placement file, professional affiliations, honors, and special skills, abilities, and knowledge.

- When identifying your experiences—academic, teaching, and life—do so in *reverse chronological order*, listing your most recent degree or your current position first. (See sample résumé in Figure 10.1.)

- Be absolutely truthful; avoid any distortions of facts about your degrees, experiences, or any other information that you provide on your résumé.

- Take time to develop your résumé, and then keep it current. Do not duplicate hundreds of copies;

Richard Da Teacher
1993 Schoolhouse Drive
Dewey, CA 95818

OBJECTIVE:	Secondary school teaching position in English/language arts
EDUCATION:	California Single Subject Teaching Credential
	California State University, Sacramento—2004
	Bachelor of Arts Degree in English
	California State University, Chico—2004

RELATED EXPERIENCES:

2/04–6/04	*Student Teaching.* Valley High School, Elk Grove Unified School District, Elk Grove, CA Taught one 10th-grade English class and two classes of junior literature, each class of 30–34 ethnically diverse students. Advised school German club. Coached girl's volleyball team.
9/03–12/03	*Student Teaching.* Eddy Middle School, Elk Grove Unified School District, Elk Grove, CA Planned, developed, and implemented interdisciplinary thematic lessons for 7th- and 8th-grade students in 2-hour humanities blocks. Year-round scheduling of students was experienced. Planned and taught a literature unit on *The Courage of Sarah Noble* with a multicultural emphasis. Paid assistant in after-school tutoring program.
9/02–2/03	*Teacher Aide.* Premier Day Care Center, Dewey, CA. Worked in teaching and supervisory positions with ethnically diverse children from kindergarten through grade 6. Planned weekly thematic activities for all children.

OTHER EXPERIENCES AND ABILITIES:

- Volunteer at California Reading Association Conference, Fall 2002.
- Paid editor of MA theses, Department of English, California State University, Sacramento, academic year 2002–2003.
- Musical ability—Have played saxophone and other reed instruments for more than 14 years; can read any type of music. Six years of professional work experience in the music recording industry.
- Travel experiences to Austria, Denmark, Germany, Holland, Sweden, and Switzerland.
- Speaking and writing ability in English, German, and Spanish. Speaking ability also in American Sign.

REFERENCES:

- Dr. Patricia Englisia, University Supervisor of Student Teaching, California State University, Sacramento (916) 278-7020.
- Mr. Ray Combs, Cooperating Teacher at Valley High School, Elk Grove, CA (916) 778-8900.
- Ms. Gloria Evans, Cooperating Teacher at Eddy Middle School, Elk Grove, CA (916) 777-2496.

FIGURE 10.1 ● Sample Teaching Résumé

produce a new copy each time you apply for a job. If you maintain your résumé on a computer disk, then it is easy to make modifications and print a current copy each time one is needed.

- Prepare a cover letter to accompany your résumé that is written specifically for the position for which you are applying. Address the letter personally but formally to the personnel director. Limit the cover letter to one page, and emphasize yourself, your teaching experiences and interests, and reasons that you are best qualified for the position. Show a familiarity with the particular school or district. Again, if you maintain a generic application letter on a computer disk, you can easily modify it to make it specific for each position.

- Have your résumé and cover letter edited by someone familiar with résumé writing and editing, perhaps an English-teaching friend. A poorly written, poorly typed, or poorly copied résumé fraught with spelling and grammar errors will guarantee that you will not be considered for the job. In addition to avoiding misspellings, check for inaccuracies and omissions. Keep a consistent format. Leave some white space; do not overcrowd the page.

- Be sure that your application reaches the personnel director by the announced deadline. If for some reason it will be late, then telephone the director, explain the circumstances, and request permission to submit your application late.

■ The In-Person Interview

If your application and résumé are attractive to the personnel director, you will be notified and scheduled for a personal or small-group interview, although in some instances the hiring interview may precede the request for your personal papers. Whichever the case, during the interview you should be honest, and you should be yourself. Practice an interview, perhaps with aid of a video camera. Ask someone to role-play an interview with you and ask you some tough questions. Plan your interview wardrobe and get it ready the night before. Leave early for your interview so that you arrive in plenty of time. If possible, long before your scheduled interview, locate someone who works in the school district and discuss curriculum, classroom management policies, popular programs, and district demographics with that person. If you anticipate a professionally embarrassing question during the interview, think of diplomatic ways to respond. This means that you should think of ways to turn your weaknesses into strengths. For instance, if your cooperating teacher has mentioned that you need to continue to develop your room environment skills (meaning that you were sloppy), admit that you realize that you need to be more conscientious about keeping supplies and materials neat and tidy, but mention your concern about the students and the learning and that you realize you have a tendency to interact with students more than with objects. Assure someone that you will work on this skill, and then do it. The paragraphs that follow offer additional specific guidelines for preparing for and handling the in-person interview. As you peruse these guidelines, please know that what may seem trite and obvious to one reader is not necessarily obvious to another.

You will be given a specific time, date, and place for the interview. Regardless of your other activities, accept the time, date, and location suggested, rather than trying to manipulate the interviewer around a schedule more convenient for you.

As a part of the interview you may be expected to do a formal but abbreviated (10–15 minutes) teaching demonstration. You may or may not be told in advance of this expectation. So, it is a good idea to thoughtfully develop and rehearse a model one that you could perform on immediate request. Just in case it might be useful, some candidates carry to the interview a videotape of one of their best real-teaching episodes, such as one that was made during student teaching.

Dress for success. Regardless of what else you may be doing for a living, take the time necessary to make a professional and proud appearance.

Avoid coming to the interview with small children. If necessary, arrange to have them taken care of by someone. Arrive promptly, shake your dry hands firmly with members of the committee, and initiate conversation with a friendly comment, based on your personal knowledge, about the school or district.

Be prepared to answer standard interview questions. Sometimes school districts will send candidates the questions that will be asked during the interview; at other times, these questions are handed to the candidate upon arrival at the interview. The questions that are likely to be asked will cover the following topics:

- *Your experiences with students of the relevant age.* The committee wants to be reasonably certain that you can effectively manage and teach at this level. You should answer this question by sharing specific successes that demonstrate that you are a decisive and competent teacher.

- *Hobbies and travels.* The committee wants to know more about you as a person to ensure that you will be an interesting and energetic teacher to the students as well as a congenial member of the faculty.

- *Extracurricular interests and experiences.* The committee wants to know about all the ways in which you might be helpful in the school and to know that you will promote the interests and cocurricular activities of students and the school community. Be sure to include any relevant coaching experience or interests.

- *Classroom management techniques.* You must convince the committee that you can effectively manage a classroom of diverse learners in a manner that will help the students to develop their self-esteem.

- *Knowledge of the curriculum standards and the subject taught at the grade for which you are being considered.* The committee needs to be reasonably certain that you have command of the subject and its place within the developmental stages of students at this level. This is where you should show your knowledge of national standards and of state and local curriculum documents.

- *Knowledge of assessment strategies relevant for use in teaching at this level.* This is your place to shine with your professional knowledge about using rubrics and performance assessment.

- *Commitment to teaching at this level.* The committee wants to be assured that you are knowledgeable about and committed to teaching and learning at this level as opposed to just seeking this job until something better comes along.

- *Your ability to reflect on experience and to grow from that reflection.* Demonstrate that you are a reflective decision maker and a lifelong learner. If you are asked about your weaknesses, you have an opportunity to show that you can effectively reflect and self-assess, that you can think reflectively and critically, and that you know the value of learning from your own errors and how to do so. Be prepared for this question by identifying a specific error that you have made, perhaps while student teaching, and explain how you turned that error into a profitable learning experience.

Throughout the interview you should maintain eye contact with the interviewer, demonstrating interest, enthusiasm, and self-confidence. It is very important that you research the school, district, and position and prepare questions for your interviewer(s). When an opportunity arises, ask one or two planned questions that demonstrate your knowledge of and interest in the position and the community and school or district.

When the interview has obviously been brought to a close by the interviewer, that is your signal to leave. Do not hang around, which is a sign of lacking confidence. Follow the interview with a thank-you letter addressed to the personnel director or interviewer; even if you do not get the job, you will be better remembered for future reference.[6]

Once you are employed as a teacher, your professional development continues. The sections that follow demonstrate ways in which that can happen.

■ PROFESSIONAL DEVELOPMENT THROUGH REFLECTION AND SELF-ASSESSMENT

Beginning now and continuing throughout your career, you will reflect on your teaching, and you will want to continue to grow as a professional as a result of those reflections (growth is not so likely unless self-initiated and systematically planned). The most competent professional is one who is proactive, that is, who takes charge and initiates his or her own continuing professional development. One useful way of continuing to reflect, self-assess, and grow professionally is by maintaining a *professional journal*, much as your students do when they maintain journals reflecting on what they are learning. Another is by continuing to maintain the professional career portfolio that you began assembling early in your pre-service program and finalized for your job search (as discussed earlier in this module). Some teachers maintain *professional logbooks*, which serve not only as documentation of their specific professional contributions and activities, but also as documentation of the breadth of their professional involvement. Some teachers maintain research logs as a way of recording questions that come up during the busy teaching day and as a way of establishing a plan for finding answers. The *research log* strategy can be of tremendous benefit to you in actively researching and improving your classroom work, but also it can be of interest to colleagues. Finally, working in

teams and sharing your work with team members is still another way of continuing to reflect, self-assess, and grow as a teacher.

■ PROFESSIONAL DEVELOPMENT THROUGH MENTORING

Mentoring, one teacher facilitating the learning of another teacher, can aid in professional development.[7] In what is sometimes called *peer coaching*, a mentor teacher volunteers, is selected by the teacher who wishes to improve, or is selected by a school administrator, formally or informally. The mentor observes and coaches the teacher to help him or her improve in teaching. Sometimes the teacher being coached simply wants to learn a new skill. In other instances, the teacher remains with the mentor teacher for an entire school year, developing and improving old and new skills or learning how to teach with a new program. In many districts, new teachers are automatically assigned to mentor teachers for their first, and sometimes second, year in an induction program.

■ PROFESSIONAL DEVELOPMENT THROUGH IN-SERVICE AND ADVANCED STUDY

In-service workshops and programs are offered for teachers by the school, by the district, and by other agencies such as a county office of education or a nearby college or university. In-service workshops and programs are usually designed for specific purposes, such as to train teachers in new teaching skills, to update their knowledge in content, and to introduce them to new teaching materials or programs. For example, Baltimore City Public School (MD) provides a systemwide professional development program for teachers of grades 6–8, administrators, and staff at its Lombard Learning Academy Demonstration Center. The Lombard Learning Academy is a school-within-a-school located at Lombard Middle School. Cohorts of 5 to 10 teachers from other schools in the district visit the Academy for 5-day periods to observe instruction, practice strategies, and hone their skills in the use of technology.

University graduate study is yet another way of continuing your professional development. Some teachers pursue master's degrees in academic teaching fields, while many others pursue master's degrees in curriculum and methods of instruction or in educational administration or counseling. Some universities offer a Master of Arts in Teaching (MAT), a program of courses in specific academic fields that are especially designed for teachers.

■ PROFESSIONAL DEVELOPMENT THROUGH PARTICIPATION IN PROFESSIONAL ORGANIZATIONS

There are many professional organizations, local, statewide, national, and international. The organizations are usually discipline-specific, such as, for example, the National Council for Teachers of English (NCTE), the International Reading Association (IRA), the National Council of Teachers of Mathematics (NCTM), the National Council for the Social Studies (NCSS), and the National Science Teachers Association (NSTA). In most states there is a statewide organization, probably affiliated with a national organization. In addition, there are the National Education Association (NEA), the Association of American Educators (AAE), and the **American Federation of Teachers (AFT).**

Local, district, state, and national organizations have meetings that include guest speakers, workshops, and publishers' displays. Professional meetings of teachers are educational, enriching, and fulfilling for those who attend. In addition, many other professional associations, such as those for reading teachers, supply speakers and publish articles in their journals that are often of interest to teachers other than the target audience.

Professional organizations publish newsletters and journals for their members, and these will likely be found in your college or university library. Sample periodicals are listed in Figure 8.2 (Module 8). Many professional organizations have special membership prices for teachers who are still college or university students, a courtesy that allows for an inexpensive beginning affiliation with a professional association. For information on special membership prices and association services, contact those of interest to you. See addresses in Module 3.

■ PROFESSIONAL DEVELOPMENT THROUGH COMMUNICATIONS WITH OTHER TEACHERS

Visiting teachers at other schools; attending in-service workshops, graduate seminars, and programs; participating in teacher study groups[8] and meetings of professional organizations; participating in teacher networks;[9] and sharing with teachers by means of electronic bulletin boards are all valuable experiences, if for no other reason than talking and sharing with teachers from not only across this country but from around the world. These discussions include a sharing of not only "war stories" but also ideas and descriptions of new programs, books, materials, and techniques that work.

As in other process skills, the teacher practices and models skill in communication, in and out of the classroom. This includes communicating with other teachers to improve one's own repertoire of strategies and knowledge about teaching as well as sharing one's experiences with others. Teaching other teachers about your own special skills and sharing your experiences are important components of the communication and professional development processes.

■ PROFESSIONAL DEVELOPMENT THROUGH SUMMER AND OFF-TEACHING WORK EXPERIENCE

In many areas of the United States there are special programs of short-term employment available to interested teachers. These are available especially, although not exclusively, to teachers of physical education, mathematics, science, and social studies and are offered by public agencies, private industry, foundations, and research institutes. These institutions are interested in disseminating information and providing opportunities for teachers to update their skills and knowledge, with an ultimate hope that the teachers will stimulate in more students a desire to develop their physical fitness, to understand civic responsibilities, and to consider careers in science and technology. Participating industries, foundations, governments, and institutes provide on-the-job training with salaries or stipends to teachers who are selected to participate. During the program of employment and depending on the nature of that work, a variety of people (e.g., scientists, technicians, politicians, businesspersons, social workers, and sometimes university educators) meet with teachers to share experiences and discuss what is being learned and its implications for teaching and curriculum development.

Some of the programs for teachers are government-sponsored, field-centered, and content-specific. For example, a program may concentrate on geology, anthropology, mathematics, or reading. At another location, a program may concentrate on teaching, using a specific new or experimental curriculum. These programs, located around the country, may have university affiliation, which means that university credit may be available. Room and board, travel, and a stipend are sometimes granted to participating teachers.

Sources of information about the availability of programs include publications and Web pages of professional organizations, the local chamber of commerce, and meetings of the local or regional teacher's organization. In areas where there are no organized programs of part-time work experience for teachers, some teachers have successfully initiated their own by establishing contact with management personnel of local businesses or companies.

■ PROFESSIONAL DEVELOPMENT THROUGH MICRO PEER-TEACHING

Micro peer-teaching (MPT) is a skill-development strategy used for professional development by both pre-service and in-service teachers. Micro peer-teaching is a scaled-down teaching experience involving a:

- Limited objective
- Brief interval for teaching a lesson
- Lesson taught to a few (8–10) peers (as your students)
- Lesson that focuses on the use of one or several instructional strategies

Micro peer-teaching can be a predictor of later teaching effectiveness in a regular classroom. More importantly, it can provide an opportunity to develop and improve specific teaching behaviors. A videotaped MPT allows you to see yourself in action for self-evaluation and diagnosis. Evaluation of an MPT session is based on:

- The quality of the teacher's preparation and lesson implementation
- The quality of the planned and implemented student involvement
- Whether the instructional objective(s) was reached
- The appropriateness of the cognitive level of the lesson

Whether a pre-service or in-service teacher, you are urged to participate in one or more MPT experiences. Formatted differently from previous exercises in this book, Exercise 10.2 can represent a summative performance assessment for the course for which this book is being used.

EXERCISE **10.2**

■ Pulling It All Together—Micro Peer-Teaching IV

Instructions: The purpose of this exercise is to learn how to further develop your own MPT experiences. You will prepare and teach a lesson that is prepared as a lesson presentation for your peers, at their level of intellectual maturity and understanding (i.e., as opposed to teaching the lesson to peers pretending that they are public school students). Forms A, B, and C appear on pages 303–305.

This experience has two components:

1. Your preparation and implementation of a demonstration lesson.

2. Your completion of an analysis of the summative peer assessment and the self-assessment, with statements of how you would change the lesson and your teaching of it were you to repeat the lesson.

You should prepare and carry out a 15- to 20-minute lesson to a group of peers. The exact time limit for the lesson should be set by your group, based on the size of the group and the amount of time available. When the time limit has been set, complete the time-allowed entry (item 1) on Form A of this exercise. Some of your peers will serve as your students; others will be evaluating your teaching. (The process works best when "students" do not evaluate while being students.) Your teaching should be videotaped for self-evaluation.

For your lesson, identify one concept and develop your lesson to teach toward an understanding of that concept. Within the time allowed, your lesson should include both teacher talk and a hands-on activity for the students. Use Form A for the initial planning of your lesson. Then complete a lesson plan, selecting a lesson plan format as discussed in Module 4. Then present the lesson to the "students." The peers who are evaluating your presentation should use Form B of this exercise.

After your presentation, collect your peer evaluations (the Form B copies that you gave to the evaluators). Then review your presentation by viewing the videotape. After viewing the tape, prepare

- A tabulation and statistical analysis of peer evaluations of your lesson.
- A self-evaluation based on your analysis of the peer evaluations, your feelings having taught the lesson, and your thoughts after viewing the videotape.
- A summary analysis that includes your selection and description of your teaching strengths and weaknesses as indicated by this peer-teaching experience and how you would improve were you to repeat the lesson.

(continued)

■ TABULATION OF PEER EVALUATIONS

The procedure for tabulating the completed evaluations received from your peers is as follows:

1. *Use a blank copy of Form B for tabulating.* In the left margin of that copy, place the letters N (number) and σ (total) to prepare for two columns of numbers that will fall below each of those letters. In the far right margin, place the word *Score.*

2. *For each item (a through y) on the peer evaluation form, count the number of evaluators who gave a rating (from 1 to 5) on the item.* Sometimes an evaluator may not rate a particular item, so although there may have been 10 peers evaluating your MPT, the number of evaluators giving you a rating on any one particular item could be less than 10. For each item, the number of evaluators rating that item we call N. Place this number in the N column at the far left margin on your blank copy of Form B, next to the relevant item.

3. *Using a calculator, obtain the sum of the peer ratings for each item.* For example, for item a, *lesson preparation evident*, you add the numbers given by each evaluator for that item. If there were 10 evaluators who gave you a number rating on that item, then your sum on that item will not be more than 50 (5×10). Because individual evaluators will make their X marks differently, you sometimes must estimate an individual evaluator's number rating—that is, rather than a clear rating of 3 or 3.5 on an item, you may have to estimate it as a 3.2 or a 3.9. In the left-hand margin of your blank copy of Form B, in the σ column, place the sum for each item.

4. *Now obtain a score for each item, a through y.* The score for each item is obtained by dividing σ by N. Your score for each item will range between 1 and 5. Write this result in the column in the right-hand margin under the word *Score* parallel to the relevant item. This is the number you will use in the analysis phase.

■ PROCEDURE FOR ANALYZING THE TABULATIONS

Having completed the tabulation of the peer evaluations of your teaching, you are ready to proceed with your analysis of those tabulations.

1. To proceed, you need a blank copy of Form C of this exercise, your self-analysis form.

2. On the blank copy of Form C, there are five items: Implementation, Personal, Voice, Materials, and Strategies.

3. In the far left margin of Form C, place the letter σ for the sum. To its right, and parallel with it, place the word *Average.* You now have arranged for two columns of five numbers each—a σ column and an *Average* column.

4. For each of the five items, get the total score for that item, as follows:
   a. *Implementation.* Add all scores (from the right-hand margin of blank Form B) for the four items a, c, x, and y. The total should be 20 or less (4×5). Place this total in the left-hand margin under σ (to the left of *1. Implementation*).
   b. *Personal.* Add all scores (from the right-hand margin of blank Form B) for the nine items f, g, m, n, o, p, q, s, and t. The total should be 45 or less (9×5). Place this total in the left-hand margin under σ (to the left of *2. Personal*).
   c. *Voice.* Add all scores (from the right-hand margin of blank Form B) for the three items h, i, and j. The total should be 15 or less (3×5). Place this total in the left-hand margin under σ (to the left of *3. Voice*).
   d. *Materials.* Add all scores (from the right-hand margin of blank Form B) for item k. The total should be 5 or less (1×5). Place this total in the left-hand margin under σ (to the left of *4. Materials*).
   e. *Strategies.* Add all scores (from the right-hand margin of blank Form B) for the eight items b, d, e, l, r, u, v, and w. The total should be 40 or less (8×5). Place this total in the left-hand margin under σ (to the left of *5. Strategies*).

5. Now, for each of the five categories, divide the sum by the number of items in the category to get your peer evaluation average score for that category. For item 1 you will divide by 4; for item 2, by 9; for item 3, by 3; for item 4, by 1; and for item 5, by 8. For each category you should then have a final average peer evaluation score of between 1 and 5. If correctly done, you now have average scores for each of the five categories:

(continued)

Implementation, Personal, Voice, Materials, and Strategies. With those scores and evaluators' comments you can prepare your final summary analysis.

The following table includes three sample analyses of MPT lessons based *only* on the scores—that is, without reference to comments made by individual evaluators, although peer evaluators' comments are important considerations for actual analyses.

Sample Analyses of MPTs Based Only on Peer Evaluation Scores

Teacher	Category/Rating					Possible Strengths and Weaknesses
	1	2	3	4	5	
A	4.2	2.5	2.8	4.5	4.5	Good lesson, weakened by personal items and voice
B	4.5	4.6	5.0	5.0	5.0	Excellent teaching, perhaps needing a stronger start
C	2.5	3.0	3.5	1.0	1.5	Poor strategy choice, lack of student involvement

 To access this exercise online, go to the Companion Website at **www.prenhall.com/kellough**.

EXERCISE 10.2A

■ Form A

MPT Preparation

Form A is to be used for initial preparation of your MPT lesson. (For preparation of your lesson, study Form B.) After completing Form A, proceed with the preparation of your MPT lesson using a lesson plan format as discussed in Module 4. A copy of the final lesson plan should be presented to the evaluators at the start of your MPT presentation.

1. Time allowed:

2. Title or topic of lesson I will teach:

3. Concept:

4. Specific instructional objectives for the lesson:

    Cognitive

    Affective

    Psychomotor

5. Strategies to be used, including approximate time plan:

    Set introduction

    Transitions

    Closure

    Others

6. Student experiences to be provided (i.e., specify for each—visual, verbal, kinesthetic, and tactile experiences):

7. Materials, equipment, and resources needed:

 To access this exercise online, go to the Companion Website at **www.prenhall.com/kellough**.

Peer Evaluation

Evaluators use Form B, making an *X* on the continuum between 5 and 1. Far left (5) is the highest rating; far right (1) is the lowest. Completed forms are collected and given to the teacher upon completion of that teacher's MPT and are reviewed by the teacher prior to reviewing his or her videotaped lesson.

To evaluators: Comments as well as marks are useful to the teacher.

To teacher: Give one copy of your lesson plan to the evaluators at the start of your MPT. (*Note:* It is best if evaluators can be together at a table at the rear of the room.)

Teacher _____ Date _____

Topic _____

Concept _____

1. Organization of lesson	5	4	3	2	1
a. Lesson preparation evident	very		somewhat		no
b. Lesson beginning effective	yes		somewhat		poor
c. Subject-matter knowledge apparent	yes		somewhat		no
d. Strategies selection effective	yes		somewhat		poor
e. Closure effective	yes		somewhat		poor

Comments

2. Lesson implementation	5	4	3	2	1
f. Eye contact excellent	yes		somewhat		poor
g. Enthusiasm evident	yes		somewhat		no
h. Speech delivery	articulate		minor problems		poor
i. Voice inflection; cueing	effective		minor problems		poor
j. Vocabulary use	well chosen		minor problems		poor
k. Aids, props, and materials	effective		okay		none
l. Use of examples and analogies	effective		needs improvement		none
m. Student involvement	effective		okay		none
n. Use of overlapping skills	good		okay		poor
o. Nonverbal communication	effective		a bit confusing		distracting
p. Use of active listening	effective		okay		poor
q. Responses to students	personal and accepting		passive or indifferent		impersonal and antagonistic
r. Use of questions	effective		okay		poor
s. Use of student names	effective		okay		no
t. Use of humor	effective		okay		poor
u. Directions and refocusing	succinct		a bit vague		confusing
v. Teacher mobility	effective		okay		none
w. Use of transitions	smooth		a bit rough		unclear
x. Presentation motivating	very		somewhat		not at all
y. Momentum (pacing) of lesson	smooth and brisk		okay		too slow or too fast

Comments

 To access this exercise online, go to the Companion Website at **www.prenhall.com/kellough.**

EXERCISE 10.2C

■ Form C

Teacher's Summative Peer Evaluation

See instructions within Exercise 10.2 for completing this form.

1. Implementation (items a, c, x, y)	5	4	3	2	1
2. Personal (items f, g, m, n, o, p, q, s, t)	5	4	3	2	1
3. Voice (items h, i, j)	5	4	3	2	1
4. Materials (item k)	5	4	3	2	1
5. Strategies (items b, d, e, l, r, u, v, w)	5	4	3	2	1

Total = _____

Comments

 To access this exercise online, go to the Companion Website at **www.prenhall.com/kellough.**

POINTS TO PONDER

1. Do you believe that teachers' salaries should be tied to student achievement?

2. In 1998, young teachers (ages 22 to 28) earned an average of nearly $8,000 less per year than did other college-educated people of the same age cohort. Further, for teachers in the 44 to 50 age range, the gap was three times greater than for their counterparts in other occupations. Worse yet, teachers of that age range (44 to 50) who had master's degrees earned an average of more than $32,000 less than did their nonteacher counterparts with master's degrees.[10]

3. If offered by a district or requested by your school principal, would you accept a job teaching a subject that is out of your field of training?

4. Would you be willing to have your surgical operation performed by an unlicensed surgeon? Would you be willing to be defended in trial by an unlicensed attorney? Would you be willing to insure your automobile with an unlicensed insurance agent? Would you be willing to leave your child each day in the care of an unlicensed teacher?

5. Some teachers become disenchanted working in a profession where they see no opportunity to improve their salary through merit. They argue that in most other careers there is at least the option of requesting a raise, and if you perform well you can get a bonus or promotion. That just isn't the case in teaching.

■ SUMMARY

Because teaching and learning go hand-in-hand, and the effectiveness of one affects that of the other, the final two modules of this book have dealt with both aspects of the "how well" component of teacher preparation—how well the students are learning and how well the teacher is teaching. In addition, you have been presented with guidelines about how to obtain your first teaching job and how to continue your professional development. Although you have not been told everything you will ever need to know about the assessment of teaching and learning, or about other aspects of public middle school and secondary school teaching, about finding a job, or about continuing your professional development, we have addressed the essentials. Throughout your teaching career you will continue improving your knowledge and skills in all aspects of teaching and learning.

We began this book by providing input data about schools and teaching and then proceeded to guide you through additional ways to collect and share data as well as ways to process those data into your own plans for teaching. Now you are ready for the highest application of your knowledge and skills—a full-time teaching position, where you are paid for teaching.

You have arrived at the end of this text! We thank you for allowing us to be a part of your quest to become a competent teacher. We hope your quest has been and will continue to be enjoyable and profitable, and we wish you the very best in your new career. Teaching is a profession to be proud of. We welcome you to it!

■ MODULE 10 **POSTTEST**

Multiple Choice

1. Which one of the following is evidence that a teacher-candidate is not ready to be granted a teaching credential?
   a. The candidate is able to plan lessons independently.
   b. The candidate demonstrates enthusiasm for teaching.
   c. The candidate has irregular attendance and gives excuses when evaluated.
   d. The candidate is open and responsive to suggestions for improvement.

2. Which one of the following is a positive indicator that the teacher-candidate is ready to be granted a teaching credential?
   a. The candidate overreacts to student misbehavior.
   b. The candidate's knowledge of subject matter is superficial.
   c. The candidate has effective activities planned for emergency situations.
   d. The candidate typically has but one instructional activity for an entire class period.

3. Professional field experiences include
   a. assisting credentialed teachers in the classroom.
   b. student teaching.
   c. internship.
   d. any of the above

4. Of the following, which are you expected to possess when entering the student-teaching phase of your professional training?
   a. an understanding of youth and how they learn
   b. a repertoire of teaching skills
   c. a command of subject matter
   d. all of the above and more

5. As a student teacher you are expected to
   a. be prompt with all assignments.
   b. abide by the routines of the host school.
   c. make arrangements when you will be late or absent.
   d. all of the above and more

6. While student teaching, the legal responsibility for day-to-day activities in the classroom belongs to
   a. the parents of the students in the classroom.
   b. the credentialed cooperating teacher.
   c. the adult classroom aide.
   d. the student teacher.

7. While at their teaching assignments, student teachers should dress
   a. casually.
   b. professionally.
   c. however teachers at the school dress.
   d. however they dress when not at the school.

(continued)

8. Data in your professional résumé should include
   a. name, address, telephone number, education, professional experience, and credentials.
   b. name, address, marital status, photograph of yourself, education, professional experience, and credentials.
   c. name, address, age, height, weight, marital status, number or names of children at home, and a personal photograph.
   d. name, address, phone number, marital status, professional experience and credentials, location of placement file, professional affiliations, and honors received.

9. During a professional employment interview, it is recommended that you
   a. avoid eye contact with the interviewer.
   b. be a few minutes late for the appointment.
   c. dress casually to demonstrate that you are relaxed and in control.
   d. none of the above.

10. The practice of assigning an experienced teacher to mentor a first-year teacher is called
   a. inclusion.
   b. induction.
   c. indignation.
   d. distance learning.

Short Explanation

1. During your student teaching, suppose you should try out a new teaching technique and it fails miserably for you. Describe what you should do.
2. Identify three danger signals that a cooperating teacher needs to be alert for to try to prevent a student teacher from getting into serious teaching trouble.
3. Identify and explain three ways that you can prepare yourself to be more hirable.
4. Explain why it is that most professional educators will recommend that you join a professional organization in your teaching field.
5. Identify five ways a teacher can continue to grow professionally.
6. Explain why you agree or disagree with the statement that there is a direct correlation between discipline problems and how well prepared the teacher is.
7. What would you do if during your student teaching your cooperating teacher tells you that a strategy you have planned will not work?
8. While student teaching, will you expect to have student papers to take home to read and grade? Why or why not?
9. Explain the role of reflection and self-analysis during your student teaching.
10. Explain how many hours a week of your time you expect your student teaching will require of you.

Essay

1. Explain why you agree or disagree that classroom observations and theory courses in education should precede the student-teaching experience in teacher preparation.
2. Identify and define the categories by which teacher effectiveness is determined.
3. From your current observations and fieldwork related to this teacher preparation program, clearly identify one specific example of educational practice that seems contradictory to exemplary practice or theory presented in this module. Present your explanation for the discrepancy.
4. Describe any prior concepts you held that changed as a result of the experiences of this module. Describe the changes.
5. Explain why teaching is considered to be a profession. Explain when, if ever, it is not a profession.

 To access this posttest and the answers online, go to the Companion Website at www.prenhall.com/kellough.

■ SUGGESTED READINGS

Backes, C. E., & Backes, L. S. (1999). Making the best of a learning experience. *Techniques: Making Education and Career Connections, 74*(5), 23–24.

Chenfeld, M. B. (2004). Metaphors of hope, *Phi Delta Kappan, 86*(4), 271–275.

Cramer, G., & Hurst, B. (2000). *How to find a teaching job: A guide for success.* Upper Saddle River, NJ: Merrill/Prentice Hall.

Graham, P., et al. (Eds.). (1999). *Teacher/mentor.* New York: Teachers College Press.

Jupp, J. C. (2004). Culturally relevant teaching: One teacher's journey through theory and practice, *Multicultural Review, 13*(1), 33–40.

Kellough, R. D. (2001). *Surviving your first year of teaching: Guidelines for success* (2nd ed.). Upper Saddle River, NJ: Merrill/Prentice Hall.

Kottler, E., et al. (1998). *Secrets for secondary school teachers: How to succeed in your first year.* Thousand Oaks, CA: Corwin Press.

Lester, J. H. (2003). Planning effective secondary professional development programs. *American Secondary Education, 32*(1), 49–62.

Lowenhaupt, M. A., & Stephanik, C. E. (1999). *Making student teaching work: Creating a partnership.* Fastback 447. Bloomington, IN: Phi Delta Kappa Educational Foundation.

Lyons, N. (Ed.). (1998). *With portfolio in hand.* New York: Teachers College Press.

Martin, D. B. (1999). *The portfolio planner: Making professional portfolios work for you.* Upper Saddle River, NJ: Merrill/Prentice Hall.

McEwan, E. K. (1998). *How to deal with parents who are angry, troubled, afraid, or just plain crazy.* Thousand Oaks, CA: Corwin Press.

McLaughlin, M., et al. (1998). *Portfolio models: Reflections across the teaching profession.* Norwood, MA: Christopher-Gordon.

Michie, G. (2004). Teaching in the undertow: Advice for new teachers on resisting the pull of schooling-as-usual. *Rethinking Schools, 18*(4), 18–21.

National Opinion Research Center. (1998). *Questions parents ask about schools.* Chicago: Author.

Newman, J. M., et al. (1998). *Tensions of teaching: Beyond tips to critical reflection.* New York: Teachers College Press.

Notman, T. S., & Megyeri, K. A. (1999). To student teach. *English Journal, 88*(4), 20–25.

Oakley, K. (1998). The performance assessment system: A portfolio assessment model for evaluating beginning teachers. *Journal of Personnel Evaluation in Education, 11*(4), 323–341.

Sparks, D. (2004). The looming danger of a two-tiered professional development system. *Phi Delta Kappan, 86*(4), 304–306.

Torreano, J. M. (2000). *500 Q&A for new teachers: A survival guide.* Norwood, MA: Christopher-Gordon.

Trubowitz, S. (2004). The why, how, and what of mentoring, *Phi Delta Kappan, 86*(1), 59–64.

Van Wagenen, L., & Hibbard, K. M. (1998). Building teacher portfolios. *Educational Leadership, 55*(5), 26–29.

Wasonga, T. A. & Piveral, J. A. (2004). Diversity and the modeling of multicultural principles of education in a teacher education program, *Multicultural Perspectives, 6*(3), 42–47.

Wilder, A., & Croker, D. L. (1999). How can we better train our student teachers? *English Journal, 88*(3), 17–21.

Wong, H. K., Britton, T. & Ganser, T. (2004). What the world can teach us about new teacher induction, *Phi Delta Kappan, 86*(4), 379–384.

■ ENDNOTES

[1] R. Fulghum, Pay Attention. In Richard Carlson and Benjamin Shield (Ed.), *Handbook for the Soul* (Maine: G. K. Hall & Co., 1995).

[2] See, for example, P. J. Hallman, *Field-Based Teacher Education. Restructuring Texas Teacher Education Series 1* (Austin, TX: Texas State Board for Educator Certification, 1998); and L. Huling, *Early Field Experiences in Teacher Education*, ED429054 (Washington, DC: ERIC Clearinghouse on Teaching and Teacher Education, 1998).

[3] R. P. Johanson et al., *Internet and List-Serves to Support the Student Teaching Semester* (Paper presented at the Annual Meeting of the American Association of Colleges for Teacher Education, Washington, DC, February 24–27, 1999).

[4] C. Shakesaft, *Educator Sexual Misconduct: A Synthesis of Existing Literature* (Washington, D.C.: U.S. Department of Education Office of the Under Secretary, Policy and Program Studies Service, June 2004). Report # ED-02-PO-3281. Available at: **http://www.ed.gov/rschstat/ research/pubs/misconductreview/report.pdf**.

[5] You may be interested in several articles about portfolios in the theme issue of *Teacher Education Quarterly 25*(1) (Winter 1998).

[6] For additional suggestions for preparing for a teaching job interview, see Internet Web site **http://www.teachnet.com/**.

[7] For additional information, see The International Center for Information About New Teacher Mentoring and Induction at **http://www.teachermentors.com/MCenter%20Site/AdviceBegTchr.html.** and a description of California's Beginning Teacher Support and Assessment (BSTA) Program at **http://www.ccoe.k12.ca.us/coe/curins. sbtsa/**. See also A. Gratch, Beginning Teacher and Mentor Relationships, *Journal of Teacher Education 49*(3), 220–227 (May/June 1998).

[8] See, for example, G. Cramer et al., *Teacher Study Groups for Professional Development*, Fastback 406 (Bloomington, IN: Phi Delta Kappa Educational Foundation, 1996).

[9] See, for example, A. Lieberman and M. Grolnick, Networks, Reform, and the Professional Development of Teachers, in A. Hargreaves (Ed.), *Rethinking Educational Change with Heart and Mind*, Chap. 10, pp. 192–215 (Alexandria, VA: ASCD 1997 Yearbook, Association for Supervision and Curriculum Development, 1997).

[10] Source of the data: Quality Counts 2000, *Education Week XIX* (18), p. 8 (January 13, 2000).

Glossary

A

Ability grouping The assignment of students to separate classrooms or to separate activities within a classroom according to their perceived academic abilities. *Homogeneous grouping* is the grouping of students of similar abilities; *heterogeneous grouping* is the grouping of students of mixed abilities.

Academies Private secondary schools that prepared students for a number of fields. The first academy was founded in Philadelphia by Benjamin Franklin in 1751.

Accommodation The cognitive process of modifying a schema or creating new schemata.

Accountability Reference to the concept that an individual is responsible for his or her behaviors and should be able to demonstrate publicly the worth of the activities carried out.

Adolescence The period of life from the onset of puberty to maturity, terminating legally at the age of majority, generally the ages of 12 to 20, although young or early adolescence may start as soon as age 9.

Advance organizer Preinstructional cues that encourage a mental set; used to enhance retention of content to be studied.

Advisor-advisee Common to many middle schools and increasingly in high schools, the program (sometimes referred to as *homebase* or *advisory* program) that provides each student the opportunity to interact with peers about school and personal concerns and to develop a meaningful relationship with at least one adult.

Affective domain The area of learning related to interests, attitudes, feelings, values, and personal adjustment.

Aims The most general educational objectives.

Alternative assessment Assessment of learning in ways that are different from traditional paper-and-pencil objective testing, such as a portfolio, project, or self-assessment. See *authentic assessment*.

American Federation of Teachers (AFT) A national professional organization of teachers founded in 1916, currently affiliated with the American Federation of Labor and Congress of Industrial Organizations (AFL–CIO). It was recently merged in at least two states with the NEA.

Anticipatory set See *advance organizer*.

Articulation Term used when referring to the connectedness of the various components of the formal curriculum—*vertical articulation* refers to the connectedness of the K–12 curriculum, and *horizontal articulation* refers to the connectedness across a grade level.

Assessment The relatively neutral process of finding out what students will or have learned as a result of instruction.

At-risk General term given to a student who shows a high potential for not completing school.

Authentic assessment The use of assessment procedures (usually portfolios and projects) that are highly compatible with the instructional objectives. Also referred to as *accurate, active, aligned, alternative, direct,* and *performance assessment.*

B

Behavioral objective A statement of expectation describing what the learner should be able to do upon completion of the instruction.

Behaviorism A theory that equates learning with changes in observable behavior.

Block scheduling The school programming procedure that provides large blocks of time (e.g., 90 minutes or 2 hours) in which individual teachers or teacher teams can organize and arrange groupings of students for varied periods of time, thereby more effectively individualizing the instruction for students with various needs and abilities.

Brainstorming An instructional strategy used to create a flow of new ideas, during which judgments of the ideas of others are forbidden.

C

CD-ROM (compact disc—read only memory) Digitally encoded information (up to 650MB of data that can include animation, audio, graphics, text, and video) permanently recorded on a compact (4.72 inch, 12 cm in diameter) disc.

Character education A program that focuses on the development of the values of honesty, kindness, respect, and responsibility.

Charter school A school that is "an autonomous educational entity operating under a charter, or contract, that has been negotiated between the organizers, who create and operate the school, and a sponsor, who oversees the provisions of the charter".

Clarifying question A question used to gain more information from a student to help the teacher better understand a student's ideas, feelings, and thought processes.

Classroom control The process of influencing student behavior in the classroom.

Classroom management The teacher's system of establishing a climate for learning, including techniques for preventing and handling student misbehavior.

Closure The means by which a teacher brings the lesson to an end.

Coaching See *mentoring*.

Cognition The process of thinking.

Cognitive disequilibrium The mental state of not yet having made sense out of a perplexing (discrepant) situation.

Cognitive domain The area of learning related to intellectual skills, such as retention and assimilation of knowledge.

Cognitive psychology A branch of psychology devoted to the study of how individuals acquire, process, and use information.

Cognitivism A theory that holds that learning entails the construction or reshaping of mental schemata and that mental processes mediate learning. Also known as *constructivism*.

Common planning time A regularly scheduled time during the school day when teachers who teach the same students meet for joint planning, parent conferences, materials preparation, and student evaluation.

Compact disc (CD) A 4.72-inch disc on which a laser has recorded digital information.

Comprehension A level of cognition that refers to the skill of understanding.

Comprehensive high school Schools that offer college preparatory, general, and vocational tracks.

Computer literacy The ability, at some level on a continuum, to understand and use computers.

Computer-assisted instruction (CAI) Instruction received by a student when interacting with lessons programmed into a computer system. Known also as *computer-assisted learning (CAL)*.

Computer-managed instruction (CMI) The use of a computer system to manage information about learner performance and learning-resources options in order to prescribe and control individual lessons.

Concept map A visual or graphic representation of concepts and their relationships; words related to a key word are written in categories around the key word, and the categories are labeled.

Constructivism See *cognitivism*.

Continuous progress An instructional procedure that allows students to progress at their own pace through a sequenced curriculum.

Convergent thinking Thinking that is directed to a preset conclusion.

Convergent thinking question A low-order thinking question that has a single correct answer such as a recall question.

Cooperative learning A genre of instructional strategies that use small groups of students working together and helping each other on learning tasks, stressing support for one another rather than competition.

Core curriculum Subject or discipline components of the curriculum considered as being absolutely necessary. Traditionally these are English/language arts, mathematics, science, and social studies/history.

Course A complete sequence of instruction that presents a major division of a subject matter or discipline. Courses are laid out for a year, semester, a quarter, or, in the case of minicourses or intensive courses, a few weeks.

Covert behavior A learner behavior that is not outwardly observable.

Criterion A standard by which behavioral performance is judged.

Criterion-referenced assessment Assessment in which standards are established and behaviors are judged against the present guideline, rather than against the behaviors of others.

Critical thinking The ability to recognize and identify problems, to propose and to test solutions, and to arrive at tentative conclusions based on the data collected.

Cueing question When a teacher goes backward in a questioning sequence to cue students.

Cultural competence As defined by Diller and Moule, cultural competence "is the ability to successfully teach students who come from cultures other than your own. It entails mastering complex awareness and sensitivities, various bodies of knowledge, and a set of skills that, taken together, underlie effective cross-cultural teaching."

Culturally sensitive pedagogy A student-centered approach that integrates the students' cultural beliefs, traditions, and values into the teaching/learning process while emphasizing integration, critical thinking, and community involvement.

Culture Simply stated, culture is shared, learned behavior. It shapes values, beliefs, traditions and mores. Our cultural heritage determines who we are and helps us to make sense of the world.

Curriculum Originally derived from a Latin term referring to a race course for the chariots, the term still has no widely accepted definition. As used in this text, curriculum is that which is planned and encouraged for teaching and learning. This includes both school and nonschool environments, overt (formal) and hidden (informal) curriculums, and broad as well as narrow notions of content—its development, acquisition, and consequences.

Curriculum mapping The initial step in the process of designing integrated curriculum where middle and high school teachers list out what they each teach in their disciplines in a calendar year.

Curriculum standards Statements of the essential knowledge, skills, and attitudes to be learned.

D

Dame school The first schools, run by women in their homes during the Colonial Era. Reading, writing, and basic math skills were taught.

Deductive learning Learning that proceeds from the general to the specific. See also *expository learning*.

Detracking An effort to minimize or eliminate separate classes or programs for students who are of differing abilities.

Developmental characteristics A set of common intellectual, psychological, physical, and social characteristics that, when considered as a whole, indicate an individual's development relative to others during a particular age span.

Developmental needs A set of needs unique and appropriate to the developmental characteristics of a particular age span.

Diagnostic assessment See *preassessment*.

Didactic teaching See *direct instruction*.

Differentiated instruction Varying the methods and content of instruction according to individual student differences and needs.

Direct experience Learning by doing (applying) that which is being learned.

Direct instruction Teacher-centered expository instruction, such as lecturing or a teacher-guided group discussion.

Direct intervention Teacher use of verbal reminders or verbal commands to redirect student behavior, as opposed to nonverbal gestures or cues.

Direct teaching See *direct instruction*.

Discipline The process of controlling student behavior in the classroom. The term has been largely replaced by the terms *classroom control* or *classroom management*. It is also used in reference to the subject taught (e.g., language arts, science, mathematics, and so forth).

Discovery learning Learning that proceeds from identification of a problem, through the development of hypotheses, the testing of the hypotheses, and the arrival at a conclusion. See also *critical thinking*.

Divergent thinking Thinking that expands beyond original thought.

Divergent thinking question Open-ended (i.e., usually having no singularly correct answer) higher-order thinking questions (requiring analysis, synthesis, or evaluation), which require students to think creatively, to leave the comfortable confines of the known and reach out into the unknown.

Downshifting Reverting to earlier learned, lower-cognitive-level behaviors.

DVD (digital versatile disc or digital video disc) Media storage device like a CD-ROM but with a much greater storage capacity.

E

Early adolescence The developmental stage of young people as they approach and begin to experience puberty. This stage usually occurs between 10 and 14 years of age and deals with the successful attainment of the appropriate developmental characteristics for this age span.

Eclectic Utilizing the best from a variety of sources.

Effective school A school where students master basic skills, seek academic excellence in all subjects, demonstrate achievement, and display good behavior and attendance. Known also as an *exemplary school*.

Elective High-interest or special needs courses that are based on student selection from various options.

Elementary school Any school that has been planned and organized especially for children of some combination of grades kindergarten through 6. There are many variations, though; for example, a school might house children of preschool through grade 7 or 8 and still be called an elementary school.

Empathy The ability to understand the feelings of another person.

English classical school These schools provided a free public education for all students. They first opened in Boston in 1821 and offered a practical curriculum.

English Language Learners (ELLs) Students whose first language is other than English who are in the process of developing English language proficiency.

Equality Considered to be the same in status or competency level.

Equity Fairness and justice, that is, impartiality.

Evaluation Like assessment, but includes making sense out of the assessment results, usually based on criteria or a rubric. Evaluation is more subjective than is assessment.

Evaluative question A question that requires students to take a stance on some issue.

Exceptional learner A child who deviates from the average in any of the following ways: mental characteristics, sensory ability, neuromotor or physical characteristics, social behavior, communication ability, or multiple handicaps. Also known as a child with special needs.

Exemplary school See *effective school*.

Exploratory course A course designed to help students explore curriculum experiences based on their felt needs, interests, and abilities.

Expository learning The traditional classroom instructional approach that proceeds as follows: presentation of information to the learners, reference to particular examples, and application of the information to the learner's experiences.

Extended-year school Schools that have extended the school-year calendar from the traditional 180 days to a longer period, such as 200 days.

Extrinsic motivators Motivation of learning by rewards outside of the learner, such as parent and teacher expectations, gifts, certificates, stamps, and grades.

F

Facilitating bahavior Teacher behavior that makes it possible for students to learn.

Facilitative teaching See *indirect instruction*.

Family See *school-within-a-school*.

Feedback Information sent from the receiver to the originator that provides disclosure about the reception of the intended message.

Flexible scheduling Organization of classes and activities in a way that allows for variation from day to day, as opposed to the traditional, fixed schedule that does not vary from day to day.

Focus question A question that is designed to focus student thinking.

Formative assessment Evaluation of learning in progress.

For-profit school A public school that is operated by a for-profit company.

Full-service school A school that serves as a hub for quality education and comprehensive social services.

Fundamental school A school that specializes in teaching basic skills.

G

Generalizations General statements that can help explain commonalities shared to some degree with individuals who belong to various microcultures.

Goal An idea an individual intends to reach or hopes to accomplish.

Goal, course A broad generalized statement about the expected outcomes of a course.

Goal, educational A desired instructional outcome that is broad in scope.

Goal, student A statement about what the student hopes to accomplish.

Goal, teacher A statement about what the teacher hopes to accomplish.

Goals 2000 A reform initiative started in 1989 when then President George Bush convened all the governors to discuss the state of education. The resulting six national education goals were modified and became know as Goals 2000 under President Clinton.

H

Hands-on learning Learning by actively doing.

Heterogeneous grouping A grouping pattern that does not separate students into groups based on their intelligence, learning achievement, or physical characteristics.

High school A school that houses students in any combination of grades 9–12.

High-stakes assessment An assessment is called high stakes if use of the assessment's results carry serious consequences, such as if a student's grade promotion rests on the student's performance on one test, or the student's gradu-

ation from high school rests on the student's performance on a single test.

Holistic learning Learning that incorporates emotions with thinking.

Homogeneous grouping A grouping pattern that separates students into groups based on common characteristics, such as intelligence, achievement, or physical characteristics.

House See *school-within-a-school*.

I

Inclusion The commitment to the education of each student with special needs, to the maximum extent appropriate, in the school and classroom the student would otherwise attend.

Independent study An instructional strategy that allows a student to select a topic, set the goals, and work alone to attain them.

Indirect instruction Student-centered teaching using discovery and inquiry as learning strategies.

Individualized instruction The self-paced process whereby individual students assume responsibility for learning through study, practice, feedback, and reinforcement with appropriately designed instructional modules.

Individualized learning Self-paced instruction which is modified to meet the needs of individual students. Accommodating students with special needs can be accomplished by modifying lessons.

Inductive learning Learning that proceeds from specifics to the general. See also *discovery learning*.

Inquiry teaching Like discovery learning, except the learner designs the processes to be used in resolving the problem.

In-service teacher Term used when referring to credentialed and employed teachers.

Instruction Planned arrangement of experiences to help a learner develop understanding and to achieve a desirable change in behavior.

Instructional module Any freestanding instructional unit that includes these components: rationale, objectives, pretest, learning activities, comprehension checks with instructive feedback, and posttest.

Integrated curriculum Curriculum organization that combines subject matter traditionally taught independently.

Interdisciplinary instruction Instruction that combines subject matter disciplines traditionally taught independently.

Interdisciplinary team An organizational pattern of two or more teachers representing different subject areas. The team shares the same students, schedule, areas of the school, and the opportunity for teaching more than one subject. Also called *interdisciplinary teaching teams*.

Interdisciplinary thematic unit (ITU) A thematic unit that crosses boundaries of two or more disciplines.

Interdisciplinary thematic unit (integrated unit) A team representative of several disciplines: English/language arts, mathematics, science, social studies/history, and so forth, plan collaboratively and create unit plans that integrate their content areas by making relevant, meaningful connections across the curriculum.

Intermediate grades Term sometimes used to refer to grades 4–6.

Internalization The extent to which an attitude or value becomes a part of the learner. That is, without having to think about it, the learner's behavior reflects the attitude or value.

International Baccalaureate School A school with a curriculum approved by the International Baccalaureate Organization (IBO), a worldwide nonprofit educational foundation founded in the 1960s and based in Switzerland.

Interscholastic sports Athletic competition between teams from two or more schools.

Intervention A teacher's interruption to redirect a student's behavior, either by direct intervention (e.g., by a verbal command) or by indirect intervention (e.g., by eye contact or physical proximity).

Intramural program Organized activity program that features events between individuals or teams from within the school.

Intrinsic motivation Motivation of learning through the student's internal sense of accomplishment.

Intuition Knowing without conscious reasoning.

J

Junior high school A school that houses grades 7–9 or 7–8 and that has a schedule and curriculum that resemble those of the senior high school (grades 9–12 or 10–12) more than they do those of the elementary school.

L

Latin grammar school In 1635 the first secondary schools were founded in Boston. In the Latin grammar schools young boys between 7 and 14 years of age received an education focusing on the classics.

Lead teacher The member of a teaching team who is designated to facilitate the work and planning of that team.

Leadership team A group of teachers and administrators, and sometimes students, designated by the principal or elected by the faculty (and student body) to assist in the leadership of the school.

Learning The development of understandings and the change in behavior resulting from experiences. For different interpretations of learning, see *behaviorism* and *cognitivism*.

Learning center (LC) An instructional strategy that utilizes activities and materials located at a special place in the classroom and is designed to allow a student to work independently at his or her own pace to learn one area of content. See also *learning station*.

Learning modality The way a person receives information. Four modalities are recognized: visual, auditory, tactile (touch), and kinesthetic (movement).

Learning resource center The central location in the school where instructional materials and media are stored, organized, and accessed by students and staff.

Learning station (LS) Like a learning center, except that where each learning center is distinct and unrelated to others, learning stations are sequenced or in some way linked to one another.

Learning style The way a person learns best in a given situation.

Least restrictive environment Under Public Law 94-142, the Education for All Handicapped Children Act—IDEA emphasized the normalization of the educational environment for students with disabilities. The legislation requires provision of an environment that is as normal as possible.

Lesson A subdivision of a unit, usually taught in a single class period or, on occasion, for two or three successive periods.

Looping An arrangement in which the cohort of students and teachers remain together as a group for several or for all the years a child is at a particular school. Also referred to as *multiyear grouping, multiyear instruction, multiyear placement,* and *teacher-student progression.*

M

Magnet school A school that specializes in a particular academic area, such as science, mathematics and technology, the arts, or international relations. Also referred to as a *theme school.*

Mainstreaming Placing an exceptional child in regular education classrooms for all or part of the school day.

Mandala A diagram, usually circular, with spiritual and ritual significance.

Mastery learning The concept that a student should master the content of one lesson before moving on to the content of the next.

Measurement The process of collecting and interpreting data.

Mentoring One-on-one coaching, tutoring, or guidance to facilitate learning.

Metacognition Planning, monitoring, and evaluating one's own thinking. Known also as *reflective abstraction.*

Micro peer-teaching (MPT) Teaching a limited objective for a brief period to a small group of peers for the purpose of evaluation and improvement of particular teaching skills.

Microcultures Also referred to as microcultural groups, subcultures, or subsocieties are groups whose members share certain cultural patterns. Individual's cultural identities are based on their identity with or membership in a variety of microcultures including: race, ethnicity, religion, gender, age, socioeconomic status, ability and language.

Middle grades Grades 5–8.

Middle level education Any school unit between elementary and high school.

Middle school A school that has been planned and organized especially for students of ages 10–14.

Minds-on learning Learning in which the learner is intellectually active, thinking about what is being learned.

Misconception Faulty understanding of a major idea or concept. Also known as a *naïve theory* and *conceptual misunderstanding*.

Modeling The teacher's direct and indirect demonstration, by actions and by words, of the behaviors expected of students.

Multicultural education A deliberate attempt to help students understand facts, generalizations, attitudes, and behaviors derived from their own ethnic roots as well as others. In this process, students unlearn racism and biases and recognize the interdependent fabric of society, giving due acknowledgment for contributions made by its members.

Multilevel instruction See *multitasking*.

Multilevel teaching See *multitasking*.

Multimedia program The combined use of sound, video, and graphics for instruction.

Multiple intelligences A theory of several different intelligences, as opposed to just one general intelligence; intelligences that have been described are verbal/linguistic, musical, logical/mathematical, naturalist, visual/spatial, bodily/kinesthetic, interpersonal, and intrapersonal.

Multipurpose board A writing board with a smooth plastic surface used with special marking pens rather than chalk. Sometimes called a visual aid panel, the board may have a steel backing and then can be used as a magnetic board as well as a screen for projecting visuals.

Multitasking The simultaneous use of several levels of teaching and learning in the same classroom, with students working on different objectives or different tasks leading to the same objective. Also called *multilevel teaching*.

N

Naïve theory See *misconception*.

National Education Association (NEA) The nation's oldest professional organization of teachers, founded in 1857 as the National Teachers Association and changed in 1879 to its present name. Recently merged in at least two states (Montana and Minnesota) with the AFT.

No Child Left Behind (NCLB) Landmark legislation that promises to improve student achievement and change the culture of America's schools while providing equal educational opportunity for all students. It became law on January 8, 2002.

Normal school The first teacher education programs designed to prepare teachers to teach.

Norm-referenced Individual performance is judged relative to overall performance of the group (e.g., grading on a curve), as opposed to being criterion-referenced.

O

Objectives Instructional objectives are statements describing what the student will be able to do upon completion of the instructional experience.

Orientation set See *advance organizer*.

Overhead projector A teaching tool that projects light through objects that are transparent.

Overlapping A teacher behavior where the teacher is able to attend to more than one matter at once.

Overt behavior A behavior that is outwardly observable.

P

Partnership school A school that has entered into a partnership agreement with community business and industry to link school studies with the workplace.

Peer-tutoring An instructional strategy that places students in a tutorial role in which one student helps another learn.

Performance assessment See *authentic assessment*.

Performance-based instruction Instruction designed around the instruction and assessment of student achievement against specified and predetermined objectives.

Performance objective See *behavioral objective*.

Phonics The application of sound-symbol relationships to the teaching of reading.

Portfolio assessment An alternative approach to evaluation that assembles representative samples of a student's work over time as a basis for assessment.

Positive reinforcer A means of encouraging desired student behaviors by rewarding those behaviors when they occur.

Preassessment Diagnostic assessment of what students know or think they know prior to the instruction.

Pre-service teacher Term used when referring to teachers in training, as opposed to in-service teachers; teachers who are employed.

Probationary teacher An untenured teacher. After a designated number of years in the same district, usually three, upon rehire the probationary teacher receives a tenure contract.

Probing question Similar to a clarifying question, the probing question requires student thinking to go beyond superficial first-answer or single-word responses.

Procedure A statement telling the student how to accomplish a task.

Psychomotor domain The domain of learning that involves locomotor behaviors.

Q

Question-answer relationship (QAR) A strategy used to question students about reading material that involves asking questions and providing one of three types of cues: "right there", "search and think", or "on your own."

R

Realia Real objects used as visual props during instruction, such as political campaign buttons, plants, memorabilia, art, balls, and so forth.

Reciprocal teaching A form of collaborative teaching where the teacher and the students share the teaching responsibility and all are involved in asking questions, clarifying, predicting, and summarizing.

Reflection The conscious process of mentally replaying experiences.

Reflective abstraction See *metacognition*.

Reliability In measurement, the consistency with which an item or instrument is measured over time.

Rubric An outline of the criteria used to assess a student's work.

Rules In classroom management, rules are the standards of expectation for classroom behavior.

S

Schema (plural: schemata) A mental construct by which the learner organizes his or her perceptions of situations and knowledge.

School-within-a-school Sometimes referred to as a *house, cluster, village, pod,* or *family,* it is a teaching arrangement where one team of teachers is assigned to work with the same group of about 125 students for a common block of time, for the entire school day, or, in some instances, for all the years those students are at that school.

Secondary school Traditionally, any school housing students for any combination of grades 7–12.

Self-contained classroom Commonly used in the primary grades, it is a grouping pattern where one teacher teaches all or most all subjects to one group of children.

Self-paced learning See *individualized learning*.

Senior high school Usually a high school that houses only students in grades 9–12 or 10–12.

Sequencing Arranging ideas in logical order.

Simulation An abstraction or simplification of a real-life situation.

Socratic questioning Named for the Athenian teacher, Socrates, a questioning strategy where a teacher asks students a series of questions and encourages students to develop their own conclusions and draw their own inferences.

Special needs student See *exceptional child*.

Special transitional school A one-year school designed to help recent immigrant students feel welcome and self-assured and to succeed in learning to read and write in English.

SQ3R A study strategy where students survey the reading, create questions, read to answer the questions, recite the answers, and review the original material.

SQ4R Similar to SQ3R, but with the addition of recording, the students survey the reading, ask questions about what was read, read to answer the questions, recite the answers, record important items in their notebooks, and then review it all.

Standards See *curriculum standards*.

Stereotypes Absolute and inflexible descriptions of groups of individuals that ignore individual differences.

Student teaching A field experience component of teacher preparation, traditionally the culminating experience, where the teacher candidate practices teaching children while under the supervision of a credentialed teacher and a university supervisor.

Summative assessment Assessment of learning after instruction is completed.

T

Teacher leader See *lead teacher*.

Teaching See *instruction*.

Teaching style The way teachers teach; their distinctive mannerisms complemented by their choices of teaching behaviors and strategies.

Teaching team A team of two or more teachers who work together to provide instruction to the same group of students, either by alternating the instruction or team teaching simultaneously.

Team teaching Two or more teachers working together to provide instruction to a group of students.

Tech prep high school A school that has a 4–2 coordinated curriculum that is articulated from grades 9–12 to the first two years of college, leading to an associate of applied science degree.

Tenured teacher After serving a designated number of years in the same school district (usually three) as a probationary teacher, upon rehire the teacher receives a tenure contract, which means that the teacher is automatically rehired each year thereafter unless the contract is revoked by either the district or the teacher and for specific and legal reasons.

Terminal behavior That which has been learned as a direct result of instruction.

Thematic unit A unit of instruction built on a central theme or concept.

Theme school See *magnet school*.

Think-time Providing students with sufficient time to take things in and think about them before expecting them to react to them. See also *wait time*.

Tracking The practice of voluntary or involuntary placement of students in different programs or courses according to their ability and prior academic performance. See also *ability grouping*.

Traditional teaching Teacher-centered direct instruction, typically using lectures, discussions, textbooks, and worksheets.

Transition In a lesson, the planned procedures that move student thinking from one idea to the next or that move their actions from one activity to the next. With reference to schooling, transitions are the times when a student moves from one level of school to the next.

U

Unit A major subdivision of a course, comprising planned instruction about some central theme, topic, issue, or problem for a period of several days to several weeks.

Untracking See *detracking*.

V

Validity In measurement, the degree to which an item or instrument measures that which it is intended to measure.

Village See *school-within-a-school*.

W

Wait time In the use of questioning, the period of silence between the time a question is asked and the inquirer (teacher) does something, such as repeats the question, rephrases the question, calls on a particular student, answers the question him- or herself, or asks another question. Also referred to as *think-time*.

Whole-language learning A point of view with a focus on seeking or creating meaning that encourages language production, risk-taking, independence in producing language, and the use of a wide variety of print materials in authentic reading and writing situations.

Withitness The teacher's timely ability to intervene and redirect a student's inappropriate behavior.

Y

Year-round school A school that operates as is tradition, that is with 180 school days, but the days are spread over 12 months rather than the usual 10. Most common is the 9-weeks on, 3-weeks off format.

Young adolescent The 10- to 14-year-old experiencing the developmental stage of early adolescence.

Author Index

Page numbers followed by an "n" and a number indicate endnote entries.

Subject Index

Page numbers followed by an "n" and a number indicate endnote entries.

indirect, 312

individualized, 312

inquiry teaching, 184–187

integrated, 135

interdisciplinary, 312

learning styles and, 36–38, 40–41

methods of, 21–22

performance-based, 108, 120–121, 314

principles of, 171–173

student differences and, 41

Instructional components, of lesson plans, 143–145, 154, 156

Instructional materials. *See* materials

Instructional module, 312

Instructional objectives, 92, 108, 314

classifying, 113–118

curriculum and assessment, 108–109

instructional plan, 126, 129, 133

lesson plans, 145, 150

preparing, 110–113

student teaching, 291

teacher talk, 202

Instructional planning, 91–92, 120–121, 125–126

aims, 108

collaborative planning, 102–103

components of, 92–93

content outlines, 103–104

controversy, 104–107

course planning, 93–97

curriculum integration, 134–139

goals, 108

instructional objectives, 108–118

instructional unit, 132–134

learning and, 120

lesson plan construction, 143–145

lesson plan elements, 145–164

lesson plan rationale and assumptions, 140–143

multitext and multireading approaches, 101

printed materials, 101–102

process, 126

syllabus, 126–132

taxonomies, 118–120

textbooks, 98–101, 102

thoughtful and thorough, 92

Instructional procedures, 133

Instructional strategies. *See* student-centered instructional strategies; teacher-centered instructional strategies

Instructional tools, computer-based, 245–248. *See also* materials

Instructional unit, 132–134

Integrated curriculum, 135, 312

Integrated inquiry activity, 185

Integrated instruction, 135

Integrated learning, 191–194

Integrated thematic unit, 132, 313

Integration, 93

Intellectual cautiousness, 198 n.14

Intelligence, 198 n.14, n.16

Intelligence quotient (IQ), 45

Intelligent behavior, 182–184

Interactive lectures, 228–229

Interactive phase of instruction, 16

Intercom announcements, 69

Interdisciplinary curriculum, 312

Interdisciplinary inquiry activity, 185

Interdisciplinary instruction, 312

Interdisciplinary teams, 11–12, 312

Interdisciplinary thematic team teaching, 137

Interdisciplinary thematic unit (ITU), 132, 136–139, 185, 263, 312, 313

Intermediate grades, 313

Internalization, 115, 116, 313

International Baccalaureate School, 8, 313

Internet, 234–236

community service learning, 17

instructional objectives, 93

learning styles and multiple intelligences, 40

sample sites, 19

student-centered instructional strategies, 176–177

Internship, 289

Interpersonal intelligence, 39

Interpretive thinking, 52 n.28

Interruptions, 65, 69–70

Interscholastic sports, 313

Interstate New Teacher Assessment and Support Consortium Standards, The, 18

Intervention, 77–78, 79, 313

Interviews, 63–64, 298

Intramural program, 313

Intrapersonal intelligence, 39

Intrinsic motivation, 72, 216, 313

Introductory activities, 133

Introductory overviews, in textbooks, 101

Intuition, 313

Invention or concept development learning phase, 38

Inventiveness, 198 n.14

Investigation, 198 n.14

Looping, 11, 313
Loud talk, 79
Lying, 76

Macroclasses, 12
Macroperiods, 12
Magnet schools, 8, 313
Mainstreaming, 42, 313
Man: A Course of Study (MACOS), 135
Management. *See* classroom management
Mandala, 313
Manipulating, 116–117
Maps, in textbooks, 101
Marking, 130, 264–266. *See also* grading
Master of Arts in Teaching (MAT), 299
Mastery learning, 109, 313
Matching, 274
Materials
    audiovisual, 247
    commercial, 124 n.11
    computer-based, 245–248
    copyrighted, 247–248
    instructional plan, 129, 134
    lesson plans, 145, 160
    maintaining, obtaining, and using, 69
    organization and administration of, 65
    printed, 101–102, 234–241
Materials manager, 129, 181
Mathematical intelligence. *See* logical/mathematical intelligence
Mathematics
    curriculum standards for, 94
    lesson plan sample, 151–152
Meaningful learning, 119–120, 216–217
Measurable objectives, 112–113
Measurement, 256, 313
Media tools, 241–245
Meetings, class, 73–75, 126
Memorization, 228
Memory strategies, 192
Mentoring, 178–179, 299, 313
Metacognition, 183, 198 n.14, 261
Microcultures, 33, 313
Micro peer-teaching (MPT), 24, 219, 228–229, 269, 288, 301–305, 313
Middle grades, 313
Middle level education, 8, 314
Middle school concept, 8
Middle school movement, 8

Middle schools, 1, 2–3, 314
    community resources, 17–18
    contemporary, 7
    creation of, 4–5
    curriculum modifications, 13
    decision-making and thought-processing phases, 16–17
    diversity, 14–16
    educational reform, 6–7
    emergent overall picture, 18–20
    organization of, 7–9
    problems and issues in, 19, 20
    structuring, 10–13
    trends and practices in, 19, 20
    See also assessment; classroom management; instructional planning; materials; media tools; professional development; schools; student achievement; student-centered instructional strategies; teacher-centered instructional strategies
Middle school students, 31–32, 48–49
    adolescence, 32–33
    character development, 47–48
    culturally and linguistically diverse students, 43–44
    culture and education, 33–35
    diversity, 35–36
    English Language Learners, 44
    exceptional students, 41–42
    gifted and talented students, 45–46
    learning capacities, 38–41
    learning cycle, 38
    learning styles and teaching implications, 36–38
    multitasking, 48
    recalcitrant students, 47
    student differences, 41
    students willing to learn, 46
    students with special needs, 42–43
    success for all students, 44–45
    See also students
Minds-on learning, 173, 314
Misbehavior
    categories of, 75–77
    classroom management, 61, 75
    direct and indirect intervention, 77–78
    success stories, 77
    teacher-caused, 78–80
Misconceptions, 179, 314
Mission statements, exemplary, 15
Mistakes, avoiding, 80–85
Mnemonics, 228